AF663281

ENGINEERING EDUCATION

Perspectives, Issues and Concerns

Engineering Education

Perspectives, Issues and Concerns

Editor
Rajarshi Roy

SHIPRA

All right reserved. No part of this publication may be reproduced, stored in a retrival system, or transmitted in any form or by any means, electronic, mechanical, photocopying, recording or otherwise, without the prior written permission of the Publishers.

ISBN: 978-81-7541-505-8

First Published in India in 2009

Engineering Education: Perspectives, Issues and Concerns

© Contributors/Editors

Published by :
SHIPRA PUBLICATIONS
115-A, Vikas Marg, Shakarpur, Delhi-110092 (India)
Tel. : 91-11-65277210, 22500954, Fax : 91-11-22458662
Email : info@shiprapublications.com
www.shiprapublications.com

Foreword

National Institute of Technical Teachers' Training and Research, Kolkata, abbreviated as NITTTR-K, the first of its kind, started its journey in January 11th, 1965 as Technical Teachers' Training Institute (TTTI), Calcutta, and was set up by the then Ministry of Education, Government of India. Since then the Institute is enjoying its status as an autonomous Institute, with full fund by the Govt. of India. Presently it is functioning under the Ministry of Human Resource Development of Government of India with its changed name and mandate since 20th October 2003.

The primary aim of the institute is to develop Engineering vis-à-vis Technical Education system with focus on Engineering Education.

As per our Mission Statements, we are committed to:

- Conduct quality programmes and projects to train manpower for development of technical education system in India and abroad
- Undertake postgraduate programmes and research activities in content, process, policy and delivery, related to frontiers of technology
- Develop innovative curricula and instructional resources to groom creative and critical thinking
- Integrate the world of work with technical education system
- Offer extension services and consultancy to the satisfaction of the stakeholders of technical education system
- Enhance partnership with similar national and international organizations
- Perform advisory and catalytic role in transformation of Technical, Vocational Education and Training (TVET) System.

Today it is a proven fact that irrespective of levels, types and forms, according to modern educational psychology, students hold the central position in the formal system of education. Actually the entire system of education runs for the betterment of students in various dimensions.

Engineering, technological as well as Technical education differs from rest of the education gamut, so far the nature of students' development and participation in pedagogical process is concerned. It is often argued that while in the other segments of education, the basic objective of educational instruction is to develop theoretical knowledge, the central emphasis in technical education is to develop certain specific skill among the students, apart from knowledge

However skill cannot be imbibed in isolation. The basic philosophy of skill-development stress on the principle that any theory (or the theoretical knowledge) should be followed by appropriate practice. These are considered under 'cognitive' and 'psychomotor' domain of educational objectives, respectively, under various sequential sub-domains. However all these activities, i.e., developing the level of knowledge in the specific subject area and competency over certain specific skill will go in vain until and unless the student is having a strong positive attitude and interest towards the subject of study. Infact, effectiveness and acquisition of knowledge by the student largely depend upon sequel of factors and variables.

The domain, engineering education aught to be a subject of scrutiny, so far the dissemination strategies and tactics are concerned. Infact the very gamut is a 'special' one. Changes brought about various government and industry based inquiries and studies into engineering education have often proved to be too little and often inappropriate. In many ways studies into engineering education have resulted in producing many educational benchmarks and yet not addressing issues of dissatisfaction.

In the venture, the first volume on '*Engineering Education: Perspectives, Issues and Concerns*' is brought up. The volume is edited by my colleague, Dr. Rajarshi Roy from the Department of Education. The volume focuses over specific four dimensions, namely, **Redefining Engineering Education, Innovative approaches in Engineering Education, Organizational Climate and ICT in Engineering Education**, and **Revisiting Curricula in Engineering Education**. This first volume incorporating numerous contributions from the authors across the world. The volume addresses the international audience interested in Engineering Education. I believe, the volume will be considered a useful document for those interested in the very gamut of Education.

S. K. Bhattacharyya
Director
National Institute of Technical Teachers' Training and Research, Kolkata
(*Under Ministry of Human Resource Development, Government of India*)

Introduction

Engineering education, in Asian context, is yet to be defined, though the popular web definition of engineering education characterizes it as 'the activity of teaching engineering and technology, at school, college and university levels'. The goal of engineering education is to prepare people to practice engineering as a profession and also to spread technology literacy, increase student interest in technical careers through science and mathematics education and hands-on learning. Engineering education often begins with technology education in K-12 schools and is continued at college and university. (Douglas, Iverson & Kalyandurg, 2004). Engineering education is a part of the STEM initiative in United States public schools. The National Science Foundation is supporting research in Engineering Education through the National Centre for Engineering and Technology Education among others. Service Learning in engineering education is gaining popularity within the variety of disciplinary focuses within engineering education including mechanical engineering, construction science, computer science and engineering, electrical engineering, and other forms of related education...'

It is probably the very form of education, which is not restricted within cognition, and accords, as like performing arts, weightage on conative (or psychomotor) as well as affective domains of learning, which makes the system distinct. Experiential learning proves close relationship between engineering education and development, in its true sense, due to which availability of engineers per thousand population in a given society and nation are taken as major index of development. Unfortunately, sudden and huge proliferation of engineering education, though has given raise the percentage of engineers in oriental societies and thereby helped to raise up in the developmental index, however in real sense, development in specified segments is lacking due to non-integration of engineering education with the economy and society, often resulting a 'fallacy of development'.

So far the pedagogical dimension of engineering education is concerned, problem-issues questions the relevance of the very gamut of education, often appearing theoretical and lacking practical orientations. In recent days, a sudden crisis is experienced across globe in financial context, which is having adverse impact over the economy as well as on the social facets, including technical and engineering education, in some East Asian countries (Albett & Slengesol

2000), which help emerging some doubt in efficacy of investment in education in general and engineering education in particular. It is a proven fact that status of engineering and technical education is having a direct bearing with economy of a nation, and as analyzed by Tilak (2001), it is neither lack of education or over education, which results to economic crisis in Asia and Pacific. It is also a fact that higher education [to which engineering education is one of the major component] act as a 'safety valve' to absorb the shock of economic crisis; and the value of education to deal with disequilibria is very vital (Schultz, 1975, 1990). Therefore it may be expected that the shock is not a permanent phenomenon, and it could be solved shortly. On the other hand, education in general, and engineering-cum-technology education in specific is having a high potent for development. As such, engineering education directly contributes to development, and development of the economy leads to further development in education. There remains a cyclic causal-effect relationship between the two factors, which ultimately leads to progress.

In contemporary economic analysis, the emphasis has, to a considerable extent, shifted from perceiving capital accumulation in primarily physical terms to viewing it as a process in which productivity of human beings is integrally involved (Sen, 2000). For example, through education, learning and skill-formation, people can become much more productive in course of time, and this contributes a lot over the process of economic expansion. In recent studies of economic growth, often influenced by empirical readings of the experiences of Japan and the rest of East Asia as well as Europe and North America, there is much greater emphasis over 'human capital'. Human capital helps enhancing the human capability, and in consequence, enhances the social and economic indicators of human development. Engineering education directly contributes for human development. This is the very segment of education, which has its immediate impact over the society at large. Research in this domain also helps to bring structural change in the society. Therefore with a view to achieve development, proper attention is needed over engineering education and research.

Education (including both soft and hard skill) makes the human beings more efficient in production of commodity or in extending services, which is a human capital. These should add value to economy and also to the income of a person. But even with the same level of income, a person may benefit from education – in reading, communicating, arguing, in being able to choose from alternatives in a more informed way, in being taken more seriously by others. The benefit of education thus exceeds its role as human capital in producing commodity. In consequences, if a person can become more productive in making commodities through better education, better health and so on, it is not unnatural to expect that he can, through these means, also directly achieve more and have the freedom to achieve more to lead his life. In this way, the process of development follows a rotating cycle and thereby accelerates the rate of development.

The present volume incorporates chapter-contributions, having direct bearing for the development and enrichment of engineering education from Gestalt perspective. Contributors of the volume are from different corner of the globe. Though it was a difficult task to classify the contributions, however, keeping in view the major broad areas and focal-line of the papers, those are classified under four sections, viz., 'Redefining Engineering Education', 'Innovative approaches in Engineering Education', 'Organizational Climate and ICT in Engineering Education' and the last is 'Revisiting Curricula in Engineering Education'. The other pertinent dimensions of engineering education are expected to be brought up in the next volume.

Rajarshi Roy

Contents

Part III
Organizational Climate and ICT in Engineering Education

Part IV
Revisiting Curricula and Allied Issues in Engineering Education

List of Tables

List of Figures and Pictures

Figures

Pictures

Part I

Redefining Engineering Education

1

Humanizing Engineering Education for the Twenty First Century

Josef Rojter

The arena of engineering education has been, for over 150 years, a subject of scrutiny. Changes brought about various government and industry based inquiries and studies into engineering education have often proved to be too little and often inappropriate. In many ways studies into engineering education have resulted in producing many educational benchmarks and yet not addressing issues of dissatisfaction, in Australia, with engineering graduate core attributes.

Issues of professional engineering education are not unique and many of these are found in the education of other professions (Aulich, 1990). It seems to be the nature of the beast of professional education as a whole since epistemology of professions is generally a multidisciplinary one and, among professions, the engineering profession is the most in multidisciplinary of all. Though this article concentrates on Australian environment, it is not restricted to it. Issues of engineering education and profession found in Australia have resonance in Britain, United States, New Zealand and Canada—areas of once a British Empire settled by the inhabitants of the British Isles.

Background

The recognition the strategic role that engineering professions play in the economy and public welfare has ensured that the profession and its formation has been subject of public scrutiny. Professor Richard Morrow (1994, p. 17), the past chairman the National Academy of Engineering in the United States referring to the strategic value of engineering professions to national economic and social welfare commented, *"The nation with the best engineering talent is in possession of the core ingredient of comparative economic and industrial advantage."*

The Royal Society of the Arts (Weingart, 1978) had raised the problems of the relevance of engineering education way back in 1853. Major national inquiries and reviews by Mann (1919, p. 50), Grinter (1955), Augustine (1994), Dowell (1998) in the United States, Finniston (1980) in Britain, Moorehouse (1964), Williams (1988), Johnson (1996) in Australia have ensured that educational issues in professional engineering stayed in the spotlight. The issues of engineering education were time invariant. Engineering graduates were seen to be lacking the attributes, skills and knowledge necessary for a high level of innovation, and for the management of technology and human resources in the production of goods and services, as well as the entrepreneurial skills necessary in the commercial world. A survey conducted in Australia of employers to determine employer perceptions of engineering graduates from Australian universities showed that 97 per cent of employers felt that engineering graduates from Australian universities lacked an adequate knowledge and skills base to meet the future needs of the engineering workforce (Johnson 1996). Both the Finniston Inquiry in Britain and the Williams Review in Australia linked the deficiencies and inadequacies of engineering practice to engineering education. Shortcomings in engineering practice were identified in the areas of innovation, research and development, design and technical improvisation.

Many of the recommendations of the studies and reviews for improving engineering education were, to some degree, implemented but that did not address the divergence between professional engineering practice and education. Computer and information technology revolution was incorporated into engineering curricula and provided new tools for greater and quicker access to data bases, greater exactitude in engineering analysis and design, and widened the audience with whom the engineer communicated. Yet, despite these new tools, these educational issues in engineering remained and, if anything, the introduction of computer and information technology further consolidated the technical dimension of the engineering curricula.

The point is that the changes in engineering education are either too slow or are of the wrong kind to address the workplace and social demands of engineering graduates. These issues are part of overall problems facing engineering education. These are:

1. Mismatch of the skills and knowledge of engineering graduates and the type of skills and knowledge needed in the workplace;
2. Engineering education (and therefore profession) does not present an attractive option
3. Relatively high attrition rates of students undertaking engineering courses at Australian universities. Engineering enrolment of commencing students represents 7.5 per cent of total commencing enrolment at Australian universities, yet engineering graduates account for only 5.7 per cent of all

graduates in Australia (Department of Education, Training and Youth Affairs, 2000);

4. There exists a gender imbalance slanted towards boys among engineering students. Gender imbalance in the engineering profession makes the discipline less attractive to prospective female students; only 10.6 per cent of the engineering intake into Australian schools and faculties of engineering are women (Department of Education, Training and Youth Affairs, 1998);
5. Rigid entrance requirements into engineering courses. Entry into engineering courses in Australia requires passes in physical sciences and mathematics in the final year of secondary schooling. These requirements exclude the majority of secondary students from engineering education;
6. Rigid engineering curricula that is excessively positivist in character and generally ignores social, political, environmental and economic dimension is of professional engineering work;
7. Inappropriate academic recruitment. Academics into engineering schools and faculties are generally recruited on the basis of their research degrees and research practice and such practice seems to downplay the vocational nature of the profession.

Problem Context of Engineering Education

There are two main problems facing the engineering profession in Australia (and elsewhere) as far as professional education is concerned. One problem relates to the skills and knowledge acquired during the period of formal professional engineering education, and have been found wanting to meet the demands of the workplace. Another problem relates to perceptions of the engineering profession, which has translated into a lack of attractiveness of engineering as a course of study, as evidenced by the long tail of entrants into engineering courses with relatively poor academic preparation and abilities, and the gender imbalance that exists within the profession.

Woolnough (1994) showed that in Britain the rate of growth in engineering enrolments has not kept up with the expanding sector of higher education. The increased industry demand for professional engineers in Britain has been accompanied by a relative decline in enrolment in engineering courses. Department of Education and Employment [DfEE] (2000) estimated that the annual growth in professional engineering jobs in Britain for the period 1998-2009 is in excess of 2 per cent per annum. Taking into account professional engineers leaving or retiring from professional work, it would necessitate a growth of enrolment in engineering close to 5 per cent per annum. This has led Richard Wilson (2005) to comment that the increasing demand for professional engineers in Britain cannot be met. Huband (2007) points out to the decline in relative engineering enrolments in the United States. Since 1965 the decline in engineering enrolment in the United States has been observed to be less than 3 per cent of the total higher education enrolment. This has led to almost a critical shortfall in supply of professional engineers in the United States (Hutchinson *et al.*, p. 39), (National Science Foundation 2004). The enrolment in engineering courses has fallen by 40 per cent in Denmark (Ellis, 1991, p. 36), 35 percent in Switzerland, and 10 per cent in the Netherlands and Norway (Thulstrup, 1999, p. 16). Though the rate of annual growth in engineering enrolment in Australia over the period 1983-2004 was 4.3 per cent, it lagged behind the overall growth in enrolments at higher education institutions for the same period. The overall growth in Higher Education enrolments in Australia was 5.6 per cent with disciplines such as Business and Economics, Law, and Science registering annual growths in enrolment, of 7.0 per cent, 8.0 per cent and 5.6 per cent respectively (Department of Education, Training and Youth Affairs, 2005). There is a definite trend of people entering higher education who in growing proportion disregard engineering as an attractive option for study.

The relative lack of attractiveness of engineering as courses of study is not new. This has been identified in Australia since 1950's onwards by, among others, Moorhouse (1964), Williams (1988) and Johnson (1996). Though the entry scores into engineering courses at the more prestigious universities such as Sydney, Melbourne, Monash, New South Wales and Queensland are high, they are lower than the entry scores to other professional courses such as medicine and law at these universities. There is also a long tail of students with relatively poor academic achievements entering engineering courses at the less prestigious universities (Department of Education, Training and Youth Affairs, 2005). The minimum score for entry into engineering courses at the Victoria University, for instance, would not meet entry requirements for any courses at the abovementioned universities.

Thus there seems to be, as far as the engineering profession is concerned, issues concerning both sides of the professional engineering educational spectrum. The lack of attractiveness of engineering as a course of study has ramifications on the status of the profession with a visible synergism between these two factors. It is difficult to disengage the standing of the engineering profession from engineering education. It is not clear whether it is engineering education that fails to attract a client group because of the standing of the engineering profession, or whether the poor standing of the engineering profession is the result of the lack of attractiveness of engineering education. The exit part of professional engineering education does not, seemingly, meet needs of professional engineering work. The problem therefore needs to be attributed to the professional engineering education and assumptions on which the design and implementation of engineering curricula are based.

Educational Issues in Engineering Profession

The shortcomings in professional engineering practice in Australia have been widely identified and documented (Dowell, E., Baum, E., and McTague, J. 1998), Williams (1988), Johnson (1996), Beswick, D., Julian, J., and Macmillan, C. (1988), and Bothwick, S., and Murphy, T. (1998). Studies undertaken to establish the relationship between the knowledge derived from engineering education and the knowledge applied in professional work have shown a divergence between the worlds of professional education and professional work.

Key conclusions and recommendations proposed by the Williams Committee, in the 1980's, called for changes in contemporary engineering education. These were based on the identification of contemporary demands on professional engineering practice and were:

(a) Technology has technical and human aspects. The nations undergoing the greatest rate of technological change have an understanding of the human aspects of technology. There were many Australian employers who did not appreciate the dual nature of technological change: this was also true of many practicing Australian engineers;
(b) The attrition rate of engineering students enrolled in engineering degree courses was relatively high in comparison to students enrolled in other professional courses;
(c) Engineering schools and faculties were more responsive to the changes and demands in engineering science and the equipment associated with engineering science than to changes in engineering practice. Too little emphasis was placed, in engineering curricula and research, on the human aspects of technology; and
(d) Engineering schools and faculties in Australia were lacking innovation in designing and introducing unconventional programmes in engineering curricula.

Among the many recommendations put forward by the Williams Committee, the most relevant to this study were concerned with engineering curricula at Australian universities. These recommendations called for the development of appropriate engineering curricula to meet the needs of engineering practice. The report also identified the need for change in the organizational structures of engineering schools and faculties in order that such recommendations could be accepted and implemented. The recommendations suggested that:

- Engineering students needed greater exposure to the art of technology rather than the current emphasis on the science of technology;
- Engineering curricula needed to pay greater attention to communication skills, and management and financial literacy;

- Engineering curricula needed to evolve as part of a business context;
- Engineering academic staff members needed to develop closer links with the employers of engineers in order to ascertain organizational engineering demands and to evaluate how these demands connect to current engineering education;
- Engineering research at universities ought to take the path of multidisciplinary group research. This would reflect the true multi-variat nature of engineering; and
- Engineering education needed to be expanded to meet the expected demand for graduate engineers. It was suggested that an annual growth of 3 per cent of engineering graduates would be the bare minimum to sustain engineering activity in Australia. Such expansion had to be accompanied by a 14 per cent increase in investment in staff, spatial resources, and equipment.

A survey done by Vollmer in Germany, of 1200 graduates in mechanical engineering showed that engineering education contributed 50 per cent of the knowledge of engineering sciences required to perform well in a job, and only 2 per cent of the non-technical skills required in engineering practice (Muller, H.D. and Collet, M. 1995). The same German study also showed that 48 per cent of mechanical engineering graduates worked initially in production—related areas and 24 per cent worked in research and development. Five years after graduation only 14 per cent of mechanical engineers worked in the production—related areas and 4 per cent of mechanical engineers worked in the area of research and development. There is an evident diffusion of professional engineers from the technical areas. A study of employers, in Britain, disclosed dissatisfaction with cognitive skills and knowledge British graduates developed in the course of their engineering studies (Glover, I.A. & Herriot, P., 1982). The Finniston Inquiry, earlier, revealed the following attitudes and opinions:

- The employers had great difficulties in recruiting the appropriate engineering graduates suitable for the areas of production. There were however no such difficulties in recruiting suitable engineering graduates for research and development; and
- Engineering graduates tended to be less ambitious than graduates from other professional fields such as law, business and accountancy. Engineers were therefore less likely to be promoted within an organization and were therefore more exposed to the vagaries of the market and more likely to be retrenched during economic downturns. The relatively high unemployment of engineers in comparison to the other professions would be to the detriment of the professional engineer's status, and would influence the quality and quantity of intake into engineering courses (Wilenski, H., 1964).

A similar study was undertaken in Australia to establish the relationship between the cognitive skills derived from professional engineering education and the nature of professional work. Private firms and government organizations at commonwealth, state and municipal levels were surveyed and the results of these surveys showed that the employers were generally satisfied with the knowledge engineering graduates possessed in the areas of basic sciences, engineering sciences and disciplinary technical engineering practice (Bothwick & Murphy, 1998). Concerns were expressed at the lack of the following attributes among Australian engineering graduates:

- Knowledge of industrial relations and management of people;
- Knowledge of management of costs and resources;
- Knowledge of engineering as part of the broader business context; and
- Skills in written and oral communication.

German, British and Australian studies observed a mismatch between the knowledge imparted in professional education and in engineering practice.

Professional Engineering Workplace Discourses

Like for any professional education, the educational programme for professional engineers must be designed with the view of meeting both the demands and needs of professional workplace and the social identity and a culture of the engineering profession. These needs often conflict since employer needs and demands are directed towards profits and a professional identity is embedded in service not only to employers but also to the community, environment and social well-being.

Engineering profession is a profession that highly embedded in both public and (increasingly) private. The withdrawal of government participation in Britain and Australia in building and managing public infrastructures such as energy, water supply and manufacturing has led to the de-engineering of public and statutory organizations. The proportion of professional engineers employed within government and semi-government sector has fallen from above 70 per cent in the early 1980's to less than 30 per cent. In the United States 77 per cent of professional engineers are employees of organizations. In the late 1960's the proportion of engineers, in Australia, who were employed in the public sector was in the vicinity of 80 per cent. By 1993, 80 per cent of professional engineers in United States (National Engineers Register, 1994) and 60 per cent of engineers in Australia (Johnston, 1994] were employed in private industry (National Engineers Register 1994), (Johnston, 1994, p. 13). One would thus expect an increasing influence of private industry over the shaping of engineering education. In the past, such influence over professional engineering educational discourse has been fairly common through external membership of course advisory panels and could be argued that it was partially responsible for emergence of the scientifically trained engineer which coincided with the transformation of small enterprises into large manufacturing concerns. It was the emergence of the large manufacturing concerns that could afford to exploit scientific knowledge for practical purposes and make money (Layton, 1976).

Despite the presence of industry on course advisory committees engineering education has produced less than a satisfactory product for both the industry and the engineering profession. One reason is the polyvalent nature of professional engineering practice and the two or three industry representative cannot reflect the broad discourse of professional engineering. Another reason is attributable to tensions arising due to differing values between engineering professions and organizations that employ them.

Larson (1979) identified a significant growth in the diversity of engineering work that was not reflected in engineering curricula. The technical and scientific focus of engineering education was seen to be increasingly out of touch with the practical world of professional engineering work. The transformation of engineers from the technical to human realms altered the role of professional engineering work and has been a part of an evolutionary process in the professionalization project since the late 19th century (Hotchkiss, 1935), (Cross, 1980). Florman (1996) pointed to the fact that professional engineers were recruited to play a significant role in administration and management, leaving the technical aspects of work to other technically qualified workers. In the United States only 60 per cent of working professional engineers has any direct connection with the technical aspect of engineering work. Arthur (1993) shows a diffusion from the technical to the human dimension of professional engineers in Britain where 25 per cent of engineering graduates enter employment in industries such as tourism, sales, public relations and marketing, industries which lie well outside what is considered to be classical engineering activity. An early 1970's survey conducted in Australia by the Department of Labour and National Service (1973) of the engineering profession showed that 40 per cent of professional engineers were engaged in functions such as planning, research and development, design and teaching that drew heavily on technical knowledge and skills. The remaining 60 per cent of professional engineers participated in activities such as management, production, maintenance, sales and marketing where the need for technological skills and knowledge receded into the background. Deans (1999) refers to a survey of mechanical engineering graduates in New Zealand, which revealed that in the course of their careers mechanical engineers migrate towards management positions. Within 15 years of leaving university, 80 per cent of mechanical engineers were employed in management positions. Beder (1989) using engineering employment data taken in the United States, Britain and Australia confirms that between 30 and 40 per cent of professional engineers are engaged in management. The Vollmer Survey in Britain [p. 105-9] involved a large sample of several thousand recent engineering graduates and engineering graduates who had been in the workforce for 5 or more years. The survey revealed that for engineering graduates of less than 2 years standing, 48 per cent worked in production related areas and 24 per cent in research and development. Interviews with the same engineers five years later showed that only 14 per cent remained in the production related areas and only 4 per cent in research and development (Muller and Collett, 1995).

As largely an employee profession there are tensions often associated with the difference between professional and employer values. This is a particular issue for professional engineering education providers who see themselves as fostering, through education, professional values. Employers have a strategic stake in the professions because the growth of business and profitability is dependent on the competence and integration of its professional workforce into their organizations. To many employers, the professions represent a highly educated and skilled workforce, but are still a part of the employee population. The integration of professions into organizational missions and objectives cannot be complete if the professional occupation retains a strong identification with professional values and identity. A structural conflict of values exists between organizational values, which are directly driven by the economic imperatives, and professional commitments that are based on notions of service, welfare and safety. These conflicting values lead to tensions in the workplace which may be overt but are more often implicit in workplace relationships. Beder (1989) observed four major areas of tension for professional engineers employed in organizations as the result of differences in values between professional engineers and the employing organizations. She framed these areas of conflict in terms of goals, incentives, control of work, and influence over outcomes. This is shown in Table 1.1.

Table 1.1: Contrasting Values of Employer: Organizations and Professions

	Organizational Values	*Professional Values*
Goals	Developing products and services for the markets	Maintenance of standards of technical competence
Control	Generally hierarchical, values are asserted and developed at the higher echelons of organizations	Generally organized along collegial lines. Professions tend to represent democratic culture.
Incentive	Pay rises and promotion through organizational ranks	Collegial recognition and acclamation.
Influence	Official position within the organization.	Recognition of expertise and possession of special knowledge and skill base.

In reality, professional discourses in employer organizations often tend to be subjected to organisational objectives. This is most commonly the case in the engineering profession where organizations serve as infrastructures to professional engineers. In such cases professional engineers are assimilated into organisational ways of working and entrepreneurship. Where this occurs, engineering professionals become locked into the employer organizational structure to the extent that individual professional engineers derive their status from the employing organization. In such cases professional accountability in engineering tends to take on secondary importance to careers and organizational matters. The process in which organizational values predominate over professional values is not just one of assimilation, but a kind of protective self-interest which is focused on shaping the infrastructure in ways that support professional practice.

An American study (Zussman, 1985) of the role, professional engineers play in employer organizations, showed that professional engineers employed in enterprises and organizations were more concerned with organizational than professional values and objectives. This study complemented an earlier study which suggested that the ideas and values of professional engineering discourse in the workplace were being shed (Prandy, 1965). In this earlier study, Prandy (1965) observed that professional engineers in Britain were more sensitive to the needs and demands of their employers than their career and professional engineering issues. They were more concerned with the possibility of being dismissed by their employers than being expelled from professional associations. In the United States professional engineers also exhibited a greater sense of loyalty to their employers than to their profession, though not necessarily out of fear of consequences. Engineers were generally unconcerned about the opinions of other members of their profession who were outside their organization and they gave overriding precedence to company-profits over notions of professional commitments (Goss, 1969). This can be contrasted with the more autonomous professions, such as law and medicine, where collegial accountability is still observed. There was greater work satisfaction among professional workers employed in organizations when the professional discourse retained a commitment to professional ideals and values, especially in relation to work autonomy. Wilenski (1964) in his study of professional work found that the greatest work dissatisfaction among the professional workforce was found among professional engineers where they had little participatory role in decision-making process concerning their work. Participation in decision-making has been shown to be an important component in work satisfaction for professions embedded in organizations (McGregor, 1960).

Larson (1979) suggests that the commitment of employing organizations and bureaucracies to rational processes entrapped engineers, and blended engineers and bureaucratic rationality in ways that worked against the engineering profession. This close identification with bureaucracies provides individual engineers with high bureaucratic status within an organization but at the expense of the profession as a collective, of its professional autonomy and its control over professional markets. For the engineering profession, its continuous links with employing organizations and their bureaucracies has led to a synergy of entrapment. This organizational framework acts as a medium for professional engineering discourse. It has important epistemic implications for the discourses of professional engineering education. This 'capturing of the engineering profession by discourses of business' means that workplaces' knowledge practices (such as knowledge of organizational behaviour) constitute a substantial portion of professional engineering discourse (Goldman, 1991, p. 124-5). If this diversified and blended knowledge base in engineering is to inform the preparation of young engineers, there is a need for the incorporation of subjects that deal with management and organizational behaviour as a part of the engineering curriculum.

Perceptions of Engineering Profession and Engineering Education

The attractiveness of the engineering profession is governed by how the prospective entrants perceive engineering as a profession and as a course of study. Albert Einstein perceived engineering to belong to the logical empiricist philosophy, which eschewed free inventions from human intellect and relied strictly on empiricism (Howard, 2005).

The engineering profession has had a relatively poor status and this view has been carried into the self-perception of members of the engineering professions. In the mid sixties, during the most intense time of the cold war period in the United States, when there was a strong empathy with science and technology in the belief that these could address human, economic and political issues, the engineering profession did not have a high professional profile in the community. Professional engineers were more likely to be valued on the basis of their expertise rather than as members of a profession. In a study of occupations and professions Wilenski (1964) found that professional engineers had also negative perceptions of themselves. He called the engineering profession an 'alienated profession'. Amongst the professions surveyed, professional engineers exhibited the highest dissatisfaction with their occupation, though not with their work (McGregor, 1960). These self-perceptions of engineers were widespread across the fields of employment of professional engineers: in industry, engineering consulting firms and academic departments at universities. The engineering profession, in comparison to other professions, had relatively low self-esteem. American surveys conducted by the National Academy of Engineering showed that the engineering profession lacked identity, and that many people could not distinguish between engineers, technicians and scientists (Ahlstrom, 1982). Braham (1992) in his study of the attractiveness of engineering as a course of study among the young mentions an American surveys of public attitudes towards professional engineers, which shows the low esteem in which the public holds professional engineers. Engineers were perceived as having poor social skills, being self-absorbed, loners and rigid in mind. Hilton and Lees (1988) place the blame on the lack of appreciation of the engineering profession on the poor marketing of the profession. Engineers were isolated from the mainstream of the society because they were associated with engineering failures, the nature of engineering work being such that failures could not be associated with particular persons and the blame shifted to the profession.

In terms of public perceptions, the engineering profession in Australia has not marketed itself well. Yates (2000), in a discussion paper on the status of engineers in Australia, noted that professional engineers have failed to market themselves as a profession and are responsible for much of the perception as an alienated technical and scientific occupation that is sometimes associated with technical trades. Beder (1989) using a survey conducted in 1992 by the Institution of Engineers, Australia points to the amorphous nature of the engineering profession in Australia the Australian public could not distinguish between the activities of different engineering disciplines. This was borne out by subsequent surveys conducted by I.E. Aust., which showed that beyond the construction of machines and buildings, the Australian public had little knowledge and appreciation of what engineers did (Diedrich, 1996 & 2000). The public profile of the engineering profession in Australia is illustrated in Table 1.2. These perceptions of engineering are somewhat contradictory and reflect uncertainty concerning the nature of the engineering profession. The positive perceptions of translating ideas into reality and coping well with weighty responsibilities are not congruent with the negative perceptions of engineers as being too theoretical and not senior management material.

Table 1.2: Perceptions in Australia towards the Engineering Profession

Positive Perceptions	*Negative Perceptions*
Trustworthy	Conservative, pedantic and aloof
Copes well with weighty responsibility	Too theoretical, lacks practical skills
Translates ideas into reality	Tends towards rigid, outdated management style
Represents a source of ideas and technologies	
Acts as a bridge between management and workers	Has problems communicating with workers
Keeps government and big business honest	Not senior management material

The alienation of the engineering profession was also evident among engineering undergraduates. In this case, however, the dissatisfaction had little to do with the engineering curricula and education, but rather with ignorance concerning the final destination of engineering graduates.

A study done by Shulman (2005), a member of the Carnegie Foundation for the Advancement of Teaching, on perceptions of professional engineers among students to a question of 'what is an engineer?' produced a responses *...An Engineer is someone who uses math and science to mess with the world by designing and making things that other folks can use (pause)...'And once you mess with the world, you're responsible for the mess you made.* A survey in Britain, by Industry Ventures, of 2700 final year engineering undergraduates, showed that the majority of students had no idea what engineers did. An earlier study conducted in the United States showed that the majority of engineering students had only vague notions of engineering work (Ritti, 1971).

The motives for studying engineering were not clear in the survey of engineering students in a study Durcholz (1979) performed in the United States. As a result of his study Peter Durcholz commented: *As I continued to interview students, it was clear they were puzzled about what their chosen career would lead them to in the way of work.* Hutton and Gerstl (1995, p. 142) in an inquiry into why students in the United States chose engineering as their discipline of study, found that a third of the students chose engineering due to the influence of a role model. A quarter of the students undertook engineering studies because they saw engineering as a path to management and a further third of the students studied engineering because they felt they had a technical disposition and mechanical aptitude. Interestingly, Hutton and Gerstl observed that student perceptions of engineering did not show common themes, reflecting a general confusion about the nature of engineering work. Skobrook (2006) commented that students' preconceptions of engineering and engineering studies in Britain were not matched by the reality.

Perceptions of engineering professions manifest confusion because of the multi-variant discourses of professional practices.

Traditional Shape of Engineering Education

Professional engineering education owes much of its structure to positivism championed by Saint Simon and Auguste Comte who saw science as a vehicle for unifying knowledge and predict the behaviour of the physical (and social) world (Carr, 1964). It sat well in the 19th century embroiled in industrial revolution and the rise of capitalism in an era of rationalism spawned by positivistic ideas. Rationalism relied on empirical measurements and analytical precision and differentiated the technical worldview from cultural and social orientations. The language derived from science suited the ideas of rationalism which relied on predictability. The language was associated with objectivity, impartiality and discouraged thought and political aspects of science. Science and the scientific knowledge provided the space for locating both a scientist and an engineer.

However engineer is not restricted to 'doing science'. Johnstone observed that the nature of real world engineering. *Basically an engineer is not trying to do science; he is doing engineering which is something different. The science he uses is means to an end, and its quality as science is irrelevant as long as it works. A scientist is judged by his publications but an engineer is judged by his large-scale achievements. He can be a great engineer without having published a word. Does anyone remember what Brunel wrote? What we remember is that he built the Great Western Railway and the Great Eastern Steamship. In short engineers are not second hand citizens in the empire of science; they are the masters of an empire of their own of which science is only a part.*

This science-centred view is the most acceptable in engineering education and constructs a model of a science-dominated engineering education. The view of science as a predominating knowledge base in engineering practice and education has had a negative effect on the engineering profession. The confusion between science and engineering has adversely affected the engineering profession. A survey (Department of Labour and National Service, 1973, p. 33) revealed that the general community viewed that scientists contributed more to the welfare of a society than professional engineers. This is despite the fact that when the work roles of scientists and engineers were examined by Hilton and Lee (1988), it was the engineers who were recognised for the social role they played in improving social conditions.

Attributes represent special characteristics associated with particular social and occupational groups. In the case of professional occupations, such as professional engineers, the professional attributes can be understood in terms of professional practice and professional knowledge. In engineering, the proximity of engineering to science and technology is important in the conceptualization of professional engineering attributes. Professional engineers, if not doing science, use science in their technical discourses. These technical discourses are often embedded in the practice of technology which often is interpreted in a highly positivist terms and such interpretation of technology finds its way in the curricula constructs. The view of science, expressed by Alfred North Whitehead (Carr, 1964, p. 3) as a static body of knowledge which does not care to explain its meanings to a post-modern view, based on ideas of Karl Popper, of a body of knowledge which relies on competing and often contradictory models that are accommodated through a process of accreditation (Ziman, 1991). Thus science is a body of knowledge constructed through a process of evolutionary epistemology. However, technology can also be viewed through the prism of post-modernism.

Locke (1984) defines technology as an activity associated with the art of increasing economic production. In this definition technology is both coherent and incoherent as it is entangled with many things and therefore tangible. The post-modernist view of technology is no longer positivist because it deals simultaneously with technical, scientific, economic, social, political, cultural, ethical and environmental issues. The association of engineering with technological change gave the profession a strategic role in the economy since technological change was driven by economic imperatives. Solow [in Bothwick and Murphy, 1998] connected engineering through technology to the economy in which science and technology underpin the growth of knowledge-based industry. The focus of engineering education has been, and to some extent still is, based on a 'technology paradigm', drawn from the historical formation of the profession.

Yet such a technology paradigm in its educational implementation has shown to produce engineering graduates who lacked (Lang, J.D., Cruise, S., McVey, F.D. and McMasters, J, 1999, p. 47):

- Strong communication skill;
- Broad perspectives, such as social, environmental, cultural, political and ethical issues, concerning the profession;
- Ability to bridge the realities of engineering science and the professional engineering practice.

Towards New Curriculum Paradigm

There is a body of core knowledge that bestows each engineering discipline with its unique characteristics. Chemical engineers need to be familiar with unit operations and stage and rate processes, mechanical engineers need to apply laws of motion and thermodynamics to problems involving conversions between work and energy. However, core knowledge aside, there is in engineering curricula large tracts of disciplinary knowledge, often exceeding more than half the curriculum, which has been introduced on beliefs and assumptions of professional engineering discourses. Since curricula structures for the same engineering disciplines vary between universities, it can be assumed that the assumptions and beliefs of course designers and their course advisory committees concerning professional engineering work vary. It has been stated (Turns, Atman, Adams, and Barker, 2005, p. 28) that there is no universally acknowledged and accepted characterization of engineering knowledge.

Professional engineering discourses have a lot to do with the implementation and management of change. Like all occupations, engineering is not immune from change but rather due to its proximity to change it is both the parent and the child of change. Professional engineering discourses are thus in flux. The new curriculum must meet changes in professional engineering discourse. The view of professional engineering as applied science is anachronistic and one must look towards future evolution of the profession. There are three identifiable evolutionary stages in engineering practice, shown in Figure 1.1. It is seen that science has had diminishing role in the professional practice. Though science, which was placed in the foreground of engineering practice during the industrial age of the nineteenth and twentieth centuries, will still be important but is likely to play a less important role and be overtaken by social issues. It is the post-industrial engineering discourses in workplaces which are relevant to the future directions of engineering education. The common perception of the engineering profession as an occupation which is intertwined with science, technology and economy played a significant role in influencing the type of attributes and the knowledge base that engineering profession needs to have. It has been important in the conceptualization of professional engineering attributes. However strict associations with science and the narrow technology perspective do not meet the needs of the profession to provide the type of service both employers and the society need and deserve. In the United States, the definition of the professional engineer was linked to the application of advanced levels of knowledge.

Pre-industrial Revolution	*Early to Middle Industrial Revolution* ⟶	*Late to Post Industrial Age* ⟶
Technical application is based on trial and error procedures. Knowledge is standardized on the basis of past engineering successes, though such standardization is generally restricted to the developer of engineering successes and his pupils and apprentices. The practice of engineering is thus based on Formalized Procedural Knowledge	This period begins in the late thirteenth century and in engineering it reflects technical application based on scientific methods and discovery. There is greater incorporation of science into practice and engineering knowledge base accompanied by the formation of first scientific engineering educational institutions in France and England in 17th and 18th centuries. Engineers took on the role of managers and innovated management techniques	This period covers the timeline from mid-nineteenth century onwards. Science continues to have impact on the technical application in engineering. However the technical nature of engineering practice is increasingly supplemented by economic, environmental and social consideration.

Fig. 1.1: Evolution of Engineering Practice

The American Engineering Council constitution described professional engineering as an occupation that applied ...*the science of controlling the forces and utilizing the materials of nature and the art of organizing and directing human activities in connection therewith* [Hotchkiss, 1935, p. 311]. The American Engineering Council thus defined professional engineering in the broad terms of science, technology, design, management and human activities. Professional Engineering was no longer narrowly confined to solving human problems in terms of matter and energy but had to do with the improvement of the human condition. In observing professional engineering workplace discourses Edwin Layton (1971) saw, in the early 1970's, engineers as all rounded professionals. He placed the engineer not as a corporate professional but as a social professional and described the professional engineer as:

- An agent of technological change which is essential to human progress;
- A free thinker who takes an arbitrary social class position; and
- A socially responsible practitioner who will ensure that the technological change is for the common and individual benefit.

Associating engineering purely with the practical application of science has locked the engineering profession with pure and applied science, and positions the profession into a strictly technical dimension. It acted against the interest of the engineering profession because it becomes difficult for the profession to distinguish itself from science, without accounting for the non-scientific dimensions of professional engineering work. Attributing professional engineering to just the technical dimension is problematic for the profession because it is difficult for it to differentiate the profession from other occupations within the engineering workforce.

The scientific context of professional engineering discourses does not necessarily translate into the application of scientific method in the context of work. There is a need for reflection and judgement which, like in other professional work, places reflection-in-action in the foreground of professional engineering work discourse. Koen (1984, p. 150-158) describes professional engineering reflection-in-action as an occupational activity that defines the engineering method and which contrasts with the scientific method in professional engineering work. The engineering method is based on engineering heuristics, which are applied in poorly understood situations. These heuristics encapsulate ambiguities and provide approximations that facilitate problem solving and they cannot guarantee perfect, or even any solutions. Typical examples of engineering heuristics can be found in the applications of rules of thumb, safety factors and risk analysis, and, as such, the engineering method underpinned by engineering heuristics resembles professional discourses in other professions, such as medicine and law. When the discourse of professional engineering workplaces diverges from the engineering discourses at universities, a deficit in professional engineering knowledge is produced.

The state, students and employers represent these major stakeholders each of which have different expectations of the profession, and hence, of engineering education. Employers want (Table 1.3) professional engineers to exhibit proficiency, knowledge and literacy in areas of social sciences, environmental issues and ethics, and to possess the attributes and skills that are the characteristics of professional practice and well-rounded education.

Table 1. 3: Demands on the Engineering Profession

Customers and Stake-Holders of the Engineering Profession	*Service and Product Required from Engineering Profession*
Students	Marketable skills and knowledge necessary for future engineering work. Preparation for life-long learning on entering professional work
Employers	Professional engineers need to possess the following attributes: 1. Technical literacy and competence; 2. High level of communication and interpersonal skills; 3. Inquiring and curious mind; 4. High motivation; 5. Economic, social and environmental literacy; and 6. Professional and ethical attitude in the workplace.
State: Public and Society	In addition to the attributes required by the employers, professional engineers need to: 1. Have political awareness; 2. Possess a sense of social responsibility; and 3. Reflect as a group the gender and ethnic distribution in the society.

The human dimension of new professional engineering discourses was recognized in the inquiry into engineering education in Australia (Johnson, 1996, p. 47). In its executive summary it stated:

> ...The present emphasis placed on engineering science resulting the graduates with high technical capability, has often acted to limit their appreciation of the broader role of engineering professionals. Graduates must understand the social, economic and environmental consequences of their professional activities if is to fully assume its expanding responsibilities...Engineering education must be more outward looking, more attached to the real concerns of communities. Courses should promote environmental, economic and global awareness, problem solving ability, engagement with information technology, self-directed and life-long learning... on a sound base of mathematics and engineering technology.

This was convergent with recommendations issued by the Australian Science and Technology Council [ASTEC] (1996) which declared that engineering schools and departments should ensure that engineering graduates are equipped to understand the social, economic and environmental consequences of their profession; activities. Both the summary and the ASTEC declaration pointed to a paradigm shift in engineering education from scientism to more holistic notions of what Germans refer to as *wissenschaft* or *bildung*—the business of knowledge.

The inclusion of human elements such as humanities and social sciences to engineering curricula makes sense if professional engineering practice in the post-industrial world is to be met. It strengthens and broadens professional knowledge. Professional engineers though often creators and dreamers in workplace discourses have taken on the tenancy of the scientific culture based on pragmatism and valuing the precise in the educational discourse. UNESCO, over three decades ago, linked engineering practice with social responsibility (Hardy, 1992). The introductory remarks of this report challenged scientific hegemony over engineering education and suggested broader engineering curricula that incorporated humanities and social sciences. Follow up UNESCO reports (1968, 1970 and 1974) —warned that the profession of engineering was in danger of marginalization if the present trend of scientification of engineering curricula continued and engineering education failed to acknowledge and address the problems of human beings. Solomon [1996, p. 28] noted that professional engineers in Australia lacked the cultural references needed in leading large organizations. The reviews and inquiries into the engineering profession and education in United States (Grinter 1955 & Augustine 1994), Britain (Finniston 1980) and Australia (Williams 1988, Johnson 1996) identified the lack of emphasis on social sciences and humanities in engineering curricula as a source of structural weakness in engineering education. It led to both a knowledge deficit in the engineering knowledge base and the marginalisation of the engineering profession. The Green Report (Doeell *et al.*, 1998) commissioned by the American Society for Engineering Education noted that humanities should be expanded in current engineering education in order to provide the graduate engineer with the diversity of skills needed in the workplace. The lack of visible participation of professional engineers in public issues and concerns sent out distorted signals to the public concerning engineers and engineering work. Beswick [1998, p. 129] in the study of the engineering profession in Australia demonstrated that both practising engineers and their employers agreed that the expansion of social sciences and humanities in engineering curricula was needed to enhance the knowledge base necessary for workplace competency. This could be achieved at the expense of science subjects occupying a larger part of the engineering curricula than was strictly necessary. There is also a sociological dimension concerning the relation of the engineering profession to work. Wilenski (1964) showed that the overemphasis on science-based knowledge in engineering curricula has produced professional engineers who under-perform at work and have lower esteem and aspirations. Braham [1992, p. 77] has pointed to a survey conducted in the United States of public attitudes towards professional engineers that showed the profession as one that was composed of people who lacked social skills, were inflexible in mind and related poorly to the rest of the society. Engineers, in the academia, have far too often taken of a negative position to 'soft' humanities. Hardy [1992, p. 558] saw the low time allocation to humanities and social sciences within engineering curricula as a major weakness of engineering education because it confined engineering education to the technical world.

The expansion of humanities and social science components of engineering curricula needs to be seen not only as a vehicle for expanding the professional engineer's knowledge base, but as a process by which the cognitive skills of engineering graduates are enhanced (Elms, 1992), (Florman 1994, p. 13). Vesilind (1978, p. 376-379) observed that the people-orientation of engineering work were discourses of social activity and justified the knowledge acquisition from the disciplines of social sciences. In aptitude and intelligence tests of senior undergraduate and graduate students in humanities and social science, and engineering students, Hudson (1975) showed that engineering students performed better on convergent thinking, whereas humanities and social students were superior in divergent or lateral thinking. Convergent thinkers exhibit high ability in solving a problem, if such problems are well defined. Divergent thinking capabilities are concerned with identifying a problem and framing the problem in a context. It is divergent thinking that underpins the cognitive skills identified to be in short supply among engineering graduates but much needed in professional engineering work. The presence of humanities and social sciences in engineering curricula counter the positivist and utilitarian attitudes that are derived from purely scientifically-based education and with which the engineering profession is associated in the public perception. Other studies by Paulsen and Wells (1998, p. 365-384), in the United States, indicate that engineering students are more conformist and less critical in questioning and confronting knowledge than their peers studying humanities and social sciences. They are more conformist and have a view that knowledge is linear, certain and consists of a simple collection of facts. This is at odds with post industrial and post-modern perception of a highly globalized world.

Introduction and expansion of humanities and social sciences in engineering curricula is not particularly revolutionary. In France, the subject of Literature is compulsory part of engineering curriculum in all the 232 French engineering schools and faculties Didier, 2000, p. 330). In France, the

Commission des Titre D' Ingenieurs (CTI), which protects the engineering title, recommended in 1995 that engineering schools were expected to provide a general education consisting of foreign languages, economic, social and human sciences. Grinter (1955) suggested that 30 percent of engineering curriculum in the United States be allocated to social sciences and humanities. Gunther Heitmann (1995, p. 138) an editor of the European Society for Engineering Education (SEFI) Journal, suggested that at least 20 percent of engineering curricula be allocated to humanities and social sciences. The American Society for Engineering Education was in full agreement with the Accreditation Board for Engineering and Technology (ABET) that at least 12.5 percent of undergraduate engineering curricula should be set-aside for humanities and social science subjects. This allocation did not include management or communication subjects and reflected the Accreditation Board for Engineering and Technology philosophy that professional engineering discourses require knowledge and understanding of the social, ethic, economic and safety dimensions of successful engineering practice [ABET (Accreditation Board for Engineering and Technology, 2002]. In Germany some, of the pre Bologna Declaration in engineering courses allocated 39 percent of the engineering curriculum to non-technical subjects (Hutton and Lawrence, 1982). Of this 27 percent consisted of pure humanities, foreign language studies and written communication skills. Since management and administration knowledge is derived from social sciences, management was not considered as a separate entity from social sciences.

In examining future directions of engineering education, Goldman (2004, p. 168) raised questions such as:

- What will professional engineering be like in the twenty first century?
- What should the purpose of engineering education be?
- Should vocational and humanistic education be reconciled?

The model of professional engineering discourse, shown in Fig. 1.1 exemplifies a steady drift from positivist scientific empiricism to one of social and humanistic constructivism. It is not difficult to argue that engineering educational discourses should follow the diffusion path towards humanism and constructivism.

Conclusion

Current engineering curricula produce engineering graduates who are celebrants of technology and, as such, do not meet the needs and demands of employers, society and the engineering profession. This restricted role to technology providers renders the engineering profession invisible to the public eye (Fawcett and Roberts, 2001, p. 61). To open up professional education it is argued here that engineering education need to made more socially relevant through the incorporation of disciplines dealing with human affairs into the professional curriculum. This can be achieved through shaping the curriculum into a more constructivist pedagogical modes, which incorporate critical theories.

Educational paradigm shift is achievable if the educational curriculum has a philosophical basis. Much of science, medicine and law educational curricula constructs owe are indebted to philosophies of science, medicine and law respectively. It has been suggested by Sinclair and Tilson (1979, p. 252) that the confusion of focus of engineering education is attributable to the lack of a proper philosophical base of engineering, which can provide guidelines. Notions of the importance of philosophy of engineering-to-engineering education have been raised in some quarters (Goldman 2004), (Sinclair and Tilson 1979), (National Academy of Engineering [NAE], 2004), (Royal Academy for Engineering [RAE], 2007). Both the National Academy of Engineering in the United States and the Royal Academy for Engineering in Britain has devoted many of their activities to philosophy of engineering. Yet despite Goldman (2004) arguing that there exists a philosophy of engineering, cursory readings of literature suggests it to be a work in progress.

The construction of a new paradigm of engineering education would thus require curriculum designers who are not only attuned to the changes in professional practice but also participate in developing engineering philosophy. They must be men and women who are not only literate in disciplines outside their areas of specialised research fields, they must also be active in applied professional practice and be politically courageous to challenge the universities' increasing emphasis towards what Lyotard (1984) calls 'performative knowledge'.

Unlike the higher status of the more autonomous professions of medicine and law, engineering has derived its social status from university and (to some extent), specifically, scientific education. Engineering faculties have increasingly been associated with applied science with the demise of many Applied Science faculties at Australian universities. This has resulted in the narrowing of engineering education, which has become increasingly scientific in nature where scientific norms predominate. Increasing proximity to science has in many cases resulted in the loss of identity of engineering at universities in terms of research, staff recruitment and autonomy as a separate intellectual discipline. In intellectual terms there are of course positives in scientific engineering as an intellectual discipline and discourse but these are offset by the fact that engineering discourses in practice demand attributes that are not mostly found in science. The universities as institutions, therefore, act as an impediment to wholesome changes in engineering curricula. Engineering schools and faculties have become cultural artifacts at universities with predominating norms of science. The engineering schools and faculties are composed of academic staff members who were recruited, and continue to be recruited, on the basis of predominating scientific norms. The adoption of engineering curricula, which shift away from scientific norms towards a professional practice orientation, necessitates a paradigm change within the faculties and schools of engineering from the current culture that embraces scientific norms; these also present an obstacle in developing a problem or target oriented engineering curriculum with an emphasis on design which is not inclusive of scientific norms. Unlike the faculties of law and medicine at universities, engineering schools and faculties were reluctant to recruit full time academic staff from the ranks of practising professional engineers. Engineering at universities finds its identity in the paradigm of science, though its professional paradigm has also much in common with the scholarship found in humanities and social science, art and design and applied art. For the engineering profession to contribute to the economic, social and environmental welfare of the community, the educational paradigm for the profession needs to recognize that science is only one of the cornerstones of the professional work, and therefore construct educational programmes more inclusive of non-scientific knowledge and skill bases. To do so, the hegemony of science in engineering education needs to be shed.

2

Engineering Education

Finding the Meaning

Mariana Ruiz Morales

'Tell me and I shall forget,
Show me and I shall remember,
Involve me and I shall understand'

— *Chinese Proverb*

Engineering education encompasses basic sciences, technology and human studies in a complex mixture to create new products, machines, structures and processes. Such a diverse and rich field of study would be expected to attract self-motivated and truly committed students. But experience has shown this is not always the case, especially for first-year students who need to deal with subject of basic sciences, which seldom make sense to them for their future career.

Engineering is, in fact, a field of study that requires a holistic way of understanding reality that goes beyond theoretical knowledge and practical skills. Professors, especially in first-year engineering, need to promote the conditions that lead to a more meaningful engineering study and practice, including the commitment with the social and the natural environments.

This chapter aims to discuss some of the factors that promote Motivation in Engineering Education. It begins with a theoretical background and then presents a differentiation between intrinsic and extrinsic motivation. The section entitled 'Intrinsic Factors of Motivation' includes personal traits like attitudes and feelings that affect motivation in students, whereas the section 'Extrinsic Factors of Motivation' covers the importance of healthy interpersonal relationships as well as educational strategies and classroom activities that help students to find the meaning in study and practice.

Motivation and the Practice of Human Development

The evolution on engineering education has been assessed by several authors who agree on the need of objectives that include not only technical factors but also inner aspects of the person (Rompelman, 2000; Yrjänheikki and Takala, 2001). One of the means to address these new objectives is provided by the practice of Human Development.

Human Development is understood as the nomination for the scientific approach that encompasses philosophy, psychology, sociology and anthropology towards the understanding of the fully functioning being, and the mechanisms that encourage personal growth. The concept emerges from the theoretical basis of Humanistic Psychology, Phenomenological Philosophy and the Person-Centered Approach (Bogantes, 1993; Lafarga and Gómez del Campo, 1986; Watson *et al*. 2002).

The basic principle sustaining this scientific approach is the belief of an ever changing state of growth that leads the person to actualize his full potential. This implies fully experiencing feelings and reactions to perceive reality, and, with this information, taking the best course of action in every given situation (Guay *et al*., 2000; Lafarga & Gómez del Campo, 1986).

Self-actualization

The term self-actualization was developed by Abraham Maslow and is defined as the basic organismic tendency to move towards the realization of the inherent potentials of the human being (Watson *et al*. 2002). It means that there exists a basic potentiality in every person that leads him towards completing or actualizing his full being. Under this principle, given some facilitating conditions, a person can find by himself the best alternatives of functioning that will lead to wholeness and optimal results in life.

Internal motivation could be understood, therefore, as the consequence of self-actualization (Hendriks & Van Snippenburg, 2002), i.e., the inner force that drives a person to persist in the achievement of his objectives. It is thought that, given the proper conditions in the engineering study and practice, this internal motivation will lead towards the promotion of critical and analytical skills as well as and the personal interest required to develop new products, processes, and ways of doing things.

As motivation leads to the development of human potential, authors have found that the person is more sensitive and responsible, with a greater decision making capacity and a more harmonious development of his capacities (Bohart, 2000; Strawbridge 2001). It is also thought that meaning must be found in the harmonious relationship of technology advances with cooperation and social responsibility, as these values include the acceptance of commitment towards the achievement of personal goals.

Authors have related motivation to several constructs like emotion, performance, self-concept and self-efficacy (Bong & Skaalvik, 2003), engagement (Shaufeli *et al*., 2002) and even defined it as a mixture of ambiguous behaviour components with social and mental origins (Hendriks & Van Snippenburg, 2002).

Motivation is strongly linked with self-reliance and satisfaction, which are related to the feelings of worth and confidence in who we are, what we know and what we feel we are good for, which motivate the student to achieve new goals that bring fulfillment (internal motivation). It could be considered as a consequence of the way reality is perceived and understood. Free access of information leads to finding more mature meanings of the experience, making decisions on a better basis and finding the meaning of the actions taken.

Intrinsic Factors of Motivation

As it has been stated, internal motivation is a consequence of the self-actualization principle, which can arise given the proper conditions within the person. This conditions were stated by Carl Rogers (1978) and include Congruence, Openness to experience with acceptance (unconditional positive regard), and Empathy, which could in fact be considered as attitudes towards life and its challenges.

Openness to experience

A person that is open to experience functions better because he perceives situations and events in complex and rich forms that lead to the realization of his inner potential (Pearson, 1974). Openness also means to accept experience with unconditional positive regard, and it has been observed that such an attitude promotes emotional intelligence, social learning, and decision making with liberty and responsibility (Mayer & Cobb, 2000).

Congruence

Congruence is defined as the harmonious and integrated functioning of the organism, within which, the person can attend to his needs of development (Ortega & Mariño, 1997). Congruence has been broadly studied by several authors such as Behr and Becker (Watson, 2002).

Congruence can also be defined as the attitude of genuineness. It means a transparent experiencing, with no alterations of reality; that encompasses honesty with one's self and lessening discrepancy on what one thinks and feels. Congruence is also understood as the transparency in the actions and the main source of awareness. From phenomenological point of view, the person needs to be aware of his liberty and his responsibility of living the life he chooses in order to assume the consequences and achievements of his actions, and thus, feel motivated to further achievements.

Empathy

The attitude of empathy could be defined as the capacity to observe and understand the own feelings and such of another person. It is greatly related to the attitude of openness, in terms of being able to accept reality and its challenges. Empathy is an important element for interpersonal relationships and will be further discussed in the next section specifically related to the professor-student relationship.

Extrinsic Factors of Motivation

The following section pretends to show the importance of healthy interpersonal relationships as well as the appropriate classroom activities required to help students to find the meaning in engineering study and practice. The need for educational strategies that help students to be more efficient in the use of their creative potential in order to find and chose, with flexibility, the best option in any given situation, is also assessed.

Student-Professor Relationship

The role of the professor in engineering has evolved from being a source of knowledge to be a role model and a promoter of students, human development, as he might set the conditions either to facilitate or to obstruct the experiencing ability that will provide students with the elements to be able to acquire information in its fully and complete sense. Given this ability, engineers can live in a more productive and satisfactory way if they feel that, in any given situation, they can perceive the more subtle details and use this information to make better decisions for themselves and the company, which they work for.

The feelings of worth, appreciation and understanding, are also a keen aspect of motivation. It is, therefore necessary to acknowledge the roll of the professor who, living these attitudes towards his students, can promote constructive feelings in them.

The attitude of empathy is an important element in the student-professor relationship, as it can lead to confidence and a more mature and communicative environment. Students need to be empathetically understood, and communication of this understanding has to be achieved, in order to promote a better relationship. Communication and the manner of relating are the keys to a successful educational experience for engineering undergraduates, because it sets the basis of healthy organizational behaviour. The relationship student-professor should be considered as a true encounter, with an open environment in which it is safe to explore and express what one thinks and feels, in which all the richness of experiential information can be of use. This kind of relationship is the basis of cooperative work and the understanding of group dynamics, two aspects that are nowadays of major importance in the engineering practice.

Empathy is related to acceptance, understood as the openness to the own experience as well as such of others in an environment of warmth and recognition of reality and life circumstances. Acceptance is a requirement for a successful engineering education, from the positive regard that students need to experiment in order to develop self-prizing, to the committed appraisal of others. Better engineering professionals are those that manifest an acceptant attitude towards people in complex situations, with no denial of the point from which they start, which enables them to work more efficiently from there.

Several authors have studied the attitudes and feelings of engineering students (Rompelman, 2000; Ruiz, 2007; Yrjänheikki & Takala, 2001) and of working engineers (Roy *et al.*, 2006). They have found that class activities make a difference in students' development and that there are numerous strategies to impart engineering education besides the direct mode of instruction-transaction, such as the distance mode of instruction in which the student needs to be strongly motivated in order to commit with learning by himself.

Some class activities and educational strategies used in engineering:

The Project

This is one of the most widely used educational strategies in engineering schools. The completion of a final Engineering Project is usually required for graduation or as a requirement in one or more subjects. It is understood as the generation of new ideas or ways of applying existing ideas in the solution of problems or in the creation of something that solves, prevents or controls any adverse effect in engineering systems. Projects help future engineers to apply concepts and techniques to real situations in which they come up with original proposals to make things work better for the individuals and the community.

The use of projects contributes to the development of responsibility since the student takes an active role on the solution of problems. He feels that he is no longer an observer but also an actor responsible for changing what is wrong, which would be an important objective of engineering education and a source of motivation.

Even if the use of projects as an educational strategy has many advantages, there are several factors that obstruct its proper use, such as the following:

1. Lack of resources such as time for the adequate project development. Usually, engineering schools are under pressure to cover theoretical concepts in short periods of time, living short edge for the project work and assessment.
2. Lack of a physical space where the group working in a project can work together with the required tools.
3. Lack of project advisors with dedicated time to work with project teams.

It is therefore necessary to take into account these requirements when expecting students to complete meaningful projects and hence, increase motivation in engineering study.

The Creative-Desire Based Learning

Most educators have heard of the popular educational strategy called 'Problem Based Learning' (PBL). With this technique, students are faced with a problem that has to be studied for a long time in order to find possible solutions. Even if this technique is thought to promote the ability to confront real problems in the future, it would be more interesting to achieve goals with another motivation than a problem because, since alternatives are usually difficult to find and students have a short attention spam, they usually get frustrated and loose motivation after some time of working with a problem. It happens that when students are faced with a problem, they try to find the easiest and fastest way of getting over with it with little effort.

Another shortcoming that has been found in this strategy is in the semantics. The word 'problem' has a negative connotation, something everybody wants to avoid. Since childhood, many relate 'school' with 'problems' which causes a barrier to creativity, innovation, and job enjoyment.

A suggestion would be to change to a more optimistic way of facing challenges. Instead of handing out problems to students, start by showing examples of how technology and science has been the basis for meeting a technical or social requirement, from the discovery of cooking food to the construction of personal computers. Many times, technology develops not in order to solve a problem but as a 'creative desire'. So the proposal would be to apply the technique of 'Creative Desire Based Learning' in conducting class activities with engineers. This technique promotes motivation and commitment nurtured by the will of achievement of new ideas and products. Using this strategy, the course instructor reinforces creativity by helping students to find new relationships between several variables such as those present in real situations.

The Experiment

Not as popular as other strategies in engineering schools, experiments are extremely useful as they lead students to deeply comprehend concepts or situations, and participate in an active way developing new products and processes. Depending on the sort of experiment proposed, students could also develop manual skills, intellectual abilities such as analysis and decision-making and values like teamwork, respect for life, and so forth. In the quest for success with an experiment, engineering students might find the required motivation to keep on going with study and practice, but the need of proper tools, space and advisor services has to be met.

Two examples of experiments that have been used with success in capturing interest of engineering students are the following:

1. Home Composting

Even if composting has gained popularity in recent years, it is still a little known practice among college students who usually feel it is too complicated or useless. Giving students the basis for conducting an experiment on the production of home composting and reviewing advances in a few weeks has proven good results in motivation and achievement of several objectives:

(a) Students feel they can actually do something to solve environmental problems, since they reduce pollution caused by organic waste.
(b) They find out there are unexploited resources if one learns to see waste from a different point of view.
(c) Values such as responsibility and care for life are reinforced.
(d) Manual skills are developed as well as intellectual.

2. Simulation of Production Systems

Computer simulation promotes the development of abilities such as the comprehension of large amounts of data and the interrelationship of variables included in complex systems. The skills acquired via simulation modeling are not restricted to the mathematical and analytical areas. Abilities such as intuition, openness, and critical thinking, and values such as responsibility and tolerance have been increasingly observed in students as well as their motivation for pursuing a professional career in engineering.

It has also been proven that simulation affects students' cognitive process as it promotes the enhancement of higher-order thinking strategies, and help students to develop intuition and awareness of the environment simulated, integrate information, think creatively, and solve complex problems, all major components of motivation.

Conclusion

This chapter has aimed to discuss motivation in order to better understand its origins and the ways to promote it in engineering students. It is stated that even if motivation is a personal attitude derived from an inner force, it can be promoted by the professor and his relationship with students, as well as the variety of educational strategies chosen for class sessions.

Knowledge of the students' interests and the understanding of their needs and wills can guide educators to make the best decisions with flexibility and empathy. A helpful guideline would be to consider the following as a main objective of engineering education: To nourish the capacity of understanding the world's functioning as a whole, with a deep comprehension of the human experience and the consequences of one's actions as professionals and agents in the world.

3

Collaborative Writing Tools in Engineering Educati on

Challenges for Knowledge Management and Sharing

João Batista Bottentuit Junior and *Clara Pereira Coutinho*

The profile of engineers has been gradually changing, which means that nowadays professionals have to dominate more competences and technologies in order to have a multidisciplinary and transversal curriculum. This professional uses a variety of information and communication technologies (ICT) that use the Internet to perform or complement their daily activities.

The first generation of the Internet had as main characteristic the amount of available information. However, the user's role in this scenario was only of viewer of what was happening in that particular web page, as he didn't have authorization to change or edit the content. In the first stage, the services available on the Internet appeared and spread fast, creating new jobs and economic markets. One example of this is the e-commerce, which developed a new business pattern as it made companies triple their profit. This stage can be called Web 1.0. Web 1.0 was very expensive to users, because most services were paid and controlled through licences; the systems were only available to those who could afford online transactions and buy software to create and maintain sites.

Web 1.0 led to great advances in accessing information and knowledge, but the philosophy behind the global network concept was of an open space, without 'owner' or person who controlled the access or content. The idea of making this a democratic environment was always present and the technological evolution allowed an increase in the number of users only possible due to the increase of the network bandwidth, the possibility to publish information on the web in an easy, fast way, regardless of specific software, programming language or additional costs.

Along with the changes of paradigms to Web 2.0, it exists huge and varied online applications for several aims, the use of these resources grows as the users produce information, sharing their knowledge through the Internet, in an easy, fast way. Within this new generation of the Internet called Web 2.0, concepts like Blog, Wikipedia, Podcast, Orkut, Del.icio.us, Skype, Messenger, Linkedln are a few examples of tools of systems available on the global network (Richardson, 2006).

Many users didn't notice that the Internet had changed its paradigms, due to the fast change process. The philosophy with Web 2.0 is different as people create their own documents and automatically publish them on the web, without having knowledge of programming or of computer environments.

A wiki is a website for collective work of several authors; It is similar to a blog in its logic structure, but it also allows to add, edit or remove content created by other authors (Schwartz *et al.*, 2004; Tonke, 2005; Qian, 2007). The wiki is already used in several countries and for several purposes, which means it can be used in schools or in companies for share or knowledge management. The wiki concept became popular with the creation of Wikipedia* that grows everyday with the voluntary contribution of specialists in various fields and according to Schons, Silva & Molossi (2007) has 3, 5 millions of articles and more than 720 million words in 205 languages and dialects (see picture 3.1). According to the same authors, its content is voluntarily created and modified. Although there is a lack of 'top-down' quality control and a strict hierarchy, many articles have good quality, which was proved by Nature magazine. This British magazine submitted 50 scientifical notes of Wikipedia and Encyclopaedia Britannica to be evaluated by specialists, who came to the conclusion that just 10 per cent of more than a thousand of doctors or researchers connected to Nature had written to Wikipedia. Through this analysis it was also possible to assume that people without any technical knowledge had written the majority of the notes. But the research had 42 corrections, showing a rate of four incorrect notes in Wikipedia and three incorrect ones in Britannica. The specialists also found four serious mistakes in each encyclopaedia, 162 omissions and false truth in Wikipedia and 123 in Britannica. These results confirm that both are very similar regarding mistakes and reasons.

In this chapter, we present the context for the new profile of engineers, pointing out the technological transformations and the effect that the Internet has on teaching and learning activities. Within this scope is the wiki, as it is an advantage when creating or managing information essential to the success of engineering projects.

Wikis

To Moura (2006) wiki is a Hawaiian word 'wikiwiki' that means 'very fast' or informal. In 1995, Ward Cunningham created the wiki, imagining a web page where it was possible to have a cooperative and open edition. Following this idea, it was built the first wiki software as well as other similar actions.

* www.wikipedia.org

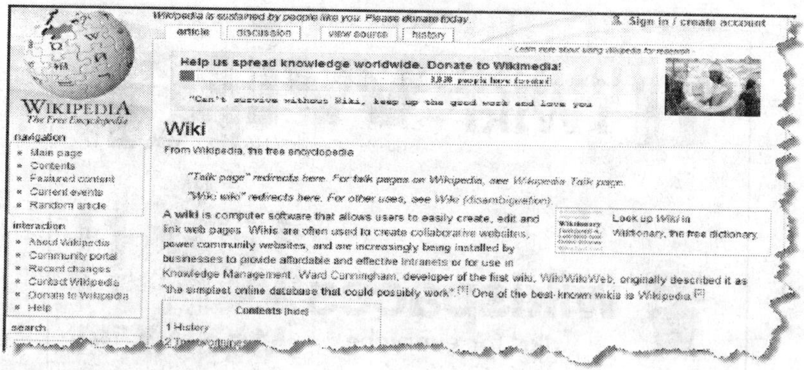

Picture 3.1: Wikipedia

Wikis can be of a commercial or open source (open code) type. Most companies prefer to work with the commercial software as, in an Intranet environment, only those who are logged on the wiki can access contents and data is secure against losses on the company servers.

Some of the commercial softwares are (see picture 3.2):

- Confluence Enterprise Wiki [http://www.atlassian.com/software/confluence/]
- SocialText [http://www.socialtext.com/]

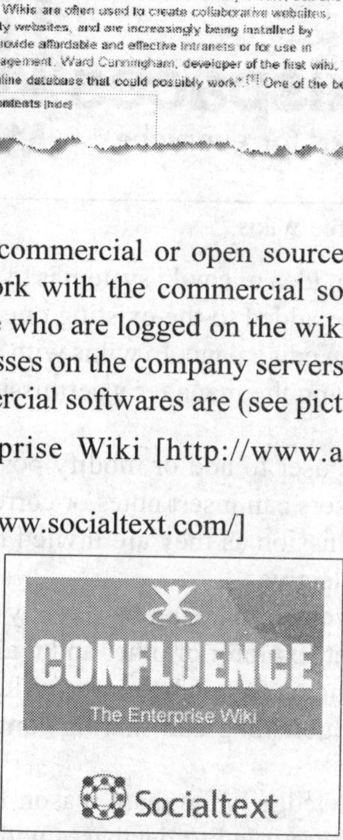

Picture 3.2: Examples of Paid Wikis

Some of the open source softwares are:

- Wiki.Com [http://wiki.com] works as a search engine of other wikis and as an environment to create free wikis. It is part of google
- MediaWiki [http://www.mediawiki.org/wiki/MediaWiki]
- Twiki [http://www.twiki.org/]
- Wikispaces [http://www.wikispaces.com/]
- Wikia [http://www.wikia.com/wiki/Wikia]

Leuf and Cunningham (2001, p. 14) defines a wiki as a 'free expansive collection of web pages connected in an hypertext system to store and modify information – a database, where each page can be easily edit by any user

Picture 3.3: Examples of Free Wikis

with a browser'. The main idea of a wiki system is to change any original text, so new knowledge can be added to the existing one, which means that in an open wiki each person can edit a page. In wikis with a restrict access, only the persons logged on or having the manager's permission can add new contents or new texts.

The wiki allows the user to add or modify posted texts and every time there is a new post, all users can insert notes or correct it. They don't need to ask for the author's permission as they are invited to give their contribution and the final result is collective.

In practice, it is a website that can be directly edit from a navigational structure, such as Internet Explorer or other and it allows the creation of new web pages only by clicking on certain buttons to write a text, as if it was a word processor. Wikis allow publishing and sharing content on the web in a very easy way.

The search for knowledge is the main reason for the existence of wikis and the willingness to share it led to databases with information that can be read and modified by those who know about a specific subject. These databases are important to the persons who participate in a wiki and they are important when all members of a group share knowledge between each other.

Although several support tools for collaborative work have already been tested, wikis are one of the most promising technologies that allow implementing a collaborative technique on the work group in virtual environments. A wiki is a website produced by several authors through a collective work.

It allows the creation of new web pages only by clicking on certain buttons and by writing a text, as if it was a word processor. Wikis allow publishing and sharing content on the web in a very easy way (Schwartz *et al.,* 2004; Qian, 2007).

According to Leuf and Cunningham (2001) wikis can be used in two different writing modes or styles of usage: the document mode and the thread mode. In document mode contributors create collaborative documents and in the thread mode contributors carry out discussions in the wiki environment by posting signed messages. Although there is still few research regarding educational uses of wikis, findings support the use of this tool for collaborative learning (Wijekumar, s/d/; Augar *et al.,* 2004; Gomes, 2006; Faquetti and Alves, 2006; Santamaria and Abraira, 2006; Coutinho and Bottentuit Junior, 2007a; Coutinho and Bottentuit Junior, 2007b).

The most spread use of wikis is known in literature as wikis interclase (Santamaria and Abraira, 2006, p. 376) and consists in the creation of a repository or a collaborative database by a group of students that attend the same subject or course. The wiki can be used so students can develop a project in small groups, can work a part of a collaborative class project or so they can create and maintain the website of the subject or course. (Santamaria & Abraira, 2006, p. 376). Thus give this tool the following educational potentialities:

- To dynamically interact and cooperate with students;
- To exchange ideas, create applications, purpose work guidelines for certain goals;
- To recreate or make glossaries, dictionaries, textbooks, manuals, repositories of classes, topics, meetings etc;
- To make structures of shared, collaborative knowledge that can create learning communities;
- Inclusion in edublogs, because they complement each other despite being different in their creation;
- To check all modifications, allowing the professor to evaluate for improvement;
- Students can create, edit or delete a posted text, being responsibles since they are logged on;
- Wikis can be used to create a work schedule or to develop projects;
- The use of wikis leads to a decrease in the use of media such as the telephone and e-mail, because a colleague can search for information on the wiki before asking about it.

Wikis have quickly increased and they were used in areas such education, namely in teaching and distance learning; in business, as co-workers share knowledge and in engineering and management as a tool for projects management, etc.

Some Contexts of Use

Santamaria and Abraira (2006) define some contexts of use for wikis: the first is the willingness to **write**. In our society, this skill is very important, as it represents not only the ability to write but also the ability to understand or recognize when a mistake is commited. Wikis allow people to write for their profit as well as for their teammates.

Portfolios have also been improved through media. Wikis help people to organize digital material and to connect them in hypertext networks.

As far as **collaborative knowledge** is concerned, groups can use wikis to create a database of shared knowledge. Therefore, they can develop a project as a group, can work a small part of a class project and can maintain the website of the course.

In **research coordination and cooperation**, wikis allow people to be in different places when building a collective digital space of ideas, articles, data, documents and research results. Researchers can also use wikis as a notepad of their main ideas.

As a way to perform a **curricular and interdisciplinary coordination**, wikis allow the persons involved (professors, directors, co-workers, etc) to organize together classes, schedules, evaluation and distance coordination without the need of using books or registers.

Events coordination through web: many universities organize symposiums and congresses, scientifical and professional meetings through wikis. One advantage of using them is the ability to edit the content and layout without having much knowledge of it.

Time and project management is also important. Wikis are one of the best tools to manage a project in several fields. We will approach this subject on the next topic.

Some contexts of use will be thoroughly presented. In a recent study done by Coutinho e Bottentuit Junior (2007a), a wiki was used for the work of a master degree subject in Educational Technology at the University of Minho, in Portugal. The wiki was the repository of the class and it was built by all students that worked together on a specific topic of the subject. The final evaluation of this experiment showed how important the collaborative work was (the students had the chance to learn from their partners and consult their material) and the final product was a data repository, which can be consulted and used online by those interested in different areas.

This repository [http://claracoutinho.wikispaces.com] was also a communication method between students and professor, as comments and evaluations could be seen by all class, allowing the students to correct their mistakes and improve their contribution to collaborative knowledge (see picture 3.4).

Another context used for wikis is personal sites or class/group sites. Paulo Marques, professor of the Department of Informatics Engineering in the University of Coimbra (Portugal), uses the wiki [http://pmarques.dei.uc.pt/wiki/Paulo_Marques] as a personal site. In this wiki we are able to check

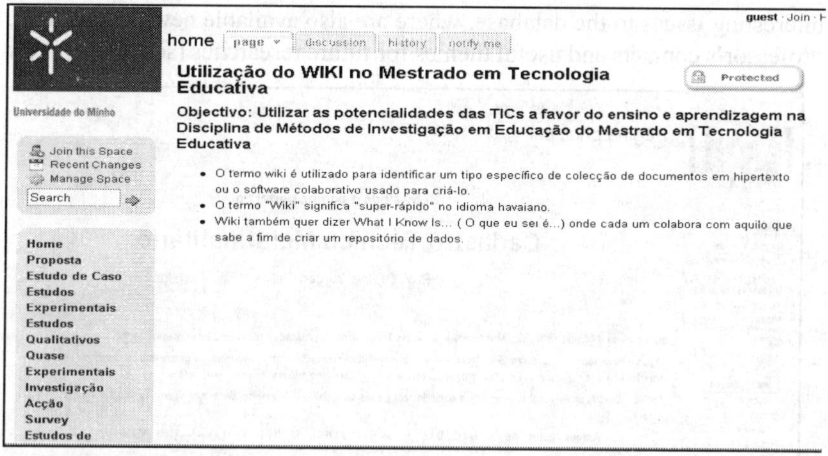

Picture 3.4: Main Page of the Wiki of a Subject

personal information, his education, professional experience, publications, projects and information about the subjects he teaches. The advantage of having a wiki is that the keywords are always hyperlinked and users can always see the updates by clicking on the botton *related changes* or through a RSS (see picture 3.5).

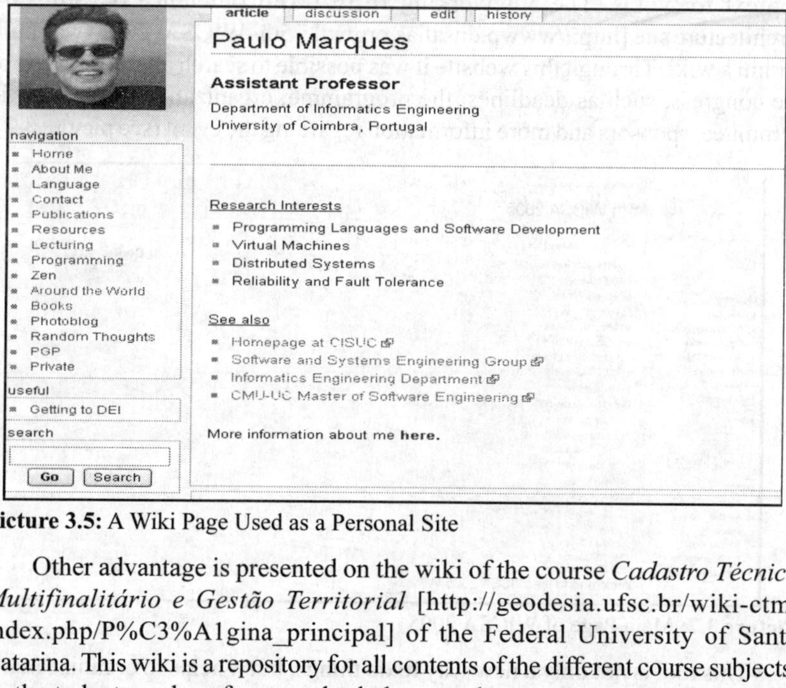

Picture 3.5: A Wiki Page Used as a Personal Site

Other advantage is presented on the wiki of the course *Cadastro Técnico Multifinalitário e Gestão Territorial* [http://geodesia.ufsc.br/wiki-ctm/index.php/P%C3%A1gina_principal] of the Federal University of Santa Catarina. This wiki is a repository for all contents of the different course subjects. Both students and professors who belong to the group can consult and add interesting issues to the database, where are also available news of that area, professor's contacts and useful themes for future researches (see picture 3.6).

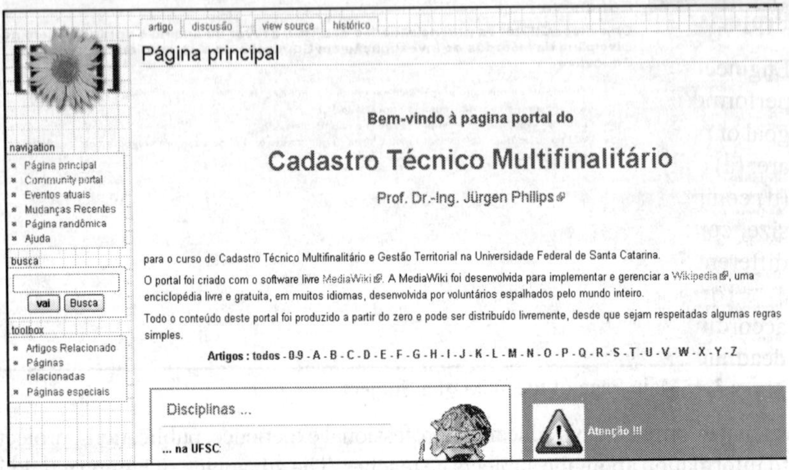

Picture 3.6: Page of a Wiki Used as a Repository

Events and congresses management, as it was already mentioned, is also a context for wikis. The 5th Working IEEE/IFIP Conference on Software Architecture site [http://wwwp.dnsalias.org/wiki/5th_WICSA_2005] was built within a wiki. Through this website it was possible to search all information of the congress, such as deadlines, the programme, organization and scientific commitee, sponsors and more information regarding the event (see picture 3.7).

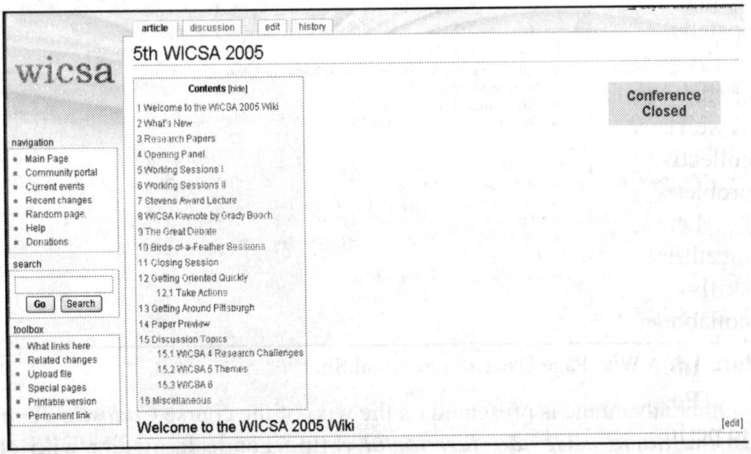

Picture 3.7: Main Page of WICSA 2005

This tool is not only a new way to do things, but it helps to organize many ideas of different groups from a company, regardless its size and number of employees. The wiki managed to have many users in many companies in such a short time, because the productivity of a department increases a lot.

Projects Management with Wikis

Engineering uses projects methodology in most of its services, as tasks are performed by a multidisciplinary group that shares its knowledge to build a goal or product. Nowadays, there are several projects within engineering, some are: (a) civil engineering; (b) research; (c) products and systems development; (d) commerce; (e) environmental impact, etc. They can also change as far as size, complexity, subject, and types of activity are concerned. They involve different groups of persons and they have a clear beginning and end.

To Brand (1998) a project is a non-repetitive, planned job performed according to specific techniques and with pre-defined costs, investments and deadlines. A project can be also defined as a complex, extensive work, which is performed with the cooperation of several departments of a company and eventually of other persons.

Team members do the project management, including power and tasks division and this should be a clear process in evaluation and observation. To accomplish it, they should use management systems for project development to record tasks division and distribution, deadlines, information register, lists from the team members, representatives and partners e-mails. Wikis are software capable of store all this data fast and in a practical way, as they offer a rich and simple environment for information management. The best things about them is the fact that they are free (open source) and allow all users to have login and passwords, making possible to secure and recover all posted contents.

A wiki system creates an interactive space, where information of engineers or students teams can be managed. It can also lead to a collaborative learning as well as to a connection between the different project levels. It promotes the collective growth of a certain matter, giving simple solutions to complex problems through a collaborative hypertext construction.

Learning or collaborative work occurs when two or more persons perform together an activity that aims to define a goal, search a theme or improve skills. For Panitz (1996) e Zañartu (2003) the elements that define a collaborative activity are:

Individual Responsibility: each person is responsible for the group work;

Positive Interdependence: each person of the group depends on the other to perform the job;

Cooperation Skills: the persons involved should learn about team work;

Promoting Interaction: interaction between the persons of the group can develop richer relationships and effective learning processes;

Group Process: periodically, it is realized the reflection and evaluation of the process to proceed the necessary changes;

The use of wikis leads to the idea of connection, as Siemens (2004, p. 1) believes *'connection is guided by the idea that decisions are based on principles that quickly change'*. Therefore, we can change already posted information, creating a new space of continuous learning through exchange of knowledge. Siemens (2004, p. 1) describes some principles of connection that are similar to wikis functionality:

- Learning and knowledge are based on several opinions.
- Learning is the process of connecting specialized persons or information sources.
- Learning can also be done through non-human's methods.
- The ability to learn more is more critical than what is actually known.
- It is necessary to create and maintain connections in order to make easier continuous learning.
- It is important to have the skill of noting connections between different areas, ideas and concepts.
- Update ('currency' — an accurate and updated knowledge) is the goal of all learning connection activities.
- To make a decision is a learning process. To choose what to learn and to understand the meaning of information is to be able to note through a changing reality. Although there is a correct answer now, this can be wrong tomorrow due to changes of the conditions that affect information and decision.

The advantages of using wikis when managing projects are the possibility to define objectives for the project and their accomplishment, allowing all participants to understand, share and approve the responsibilities along the different stages. This leads to a logical approach to planning and encourages more stricted calculations, it gives all necessary means for supervision and control, and it gives security to management by showing the control of all accomplished stages and the remaining ones.

Conclusions

Information and communication technologies along with new computer technologies have influence upon society and the education of the engineer is directly influenced by it. The inclusion of wikis in learning processes is a natural path that an engineer can take to learn in a society of knowledge.

The student, future engineer, will work in a market of social and technological change and he creates his concepts and knowledge through situations that represent his expectations and allow him to contact a technological world.

Wikis are very successful in this venture because they are simple, efficient and easy to use, learn and implement. They make the content available to the persons all the time without costs.

Although there are several softwares for project management, wikis alone can be the first choice as they are simple, with open code, which means that besides not demanding a licence payment, managers can change their layout and structure. Wikis are a cheap solution to project management, cooperation and they solve communication problems or obstacles.

4

Design and Production Engineering

Some Moving Frontiers of the Engineering Education in Brazil

Beany Guimarães Monteiro and *Roberto Bartholo*

Engineering: Design under Constraint

A recent important study of the National Academy of Engineering (2004) in the United States of America recognizes that engineering is, since its origins, 'A profoundly creative process', and suggests a very provocative definition: 'A most elegant description is that engineering is about design under constraint'.

This definition advances a significant connection in the practices of engineers and designers, which is possibly the core aspect of any education intended to correspond to the one proposed by the National Academy of Engineering: 'The engineer designs devices, components, subsystems, and systems'. That is to say, there should be a significant overlapping zone between education processes of both engineers and designers. One positive consequence, at least, from that proposition is that there is ground for a fertile interdisciplinary interaction.

According to the study of the National Academy of Engineering, the activity of an engineer is directed to the creation of 'a successful design'. Concerning the meaning of this success, the study provides important indications: 'In the sense that it leads directly or indirectly to an improvement in our quality of life and must work within the constraints provided by technical, economic, business, political, social, and ethical issues'.

Exploring the overlapping zone between the education processes of engineers and designers, we observe more than the enlargement of the technical education *stricto sensu*. Educating in this zone is not reduced to the incorporation of a bunch of technical skills (though, of course, they are relevant). This zone of interface provides the future engineer with a broader capacity of problem solving as they learn to autonomously identify, formulate and structure problems.

This chapter is focus on the meaning of this interface between engineering and design for education and a Brazilian empirical case has been, in which that interface is explored with emphasis on problems and topics of social interest.

The perspective brings up to date some provocative ideas from a classical work by the Brazilian anthropologist G. Freyre (1987), who lists different types of engineering and gives priority to social engineering, which '... is concerned more with the creation of new ways and styles of social living than with the adaptation of a social group behaviour to pre-defined norms of social living'. Similar to what occurs to the other types of engineering, Freyre claims that every social engineering project starts with a problem.

Possible importance of what is call *social interest design*, that could be identified as a work field of social engineering, as conceived by Freyre in the education process of engineers in the contemporary world is highlighted.

The study of the National Academy of Engineering denies that engineering is only about applied science and states that 'Technology is the outcome of engineering; it is rare that science translates directly to technology, just as it is not true that engineering is just applied science' (*op. cit.*). It is clear that some components and processes are characteristic of engineering and technology.

What is critical in contemporary world, however, is that 'Innovations are occurring at an astonishing pace, especially those in information and communications technology, which are most apparent to the public, and this has important implications for engineering practice and engineering education in the future.' (in National Academy of Engineering, op. cit).

This text is intended to indicate innovative possibilities in the engineers' education process. It is understood that the interface engineering/design, (and more specifically production engineering/*social interest design*) opens those possibilities. Design enables the actualisation of ideas, making them concretely available in their diverse possibilities. Social interest in turn concerns the inter-human space, where there are asymmetric reciprocities determined by will, knowledge and power. That evokes the relational nature of human condition, which is not only technically but also, and mainly, ethically shaped (Bartholo, 2003).

The recommendations of the National Academy of Engineering (2005) are that 'Technical excellence is *the* essential attribute of engineering graduates, but those graduates should also possess team, communication, ethical reasoning, and societal and global contextual analysis skills as well as understand work strategies'.

Thus the study of the National Academy of Engineering (2005a) aims at 'reengineering' the engineering education system, but without losing 'The essence of engineering: the iterative process of designing, predicting performance, building, and testing', which 'should be taught from the earliest stages of the curriculum, including the first year'.

Here the perspective is in agreement with those recommendations so that 'The engineering education establishment should strengthen the ties binding engineering education to practice not only through curricular design and provision of co-curricular activities, but through the experiences of engineering faculty in industrial research, product design, and/or production' (National Academy of Engineering, 2005b).

It is argued that *social interest design* is a fertile field for the integration of pedagogic experiences of designers and engineers' education processes. The Brazilian case presented corroborates that view: the academic cooperation between the Programme of Production Engineering of COPPE/UFRJ and the Department of Industrial Design of the Fine Arts of UFRJ with initiatives in teaching, research and extension.

Social Interest Design: A Possible Interface between Production Engineering and Industrial Design

In a special edition of the *Journal of Design Research* the professor of the Engineering School of MIT, L. Bucciarelli (1996), claims that the issue of *design as a social process* should be approached with special emphasis on how social values and norms have consequences in choices and specifications of product form and functioning. The proposal of a *social interest design* seems to be in agreement with Bucciarelli's approach.

The *social interest design* is linked to an ethical commitment and a cognitive intention: a situated practice of design and the rooting of the different kinds of knowledge in their *original symbolic sites* both converging on the consolidation and enlargement of the cultural and relational human heritage (Zaoual, 2005; Zaoual, 1999). Because of that and because of the priority ascribed to the alterity and vulnerability, it is possible to refer social interest to ethical commitment and responsibility.

Our theoretical conceptions are based on a reference framework that understands design as a reflexive practice and highlights it as an element of dialogue between designers and the project context. Situating a problem is a process in which one aims at a question and its context is framed according to the intention. Considering this perspective, a good design process may be understood as a reflexive dialogue with the situation, according Schön (1983).

To Cross (1999), drawing is an important tool of the natural design process, but the understanding of this importance in design constitution and essence has only recently become a subject of inquiry in researches about design. Drawing, or a set of drawings, is necessary to provide a model of the object, product. In Renaissance, some of Leonardo da Vinci' s projects show that drawing is not only an important tool of communication, but also a tool to express free thought, reasoning and cognitive process. By allowing representing many design aspects at once, the sketch allows the dialogue of those aspects in the drawing and in their conception.

Zaoual (1999), opposing the universalising pretension of inherent criteria to homo economicus' instrumental rationality with homo situs' valorative, substantial and situated rationality, following his concept of bio-cultural rooting in original symbolic sites, states that each problem a community faces will have an unpredicted and unexpected development. This unpredictability is the result of people's creative action. It follows that, as a corollary, human development as situated development will be intrinsically plural, and the existence of diversity is the most significant index of the fact that alterity is preserved and corroborated as an ethical value.

Buber (1982) believes that human development, seen as the happening of novelties brought by ruptures, is not determined by any constraint of the future, which would make the present the result of an 'inverted prophecy'. Our futures are non-deterministic possibilities. That is why they are relative to our present ethically responsible acts. Given this perspective, the insecurity resulting from the acceptance of a radical unpredictability of the possible futures is replaced by the security of the possible pacts agreed in the inter-human space: solidarity, commitment and friendship of interpersonal and community relational attachments.

In sum, the proposal of a Social Interest Design points to the necessity of recovering the capacity of forming and establishing relational attachments of solidarity, in a social reality where the predominance is fragmentation, individualism and consumerism. That recovery can be enhanced by our creativity, making the impossible possible. The implications are that we will not be deluded by the authority's argument that things must continue to be the way they are and that we will be able to recognize that correction and success are only instrumental criteria, always preceded and surpassed by criteria of ethical and valorative commitment to Good, Beauty, Truth and Justice.

The connection of the engineer's education process to the practice of *social interest design* leads to the articulation of various experiences and competences in an intra-university level and in an extra-university level (i.e. between the university and groups of interest). This dialogical opening to other knowledge areas can be significant for the communicative dimension of the engineer's education process, emphasized in the study of the National Academy of Engineering: 'A strategy for realigning engineering education must be developed within the contexts of understanding the elements of engineering and recognizing the importance of constant communication with the public and engineering community stakeholders on the goals of education' (National Academy of Engineering, 2005b].

The interface *production engineering/social interest design* may contribute to move frontiers of knowledge in contemporary engineering, towards the multiplication of information in systematized fields of knowledge. Besides, it may contribute to redefine *constraints.* That is a strategic question for the pedagogic project of the engineer's education, if we take into account the possibility of learning relations renewing the capacity of dialogue and intervention in reality. This effort may be optimised by a *co-design activity*, similar to what Manzini and Vezzoli (2002) suggest. This means the formulation of theoretical frames and a dialogical perspective on research and projects, establishing relational ties between interlocutors; which goes beyond merely instrumental relations with objects of knowledge and experimentation.

The *social interest design* is accomplished in *co-design*, thanks to the fact that designers have their responsibilities based not only on considerations about technique or form, but also, and primarily, on ethical judgements about methodologies (Papaneck, 1973). In this perspective, the first thought must be if the projects or products deserve attention. For engineers and designers to be able to make that evaluation, it is essential to include this ability in their education.

However, *social interest design* is still about design. And we believe that *drawing* is a critical element playing an important role in this mediated pedagogic process (Cross, *op. cit.*). In this process, *drawing* has a double role. Firstly it assists in problem structuring through the solutions it brings to light; secondly it allows a concise recognition of the characteristics and properties of a certain solution. Those processes of solution structuring and construction are in a very significant way mediated by the *drawing of sketches* that enable interaction between different stakeholders.

In a research about clothing design, the design of the pilot piece can be understood analogously to Illich (2002) thinks the alphabet as an intellectual technology that has its applications optimized by instrumental technologies: parchment, paper and press. In the same way instrumental technologies such as CAD—*Computer Aided Design*—optimise the production of various artefacts (Monteiro, 2004).

In this analogy, it is important to say that neither press nor CAD promotes or creates the critical rupture; they optimise it. This rupture occurs primarily in the immaterial plan, in the conception of the text or of the pilot piece; they are immaterial technologies. The interpretation and translation of design into artefacts can be considered implications of the intellectual technology generated in the conception, development and fabrication of the product (Monteiro, *op. cit.*). And in this context, designers bring creation, visualization and communication instruments and act as mediators of several stakeholders, working on solutions with them, who know their own reality, co-designing (Manzini, 2007). Designers' position in this analysis is in the ethical judgement of methodologies and in the choice of what kind of well-being they want to promote. For that, they must use and promote the use of adequate instruments. (Silva, 2007). According Manzini (2007),

> 'The idea of well-being is a social construct: it takes shape over time according to a variety of factors. The idea of well-being dominant today in the west and widely diffused throughout the world was born with the industrial revolution. It has changed with the evolution of society and now appears as an articulate set of visions, expectations and assessment criteria which undergo continuous adaptation, but with a persistent common characteristic: that of linking expected and perceived well-being with the availability of a growing quantity of products and services.
>
> Today we know that this idea of well-being leads to an intrinsically unsustainable consumption of environmental resources. We know that because of this, given the limits of our planet, this way of thinking and consequently behaving must change over the coming years. In fact, we can see today that in many ways this change is already happening and that other ideas of well-being are emerging. The timing and the way in which this transformation process will come about are, however, still a completely open question. Faced with this transformation, our common problem — that is the problem for the entire worldwide community — is to facilitate a change that can take place in the least dramatic way possible. Our common design aspiration is, or should be, to foster conditions such that this can come about from choice and not from necessity. In other words: by the attraction of new opportunities and new ideas of well-being, rather than under the force of catastrophic events'.

In the next section we talk about the empirical case, consequence of the particular cooperation between LTDS—Laboratory of Technology and Social Development (Production Engineering, COPPE/UFRJ) and LIDIS—Interdisciplinary Laboratory of Social Interest Design (Industrial Design, EBA/UFRJ).

A Case of Cooperation between Engineering and Design in the Federal University of Rio De Janeiro

The Graduate Programme of Production Engineering (COPPE/UFRJ) is presently organized in three areas or research lines: Management and Innovation (GI); Operational Research (PO); and Evaluation of Industrial and Technological Projects (APIT). GI is the most connected to *design;* it has incorporated the old area of concentration, Product Engineering, in which most of the activities in the interface engineering/design of the graduate programme were accomplished since the beginning of the programme. GI develops studies related to the processes of innovation, dissemination and implementation of technological changes in several economic sectors (manufacturing and services). The techno-methodological perspective of this area is solidly founded on multidisciplinary approaches. GI curriculum includes the following disciplines: Project, Product and Process Development; Information Engineering; Strategic Studies; Social Initiative Management, etc.

The course of Industrial Design of the Fine Arts School (DI/EBA/UFRJ) sees the professional activity of Industrial Design as the creation, analysis and development of formal concepts of industrial products. According to this conception, the professional works with design methods and specifications that optimise the function, value and appearance of the product, for the mutual benefit of producer and user, and respect for the environment. This course offers two qualifications: Product Project and Visual Programming. Students choose one of them at the moment they enrol in the selective process. The qualification 'Product Project' has the objective of providing a solid basic education in the area of Industrial Design, so that students are able to evaluate and define the user/object relations through the mastering of project techniques, bidimensional technical representation, physical model construction and electronic mock-ups, besides the knowledge about industrial processes of fabrication. The qualification 'Visual Programming' has the objective of preparing the professional that will work in the following areas:

System in Design, Photo Design, Interactive Hypermedia Design and Narrative Illustration.

The laboratories LTDS and LIDIS are developing a tight academic cooperation. This cooperation results in activities of teaching, research and extension, whose main objectives are shortly described below.

The *Creative Communities and Sustainable Lifestyles—CCSL* (Meroni, 2007) project intends to investigate practices of social innovation in communities and their implications for the promotion of sustainable life styles in several contemporary urban contexts. The structure of the project is a collection of case studies, from different contexts. Existent experiences in the European Union are compared with cases in three developing countries (Brazil, India and China). The project is not limited to a simple identification and collection of significant experiences, though it is aimed at discussing the possibilities and conditions for the implementation of the original formulation in a way that the original experiences be significant in different contexts. Learning with these experiences of social innovation may contribute to the dissemination of sustainable life styles in the contemporary world.

The CCSL project was developed by Ezio Manzini from the Polytechnic (Milan) and François Jégou from Strategic Design Scenarios (Brussels). It is an initiative of *Task Force on Sustainable Lifestyles,* linked to multilateral cooperation programmes of the United Nations, members of the *10 Year Framework of Programmes on Sustainable Consumption and Production*, commonly known as *Marrakech Process*. In the frameworks of the CCSL project, four similar scenario-building exercises are being held in Brazil, China, Europe and India with groups of students from different local design schools.

In Brazil the local partner in the CCSL project is LTDS, which has been working in interaction with LIDIS. An integrated work group was composed of graduating students in Design (DI/EBA), Master's students in Production Engineering (PEP/COPPE) and *stakeholders* from the initiatives considered relevant to the project. Professors from LTDS and LIDIS also participated actively in the CCSL project.

The activities of this work group unfolded in three scenarios with different foci: *food, neighbourhood and co-housing.* The elaboration of these scenarios are based on the composition of a *storyboard,* with concise text, visual schemes and a panel with photos of a certain initiative, all inserted in a *blog*. For the photographs to be taken, sketches of the most characteristic scenes of each scenario are done. These sketches become a reference for the participants of each scenario to develop their own storyboard. Sketches play a key role in communicating the most representative ideas of each scenario and in organizing the scenarios. They are essential elements for the integration of the stakeholders participating in the project. Possible implications of the elaboration of these scenarios:

- Generate initiatives and projects aiming at the development of sustainable products and services, with focus on the local reality.
- Identify the social, interpersonal and human relations, which enable the sustainable solutions.
- Identify conditions that may make the implementation of these initiatives in other sites possible.
- Identify the urgent conditions of these initiatives, in relation to the basic concepts of the CCSL project, which are:
  (i) creative communities;
  (ii) Sustainable life styles;
  (iii) Social innovation.

For the development of creative solutions in the process of scenario-oriented Design, sketches gain the role of a project tool. This role, which is in the origins of Industrial Design teaching, had lost some space for computer tools of project support, such as CAD (Computer Aided Design). With those computer resources, students resist or have difficulties to express their ideas with sketches. Thus, the methodology proposed by the scenario-oriented Design leads to the return of sketches in the attempt of creative solutions. CAD is a finished tool and its functions are organized in packages that correspond to the project phases and to the project commercial rates. As the development of sustainable solutions is realized in a specific situation, those packages are not useful; it is necessary to visualize the idea in the situation. That is why sketches are such a valuable means of communication: the ability to express ideas through sketches means the possibility of improvising situated responses. It does not mean drawing as an art piece (which would require a higher level of qualification from the designer), but as a means of expression and communication, which implies that the ability of drawing is a requisite almost as universal as the verbal communication. These are the results obtained from the participation of under-graduate students in Design and graduate students in Engineering in the CCSL project:

- a higher capacity of response to the matters of the situation;
- A more skilful creative expression due to the enlargement of communicative resources.

The attachment of LTDS and LIDIS to the CCSL project has implications for the teaching activities in the graduate courses of production engineering (mainly for the Master's course) and also for the design graduating course of EBA. That not only concerns the direct participation of students in work groups such as the one mentioned in this article. It also concerns the internalisation of learning and products from the different phases of the project into disciplines of the curriculum (such as Ergonomics, Product Project, Management and Methods in Design) and the elaboration of final works and Master's dissertations in the thematic areas open by the project.

As a logic result, a new research line is being developed, integrating vertically graduating and graduate activities in the Federal University of Rio de Janeiro in the area of *strategic design, design for sustainability, and design for social innovation, with a focus on scenario building and solution development.*

This initiative is in agreement with the priority given by the Brazilian government to the generation of human resources and the promotion of *design as a strategic sector for the Brazilian development.* That priority is attributed by the agencies of research promotion and support of the Ministry of Education and Ministry of Science and Technology, through their policy on science, technology, innovation and industrial development.

The theoretical-methodological perspective of that research line is according to the ideas of Professor Ezio Manzini from the Polytechnic of Milan, once it assumes that 'Design strategies address the pressing issue of the culture of consumption and require thinking beyond 'the product' (Manzini, 2002). At this point it becomes important to consider a number of 'leapfrog' strategies and product-service systems that suggest ways of achieving welfare, which does not necessarily involve material, tangible products. These strategies demand innovative design thinking with the ability to confront and overcome cultural and economic norms. The exercise of building scenarios and the development of solutions are supported by the images, which play a central role in the interaction of designers, production engineers and other stakeholders. These images usually do not exist and need to be created and developed. In this process, design gets pedagogic and communicative relevance by expressing ideas, identifying problems and solutions through graphic representation.

An important consequence of the activities promoted by the partnership between LTDS and LIDIS is the coming of Professor Ezio Manzini to Brazil in the second semester of 2007, sponsored by the School Programme of High Studies of the governmental agency Coordination for Improvement of Higher Education Personnel (CAPES) of the Ministry of Education. During his visit, Professor Ezio Manzini will offer a graduate course in PEP-COPPE, open to other Brazilian design and production engineering graduate courses, thanks to resources of distance education mediated by computer.

The course *Design, Social Innovation and Sustainable Development* to be given by Professor Ezio Manzini has two objectives.

To give the participants the opportunity to have a theoretical and practical insight in the strategic design tools, as they are implied in promoting social innovation in everyday life.

To increase the participants' capability to recognize promising cases of social innovation and develop enabling solutions in order to enhance these cases and promote their consolidation and dissemination.

The course will have two modules. The first one has a theoretical standpoint and establishes guidelines to identify promising cases of social innovation for sustainable development. The second one focuses on the discussion about some cases gathered by the participants in the meantime between the two modules. The second module aims at formulating intervention projects along the lines of design-oriented scenario building. The chapters' contents are articulated in 5 steps.

Sustainability: Systemic change and social learning process. The transition towards sustainability will be a social learning process thanks to which human beings will learn how to live well, consuming far fewer environmental resources and regenerating the quality of the contexts, in which they happen to live. To do that a systemic change is needed at both the global and the local scale.

Ways of Living: Product-based and context-based well-being. The idea of well-being, the traditional, unsustainable product-based well-being, is changing. A new idea, defined as access-based well-being is emerging. Unfortunately, this new vision on well-being, as it is appearing now, is even more unsustainable than the old one. The on-going change has to be changed and re-oriented towards the search for a well-being based on the qualities of the whole context of life.

Social Innovation: Creative communities and diffused social enterprise. Contemporary society emits different, contradictory signals. Among these are the very promising ones of groups of people inventing sustainable ways of living. Some of the practical ideas produced by creative communities consolidate and last in time. Some of them are reproduced in other contexts. All of them have to be considered as experimentations of possible futures.

Emerging Scenarios: Active well-being and distributed economies. Today, creative communities and diffused social enterprises are minorities. Nevertheless, a closer view shows that they are linked to powerful drivers of change. Considering these links, their real potentialities emerge and a new scenario appears: the scenario of the multi-local society, based on a new sense of place and on the ideas of active well being and distributed economies.

Enabling Systems: Bottom-up, top-down and peer-to-peer interactions. Creative communities and diffused social enterprises are complex and delicate social organizations. For this reason their origin and their existence cannot be planned. But something can be done to make them more probable. A favourable environment can be generated. Supporting services, products, spaces and communication tools can be designed.

Design and Social Innovation Virtual Institute — IVIS

As a consequence of these projects and considering the experience of LTDS with the theme, the Design and Social Innovation Virtual Institute — IVIS — was founded. The IVIS is a virtual space for the discussion and construction of proposals relative to social innovation in Brazil. That is an initiative of researchers from different areas and universities of the country, connected by a virtual platform of collaborative communication. With this tool (the virtual platform), the Institute discusses the role of design in the process of social innovation, by means of the formulation of a methodology committed to the situated and sustainable development.

The first step of this initiative is to elaborate a methodology of collection and understanding of social innovation practical cases in the Brazilian context, constantly feeding back to the concerned theoretical reflection.

The IVIS was the result of discussions held throughout the Seminar of Design, Social Innovation and Sustainable Development, promoted by the Programme of Production Engineering of COPPE/UFRJ with the support of the School of High Studies of CAPES, in September 2007. In this meeting researchers from several universities discussed the methodology, presented by Professor Ezio Manzini about creative communities and sustainable life styles, and showed interest in exploring this view under the Brazilian perspective. Since then, efforts started to converge on the creation of a virtual platform that allowed discussions to continue independently of in-person meetings.

Then, based on the previous experience on 'moderation' of the Tourism Virtual Institute— IVT, the Social Development and Technology Laboratory— LTDS—of the Programme of Production Engineering of COPPE/UFRJ organized the necessary infrastructure so that more than eight institutions permanently collaborated in the understanding of social innovation in Brazil.

As several studies show, Manzini's and Jégou's stand out, the decisions made at project fase have consequences amplified by mass production. The well-being, according to Manzini (2007), was understood in the historical process of society development as if less work (physical and mental demand) to man equaled greater well-being. However, this logic perpetuates the dissociation of man from his participation/role in the construction of his context of life. It promotes an impersonal, fragile well-being of product-based solutions that legitimize consumerism as an answer to most of the problems and accentuates the social inequality when restricts the accessibility of actors to resources (natural ones, information, work, values, culture, products, services). That way disintegrates relationship values, which aggravates the deconstruction of social fabric. The result, therefore, in an unsustainable society, is that more and more the reversion of the state of inequality is not feasible. That reality is showing to be opposite to the establishment of a real and solid well-being.

The designer has a potential competence to promote the active well-being in which the actor becomes an active agent of the construction of his/her context of life, localized in his/her original symbolic sites. Changes in how people organize themselves and communicate point to the appearance of a context more propitious to social innovation that enables the active well-being. And in this new context, the designer brings creation, visualization and communication instruments, and acts like a mediator of actors, co-working with these actors connoisseurs of their own reality, co-designing, according Manzini (2007).

The designer-role in this analysis is in the ethical judgement of methodologies and in the choice of which well-beign he/she wants to promote for that the designer must utilize and promote the use of proper instruments Papaneck (1973).

The cases of Creative Communities demonstrate that a project can multiply positive experiences. However, there are differences not yet clarified between national and international cases. Such diversity needs to be studied so that the Creative Communities can be correctly identified and replicated. Here, once again, the badly executed designer's work on the identification of a case can have catastrophic dimensions when reproduced numerous times. It must be assured that the case promotes a sustainable lifestyle (Silva, 2007).

The goal of IVIS is, therefore, to look for, in a dialogic discussion between people, these differences that characterize and differentiate the cases of Brazilian reality from international ones.

Design and Innovation for Popular Entrepreneurship

The partnership between LTDS and LIDIS also has important consequences in university extension projects, which may use design in popular entrepreneurships. The developed extension projects respond to the demand of the popular entrepreneurs.

The actions of the partnership LTDS and LIDIS are founded on the intellectual technology generated in the conception and production of artifacts of different production chains (such as handicraft, clothing manufacture, art, culture and leisure). This intellectual technology exists to support the development of new products, value aggregation to existent products, work and income generation, and the intensification of design use in other popular entrepreneurships.

The activities developed include:

- Mapping and classification of popular entrepreneurships in incubators of Rio de Janeiro according to the type of entrepreneurship, business plan and estimated return (income generation and personal satisfaction).
- Organization of Innovation Workshops about the process of artifact development: inspiration sources; colours and shapes; materials and fabrication processes; finishing; wrapping; representation techniques; work exposition and presentation; product certification and registration.
- Planning, organization and promotion of public events to show the activities developed in these Workshops, in order to stimulate the interaction between them and the community.

Its purpose is to give the entrepreneurs who are at incubation period, the role of co-designers of its own business. This requires the construction of enabling tools of a possible and desirable vision of future for this entrepreneurship, and enabling systems, through services, products, spaces and tools of communication as support.

Design and Innovation is organized in fourteen design workshops, which have a characteristic theme related to the productive chains, defined together with the entrepreneurs, by whom shared strategies and partnerships are identified. These strategies and partnerships are organized in scenarios and worked relative to each entrepreneurship. The three last workshops are turned to organization and implementation of a public event.

In this first edition the target public was constituted of entrepreneurs from the productive chains of Culture, Gastronomy and Tourism, and Service.

The four workshops of module 1 were organized based on a survey of the main activities of the productive chain and entrepreneurship, in an analysis of the main problems and differentials, with focus on developed products and services. Their main objectives were to develop a perception of the culture surrounding and in interaction with the entrepreneurs and a critical view about the present conditions, as the first step to promote the capacity of contributing to the cultural valorization and recovery and of visualizing promising potential strategies. From that attempt was made to construct a platform of values to formulate a vision of future possibilities: exploring solutions and strategies, based on visual elements, scenarios.

Modules 2 and 3 (seven workshops) aimed at assisting the creation and development of contextualized strategies in order to help entrepreneurs to optimize their contacts with partners, favouring synergies between entrepreneurs and partner institutions, in the offer of specific activities and enabling systems for their entrepreneurship.

In module 4 (three workshops) attempt was made to identify, for each emergent strategy, the promising partners that could contribute to its accomplishment. This process revealed the potentialities and resources in the place (people, organizations and institutions rooted in the territory) as well as potential external partners. The process of partnership construction consists in analysing potential partners and plans, their participation in the planned strategies. The groups of entrepreneurs organize a partially autonomous net, in which some connections derive from the institutional net of the incubator, but some others emerge from the context. That is a community-oriented process, so the methodological structure and tools reflect the premises of finding partnerships and solutions next to the group, reinforcing existent or potential connections with the group community.

Each group of emergent ideas from modules 1, 2 and 3 constitute a structure for a scenario. A scenario pre-suposes more than a visual synthesis of what emerges with the instrument of future description; it subsumes the interpretation of the results. This task is performed by the designer (Penin, 2006).

To draw these scenarios, the instruments proposed by Penin (2006) were used. The instruments of present description are highlighted. Their objective is to describe and analyze the focus-activity of the productive chain and establish the relevant aspects for the project. This instrument is attached to a recovery of the cultural origins of the entrepreneurship and to a consolidation of the business identity. The second instrument is of future description and strategy clusters. These instruments introduce questions to stimulate a profound description of aspirations, identifying them with elements lost in day-by-day reality in the attempt to accomplish the imposed aspirations. The answers to these questions start by setting the strategies of the group of entrepreneurs, outlining the scenario structures. The next step is to identify, for each emergent strategy, the promising partners that can contribute to its accomplishment. This process reveals the potentialities and resources in the place (people, organizations and institutions rooted in the territory) as well as potential external partners. A colour code is introduced to differentiate the potential category of partners: institutions, associations and groups, individual and private initiatives. The result of the instrument of Future Description is a series of experimental strategies and potential partners derived from these strategies, to be discussed collectively and in groups according to a theme in a separate board: Group of Strategical Instruments.

The potential partners identified in the *Scenario Construction* are mapped according to their proximity with the community: resources present in the context that may be connected to the initiative, in a deliberate effort to maximize connections with members of local communities, identifying potential partners in the context; and their *categories*: individuals, associations and groups (third sector), institutions (public administration, schools and universities) and private initiative.

Then, each potential partnership is categorized according to its related aspect of the strategy: production, commercialization, internal organization, vocational education and training, and communication. At last, the potential partners are classified according to the priority the partnership represents for the strategy. This process also helps to understand the sequencial steps necessary to reach the established goals.

The study of scenarios, from a shared theme, makes it possible for the entrepreneur himself/herself to bring up his/her own theme proposal—a very important step for the perception of one's capacity of making changes. The co-design process favours a better relationship between entrepreneur and his/her business, the process of incubation and his/her professional acting, modifying traditional concepts of marketing and design. It permits the perception of an active role in improving his/her entrepreneurship, as well as his/her daily life and favours synergy between different initiatives from other entrepreneurships at different stages of the incubation process. Finally, that augments the designer acting field and favours the access of popular entrepreneurship to design.

Conclusions

In this chapter an experience in engineering teaching is presented, developed in the Federal University of Rio de Janeiro, and interpret it taking as a theoretical reference the framework presented by the National Academy of Engineering of the United States of America, concerning its prospective studies about engineers' education.

Considering the provocative proposition of the study of the National Academy of Engineering that *engineering is about design under constraint*, attempt has been made to highlight the interface between production engineering and design in engineers and designers' education processes. It is claimed that design plays a pedagogic role (particularly the *sketches*), by allowing the visualization and communicative expression of theoretical propositions. Not intending to transform engineers into designers; our proposal is to make them familiar with the use of this tool as an element of communicative mediation and idea visualization in interactions between different professionals and stakeholders.

It is observed that the Design students who participated in the Creative Communities for Life Styles project and who had access to the scenario-based methodology, during the project discipline in the course of Industrial Design in the School of Fine Arts, developed independent and more creative solutions than those who were guided by traditional project methodologies. The authors believe that those traditional methodologies ascribe to the teacher a prescriptive role of telling students what they have to do. Conversely, because the proposed methodology is the result of a personal research of each student, it provides him or her with a commitment to the solutions of their project in a way they become responsible for it. The propositions were corroborated by the students' recent performance in projects of scientific initiation during the school year of 2006/2007.

These activities of university extension have as main partners the Popular Entrepreneurship Incubator and the Afro-Brazilian Incubator (IA) of the Palmares Institute of Human Rights (IPDH). The interaction of the work groups of LTDS and LIDIS with the facilities of IA encompass the following productive chains:

- commerce and services;
- clothing manufacture;
- tourism;
- handicraft;
- art and culture;
- gastronomy;
- marketing and social service.

Another important partnership is with the Incubator of Popular Entrepreneurship (IEP) of the city of Nova Iguaçu, in the metropolitan area of Grande Rio.

The meeting and dialogue with the partners were fundamental to elicit expectations and demands to be considered in the definition of the Innovation Workshops, organized around the following suggested themes:

(i) artifact creation and development,
(ii) inspiration sources,
(iii) colours and shapes,
(iv) product and process development,
(v) wrappings,
(vi) visual identification and
(vii) certification.

The Innovation Workshops have their own dynamic in each productive chain. To understand these activities, field observations are conducted, followed by photograph taking, filming and recorded interviews. The observation of each activity is based on the elaboration of visual schemes. The sketches drawn in A4 paper representing the main points of each entrepreneurship serve as a map to guide the observations of these field activities.

The horizon of expectations open by the extension activities of LTDS and LIDIS is concentrated on the conjoined development of solutions adequate to product presentation; difference making; market expansion; product and work valorisation; and the internalisation of knowledge of design as a strategic element in the incubation of entrepreneurships.

In the extension activities developed by LTDS and LIDIS association, Innovation Workshops are an active exercise of *co-design*. These workshops enhance *situated innovation*, rooted in the popular culture. They also underlie the production of an instructional material that, supported by the communicative resources of *e-learning*, can be additional help in the consolidation, autonomy and auto-organization of a series of entrepreneurships of social interest. In this way they contribute to the situated and sustainable development, following the guidelines in Manzini (2002).

Finally, the Brazilian case presented illustrated the opinion that the moving frontiers in the engineering education should not only be understood as an expansion of activities under the same fixed constraints. Moving frontiers in the engineering education should mean primarily changes in those constraints.

5

The Contribution of Socrates Thematic Networks to Mutual Recognition of Engineering Study Programmes Across Europe

Claudio Borri, Elisa Guberti and *Francesco Maffioli*

Every year, hundreds of thousands of people in Europe take the opportunity to study abroad or work on European projects supported by the SOCRATES Programme of the Directorate General (DG) Education, Audiovisual and Culture (EAC) of the European Commission. ERASMUS is the higher education Action of SOCRATES II programme, as well as of the Lifelong Learning Programme as it is denominated for the next period (2007-2013). It seeks to enhance the quality and reinforce the European dimension of higher education by encouraging transnational cooperation between universities, boosting European mobility and improving the transparency and full academic recognition of studies and qualifications throughout the European Union.

SOCRATES—ERASMUS

In this framework Thematic Networks (TN for short from now on) are one of the main innovations of the Socrates-Erasmus programme. They were created to promote forward-looking, strategic reflection on the scientific, educational and institutional issues in the main fields of higher education. Generally speaking, a Thematic Network is a co-operation between departments of higher education institutions and other partners (e.g. academic organisations and/or professional bodies), with the main aim to identify how to enhance quality and to define and develop a European dimension within a given academic discipline or study area. Alternatively, it can take up a topic of an interor multidisciplinary nature, or other matters of common interest, such as university management or quality assurance. Co-operation within Thematic Networks is expected to lead to outcomes which will have a lasting and widespread impact on universities across Europe in the field concerned.

Thematic Networks in Engineering Education and Their Contributions

So far as Engineering Education (EE for short from now on) is concerned several TNs have been operational during the last decade. Here the characteristics of three of these projects, investigating themes of transversal interest for the whole of EE, whereas other TNs have been targeted only to specific branches of EE (e.g. Civil Egnineering, Computer Engineering, Agricultural Engineering) has been outlined. These three projects are: H3E2, E43 and TREE4.

H3E Thematic Network (Higher Engineering Education for Europe) 1998-2000

The aim of H3E, a Thematic Network active in the period 1998-2000, has been that of contributing to the development of a European Dimension within Higher Engineering Education through reflections and actions. This work has been carried out in co-operation among Engineering Education Institutions' and Students' associations in order to:

(a) Put forward the common elements that existed across European Higher Engineering Education Systems in the following six main challenging areas:
   - Motivation for Higher Engineering Studies
   - Types and Forms of Higher Engineering Education and Core Curricula
   - Quality Assurance and Mutual Recognition
   - Internationalisation
   - Educational Methods to foster Life-long learning
   - Continuing Education

(b) Act in favour of a co-ordinated approach in facing future challenges.

(c) Support the following specific case studies likely to bring added value and enrich the work carried out in connection with points above.
   - JEEP Teams—Joint European Engineering Project Teams
   - Pie—Plastics in Engineering
   - Protect—ProTecT Consortium: Technical Textiles.

For instance, so far as the 'Quality Assurance and Mutual Recognition' theme is concerned (see point a. above), it is well known that there is a wide range of types and forms of Engineering Education in Europe. This is so both within any individual nation and between the various European countries. Moreover, practices on quality assurance and on the recognition of qualifications also vary greatly between countries.

The Working Group (WG) of H3E on 'Quality Assurance and Mutual

Recognition' investigated how far it is possible to classify, into a relatively small number of basic types, the various curricula and schemes of tertiary professional training. The declared aim was that of facilitating mutual recognition (more than what was usual at that moment): this WG of the H3E project seeked to catalyse the interaction of the many bodies involved. One of the results of the work was also a proposal for a European system of accreditation of EE and suggestions on how it could be implemented in practice.

E4 Thematic Network (Enhancing Engineering Education in Europe) 2000-2004

Given the interest of the European Engineering Education Community in the topics approached by H3E it was considered strategic to go on with a new Thematic Network which was active in the period 2000-2004. The new project was named E4 (Enhancing Engineering Education in Europe) and was managed from its very beginning by an Executive Bureau formed by the authors of this paper.

Among all TN projects approved and running under SOCRATES II, E4 offered a wide perspective over all Engineering/Technology education fields covering relevant and transversal issues, deliberately chosen to be not branch specific. Innovative contributions to international dimension and curriculum development, high standards, quality insurance and accreditation, use of ICT tools were the main topics of interest and were articulated into the following five Activities of E4:

1. Employability through innovative curricula;
2. Quality assessment and transparency for enhanced mobility and trans-European recognition;
3. Engineering professional development for Europe;
4. Enhancing the European dimension;
5. Innovative learning and teaching methods.

In particular Activity 2 (Quality Assessment and Transparency for Enhanced Mobility and trans-European Recognition) was targeted to a key issue, essential for the development of the European dimension of engineering education, from the point of view of all stakeholders (academia, enterprises, students, Society): namely, the way and means to enhance recognition throughout Europe, with the main aim to ensure employability and (physical and virtual) mobility of engineers.

In order to let the great diversity of educational systems throughout Europe to be an asset for, and not an obstacle to recognition, the stress was shifted from requirements on the curriculum to requirements on the 'competences' of the graduates. As a prerequisite, each educational institution had to complete information on itself and strive for the maximum transparency. In many European countries, this is already ensured by Quality Assurance procedures, suggested (or imposed) to EE institutions in order to validate the learning opportunities they offer; and supported by Quality Assessment bodies, managed by the competent Ministry and/or by professional associations

The development of lists of 'Qualification Attributes' to measure the competencies of each 'type' of engineer, and the generalization of 'Quality Assurance' procedures will make the issue of Trans-European recognition of courses and degrees, also for professional purposes, much simpler to tackle.

In parallel, the development of a European permanent 'Observatory' of these assessment bodies (ESOEPE: European Standing Observatory for the Engineering Profession and Education[5]) helped to provide a path to a smooth form of 'accreditation' through mutual trust and bilateral agreements.

As already anticipated, Activity 2 of E4 TN relied and capitalised on the work already done by Working Group 2 of H3E, trying to move gradually towards a more experimental phase.

The first commitment of A2 was that of being actively present in ESOEPE, the Standing Observatory which resulted from the contacts established by WG2 of H3E also outside the Academic world through the two European Workshops on Assessment of Engineering Programmes (EWAEP1: The Hague, 3-5 December 1998; EWAEP2: Paris, 17-19 June 1999).

The other immediate commitment of A2 was that of updating and extending the state-of-the-art Report of WG2 of H3E. The three Chapters of Volume B of the set of six volumes collecting the results of E4, constitute three independent (albeit correlated) documents.

These three documents (and all other E4 documents) needed to rely on a Glossary of the most important terms in higher education, to clarify and standardise their use by E4. The A2 group was very active in the preparation of such a tool. As matter of fact the E4 Glossary has become a well known reference document for the EE community in Europe and has continued to evolve within the successor of E4: the TREE Thematic Network.

TREE Thematic Network (Teaching and Research in Engineering in Europe)

Thanks to the success of E4, the University of Florence was invited by the European Commission to continue to manage this important activity with a follow-on project considering in particular the synergies between education and research in faculties of engineering in Europe. In September 2004, the TN TREE (Teaching and Research in Engineering in Europe) was launched with a substantial partnership of some 115 engineering schools.

The four main activities within TREE have been:

1. Line A: *Tuning*. Fine-tuning new curricula for the two-tier structure of higher education; developing tools for quality assessment, assurance, and accreditation; extending ECTS;
2. Line B: *Education and Research*. Monitoring the status and promotion of doctoral studies; promoting the role of research activity in engineering education; endorsing the value of research-oriented project work;
3. Line C: *Enhancing the Attractiveness of EEE*. Attracting young people, especially women, to engineering education with special initiatives such as joint/double degrees;
4. Line D: *Sustainability*. Sustaining engineering education institutions by developing continuing education, open, and distant learning opportunities; studying ways to make valuable tools, identified during the TN.

The transition from E4 to TREE suggested the necessity to prepare real 'instruments' to reinforce the European dimension of the studies in engineering, without however diminishing the importance of continuing with study activities about various key issues. We have to keep in mind indeed the dynamics of the situation favoured by so called Process of Bologna, of a major mobility of the students thanks to Erasmus, etc. The potential beneficiaries of the TREE activity, with its rich set of results available since the end of 2007, will not only be the faculties of Engineering in Europe, students and professors, but also the academic associations, the enterprises, the national and international agencies for accreditation, and all other stakeholders.

Related Projects

Tuning

The project Tuning Educational Structures in Europe is at the heart of the Bologna Process. It actually links the political objectives set in the Bologna Declaration of 1999 to the higher education sector. 'Tuning' is a project developed by and meant for higher education institutions in much diversified fields.

The Tuning project focuses not on educational systems, but on educational structures and content of studies. Whereas educational systems are primarily the responsibility of governments, educational structures and content are that of higher education institutions. As a result of the Bologna Declaration the educational systems in all European countries are in continuous evolution. This is the direct effect of the political decision to harmonise different national systems of higher education in Europe. For Higher Education institutions these reforms mean the actual starting point for another discussion: the comparability of curricula in terms of structures, programmes and learning methodology. In this reform process the required academic and professional profiles and needs of Society play an important role.

The main aim and objective of the project is to contribute significantly to the elaboration of a framework of comparable and compatible qualifications in each of the (potential) signatory countries of the Bologna process, which should be described in terms of workload, level, learning outcomes, competences and profile. The Tuning project has developed a methodology and a common language, reflected in the Berlin Communiqué (19 September 2003), which can serve as a common basis, and will make it possible to develop an overarching European framework of qualifications.

In the third phase (2005-2006), three major tasks are foreseen. The first task of this new project is to validate and to consolidate the outcomes of the Tuning pilot project, phases 1 and 2.

Although not included into the set of disciplines experimenting the Tuning methodology, EE was soon felt as a mandatory field to consider. The TN E4 then decided to promote a Synergy Group in EE aimed at exploring the implications of the Tuning methodology for EE. The group included experts from E4, TUNING, and EUCEET, and produced a study included among the outputs of E4 (Volume D) and also available via the web site of TREE (Archives).

TechnoTN

Since many topics studied within E4 were obviously of interest in areas of tertiary education different from Engineering, the third author of this contribution proposed in 2004 to the DG EAC to establish an 'Archipelago' of TNs in the scientific and technological fields of education, such as Chemistry (RCTN), Physics (EUPEN), Food (IsekiFood), Agricultural Engineering (USAEE), Civil Engineering (EUCEET), and many others. The main task of this archipelago of TNs denominated TechnoTN would have been to organise a Forum in each year where hot topics of transversal interest for all the TNs involved could be debated. This project was accepted by the DG EAC and partially funded from 2005 to 2007. At the moment of writing the chapter, TechnoTN have run four Fora from 2004 to 2007, and the plenary presentations as well as the results of the discussion sessions of each of the Fora can be looked at in the web site of TechnoTN www.upv.es/TechnoTN.

EUR-ACE

A rather novel way of international accreditation of engineering degree programmes has been elaborated by the EUR-ACE project. The rich experiences accumulated in decades by national bodies like the French 'Commission des Titres d'Ingénieur' and the British Chartered Engineering Institute are capitalised and exploited to create a consistent accreditation system of engineering education at the continental scale. Indeed, while international accreditation systems exist or are being established in other areas and continents, European engineering still lacks one: and on the global job market this puts the European engineer in an objectively weaker position. The success of the EUR-ACE project has shown that there is a great interest towards accreditation procedures in the engineering field and also a need for a European accreditation system. A non-profit association has been formed to follow the implementation phases of the EUR-ACE proposal denominated ENAEE, for European Network for Accreditation of Engineering Education. The readers are referred to the web site www.enaee.eu. the author, are confident that the project results will find increasing support across Europe and that a coordinated accreditation system will be established covering most European countries.

The Mission of a Future TN

A (certainly not exhaustive) list of key questions for European EE to be addressed in the near future is:

- Is European EE in general competitive worldwide?
- Is the third (i.e. doctorate) level attractive for European as well as non-European students?
- How should the Bologna Process better evolve (for EE)?
- Which new (and classical) study programmes have to be promoted?
- Which are the demands of Industry to enhance competitiveness and innovation?
- How can EE Institutions be protagonists in the need of Continuous Professional Development of engineering professionals?
- How to build the responsibilities of graduates concerning sustainable development?

In order to help coping with these (and other) challenges the authors believe that a new TN could be instrumental. Taking advantage of the work done in the recent past by the TNs described before (H3E, E4, and TREE), it could articulate its activity into the five working groups (WG), trying to move forward in the identification of true instruments for enhancing EE in Europe.

A first WG to be devoted to the Attractiveness of EE. It is in fact widely believed that Europe will face a shortage of engineering graduates in the near future with respect to the demand of industry. Examples of good practice in attracting the best young graduates of secondary schools to EE have to be collected in order to arrive at guidelines to be proposed to engineering faculties. Another aspect is the increasing importance of offering good opportunities for the pedagogic formation of teachers, a mandatory instrument for an effective formation and for retaining good students. Another set of guidelines should identify instruments for widening the participation of underrepresented groups, in particular female students. Facilitating students' mobility is another aspect for which examples of good practice must continue to be collected, as requested by students themselves as well as from the labour market. Finally the importance of offering early enough in the curriculum to students an appreciation of the most stimulating aspects of the engineering profession, in order to emphasise satisfaction more than just economic rewarding.

Another WG addressing tools for the full exploitation of the learning potential of students. One key aspect is techniques for the formation of good learners, able to cope with the ever-changing challenges of their future professional life. Another is the correct implementation of the Bologna Process, which still appears to be implemented in too many different ways across Europe, thus creating hindrances to students' mobility, instead of the opposite. The effective use of ICTs, in particular of distant learning opportunities, to make both teachers and learners activities more productive should also be considered. A particular emphasis has to be devoted to the peculiar characteristics of the third (i.e. doctorate) level of EE, its strong relations with research activity at European engineering faculties, its relevance for enhancing the innovation potential of European industry, its attractiveness for non-European students.

A third WG to be concerned with non-technical aspects of the formation. The increasing complexity of engineering projects in our globalised world does in fact require that engineering graduates, without being, at least after the first level of study, experts themselves, have a certain degree of non-technical 'skills' in order to be productive in the working environment. These skills include the capacity of understanding the legal implications of projects, their managerial requirements, and the evaluation of their costs. A special role, probably to be developed at the second level of tertiary education, is played by the formation of entrepreneurship. Anther key aspect of non-technical formation is the building of responsibilities, not only towards the enterprise where one is working, but also towards the whole Society.

A fourth WG should be targeted to Continuing EE (CEE) and how to make it work to the advantage of the economic world as well as that of Universities themselves. Among the aspects to be studied here we find: effective management of CEE opportunities, the role of ICTs in this activity, the importance of work-based learning opportunities, adult education models, validation of non-formal learning.

The fifth WG should be concerned with quality assurance and assessment (QAA) and Accreditation within the Bologna Process. Updated guidelines for QAA activity at European engineering schools should be offered, stressing their importance for increased transparency and mutual recognition among EE Institutions. The importance of a European system for accreditation of EE does not need to be stressed again: the path towards this goal provided by the

EUR-ACE project should be considered, in order to suggest improvements and to promote its acceptance by an increasing number of study programmes in all European countries.

Concluding Remarks

The Thematic Networks, with the support of the DG EAC of the European Commission, have contributed during all these years in many aspects of general interest for tertiary education: harmonising the studies, the development of life-long learning, the effective use of ICT, appraisal of the quality, accreditation, innovation of the learning methods, and last but not least, the birth of a network of institutions trusting each other. It is the firm opinion of the authors of this contribution that such a precious set of results must be exploited as fully as possible in the near future, by promoting new projects and/or the birth of European associations actively involving all stakeholders of EE, and committed to the enhancement of the European Higher Education Area, in particular in technology oriented fields. In fact, even if a lot has been achieved, the rapid evolution of our globalised economy presents continuously new challenges to European EE institutions, to be tackled with better and better tools. Designing such tools and disseminating guidelines for their adoption is the important task of a future TN devoted to the enhancement of EE in Europe.

6

Technology and Education for Human Resource Development in Asia-Pacific

Anjana Paira and *Rajarshi Roy*

The Social Scenario

> 'Freedom has a thousand charms to show,
> That slaves however contended, never know.'
>
> —*William Cowper* (18th century BC)

In a world of unprecedented increase in overall opulence, millions of people living in reach and poor countries are still not free. Even if they are not technically slaves, they are denied elementary freedom and remain imprisoned in one way or another, by economic poverty, social deprivation, political tyranny, or cultural authoritarianism, and are thereby denied with technological development. The basic aim of development is to spread freedom and its thousand charms to the 'un-free', living across the world.

Freedom is at once the ultimate goal of social and economic arrangements and the most efficient means of realizing general welfare. Technological development is the pivotal means in the path of development. Social institutions like *educational organizations of varied kinds* and *levels, market, political parties, legislatures, the judiciary,* and *the media* — all contribute to the development through enhancing the individual freedom and are in turn sustained by social values. Therefore technology, education, values, institutions, development and freedom—all are all closely related and linked together in an elegant analytical framework. In this frame, one of the important sub-cycle is rotating with massive speed, centering round the variables—*technology* and *education*, which in its' turn, giving a dynamism towards the entire frame.

Technology and Education

> "Existing educational institutions were created to meet the need of a society that is first disappearing. We need new educational organizations that can

> exploit the new technologies to meet the need of twenty-first century. Economic development will depend as much on the success of creativity and supporting such organizations, as on establishing the technological infrastructure. It is critical to get this right because those countries that harness the power of multimedia communication for education and training purposes will be the economic powerhouses of twenty-first century. The development of modern communications and information technologies is becoming a major instrument for widening access to education and training on a cost-effective basis while also enhancing its quality."
> —*Tony Bates*

It should be accepted by almost each and every hand that at the present juncture we are suppose to think in global perspective. The world is 'expanding' due to advancement in communication technology. From economic point of view, the world is polarized in two extreme poles—the *developed world* and the *developing world.* Economically self sufficient countries are termed as developed countries, where as the rest became known as developing countries. Self-sufficiency of a country depends on the economic stability[1]. Therefore every nation thrives on enhancing their economic condition. Today it is an axiom that economic self-sufficiency is the precondition of development.[2] various research studies[3] and statistics reveals that developed countries posses almost a cent percent literacy among their population. However exceptions are also there. A glance perusal of the situation of the Gulf countries reveals that though they are rich, but not always developed, due to lack of literacy[4]. Recent history of those countries advocates that due to lack of education, they failed to keep up their economic stability and richness. Lack of education is one of the major causes of wastage and deteriorated economic condition. So it may be assumed that education among the mass leads to development and enhance economic condition, which is further necessary to keep up to enjoy the developmental effect.[5] The argument may be more clear if we can have a comparative sketch of index of education and index of economy[6] of a bunch of nations in Asia as given in the table 6.1, where a high positive correlation is visible between the two major indicators of human development.

The Experience of Asia and Pacific in 21st Century

The region of Asia and the Pacific consist of huge number of small and large countries over a vast area of the world. As a result, a diversified culture, people, and developmental patterns can be observed here. The region covers almost half of the world population and almost 70 per cent of the population of the developing countries. However it accounts for only one-tenth (1/10th) of the world's gross national product (UNDP, 1999). The region includes the largest countries of the world (viz. China, India) and some of the smaller countries such as Bhutan. The region also includes countries with varied economic condition. The poorest countries (such as Bhutan and Cambodia) and the affluent countries viz. Singapore, Japan, Korea are also included in the very region.

Table 6.1: Education and Economic Development in Asian Countries

Country Name	*Education Index*	*GDP Index*
Bhutan	0.33	0.45
Bangladesh	0.38	0.39
Pakistan	0.41	0.46
Nepal	0.45	0.40
India	0.54	0.47
Cambodia	0.64	0.43
Maldives	0.66	0.89
Myanmar	0.74	0.41
Indonesia	0.78	0.59
China	0.78	0.57
Malaysia	0.79	0.73
Vietnam	0.82	0.47
Srilanka	0.82	0.54
Thailand	0.83	0.70
Honking	0.83	0.92
Singapore	0.85	0.94
Philippines	0.90	0.59
Japan	0.94	0.92
Korea	0.95	0.82

Source: UNDP, Human Development Report-2001, Oxford University Press, New Delhi.

So far the economic potentialities of these countries are concerned, a change is perused in due course of history, which is mostly guided by colonial rule (Tilak, 2001). Most of the models of educational development in the region are either borrowed or imposed by colonial rulers. The existing system of education and development in China and India, respectively, advocates the fact. However most of the countries in this region can adopt the imported models to their local environments, purely due to effective market pressures in some countries, and partially a more authoritarian approach to education in others (Papanek, 1988). Irrespective of waive of globalization, several of these countries are by nature religious and remains tradition-bound societies in modern, technologically developing world. Besides, most of these countries are having their own historical and unique cultural background, bracketing their respective social, political, and economic institutions to inspire and guide its developmental goals (Huq. 1975).

Globalization-IT-Market: The Triangle

In the past around fifteen years, the significant factor in every sphere education occurred, almost in every corner of the globe, which may be termed as explosion of education in consonance with LPG.[7] The extent may be experienced in different ways where, in some cases, the rate of explosion is quite higher whereas in some other zones, the rate is lower enough. Due to one-world culture[8], the direction of educational planning attracts Asian nations, irrespective of their lacuna and potentialities, to adopt almost a uniform approach. The trend started during the early nineties of the last century. The trend continues. Since then the pace of education and development carried out in such a way that at this very moment it is difficult to predict the change of development. However a few components of the development is quite well reflected. These are — impact of globalization (tagged with liberalization and concerns of human development), revolution in information technology, and the neo liberal market philosophy (Tilak, 2001), coupled with economic monetarism.[9] Globalization, started during nineties of the last century, has been spreading extensively all over the world. Right now it is felt that it may neither be feasible, nor desirable for any country to remain outside the truly global phenomenon of globalization, which is regarded as a threat as well as an opportunity (Streeten, 1998). Along with globalization, liberalization and competition —both at national as well as at international level, is bound to increase which will further help in increasing knowledge as well as its flow, both in and out, so far human resources are concerned. Developing countries are supposed to face the problem of brain drain, as 'competition for quality graduate will remain fierce' (Task Force on Higher Education and Society, 2000). The competition will lead to diversified product and also services. Both, the service and product will require more (soft and hard) skilled manpower, which surely puts a tremendous impact over the economy across the nations. Therefore the concerns for globalization should include human power, and as a result the nature of globalization may also show some new vista in economy and human development in near future.[10]

In the changed paradigm, higher education is supposed to be influenced by the globalization, which may lead to internationalization of higher education, and to be more specific, trans-nationalization, where the role of education (as a vehicle to carry on heritage) may disappear. This will be more a fact in developing countries, and, as can be assumed, are not necessarily beneficial for developing countries; moreover, these may be responsible factors for damaging consequences. The possibilities are anticipated as follows:

> "...It can lead to unregulated and poor quality of higher education, with the world wide marketing of fraudulent degrees or other so called higher education credentials; franchise Universities have also been problematic, where the parent university meets quality and standards, set in home country, but offers a substandard education through its franchised programmes in other countries..."[11] (*Task Force on Higher Education and Society 2004*).

Next to globalization, it is assumed that *revolution in the sphere of information technology* holds a major importance. The 'hybrid-technology', involving both hardcore and software, is providing numerous avenues for rapid dissemination of information, which was not anticipated, perhaps even a decade ago; this results to massive influence over varied dimensions of life

— social, cultural, economy, and ultimately, on overall psyche. In this age technology appears as the single most important determinant of progress for any nation. Unwillingness or inability to use, master and to adopt modern technology in the 'developing' countries like ours, may widen the disparities between the richer and poorer countries, continents, even within countries, regions, and people. Therefore it is desired to pay special attention on developing *technology,* and on its *extensive spread.* In this context it is worth-noting that though 'open learning system' use a wider variety of technology, however, the system cannot completely substitute teacher. Spread of technology in general, and information technology in specific, including Internet, fax, telecommunication and etc. might increase the thirst for knowledge and information, which would have far reaching implications on education (Roy, 2002). Awareness is already visible across the nations where some of the developing societies have begun thinking of not merely to be literate, but also of becoming computer literate — which is considered as an essential precondition for development (Mazumder, 1998). Obviously such literacy is expected to be the underpinning factor for revolutionary changes in the system of education (Tilak, 2001).

Finally the *neo liberal market philosophy, coupled with economic monetarism* is appearing as an influential phenomenon since a decade, which is controlling the state welfare politics of the developing countries (Jakobeit, 1999).

Educational development is one area where all these three major factors are playing an influential role and thereby trying to keep a stringent control over the system and structure of education, irrespective of its type and level.

A glance perusal to the Human Developmental Indicators reveals wide disparity among the nations in Asia and Pacific region. A review of Asian experience, with its diverse types of educational policies and varied levels of educational development, can be hoped to offer a wide range of positive and negative lessons for policy makers and educational planners in this region in relation to the respective countries. No uniform approach be wise to advice for the cluster of nations from this region due to sequels of socio-economic factors. Experiences reveals that 20th century perused an educational miracle all over the world with an unprecedented explosion in the number of literates, illiterates, student enrolment, schools and other institutions, teaches, and in the public expenditures. It is really difficult to imagine any comparable period in world history when the expansion of education was so rapid. In the 20th century, modern education system was established almost everywhere and the spread of modern economic growth, since then have noticing accelerated. Asian countries also experienced tremendous growth, especially in Japan, China, India, Burma, Indonesia, Thailand and Philippines. This further

Table 6.2: Human Developmental Indicators in Asia and Pacific Region (Status of Various Nations in Asia Pacific in Terms of Selected Indicators of Human Development)

Sl. No	Nations	Life Expectancy at Birth (Years)(2001)	Adult Literacy Rate (%age 15 Years and Above 2001)	Combined Enrolment Ratio (%) 2000-2001	GDP per Capita (PPP US $) (2001)	Life Expectancy Index	Education Index	GDP Index	Human Development Index (HDI) Value (2001)	GDP per Capita (ppp US $) Rank Minus HID Rank	Rank among Asian and Pacific Countries in Terms of GDP
1.	Bruni Darussalam	76.1	91.6	83	19210	0.85	0.89	0.88	0.872	–4	33
2.	Cambodia	57.4	68.7	55	1860	0.54	0.64	0.49	0.556	9	19
3.	China	70.6	85.8	64	4020	0.76	0.79	0.62	0.721	–2	11
4.	Fiji	69.3	93.2	76	4850	0.74	0.88	0.65	0.754	11	9
5.	Honking, china (SRA)	79.7	93.5	63	24850	0.91	0.83	0.92	0.889	–11	1
6.	Indonesia	66.2	87.3	64	2940	0.69	0.80	0.56	0.682	2	14
7.	Korea, Rep. .of.	75.2	97.9	91	15090	0.84	0.96	0.84	0.879	7	4
8.	Lao Peoples' Dem.Rep.	53.9	65.6	57	1620	0.48	0.63	0.46	0.525	10	22
9.	Malaysia	72.8	87.9	72	8750	0.80	0.83	0.75	0.790	–2	5
10.	Mongolia	63.3	98.5	64	1740	0.64	0.87	0.48	0.661	25	21
11.	Myanmar	57.0	85.0	47	1027	0.53	0.72	0.39	0.549	28	25
12.	Papua New Guinea	57.0	64.6	41	2570	0.53	0.57	0.54	0.548	–12	16
13.	Philippines	69.5	95.1	80	3840	0.74	0.90	0.61	0.751	19	12
14.	Samoa (West)	69.5	98.1	71	6180	0.71	0.89	0.69	0.775	4	7
15.	Singapore	77.8	92.5	75	22680	0.88	0.87	0.91	0.884	–7	2
16.	Thailand	68.9	95.7	72	6400	0.73	0.88	0.69	0.768	–2	6
17.	Vietnam	68.6	92.7	64	2070	0.73	0.83	0.51	0.688	21	17
18.	Bangladesh	60.5	40.6	54	1610	0.59	0.45	0.46	0.502	7	23
19.	Bhutan	62.5	47.0	33	1833	0.62	0.42	0.49	0.511	5	20
20.	India	63.3	58.0	56	2840	0.64	0.57	0.56	0.590	–12	15
21.	Iran, Islamic Rep.	69.8	77.1	64	6000	0.75	0.73	0.68	0.719	–29	8
22.	Maldives	66.8	97.0	79	4798	0.70	0.91	0.65	0.751	7	10
23.	Nepal	59.1	42.9	64	1310	0.57	0.50	0.43	0.499	8	24
24.	Pakistan	60.4	44.0	36	1890	0.59	0.41	0.49	0.499	–7	18
25.	Srilanka	72.3	91.9	63	3180	0.79	0.82	0.58	0.730	13	13

Source: Cit in University News, vol. 42, Nos. 10, 13, 18, 21 and 28, AIU Publications; New Delhi.

contributed to the rapid growth of education, irrespective of levels. However the development is not uniform at all. The massive expansion of education contributes significantly to the socio-economic development of the countries in the region. Education has been a crucial factor of the economic miracle in (East) Asian countries (World Bank, 1993). In contrast, relatively low literacy and educational level of the population in south Asian countries are considered as major bottleneck when it comes to reducing poverty, improving economic distribution, and to achieve progress in terms of socio-economic development. Good many developmental research over Asian countries in relation to education and economy revels that returns to education in Asian countries are high not only on their own, but also in comparison with other regions of the world, and apart from monetary terms, the contribution of education to productivity of the workforce is well demonstrated in manufacturing sector.[12] The findings reveal a direct relationship between economic and social benefits. The contribution of education in various facets of development in Asia and Pacific region is exclusive, and all pervasive on the individual and social lives of the people. It is not only a human right but also a prerequisite for demanding human rights.[13]

In recent days a sudden crisis is experienced in financial context, which is having adverse impact over the economy as well as on the social facets, including technical education, in some East Asian countries (Albett & Slengesol 2000), which help emerging some doubt in efficacy of investment in education. It is a proven fact that status of technical education is having a direct bearing with economy of a nation, and as analyzed by Tilak, 2001 (Op. cit.) it is neither lack of education or over education which results to economic crisis in Asia and Pacific. It is also a fact that higher education act as a 'safety valve' to absorb the shock of economic crisis; and the value of education to deal with disequilibria is very vital (Schultz, 1975, 1990). Therefore it may be expected that the shock is not a permanent phenomenon, and it could be solved shortly. On the other hand, education in general, and technology education in specific is having a high potent for development. As such, technical education directly contributes to development, and development of the economy leads to further development in education. There remains a cyclic causal-effect relationship between the two factors, which ultimately leads to progress.

Education, Technological Education and Socioeconomic Development

Right now, countries in Asia and Pacific region are possessing varying stages of socio-economic development from *developed*, to *newly industrializing*, to still *under developed*; where some of the countries are characterized as *'modern'* some are still *'traditional'*. They differ on various developmental indexes; for example, on the *economic indicators*, such as their market potentiality,[14] *standard of living* (measured with the help of *gross national product*, abbreviated as GNP), *per capita income*, *social indicators* like *life expectancy, health status,* and other major developmental indicators viz. *poverty* and *income inequalities*-which widely differs across sub—region, and between the countries. Demography and political situations also varies significantly in the region, all of which possess a tremendous impact over the system of education in general, and over technical education, in particular, with a synergic impact. In its existing scenario, even developing countries can also afford to make appropriate investments in education and thereby achieve economic miracles (Tilak, 2001). However one of the most notable differences can be pressured so far the quality of education prevails in the region. The experience of majority of the developing countries reveals a comparatively high pupil-teacher ratio, which ultimately leads to high dropout, low retention, and lower promotion rates, and finally lowers the level of students' achievement.

Table 6.3: Status of Various Nations in Asia and Pacific Region in Terms of Expenditure on Education, Expenditure on Research and Development and Availability of Scientists and Engineers

Nations	*Public Expenditure on Education As % of GDP (2001)*	*R&D Expenditure As % of GDP (2001*	*Scientist and Engineers in R&D (Per Million People) (2001)*
Brunei Darussalam	4.8	–	–
Cambodia	1.9		
China	2.1	1.0	545
Fiji	5.2	–	50
Honking, china (SRA)	–	0.4	93
Indonesia	1.0	–	130
Korea, Rep. of.	3.8	2.7	2319
Lao Peoples' Dem.Rep.	2.3	–	–
Malaysia	6.2	0.4	160
Mongolia	2.3	–	531
Myanmar	0.5	–	–
Papua New Guinea	2.3	–	–
Philippines	4.2	–	156
Samoa (West)	4.2	–	–
Singapore	3.7	1.9	4140
Thailand	5.4	0.1	74
Vietnam	4.0	–	247
Bangladesh	2.5	–	51
Bhutan	5.2	–	–
India	4.1	1.2	157
Iran, Islamic Rep.	4.4	–	590
Maldives	3.9	–	–
Nepal	3.7	–	–
Pakistan	1.8	–	69
Sri Lanka	3.1	0.2	191

Developmental Problems

Though education, as argued in the preceding sections of the paper, is the vehicle for development, however there remains various problems in the process of its execution. Priority towards education — in terms of level is not well thought of in many nations in the Asia and Pacific region. A major disparity prevails among them so far gross enrolment ratio is concerned.

Experience in the Asia and Pacific region, as observed from various national and international reports, reveals that the policies related to globalization results to numerous situations so far the economy of the nations are concerned. It appears that those countries are in a better position to raise their human resource and economy during last decade, which had a sizable investment over higher/technical education (Khan, 1998). Globalization did not yield desired results to countries with low and inadequate levels of investment in higher and technical education, which is mirrored through their low educational levels of the workforce. Vietnam, Laos and Cambodia may be the examples in this direction, whereas countries like Korea, Thailand, Indonesia and Philippines did able to raise their economy a lot, by increasing the expenditure over education. This again proves that success depends upon capacity to compete in international market and also require highly skilled manpower, which is an output of technical education system, with a strong base (Tilak; 2001). Countries those have succeeded in the era of globalization are those who did able to built up the capacity to develop, and thereby mobilize the knowledge needed to produce new information-based goods and services, to adopt new innovative methods of production, public education, worker's training, and more Government investment in research and developmental activities (Carnoy, 1995). Empirically, it was found that globalization has contributed to eradicate poverty and inequalities in eastern Asia, which is not true for western part of the sub-continent (Khan, 1998). The underlining reason can be traced in differences among pattern of investment in education, particularly at tertiary level.

With a view to raise the standard of manpower and thereby to enhance their potentialities, the so-called developing countries in Asia and Pacific need to adopt appropriate policies for expansion of (skill) education, keeping in view the emerging needs of the nation and the region as well. The technology education, which comes under the preview of higher education, therefore need to be given proper weightage. Sudden and huge-expenditure, massive proliferation of the technical education system, and enhanced enrolment without carrying out any future manpower requirement survey should no way be helpful for enhancing the standard of human resource. Rather such attempt will invite different sorts of problems with different magnitude (which is presently experienced by the country like India). Proper planning is inevitable so far education in science and technology are concerned. It has been observed, while

East Asian economy have been successfully build up huge stock of human capital and utilizing those for national development, India being the third largest reservoir of scientific and technical manpower in the world, is yet unable to reap sizable economic benefits. Science and technology education will become futile, until and unless it is tagged with research and development (R&D) activities. Therefore apart from supplying sufficient 'fresh-blood' on technical education, research and innovation should also be enhanced. Experience of Japan can be taken up as a model by the rest of the world, which, even being an Asian Country, excelled its economy, and is much ahead, not only of other countries in Asia, but also of other developed countries in the world. This becomes possible with an investment of nearly 3 percent of GNP over R&D activities, along with a strong feeling of nationalism among the cross section of the population.

Human Capital: The Expression of Freedom

In contemporary economic analysis, the emphasis has, to a considerable extent, shifted from perceiving capital accumulation in primarily physical terms to viewing it as a process in which productivity of human beings is integrally involved (Sen, 2000). For example, through education, learning and skill-formation, people can become much more productive in course of time, and this contributes a lot over the process of economic expansion. In recent studies of economic growth, often influenced by empirical readings of the experiences of Japan and the rest of East Asia as well as Europe and North America, there is much greater emphasis over 'human capital'. Human capital helps in enhancing the human capability, and in consequence, enhances the social and economic indicators of human development. Technical education directly contributes for human development. This is the very segment of education, which has its immediate impact over the society at large. Research in the very domain also helps to bring structural change in the society. Therefore with a view to achieve development, proper attention is needed over technical education and research.

Education (including both soft and hard skill) makes the human beings more efficient in production of commodity or in extending services, which is a human capital. These should add value to economy and also to the income of a person. But even with the same level of income, a person may benefit from education—in reading, communicating, arguing, in being able to choose from alternatives in a more informed way, in being taken more seriously by others. The benefit of education thus exceeds its role as human capital in producing commodity. In consequences, if a person can become more productive in making commodities through better education, better health and so on, it is not unnatural to expect that he can, through these means, also directly achieve more and have the freedom to achieve more to lead his life. In this way, the process of development follows a rotating cycle and thereby accelerates the rate of development.

In the twenty-first century, not only the people of the Asia and Pacific, but all over the world having high hopes that new technologies, mostly in the sphere of information technology, will lead to the healthier lives, great social freedom, increased knowledge (not mere information) and more productive livelihoods. Though at the end stage of the last century, (to be more specific, since 1990s), massive gain was achieved by some nations in the wave of globalization, which was the output of technological breakthroughs, but time has come to rethink over the supremacy of market and technology. Market is a powerful vehicle of technological progress; but not powerful enough to create and thereby to defuse the technologies needed to irradiate poverty in SAARC and other zones. Affluent societies may gain especially high rewards from new technologies, but they also use to face several challenges in managing risks.

Post Script

As reflected from the present scenario, what actually happening is the *technology revolution* and *globalization* is *creating a network.* This network is the mode of creation and diffusion of technology. In the networking-paradigm, national policies still coming on the way. Even the poorest countries like Bhutan also need to implement policies, which encourage research, development and innovation, access and development of advanced skills. It is national policy, not the national charity, which will determine whether new technologies are really becoming tool for human development everywhere or not. Commitments under Trade Related aspects of Intellectual Property Rights (TRIPS) of World Tread Organization (WTO), to promote technology-transfer to developing countries are appearing as mere paper-promises, and are often neglected in implementation. The basic form of development is "creativity", which generates the potentialities of techno-capabilities. The ultimate significance of the present networking (between globalization and technology) age is that it can empower people by enabling them to use and contribute to the worlds' collective knowledge. Recent Human Development Reports utter that richest one percent of the world population owns as much as fifty-seven percent of the resources and income. Therefore the role of technology in creating and generating resources is expected to follow the path whereby inequalities between rich and poor, developed and developing, be minimized. Every technological advancement possesses potential benefits and risks and also possesses widely varying capacities to handle those risks. The third world countries, as recent experiences says, becomes the worst sufferers of such risks. Technology in coming days is expected to eradicate the inequalities in absorbing or in preventing the risks of technological development.

Notes

1. Apart from human resources, as Professor Sen perceives, economic stability helps in maintaining congenial climate, within which fruits of self-sufficiency ripe.
2. Development depends upon four basic components—viz. *Independence, cooperation, enhanced skill* and *growth in production rate.*
3. Most of these studies are carried out in the disciplines—Economics and International Relations.
4. Though literacy is one of the major indicators of formal education, however it cannot be considered synonymous with education.
5. 'Welfare-Economics' stressed the very concept.
6. Among many others, gross domestic product is a component of economic-index, which estimates human development.
7. It is the abbreviation of Liberalization, Privatization and Globalization.
8. A visible indicator of Globalization, which breaks down the barrier among the nations, so far their market-economy, is concerned.
9. Activities performed by WTO in the economic policy perspectives of the member countries of UNO, which appear as a compulsion to the members.
10. Though at present, it is mere a hypothesis, however experience of some developing countries, which achieved comparatively advanced position, justify deducing such hypothesis.
11. Consequences has already been faced by countries like India, which compel the Government to frame preventive rules.
12. Such studies are carried out by the scholars in India and abroad.
13. Protection of Human Rights requires proper communication. Without education (3 Rs-Reading, writing and arithmetic) it is difficult to communicate the incident of violation of Human Rights, and thereby difficult to assure it.
14. Two major countries in the region-China and India hold a sizable portion of world market.

Part II

Innovative Approaches in Engineering Education

7

Classroom Usage of Science Fiction to Enhance Engineering Education

Thoughts and Techniques

A.E. Segall

Considering the various tools used by educators to teach their respective subjects, there is truly a vast arsenal at our disposal. While the arsenal may be vast and varied, there must ultimately be a good fit with the targeted subject, lest the educator 'loose' the student's interest in the process. For example, historical reenactments in the classroom are an excellent way of teaching history in a fun and exciting way by mixing the requisite (and boring) names and dates with lasting impressions. Moreover, historical novels, movies, and of course, television have become major sources of information and unfortunately, misinformation as well. While it is doubtful that reenacting major engineering feats and breakthroughs (or even a popular TV show about engineers solving major problems) would do much for engineering education or recruitment, that does not mean that the medium cannot contribute. In fact, with special effects now creating dazzling and lasting images, fiction, and more specifically, Science Fiction or SF opens up a vast arsenal for engineering instruction. Unfortunately and despite the obvious promise of the genre and all of its inherent possibilities, Science Fiction has not been integrated with engineering education to any appreciable extent.

The absence of SF in the classroom is truly regrettable since a potent combination of theory and imagery has great potential to help students at all levels to 'get it.' Sadly, this is especially true in the early 'core' classes where there may be a real conflict between the student's original concepts of engineering, and a curriculum overly saturated with math and physics. This conflict and the ensuing disconnect is often further irritated by the distinctly theoretical and very non-practical implementation of both topics in the entry level courses. Unfortunately, this attitude also permeates higher levels as well as evidenced by overly theoretical and derivation driven graduate level curricula. In fact, It can be remembered that taking a graduate level course on numerical methods where each presumably practical technique was derived and then instead of doing examples, the instructor proceeded to do proof after proof; the instructor was truly shocked beyond belief when the class of mainly engineers had the audacity to ask for practical examples. While not as bad (at least in my opinion), engineering education also suffers from the same or similar attitudes when derivations are deemed far more important than examples and the practical application of the knowledge. This is not to say that theory and such do not have a place in engineering education, only that there must be a good mix or we will end up with great designs that can never be fabricated. Moreover, an actually fun connection between concept and application via SF could actually help change the very perceptions of the engineering profession throughout society.

Given these important issues and the potential benefits of SF, its absence in the engineering classroom represents a significant loss of valuable resources and opportunities for enhancing engineering education, as well as attracting new students to the profession. Surprisingly, the application of science fiction in education is not a new concept in any way, shape, or form with science and physics educators long recognizing Science Fictions' intrinsic value for teaching basic principles[1-3] at the undergraduate level. Since physics is certainly the foundation for engineering, the obvious question becomes: why not use science fiction to enhance and illustrate engineering as well? Clearly, the answer is that SF can and should be used to convey a wide range of concepts from basic mechanics all the way up to advanced design and analysis. In fact, the importance of such usage cannot be overstated for a number of reasons. Firstly, SF's creation of lasting mental images to the underlying theory will help students through the seemingly abstract core physics, math, and mechanics classes. As pointed out in earlier studies, a potent combination of theory and visual imagery could easily provide a critical nudge to help students to 'get it'[4], especially in the early classes where many of their impressions about the profession and what it entails are formed. Another advantage is that a visual and fun connection between concept and application may also help avoid a 'disconnect' between their original (and arguably, often very erroneous) idea of what the profession of engineering entails and the freshman and sophomore curriculum that quickly plunges into math, physics, and chemistry without a clear linkage to anything related to engineering and design.

From a purely technical standpoint, the use of SF in the classroom clearly offers many possibilities. However, limiting the use of Science Fiction to just teaching basic mechanics principles may be an underutilization of a very powerful medium since other equally important opportunities also exist. For a most telling instance, a recent Harris Poll[5] revealed that '*People do not think of engineers as researchers, inventors, and discoverers—they attribute these functions to scientists.'* Unfortunately, this misperception is widespread as epitomized by the typical class answer to the age-old question: is the Professor in the campy and well-know, 1960's television show, Gilligan's Island a Scientist or Engineer? As can be expected by the tone, the answer to this intriguing question is almost universally 'Scientist,' even though it is clearly wrong! While the professor is certainly knowledgeable in scientific theory, he is clearly able to translate this knowledge into practical solutions — the very definition of engineering! Since this appears to be one of many misperceptions about engineering that helps to reduce the number of prospective students, why not use the medium to illustrate the many contributions of engineering and hopefully create a more positive image of the profession? Moreover, why not use the class to help recruit students to the profession by showing the many exiting aspects of the profession not usually seen in TV and movies. Finally, why not use the same techniques to teach others in a fun and interesting way about the engineering concepts they unknowingly encounter every day?

Figure 7.1: Was the Professor on Gilligan's Island a Scientist or Engineer? You can decide for yourself, but I will give you a subtle hint: Yes!

While Science Fiction can certainly be used to help teach basic theory and its engineering implantation via design and analysis, the influence of SF can be much greater. In fact, another underutilized aspect of science fiction in engineering education revolves around technology and societal issues[6-7] and the underlying ethical considerations that go with them. Given our limited resources and the interrelated global problems of food, water, energy, climate change, and pollution, these issues should be included in engineering education.

In this regard, Science Fiction is a 'natural' since it can easily (but not always accurately) depict a wide range of 'what ifs' as already demonstrated in classroom exercises that are discussed below[8-10]. Although not usually considered to be an integral part of an engineering education, ethical and societal considerations are also essential; years ago I was struck by a passage in Alexander Solzhenitsyn's *Gulag Archipelago* that describes his arrest and restraint in handcuffs that were designed to painfully cut into the wrist with the slightest movement. Solzhenitsyn asked a truly haunting (and ultimately inspiring) question in wondering if the designer truly believed that the handcuffs would only be used against bad people who deserved the pain they inflicted. Obviously, the teaching of ethics represents a unique set of challenges, as it is very hard to consider all possible situations and ramifications. Given these complexities, an attainable goal is to get the students thinking about societal and ethical issues with the belief that once the thought process is started, it cannot be stopped no matter how hard they try! Hopefully, the next generation of engineers will at least be able to more-fully contemplate and understand the ethical and societal implications of their actions.

Background

Obviously, the potential for SF to enhance the engineering curriculum is significant with many possibilities for both technical and societal/ethical topics. In this treatise, these possibilities will be explored with two well-known science fiction stories (a movie and a TV series) used to illustrate potential teaching approaches. However, it is not the desire of this work to dictate style or form with one notable exception that pertains to delivery; *the class must be fun and the material engaging or else the class is no better than any other 'dry' lecture and the students will ultimately be lost!* As such, one must have a passion for the material and hopefully, the genre of SF as well. Moreover, the humorous and discussion-like style of this study is intended to reflect how the various topics can be conveyed to the students during the class in a fun and engaging manner. With this approach in mind, a series of tried and tested examples will be given illustrating how one could use the topics and genre in engineering education. It is hoped that these illustrations will serve as a guide and spur many new innovations that can help improve engineering education in the years to come.

Finally, it should be noted that the class has been evolving since its inception and has been taught at two very different schools. For the first two-years, the class was taught as the 2-credit ENG 280, Science Fiction in Engineering at Clark College (Vancouver, Washington) while the author was faculty at Washington State University Vancouver (WSUV); because WSUV was restricted at the time to upper division undergraduate and graduate level courses only (2+2 system), it was not feasible to teach the science fiction course to freshman engineering students as originally intended. During the past 5-years, the course has been offered as a 1-credit first-year seminar (Engineering Science 121s, Science Fiction in Engineering) at the Pennsylvania State University with approximately 100+ students enrolled to-date. In both instances, the course was open to all majors with no math, chemistry, or physics requirements. For the Penn State version of the course, a new series of interactive PowerPoint notes have been developed to help keep the students engaged and learning instead of copying detailed diagrams; while it has been said that power corrupts, and that PowerPoint corrupts absolutely, the downloadable notes have allowed the students to get all pertinent details without having to make the Faustian choice between writing it all down and understanding the material. These notes and their interactive components have also more than proven themselves in other technical courses at the undergraduate and graduate levels.

Class Format

Because of the inclusion of all majors at both schools, the class format consisted of demonstrations (with movies), some lecture including a very limited use of equations and diagrams, and extensive discussions. Using a 1-2 hour class period, a brief introduction to a movie combined with a listing of key points to observe was first used to prime the students. The class was then allowed to watch the movie without any interruptions unless a significant point had to me made. Following the in-class presentation, the class was then asked to describe and explain at least five events in the movie where they first felt that the laws of physics/engineering were observed and/or violated. The students were also asked to highlight and discuss any technology and society and/or ethical issues that were raised by the story. The one-to two-page essays were collected the following class and were primarily intended to help spur thought and discussion. The class following each presentation was entirely devoted to discussions and demonstrations. In addition, demonstrations that included lasers and an octopus-like robot were also arranged to show SF concepts that have become reality.

While the collected essays accounted for 50 per cent of the student's grade, the accuracy of their review of the underlying physics and engineering was not used as a basis for their score. This is an important point since the purpose of the course is to help teach basic engineering concepts and not to evaluate existing knowledge. Class participation accounted for another 10 per cent of the grade with the remaining 40 per cent of the grade awarded for a term paper collected during the final class. For this paper, students were expected to choose (or assigned) a science fiction book such as H.G. Well's War of the Worlds not covered in class and analyze the story for its accuracy and any pertinent technology versus society issues invoked. The students were expected to incorporate the concepts and issues raised in the classes so the technical accuracy of their paper and the discussions contained within were evaluated to some degree.

Illustrations and Examples

The remainder of this text will be devoted to a few examples of classroom topics and lectures using SF to enhance engineering education, as well as recruit or retain potential students when an open class format is used. As stated earlier, the sky is the limit (as with SF itself) in terms of what can be taught and how it is implemented in the classroom. However, and as stated earlier, the class must be made fun or else the overall goals are less likely to be achieved! With this in-mind, the 1997 movie 'Independence Day' (ID4, Paramount Pictures) was chosen to be an integral part of the SF class for freshmen/sophomores of all majors; interestingly, the idea for the course was actually spawned while watching this movie with my children. As will also be shown below, the Hugo award-winning Star Trek episode 'The Menagerie' was also be used as a starting point to discuss societal and moral implications of engineering, as well as review various topics in engineering including the universally loathed Dynamics.

Mechanics

ID4 was chosen in part because of its 'looseness' with the laws of nature and engineering, not to mention its stunning visual effects that create a great opportunity to leave a lasting and hopefully educational impression. As mentioned earlier, there are numerous topics and sub-topics that can be explored using science fiction; 'Independence Day' definitely hits on many of the major themes and can be readily used to illustrate a number of points integral to engineering practice. For instance, as the alien's evil plot unfolds, a number of extremely large ships descend to the surface and silently hover over earth's major cities as shown in Fig. 7.2. Based on estimates[11-12] of the mass of one ship to be ~$9\text{x}10^3$ kg and assuming a diameter of approximately 24 km, the concepts of both static equilibrium and pressure can be poignantly explored. Obviously, for the ship to remain stationary over any given location, it must exert a downward force on the ground (and the ground back up on to the ship) equal to the total weight of the craft. A simple animated cartoon using PowerPoint and/or the more commonplace chalk-and-talk can illustrate this point so that the concept of static equilibrium can be explored. While this may represent a rudimentary 'statics' concept that is easily understood by most sophomores, the distribution of this force and the consequences might go unexplored. Given the force required for equilibrium and the diameter of the ship, the resulting pressure (if assumed uniform) would be a staggering 21 times our normal atmospheric pressure and would easily crush the hapless inhabitants below; the death ray was not even needed! An instructor can then proceed to discuss pressure and the concept of distribution of force over an area. Once these concepts are understood by the students, the discussion can be further expanded to include stress as a measure of the intensity of a force over a given cross-section for a solid.

More advanced concepts such as conductive and radiative heat transfer can also be explored by reviewing key scenes of the movie. One such exhilarating sequence involves the residents of Los Angeles attempting to quickly escape the city using the freeways (a major falsity in and of itself). One of the movies main characters is trapped in a tunnel with her son and dog and fortunately able to find refuge from the alien destructive plasma-like weapon in a utility room with a metal door. Under the assumptions that the plasma is at least 2200°C and the steel door is 50 mm thick, classroom calculations can easily show that the door will reach at least 1900°C within 2-3 minutes. Given the door's temperature and a conservative estimate that approximately one-half of the total radiative flux will reach anyone inside, the unfortunate inhabitants would quickly be 'barbecued'. Discussion can also be held about the differences between a solid steel-door where thermal conduction governs and a more likely hollow door scenario where radiation between the panels could ultimately allow a faster heat-up. Numerical simulations and animations using finite-element methods are an excellent way to further illustrate these important points, as well as expose the students to a extremely useful and increasingly commonplace engineering tool.

Figure 7.2: Concepts of Equilibrium and Pressure Underlie the Alien's Successful Effort to Ruin New York's Day

There are many other aspects of engineering (and the underlying physics) that can be discussed in class if desired. Given the current concerns about energy and the climate, the lectures can also discuss the staggering energy required to levitate the behemoth ships, as well as the massive amount of heat that would need to be dissipated using any of our current energy production concepts. Topics such as the aerodynamics of the motherships and the energy required propelling them into and through the atmosphere are other engineering realities glossed-over in the movie. Other discussions can delve into the structural aspects of ship construction and the materials required sustaining the stress and thermal loads encountered. Finally, concepts of potential energy can also be explored by discussing the tremendous impact energy sustained by the earth when the ships are taken down; in reality, the humans are falsely victorious since each impact might have an energy equivalence in the ~400 megaton range with massive amounts of debris helping to create a nuclear winter.

While Star Trek (Paramount Home Video) episodes were primarily used to highlight societal and ethical issues as will be discussed in the next section, they also contain many opportunities for the technical side of engineering. In this regard, the universally reviled, sophomore dynamics class can also benefit from the use of science fiction since the Starship Enterprise shown in Figure 7.3 can be used to illustrate dynamics and concept of a mass acceleration diagram (MAD). While an animated PowerPoint demonstration could easily show the ship, its MAD, and how the Enterprise should be spinning out of control with the off-CG thrusts, this might not aid understanding as much as desired. In this situation, a simple prop and hands-on experiment seems to have a far greater impact on student understanding. To begin the demonstration, a large book is placed on a flat surface with the outline of the Starship Enterprise centrally pasted on the centre of the book so their CG's align. The book is then placed on a desk and a student is asked to push it with their finger aligned at either the CG or the engine pods. When pushed along the CG, the book translates as expected and the students are generally not impressed. However, when their fingers are aligned with the engine pod and the ship begins to spin, the MAD diagram truly begins to come to life. The moral of the story is that simple props and demonstrations, especially kinesthetic or hands in nature on can make a big difference.

Computers (especially Artificial Intelligence), mass, and energy concepts, as well as new propulsion system and the engineering challenges can also be discussed. It should be noted that common engineering (and physics) concepts such as force, acceleration, and inertia can be discussed and visually explored using many science fiction stories since motion and flight (terrestrial and space) are common themes. However, lower-brow, albeit still entertaining cartoons such (Roadrunner, Bugs Bunny etc.) are also great ways to illustrate many of the basic concepts of dynamics.

Technology and Society

While hopefully creating lasting links between engineering theory and practice, equally important concepts of technology and society can also be explored using SF in lectures. In this respect, both ID4 and Star Trek present a number of useful seeds for insightful discussions. For instance, analogies between the

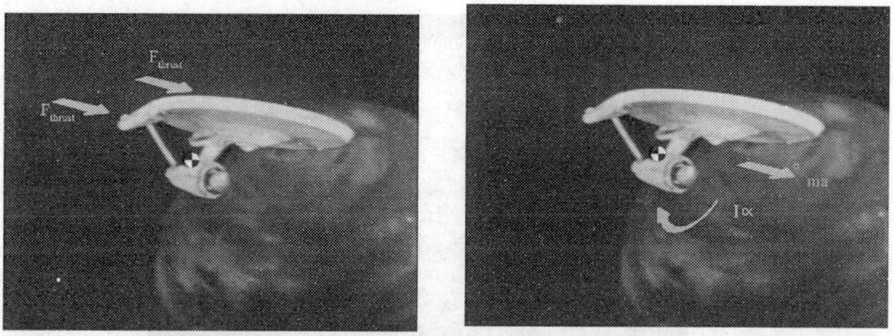

Figure 7.3: The Off Center-of-Gravity Thrust will Truly Cause the Starship Enterprise to Travel at Dizzying Speeds

aliens' in ID4 and their locust-like behavior of moving from planet to planet and using all resources and our own throwaway culture can be easily drawn. While most students are skeptical that we act in a similar fashion, a simple review of history and the self-destructive behaviours of the Anasazi (Southwest US), the inhabitants of Easter Island, and/or the Mayans can be eye opening. What are the ethics of stimulating an ever-increasing consumer demand when the result is increased pollution, possible long-term or irreversible environmental changes, and diminished resources? How can the profession of engineering help create a balance between economic prosperity and the limited resources of the earth? Can science and engineering ultimately solve all problems as many assume or hope? As illustrated by our inability to cure the AIDS virus or harness fusion power after many decades of research, we are a long way off from Scotty's and Dr. McCoy's ability to use technology to solve any problem in an hour or less.

The Hugo award-winning Star Trek episode 'The Menagerie' can also be used to illustrate our increasing dependence on technology and the problems that can arise when we lose the ability to manufacture or repair as suffered by the bigheaded inhabitants of Talos IV (Figure 7.4) after a horrific war. Compelling stories such as 'The Menagerie' also highlights the pitfalls of a society overly dependent on technology that is not understood by a vast majority of users. While many might 'scoff' at the idea of losing important skills and technology even if we grow big heads like the Talosions, how many could start a fire without a match? When asked, most students know that rubbing two sticks together will create friction that can start a fire. However, when required by circumstance to try such a feat, few if any could actually do it even if their life depended on it.

As mentioned earlier, the classes were taught in an open format with all majors welcome. This actually served a three-fold purpose in that it can help engineers better connect with their majors and the materials (per the original intent), as well as expose other students to the possibilities of an engineering career. However, in addition to being a recruiting tool, the SF class can also

Figure 7.4: Even Big Heads with Pulsing Veins could not Help the Poor Talosian Race

serve to better educate everyone to the engineering and yes, scientific concepts that they use and encounter every day. Perhaps these methods and insights can eventually lead to required engineering and science courses for all college students to help balance a liberal arts education.

Student Feedback

At this point in time, the class has been taught for 7 years at two universities. Based on an 'exit' discussion held on the last day of the course, the following feedback has been received. In general, the students felt that the class was worthwhile in terms of illuminating the important role of engineering and basic concepts. While the class did not necessarily convince any students to change their major (the vast majority of students were already in engineering), all of the students did report a greater appreciation of the role of engineers and some basic engineering concepts. *In fact, (and perhaps most importantly), most of the students now believe that the 'Professor' was an engineer and not a scientist.*

In terms of understanding and visualizing basic engineering concepts, the engineering students stated that they believed they were better equipped to take their courses. More importantly, the students indicated that they could to some extent, see a link between their original vision of engineering and current coursework. Since the students will go to a variety of engineering majors and schools (in the 2+2 system in Washington State) to complete their degrees, it is not feasible to track the success and grades of the students. Not surprisingly, a majority of the students (especially non-engineering majors) preferred that the use of equations be kept to a minimum with an emphasis placed on more physical demonstrations such as the simple hands-on experiment for the somersaulting motion of the enterprise.

Assessment

While the 2+2 system in Washington State limited the ability to track the success of the course in terms of teaching engineering theory and student retention, traditional 4-years programmes such as at Penn State have far greater latitude to do so. In addition to tracking student success and opinions at the end of each semester, it is also recommended that a basic questionnaire be developed and given to the students at the beginning and end of the class. The purpose of the questionnaire will be to assess changes in the students understanding of basic engineering principles. However, when crafting the questions and developing the course, great care must be taken to avoid teaching to the evaluation or directly covering any given questions. Some possible evaluation questions in a multiple-choice format are as follows for the suggested open-class atmosphere that includes both engineering and other majors:

1. If a person is standing on the surface of the earth, what force must be exerted by the earth to avoid having them crash to the centre?
   A. Any force up to the persons weight
   B. Any force greater than the persons weight
   C. The person's weight
   D. None of the above
2. Two equal sized trays of water are placed in a freezer at –10°C? If one tray is at 50°C and the other is 75°C, which one is more likely to freeze first?
   A. 50°C
   B. 75°C
   C. Both the same
   D. None of the above
3. A 500 kg body at a height of 100 m and a 100 kg body at height of 500m are both dropped to the ground. Neglecting air resistance, which body will do more damage at impact?
   A. 500 kg
   B. 100 kg
   C. Both the same
   D. None of the above
4. If both are dropped from the same height, which one will hit first if air resistance is neglected?
   A. 500 kg
   B. 100 kg
   C. Both the same
   D. None of the above
5. Is the Professor on 'Gilligan's Island' a scientist or engineer?
   A. Scientist
   B. Engineer
   C. None of the above

When asking these questions at the beginning and end of the course, it should be emphasized that the answers will not influence the students' grade. Furthermore, it is recommended that each answer be followed by a brief explanation to help frame the mind and intent of the student.

Conclusions and Recommendations

Since special effects creating dazzling and lasting images of engineering principles (or, as is often the case, what is not really possible), Science Fiction opens up a vast arsenal for enhancing engineering instruction. Unfortunately and despite the obvious promise of the genre and all of its inherent possibilities, SF has not been integrated with engineering education to any appreciable extent until now. Given its inherent possibilities, a new teaching paradigm has been conceived that uses Science Fiction as found in the literature and movies to help enhance engineering education. To-date, this paradigm has been incorporated into two similar courses intended for entry-level students. While there are many facets to this paradigm as encapsulated in the new courses, the primary reasons behind their inception were to help illustrate basic engineering principles and create a positive image of engineering. The courses also served a useful purpose in that they can highlight many important, albeit neglected, issues of man, technology, and society. If an open course format that allows all majors is used, it may also aid in recruitment of students to the profession. Student feedback indicates that the Science Fiction approach is capable of reaching and teaching a wide spectrum of students. Given the critical need to maintain an innovative and technically capable engineering force, the use of Science Fiction in engineering education should be encouraged.

Finally, when teaching the concepts discussed earlier, and regardless of the audience, the class and subject matter can and should always be made fun and interesting. This is essential to help teach the concepts, as well as avoid ruining what could be fun movies and stories. In addition to tracking student success and opinions, it is also recommended that a basic questionnaire be developed (tailored to a specific major if needed) and given to the students at the beginning and end of the class. The purpose of the questionnaire will be to assess changes in the students understanding of basic engineering principles. When crafting the questions and developing a SF oriented course, great care must be taken to avoid teaching to the evaluation or directly covering any given question as with any course. When asking these questions at the beginning and end of the course, it should be emphasized that the answers will not influence the students' grade. Furthermore, it is recommended that each answer be followed by a brief explanation to help frame the mind and intent of the student.

References

1. Dubeck, L.W., Moshier, S.E., and Boss, J.E., (1995). Using Science Fiction Films to Teach Science at the College Level. *Journal of College Science Teaching*, 25, 46-50.
2. Dubeck, L.W., Bruce, M.H., Schmuckler, J.S., Moshier, S.E., and Boss, J.E. (1990). Science Fiction Aids Science Teaching. *Physics Teacher*, 28, 316-318.
3. Dubeck, L.W., Moshier, S.E., and Boss, J.E. (1993). *Fantastic Voyages: Learning Science through Science Fiction Films*. New York: Springer Verlag.
4. Campbell, M.E. (1999). Oh, now I get it! *Engineering Education*, 88, 381-383.
5. Harris Poll (ASME News Vol. 17, No. 10).
6. Dick, K.J., and Stimpson, B. (1999). A Course in Technology and Society for Engineering Students. *Engineering Education*, 88, 113-117.
7. Wilson, R. (1973). Bridging the Gap between Technology and the Humanities. *Engineering Education*, 63, 349-351.
8. Segall, A.E. (2002). 'Science Fiction in the Engineering Classroom to Help Teach Basic Concepts and Promote the Profession,' *Engineering Education,* 91, 419-423.
9. Segall, A.E., (2002). Science Fiction in Engineering Instruction: To Boldly Go Where No Educator has Gone Before. *Proceedings of the 2002 ASEE Annual Conference*, Montreal, Canada.
10. Segall, A.E. (2007). Science Fiction in Engineering Instruction: the Final Frontier? *Proceedings of the 2007 International Conference on Engineering Education — ICEE 2007*, Coimbra, Portugal.
11. Krauss, L.M. (1996). The Physics of Star Trek, New York: Harperperennial Library.
12. Krauss, L.M. (1998). Beyond Star Trek—Physics from alien invasions to the end of time. New York: Harperperennial Library.

8

Improving Teaching and Learning Process through Computational Resources

New Approach

Edson Pedro Ferlin, Nestor Saavedra and *Valfredo Pilla Jr.*

The 21st century brought two great challenges to scientific and technologic careers. The first one is the low demand for this kind of programmes; a phenomenon most accentuated at the OCDE members. Several multinational enterprises development centres are now placed on emergent countries, like Brazil, India and China. This picture could be due to a common sense that 'engineering is a hard, difficult course and the financial reward is poor'. These kind of ideas make people choose business careers, which increase the myth. All of this has make teachers, universities and even employees to think: but, what's happening?

From what concerns to us, teachers, it's easy to enumerate several points: boring and few interactive classes, courses that put in first place the number of (not enumerable) subjects, instead the real learning of them by students. The major part of this fault becomes the fact that the teaching-learning process is centered exclusively on the teacher, the only one that, supposedly, has the knowledge. This is a paradigmatic point of view, surviving form decades, and needs to be changed. This breakdown should be easy and continuous, followed by a change of mind at the educational systems, and now taking into account new technologies on science education, like internet, multimedia facilities and so on.

The first of the new technologies, the internet, composes the second challenge of this century. At the first view, the internet has an uncommon number and kind of information. Student usually thinks that classes are not more necessary, once the information can be discovered and assimilated by a single click on the computer's mouse. On the other hand, these billions of kinds of information are not classified and, the worst picture, without someone to tell him what is true or not. The teacher must use internet on his classes, in order to make them more interactive, participative and dynamical, once this is a tool used currently by students. So, this is a new challenge to today's teachers: how to classify the vertiginous number of information? How to make classes necessary to students? How to make students, once again, motivated to discover, learn and to argue with teacher and other students?

In the search of how to make a more effective teaching-learning process, the engineering courses of UnicenP has been carrying on several initiatives based on interdisciplinary and computational resources. These initiatives include a new view of the 21st century student by teachers, multidisciplinary projects and classes and a significant use of computational resources through the entire programme.

Teaching-Learning Process

The meaning of teaching puts the teacher as the main player and the responsible for the process. All the activities point to his person, his qualities and abilities. By the other side, the act of learn, which means search information, acquire abilities, assimilate changes, modify position and behaviour, break paradigms, is focused on the student[1].

At the engineering courses of UnicenP, the centre focus is the learning of the students upon the teaching of the teachers. The efficiency of a teaching process can be estimated by how much students are able to assimilate the subject on discussion at a given period. The teacher resources that must be used to increase student learning are innovative teaching strategies, alternative evaluation process and the relation surrounding both, teacher and student, a relation with social and emotional components that should be taken into account. The teacher becomes the player that make easier to student about how to learn, so the teacher is a mediator between student and knowledge. The teacher role is not to teach some subject in particular, but teach the student about how to learn that subject, not more just proclaim and transmit information, but create conditions to student acquire and assimilate the information. The pedagogic process based in a passive absorption of subjects should be replaced by another one, based on an active and intensive relation between student and the teacher-mediator, which would organize significant learning experiences[2].

The desire to break the traditional classes dominated only by the teacher and stimulates bigger participation, initiative and responsibility by the students carries to a teaching process centered on learning. The whole class, composed not only by the teacher, but also with the students, becomes the responsible by the teaching learning process.

Teacher Student Relationship

The concern with the student learning and not with the teacher teaching is determinant on main directions of relationship within classes. Some ways to make easier the student learning are based on certain kinds of behaviours inside the relationship between teacher and student, as teacher's reliability, in the sense that the student feels make out by a person who is not judging him.

The teacher has a direct influence upon the classes' pictures, relationship with students and their adaptation on learning skills of them. This requires an effective way of teacher's actuation, in order to provide students all support necessary for their growing and effective learning, also. As examples of effective actuation, which requires alternative strategies of teaching, we have a preliminary discussion of the discipline programme, division of the class in several groups of discussion and studies and weekly periodical hours to students to meet the teacher to provide the adequate support.

In the particular context that the programme is inserted, the Law of Directions of Brazilian National Education (LDB), stated in 1996, has defined the Brazilian organization among the levels of student formation. Beside this, it has also defined the students′ profile when they are starting their undergraduate programmes. At that time, the Engineering programmes are not able to handle with these changes and several adaptations have become necessary, because the LDB has idealized a student profile that not exists in reality. This kind of student has demonstrated on recent past years several difficulty on skills like maths, abstraction and reading comprehension. However, we can wait that students find the solution by themselves, and some efforts are carried out at the Computer Engineering Programme of UnicenP, in order to improve first year student's adaptation to the new skills and abilities required in an Engineering undergraduate programme. Some of these efforts[3] are described below:

Motivation of the Teaching Body

The professionals compose the teaching body have solid experience on both, teaching and professional range of actuation. As the student profile is not exactly the expected, some adaptations in the way on how to handle with the classes are necessary, without lack of rigor on at student formation. A remarkable character of the two first year's teachers is that the majority of them have recently had experiences with high school students. This fact makes possible a easier communication between these teachers and the students.

The hand of the UnicenP created the CEAP (Pedagogic Support Centre) in order to provide support to teacher on how to structure classes and lessons and how to make a better use of the new multimedia possibilities. Every January month, when the teachers are coming back from vacations, the CEAP organizes the Teacher Development Course, where we have discussions about new and innovative strategies and abilities to increase the teaching-learning process.

Classical Books Reading Comprehension

One remarkable difficulty that student bring with them is that one about reading comprehension about technical or non-literature. This also increases another difficulty, which is how to express yourself by oral or written way. The comprehension of the state-of-the-art technical literature is also damaged. Instead the major difficult Uni form hyper be the comprehension of the technical concept, it becomes the comprehension of what is really written on the text.

Since 2005 it was decided that student has to read one classical book by semester. At the end of the semester, on the last test of each discipline, a question about the semester book is included. The results points to an increasing interest of the students by reading and, as a consequence, their texts comprehension.

Basic Math's Introductory Course

offering of this course is necessary due to the background diversity of the first year incoming student. So, the course intends to provide the basic mathematical skills in order to make student able to get on along his first year at the university. For example, in a Physics class about free fall motion, the major difficulty should be the physical concepts and not how to handle with a equation involving square factors.

The course is carried on along the first semester of the first year. The programme was elaborated by the Physics, Calculus and Linear Algebra teachers, taking into account the previous knowledge of the students, their major difficulties and the sequence of how these difficulties appears along the year.

To conclude this section, as could be seen, the related efforts are mainly concentrated on the first and second year students, because among these students we have the bigger rate of dropout. This character appears due to two facts: a previous wrong choice of career and, even choosing correctly, students often feel loss himself at the beginning of the course. To help them, such types of activities and support become more necessary since the today's young student has been demonstrating less maturity than of the past.

The Theory-Practice Partnership

This section has for objective to present our agreement regarding the theory-practice what we are developing using these concepts and applying in the Computer Engineering Programme.

The theory is the base for the practice, and it in turn develops, justifies and it experiments new concepts that become new theories or formularizations providing new a practice, and thus successively.

In this way, this theory-practice binomial should to produce an ascending spiral, representing the knowledge that is being added by the student to the long of the process. This must be given to the long of the years, in way that is a solid and consistent process for the formation of the professional that it is being helped in the development of the technical-scientific knowledge of the student.

In Figure 8.1 one may observe that the Theory by means of the experiments and projects produces the Practice that consolidates and strengthens the knowledge. On the other hand the Practical one through the comparison/ discussion, results, considerations and conclusions, adds new elements to the Theory, propitiating new ways of teaching, also with new tools produced in this process.

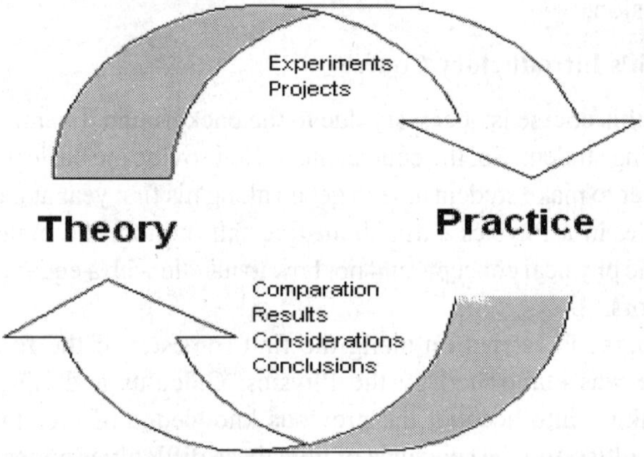

Figure 8.1: Theory-Practice Partnership

The Computer Engineering Programme

The Computer Engineering Programme[4], at UnicenP, has an annual serial structure, being offered in two turns: early and nocturnal. The programme offered in the early turn has foreseen duration of four years and the nocturnal duration five years. The curriculum of both programmes contains the same courses, differing only in the distribution along the period of duration of the programme. The daytime programme had beginning in the year of 1999 and the nocturnal programme in the year of 2000. Both the turns have a total of 4210 hours, including 160 hours of traineeship, 80 hours to the Graduation Thesis and 50 hours to complementary activities, like research, participation in congress and symposiums, etc.

The curricular structure congregates the set of courses in two great areas of Professional Formation (hardware and software)[5], together with courses of the area of Basic Formation (Calculus, Physics, and others), of Human Formation (Humanities), Management Formation (Enterprise Management and Management of Projects) and Specialty Formation.

The pedagogic guideline is described in the Pedagogic Project of the Computer Engineering Programme at UnicenP[6].

It is better to deal with the two areas simultaneously since the projects involve hardware, software and an application.

Since the first programme series the students have in the curriculum of the Computer Engineering Programme, courses of both hardware and software areas, beyond the basic area that include Physics, Chemistry and Mathematics.

This makes possible that the professors elaborate multidisciplinary projects, with the intention of defrag the knowledge that the student is acquiring by means of the multidisciplinary experimentation. However, many times this is not possible, because at this moment enters in scene the diverse disciplinary projects, that has a more restricted target, but that promote the consolidation of the theory by means of the experimentation, many times empirical, but that inside of a narrower base, wakeup the students to know to make it, using the available tools.

Beyond this intra-series approach, also a bigger inter-series relationship was looked where the students apply and use all the knowledge the previous series in a project of the next series making with that the student breaks the paradigm of the segmented knowledge for a more systemic and integrated approach, knowing that he or she is in a process, that to the end of the course, a base for the good professional performance will propitiate it[7].

In the Computer Engineering Programme at UnicenP, we have created a favourable environment so that this Theory-Practice evolution happens in a gradual and solid form, not only in the courses of programme, but also in others initiative as curricular job experience, extension projects and scientific initiation, AVIN, Engineering Games, tutorial sessions for first year students, that if they have shown of extreme value in this teach-learning process[8-9].

It fits to stand out that this has brought benefits to the programme as a whole, as much for the student staff and the faculty, that it had that to change the form as approached it courses it and of as this if it related with excessively. Obviously this also affected the way as the professor was integrated in the process, therefore it had that to leave to think that it was a passive element, therefore he or she judged that it did not influence at all, to become an active subject, increasing its compromise with the programme, suggesting new ideas, partnerships, projects.

One another aspect with high influences in this new vision, in the majority of the times the professor minister its courses in more than one series, and this creates a sequence of knowledge and the way as to relate the knowledge of its course them in order to create a bridge between the series and contents, also producing a feedback of more advanced courses in the programme to the more basic courses, always respecting the area of affinity between its courses.

As secondary factor we have a reduced and more harmonic faculty, what makes possible a bigger integration and contact between the professors. Another point of prominence is that each course is thought and elaborated in view of the Computer Engineering Programme, of this form we obtain contents directed and with the approach for the profile of the programme, this makes with that the courses have its development thinking about an only focus that to form a Computer Engineer.

It is important to be pointed out that since the first series the student is treated as a 'professional in training', because he our she has to perceive that he or she should be involved with the programme, so that to the end of this process it has the complete formation.

Fist Year

A course that establishes diverse bridges between knowledge is Computer Engineering Project course. The concomitant courses as Algorithms and Computer Programming, Computer Foundations, Electronics, Physics and Calculus work several theoretical concepts that are applied in final project of Works on Computer Engineering Project. Works on Computer Engineering Project develops a contact with the practical activity of engineering (the question of the construction of a viable solution for a real problem, exactly which it is a simple solution) using tools that compose the nucleus of the Computer Engineering Programme, with hardware and software.

An example: to make possible simple experiments integrations were carried through parallel interface of a personal computer. The concepts were tested by hardware and software with direct integration, with assemblies of the whole system in proto-o-board. For in such a way basements were carried through others courses and some one in the Computer Engineering Project course, as the use of the parallel interface. We noticed that these experiments could be safer and trustworthy if a protection system was installed in the interfaces parallel. This protection if transformed into a set of kits that it started to be used in this course and others. Then, the dedicated initial effort in the projects to the protection of the computer was transformed into more dedicated time to the study of the specific digital hardware and the system of parallel interface in itself. Modifications in these interfaces had been produced resulting in new versions that allowed a minimum of implementation of hardware, as Analog to Digital interfaces, step motors interfaces, etc (Figure 8.2). Thus, more complex experiments could have been elaborated and the focus of the work of disciplines could be dislocated for these works in time of the test in the basic hardware. However, the beddings of digital interface are not forgotten or despised, but the time dedicated to its operation was reduced. Thus, more time can be dedicated to the study of more advanced subjects without disdaining the recital.

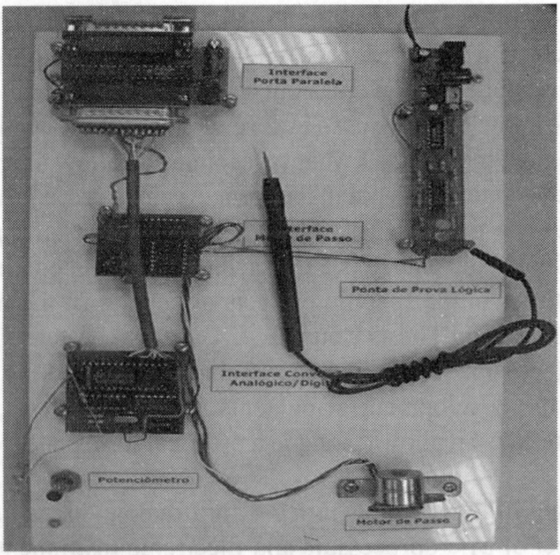

Figure 8.2: Kits for Interface with the Parallel Port

As a more advanced application example we may cite the project of a ballistic launcher with computer control (Figure 8.3). Operational software allows setup the angle and strength of the ballistic launching. The system is plugged to parallel interface. This interface is previously studied in Electronics course too. The Algorithms and Computer Foundations supply the theoretical and practice foundations for the interface software development. At last, Physics develops the concepts of movement, speed, acceleration and strength. The result of such system is to make possible a better comprehension of the individually developed concepts at the courses. Moreover, the system may be used as an accelerating learning tool in the Physics course, because with the launcher the student can verify in practice the specific concepts with direct experiments in the equipment.

Figure 8.3: Ballistic Launcher

Still, the Computer Engineering Project course develops the concepts of technical documentation: reports, technical papers, monograph. These knowledge are applied in several courses with experimental contends, like Physics. These knowledge are used in several other courses with experimental contends, like the Physics itself what saves time and allow the professor work with focus in the content and not in the form. Again, a profit is had associating the knowledge to the practical activity. The methodology itself applied to project development inside the course is é understated as practiced knowledge to be reused many times in the specific projects of courses of the next series and same in the Graduation Thesis Course.

The interfaces initially developed to Computer Engineering Project course are useful in the development of contents of others courses, as Computer Foundations, because it allow testing in a practical form concepts in a fast and direct form.

The domain of the concepts reflects, for example, in the development of the final project of Microprocessors and Electronic Instrumentation courses, developed in partnership. The base of these projects is of microprocessors systems that iterates with analog processing systems and interfaces to computer. The concepts of computer interface are reviewed and adjusted for a new higher level of communication, the USB.

Second Year

In Digital System course the technology have been used with intention to represent the different levels of abstraction that projects can be developed. The application of digital projects techniques using low and medium integration levels is a tool to concept the physical environment influence (electronic) in the projects. The practice in these projects allows students to verify electronic limits.

Based in this experimentation students can model the systems whose practical functioning was already known and well tested in more complex systems elaboration. Thus, the use of VLSI devices and hardware description language allow to elaborate systems that have electronic coherence added with conventional functions, both characteristics are present in low and medium integration level projects with logic structure developed using VLSI technology, as well relating the test procedures applied in the first and the second. Becomes possible, in this second stage, the elaboration of very complex systems with a strong reference to the simple systems, being possible to students know what are the real difficulties to implement in the physical world and the relation between function and logic theory associated to 'assembly' (like a puzzle) where the pieces are previous studied/manipulated structures.

Figures 8.4 and 8.5 presents two developed kits to aim the systems project. The kit FPGA shown in Figure 8.4 is a project used in Computer Architecture and Organization course in the project of Direct Computer Interface Systems, like ISA and EISA, where again becomes available know base to other projects in another courses. The kit shown in Figure 8.5 presents an automatic system to test combinatorial and sequential logic circuits.

Another project that is based in this kit is the microprocessor, where architecture, machine language and application are developed in a common form integrating Digital Systems and Computer Architecture and Organization. A project is the base, again, to application in other courses.

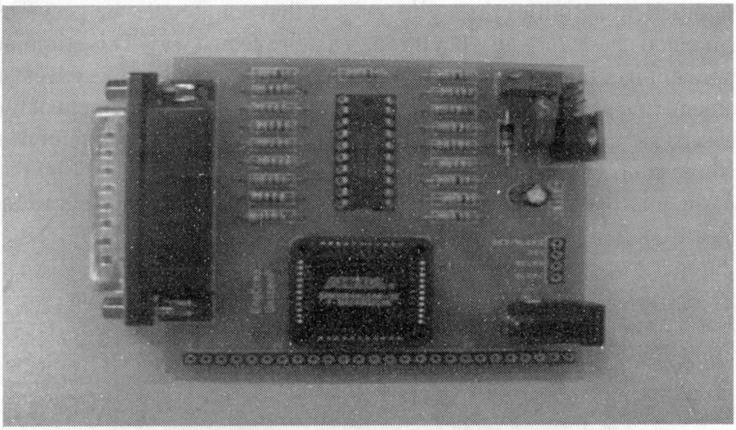

Figure 8.4: FPGA KIT

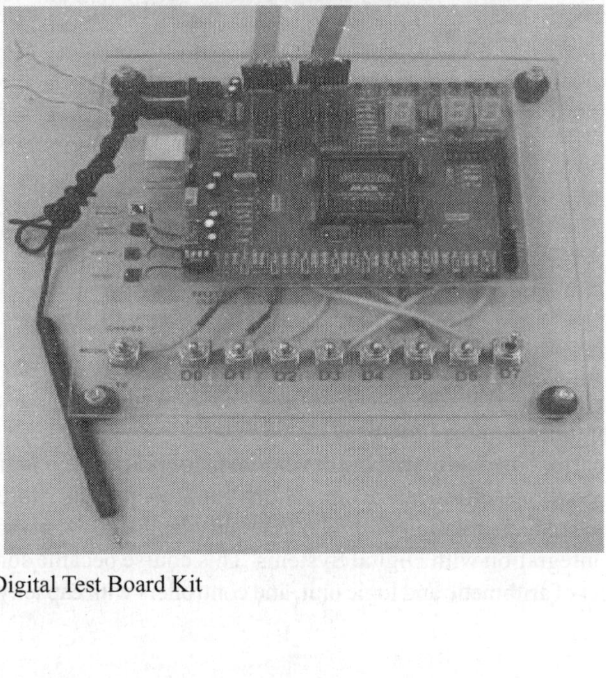

Figure 8.5: Digital Test Board Kit

Third Year

Another example of theory-practice interaction in our Computer Engineering Programme occurs in Microprocessor course.

Initially the microcontrollers contents were experienced through simulation and assembly in proto-o-boards. Despite we have microcontrollers commercial didactic kits, these kits allow a very limited interaction level. Thus, the results obtained from practical activities was projected and a low cost kit that is available to students that is assembled to become a complement for the practical activities through a project that congregate the previously experimented characteristics, but through a more robust way. This stimulated the application of microcontrollers in another courses project, like Electronic Instrumentation and Software Engineering, allowing the development of more complex systems. Thus was possible to define common projects between these three courses, approaching multidisciplinarity contents. The Figure 8.6 shown the microcontroller minimum system kit developed on programme.

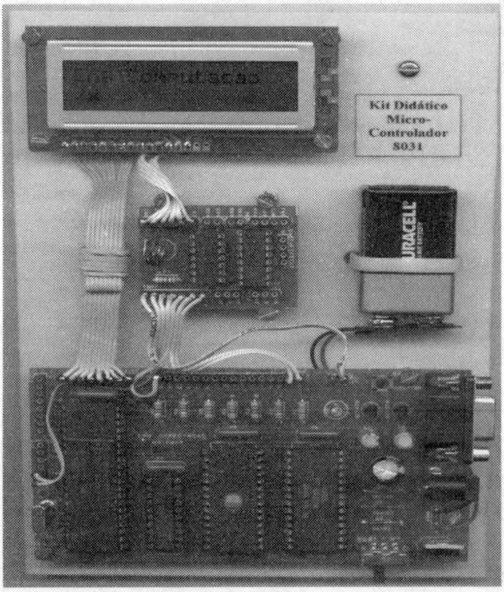

Figure 8.6: 8051 Microcontroller Kit

Thus it was possible to verify that the consequence is a complexity increment in final graduation projects.

A recurrent difficulty was the development of practical content correlated with the concepts of processor operational and control structures, machine cycles and students relation with x86 assembly language. The approach used involves integration with Digital Systems. This course became some contents like project of arithmetic and logic unit, and controllers with capacity to interpret machine language instruction, using as conventional integrated circuits SSI, MSI and VLSI as FPGAs, what allow a complete system integration (including memory).

The students have the opportunity to apply the mathematical and physics knowledge using a completely microprocessed system developed by themselves which have complete domain. Thus can exercise other courses' knowledge through a practical way.

Fourth Year

The Graduation Thesis course is an individual work developed by students[10]. The Graduation Thesis has its objective to allow the last year student the chance to use, prove and to strengthen the knowledge acquired along the Programme in an interdisciplinary project. This opportunity is materialized by a project development, reconciling theory and practice and under the supervision of a professor and with the evaluation of a Board of Examiners, composed by at least three professors of the Programme. The project involves both hardware and software development applied to an engineering problem solving.

This is the final opportunity for the student to improve its knowledge uniting the practice with theory inside the programme.

Others Activities

Several extra classroom activities are offered to the students as complementary chances for this theory-practical integration. Some are obligatory as the prescribed period of training and others are optional, as the monitorship work, participation in lectures, courses and projects of extension. Some of them will be detailed on next sections.

This process is being developed since the first year of implantation of the programme, in 1999[4], and with passing of the time, it was evidenced that we are getting resulted entertainers, in virtue of whom the students are each time more present in the activities and projects, and of that the professors participate actively of the programme, in the most diverse activities.

The practice makes with that the theory pass to have meant for the students, beyond the motivational factor and even though of dispute, in the direction of that the students want to present a work with more resources and functionalities of that of the too much pupils, and that is to healthful in the academic environment.

The practice awakes the students for the experimentation, in which always we have the possibility of the error. The error becomes a generating element of new discoveries in the learning, and through the rightness and errors the students will search assist with the professor, course monitor, or same with other students, becoming the act to learn a life experience, therefore there is human relationship involved.

But the practice must be linked to a theory, formularization or thesis, so that the student can prove or refute, provoking new discoveries and rearrangements in order to acquire new knowledge.

However the professor must have closed attention to the signals generated for the students in order to help them and to direct them in this environment of discoveries and reformulations. Moreover the professor must use the practice as a booster element for new theories, justifying the persistence and effort of the students in the search of new knowing, not only as a verification of that to that true age, but that it was the beginning of a new theory-practice process.

This shows to be necessary an approach closer to the know, how making possible the student to try and to produce new knowledge, taking for base the knowledge acquired through the theory (classroom) and tested/tried (laboratory).

But this only starts to have concrete effect when the student lives deeply the problem and interacts with the solution in the practice; therefore she is using more one form of acquisition of knowledge recurrent of this practical experience, also developing the psychomotor ability. The four pillars of the education are to apprehend to know, to learn to make, to learn to live together and to learn to be.

When the theory is developed belong to the practice, the learning is developed in these pillars, therefore the student acquires the knowledge, makes it solid with the practice, works on the relationship with other students and professor, beyond to acquire the auto-confidence for the solution of the problems and also about itself.

Multidisciplinarity at the Computer Engineering Programme

Computers have many applications in such different areas as Medicine, Biology, Automotive and Security. Instead of being presented as based as a CPU-Display-Keyboard-Mouse model, they are presented as an electronic device, with an internal microprocessor, analyzing any systems behaviour and performing a real time data transmission. One can spell out applications as physical activities to monitor or many others where computers interact with the system control, as engine fuel injection, security systems based on human patterns, and so on. Those applications involve not only knowledge about microprocessors and electronic devices, but one must include on it other areas as Physics, Chemistry and Mechanics. It should be emphasized that, in a conception of a electronic device with focus on market, on must carry knowledge on normative and administrative questions.

Based on this multidisciplinary world, engineering programmes should follow the same evolution line, inspired by research centres and corporations, with a view to be focused on graduated students collocations in the job market, once employers have been preferred to give a collocation to pre-qualified people, instead of invest time and money on training one. Thus is very important that students start to apply their knowledge during the engineering programme, mostly in extra-class activities.

Among the activities that UnicenP's Computer Engineering Programme is carry on, that be detailed on this work, one can cite the following:

- Integrated projects among courses (multidisciplinary works), promoting integration among teachers and students;
- Computer Engineering Project course, that involves a conception and realization of a project in the initial year of the programme;
- Engineering Games, involving students of the first and second year, besides the Electrical, Mechanical and Civil Engineering students;
- Graduation Thesis;
- Annual Integrated Examination. Take part of this examination students of third year and higher, in order to evaluate how is going on the acquired knowledge by them;
- Scientific Initiation Projects;
- Operational Structure Maintenances, where specialized workers do the laboratory support and conservation, development of projects, electronic didactics tools and other related projects;
- Monitor collocations offers in the laboratories;
- Supervised trainings, evolving a project realization in the UnicenP;
- Scientific research projects;
- Extra-classes projects in partnership with enterprises;
- Monitor (pupil) activities in courses;
- Academic events;
- Talks and lectures with invited speakers as graduated students, companies CEO's, and other professionals on related areas.

Those activities aimed to produce the multidisciplinary students' formation. Due to mass and intense participation of professors, dean, technical and support personel, a quality students group used to be sent up. Some of these activities will be detailed in this section.

The Multidisciplinary Works

One of the ways to obtain the multidisciplinarity is by the development of multidisciplinary works, involving several courses, as for example the project of an ISA card for communication between computers. This work involved the courses of Computer Architecture and Organization, Digital Systems and Computing Foundation and Programming and Teleinformatics[11-12], which are courses of the second year programme. Another example is the analog data acquisition system produced by sensors and transducers, a partnership development of Microprocessors and Electronics Instrumentation of the third year. In the Microprocessors course the students develop the digital part of the system and its firmware and, in the Electronics Instrumentation the analog interface and the specific software for data acquisition.

The Computer Engineering Project Course

This kind of multidisciplinarity happens since the early series of the programme and begins with the Works on Computer Engineering Project Course[13], a first year course. In this course the student is faced with the multidisciplinarity soon early, therefore in the end of the first semester they have to define a simple project that will be developed in the second semester. This multidisciplinary project should cover the knowledge of the first year courses, for example using the physics, electronics, algorithms and logics knowledge. In this year, a computer controlled robot is under development, and will be used for development of the knowledge of Physics, for the mechanic parts, Electronics for the motors driving circuits and for communication with a computer, Algorithms and Computer Programming and Mathematics Logic for the computer programme development, using the C programming language studied in the Algorithms and Computer Programming course.

The UnicenP Engineering Games

The UnicenP Engineering Games[8, 9, 14] is other adopted resource in the Engineering Programmes at UnicenP, among themselves the Computer Engineering Programme where the students have the possibility of the experiment in practice and in a playful form the several concepts and knowledge in a extra-class activity, but that finished reverting in beneficiation for the student who participate in of this activities. It is allowed for the participation of students of the first and second year. This activity occurs since the implantation of the programme in 1999.

Besides it is a voluntary activity, because the student is free to choose to participate or not, the frequency has been well above of the expected, confirming the initial proposal that the practical activities excite the students The students come to the UnicenP in a Saturday, a day without classes and they remain from 7h30 to 17h00 carrying through technical-scientific tasks, together with the playful side and also psycho-motor.

The Figures 8.7 and 8.8 presents an example of task, that it is consisted of mounting a small hydroelectric plant, using simple materials.

Integrated Evaluation (AVIN)

The AVIN (Integrated Evaluation), described in[15-16] is another element yet incorporated when elapsing of the course to propitiate them an ample vision of the programme and courses. The Integrated Evaluation (AVIN)[10],

Task – Hydroelectric Plant

The team must to build a small hydroelectric plant in the slope, if front of the beige block. The water used for electrical energy generation must be unloaded in the pluvial water collector in the slope base.

Task Report

The report must be write based on the ABNT standard, and must to contain

- Tank emptying forecasting, with calculus annotations;
- Forecasting of the electric motor power supplied by the water;
- Occurred difficulties;
- Suggestions for improvement of the small plant functioning;
- Conclusions.

Each team must to submit its small plant to test until 11 h 30 min. The test will to evaluate the tank emptying time and the electric power produced by the motor. The team must to stamp its number in the tank.

Supplements

- Flexible hose
- 2 bucket (20 liters);
- Fast drying epoxy;
- Fast glue;
- Empty soda thin can;
- Cork;
- PET bottle (2 liters);
- Electric motor.

Figure 8.7: Description of the Hydroelectric Plant Task.

also has as objectives the diagnostics of the skills and competences of the students, to evaluate the curricular integration of the courses and to promote a reflection about the programme pedagogic way, as presented in[13].

The AVIN is constituted of a discursive test, composed by 10 questions involving multidisciplinary projects with total duration of 5 hours. The subjects treated in the questions are the contents seen until the year where the student is registered. However, the AVIN is only applied from the third year of the programme, exactly to be able to evaluate the integration between the basic contents of engineering and the specific professional contends of the computation engineering area. The tests are elaborated and corrected for the faculty of the Computer Engineering Programme, having in mind the multidisciplinarity. The tests had been elaborated taking in consideration the degree of difficulty of each question, what it makes possible one better distribution in terms of results.

Figure 8.8: Hydroelectric plant assembly

<table>
<tr><td colspan="3">A circuit for driving a 120 VAC lamp was designed as in the figure below. The lamp is controlled by software, using the PC parallel port (D0-D5 outputs). Are requested:
(a) Determine the logic equation of the lamp L1 control. (4, 0 points)
(b) Design the maximum and minimum resistor value, such that L1 be ON when the command is sent via parallel port. The devices features must not be damaged. (6, 0 points)</td></tr>
<tr><td>Transistor 2N2222A features:
VBE saturation = 0,7V VCE saturation = 0, 2V Vb saturation = 100 mV
ICmax = 500 mA
VCE max = 50 V</td><td>Relay features:
Voperation = 12 V
Resistance = 240 Ω</td><td>Logic gates features:
VO = 5 V
I O max = 4 mA</td></tr>
<tr><td colspan="3">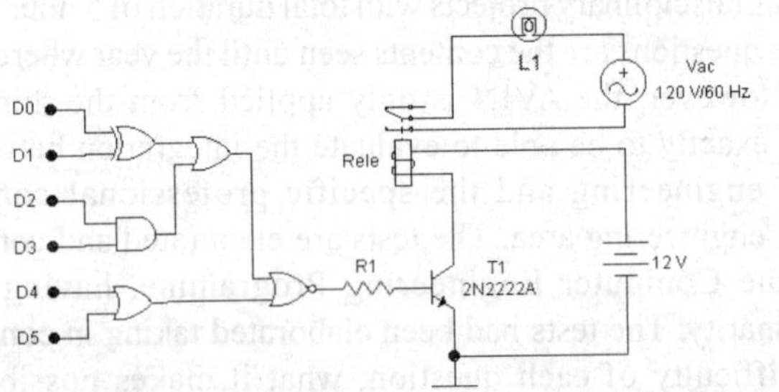
</td></tr>
</table>

Figure 8.9: AVIN Question Example

In this evaluation the student can get the solution of the presented problems and to identify its deficiencies to them and with this can correct them before she pass for other year.

The participation is voluntary, but it has been very good, around 80 per cent of attendance. It also supplies information to the professors regarding the treated knowledge, making possible adjustments of the didactics to improve the exploitation.

To follow we show an example of question of the AVIN, Figure 8.9, which in this in case involves the courses of Electronics, Digital Systems and Architecture of Computers.

Didactic Electronic Kits

One of the resources to make possible a bigger multidisciplinarity is by means of the use of electronic kits, that it comes being developed for the course, as for example: A/D converter, system with Microcontroller 8031 and others. Kits makes possible to develop bigger projects in the courses; therefore they have a reduced time of assembly and a small possibility of problems with the electric connections. The course can also use this material in the classroom activities, extra classroom and in the diverse works. Using the A/D converter module a programme can for example be developed for monitoring and management of devices by means of the acquisition of a signal proceeding from converting circuit A/D that is connected to the parallel port of the computer, where will be used knowledge of courses of digital systems, Architecture and Organization of Computers, Teleinformatics, Computation Principles and Programming, as well as the knowledge from previous years.

Graduation Thesis

The Graduation Thesis[10] has as aim to provide to the students of last year the opportunity to use, to prove and to strengthen the acquired knowledge to the long one of the programme by means of a multidisciplinary project, consolidating the concepts, fundaments, formularizations and applications studied during the programme. This project is developed under orientation of a professor, and with evaluation by an examiners board, composed at least by three members of faculty.

Besides evaluating the level of preparation of the learning for the professional practice, the Graduation Thesis of the Computer Engineering Programme also can be used as an instrument of evaluation of the teaching learning process, of the curricular structure and the of programme itself, therefore it allows to evaluate the integration between discipline of the course in a multidisciplinary project.

The Graduation Thesis is annual, constituted by two semesters, and just can be carried through by the students who are registered in the course named

'Graduation Thesis'. The course spend 80 hours of work, included the orientation and defense besides the examiners board, and the extra-classroom development.

The theme of project can be freely choused by the student from the themes proposed by the professors or from self proposition, since that approved for the Graduation Thesis Committee. The subject obligatorily must approach the topics, disciplines and treated in the Computer Engineering Programme, being desirable that the use of these topics be as ample as possible.

The Graduation Thesis course must to enclose the two main areas of the programme — hardware and software — in a proportion of at least of 20 per cent from each area, allowing the future engineer to consolidate the knowledge acquired in the programme.

Scientific Research Projects

One of the features of the Engineering Programme at UnicenP is, since the first year, provide a practice vision of the challenges that the students will find in their professional lives. Proposals of Science Research Projects are available to the students yearly. These proposals can be practical activities like the automation of physics laboratory experiments, development of acquisition and data handling systems for different areas, or research activities like the development of a parallel process scheduling method at a parallel computing cluster or the implementation of logic programmable reconfigured systems.

These projects involve acknowledgments in many courses and provide to the students a greater contact with the Engineering Programme, because they do the project out of classroom, staying in integration with teachers, employees and trainees at the university. Moreover, the Science Research Projects aim that the students do not develop a known project, but search for theory basis to develop a new methodology that solve a problem.

Some projects have one or more guide teacher and aim to develop in the students the scientific research practice, contributing to their academic future.

For example, a Science Research Project done was the 'Pressure measurement acquisition system to visualization and processing on the computer'[17] assists a hydraulic laboratory experiment of the Civil Engineering Programme, doing the measure of pressure in real time at two points of a tube, allowing the graphic visualization of water hammer phenomenon. The projected device can be seen at Figure 8.10.

Supervised Trainings

The students can validate their curricular job experience doing a supervised training at the Computer Engineering laboratories, otherwise, working at any company.

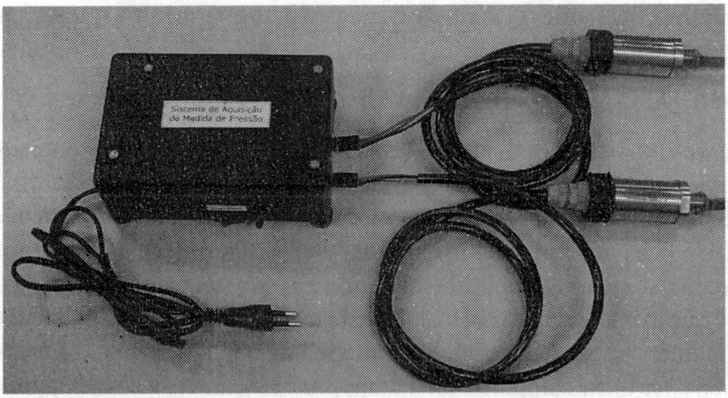

Figure 8.10: Pressure Measurement Acquisition System

The fact is that, doing the training at the university and using the resources of the programme, the students are in a process of multidisciplinarity, because they apply many concepts that was learned in courses, or that they are learning now, in a training project development, therefore, doing a research activity too.

One or more students working at the same project can do the training at the university and they want a supervisor teacher.

For example, a training project done was the 'Portable digital mini-osciloscope based on a PIC microcontroller'[18]. This project consists in a device with restrict functions to analysis electric signals and shows in a graphic LCD display, working as a low cost oscilloscope to do simple tests. The device is shown in Figure 8.11.

Figure 8.11: The Mini-osciloscope

Examples of devices developed for others programmes are: An interface to automatic read data from meteorologic station, developed to Civil Engineering

Programme, and the system for measure the 6 minutes test, used in Physiotherapy Programme.

Computer Assisted Experiments at Physics Laboratories

It is a well known fact that first years students of technology courses have difficulties on how to describe a physical situation, or trying to identify which are the relevant parameters to take into account or how to describe mathematically the system behaviour, in order to be able to analyse the outcome of an experiment and predict something about the system. One way to face this problem is by using computer simulations, which have been established as an efficient way to make learners improve their physical modelling about a system. This could be achieved once those computer simulations provide learners with the opportunities to test the understanding about a physical phenomenon by proposing and testing alternative hypotheses[19]. In this way, they can also test and learn about the causalities relations among the parameters of the given situation[20].

However, computer simulations can abstract totally students from the real world, in a sense that lots of subtle aspects as friction, air resistance and viscosity, are neglected or not modelled in a convenient way. This is why some researchers[21] claim that computer simulations should not replace the first laboratory contact, in order to avoid this lack of contact with the reality. As a pre-established model, ignoring new facts that could emerge from experiments, computer simulations could affect the students' development about scientific discovery.

This project intends to integrate computer simulations with real Physics laboratories experiments, but in an interactive way, where the student can perform a computer simulation *before* its interaction with the real experiment, to predict the system's behaviour. Manipulating the experiment, the student is going to see, on a computer monitor, the real time measurements of the relevant variables of the proposed situation. Besides this interactivity, the computer will not be a substitute to the calculations and measurements, once this certainly could be a wrong strategy, as this procedure avoids learning about how to precede data manipulation on a laboratory. However, the computer-assisted experiment will be a bridge between the real physical situation founded on an experiment and the textbooks Physical approaches.

The procedure is described below:

- The student receives the description of a physical situation and is asked to predict the behaviour of some parameters.
- The student performs a computer simulation to confront with his prediction.
- After that, he performs a real experiment in a Physics Laboratory. This experiment is computer — assisted, however the student is able to observe the real time evolution of physical quantities.

- The student analyses both results and elaborate conclusions about the results of the experiment.
- The conclusions are discussed with an instructor.

Developed Computer Assisted Experiments

This topic will being explain the construction of three measurement applications for physics laboratories: one impact transducer, one complex pendulum and an air track. These equipments are developed to assist practical physics experiments and to become easier to understand these physics phenomena.

Air Track Linear Displacement, Velocity and Acceleration

Linear Displacement phenomena experiments are carried through an air track. The objective is to measure displacement of an object without attrition loses. Nowadays the experiments carried through at physics laboratories have photointerrupters sensors. This type of sensors does not allow continuous measurement, they work only starting and stopping a chronometer. These sensors are placed with a previous known space between them, with that is possible to obtain the object velocity through simple formulas. However these velocities are only average speed between the start and stop photointerrupters, and do not show the results we want to know. Despite of these, sensors allow a great number of experiments in which they have a major problem that only can measure average speeds. We propose an acquisition system that measures the car's position in real time. This system must be mounted without devices on the car that could cause an overweight that produces errors in the measures.

For this reason, the displacement was measured through an optical system based on photoemitters and photoreceptors placed on the air track extremities. The principle of actuation is that the light emitted by the photoemitter is reflected on the car over air track and returns to photoreceptor. The point where the light returns to photoemitter is proportional to distance of reflection, this principle is shown in Figure 8.12, the distance of the first object is less than the second object and the points of distance reflection are different for the two situations.

This system is known as PSD (Position System Device) and is very used in industrial applications. It was connected one sensor on each extremity of air track to obtain position from each car, (Figure 8.13).

The PSD sensor has an exponential response. There are two ways to obtain the displacement though sensor response. First is use a table that has displacements values for sensor response values, this method is very poor and can cause serious errors. The best method is to use a logarithm amplifier to obtain a linear response. The last step is to convert an analog value to digital, analyze this value and send it to computer; these works are made by a microcontroller.

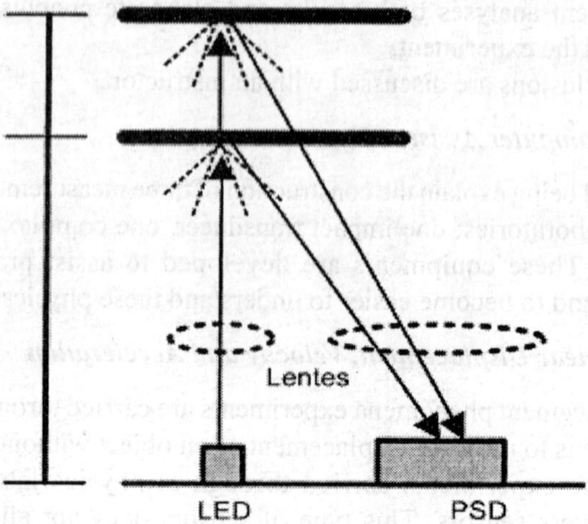

Figure 8.12: The Reception Point Comply with Object Distance

Microcontroller communicates with software develop to simulate the air track functioning. This software obtain information about position of cars and can make a series of calculus to obtain other information like velocity, instantaneous and average, acceleration. Averages can be defined over two position points or time interval. Also the curves of theses information are presented by a graphical way. The air track image with real time actualization show the displacement of cars. The software main screen one shown in figure 8.14.

Linear Impact Transducer

In a collision between two objects, these ones exert forces of great intensity one over other at a short time interval. These forces are internal to the system and are significantly bigger than any external force during the collision. The total linear moment before and after the collision remains constant, however, the total kinetic energy of the system remains constant only in an elastic collision. During the experience, the speeds of two objects (cars), moving itself over an air track without attrition, are measured before and after a collision frontal for the elastic and inelastic collisions.

Currently, the experiments are executed over the air track, where are positioned two cars. The first one starts the experiment with an initial velocity, (*v1i*), known through a pair of photo-interrupters. After a few time, the first cars shocks with the second one, initially in rest. The final speed (*v2f*) is obtained through other two photo-interrupters, these ones located at the end of the air track. This experiment is detailed in Figure 8.15. With the physical relation between moment and energy, one can obtain the power of the shock between two cars, therefore, this is and indirect method of measuring these value.

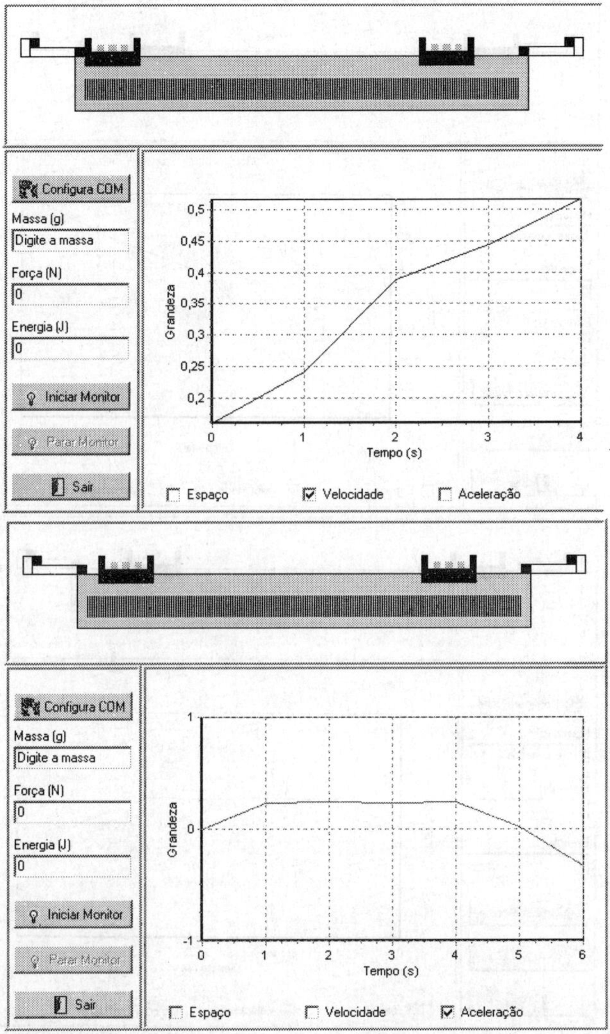

Figure 8.13: Each Extremity has a Sensor to Monitor the Car Displacement

To provide a direct form to measure the force exerted by first car over the second car, it is necessary to use a sensor that receives the impact from the car at the end of track. This form will not lead a significant loss in the mobility of cars in the diverse experiments that are developed over the air track.

The impact sensor must be robust since it receives impact right-handers from objects. Being necessary its correct setting too. The precision and band of measure are also essential factors in the experiments. Based on this information, it defined that the best type of sensor would be the LVDT

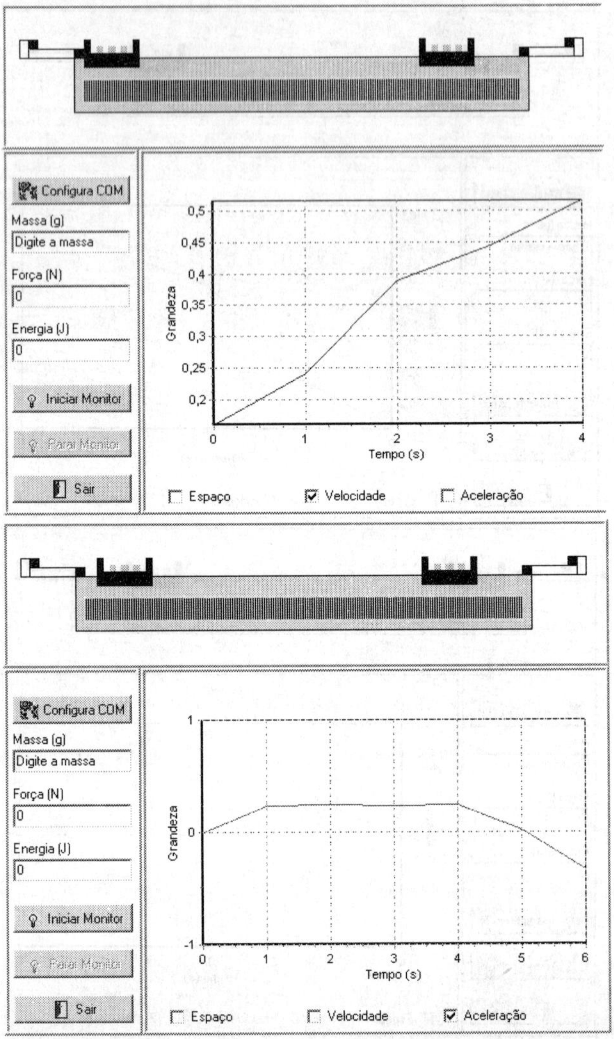

Figure 8.14: Software Interface, Showing Velocity and Acceleration

(Linear Variable Differential Transformer). The LVDT is an important and common sensor for displacement in the industrial environment. An LVDT consists of three coils of wire wound on a hollow form. A core can slide freely through the centre. The inner coil is excited and while core moves a current is inducted on secondary coils. It is shown in Figure 8.16. LVDTs have a great linear range from ± 25 cm down to ±1mm, and have a rapid time response.

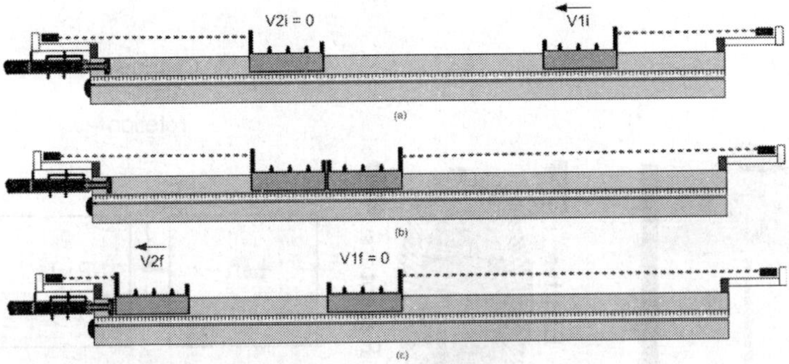

Figure 8.15: Collision Experiment

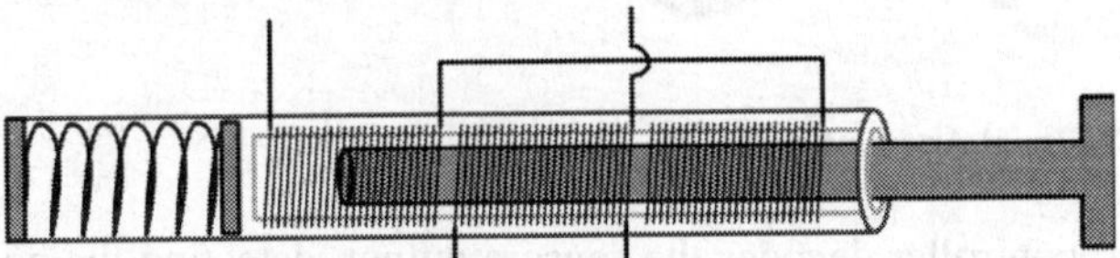

Figure 8.16: LVDT Internal Structure

Dumped Pendulum Oscillations

The practical studies of oscillated displacement have simpler example of the standard pendulum. However this type of movement has a great number of variables and normally it is of difficult understanding for students. Aiming to improve the experiments carried through in the practical physics classes we develop a data acquisition system for this experiment and software that realize a simulated experiment showing the main principles, like: frequency constant, damping curve.

The practical classes of oscillatory motion has a great number of manual actions that made constant errors and difficult to understand for students. Nowadays, a student drops the pendulum with known amplitude in the same moment that other student start a chronometer, it stops when pendulum complete one period.

This part was developed with the same principle of computer mouse, where disc allow and block the light beam with an angular space of two degrees. The light beam is provided by two photoemitters, it is point to two photoreceptors spaced forty-five degrees, this displacement make a delay in signal that is used to know the direction of motion.

Figure 8.17 shows the mechanical part of pendulum that coupling the sensor. Also, it is shown the led position relative to the disc. When the led's light beam crosses disc, the system recognizes a pulse. This is shown in the upper part of the figure. For the under led, the disc blocks light beam, and the system stay with zero value. The waveforms obtained by successive pulses are shown in Figure 8.17

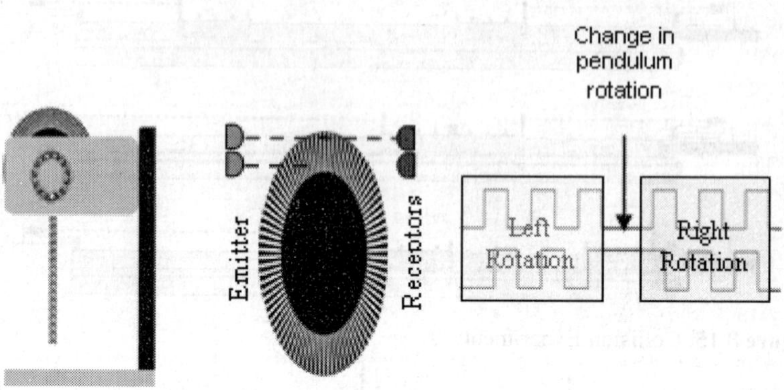

Figure 8.17: Signal Acquisition

A microcontroller decodes the sensors output, detecting the position of the pendulum. The software receives a value that represents the pendulum position referent to the rest position and calculates movement data like: amplitude, frequency and period. Also, this information about energy, potential and kinetic and damping is shown in graphs to a better understanding. Figure 8.18 presents the programme's main interface.

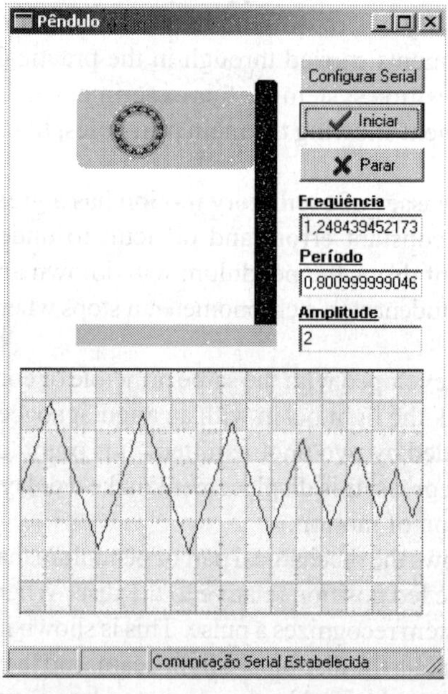

Figure 8.18: Software Interface

To conclude this section, attention is claimed to the advantages and features of the described systems:

Among the main features of the software, the following evident features may be observed:

- Clear and user-friendly interface.
- The student may observe a real time evolution of the physical quantities.
- The real-time graphics plotting avoid some misconceptions like do not distinguish between position graphic and the real car trajectory.
- It is possible make experiments to observe the mechanical energy conservation.

Among the main features of the hardware, one can evidence the following:

- The hardware was built with standard and cheap components, which makes it very useful at many institutions.
- At the air track experiment, the PSD sensors are assembled on the air track and do not on the car. This is much important in order to make a data acquisition system that does not alter the original experiment feature.
- The hardware can be easily adapted to other experiments, like collisions, linear momentum, over dumped oscillations and so on.

The main results of the utilization of computer-assisted experiments at laboratory Physics classes of UnicenP point to a significant increase in the student learning and understanding[22, 23]. The experiments make more easy and useful to explore both, the subtle and remarkable features of a given physical situation.

Internet and Multimedia Resources

Once has defined the basis of both, the teaching-learning process and the professor-student relationship, the UnicenP searched new ways of interaction, based on new technologies such as internet, intranet and multimedia projectors at each class. A brief description of these tools is made bellow.

University Portal

The University Portal is in use by the second semester of 2004. Since then, an increase of student learning has been observed. The Portal enhances de communication between class and professor also giving access to programme coordination and others professors to the information related with each one disciplines. As a result, this feature allows an enhancement of multidisciplinary activities[7]. The Portal has several resources to make the increase at the teaching-learning process. A screenshot is shown at Figure 8.19.

- The Communicator (Comunicador) allows the online contact among students and professor in order to keep them in touch to solving questions, lessons, and so on. Even each student could be contacted individually; it could be an individual orientation tool.

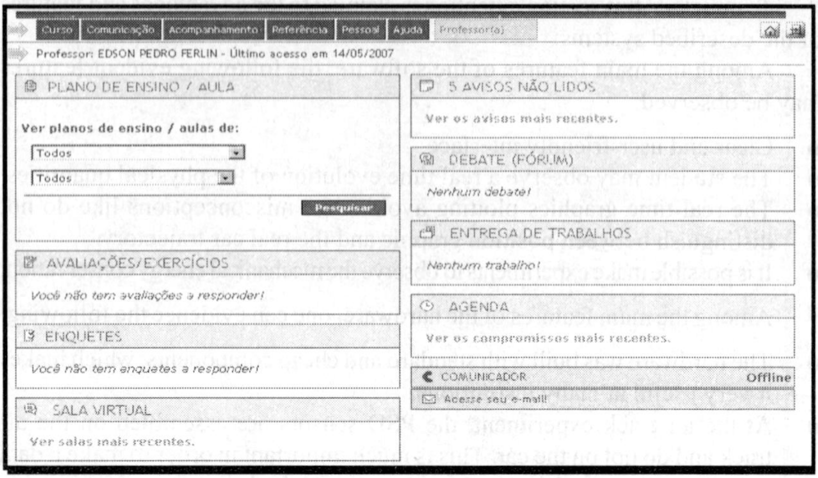

Figure 8.19: University Portal Screenshot

- The Notice Board (Quadro de Avisos) avoids the lack of information by students. It also permits to access the information whether the student is certified or not by the teacher.
- The Discipline Programme (Plano de Ensino) allows students are conscious, at the beginning and during the semester, of which topics and subjects are going to be seen, what are the evaluation criteria and what is the bibliography of the discipline.
- The Lessons (Aulas) are available at each meet between professor and class. At the Lessons, the teacher can put their videos, documents, presentations, additional bibliographic references and Internet links. A screenshot could be seen in Figure 8.20.

With these resources, student can access the next classes before the professor address. This allows a previous knowledge of the subject that are going to be in discussion at the classes, what allows student arrive at the classes more prepared to discussion of the subject and can solve some questions. The Portal can be accessed everywhere, by internet, even when the student is on travel.

Computer Engineering Course Website

Another tool that student make use is the course website (http://engcomp.unicenp.edu.br), whose screenshot is showed at Figure 8.21.

This website is complementary to the Portal, putting at disposal general information about the programme, its development, projects and activities, not involving questions relative to teaching-learning process aspects, those are Portal's attributions.

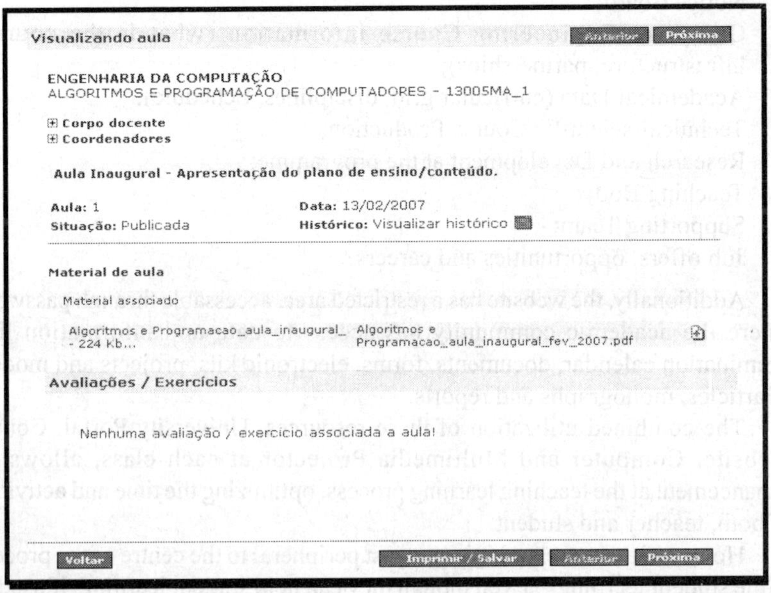

Figure 8.20: A Lessons Screenshot

Figure 8.21: Computer Engineering Course Website

The website is a large database and centralizes some information about:

- Developed activities by teachers and students (extension activities, seminars, lectures, technical visits);

- Notice Board;
- Computer Engineering Course information (what is the course, infrastructure, partnerships);
- Academical Data (curricular grid, disciplines, Schedule);
- Technical-scientific Course Production;
- Research and Development at the programme;
- Teaching Body;
- Supporting Team;
- Job offers, opportunities and careers.

Additionally, the website has a restricted area, accessable through password where the academic community has access to data and information like examination calendar, documents, forms, electronic kits, projects and models of articles, monographs and reports.

The combined utilization of these resources, University Portal, Course Website, Computer and Multimedia Projector at each class, allows an enhancement at the teaching learning process, optimizing the time and activities of both, teacher and student.

However, these technologies are just peripheral to the centre of the process of the student learning[24]. Even though they can help student learning, if used in a unadequate way, they can make class boring, classes with passive behaviour and supply more information than student can handle with. However, a challenge to nowadays professor is how to use these tools, dosing moderately each one, in order to achieve the centre of the discussion: the student learning.

Conclusion

As presented in this chapter, the Computer Engineering Programme at UnicenP is developing, since the programme beginning, multidisciplinary activities and, year after year, innovating and improvement other ways to provide an open view of the programme and of the profession to the student, using the classroom and extra-classroom multidisciplinary activities.

However, is important to stand out that the multidisciplinary process is not quick, and the results and consequences spend years, except the motivation. However, the big deal is the Graduation Thesis development, a large multidisciplinary project, in which the students have the opportunity to apply the knowledge acquired throughout the Programme and transform it in a prototype of a technologic product with high aggregated value.

In these years the students had very good improvement in the learning, what means that the acts are producing results. As example, the participation of the students in the activities of the programme, in the development of science initiation projects, the final projects quality, as also in practice over programme. Another factor is verified in Engineering Games participation, in the case of first series, and in AVIN, in the case of last series, where the students have better performances if compared with activities in the previous years, when the multidisciplinarity idea still was being implanted.

A bigger integration between the courses and activities in the programme is in the developmental phase, eliminating to complete the idea of the segmentation that haunts the graduation programmes, and that it is and inherent characteristic to this model. However, this still goes to take some time, therefore we must breach with the established paradigm and in such a way win some obstacles on the part of the students how much of the professors. This is not a simple task but that, with planned actions and coordination, to surpass, not immediately, but the medium and long run is awaited.

References

1. Abreu, M.C. and Masetto, M.T. 'O professor universitário em aula: prática e princípios teóricos.' 8a. ed. MG Ed. Associados, São Paulo-SP, 1990.
2. Kuenzer, A.Z. 'As mudanças no mundo do trabalho e a educação: novos desafios para a gestão'. *Proceedings of IX ENDIPE*, Águas de Lindóia-SP, 1998.
3. FERLIN, E.P., SAAVEDRA, N. 'How to a High School Student becomes in Engineering Student: Efforts Carried out at Computer Engineering Programme of UnicenP' In: GC 2006—5th Annual ASEE Global Colloquium on Engineering Education Highlights, 2006, Rio de Janeiro-RJ. GC 2006—5th Annual ASEE Global Colloquium on Engineering Education Highlights., 2006.
4. Tozzi, M.J., Dziedzic, M., Ferlin, E.P., Nitsch, J.C., Rodacoski, M.,'Os Cursos de Engenharia do UnicenP'. In: COBENGE 1999—XXVII Congresso Brasileiro de Ensino em Engenharia, 1999, Natal-RN-Brasil, pp. 2662-2669, 1999.
5. Pilla Jr, V., Ferlin, E.P., Cunha, J.C., 'O Ensino de Projetos Digitais: Fundamentação Teórica, Práticas de Laboratório e a Tecnologia de Dispositivos Reconfiguráveis', In: WCETE—2004 — World Congress On Engineering and Technology Education, Guarujá/Santos — SP, 2004.
6. Ferlin, E.P., 'Projeto Pedagógico do Curso de Engenharia da Computação', UnicenP, Curitiba-PR, 2002.
7. Ferlin, E.P., Cunha, J.C., Pilla Jr, V., The Multidisciplinarity in Learning Process in the Computer Engineering Programme: A Fundamental Question. In: IEEE Proceedings of 5th Int. Conf. on Information Technology Based Higher Education and Training: ITHET 04. Istanbul, 31 May-3 June, 2004. [CDROM].
8. Dziedzic, M., Tozzi, M.J., Ferlin, E.P., Rodacoski, M., Nitsch, J.C. 'Multidisciplinary Engineering Programmes at UnicenP', In: FIE 2000-30RD ASEE/IEEE Frontiers in Education Conference, Kansas City, USA, pp. 13-16, 2000.
9. Ferlin, E.P., Tozzi, M.J., Dziedzic, M., Nitsch, J.C., Rodacoski, M., 'Primeira Gincana de Engenharia do UnicenP', In: COBENGE 2000-XXVIII Congresso Brasileiro de Ensino de Engenharia, Ouro Preto — MG, Brasil, 2000.
10. Ferlin, E.P., Pilla Jr., V., Cunha, J.C., The Gradutation Thesis in the Computer Engineering Programme at UnicenP. In: Proceedings of the 33rd ASEE/IEEE—Frontiers in Education Conference. Bouder, USA, November 5-8, 2003, [CDROM].

11. V. Pilla Jr, E.P. Ferlin, and J.C. da Cunha, 'O Ensino de Projetos Digitais: Fundamentação Teórica, Práticas de Laboratório e a Tecnologia de Dispositivos Reconfiguráveis', In: WCETE—2004 — World Congress On Engineering and Technology Education, Guarujá/Santos — SP, 2004.
13. E.P. Ferlin, 'The Computer Engineering Project Course. In: ICEE 2001 — International Conference On Engineering Education, Oslo — Norway, vol. 6B5, pp. 17-19, 2001.
14. N. Saavedra, D. Traghetta, M.J. Tozzi, Dziedzic, M., E.P. Ferlin, 'Contextualizando Física nos Cursos de Ciências Exatas e Tecnológicas: Experiências e Inovações em uma Gincana de Engenharia'. In: SNEF 2003-XV SIMPÓSIO NACIONAL DE ENSINO DE FÍSICA, 2003, Curitiba. 2003.
15. E.P. Ferlin, and M.J. Tozzi, 'The Description of the First Integrated Examination of the Computer Engineering Programme', In: ICEE 2002 — International Conference on Engineering Education, Manchester-UK, 2002.
16. E.P. Ferlin, and M.J. Tozzi, 'First Integrated Examination of the Computer Engineering Programme', In: FIE 2002-32RD ASEE/IEEE Frontiers in Education Conference, Boston, USA, 2002.
17. E. Cichaczewski, E.M. Schroeder and E.P. Ferlin, 'Sistema de Aquisição de Medidas de Pressão para Visualização e Processamento no Computador'. In: XIX Congresso Regional de Iniciação Científica e Tecnológica Em Engenharia Cricte2004, Curitiba, Brazil, 2004.
18. E. Cichaczewski, E.T. Przysiezny and V. Pilla Jr. 'Mini Osciloscópio Digital Portátil Baseado em Microcontrolador PIC'. In: Anais do XIX CRICTE—Congresso Regional de Iniciação Científica e Tecnológica em Engenharia—CRICTE2004. Curitiba, Brazil, 2004.
19. Noble, T., 'Experiment, simulation and analysis: teaching and learning in an integrated physics and mathematics class', Paper presented at the annual meeting of the American Educational Research Association, Atlanta. 1993.
20. Mintz, R., 'Computerized simulation as an inquiry tool', School, Science and Mathematic, vol. 93, 2, 1993, pp. 76-80.
21. Richards, J.., *et al.*, 'Computer Simulations in the Science Classroom', *Journal of Science Education and Technology*, vol. 1, 1, 1992, pp. 67-79.
22. Saavedra, N.; Ferlin, E.P., Cordeiro, L.F.; Cunha, J.C.; Perretto, M.; Cúnico, M. "Estudo do Movimento Acelerado em Tempo Real Através de um Sistema de Aquisição de Dados Assistido por Computador'. Proc. Congresso Brasileiro de Ensino de Engenharia (COBENGE 2006), presented at Passo Fundo, RS, Brazil, September 2006.
23. Saavedra, N.; Ferlin, E.P., Cordeiro, L.F.; Cunha, J.C.; Perretto, M.; Cúnico, M. 'Utilização de Novas Tecnologias em Ensino de Física para o Estudo do Movimento Acelerado em Tempo Real'. Presented at Simpósio Nacional de Ensino de Física (SNEF 2007) São Luis, MA, Brazil, January 2007.
24. Estes, A.C. and Welch, R.W. and Ressler, S.J. The ExCEEd teaching model. Journal of Professional Issues in Engineering Education and Practice. ASCE. October, 2005.

9

Using Theory of Change and Team Teaching to Evaluate and Improve Teaching Practice in a Control Engineering Department

A Case Study

J.A. Rossiter, L. Gray and *G. Diercks-O'Brien*

Within the UK and elsewhere[1] there is a recognised tension between research and teaching. Funding mechanisms such as the research assessment exercise (RAE) have provided income incentives to achieve a high research rating, for instance by increased publications, external recognition and research income. Paradoxically, teaching assessment (now stopped) provided no cash incentive and merely gave successful departments good advertising material. Moreover, the teaching assessment was focussed on quality assurance (QA) (e.g. effective paper work) and much less émphasis was placed on quality enhancement (QE). University promotion structures mirrored this funding scenario and as a consequence staff have been highly motivated to develop their research but see little individual benefit, apart from personal satisfaction, in improving teaching quality.

Nevertheless, there is a growing awareness within the community that this pattern is not desirable and initiatives that recognise teaching excellence have developed in the background. More recently these have been consolidated through the higher education academy (HEA) and the associated subject centres. Some research led universities are also re-introducing career paths for academics who focus on teaching and learning as opposed to subject discipline research; until recently, promotion to the senior ranks was based solely on a strong discipline research profile. However, the majority of academics and heads of department still think that only research counts and it may be a while before the culture adapts to the changing environment.

This chapter takes its motivation from this research led context and looks at the repercussions on student experience, especially in year 1 where students are most vunerable[16, 22] and need better support[2]. Specifically, a major aim for the authors is to put the needs of undergraduate students at the centre of the university again, while accepting that the majority of staff priorities will differ. In other words[7], how, in the teaching context, do we get the most out of staff who are unashamedly research focussed?

A secondary aim of the paper is to present a pilot of the 'Theory of Change' (TOC) approach[3]. TOC is an evaluation approach originating from the social sciences, which have been adopted by the Learning Development Unit (LDMU) at the University of Sheffield for the purpose of both planning, and evaluating curriculum development initiatives and projects[4]. Although the focus is on evaluation, the approach can sharpen the planning and implementation of a project or initiative. The Department of Automatic Control and Systems Engineering (ACSE) has been among the first three departments in the University to pilot the new approach to evaluation. Thus the case study will be of interest to other engineering academics wishing to plan and evaluate teaching developments within their own faculties.

Assessment of the Status Quo within ACSE

ACSE is typical of many University Departments in that market forces have encouraged a rapid move from delivering just a few degree programmes to several alternative programmes. These programmes generally share a common core, but that core is becoming smaller as the number of optional streams increases; recent changes to introduce engineering with Business Skills necessitated a loss of 2 first year core modules to make space for Business modules and updated agreements over the delivery of some two department system engineering programmes also led to reductions in common content. Due to the relatively small numbers on each systems engineering stream, a large use of service teaching is made where possible. So, for instance, ACSE students on a mechanical systems degree will take two mechanical modules per year with students from the Mechanical Engineering Department, students on electrical systems take two modules within Electrical Engineering, and so on.

Effects of Modularisation

The approach of building degree programmes by making use of groups of relevant modules that are already in existence is very efficient from the institution's perspective and also should ensure high quality teaching within individual modules, because it keeps a tight rein on the number of modules a department needs to deliver. However, the flipside is that the year 1 curriculum can become fragmented, especially with the gradual, but independent, evolution of individual modules. Thus departments have the conflicting pressures of trying to ensure a large number of coherent programmes based on a small core and many specialist modules from a variety of sources. This, in combination with changes in the student intake[10, 21], can easily cause a situation where a sizable minority of weaker students struggle[11, 17] to see their programmes as coherent; some became disenchanted and others simply fail and dropout. There is also a wide variability in the style of teaching and expectations form different departments and first year students more than later years often find this confusing.

This general pattern was replicated within ACSE[7] and moreover staff had become accustomed to having very little overview of the entire programmes and were generally content to deliver modules in isolation, as this amounted to minimal effort and allowed them to dedicate more time to research. Although staff usually delivered modules very professionally, the modularisation effect was such that students had to create links between modules themselves. Many students were simply unable to do this in their first year and needed more support[19]. ACSE was keen to give students the best possible experience and optimize their learning and thus there was a large impetus for action.

First Year Team Project

The First Year Staff Team Project was first formulated in early 2004. The first two authors and the then head (Neil Mort) of the departmental Learning and Teaching Committee (LTC) had concerns about the fragmentation of the year 1 curriculum and the knock on effect for students, some of which was being reflected in student feedback[7].

Consequently, their key objectives were to engage staff more in taking ownership of the entire curriculum and not just their own modules. By encouraging such ownership it was hoped that improvements would arise naturally from the lecturers. Such improvements were expected to include: embedding of frequent and explicit linkages between modules, to ensure a proper balance of assignments and skills development, to give better co-ordination of industrial input, to ensure coherence of each degree programme. In fact one might argue that any department should be doing all these things[15, 20], however, in practice, the activities happen sporadically and the efficacy seems more dependent on individual champions or external pressures rather than departmental policy.

In summary, the authors felt that by creating a team approach to teaching, staff would become more aware of their responsibilities beyond delivery of an individual module and more proactive in bringing about positive change. Thus, they sought to obtain funding for a project whose main aim was to create a team where staffs' contributions to year 1 teaching were through the team. As the reader may guess, this is a substantial culture shift from the typical academic who wants independence and to be left to 'get on with it'; a shift many staff could resist very strongly. Hence, the next section gives insight into a strategy for planning the project in such a way that one has a good chance of success.

Project Planning and Theories of Change

Within the University of Sheffield, there is an established fund (Curriculum development fund — this is part of the teaching quality enhancement fund) for supporting projects within learning and teaching. The monies available are relatively small, but nevertheless to ensure efficacy there is assistance from educational advisors available to help academics write their applications. The process is such that guidance is given simultaneously in what might be achievable and makes good pedagogical sense.

For the project discussed here, the educational specification (or bid)[8] was written over a course of a year and without awareness of the TOC approach. However, the TOC approach[4] was being developed simultaneously and hence was ready shortly after the project commenced. Hence, it was logical to incorporate the TOC approach into detailed planning and evaluation of the project thereafter; this also gave a good test bed to pilot evaluation and project management using TOC. Hence, this section gives an outline of a typical timeline and outcomes that were considered in applying the TOC approach to the ACSE project.

Overview of TOC

The key to the TOC approach is to look at a project over the entire lifespan and be clear at the outset about the desired long term impact. The desired impact gives a benchmark for evaluation and thus for planning and monitoring. This impact may of course vary both in time and for the different stakeholders within any project, which for this chapter are most logically students and staff. The desired impact is mapped backwards (Table 9.1) in time onto more detailed aims and objectives (short-, mid-and long-term outcomes). Other essential aspects to support the desired outcomes may be ongoing throughout the project. The intent is to manage the project using the key elements in table I as a convenient way of identifying and grouping what needs to be done.

Table 9.1: Typical Theory of Change Timeline or ACSE Project

Months	*Phases*	*Ongoing Aspects*
0	Analysis of current situation/problem	Enabling factors and resources,
12-24	Short term outcomes	Processes and activities.
24-36	Intermediate outcomes	
36-60	Long term impact	

Unpacking the Detail

Each project would elaborate on the outline in different ways. The list of Table 9.2 illustrates how the different phases/aspects might be expanded for a fairly generic project whereas a more visual flow chart is given in Appendix 3, which is specific to ACSE. The key point of this table is to use keywords and concepts to help the project leaders identify the key questions they should ask. One additional focus of TOC is on looking for effective tools to assess the impact of a project across the whole institution, thus to enable planning to direct funds in order to maximise benefit. The following section will demonstrate how this approach was mapped to the learning and teaching (L&T) project within ACSE.

Table 9.2: Typical Issues to Consider

Current Situation	Awareness of existing excellence, L&T valued less than research, always the same people doing the work, funding for innovation small/hard to get, sharing good practice poor, most staff don't know how to get things done.
Enabling Factors/Resources	Is project strategic, innovation or development? Is there effective project management? Does project meet student/staff needs? Are leaders aware of support available? Is there formal recognition for teaching developments? Are there funds available? Is there good guidance available?
Processes/Activities	Are there strategic processes already in place? What can central support services offer? Can other departments help? Students participate in new activities. Dissemination of good practice. University supports wider strategic view.
Short and Intermediate Outcomes	Improved L&T, staff gain experience, University meets external needs, staff make use of central expertise, good practice shared, depts. become more strategic, staff adopt innovative practice, staff become familiar with pedagogical theory, students have better experience, dissemination.
Long Term Impact	Raised profile of L&T, holistic view of research and teaching roles, high quality graduates imply university has enhanced external profile.

Applying Theory of Change Approach to ACSE

The reader will have noted that the TOC approach steers one away from a quick fix. Awareness of a problem must be translated into a long-term solution. This section (and appendix 3) shows how the desired long-term impact for ACSE is mapped backwards to generate the necessary actions (e.g. tables 9.1 and 9.2). The phases are given in reverse chronological order.

The Current Situation in ACSE

Although this chapter focuses on areas needing improvement, it should be emphasised that most of the curriculum is very well-received. Based on student feedback and staff observations, more students than desirable were performing poorly in year 1 and there was evidence that for several, this was due to a lack of engagement. Of more concern, many students did not see the interdependence of the topics within the year 1 curriculum and this was contributing to poor satisfaction and/or disengagement. There were also ongoing problems with performance in mathematics. The department was motivated to change these perceptions and improve student performance on a long-term.

Desired Impact in 3-5 Years

For ACSE, the intended impact was better student retention, achieved through improved student satisfaction leading to improved performance. Although not a part of the project, another knock-on effect of improved student satisfaction and progression would be good publicity. This impact could be broken down to smaller items, but for convenience of presentation the facilitating factors, which are also ongoing, impact in some sense, are described as outcomes and activities; this includes changes in staff behaviour.

Intermediate Outcomes

In order to achieve the desired impact, it was necessary to ask what the year 1 curriculum and delivery should look like. Typical outcomes were for students to: have positive perceptions of the year 1 programme, greater engagement in the material, greater achievements, improved skills, teamwork ethos and, an increased sense of belonging and being supported. This still sounds a big vague, so the TOC approach goes back a little further to ask: how might these intermediate outcomes might be achieved?

Short Term Outcomes

A number of rather obvious statements could be made as to what is required to meet the intermediate outcomes; however the TOC approach encourages project leaders to write these down clearly and thus, more importantly, provide a framework to ensure action follows.

Outcomes for Students: The list of desirable outcomes for ACSE included items such as students:

(i) being aware of the curriculum as a coherent whole and linkages/interdependencies between modules;
(ii) feeling assessment is balanced in time and style and appropriate;
(iii) feeling supported, for instance through timely quality feedback and pastoral tutoring;
(iv) feeling staff communicate effectively;
(v) perceiving the curriculum to be both interesting and relevant to the real world context.

Outcomes for Staff: In order to meet the outcomes for the students, there are parallel outcomes for the academic staff, for instance the creation of a team of teachers committed to effective communication, flexibility in their individual practice and a common goal. Evidence of the effectiveness of the team could be actions supporting the desired student outcomes such as:

(i) engagement with students;
(ii) changes to curriculum proposed and implemented;
(iii) effective liaison with and influence upon departmental committees.

Processes and Activities

Next, one might now ask what processes or activities would enable the outcomes to be met, at all stages of the project. In fact, these are rather obvious, but the TOC framework helps ensure the right questions are asked. From the students perspective some simple activities were needed such as:

(i) more group work to encourage peer learning and community;
(ii) spreading of assignment deadlines to avoid overload;
(iii) links between modules; etc. However, the bigger action lay on the academic staff to ensure these things happened as well as all the other desired outcomes.

- Staff expected to link their teaching with other modules; this required a good awareness of the content and timing of what was being taught in other modules.
- Where beneficial, staff were requested to modify their delivery to give better synergy with other modules.
- Staff should negotiate all deadlines and consider the balance in style (to ensure uniform development of key skills) and magnitude of the entire coursework load.
- Staff were encouraged to include more real world examples, especially in topics such as mathematics.
- Staff should provide the year tutor (personal tutors) information to help with pasturing and monitoring.
- Staff should take joint responsibility for the overall curriculum design. This includes being proactive in proposing changes.

Enabling Factors and Resources

The next step is to ask what resources and support already exist or is needed to help with the above activities and thus how can we ensure they happen? In ACSE the key enabling factor for effective progress was the establishment of a team approach to teaching where ownership of a module was by the team, not the module leader. Although this is technically already the case, in practice a module leader has a lot of autonomy to modify a module. The net effect of small year on year changes can soon become substantial. By having a team to look after all the modules, module creep would be monitored and directed far more actively and staff would gain a good awareness of the entire curriculum. Thus a team enables or facilitates the effective communication and negotiation which is an essential factor in this project.

The more challenging issue was to convince research active staff to give up valuable research time to attend monthly team meetings and also to take on tasks agreed important by the team. It was decided that an incentive scheme could enable this culture shift; once the benefit was demonstrated, staff should be more willing in the longer term. Therefore, three members of staff put together a bid for internal funds to pay staff an honourarium for contributions to the first year of team activities. This incentive was quite effective in persuading otherwise reluctant staff to contribute and thus was key to the early success. In the longer term, a major enabling factor will be voluntary commitment by staff to the team ethos and thus giving their additional time for free. This will require them to be convinced of the value.

The team leaders also perceived a benefit in giving team members training, for instance in team building and teaching specific skills. However, most members do not see this as central to the project and so take up was not uniform.

Intermediate evaluation of project

The University carries out formal evaluations of all projects, using the feedback of students and staff involved. For ACSE, the first formative evaluation has been produced[5]. The project will be revisited in 2 years' time to assess the long-term impact of the project. In the interim, the project leaders will be involved in a reflective cycle reviewing the original TOC and progress made with the project. These reflective interviews will assist the project team to make adjustments to the project if required. These interviews will be carried out in 6 to 12-monthly intervals. This section gives an overview of the first evaluation process and results.

Designing the evaluation

The two major stake holders in this project are the staff and students, thus an evaluation is made from each of these perspectives. Qualitative evaluation is more appropriate than quantitative, so most of the evaluation was conducted via interviews based around a well designed questionnaire (Table 9.3). Some of the required activities are simply procedural (e.g. managing coursework deadlines) so the focus here is on the more fundamental issues which reflect the desired activities, processes and outcomes, for instance:

- How the First-Year Team approach is perceived by colleagues; is the approach seen as valuable?

Table 9.3: Samples from Evaluation Questionnaire

TOC Parameters and Issues	*Evaluation Questions*
Resources/Enabling Factors	
Buy-in from staff on teaching team needed, assumption that staff will make something a priority if they see it as relevant/important to them;	Ask staff individually about their commitment, To what level is staff prepared to engage? If they don't engage, why is this?
Process used: kept meetings as brief and focussed as possible, only engaged them where the issues were directly relevant to them.	Speak to Head of LTC about his perception How do colleagues feel about changing their modules?
Buy-in at department and faculty level needed.	What has been given? Was it enough? More needed? Hard to do; time constraints?
Staff time needed. Issue of research commitment over L&T	
Desired End-of-project Outcomes	
Students perceive the year 1 curriculum as coherent. Is the curriculum taught in a coherent fashion?	Do students know that there is a first-year staff team? Do they perceive it as a coherent group? Are students aware of the assignments working as links between modules?
Students perceive the year 1 curriculum as interesting and relevant.	Feedback on real-world examples, e.g. poster project, BIC and talks from industry.
Having a year 1 staff team that is embedded and exists beyond the funded period	Will the staff team continue having regular meetings once the funding runs out

- How effectively the First-Year Team is integrated within the departmental structures for learning and teaching (e.g. integration with the LTC)?
- What progress the Team has made in addressing student satisfaction, performance and retention?
- What impact any changes implemented so far have had on student learning and whether the strategies employed by the First-Year Team have been effective?
- Should the department continue with or extend the Team approach?
- What the future direction and activities of the First-Year Team should be?

The above questions have been derived from the TOC. The purpose of the formative evaluation was to assess to what extent staff and students felt the objectives have been satisfied and provide the project team with steer towards the future direction of the project.

Summary of Evaluation Results[4]

This evaluation summarises the achievements to date, provides formative feedback and aims to ascertain whether there is merit in continuing. It is based on ten staff interviews, 22 student questionnaires, eight 3-5 minute student interviews and documentary evidence. An indicative view of the evaluation can be obtained from the selected staff comments in appendix 1. This section gives a summary; some of the more detailed data is given in Appendix 2.

The main project objective has been met. The First-Year Team met six times during 2005/6 and has implemented changes, some well beyond original remit.

- It is too early to judge the impact. Moreover some of the major changes are yet to be implemented. Student feedback is generally positive, with the exception of one new component (Business in the curriculum), which subsequently the team has decided to discontinue in its current form. There is still some, possibly unavoidable, clustering of assignment deadlines.
- The team has acted as a catalyst, introducing many positive changes, which the department had discussed previously but not progressed. However, some criticism stems from an uncertainty of the role of the Team in relation to other committees and needs clarification.
- The evidence points towards continuation of the First-Year Team, at least for another year. Indeed, this could be a useful approach for other academic departments.

One could note that the department is now looking at its committee structure, and one likely change is a move away form regular large and lengthy meetings, say of LTC, with instead many discussions being delegated down to sub-committees. The first year team is one such sub-committee that has formal recognition rather than being informal and transitory.

Quantitative Evaluation against Specific Outcomes

For completeness, this section gives details of outcomes, which can be evaluated as yes/no or with numerical data. The summary is very clearly that the project is having a positive impact. However, there remain aspects that could be improved more and some things that are difficult to resolve.

In terms of procedural issues the project has been successful on a number of counts:

(i) The programme architecture has been changed substantially. This includes new assignments, substantial modifications to some existing modules and movement of modules to different semesters;

(ii) the team argued successfully for replacing the mathematics service modules by in house mathematics modules;

(iii) There are now formal mechanisms for ensuring the balancing of workload, the balancing of skills development (including group work), inclusion of sufficient and varied real-world examples, as well as enhancements to personal tutor support and effective communication between module leaders.

In terms of data collected from student interviews and questionnaires:

(i) 86 per cent of students recognised the effort put into curriculum design;
(ii) 81 per cent felt the links between modules were effective;
(iii) the majority were very satisfied with aspects drawing in real world examples;
(iv) 82 per cent were happy with the amount of group work;
(v) all were very positive about the input of the industrial speakers and
(vi) there seemed to be recognition of the wide range of skills developed.

However, minorities were still unhappy with the workload distribution, communication with the service departments and, a number of minor individual gripes. In several cases the criticisms relate to the lack of integration of the service module; as there are six very different options each semester, integration of these is infeasible.

Future Plans

Although staff found the team based approach beneficial and many support a continuance of this project, initially a sizable minority wishes to return to a traditional model of working. This reflects the ongoing issue of how do we encourage staff to devote more time to developing their teaching and including more formative assessment[14, 16, 17] when their main drive is research. Hence, the immediate plans are to seek stronger support from senior management for embedding the project, but in a format that encourages and rewards participation as much as the extra time on research. So far the HOD and head of LTC have both been very supportive and indeed have formalized the membership of the team.

We hope that once the team has been running for 2-3 years, staff will consider it as normal, get used to and rely on the benefits and no longer consider it an extra burden. In fact, early experience is that staff are still attending meetings, as long as they are convinced that the time will be spent usefully and that they are chaired efficiently. One main aim was to create a forum for discussion where it was possible to highlight major issues. This can be done very briefly and staff input is often spontaneous thereafter.

Longer Term Impact

Since the presentation at ICEE 2007 was written, a number of other developments have occurred which reflect the long-term impact desired in the TOC model. Specifically the reader is reminded that the underlying motivation of the project was to create a team in the expectation that change would then be driven spontaneously by the team. In this section we report on some longer-term changes that have been set in motion and indicate the success of the team.

Regular Meetings and Actions

It is possible to trace through the minutes of the team meetings and identify a surprisingly large number of actions what are now embedded in the curricula and this after just two full years of operation. A list of some of these is given next for conciseness.

1. Modules changing semester.
2. Modules become more integrated.
3. A total redesign of the mathematics support and delivery in year 1.
4. Effective management of courseworks, both in timing an style.
5. More helpful guidance to personal tutors on activities that support the curriculum.
6. Course directors for each programme theme as opposed to by year.
7. Team is now embedded in departmental committee structures.

Follow on Projects

The team also identified some areas where there was the significant potential for quality enhancement and these were followed up by separate projects, developed by team members. These will be reported in full elsewhere so just a brief summary is given here.

1. Redesign of the induction week for new students to address perceived issues with student attitudes to independent learning, expectations and how to study at University. This project also considered how the induction week activities would be followed through within the curriculum (to be presented at the University of Sheffield Spotlight on L&T conference in January 2008).
2. Evaluation of a Business in the curriculum project and consideration of how to embed this initiative into the 1st year curriculum more effectively.
3. A major departmental review of the organisation of the teaching, focusing on which modules were taken by whom and when. The key aim in this was in line with that of the 1st year team, to improve cohesion and management of programmes and thus improve student experience. This review was put on the agenda by team members and they persuaded the department of the potential benefits. It is now nearly complete with changes being planned for implementation in 2008.

The student feedback on the first of these projects (delivered in September 2007) has been very positive, which is a clear indicator that the project is beginning to meet its long-term aims.

Conclusions

This chapter has demonstrated how the TOC was used to help plan and evaluate a L&T project within Engineering. We believe this mechanism is useful and easily transferable to other institutions and indeed is being adopted widely within the University of Sheffield.

The chapter also demonstrates, through the TOC evaluation, which is very positive than that the team based to teaching organisation and delivery has facilitated change where previously there was a lot of inertia. It has also encouraged staff to take a broader view of their teaching responsibilities and generally this was appreciated. Nevertheless, there are major concerns over recognition, for instance in terms of workload or how to prioritise teaching and research. These issues reinforce the commonly accepted dichotomy in research led universities. They have been partially resolved by strong support from the HOD who has placed the role on the formal duties of relevant staff. Also, perhaps stating the obvious, staff seems happy to attend meetings where they believe useful outcomes will arise, and this is a challenge to the team leader to ensure meetings are planned very carefully and run efficiently.

***Appendix* 1**

Quotes from Various Staff

Supportive: Very important to continue in order to talk about problems in an open way, make solid plans and implement them. Good idea. Important to look at coherence due to disjointedness of department. Brings people together. Better than a one-person responsibility. Vital but will depend on HoD. Essential—how would you otherwise look after the curriculum and support students? Confident that it will continue after funding has run out. Has made important contributions since it has existed, should continue but not monthly, at strategic times of the year. Will keep it, serves a useful purpose, more issues in first year, small Maths team needed, team looked hard at the curriculum.

Unsupportive: Retention is a serious issue in the department and is taken seriously by staff. Coffee time discussions, informal arrangements have worked successfully before. Up to HoD whether the team will continue to exist, cannot see reason to continue, had arm twisted to go to 1st year team meetings. No, this should be the work of the LTC. Good concept for this type of interaction but is it needed in a formalised way? Is this the right vehicle?

Appendix 2
Detailed Findings

This appendix lists some of the fine detail/comments from the evaluation, which were used to build the summary.

Are student satisfaction, performance and retention at Level 1 a priority for the department? If so, how does this priority related to other priorities, e.g. research? Departmental priorities and formal recognition are important in legitimising investment of substantial amounts of time and effort in curriculum development.

Structure and role of first year team evolved and seem well understood, even if not formally recognised.

The team-based approach was viewed as positive and valuable. It is inclusive, bringing together all staff independent of their level of seniority. Enabled focused, in-depth discussion from a cross-section of staff and all contributions were valued by the other team members. The majority enjoyed working in the team and gained a valuable insight into their colleagues' modules.

There was a view among the interviewees that typically: little or no effort had been made by teaching staff, from within and outside the Department, to make explicit connections between the module(s) they teach and the Level 1 curriculum; it is important for the Department to address these issues; the Team had acted as a catalyst for many issues that had previously been discussed, but had not been acted upon.

Observations used by the interviewees included 'joined-up', 'coherent', 'integrated', 'co-ordinated', 'strategic' and 'making sense from a student point of view'. Various members indicated that it helped them to know what their colleagues were doing in their modules, at what point which materials were taught or assessed and when and how what they were teaching was built upon by their colleagues on other modules, or vice versa.

- Strategically, the main achievements seem to be that Level 1 is now considered from a holistic perspective. The project has established the First-Year Team, which now has a good profile in the department.
- Several interviewees stated that the project has introduced an effective new approach among colleagues — one which encourages collaboration and strategic curriculum development, rather than individual curriculum development. One interviewee mentioned a stronger drive to QE enhancement rather than QA.
- Overall, despite negative comments from a couple of interviewees, the consensus was that the First-Year Team had met the expectations of those interviewed. There are some issues that have not yet been addressed fully, either by the First-Year Team or the Department and one member of staff

queried whether sufficient effort had been made to understand the student needs and the origins of the retention problem. Nevertheless, the First-Year Team has made an impressive start.

- Time constraints have been a significant factor for all members of the First-Year Team, especially as the team's effort was not being formally recognised and could be seen as duplicating work done by the LTC.
- Student feedback indicated that overall, students are fairly satisfied, but there is still work to do to provide students with a greater sense of coherence and satisfaction and to convince them that staff take an interest in them. The timing of some assignments is still problematic. Projects, the 'real-world' examples and group work are appreciated and well received.
- Two-thirds of the interviewees thought that the Team should continue whereas the others felt there are already adequate formal structures and informal opportunities. Significantly, senior staff had positive perceptions of the role and contribution of the Team.
- Some colleagues commented 'a parallel structure to the LTC', 'duplicating efforts' and 'wasting time', 'parallel structures could lead to a lack of accountability' and therefore could not see the point of a First-Year Team. Ironically, the same individuals were quite complimentary about the project, the quality of discussions and the actions and with only one exception, found the team-based approach valuable and even enjoyable.

Appendix 3
TOC Model

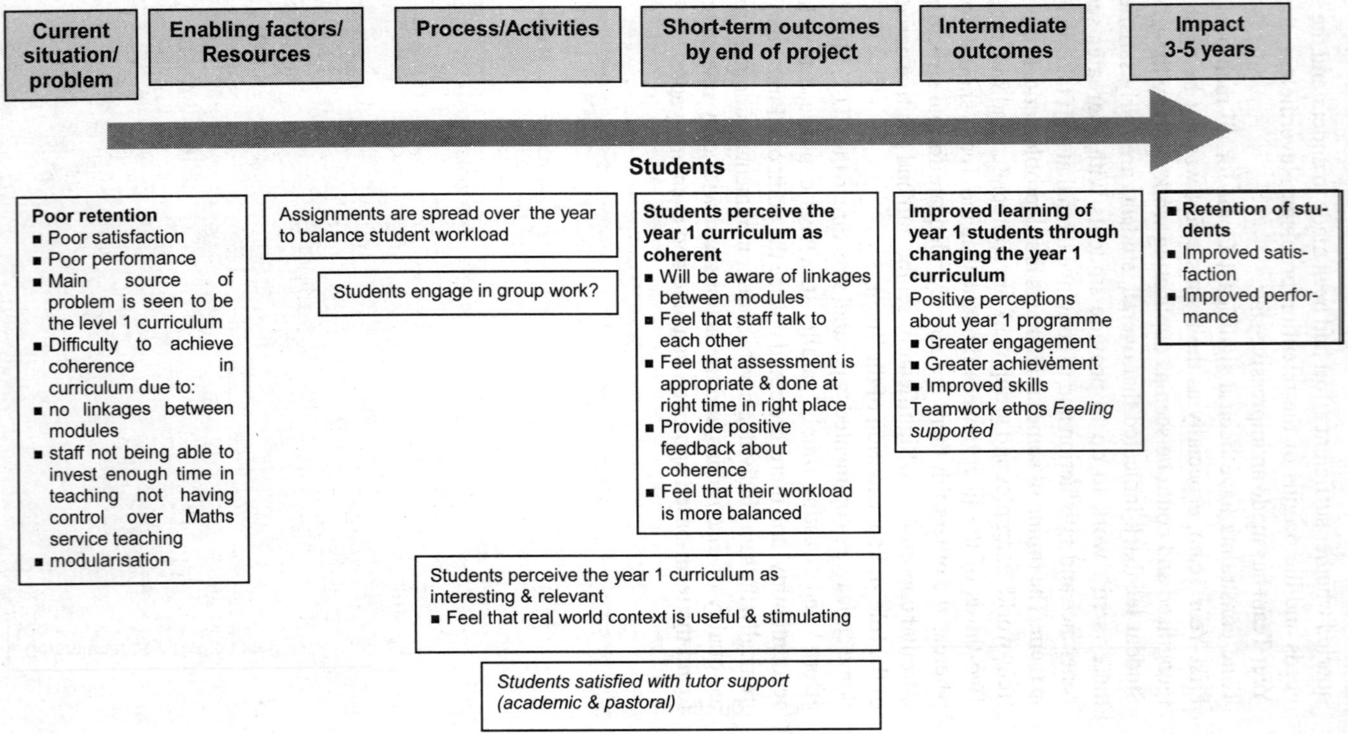

(*Contd.*)

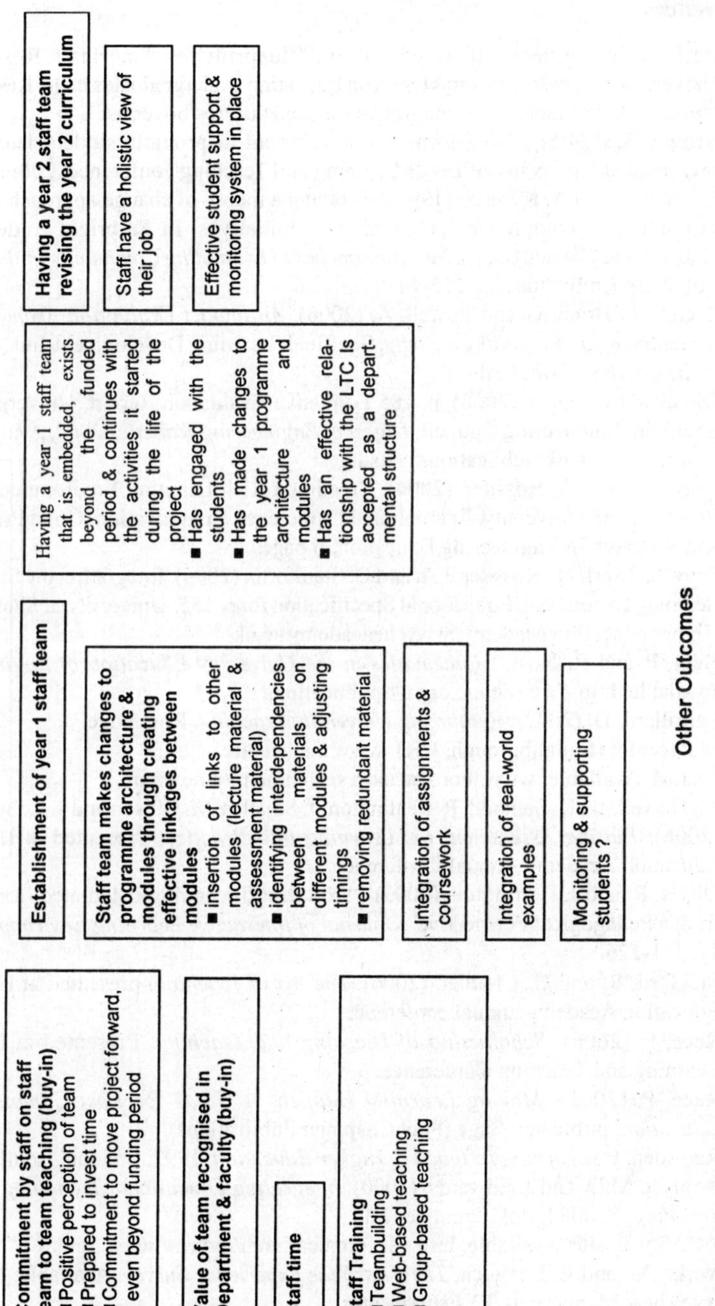

Figure 9.1: Initial Theories of Change Map

References

1. Reinventing undergraduate education: Blueprint for America's Research Universities. The Boyer Commission on Educating Undergraduates in the Research University, Available: http://naples.cc.sunysb.edu/Pres/boyer.nsf
2. Brown, S. (2006). Using formative assessment to promote student learning, presented at University of Leeds Learning and Teaching conference, 2006.
3. Connell, J. and A. Kubisch (1998). Applying a theory of change approach to the evaluation of comprehensive community initiatives, In Fulbright Anderson, Kubisch and Connell (Eds.), *New Approaches to Evaluating Community Initiatives*, Vol. 2, Aspen Institute, pp. 15-44.
4. Diercks-O'Brien, G. and Powell, A. (2006). *An Impact Evaluation Framework for Learning and Teaching Activity*, Sheffield: Learning Development and Media Unit, University of Sheffield.
5. Diercks-O'Brien, G. (2006). p. 185 Formative Evaluation Report, University of Sheffield. Engineering Council, *Digest of Engineering Statistics 2002*, Available: www.engc.org.uk/publications/statsdigest
6. Gray, L. and J.A. Rossiter. (2006). Creating a Rich Learning Environment in a Research Led University, International Conference on Innovation, Good Practice and Research in Engineering Education, 6 pages.
7. Gray, L., Mort, N., Rossiter, J.A. and D. Staniforth. (2005). Integrating the Student Learning Experience, Educational Specification for p. 185, University of Sheffield. Higher education academy, www.heacademy.ac.uk
8. Kent, P. and R. Noss, *Mathematics in the University Education of Engineers*, Available: http://www.engc.org.uk/publications
9. Laurillard, D. (2002). *Rethinking University Teaching*, Routledge.
10. Mathcentre (Loughborough, UK), www.mathcentre.ac.uk,
11. HELM: Available: www.lboro.ac.uk/research/helm/index.html
12. McDowell, L., K. Sambell, R. Penlington, J. Smailes, M. Gibson and J. Robinson. (2006). *Putting Assessment for Learning into Practice*, Presented at Higher Education Academy Annual Conference.
13. Oliver, R. and J. Herrington. (2003). "Exploring Technology Mediated Learning from a Pedagogical Perspective", *Journal of Interactive Learning Environments*, 11, 111-126.
14. Pickford, R. and H. Clothier. (2006). *The Art of Teaching*, presented at Higher Education Academy annual conference.
15. Race, P. (2006). *Scholarship of Learning and Teaching*, Presented at Leeds Learning and Teaching Conference.
16. Race, P. (2005). *Making Learning Happen: A Guide for Post-Compulsory Education*, publisher: Sage (Paul Chapman Publications).
17. Ramsden, P., *Learning to Teach in Higher Education*, 1992, London, Routledge.
18. Roblyer, M.D. and J. Edwards. (2000). *Integrating Educational Technology into Teaching*, Saddlebrook, Prentice Hall.
19. UCAS web site, Available: http://secure.ucas.com/figures/index.html
20. Yorke, M. and B. Longden, *The First Year Experience Survey*, Available: http://www.heacademy.ac.uk/FYEsurvey.htm

10

Understanding Effective Models of Audio Feedback

Andrew Middleton and *Anne Nortcliffe*

Audio feedback involves the recording and distribution of formative feedback to students. It takes many forms and addresses many specific requirements. It allows students to reflect on their work and improve it by listening to constructive messages. Ideally the design and implementation of audio feedback is encouraging, enabling students to feed their developing understanding forward into their ongoing learning and professional practise.

In this chapter we note two different approaches to audio feedback design used to support students studying Computer Networking, and Electronic and Electrical Engineering courses.

Two case studies are described that draw upon research primarily designed to find out what students think about audio feedback delivered online through a university virtual learning environment (VLE).

Earlier work (Nortcliffe and Middleton, 2007) had been inconclusive with regard to the efficacy of using audio feedback to promote learning in this context, though some students had clearly been engaged by, and had valued, the use of audio to support the development of their work. This research built upon those earlier findings and aimed to find out how audio feedback can be designed to encourage more ongoing and formative engagement.

In the first case study lab-based conversations with software engineering students were recorded: the academic and student discussed a project walkthrough and the recording was then made available in the VLE for subsequent review by the student. In the second study recordings were made of generic assessment feedback given in lecture to the entire class before being uploaded to the VLE for independent review. In both cases the impact upon the lecturer was minimal given that a portable MP3 recorder was used to capture existing feedback activities. However, the potential for formative impact upon the students was significant.

Race (1999, p. 57) warns us that innovation in assessment design should be conducted where improvement can be made, but should be conducted with care-assessment outcomes can be pivotal in the lives of our students. This chapter should therefore be considered as reflections upon ongoing work and emerging understanding towards effective design principles.

Background

The Digital Opportunity

In recent years the proliferation of MP3 players, mobile phones, and music downloads amongst students has led educators to consider the potential of integrating digital audio into their curriculum design (Windham, 2007; Meng, 2005). Digital audio's potential exists in its capacity to capture and reproduce the human voice, and the speed and ease with which it can be produced and distributed.

Digital audio production is now within the grasp of academics and students with the availability of MP3 recorders and freely available audio editing software like *Audacity* (Audacity website, 2007). Furthermore, the concurrent evolution of VLEs as content production and distribution tools, coupled with the notion of 'the Web as platform' (O'Reilly, 2005), mean that the lecturer and the student can become independent media narrowcasters (Noakes and Lomas, 2005).

Though many have seen the emergence of digital audio technologies as an opportunity to amplify existing teacher-centred models of education through the recording of lectures (Brittain *et al.,* 2006), the real opportunities exist in innovative models of student-centred learning (Lee *et al.*, 2007; Barnes and Tynan, 2007; Kirkup and Kirkwood, 2005).

Digital audio, pedagogically, is a disruptive technology—it changes what we can do, and more to the point, with a little creative thinking, allows us to improve what we do.

Feedback

Chickering and Ehrmann's (1996) 4th principle of good practice in the implementation of technology proposes that giving good feedback to students is essential because 'knowing what you know and don't know focuses your learning' and notes that there are many ways in which new technologies can provide feedback. Cooper (2000) highlights a more holistic view of assessment and how 'learning can be facilitated through challenging students to move from 'doing' assignments, to reflexive thinking about their writing.'

Sadler (1989) proposed that a key premise for formative feedback is that students must be able to 'monitor the quality of their own work during actual production' if they are to improve; they need to be able to compare their own work to feedback and understand how it applies to them. This suggests generic feedback can be valuable by providing a yard stick against which each student can measure their work.

Nicol and MacFarlane (2006) synthesised the research on good feedback to arrive at the following seven principles. They say good feedback:

1. Helps clarify what good performance is;
2. Facilitates the development of self-assessment (reflection) in learning;
3. Delivers high quality information to students about their learning;
4. Encourages teacher and peer dialogue around learning;
5. Encourages positive motivational beliefs and self-esteem;
6. Provides opportunities to close the gap between current and desired performance;
7. Provides information to teachers that can be used to help shape teaching.

Audio Feedback

Audio feedback is not new. Beyond the technology its fundamental characteristics are evident in any oral assessment where a student's work is discussed with the tutor or fellow student (Gibbs and Simpson, 2004, p. 8). With the advent of the audio cassette in the 1970s, Moore (1977) found that students preferred analogue audio feedback rather than written feedback. Other academics were also encouraged by their use of audio cassette technology to record feedback (e.g., Kirschner, 1991). Research into audio feedback delivered by cassette tape indicated its potential to promote self-reflection and bring improvement through its capacity to feed forward into subsequent assignments (Johanson, 1999). A desire to understand how audio feedback can be implemented, so that its potential to feed forward is maximised, remains and informs this work.

The recorded voice carries meaning beyond just the spoken words (Rust 2001): tone, nuance, expression, informal language and the dedicated, personal input of the academic, all carry layers of meaning difficult to find with other media, and this is indicative of the more pastoral tutor-student relationship that may be found by adopting audio feedback pedagogies. Good feedback should encourage students to act upon their feedback and (Young, 2000) has discussed the need to carefully 'foster positive self-esteem' amongst some students to ensure that feedback does not detrimentally impact their learning. It would seem particularly useful, therefore, to harness this intimate method of communication in helping students to develop. The emerging digital age offers us the potential to fulfil Rust's aspirations in providing valued and effective feedback (Rotheram, 2007).

Formative by Being Timely and Personal

Feedback is most effective when it is timely (Gibbs and Simpson, 2004, p. 19; Brown, 2001, p. 17). Though timeliness implies speediness, feedback intended to feed forward into ongoing coursework suggests that timeliness is determined by the readiness of the student as they construct their learning. In some cases this means students accessing feedback given on draft submissions or continuous assessment immediately, whilst for others it may mean 'self-regulating' (Nicol and MacFarlane, 2006) their use of feedback weeks, months or even years later as they make connections to the next assignment, module or task. For example, in our first case study feedback given in lab-based conversations is likely to be only a vague memory, obscured by time, for the many students who leave things until the last minute with their memory becoming significantly impaired; the potential impact of the valuable, formative conversation is all but lost. Accessing the conversational audio feedback, however, allows them to refresh, not just their feedback from the academic, but their own verbalised train of thought at the time of the conversation (Nortcliffe and Middleton, 2007) and so supports their re-engagement with their work. In turn, the impact of feedback is maximised further by feeding forward into their ongoing learning.

The student's autonomy in controlling the way they access their feedback implies a personalised learning context, even when the feedback is not specifically targeted at the individual. But the value of the recorded voice, especially when it is targeted at the individual, suggests that the main strength of audio feedback may be found in its personal engagement.

Assessment is often described as a 'burden' (Rust, 2001, p. 22; Race, 1999, p. 60; Powell, 1998) rather than as a formative learning opportunity. The primary concern of this chapter is not this administrative challenge, though audio feedback can bring benefits to the academic in terms of rapid and manageable turnaround. Instead we consider how digital audio can help us improve assessment by making it a richer, more engaging and formative opportunity for our students.

Methodology

In this study attempt is made to know,

- what audio feedback might offer beyond other feedback techniques?
- how audio feedback is best combined with other teaching methods?
- how, where, when and why students listened and what they did as a result of listening?
- why some students had not listened (Nortcliffe and Middleton, 2007)—eg was it disinterest in using feedback in general, disinterest in audio technologies, or related to technical barriers?

A qualitative case study methodology was adopted in order to reveal the thinking and feelings of students (Krueger and Casey, 2000, p. 7) that was not evident in the quantitative data obtained in earlier research (Nortcliffe and Middleton, 2007), which had revealed a mixed picture of engagement with the Personal Conversational audio feedback model. The same approach was used in revealing levels of interest and engagement in the second case study on generic feedback.

Three small focus group discussions, lasting on average just over 30 minutes, were run using a semi-structured discussion designed to provide orientation (Cohen *et al.,* 2000, p. 288) on the topic of audio feedback. Participants from the cohorts who had been offered the audio feedback were selected by open invitation. Users and non-users were encouraged to put themselves forward equally. The participants were mostly of a similar age and male (early 20s), whilst one was female and in her early 30s.

The discussions were facilitated by a neutral facilitator from the university's educational development unit. Two of the groups reflected on the case study 2 Generic feedback model, whilst the third group spoke about their experience of Personal Conversational feedback used in case study 1.

The groups were kept small, so that all participants could make contributions. The facilitator encouraged a permissive, relaxed environment (Krueger and Casey, 2000, p. 4) and explained that audio feedback is an emerging practice and one where there was bound to be a diversity of opinion. Consequently the ensuing discussions reflected a range of opinion. The focus groups did find consensus on a number of issues, though such qualitative findings can only be indicative.

The discussions were recorded, fully transcribed and marked up using a coding scheme designed to reflect sub-themes evident within the research questions (Miles and Huberman, 1994). These were queried to reveal patterns and themes in opinions and perceptions (Cohen *et al.,* 2000, p. 283). Students' comments were anonymised by labelling them from 'A' to 'K'.

Case Study 1: Personal Conversational Audio Feedback

This case study involves the recording of audio feedback given during the formative and summative lab-based walkthroughs of an assessment submission for individuals and groups. Each walkthrough, student-academic conversation was recorded on a portable device and distributed through the VLE. An earlier study had indicated that students preferred conversational feedback to audio comments recorded by the academic recorded in isolation (Nortcliffe and Middleton, 2007).

The rationale for this approach was that simple recordings of conversations provide students with the opportunity to make stronger connections to the feedback by reflecting on their own contribution to the walkthrough conversation, and that this later re-engagement with the conversation enriches and promotes a feed forward process significantly.

This Personal Conversation model was used on two modules:

- 18 students, typically in the 20-22-age range, were enrolled on the Level 5 Electrical and Electronic Engineering degree course with a 5:4 split of full to part-time. One of the full-time students was female, otherwise all were male. These students were required to study a semester-long module focused on Software Engineering and undertook a Software Engineering project assignment. Students had to research, design and simulate a simple quadpedal robot. The assessment consists of series of formative and final summative assessment submissions in the laboratory whereby the academic walks through the student progress.

- 41 students, typically in the 19-21-age range, were enrolled on the full-time Level-5 B.Sc. Computer and Network Engineering degree course, where there are just two female students. Students were required to study a semester-long module on how to software engineer a secure website. Students are required to self-assess and peer-assess the group work and this contributed to mark-generation for the assessment. The assessment submission was in two parts: formative walkthrough of the initial website and final formative/summative walkthrough of the final site after a four week period of maintenance.

Case Study 2: Generic Audio Feedback

Five separate generic feedback messages were distributed to Level-5 B.Sc. Computer Networks or B.Sc. Computer and Network Engineering students.

In the cohort there are 75 males and 1 female, typically 19-22 years old, but of the range 19-55. These students are required to study a placement preparation module. As part of this they were required to submit four artefacts:

- an example answer(s) to a 'killer question(s)';
- a covering letter;
- a completed job application for an actual position;
- a re-submission of their covering letter or/and job application following feedback.

Prior to the submission the students were encouraged to cultivate peer feedback on their work to improve their submission. Once submitted, the work was marked away from the students using traditional methods. The academic then noted generic issues found across the group.

Generic audio feedback for the 'killer question' submission was given and recorded in the lecture. Recordings of the separate points were made and distributed through the VLE for all to hear whether or not they had been present in the lecture.

The initial and final feedback given on the covering letter and application was 'studio' recorded and distributed through the VLE; only a handful of students turned up to the feedback seminar timetabled three weeks after the lecture course had finished. An email with written generic feedback was also sent out following the initial submission.

It was decided that individual written feedback was still the most appropriate main method of feedback in this module as it enabled the academic to highlight specific individual needs in relation to improving job applications. This visual feedback addressed grammatical errors and other specific suggestions (Huang, 2000, p. 207, also noted that grammatical errors necessitated a mixed approach to feedback). Students were also praised where they had marketed themselves effectively.

However, the academic decided that the written word on its own was not a powerful enough medium to convey the importance of some common issues. It was felt that common generic feedback might generate formative discussion amongst the students if it was facilitated well. Generic feedback, such as, 'the applications would not get past first base' combined with recommendations for improvement, was given to provoke further engagement. Audio is able to communicate the urgency of these issues through the tone and honesty of the academic voice. By integrating audio with other methods such as lectures and email, students can be reminded in a timely way to listen to recordings when writing job applications or covering letters.

Results and Discussion

Results from both case studies are discussed together and significant differences are identified in the conclusion. Students are referred to by the letter they were assigned during analysis of the data to support their anonymity. The following students were part of case study 1 who used Conversational Personal Feedback: A, G and H. The remaining students are from case study 2 (Generic Feedback).

General

All students appreciated the value of feedback and its potential to feed forward. For example student A noted, 'If you do a task and you don't get feedback after, it's like you've just written something and you have submitted it, but it's not really important… If you don't get the feedback obviously there's no point in going back and looking at the assignment you've done.' Not giving useful feedback, it would seem, can be detrimental to student levels of engagement.

Student C noted that, 'If people are happy with a mark they don't desire feedback.' If this is right, it suggests that audio feedback should be either targeted at under-achievers or else a more holistic approach should be taken where feedback is part of a broader, added value strategy focussed on feeding and connecting learning forward generally.

Students often value the chance to have one-to-one guidance: 'It would be nice if there was more personal feedback, for example if you didn't do as well as you expected on an assignment, you could sit down with someone or get personalised feedback saying, 'This is where you went wrong,' or, 'This is ok,' or, 'You didn't quite get this right.'' Personalisation is one of three themes that were clearly important to all participants and is looked at in more depth in this chapter. The themes are,

- Personalisation
- Timeliness
- Blended strategies

Personalisation

Personalisation happens through the content being targeted at an individual or through the student's perception of the feedback voice and its implicit meaning. For example A explained, 'Although it was a group thing, it felt like she was talking to me personally and I thought that was quite useful because sometimes her tone of voice, you know, suppose she had emphasised that bit, I would see the importance of that… [I would] go back to my assignment and really think, 'Yeah, maybe I should have emphasised that point more importantly than I did', you know, made it stand out.'

The students who had been offered generic feedback were also keen to talk about personalised feedback. Student F, talking about feedback in general, said that he valued it when it was personalised, 'Not just a sheet circled like a marking scheme… I take more notice of it if it's personalised. If it's not, it could be about anybody. It's not about me and what I've done. If it's written in the lecturer's own hand-writing and talking about what you wrote then it's more useful.'

> D: 'If the teacher goes to the trouble of taking their time out to do something personal, like a one to one or just writing in their own hand-writing, then I feel a bit more motivated to take on board that feedback… If [audio feedback] was personal and you knew it was there, I think I would be more inclined to listen to it.'

Those who had received the Personal Conversational Feedback believed it had made an impact on their results.

> G: 'Yes. Yes. It was directly related at you. With mine, she sat there every other week, looked at the project and said, 'What progress have you made?… Here's some suggestions to get you further on.' it really helped me out. I can't remember what I got overall, but it was definitely a 1st.'
>
> Facilitator: 'So the method of feedback really helped?'
>
> G: 'It upped my grade. Upped my grade from a 60% to over a 70% for that project. I was looking at 60% without audio feedback. With audio feedback it pushed me back into a 1st.'

The results indicate that contact with the academic, whether through lecture, seminar, tutorial or laboratory is valuable. Audio feedback can be more effective when participants are familiar to each other. Several respondents recognised how the tone and emphasis of the academic's voice communicated meaning more powerfully than the written word. Because the students had developed a rapport with the academic in class the significance of the points being made in the audio was greater.

> F: 'I think audio is more personal. I think, by audio it comes across different to if it's been wrote down on paper. Someone could say something and mean it bluntly, but you might take it in the wrong manner, whereas audio you can tell by the tone of the voice, pitching etc, whether they're being nasty, being polite, helpful. Whereas on a piece of paper it's just one [tone]. Some people take a lot of things wrongly.'
>
> D: 'It's a friendly voice and their mannerisms…'
>
> E: 'At least you know that that person knows what they on about.'
>
> G: 'When it's somebody you know, you can see and you know how they speak and you know what they mean. You've been in a lecture a few weeks and you know that when they're trying to make point about something that's a bit confusing, you kind of know what they're aiming at.'
> A:'I think you can also visualise them saying it to you.'
> G: 'Yes.'
> A: 'You actually see her in your mind talking to you, telling you that you should have done this, in a way.'

The significance of the academic's personal engagement was appreciated by some.

> D: 'If the teacher goes to the trouble of taking their time out to do something personal like a one-to-one or just writing in their own hand-writing then I feel a bit more motivated to take on board that feedback.'

Trust is important in feedback and works both ways: with personal feedback academics can gauge the impact of the feedback upon the student based upon their individual relationships.

Timeliness

The meaning and value of feedback often come with time. G commented,

> 'I thought it was strange at first. What are you doing recording me while you're talking to me?!… I have never seen this before.' But then she said, 'If you want to review what we've spoken about get yourself on the Internet. It's all recorded on an MP3. A week later, two weeks later, I'm sitting down to do a bit more work on this assignment project. I'm thinking, 'God. What did she say?' And I thought, 'It's on the Internet. Right there!"

> H: 'I listened to a couple… because it's such a long project. Again I left it 'til quite late on to get on with it—7 or 8 weeks. It was handy to go back and listen to what she'd said earlier on. How I could improve myself?'

Given that audio feedback now exists in the digital domain, understanding how and where students will use the feedback is important.

> C: 'The feedback people get with their assignments is what most people read and if you get a mark you're happy with then you just read the comments on the sheet and leave it at that.'

> B: 'Most people read the feedback as they pick it up. You're not logged onto Blackboard when you get the mark. If you got it back, when you were at a computer then you may go and do it, but unless you go out wanting the feedback then you would have just gone to a tutor.'

Students such as B said that they normally 'read the feedback and then leave it.' Often, as a paper-based exercise, the assignment is done, dusted and perhaps forgotten. Other students, discussing feedback generally, used the phrase 'in one ear and out the other' several times. Actively revisiting feedback therefore needs to be encouraged.

Blended Strategies

All focus groups reported that the students value a blended feedback approach where audio is combined with other written approaches. However it was also clear that audio by its nature promotes a semi-formal, conversational culture and these students recognised how the blended context might include corridor conversations (H), email (A, B), spontaneous tutorials (G).

> A hypothetical scenario was proposed by the facilitator in an attempt to reveal what audio could and could not achieve: If audio was the only feedback mechanism what would we gain and what would we lose?
>
> B: 'Its one of those things where I don't think it will stand as a single method of feedback, it's got to be given, with other forms, so you can't really get rid of the written notes or the [notes on the] side… We still need to get personal feedback from a tutor, emailing them questions or seeing them in person.'
>
> C: 'Again, I don't think it would work… I think less feedback would be communicated to students because a lot less students would actually go and bother to get the extra feedback if its not there in front of them. If they're happy with the mark, they are most likely to just leave it. It's what I would do anyway.'

This last comment suggests that a blended audio approach should be designed carefully in order to encourage students to use it and understand its particular value. Several students noted a surface approach to feedback that included just viewing the mark or scanning notes and marks and putting the returned assignment away in their bag (F, G). The value of feeding forward needs to be communicated well to students. Considering audio in a holistic way will improve its implementation.

In case study 1 the audio feedback was combined with an assessment grid. Students from that focus group discussed the relationship between the two tools.

> H: 'They complement each other, don't they? The criteria that she ticked off just had the basic points of what you had to do to get a certain mark. Whereas in the audio file it is explained a bit more on your specific project rather than just a general overview. What you can improve to reach a certain criteria on the sheet. One wasn't better than the other. One gave a general overview and one was specific for you. So you can use them to compare.'
>
> Facilitator: 'When you went back several weeks later did you go back to both of those things?'
>
> H: 'Yes. I went mainly to the sheet because the sheet I was using did the minimum. But then with the audio feedback I could just improve it to get a better grade.'
>
> G: 'You know where your weaknesses are with the sheet [others signal agreement] then you can go back and listen to the recording so you know what you need to do to make that naff bit better. So you got a decent mark and one part of the project letting you down: you've got a tick in the box to say try harder next time and the audio feedback to say, 'Here's what you need to do to try harder.''

The same students discussed the hypothetical situation of just having their feedback on the assessment grid.

> G: '[With no personal conversational audio feedback] I would have gone and asked [the tutor]... well maybe not actually. Lazy student factor! I would have probably been happy with 60 per cent! But because the feedback was there I used it. You know, I'm a busy guy. Most of the time I haven't got half an hour to come around the university looking for lecturers and trying to ask for help unless it's really necessary.'
>
> A: 'Yes, I would probably take the sheet to her and say, 'Could you just explain to me a bit more?' But with the audio feedback it was just there. You didn't have to call up and say...'
>
> G: 'It's just there on your computer—at home, at university. Anywhere, any time.'
>
> A: ''Cause sometimes on those grid sheets they just write '70 per cent: Good understanding of project.' I might think that what I've done is a good

> understanding, but with audio feedback she would tell me, 'If you had done this maybe…', or, 'In order to get that 70 per cent something like this should have been included.' So, in a way they complement each other. I actually think it's a good idea to have both instead of just the one. That way you can relate to the audio feedback to what's written on the actual grid sheet and see.'

This also indicates how audio feedback can reduce the academic workload and result in direct feedback being given that otherwise would not have been possible.

One of the emerging ideas in relation to a blended approach comes in understanding a wider context and opportunity for interaction around assignments:

> E: I think [audio and written feedback methods] should be combined with an opportunity to ask questions, because while you're sat there listening to a person saying things about your work you don't have the opportunity to say 'Hang on a minute. What about this?'

Conclusion

All focus groups recognised the value of personalised feedback and saw the value in the Personal Conversational model. Significantly in this model 'personal' meant both 'targeted' at the needs of a specific student and 'familiar' in terms of the academic-student relationship.

In these case studies the Generic model was not so well understood due to factors related to its timing and the organisation of the VLE. However, subsequent reflection on the focus group discussions by the authors identified that by designing it to address common issues it should be provocative and intended to generate discussions amongst peers. It can be seen therefore as a 'media intervention' (Bradley *et al.*, 2006)—'a call to action' that clearly leads into refreshed learning activity. It therefore has a feed forward use for the current cohort, and subsequently can be used to brief next year's cohort.

The design of audio feedback requires a holistic and strategic approach, needing to be understood in relationship to lectures, seminars, tutorials or laboratory. Though audio feedback can often be used in combination with other methods it should be promoted as valuable and disruptive, requiring new types of ongoing engagement from students.

The academic voice in both models was valued. Audio exists on the informal-formal continuum and so in providing sensitive, encouraging, formative feedback it is well placed.

The timely use of feedback, rather than delivery, has emerged as a valuable attribute in considering audio feedback. Students need to be encouraged to understand its significance too in order that they can benefit from this.

A blended approach was recognised and valued by all of the students. This blend may take many forms in terms of tools and methods and there is a need to understand wider informal and formal contexts too.

Software engineering projects, as in case study 1, lend themselves to audio feedback whether it is an academic or professional project. The ongoing review process is valuable to an individual or group involved in any software project research and development, because students have a chance to apply the feedback and, as Sommerville (2004) has noted, it is an effective method of picking up problems and improving systems. Audio feedback develops students because it ensures all parties involved in a software engineering project have a comprehensive understanding and record of the walkthrough; this assists the data formulation in the improvement and generation of each stage to a satisfactory conclusion (*ibid.*).

In case study 2 the importance of planning and embedding the distribution, both technically and pedagogically, became clear. The resource needs to be more easily accessible and students need to be alerted to its presence using various approaches. In this case, notifying students in a timely fashion could have been achieved by including a reminder of the guidance in email messages whilst distributing job adverts, other relevant materials and submission reminders.

Further Work

There are many other themes emerging from this work that need to be explored towards arriving at a set of audio feedback design principles. These include: listening skills for learning; how audio feedback can be understood in a wider interactive context; the value of voice; technical implementation; scalability of models; the informal-formal learning continuum and its relationship to audio.

Recommendations

The following recommendations for good practice are emerging from this work:

- Use audio feedback as part of blend of feedback methods and be clear about what can be achieved with the audio;
- Plan holistically and be clear how feedback will feed forward, and even how it can connect to other modules;
- Be clear about scalability and managing your commitment;
- Understand how students will use the feedback in a timely way and ensure that students can dip into the audio feedback as and when they need it;
- Don't neglect inter-personal development in other situations—develop trust amongst participants;

- Introduce the feedback to students effectively. Be clear,
  - Why it is valuable to them;
  - How they access it (distribution access, listening location, technology);
  - What action is required whilst listening and later on;
- Keep it short, lively, useful and usable;
- Alert students and monitor their engagement;
- Get feedback on the feedback and improve your model for *your* context—check that the feedback is personally relevant for each student.

11

Mediation in and Out of Class for Fostering Teaching and Learning Basic Sciences in Engineering

J.B. Lopes, C. Viegas and *J.P. Cravino*

In real life a professional engineer is evaluated by his performance and competence, and is asked to act in different and complex situations that involve analyzing, interpreting and anticipating results, and they should be prepared for it in college (Perrenoud, 2003). This will only be accomplished if knowledge becomes operative (Astolfi, 1992). For this to happen students must work with knowledge so that it becomes meaningful. Therefore, learning should be directed to the development of competences that will improve professional performance. Even though this concern is somehow present in the senior years, it is not common in the introductory and basic courses of the early years, in which the principal concern is to cover the subject matter as stated in the syllabus (Redish and Steinberg, 1999, Roldão, 2003) and provide enough information for the students to carry on.

Reviewing the state of the art in educational research, the need for active learning (Felder and others, 2000, Lopes, 2004, Mazur, 1997, Meltzer and Manivannan, 2002, Redish and Steinberg, 1999) in promoting students participation and responsibility strikes out. There are several efficiency factors in Science Education Research as in Engineering Education Research, involving permanent interaction among students and between students and the teacher (Crouch and Mazur, 2001, Felder, 2007, Hake, 1998, Meltzer and Manivannan, 2002, Novak and others, 1999, Ramsden, 1987, Redish, 2003), and pointing to the importance of mobilizing the prior knowledge in order to construct a more solid one (Arons, 1997). All this can be accomplish in classroom using collaborative learning (Gijlers and Jong, 2005, Heller, R.Keith, and Anderson, 1992), cooperative learning (Felder and Brent, 2007), developing project work (Bell, 2005, Cravino, 2004, Hewton, 1975), tasks to be accomplished by the students (Kearney, 2004, Lopes, 2004) associated with permanent and adequate mediation by the teacher (Hampton and Reiser, 2004, Lopes, 2004). The mediation in classroom can be harnessed to help the evolution of the student, but it can also be a powerful tool in accompanying them during their individual work.

The Bologna's perspective (CESEAR and SEFI, 2005, Gordon, 2000) of making students' active in their daily class and in improving their capability of autonomous work and responsibility, must first be acknowledged by the teachers. This means teachers have to be prepared to carry through an efficient mediation near to the students. It is much common to find teachers who are very cautious in the preparation of the material, give nice lectures and get, in fact, really good evaluations from their students. But, by doing all the hard work (to prove to the students how easy it can be) they aren't really helping their students in their construction of scientific knowledge, and so, even if students think they understand it clearly, later on they will have difficulties in applying it in different situations (Felder, 2004, Mazur, 1997, Redish and Steinberg, 1999). This means teachers should try shifting this responsibility to students, so they can build their own mental models (Redish, 1994). That is why involving students in real work from the beginning is one of the most important teacher's tasks. This work makes explicit the different traces of mediation used in a case of an introductory course (physics) in an engineering school in Portugal.

Mediation

Basically a teacher performs mediation in his classes whenever s/he proportionates the development of knowledge, know-how, or competences, and there are processes that can be more or less efficient, depending on several factors. Traditionally, expositive classes are used to developed demonstrations or complex exercises (often, purely academic) that involve mainly mathematical skills, sometimes not yet well dominated by students, in which the work of students may end up reduced to a poor transcription of what the teacher writes in the blackboard. In most cases the teacher mediation is ineffective. Even though some students seem to learn well in this environment, unfortunately this is not the case for the majority of them. In a new learning environment, more challenging, where students are involved from the beginning, learning becomes dynamic and the fundamental role is what students develop and accomplish by themselves (Felder and others, 2000, Lopes, 2004, Redish and Steinberg, 1999). In this learning environment the teacher's role is to mobilize the students' prior knowledge, with meaningful tasks which can develop the intended competences and improve their knowledge, know-how, or competences without guiding their thoughts to the easy, straight forward way, known by the teacher.

The first step towards an efficient mediation is the preparation of the curriculum. It should be based on real and interesting contexts (adapted to the students) and developed upon the prior knowledge of the students, with tasks that can develop the intended knowledge, competences, and skills.

How to Implement Mediation in the Classroom

The learning environment set up by the teacher has a crucial importance in the students' involvement and learning quality. Mediation can become more effective, for most of the students, if the teacher is able to empathize with their students, providing an active social environment (Felder and others, 2000), where students feel comfortable discussing and presenting their ideas with each other (Redish, 2003). But because students have different styles of learning there are some students who do not easily accept such participative role in the classroom. Teachers should listen to them, and be aware of their difficulties and, hopefully, gradually help them understand the benefits of becoming actively engaged. The expected results in the improvement of students' success (academic and satisfaction) is not usually immediate (Crouch and Mazur, 2001, Felder, 1995). The incitation to persist and to keep up and develop motivation are an important part of the mediation conducted with students, as well as with staff colleagues (and the teacher him/her self).

Several types of mediation can be efficiently performed both in small as in large classes (Crouch and Mazur, 2001, Felder, 1997), both in laboratories as in lectures or recitation classes (Lopes, 2004, Mazur, 1997). It can also be adapted to the intended competences we want to develop.

In order to make any class alive, students must be an integrating part of what is being developed. The profits come from the interactive environment, with argumentation generated between students, during the attempt of construction of the scientific knowledge (Engle and Conant, 2002, Scott, Mortimer, and Aguiar, 2006).

In order to do so, teachers must view students as important in the development of scientific knowledge in class and must consider their opinion, questions or proposals as they try to embrace their interests during the lecture (Engle and Conant, 2002).

Several studies state the importance of making use of peer learning and teamwork (Felder and others, 2000, Mazur, 1997). If students sense that the collaborative work developed during class with their peers is sufficiently motivating and profitable, students might continue this interactivity out of class spontaneously, by studying together, or simply discussing their doubts with each other, before resorting to the teacher. This engagement with one another will also be increased with team cooperative work (Felder and Brent, 2007), in which the teacher's mediation is crucial in order to make it work, students must understand that they are dependent on each other but can develop important social competences such as respect and autonomy, as developing teamwork skills.

It also becomes very important to make a quality assessment of the learning outcomes, on a regular basis. In order to insure its feasibility, these assessments must provide relevant results concerning the learning outcomes on the competences developed and concepts learnt, they should not be questions that involve tricks or manipulations that can easily confuse students, but rather questions that reveal deep understanding (Felder and others, 2000). Possible assessment instruments are multiple choice or short-answer questions, multiple-choice multiple-response questions, representation-translation ranking tasks, context-based reasoning problems, estimation problems, qualitative questions or essay questions (Redish, 2003).

The feedback works both ways: teachers get relevant information about their students' learning evolution and students get useful and in time information about their own personal achievements. Feedback given to students should be personal (Redish, 2003) and can function as a stimulus or a call for caution for some specific mistake or even a clue towards the solution, so students can profit and learn with it. The feedback on the formative assessment during class discussions becomes helpful not only for students (raising awareness to possible weaknesses and/or successes), but once again for teachers, providing information to help manage the curriculum in time, being able to correct some misunderstandings or faults in students's learning. In doing so, assessment is no longer an instrument for measuring mistakes but becomes a powerful tool to improve the learning process.

The type of mediation does not (necessarily) depend on the kind of class (lecture, recitation, laboratory, etc.). Most of them may be used in all kinds of class or easily adapted, but in the following section we present some general strategies that we consider more convenient to each kind of class. Our empiric study described in forgoing section points out some important traces of the mediation.

Specific Mediation Strategies According to Class's Type

The theoretical classes (lectures) involve in fact some expositive lecturing but, since students can focus their full attention for only short period of time, an efficient mediation should provide a series of different tasks to be performed during class, without a rigid pre-determine schedule (Felder and Brent, 1999, Mazur, 1997). Even in large classes, good mediation can be performed, by using cooperative work and peer instruction (Felder, 1997, Mazur, 1997).

In recitation classes (later refer as TP classes—from theoretical-practical), traditionally used to workout problems, students must also be involved in the analysis and workout solutions of the problems proposed. The scenario where teachers develop the problems in the blackboard while students transcribe has to be prevented. One of the most efficient ways of develop this type of classes is using collaborative work (Lopes, 2004), developing different kinds of problems during class, beyond traditional exercises: open ended, estimations in real situations, predict-observe-explain tasks (White & Gunstone, 1992), or cooperative work (Felder and Brent, 2007), and namely during project work (Bell, 2005, Lopes, 2004).

Students should develop experimental competences in working with the laboratory material, but also develop the important connections with the curriculum. This will be more efficient if very strict protocols (recipe experiments) are avoided (Lopes, 2004, Redish, 2003). Instead, students should face problems that need to be solved experimentally, using laboratory material.

Case Study: ISEP

This work is part of a curriculum re-design, based on research in physics education, which is being developed in an introductory physics course in an engineering school of Northern Portugal (ISEP). This curriculum has the goal of improving students' competences in their daily work with the physics subject matter and its connections with daily life, by using a diversified mediation in and out of class.

Methods

This work involves an analysis of the last four school years in the same course, always taught during the first semester of each school year. The first year represented (2003/04), was before the teaching intervention and in the two subsequent years several modifications began to take place in order to test the applicability of some efficiency factors found in a literature review on physics education research, namely the ones related with mediation. In 2006/2007 some of these changes were incorporated and integrated in a framework for curricula development and management in the classroom (the formative situation framework—FSF). Tables 11.1, 11.2 and 11.3 show the schematic development of the course over the years, for each kind of class.

Two teacher-researchers and a group of teaching assistants (that changed every year) developed this work.

The type of problems proposed to the students in their daily work, as well in assessment items, also changed, becoming less dependent of the students mathematical skills and more contextualized and focused on using the students' competences, where they needed to know what is at stake and figure out the solution by themselves. This is exemplified in Table 11.4, where some examination questions from 2003/04 and 2006/07 are shown as an example. The structure of the final exam itself also suffered considerable modifications. In 2003/04 it was divided in two parts: theoretical (with 3 questions) and practical (with 4 problems/exercises), with no separate minimum grade requirement. Last year we proposed an exam divided in 3 parts: theoretical (with 9 questions), practical (with 4 problems), each with the minimum grade of 3 points (in 20) and a laboratorial question.

Table 11.1: Summary of the Modifications in Teaching Theoretical Classes

Dimension	*2003/04*	*2004/05*	*2005/06*	*2006/07*
Students' Tasks	Applications	Discuss the conceptual questions with their neighbours	Peer instruction during discussion upon conceptual questions	Discussion upon conceptual questions, first with their colleagues and only then with the teacher. Do and Correct their neighbor's test, during discussion of the solutions. E-learning[1] Challenge: Open Problem-situation, with open participation of all.
Teacher Mediation	Exposure on blackboard. Rhetoric questions. Prompt support during class. Normal office hours for student consultation.	Conceptual questions during exposure in Power Point presentation Prompt support during class. Normal office hours for student consultation.	Stimulate discussion upon conceptual questions, first with their colleagues and only then with the teacher Credit for participating in class Prompt support during class. Normal office hours for student consultation.	Promote discussion between students with real situation and conceptual questions. (Before and after introducing a concept). Animations and some videos Predict-Observe-Explain tasks. Self-evaluation tests and discussion of the solutions. Credit for participating in class. Prompt support during class. Office hours consultation

1. The e-learning tasks is put on e-learning platform which all students can freely use and work. This e-learning platform is an additional resource.

Table 11.2: Summary of the Modifications in Teaching Theoretical-Practical (Recitation) Classes

Dimension	2003/04	2004/05	2005/06	2006/07
Synchronism with theoretical lessons	1/2weks delay	1/2 weeks delay	1 week delay	no delay
Students' Tasks	Individual work on the exercises. 2-3 Tests.	Individual work on the exercises. Weekly paper homework. Weekly e-learning task.	Autonomous work on the exercises. Weekly paper homework or e-learning task.	Project work. Autonomous collaborative work on the exercises. Weekly e-learning homework.
Teacher Mediation	Solving exercise on blackboard. Normal office hours for student consultation.	Prompt support during class. Normal office hours for student consultation. General feedback on homework and on e-learning tasks.	Collaborative discussion on the open problems. Prompt support during class. Normal office hours for student consultation. Feedback on the homework.	Collaborative discussion with the teacher supervision. Prompt support during class. Support during the development of the Project. Weekly feedback on the e-learning homework. Office hours consultation suggested by the teacher to each student.
Contribution to the final mark	15% (tests)	20% (homework and e-learning tasks)	10% for attendance and participation in class. 10% homework.	15% Project. 10% homework. 5% class participation.

Table 11.3: Summary of the Modifications in Teaching Laboratory Classes

Dimension	*2003/04*	*2004/05*	*2005/06*	*2006/07*
Synchronism with theoretical lessons	No Synchronism	No Synchronism	No Synchronism	Synchronism with the theme (chapter) being discussed
Students' Tasks	Teamwork in class, based on guided experiments. Team Report One final test on errors and uncertainties in measurements.	Teamwork in class, based on guided experiences. Prepare themselves for the experiment. Team Report One final test on errors and uncertainties in measurements.	Teamwork in class, based on guided experiences. Prepare themselves for the experiment. Team Report One final test on errors and uncertainties in measurements.	Autonomous collaborative teamwork in solving the laboratory problems. Final Project work.
Teacher Mediation	Expositive lecture about uncertainties Exercises Prompt support during laboratory. Feedback on the reports' marks Normal office hours for student consultation.	Expositive lecture about uncertainties Exercises Individual questions about students work in laboratory and experiences performed Prompt support during laboratory. Feedback on the lab reports Normal office hours for student consultation.	Expositive lecture about uncertainties Exercises Individual questions about students work in laboratory and experiences performed Prompt support during laboratory. Feedback on the lab reports Normal office hours for student consultation.	Collaborative discussion with the teacher supervision. Individual and team questions about their work in laboratory and experiences performed Prompt support during class. Weekly feedback on the lab reports. Final Project supervision. Office consultation suggested by the teacher to each student.
Contribution to the final mark	30%	30%	30%	10% Individual questions. 10% Reports. 10% Project.

Table 11.4: Examination Questions Examples

Year	Question
2003/04	Theoretical question (2 points in 20): A particle of mass m, moves along X axes under the influence of a conservative force field, being Ep his potential energy. If the particle is in the positions x1 and x2 at the instants t1 and t2, respectively, prove that if E is the mechanical energy, then: $$t_2 - t_1 = \sqrt{\frac{m}{2}} \cdot \int_{x_1}^{x_2} \frac{dx}{\sqrt{E - E_p}}$$
	Practical question (3,5 points in 20): A particle vibrates in a simple harmonic motion with the frequency of 100Hz and 3 mm of amplitude. (a) Calculate its velocity and acceleration at the middle of the trajectory and at the extremes. (b) Write an equation that expresses the displacement as a function of time, knowing that at the initial instant the particle left at the position –1,5mm, moving towards the negative extreme of the trajectory. (c) In which subsequent instant is the velocity maxim?
2006/07	Theoretical question (1 point in 20, each): (1) The body of mass m0 is put against a compress spring. When the spring is released, the body m0 moves forward without friction. Justify which of the following graphics represents the variation of the body linear motion in time? (2) A 14 ton truck frontally collides with a 2 ton's car (see the picture). Comment the following statements: A. The force the truck exerts on the car is considerably greater than the one the car exerts on the truck. B. The acceleration each one suffers is different. C. During a real collision of this kind, we can always assume a perfect elastic collision. 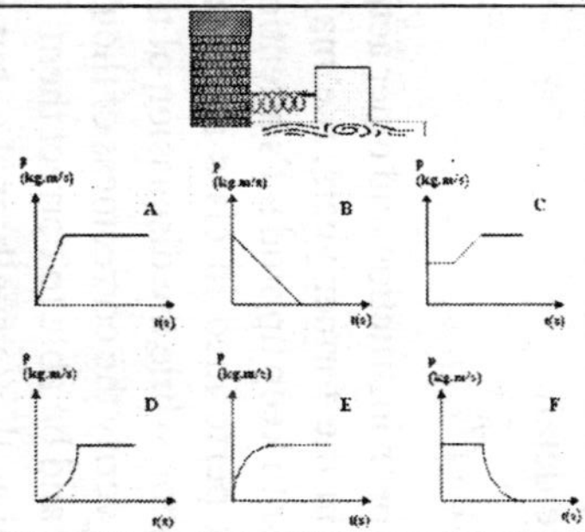
	Practical question (3 points in 20): A particle is suspended from the ceiling of an elevator through a spring and is at rest relatively to it when the elevator descends with a constant velocity of 1,5 m/s. The elevator then stops suddenly, leaving the particle oscillating with an angular velocity of 2 rad/s. Disregarding the spring's mass, can you determine: (a) The amplitude of the particle's oscillation? (b) Which will be the motion equation of the particle? (Choose the positive axis up)

Now it may be described what was done in 2006/2007, in each kind of classes, in more detail.

Theoretical Class (T)

Continuing the peer-instruction and other active learning engagement strategies, already tested in the former years, the major concern was to establish class rhythm, in order to keep up student's attention. The major introduction was the short self-tests performed in class and their immediate correction by each student's neighbor, while the discussion of the solutions was being made. They would not only verify the correctness of their answers, but also foresee different interpretations and be able to correct them. They could also gain sensibility to common mistakes they usually make, but to which they do not pay enough attention. Students were not graded for these tests' marks, only by the corrections they made and mostly by their participation in the process.

The e-learning challenges provided an opportunity for students to work together in complex problems, in which everyone could see each other's answers, and could complete them or disagree with them. The teacher would supervise their interactivity and give clues whenever she felt that was necessary.

Theoretical-practical Class (TP)

The main modification was the collaborative and autonomous work performed by the students. In each lesson they developed a different task towards their final project: 'How an elevator works'. This project provides an integrative vision of the course and stimulated the collaborative work in class, and its continuation afterwards. In these TP classes the students also discussed and solved a few problems and more classic exercises.

No synchronism was imposed on the different groups' work; in fact each group worked at their own pace, achieving their own goals, developing autonomy and responsibility. Respect for their colleagues and their ideas were promoted, in order to include everyone in the daily work.

Additionally, on a weekly basis, each student would have to perform a related e-learning task, in order to infer the success of his own individual achievements. The teacher's role was to mediate this individual and group achievements, namely in discussing certain issues at crucial moments, encouraging their performance and giving them permanent feedback of their developments, including in the homework which has individual weekly feedback. When significant difficulties emerged, a personal consultation would be scheduled with the student for an out of class office meeting with the teacher.

In the universe in study (216 diurnal students, split over 7 TP classes, taught by the different teachers—see table 11.5), we can gain some insight on the different levels of mediation performed: AB and GH classes followed the proposed methodology, KL and NV classes followed a more traditional teaching methodology, and the other classes followed a mixed strategy, in which the teacher sometimes did solve some of the problems in the blackboard. In order to realize if these differences contributed a significant difference in the results, we analyzed the achievements in all classes separately. The instruments used to collect data were: the curriculum materials; a questionnaire to students at the end of the course, the QEAME (Cravino, 2004, Ramsden, 1991), with a set of questions about students' perception about classes; interviews to students and to teachers; competence test.

Laboratory Class (LAB)

The major modification was undoubtedly the almost total abolition of guided experiments. Simpler laboratory devices were opted, which could demonstrate simple concepts that were being developed in the theoretical classes. The final part of the semester was spend developing a laboratory project, intended to solve a specific problem, in which students, with the laboratory material (or other materials), should idealized, develop and implement an experiment that could test the answer to that problem (Neumann & Welzel, 2007). In these classes the students of each TP classes were divided in two groups, with approximately 15 students each (table 11.5).

These classes had different teachers (enumerated from 1 to 7, as indicated in table 11.5), who applied the same curriculum and performed the same tasks with the students, however with differences in the mediations used, as they reported in the end of the semester.

Table 11.5: Classes Distribution of Teachers

<table>
<tr><th>Classes/Teachers</th><th>A</th><th>B</th><th>C</th><th>D</th><th>E</th><th>F</th><th>G</th><th>H</th><th>I</th><th>J</th><th>K</th><th>L</th><th>N</th><th>V</th></tr>
<tr><td>LAB</td><td>2</td><td>3</td><td>1</td><td>3</td><td>2</td><td>1</td><td>4</td><td>5</td><td>4</td><td>5</td><td>2</td><td>5</td><td>7</td><td>2</td></tr>
<tr><td>TP</td><td colspan="2">1</td><td colspan="2">4</td><td colspan="2">3</td><td colspan="2">1</td><td colspan="2">2</td><td colspan="2">6</td><td colspan="2">6</td></tr>
<tr><td>T</td><td colspan="6">1</td><td colspan="4">1</td><td colspan="4">1</td></tr>
</table>

The results in three different perspectives are presented: (i) the evolution of results accomplished over the years, (ii) the mediation differences among teachers, namely the mediation traces identified in AB and GH classes; (iii) the comparison of the impact of slightly different curriculum approaches in the development of students' competences and knowledge.

Global Analyses Over the Years

Comparing the final marks of students over the years (Figure 11.1A and 11.1B), it is clear that there is a decrease in lower marks (SM). The number of students failing the course has also been decreasing, even though the number of students who try to complete the course has been decreasing as well. It is possible that the adaptation of the degree programme to the Bologna Process, which will occur next year, may be responsible for this decrease in enrolment (due to the expected equivalences in courses).

If only the students who have tried to complete the course are taken under consideration (that is, not considering the students who did not attend the minimum number of lessons, nor those who did not take any of the two final exams) it is clear that the numerical marks have improved, specially in this last year, as shown in the Figure 2 by the numerical marks distributions (over 8 points in 20).

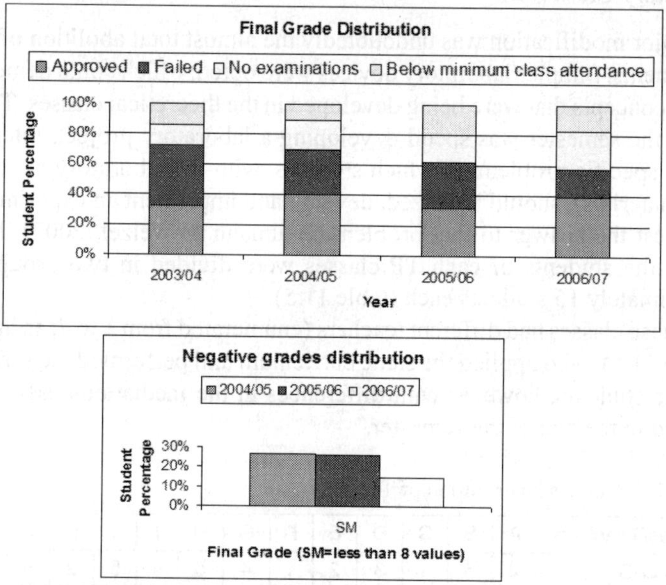

Figure 11.1A: Students' Final Status Distribution. **11.1B:** Students with Marks Below 8 (0-20 Scale).

At the end of the course, students answered an anonymous questionnaire (QEAME) in the e-learning platform. Results were compared (36 responses) with the ones obtained in the previous year (33 responses). There is an improvement in all the dimensions (Cravino, 2004) significant to this study (Table VI).

The last three indicators of the table 11.6 are related to the quality of teacher mediation, as perceived by students. It is clear that students recognize an improvement of mediation quality from 2005/2006 to 2006/2007.

In the interviews to teachers and to students, it became clear that students appreciate solving the problems by themselves, but were uncomfortable with the amount of work performed in class, referring they would rather like an intermediate solution, with the teacher solving some problems, so they would

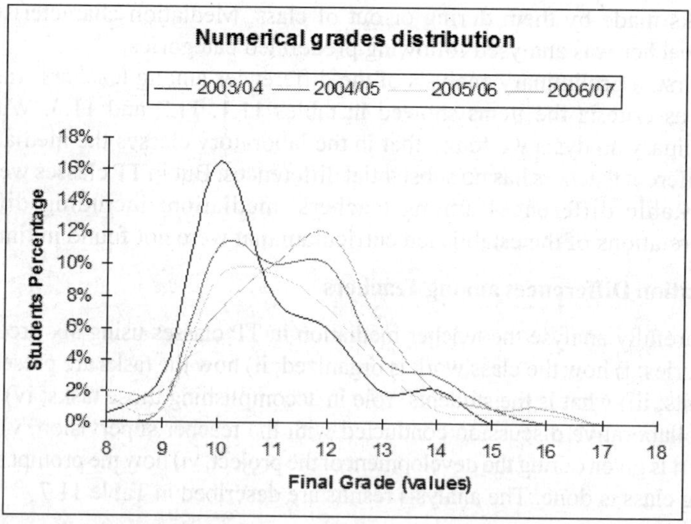

Figure 11.2: Final Results Distributions Throughout the Years

Table 11.6: Median Results Obtained in a Likert Scale (1 to 5) of Agreement (qeame)

Dimension	*2005/06*	*2006/07*
Deliberated effort towards good teaching	3,5	4
Permanent Evaluation	2,5	2,9
Permanent Interaction	3	3,4
Stimulus to the student independence	2,3	2,7

not loose so much time with it and could get more work done, that they thought was needed to get them prepared for the exam. Some of the teachers ended by doing just that, when they felt the students needed more help. Nevertheless all teachers refer that, in general, motivation in class increased, and the discussions in class were more or less participated by everyone. Another fact pointed out by the teachers was the low attendance of students in their scheduled appointments or in the personalized meetings. Some students refer they primarily seek out a colleague rather than the teacher to resolve regular doubts, and resort to the teacher only if this first resource failed. This effect is reported in the literature (Gorsky, Caspi, and Trumper, 2006), but it maybe increased by the social competences developed in classroom and the permanent discussion the students enrolled with each other.

Mediation Differences among Teachers

The data collected included personal interviews with all the teachers, during meetings and informal conversations, some students' interviews and informal remarks made by them during or out of class. Mediation characteristics of each teacher was analysed following predefined categories.

First, a preliminary analysis of the differences among teachers was done using as criteria the items showed in tables 11.1, 11.2 and 11.3. With this preliminary analysis we found that in the laboratory classes the mediation of the different teachers has no substantial differences. But in TP classes we found remarkable differences among teachers' mediation, including different interpretations of the established curriculum that were not found in time.

Mediation Differences among Teachers

We carefully analyse the teacher mediation in TP classes using six predefined categories: i) how the class work is organized; ii) how the tasks are presented to students; iii) what is the students' role in accomplishing those tasks; iv) how is the collaborative discussion conducted with the teacher supervision, v) which support is given during the development of the project, vi) how the prompt support during class is done. The analysis results are described in Table 11.7

Mediation Beyond Class

Even if an efficient mediation is being performed in class, in order to keep up engagement, especially if there is no cooperative project being developed (in these cases students' engagement might be sparkled by their colleagues), the mediation out of class becomes important. There are several ways in which this contact might be performed. We used e-mail, e-learning and office hours. Sensing that the teacher knows and is worried about the state of students' learning, they might tend to commit themselves in performing well. This kind of feedback on their homework (or other task) should be helpful in order to overcome some difficulties, but should not provide the entire solution to the problem/task. As saied before, teachers must help students in their construction of scientific knowledge, not replace them in that process. So, we carefully analyse the teacher mediation out of the classroom for each TP teacher using five predefined categories: i) Frequency and students' covered by the weekly feedback on the e-learning homework; ii) What kind of feedback is given; iii) Teacher participation in the open discussions in the e-learning; iv) Office consultation suggested by the teacher to each student; v) Students' showing up in regular office hours. The differences in the mediation performed by the different teachers are presented in table 11.8.

Teacher Mediation Traces of Teacher 1 (AB and GH classes)

Adding the data referred above to analyse teacher mediation differences, the teacher 1 perceptions on their evolution was analysed (interviewing teacher 1). This additional analysis enables us to establish some traces of mediation in AB and GH classes that seem to make a positive difference relatively to other classes.

Table 11.7: Differences in Mediation Implemented in Classroom among Teacher of TP Classes

Analysis Categories	*Teacher 1*	*Teacher 2*	*Teacher 3*	*Teacher 4*	*Teacher 6*
how the class work is organized	They worked in teams of 4-5 students, by turning to each other; The teacher would visit each group several times in each class	They worked in teams of 4-5, by turning to each other;	They worked individually or with their comate, in a traditional school tables distribution; Only in the project (at the end) they would join with their team	They worked in teams of 4-5, by turning to each other; The teacher would explain students' doubts out loud to the entire class, most of the times	They worked individually or with the colleague in the next sit, in a traditional school tables distribution;
How the tasks are presented to students	Project tasks were developed in the beginning of the class; Once finished, they would move on to the problems and exercises previously distributed	Usually they would begin with the project tasks, but when there was less time, the teacher would ask them to initiate with the problems.	In the first few problems the teacher worked them out in the blackboard with their collaboration; Brainstorm in some exercises	Before initiating each task or problem, the teacher would ask some questions to class, in order to establish a way to the solution, and then they would end by themselves	It was given a few minutes to solve each task or problem, and then asked for their contributions before presenting the solution in a projected transparency
What is the students' role in accomplishing those tasks?	Autonomous role, unsynchronized with the other teams	In most problems, only a few students participate in the discussion	In most problems, only a few students participate in the discussion	In most problems, only a few students participate in the discussion	In most problems, only a few students participate in the discussion
How the collaborative discussion is conducted with the teacher's supervision.	Most of the teams engaged in real collaboration with each other, performing peerlearning	Most of the time there was no team autonomy; some teams performed peerlearning	Little engagement in class	Most of the time there was no team autonomy and most teams clearly evidenced a leader, who would explain to their colleagues, but they were not very motivated to do team work	Little or none

(*Contd.*)

Analysis Categories	*Teacher 1*	*Teacher 2*	*Teacher 3*	*Teacher 4*	*Teacher 6*
How the prompt support during class is done.	To each team and only in crucial times and never the solution, but a clue	Sometimes the exercises were solved in the blackboard	Nearly half of the problems were developed on the blackboard	Most of the times in the blackboard; rarely in each team	After a while the teacher gave the solution in a projected transparency
What support is given during the development of the Project.	During class and with feedback on their partial achievements	During class; Many students did not meet deadlines	During class; And with feedback on their intermediate goal	During class; Many students did not meet deadlines	During class

Table 11.8: Differences in Mediation Implemented Out of Classroom among Teacher of TP Classes

Analysis categories	*Teacher 1*	*Teacher 2*	*Teacher 3*	*Teacher 4*	*Teacher 6*
Weekly feedback on the e-learning home-work.	Always, before next class	Only to the few who done it on time	Only to the few who done it on time, to the others only if they ask me	Not always	No, the teacher made a short survey of common mistakes in classroom
Kind of feedback	Clues for completing it, call for major mistakes, stimulus	Wright or wrong	Wright or wrong, occasionally the solution was given	Individual corrections were delivered	The solution
Participation in the open discussions in the e-learning	Regularly	Never	Once	Never	Never
Office consultation suggested by the teacher to each student.	Suggested every time teacher found it necessary	Sometimes, when necessary	Sometimes, when necessary	Sometimes, when necessary	No
Regular office hours	Not all students took advantage of it	Few students took advantage	Few students took advantage	Few students took advantage	Rarely

Traces of mediation used into classroom

The traces of mediation was found useful in class, in order to promote active engagement of the students with special reference to the following:

- Generate discussion in class with conceptual questions
- Provide situations and real problems in which students overcome their difficulties
- Promote peer learning
- Alternate between necessary moments of expositive lecture with engagements tasks (which should be the as varied as possible)
- Provide for regularly self-evaluation tests
- Correct their colleagues' work, while discussion is being pursuit, identifying mistakes and alternative ways of developing ideas
- Identify learning outcomes in order to fulfill any evidenced gap, and manage the curriculum.
- Provide help, guidance and explanations in crucial moments
- Resist the impulse of explaining everything, every time a student has a doubt, but give clues instead, in order to let it be the students to reach out the solution
- Supervise team discussions, stimulating everyone to participate, awarding their participation and not evaluating their faults.
- Supervise Project work, done in cooperation teams, namely helping them accomplishing the development of those social competences and specific orientations when necessary
- Stimulate their social competences, providing group autonomy, responsibility and cooperation.
- Provide students feedback on their learning outcomes
- Provide homework that are simultaneously challenging and demanding, but not too much difficult
- Diversify evaluation and give credit for the students' participation
- Evaluate how students prepare themselves to the tasks they know they have to face
- Provide the necessary resources
- Ask for their opinion on the most useful thing (in terms of their understanding) about each classes

Traces of mediation used beyond the classroom

The traces of mediation was found useful out of class, in order to keep up motivation, team engagement and persistence:

- Weekly e-learning assignments about the topics being developed (within the deadlines—until 24 hours before next class)
- Individual feedback performed by the teacher (via e-learning), in those 24 hours before next class

- In the cases of serious problems, students were called to specific office meeting (arranged according to their schedule), in order to recover the evidenced gap or misunderstanding
- Promote cooperative work outside the classroom, supervised by the teacher, with some deadlines to meet, in which they due to deliver some part of their work
- Promote collaboration work between students,
- Promote individual self and hetero-evaluation (anonymous) within teams, in order to establish responsibility in every member of the team
- Facilitate contact between teachers and their students, via email, e-learning or personal, in order to respond to doubts in specific subjects on the content of the course, doubts on the objectives or assessment on different components of the course, team problems or any others
- Promote open-problem discussions in the e-learning platform in which the answer grows with each participation, supervised by the teachers
- Award grading points to students for participating in the e-learning tasks, and not penalize them for not figuring out the right answer

Analysis of the Success of the Different Mediation Performance in TP Different Classes, in 2006/07

It can be seen in Figure 11.3, that GH class has the best pass rate and lower drop-out rate. This might be related to the fact that these students received constant feedback on their learning outcomes (always in the TP classes and almost every time in the laboratories). In sensing this attention from the teacher, they might be feel motivated to work harder, as some of them state in their interviews. In AB class this is not so clear because the majority of these students was taking this course for the second time, and had less time to accomplish the weekly tasks presented.

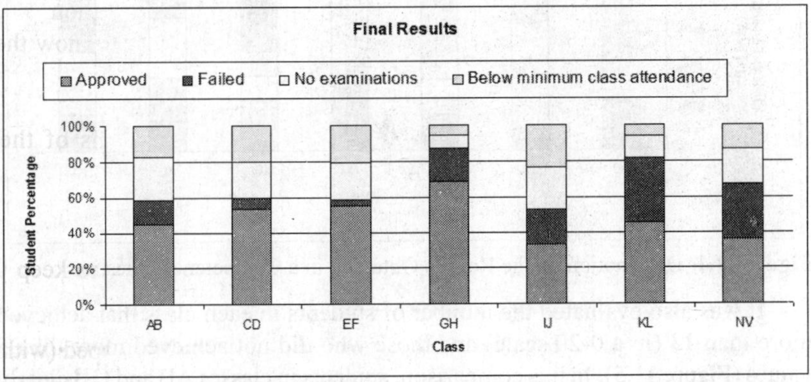

Figure 11.3: Final Results Distribution

The mediation was more significantly different in TP classes than in Laboratory. The synchronism among the topics approached in different type class (complementing the theoretical approach with practical and experimental) seems to be helpful in achieving the goal of helping students connecting the experimental procedures with the concepts being developed in the course. In this case the small differences between the mediation performed by different teachers all led to positive results, with the majority of students carrying through their final laboratory project successfully, revealing developments in specific and social competences. Even the weaker students revealed themselves positively in this final project, as was stated by more than one teacher.

Figure 11.4 shows the results of a detailed analysis of the competences test performed by the students. This test, in particular the competence question analyzed (last question present in table 11.4) involved the competences to interpret, establish relations and deduct consequences in a real situation.

In general the percentage of students who did not even try to solve the question, or in doing so did not get any tangible result, is very high, which indicates the relative difficulty students still feel in this type of questions. Nevertheless the best result is obtained in GH class. The others levels of competences results are: second level—KL class; third level,—AB, IJ, and NV classes; forth level—CD, and EF classes.

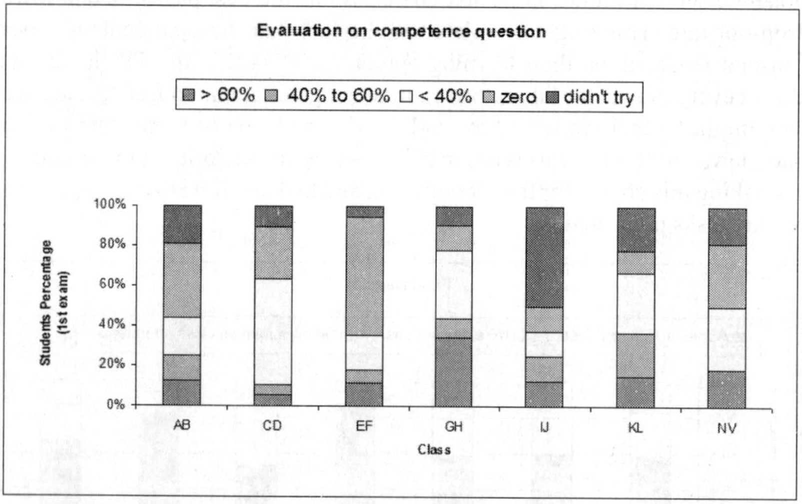

Figure 11.4: Distribution on the Results Obtained in a Competence Question

It was also evaluated the number of students in each class that achieved more than 13 (in a 0-20 scale) and those who did not achieved more than 5 values (Figure 11.5). In this comparison, students in classes AB and GH clearly performed better. Even for students who were repeating the course (majority

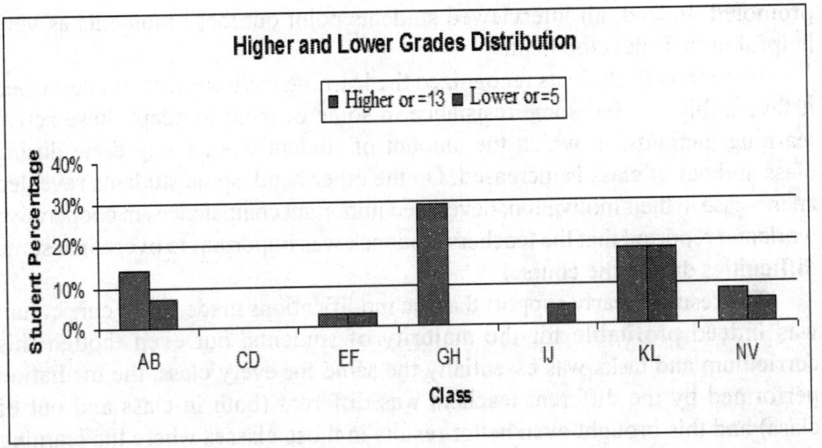

Figure 11.5: Higher and Lower Grades Comparison

of AB class and some in GH), and were not motivated at first (some had complex schedules, because of advanced courses), the results indicate that the performed mediation was able to provide some incentive to those students, as well as the others, in accomplishing the course. Some of them even became the most hard working students in class, performing every task on time, using the feedback to overcome their difficulties (including attending regularly the office hours), evidencing great evolution in the worked abilities and competences. In the KL class there was a clear teaching problem because there are a significant number of students who did not achieve more than 5 in a scale of 0 to 20. In this case the mediation performed by the teacher was not efficient, in particular for weaker students, who probably did not have enough time to think problems through, before the solution was presented.

Discussion and Conclusions

The academic results point clearly to an increase of success in the course from year to year, as measured by the final marks. There is also an improvement in the fact that the incidence of students with very low marks, and failing marks in general (below 10 in the 0-20 scale), has been significantly decreased. Also the pass rate shows substantial improvements, with a large percentage of good grades. The results, generally considered, show that the efforts contribute for a more effective teaching; producing academic results that are progressively better (pass rates). This result is consistent with the one that indicates progressively better teacher mediation, as perceived by students.

In that way, the mediation performed in the theoretical classes, the same for all students in this study, proves to be positive; most of the students who attended were involved in class and participated in the peer discussions promoted. Indeed, all interviewed students point out these moments as very helpful in their development.

Even though students recognized the learning environment and described it favourably, we felt some resistance in some of them to adapt these active learning methods, in which the amount of student work being done during class and out of class is increased. On the other hand, some students revealed an increase in their motivation, developed important competences in cooperative work and reported that the teachers feedback was important to overcome some difficulties during the course.

The results clearly support that the modifications made to the curriculum was indeed profitable for the majority of students, but even though this curriculum and tasks was essentially the same for every class, the mediation performed by the different teachers was different (both in class and out of class) and this brought even better results in those classes where the learning environment was based on autonomous real work, solving real complex problems and where teacher's mediation was diversified and centered on student's work:

(i) The academic results were equal or even better than those of classes taught in a more traditional approach;
(ii) High level competences were better developed in a larger number of students than in those classes taught in a more traditional approach.

This claim is true even though this learning environment was not yet well accepted by all students. This fact may suggest the possibility of greater developments in the students with more difficulties and in those who were already better prepared.

The differences found between the mediation performed by the different teachers were most significant in TP classes and beyond class. This might be due to several factors.

In class, most of the teachers failed to understand the importance of letting the students work out the problems for themselves and, in their goodwill, try to induce their thoughts and worked-out solutions someone (sometimes himself) already found, leaving most of the students with the minor task of replacing number in equations. This only reveals that teachers must have a better training in Science Education.

The mediation beyond class proved worthwhile, particularly for those students who perceived their advantages from the beginning and engaged in real work performed both individually and collaboratively. This kind of mediation involves more time available from the teachers. If this feedback is not done on time, or not at all, students failed to see the advantages and tend to abandon the tasks were they have more difficulties.

These results point to the fact that teachers need, not only their expertise, but also competence in science education, as well as the willpower and motivation to spend more time listening to their students. However, as the results showed, enriched teacher mediation is feasible. This claim is an important result for a practicable high quality teaching.

An important question for future work is if these active methods, even though they demand increased teacher supervision and feedback, are applicable in larger classes as well as in smaller ones. These preliminary results point to greater achievements in larger classes, but more data is needed to analyze this more accurately in the future.

In summary, results of the present study show that students do achieve better results and higher level of competences if they enroll in real work in class, mostly collaborative work, and are more motivated to continue the work out of class and that could mean that a better mediation was indeed achieved.

12

Formative Situation

A Framework for Fostering Teaching and Learning Basic Sciences in Engineering

J.B. Lopes, J.P. Cravino, C. Viegas and *C.M. Marques*

Some conferences and journals such as SEFI (European Society for Engineering Education), ASEE (American Society for Engineering Education), CESAER (Conference of European Schools Advanced Engineering Education and Research), ICEE (International Conference of Engineering Education), IJEE (International Journal of Engineering Education), JEE (Journal of Engineering Education), GJEE (Global Journal of Engineering Education), whose main objective is to provide a higher quality in engineering education, are giving the necessary impulse and are taking into account the recent developments in science education research. The topics most frequently found in engineering education literature are assessment, learning outcomes, students' prior knowledge, peer review and assessment, teamwork, skill development, students and professional's performance, curriculum developments. In fact not different from the topics found in other science education journals.

Some engineers/researchers/teachers, influenced by the research in Science Education, worried about effective teaching and learning in Engineering Schools (Ditcher, 2001; Felder *et al.,* 2000) and already obtained significant improvements using active learning (Felder & Brent, 2003; Box *et al.,* 2001), problem based learning (Benjamin & Keenan, 2007) and curriculum developments (Moesby, 2005; Mathew & Earnest, 2004; Yeomans & Atrens, 2001), or teamwork (Aman *et al.,* 2007; Felder & Brent, 2007), among many others. On the other hand, in Science Education Research several suggestions have been made to make the knowledge generated by research more useful and relevant (Bennett, 2003): there are studies of synthesis (Tiberghien, Jossem & Barojas, 1997), of meta-analysis (Hammersley, 2002) and of pragmatisation of research (Evans, 2002)[1] .

However research results have a reduced influence in classroom practices (Costa, Marques & Kempa, 2000). Trying to approach this problem, a research movement ties to go into the classroom to study in what conditions a curriculum design is really implemented and how the development of students' competences, knowledge, and attitudes is improved (e.g. Anderson & Bach, 2005; Cravino, 2004; Koliopoulos & Ravanis, 2000; Marques *et al.,* 2005; Martin & Solbes, 2001; Savinainen, Scott & Viiri, 2005). This type of studies may be more or less complete, but it is clear that it gives crucial information to develop a theoretical model, which integrates the learning and teaching aspects in real classrooms. From these researches it emerges the central importance of tasks and mediation (argumentation, classroom talk, etc.) and, also, the importance of formative assessment and student world (culture, knowledge, affective dimension, etc.), issues that are common in the Engineering Education literature. However, to produce a quality curriculum it is not enough that it is well designed, grounded and validated. It needs also to be well managed in the classroom.

This work aims to approach the problem presented above in a way that is relevant to teachers and researchers in teaching and learning basic sciences in engineering, who are interested in the improvement of teaching practices. In the line of several studies that articulate theories of learning and theories of teaching (e.g. Vermunt & Verloop, 1999), we present, elucidate and discuss a theoretical framework, that we call Formative Situation Framework (FSF), that allows:

- To articulate teaching and learning in basic sciences in engineering shools.
- To guides the choices, planning and management of teaching the basic sciences in classroom.
- To identify the main characteristics of relevant teaching practices and improve them.

So, this work is organized in the following way:

Section 2 presents the Formative Situation Framework (FSF) as a theoretical tool for fostering teaching and learning basic sciences in engineering, in particular presenting the key concepts, characterizing types of teaching, making explicit some consequences of the theoretical model.

Section 3 explains, in a general way, how can the Formative Situation Framework (FSF) be put to practical use.

Section 4 shows, with three research cases, how the Formative Situation Framework (FSF) was been put in action and developed students knowledge and competences.

Section 5 discusses how and why using the Formative Situation Framework (FSF) is relevant in engineering education.

Formative Situation Framework (FSF)—A Theoretical Tool for Fostering Teaching and Learning Basic Sciences in Engineering

Overview and Purpose of FSF

The formative situation (FS) framework is based on an implicit formulation by Astolfi, Darot, Vogel and Toussaint (1997), further developed by Lopes (2004). The FS is a theoretical framework to design a basic science curriculum and to manage it in classroom. In general, a formative situation considers teaching effort and the student learning effort/project. The teaching effort induces the learning effort/project and has two poles:

(i) the tasks and problems to propose to students;
(ii) teacher mediation.

The type of tasks, the type of mediation and the articulation between them determine the characteristics of teaching. These characteristics largely condition what knowledge, competences and attitudes can be developed in students. A multidimensional assessment of goals, approaches and learning outcomes is a process to regulate and improve teaching and learning (Fig. 12.1).

A formative situation:

(i) considers the knowledge already available from students;
(ii) gives students real opportunities to perform tasks and formulate problems;
(iii) creates an environment in which the teacher mediation is of utter importance to provide relevant information and scaffold the intended learning;
(iv) allows students to learn in a progressive and sustained way and provides the opportunities for them to use this knowledge; and
(v) induces student autonomous work.

In a formative situation, with a task reported to the situation presented and explored, students are invited to develop a mental and practical activity, using their available knowledge, and having an adequate control over the activity. The students' actual activities are conditioned not only by the tasks proposed, but also by the teacher's mediation, by students' interest and involvement, and by the material and conceptual resources used. The student's learning experience (that is, student activity in the classroom), resulting from the student's accomplishment of the tasks, is the basis for the teacher's support in helping the student appropriate, reconstruct and use a specific conceptual field of science[2]. The student's activity and the teacher's mediation, obviously interrelated, act as scaffolding for the development of student's knowledge, competences and attitudes.

Consequently, in the FS framework, the tasks and mediation are central. The tasks can mobilize the student world (the resources help and support this

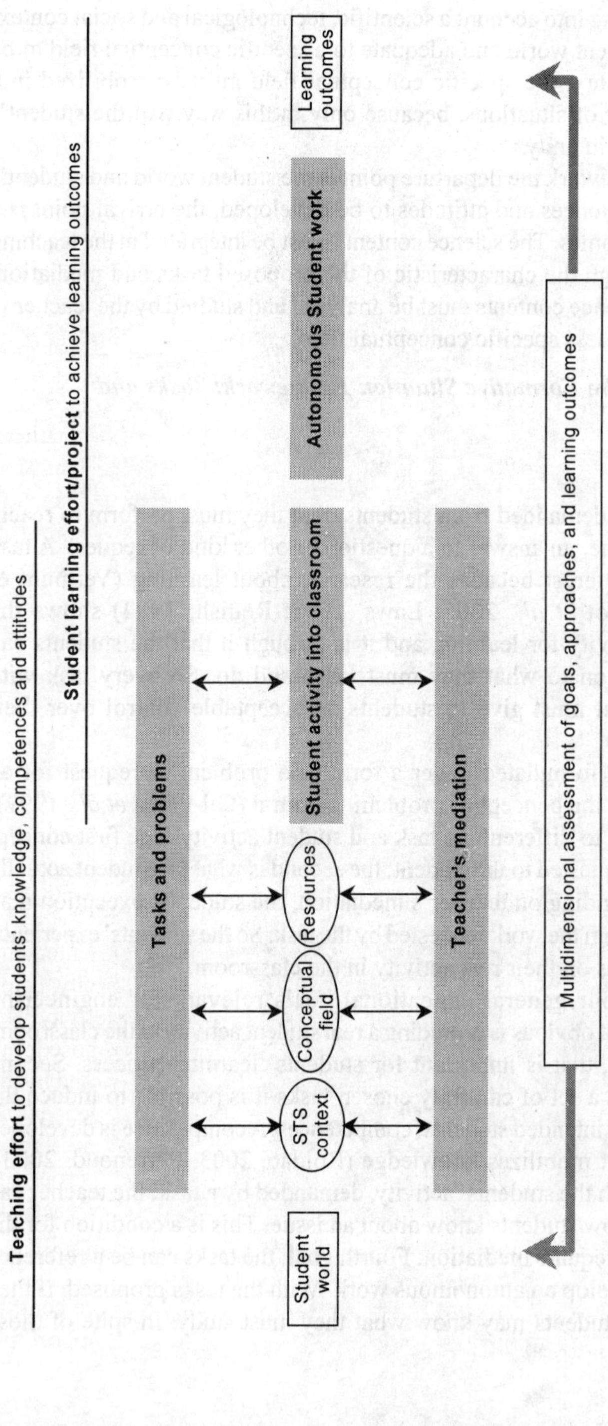

Figure 12.1: Formative Situation Framework (adapted from Lopes, 2004:166)

mobilization), taking into account a scientific, technological and social context relevant to the student world and adequate to a specific conceptual field to be learnt. In each context the specific conceptual field must be mobilized in a reasonable number of situations, because only in this way will the student's conceptual field gain unity.

In the FS framework the departure point is the student world and student's knowledge, competences and attitudes to be developed; the arrival point is a set of learning outcomes. The science contents must be integrated in the teaching and learning through the characteristic of the proposed tasks and mediation. Previously, the science contents must be analysed and studied by the teacher in terms of a more or less specific conceptual field.

Key-Concepts of the Formative Situation Framework: Tasks and Mediation

Task

A task is the work demanded from students, that they must perform to reach, within a certain time, an answer to a question or other kind of request. A task has educational interest because the research about learning (Vermunt & Verloop, 1999; Bot *et al.*, 2005; Laws, 1997; Redish, 1994) shows the importance of activity for learning and it is through it that the students can direct their attention to what they must learn and do. So every task with educational interest must give to students an acceptable control over their activity.

A task can be formulated under a form of a problem or request for an action. In any case the concept of problem is central (Gil-Perez *et al.*, 1999).

It is necessary to differentiate task and student activity. The first concept refers to what is requested to the student; the second is what the student actually does. In fact, depending on teacher's mediation, the student's execution may be very different from the work requested by the task. So the students' experience of learning depends on their real activity in the classroom.

A task has four general educational goals relevant for engineering education. The most obvious is providing a real student activity in the classroom. As we saw before, that is important for students' learning process. Second goal; only through a set of carefully chosen tasks it is possible to induce the development of the intended students' competences. A competence is developed through action that mobilizes knowledge (Roldão, 2003, Perrenoud, 2003). Third goal; through the students' activity, demanded by a task, the teacher can access what and how students know about an issue. This is a condition for the teacher to do an adequate mediation. Fourth goal; the tasks can be a reference for students to develop an autonomous work. With the tasks proposed, if they are relevant, the students may know what they must study. In spite of those tasks' general educational goals, there are obviously specific goals for each particular task. If we consider the different tasks regarding their educational function and characteristics we may classify them into five types (Table 12.1):

(i) exemplar or routine tasks;
(ii) traditional scientific process tasks;
(iii) exploring tasks;
(iv) epistemic tasks;
(v) project tasks.

As it may be seen in table 12.1, we do not consider, *a priori*, one type of task to be better than another, in the sense that all of them may be necessary. However, the types of tasks are ordered by the level of competences demanded and, consequently, by the level of competences that is possible to develop in students.

The formulation of tasks must have the following characteristics:

- It must be clear what is the action requested and its goal and it must be adequate to the characteristics of the students (student's previous knowledge, skills, attitudes and competences);
- The situation must be clearly formulated (in academic or in realistic terms) or references given to search for the main characteristics of the situation;
- The necessary resources must be appropriated and available;
- The task must demand a work and/or reflection that help scaffolding the development of student's knowledge, skills, attitudes and competences (Pea, 2004).

Each type of task may be executed in progressive levels of difficulty, abstraction, concepts involved or competences available or required. It can also be oriented so that students appropriate/construct a basic conceptual field, consolidate a conceptual field or enrich and/or extend a conceptual field.

Mediation

The mediation is, in first instance, the action (verbal and non-verbal) of the teacher in order to try to develop student's knowledge, competencies and attitudes demanded by intended curricula. The teacher's action consists in providing support for learners in complex tasks, 'that enable students to deal with more complex content and skill demands than they could otherwise handle' (Reiser, 2004). That is, teacher mediation is a work best developed in the zone of proximal development (Weil-Barais, 1994; Moll, 2002).

Mediation is not an easy issue because the teacher (and researcher) must take into account, at the same time, the cognitive, affective, relational and social-political dimensions of what happens in the classroom (Valero, 2002; Weil-Barais & Dumas-Carré, 1998). Moreover, the teacher must pay attention, simultaneously, to the following aspects (Weil-Barais & Dumas-Carré, 1998):

Table 12.1: Different Type of Tasks in Engineering Education and its Main Characteristics and Goals

Type of task	*Main characteristics*	*Main goal*	*Examples*
Exemplar or routine tasks	Oriented to show how students must work with concepts, tools, and/or devices. Oriented to training algorithmic use of concepts or basic skills with tools or devices.	Introduce the students to a conceptual field. Training students in basic skills.	Paper and pencil exercises. Manipulate devices.
Traditional scientific process tasks	Oriented to working in problem solving, experimental work or work with conceptual models in basic science. Require a considerable practical and/or intellectual effort to elaborate an answer.	Learn, enrich and/or innovate with the main and traditional scientific processes. Help students to appropriate/ construct an extended and solid conceptual field.	Problem solving. Experimental work. Modelling work.
Exploring tasks	Oriented to exploring situations or contexts, identifying problems, the need for new concepts and so on.	Help students to contact with the main problems of a knowledge area. Prepare students to use scientific knowledge in a flexible way.	Use or recognize the same concepts in different situations. Exploring a real situation.
Epistemic tasks	Oriented to working in elementary epistemic demand of scientific work or in elementary epistemic demand of engineering work.	Learn to use the basic epistemic processes demanded in scientific or engineering work.	Identify problems. Argument in a discussion. Find solutions in practical context.
Project tasks	Oriented to conceive and develop, with certain autonomy, a project. A project work requires identifying a problem, search for the pertinent information and resources, choose an approach, and find, test and develop a product addressed to a certain public.	Offer to students a part of open curriculum (choosing to study what they are interested in). Develop high level competences and attitudes, including auto nomous work.	Project a lift for a building, showing the main dimensions and technical and operational characteristics.

(i) resources and facilities to be used by the students;
(ii) languages used by himself and by the students (natural, mathematical, graphical, computational);
(iii) knowledge, competencies and attitudes from himself and from students (scientific, educational, epistemological, etc.);
(iv) science education knowledge;
(v) socio-political conceptions from himself, from students and from society (Valero, 2002).

Even though the teacher needs to present some information to the students, true mediation is not merely information transmission because, in a formative situation, information is presented only when the students are able to appropriate it. However, there are several styles of mediation that can be grouped in types of mediation. We identify five main types of mediation:

(i) informative;
(ii) interactive;
(iii) dialogic;
(iv) problem centred; and
(v) epistemic.

The characteristics of each one, the respective main goal and the main roles of teacher and students in each one are presented in table 12.2.

The types of mediation, presented in table 12.2, are characterized taking into account:

(i) How classroom talk is considered. Leach and Scott (2003) propose two dimensions to analyse the classroom talk (authoritative/dialogic and interactive/non interactive). Polman and Pea (2001) clarify the role of talk with interaction without transformative communication.
(ii) How the student's work occurs in classroom. There is a consensus that mediation is based on student work (Pea, 2004). The student work depends on the type of support given by the teacher. In particular the teacher may directly guide the students or structure and problematize their work with different nuances (Reiser, 2004).
(iii) How the classroom is considered as social system (Lemke, 1997). The information can have one origin (teacher) or multiple origins. The information flow in classroom may be directional (from the teacher to students) or there may be information flow among the students and teacher (e.g. Hoadley & Linn, 2000). Also, students may construct meaning in different ways.
(iv) How the roles of questions and situations are taken into account.
(v) How knowledge is faced. It may be seen as a finished, in construction or as an open field.

As it may be verified in table 12.2, the authors do not consider, *a priori*, one type of mediation better than another, in the sense that all of them may be

Table 12. 2: Different Types of Mediation in Engineering Education and Its Main Characteristics and Goals and the Role of Teacher or Student

Type of Mediation	*Main Characteristics*	*Main Role of Teacher/Student*	*Main Goal*
Informative	The main established concepts, laws and principles are present in the discourse. The concepts, laws and principles are structured in the perspective of finished knowledge. The situations illustrate where concepts, laws and principles work. There is a structured and appropriate discourse. The main information flow is from teacher/textbook to student.	Teacher: Present a structured, appellative and appropriate discourse. Student: listen, take notes, observe photos, representations, experiences or other resources.	Give structured information and in conditions of being appropriated.
Interactive	The main established concepts, laws and principles are present in the discourse. The concepts, laws and principles are structured in the perspective of finished knowledge. The situations illustrate where concepts, laws and principles work. There is a monitoring dimension to students' action or discourse. There are questions of short answer. The main information flow is from teacher/textbook to student.	Teacher: Present a structured, appellative and appropriate discourse with an interactive pattern. Student: listen, take notes, observe photos, experiences or other resources; execute small tasks; answer the questions posed by teacher.	Give structured information and in conditions of being appropriated and give opportunities for student to learn by himself.
Dialogic	The main established concepts, laws and principles are present in the discourse. The concepts, laws and principles are structured in the perspective of knowledge in construction. The situations are exploited with concepts, laws and principles. There is a scaffold dimension to students' action or discourse. There are open questions. The main information flow is from teacher/textbook to student. The meaning of information is obtained by dialogic interaction between teacher and students.	Teacher: Interact, dialogically, with students in order to structure their ideas or actions. Student: listen, speak, and execute tasks; control own learning.	The students become knowledge re-constructors.

(Contd.)

Type of Mediation	*Main Characteristics*	*Main Role of Teacher/Student*	*Main Goal*
Problem centred	There are a search for the relevant concepts, laws and principles already established. The concepts, laws and principles are structured in the perspective of knowledge in construction. The situations are problematized using specific knowledge. There is a challenging dimension to students' action or discourse. There are actual problems. The origin of information is multiple (teacher, textbooks, papers, software, internet, etc.). The student learns essentially by himself.	Teacher: Challenge students to find and solve knowledge based problems. Student: find and solve knowledge based problems.	The students become problem finders and solvers.
Epistemic	There is a search for the relevant concepts, laws and principles already established. There is a search for new problems, concepts, data, methods, models, systems or tools. The situations are problematized using or searching knowledge. There is a releasing dimension to students' action or discourse. There are actual problems. The origin of information is multiple (teacher, textbooks, papers, software, internet, etc.). There is information flow among participants (each one has different roles but the same status). The negotiation of meaning is frequent.	Teacher: senior epistemic subject. Student: epistemic subject in development.	The students become epistemic subjects.

necessary. However, the types of mediation are ordered by the level of exigency demanded to teacher and, concomitantly, by the level of knowledge, competences and attitudes that is possible induce in students' learning.

When teachers consider any type of mediation they must pay attention to the following aspects:

- Adapt the mediation to the student world.
- Choose the right type of mediation, in each moment, for each student, in order to maximize each student's development (Vygotsky, 1962).
- Construct a repertory of mediation resources specially adapted to the content and its nature and appropriate to the students' characteristics (Treagust, 2003).
- Assess systematically both student learning and classroom climate (Valero, 2002).

Interrelations Tasks-Mediation

In the forgoing section the importance of tasks and teacher mediation in the Formative Situation Framework are refered. Now it is necessary to make explicit how the interaction task-mediation determines the types of teaching. The main types of teaching are present in different boxes of Table 12.3.

Based on Jimenez-Aleixandre (1996) we consider that a type of teaching is determined by six factors:

(i) teaching principle;
(ii) syntax;
(iii) social system;
(iv) support system;
(v) type of tasks for students; and
(vi) learning activity induced in students.

The ensemble of the six factors determines the type of teaching. The 'teaching principle' supports the main ideas and practices of teaching. The 'syntax' is about the main rules and characteristics or pattern of what happens in classroom. The 'social system' is about how the classroom is socially organized, namely how the teacher power is exerted. The support system is about which resources are available and what is the origin of information. The type of task are characterized in preceeding section. However, it was noted that a type of teaching without tasks for students is conceivable. The learning activity induced in students' results from all the others factors.

Some aspects that may help read Table 12.3.

(i) The teaching principle is linked to mediation and does not change with task. The social system is, in general, linked to teaching principle.
(ii) A task may modify the syntax of teaching and consequently the type of teaching.

Table 12.3: Main Characteristics of Teaching Depending on Type of Mediation and Type of Tasks

Type of task	*Type of mediation*				
	Informative	*Interactive*	*Dialogic*	*Problem centred*	*Epistemic*
Without task	**P**-Teaching based on information transmission **S**-Informative lecture **SS**-Based on teacher authority **Sup**-Textbook **T**-None **L**-Accommodate contents	**P**-Teaching based on information transmission **S**-Informative lecture with interactive pattern **SS**-Based on teacher authority **Sup**-Textbook and others **T**-None **L**-Accommodate contents	**P**-Teaching enriching student's understanding supported on previous student's work and knowledge. **S**-Lecture taking into account the audience interests or gaps. **SS**-Teacher as reflective professional. **Sup**-teacher, textbooks, papers, software, internet, etc. **T**-None **L**-Reconstruct knowledge	**P**-Teaching inducing students find and solve problems knowledge based. **S**-Lecture posing/approach relevant problems. **SS**-Teacher as reflective professional. **Sup**-teacher, textbooks, papers, software, internet, etc. **T**-None. **L**-How to find problems knowledge based.	**P**-Teaching inducing students become epistemic subjects. **S**-Lecture doing the state of art in a certain domain. **SS**-Teacher and students as epistemic subjects. **Sup**-teacher, textbooks, papers, software, internet, etc. **T**-None. **L**-How to become epistemic subject.
Exemplar/ routine task	**P**-Teaching based on information transmission **S**-Informative lecture and demonstrative tasks **SS**-Based on teacher authority **Sup**-Textbook **T**-Exemplar/ routine task **L**-Accommodate or assimilate contents	**P**-Teaching based on information transmission **S**-Informative lecture with interactive pattern and monitoring students in order to give immediate direct support, help or information **SS**-Based on teacher authority **Sup**-Textbook **T**-Exemplar/routine task **L**-Accommodate or assimilate contents	**P**-Teaching enriching student's understanding supported on previous student's work and knowledge. **S**-Small dialogic lectures; assure the basic meaning acquisition. **SS**-Teacher as reflective professional. **Sup**-teacher, textbooks, papers, software, internet, etc. **T**-Exemplar/routine task **L**-Reconstruct knowledge and develop basic competences	Not very adequate or improbable match.	Not very adequate or improbable match.

(*Contd.*)

	Informative	*Interactive*	*Dialogic*	*Problem centred*	*Epistemic*
Traditional scientific process tasks	**P**-Teaching based on information transmission **S**-Informative lecture and demonstrative tasks **SS**-Based on teacher authority **Sup**-Textbook **T**-Traditional scientific process tasks **L**-Accommodate or assimilate contents	**P**-Teaching based on information transmission **S**-Informative lecture with interactive pattern and monitoring students in order to give immediate direct support, help or information **SS**-Based on teacher authority **Sup**-Textbook and others **T**-Traditional scientific process tasks **L**-Accommodate or assimilate contents	**P**-Teaching enriching student's understanding supported on previous student's work and knowledge. **S**-Small dialogic lectures; assure the basic meaning acquisition. **SS**-Teacher as reflective professional. **Sup**-teacher, textbooks, papers, software, internet, etc. **T**-Traditional scientific process tasks **L**-Reconstruct knowledge and develop basic competences	**P**-Teaching inducing students find and solve problems knowledge based. **S**-Small lectures posing/approach relevant problems. The support is based on structuring and problematizing the student work. **SS**-Teacher as reflective professional; students has control of their learning. **Sup**-teacher, textbooks, papers, software, internet, etc. **T**-Traditional scientific process tasks. **L**-Find and solve knowledge based problems in controlled context.	**P**-Teaching inducing students become epistemic subjects. **S**-Small lectures doing the state of art in a certain domain. Training basic epistemic competences. The support is based on structuring and pro-blematizing the student work. **SS**-Teacher and students as epistemic subjects. **Sup**-teacher, textbooks, papers, software, internet. **T**-Traditional scientific process tasks. **L**-Becoming epistemic sub-ject in controlled context.
Exploring tasks	Not adequate.	Not very adequate or improbable match.	**P**-Teaching enriching student's understanding supported on previous student's work and knowledge. **S**-Small dialogic lectures; Test student's ability and skills, to improve his knowledge, competences, attitudes.	**P**-Teaching inducing students find and solve problems knowledge based. **S**-Small lectures posing/approach relevant problems. The support is based on structuring and problematizing the student work.	**P**-Teaching inducing students becoming epistemic subjects. **S**-Small lectures doing the state of art in a certain domain. Training basic epistemic competences. The support is based on structuring and problema-tizing the student work.

(*Contd.*)

	Informative	*Interactive*	*Dialogic*	*Problem centred*	*Epistemic*
			SS-Teacher as reflective professional; students has control of their learning. **Sup**-teacher, textbooks, papers, software, internet, etc. **T**-Exploring tasks. **L**-Reconstruct knowledge and develop high level competences	**SS**-Teacher as reflective professional; students has control of their learning. **Sup**-teacher, textbooks, papers, software, internet, etc. **T**-Exploring tasks **L**-Find and solve problems knowledge based in open context.	**SS**-Teacher and students as epistemic subjects. **Sup**-teacher, textbooks, papers, software, internet, etc. **T**-Exploring tasks. **L**-Becoming epistemic subject in open context.
Epistemic tasks	Not adequate.	Not adequate.	**P**-Teaching enriching student's understanding supported on previous student's work and knowledge. **S**-Small dialogic lectures; The support is based on structuring and problematizing the student work. **SS**-Teacher as reflective professional; students has control of their learning. **Sup**-Teacher, textbooks, papers, software, internet, etc. **T**-Epistemic tasks **L**-Reconstruct knowledge and develop high level competences	**P**-Teaching inducing students find and solve problems knowledge based. **S**-Small lectures posing/approach real or STS problems. The support is based on problematizing the student work. To encourage student's independent thinking and work. **SS**-Teacher and students as epistemic subjects. **Sup**-teacher, textbooks, papers, software, internet, etc. **T**-Epistemic tasks. **L**-Find and solve problems knowledge based in productive context.	**P**-Teaching inducing students becoming epistemic subjects. **S**-Small lectures doing the state of art in a certain domain. To encourage student's independent thinking and work. The support is based on problematizing the student work. **SS**-Teacher and students as epistemic subjects. **Sup**-teacher, textbooks, papers, software, internet, etc. **T**-Epistemic tasks. **L**-Becoming epistemic subject in productive context.

(*Contd.*)

	Informative	*Interactive*	*Dialogic*	*Problem centred*	*Epistemic*
Project tasks	No adequate.	No adequate.	**P**-Teaching enriching student's understanding supported on previous student's work and knowledge. **S**-Small dialogic lectures; The support is based on structuring and problematizing the student work. **SS**-Teacher and student as epistemic subjects. **Sup**-Teacher, textbooks, papers, software, internet, etc. **T**-Project tasks. **L**-Reconstruct knowledge and develop high level competences	**P**-Teaching inducing students find and solve problems knowledge based. **S**-Small lectures posing/approach real or STS problems. The support is based on problematizing the student work. To encourage student's independent thinking and work. **SS**-Teacher and students as epistemic subjects. **Sup**-teacher, textbooks, papers, software, internet, etc. **T**-Project tasks. **L**-Find and solve problems knowledge based in real context.	**P**-Teaching inducing students becoming epistemic subjects. **S**-Small lectures doing the state of art in a certain domain. To encourage student's independent thinking and work. The support is based on problematizing the student work. **SS**-Teacher and students as epistemic subjects. **Sup**-teacher, textbooks, papers, software, internet, etc. **T**-Project tasks. **L**-Becoming epistemic subject in real context.

(**Legend**: **P**-principle; **S**-syntax; **SS**-Social system; **Sup**-Support system; **T**-Type of Task; **L**-Learning induced)

(iii) According to the type of mediation used for a certain type of task we have different types of teaching, as a consequence of changing the teaching principle, syntax, social system and support system.

(iv) The change of mediation type or task type determines the teaching type. On the other hand, actual changes of mediation style may occur if, even inadvertently, subtle but determinant changes in the classroom syntax, social system and/or support system take place.

The Role of Contextual Situation, Conceptual Field Network, Resources and Assessment in FSF

The contextual situation concerns putting in scene objects, events or information of scientific, technological or social nature that helps the students to understand the scientific concepts and their contexts of use. The contextual situation must be used as a permanent anchor to learning and teaching and not as fleeting illustration (for example, Stinner, 1990). So, the contextual situation must be scientific, technologic and/or socially relevant, in the sense that it is relevant to the students and appropriate to the conceptual field of science to be used. As a result the contextual situation helps develop informed and educated citizens. We can relate this issue to science-technology-society (STS) research.

The resources needed to teaching and learning may be materials, laboratory equipments, school facilities, computers, tools, communication facilities or scientific information, etc. The resources are an important way to assure the intended activity demanded by tasks. Space organization/configuration, even though it is not a resource *in strictus sensus*, assures the actual availability and usability of resources. Lemke (2005) presents an inclusive vision of the resources that are available to teaching.

The assessment is a control process that can help students, teachers, parents and society at large to know in what way the student world develop in the direction of desired knowledge, competences and attitudes. As a control process, the assessment must consider what work and effort the student does, the adequacy of tasks, the pertinence of mediation and the quality of mobilization of a specific conceptual field of science. Consequently assessment must be multidimensional in its goals, tools and approaches. Besides we note the importance of formative assessment for the mediation process. With the results of assessment the teacher may improve his/her teaching and students may enrich their learning outcomes. Some examples of recent research studies in this area are those by Etkina (2000), Bennett and Kennedy (2001) and Shepard (2002).

According to Vergnaud (1987, 1991) a conceptual field is a set of interrelated concepts (emphasis on the relational nature of scientific concepts), with a certain dimension and structure, which allows subjects to operate, approach, think and act in a more or less wide class of situation-problems. Besides, the construction/

use of the concepts is carried out according to different interconnected dimensions: systems of representation (natural language, graphical, mathematical, etc.); mental schemas (concepts' proprieties, operations with concepts, relationships among concepts, theoretical models and models of situations); set of situations/problems in which the subject can mobilize and use the concepts with meaning. The subject mobilizes, at the same time, the representational systems, mental schemas and the repertory of actions, questions and meanings attributed by the subjects to a class of situation-problems that the subjects judge appropriate because they think that the target situation-problem is similar to others that they already know (Vergnaud, 1987, 1991). A conceptual field is therefore organized around a class of situation-problems. The more inclusive the class of situations/problems used in a conceptual field, the more structured and wide it will be the respective conceptual field.

We propose a representation called 'conceptual field network' which consist in a diagram representation with three entities:

(i) central concepts,
(ii) theoretical models; and
(iii) social context of use of concepts.

In this diagram there are lines linking concepts and theoretical models among them. The social contexts of use of concepts are linked with theoretical models. Each theoretical model aggregates concepts and each of these may be linked with more than one theoretical model (see Figure 12.6). So a 'conceptual field network' encapsulates the conceptual field and contextual situations. This diagram is helpful to integrate in FSF the contents, conceptual field object of teaching and its social relevance, identifying the social context of use of concepts.

Some Consequences of FSF

First consequence. The FSF clarifies that there is not an ideal teaching type. Different types of teaching are useful for different purposes. What we propose is a combination of several types of teaching. Each combination must be different depending on the type of students and learning outcomes intended (related with aims and goals of a certain course level). As we see above the FSF can predict and characterize teaching type but cannot suggest, *a priori*, the best combination of teaching types.

Second consequence (related with the first purpose of this work). The FSF clarifies how tasks can be interrelated with mediation, how these interrelations determine a teaching type and how a teaching type is closely linked to the learning activity induced. A certain type of teaching is determined by the actual articulation between tasks proposed to students and the actual mediation done by teacher. An inadequate mediation may reduce drastically the educational potential of a task. In the limit it can render inadequate the use of a certain task. An example of the first situation is the case of an experimental work (traditional scientific process task type) that may be of little value if the mediation is of the informative type. One example for the second situation is the case of an exploring task that may be inadequate if the mediation is of the informative type. On the other hand, some types of mediation require tasks which demand high level of competences. For example, an epistemic mediation does not work with an exemplary/routine task type. So, the actual learning activity induced in students may be changed by a subtle but fundamental change of mediation type. The FSF can predict the type of teaching if we know the type of task to propose to students and the mediation style chosen. It can also predict the changes in teaching type intended if some changes occur in mediation style, for example classroom social system and/or syntax. In fact, in a teaching type all factors are aligned among them, but only four are directly observable (syntax, social system, support system, type of tasks for students). Any change in one of these factors causes a change of teaching type. So, if the teacher (even if unaware) changes one of these factors, he changes the intended mediation and consequently the teaching type.

Third consequence (related with the second purpose of this work). The FSF may help a teacher to make fundamental choices for his/her teaching. Choices about type of tasks, type of mediation, appropriate combination of teaching types, resources, and conceptual field network. With FSF it is possible to plan the curriculum of a theme, curricular unit, course or study cycle. Also FSF can help teachers in the management of the curriculum. In the next section we approach this issue carefully.

Fourth consequence (related with the third purpose of this work). Finally, the FSF allows identifying the actual characteristics of teaching. The FSF does not give direct indicators to assess teaching quality. However, it provides evaluation dimensions (the six factors that characterize a teaching type) that can guide a characterization of teaching work. With formative assessment of learning outcomes and assessment of teaching quality it is possible to improve teaching and learning quality.

How can the Formative Situation Framework (FSF) be Put to Practical Use?

The FSF provides a theoretical tool to help the preparation of the curriculum and the management of the curriculum in the classroom. It also allows the identification of the main characteristics of teaching practices. Each of these potential uses are analyse as follow:

FSF and the Preparation of the Curriculum

Concerning the preparation of the classroom curriculum, the FS framework allows the central aspects of learning and teaching of science in formal contexts to become operational (see Figure 12.2).

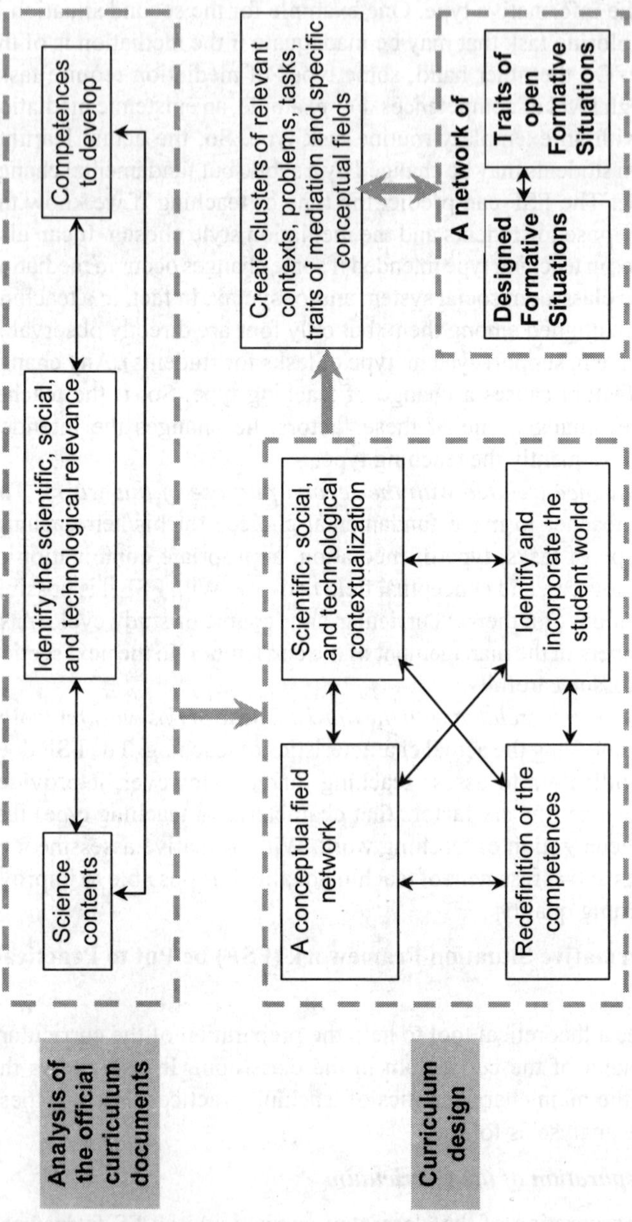

Figure 12.2: Operations to Prepare a FS Based Curriculum (Adapted from Lopes, 2004)

First, the FS framework helps to identify in the normative curricular documents the key-aspects like science contents, competences to develop and the scientific, technological and social relevance of the science contents. Then it also helps to identify a conceptual field network with three key-aspects: theoretical models, key-concepts and relevant contexts of use of the concepts. From this conceptual field network it is possible to make explicit, from the point of view of the expert, the main aspects of each specific conceptual field associated to each curricular unit to teach: key-concepts, models (theoretical and from situations), operations with concepts and models, language used, contexts to use concepts and models, historical and social contexts of production of concepts.

Second, the FS framework helps to choose the situations that allow for the contextual use of concepts by the students. The teaching and learning must be centred on tasks, strongly related to a contextual situation-problem and to a conceptual field, in order to mobilize the student world and permanently improve learning by mediation. The teacher needs to articulate the characteristics of a specific conceptual field with the competences to be developed and the identified student world with tasks and the contextual uses of the concepts. So, the contextual situation must be carefully chosen by the teacher, taking into account the students' interest, since it will condition the tasks, the development of competences and the usability of a conceptual field.

Third, after this work it is possible to create clusters of relevant contexts, problems, tasks, traits of mediation and specific conceptual field to be used. So, the first draft of the curriculum plan is a network of formative situations (only with some key-aspects identified like competences, situations, tasks, models, contextual use). Actually, the curriculum design itself is a network of formative situations. Each formative situation is adequately designed if most aspects can be anticipated with precision. When all formative situations are drafted, they must also be articulated in a network, not as a simple sequence. It is important to anticipate the possibility that the order and emphasis of formative situations may be altered, if the students' needs require that. This is why a network articulation of formative situations is better that a simple sequence.

Fourth, the specification of each formative situation through the central aspects of FS (see Figure 12.1) may become operational using a tool similar to Table 12.4. The student world cannot be completely anticipated. But some aspects are possible to anticipate: use of certain types of objects, the knowledge of certain aspects of situations, certain conceptual demands. The other aspects related to the student world can only be known during teaching. Making the conceptual field of a theme explicit involves identifying the key-concepts, models (theoretical and from situations), operations with concepts and models, language used, contexts of use of concepts and models, historical and social contexts of production of concepts. This work allows the teacher to choose and clarify the contextual situation and, above all, articulate, in a flexible way, the tasks with mediation within each formative situation. Also, it allows articulating the different formative situations. The first approach to a situation is to formulate problems based on it. The necessary resources for solving it must be available. The characteristics of the tasks to propose from students must allow:

(i) to mobilize the students' available knowledge;
(ii) approach the chosen concepts, and
(iii) develop the intended competences.

As we see above the mediation can reduce or improve the educational potential of tasks. So, the mediation, even though it cannot be entirely foreseen, must be carefully prepared to guarantee certain desired traits of teaching and learning. In Table 12.4 the vertical double arrow indicates the need for temporal articulation and the horizontal arrow indicates the need for articulation among situation-problem, problems, tasks, resources and mediation.

If a teacher prepares an enriched teaching, he/she must expect some complexity in the classroom environments This complexity may be manifested by:

(i) the self-regulation (influence on contexts choice, self-assessment);
(ii) the multiplicity of learning paths in the same educational space (manifested by the characteristics of student activity and the correspondent mediation and by the network organization of formative situations);
(iii) the mobilization of the student world to improve the knowledge, competences and attitudes to be developed.

FS Framework to Manage and to Analyse the Curriculum in the Classroom

The main goal of the curriculum management in the classroom is to improve the students' knowledge, competences and attitudes achieving the desired learning outcomes (see Figure 12.3). Obviously, the first tool to manage the curriculum is the curriculum design itself. The other tool is the FSF that guides, theoretically, the use of conceptual field network, contexts of use of concepts, and above all guides the articulation between tasks and mediation that induce student learning activity. The most sensitive aspect of curriculum management is the teacher's mediation, because it takes a particular form with each specific teacher and students, in their particular circumstances and it may change even inadvertently from one type to another, in general degrading of its educational potential.

Table 12.4: Formative Situation Specification Table

Student World (conceptions, available knowledge, life experience, interests...)				
A Specific Conceptual Field [key-concepts, models (theoretical and from situations), operations with concepts and models, language used, contexts to use concepts and models, historical and social contexts of production of concepts]				
Context (situation-problem)	**Problems**	**Tasks**	**Resources**	**Traits of Teacher's Mediation** (Traits of Informative, interactive, dialogic, problem centred or epistemic mediation type)
↕				
Students' competences, knowledge and attitudes to be developed and learning outcomes				

Note: Adapted from Lopes (2004).

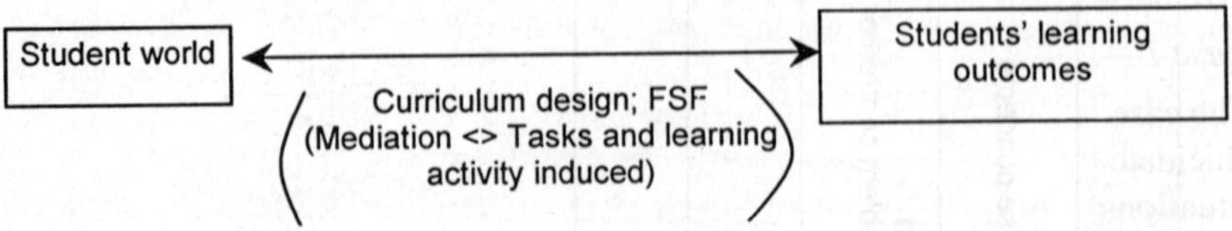

Figure 12.3: Components and Process of Curriculum Management in the Classroom Based on the FS Framework (Adapted from Lopes, 2004)

The tasks mobilize the student world, condition the desired student activity and indicate what the appropriate resources are. The accomplishment of tasks by the students allows to anchor the appropriation and use of a specific conceptual field and to develop the intended competencies, knowledge and attitudes.

The mediation of students' work helps to choose the appropriate tasks and verify if each task is clear to the students and if they correctly appropriate it. It also allows identifying the characteristics of student world, to incorporate assessment to adjust the mediation itself and to verify if the competencies, knowledge and attitudes are being developed. Through the mediation, the teacher helps the students mobilize, appropriate, reconstruct and/or use a specific conceptual field.

The FSF allows the teacher to take into account the complexity of the classroom climate, without losing the necessary control about what happens inside the classroom.

Finally the FSF may be used to analyse the curriculum management in the classroom (independently of the curriculum design nature) and identify its strengths and weaknesses. As we see in preceeding section, to characterize a teaching type we can use the six evaluate dimension proposed. With this analysis it is possible to identify the tasks type and mediation type and make the necessary adjustments if it does not correspond to the desired teaching.

Potential, Limitations and Conditions to Use FSF

The FSF may be used in formal learning contexts (e.g. engineering education in classrooms at several educational levels and institutional constraints), in informal learning contexts (e.g. science/technological museums, educational centres, entertainment centres) and in professional learning contexts (e.g. professional work contexts, professional development). The focus is student (or apprentice or professional) learning and what the teacher (or instructor or supervisor) must do, in certain conditions, to promote lasting learning.

Another important potential use of the FSF is to guide future researches in engineering education, especially if they are directed to questions of practical relevance.

The FSF has, obviously, some limitations. It is a theoretical tool that assumes that teaching must be directed to learning outcomes and these may take different forms and levels. Also, the FSF may be developed and become even more operational.

FSF in Action—Brief Reporting of Three Research Cases Using FSF

Case 1—Basic Chemistry in Environment Engineering

The case is described in Marques *et al.* (2005). With this case we intended to elucidate the role of 'conceptual field network' and the 'network of formative situations' tools to plan the curriculum in basic chemistry in environment engineering.

Usually, teaching chemistry, or other scientific area, is based on a disciplinary logic approach, which follows a sequence of topics of chemistry. In the FSF, the theoretical models, concepts and their relationships were chosen according to themes of interest to students (in this case, ecology based STS contexts) and to competences, knowledge and attitudes to develop in each curriculum unit. So, the teacher did not follow a simple sequence of topics of chemistry. Therefore, it is necessary to explicit the 'conceptual field network' for the course.

First the construction of a 'conceptual field network' allows to support and to settle a discussion among teachers of a course in order to identify and to interrelate the key-concepts, the contexts of use of chemistry concepts and the theoretical models. In fact, the 'conceptual field network' allows centring the discussion on:

(i) the main conceptual aspects;
(ii) the differentiation of the epistemological status of each conceptual entity, namely the distinction between concepts and theoretical models;
(iii) the social context of use of science concepts.

In this sense 'conceptual field network' is the first step to prepare a curriculum: settle the main curriculum options. It is also the base for future decisions on curriculum management.

As an example a 'conceptual field network' from this study in Figure 12.4 is shown.

Experience reveals that the use of this tool provides an expedite way to support a serious discussion for some time before settling it. We used the same tool with good results in physics teaching, in both university and secondary levels. Our experience shows that this tool allows for people with different academic and professional backgrounds to discuss and participate in educational tasks and research.

How to construct the 'conceptual field network' tool?

A first step can be the choice of large contexts of use of the concepts. In this research, the main large context of use of chemistry concepts is environmental problems and the correspondent science, technology and society (STS) relationships. The more specific contexts of use of chemistry concepts are (see Figure 12.4): A-Aquatic systems; B-Water environmental disasters; C-Pollution effects; D-Sustainable development. Each context of use of chemistry concepts is made operational by choosing specific situations.

The second step it is the identification of the main concepts of the course's syllabus.

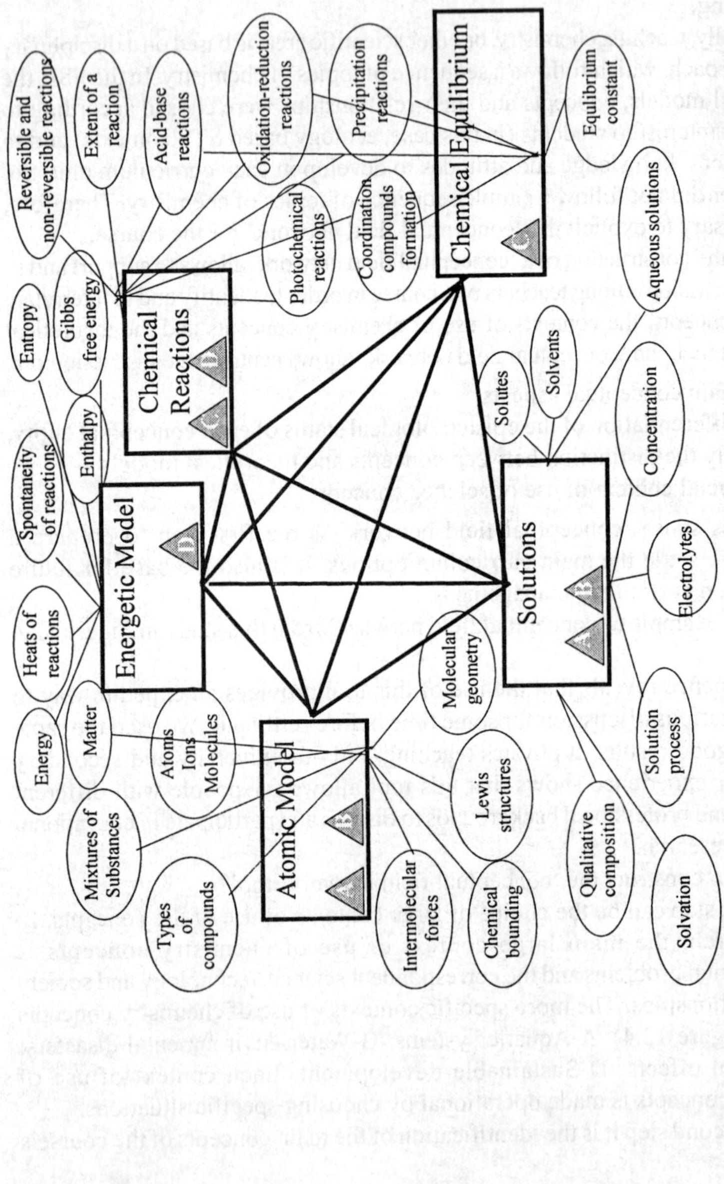

Figure 12.4: Example of a Conceptual Field Network in Chemistry. Legend: Triangles Indicate Social Contexts of Use of Concepts (A-Aquatic Systems; B-Water Environmental Disasters; C-Pollution Effects; D-Sustainable Development); Squares Represent Theoretical Models; and Ovals are Used for Key-Concepts

The third, and last step is a conceptual, Science/technological/social (STS) interrelations and epistemological discussion in order to identify and to interrelate the contexts of use of chemistry concepts, the key-concepts and the theoretical models. In this way the 'conceptual field network' supports and settles the discussion. For example, in this study the atomic model became explicit as a necessary theoretical model to support conveniently the processes and concepts related with solutions. Another example is that, in this study, the 'conceptual field network' tool clarified that some contexts of use of chemistry concepts are more adequate to approach certain conceptual aspects than others. So, the use of the same concepts in several contexts allows an extension and generalization of the student's conceptual field.

During the curriculum design the 'conceptual field network' supports the teacher's decisions. Another tool that helps in the development of the curriculum design is the 'network of formative situations', presented in the next subsection.

'Network of Formative Situations' Tool.

The elaboration of a network of formative situations has a correspondence with the contexts of use incorporated in the conceptual field network. In Figure 12.5 the main characteristics are presented [contexts of use (C), theoretical models (M), key-concepts (KC), type of tasks (T)] of each formative situation and the relationships among them. The projects to develop by students were chosen by each group of students and carried out in several phases (plan, progress report, project completion, public presentation and individual critical report) throughout the semester, in and out of the classroom.

The 'network of formative situations' is a tool to help the teacher in articulating all formative situations during the curriculum design and management. The designed 'network of formative situations' may be modified during the specification of each formative situation. Also, the 'network of formative situations' guides the teacher during the curriculum implementation and the curriculum development, because it may take different forms in the classroom, according to specific mediation and actual students' learning progress and interests. In particular, it is a guarantee that in each formative situation the students may work with concepts and models used previously, but in a new context.

The relationship among formative situations is based on the connections among contexts of use of concepts, taking into account the key-concepts and theoretical models. In spite of there being an organization, there is no unique sequence. In particular, the development of project work in the project FS, as it really occurs, may pose different curriculum choices in different editions of the course. Another characteristic of the 'network of formative situations' is determining the type of competences to develop during the course, by choosing the types of tasks to propose to students in each formative situation. In this research, one special cluster of competences are experimental competences, related to a part of the tasks proposed (see Figure 12.5).

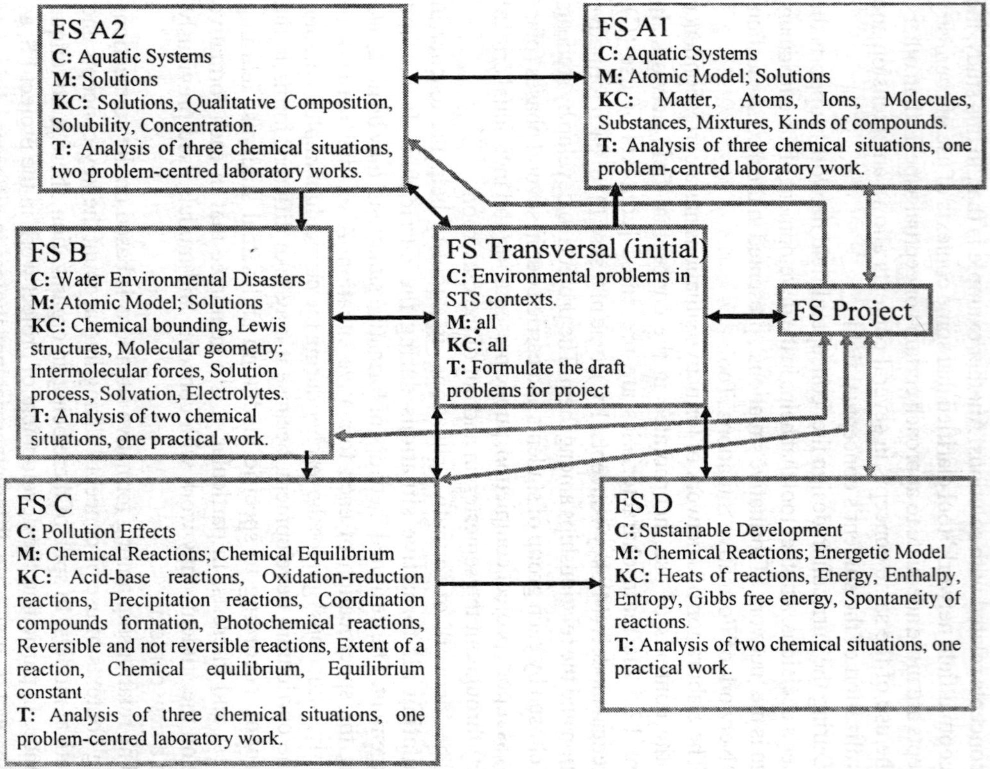

Figure 12.5: Example of a Network of Formative Situations (C Stands for Social Context of Use of Concepts, M for Theoretical Models, KC for Key-Concepts and T for Types of Tasks)

As a guide in the curriculum implementation and management, the 'Network of formative situations' helps the teacher to have a global view of the curriculum. In this way it is a permanent scaffold to revisit theoretical models and some key-concepts in different contexts of use. It also helps the teacher in deciding the best path in the network of formative situations according to the learning progress and interest of students.

Case 2—Basic Physics in University

The case is described in Cravino (2004) and in Cravino and Lopes (2003). With this case we intended to elucidate the role of 'FS specification table' tool to plan the curriculum in an introductory Physics university course based on FSF.

As part of the curriculum design the teacher produced documents detailing the design and the specification of each formative situation. As an example of specification of a formative situation is presented table 12.5 with a 'FS specification table' for the formative situation called 'The Sun and electromagnetic radiation'. This specification table follow the format described in Table 12.4. The main aspects concerning the elaboration and use of 'FS specification table' as a tool is given as follows:

The 'FS specification table', as a tool, makes operational the crucial components of the curriculum and their articulation according to the FSF. In this sense it is a permanent reference and support in the curriculum management for the main teacher's decisions. It should be used in articulation with the previously described tools (the network of FS and the conceptual field network).

The 'FS specification table' explicitly presents the main components of the curriculum: the student world, the competences, knowledge and attitudes to develop, the specific conceptual field, physical situations, tasks, resources and foreseen mediation. It indicates the main articulation among physical situation, tasks, resources and mediation (see table 12.5, in the respective columns, the crossed references indicated by the letters T, R and M). Also, the 'FS specification table' gives a good idea of the temporal duration of the physical situations to approach and of the tasks to be executed.

During the FS specification table, the hardest work is the conception of tasks, foreseeing the mediation and articulating both. This instrument is important as a tool to prepare the curriculum, but is not a tool to follow in a rigid way during the curriculum implementation. Without some flexibility the curriculum implementation does not become a formative situation. In fact, the actual mediation and the specific circumstances of teaching and learning may give the teacher indications to modify certain aspects of the formative situation or even the articulation among formative situations.

Table 12.5: Example of a Formative Situation—The Sun and Electromagnetic Radiation

Models:

Layered model of the Sun; Model of nuclear fusion in the Sun; Models of electromagnetic (EM) radiation and photon beams.

Concepts:

Energy; energy transfer by conduction, convection, radiation; nuclear fusion; heat; temperature; thermal equilibrium; energy sources and receptors; system; energy conservation; particle (atom, proton, neutron, neutrino and photon); electromagnetic (EM) radiation; frequency, wavelength and wave propagation speed.

Relationships:

Rate of energy transfer by radiation: $R = \sigma\ e\ A\ T^4$; relationship between mass and energy ($E = m\ c^2$); energy of an EM wave; relationship between energy and frequency of a wave ($E = h\ f$); propagation speed of a EM wave; relationship among frequency, wavelength and propagation speed of a wave; equation for the calculation of power ($P = E/\Delta t$); $I = P/A$.

Knowledge available from students:

Concepts of particle, mass, heat, temperature, modes of energy transfer. Atomic model of matter and subatomic particles (electron, proton and neutron). Electric charge of electrons and protons. Notions about the importance of the Sun for life on earth and as a source of most energy forms used in the planet.

Physical Situation	*Problem*	*Tasks*	*Resources*	*Teacher Mediation*
PS1: Data and schemes about the structure in layers of the Sun. [T1, T2]. PS2: Scheme of the EM spec-trum and data about the various types of EM radia-tion [T3 to T7].	Starting from the effects of solar activity on earth and its human inhabitants, under-stand how the energy is produced in the sun, how it propagates in its interior and how it is emitted to space.	T1: Analyse the different layers of the Sun and the energy transfer proce-sses that occur in these layers: radiation, convec-tion and conduction. [M1, M4; R1, R2, R3, R9] T2: Analyse the chain of reactions (p-p chain) and perform calculations about the amount of energy produced in the Sun by nuclear fusion. [M1, M2, M3, M4; R1, R4, R9] A3: Characterise the different types of EM radiation, their uses and discuss the effects on human beings. [M1, M6; R6, R9]	R1: Images of the Sun collected in the Internet and obtained form various observa-tion instruments. R2: Data about the Sun. R3: Scheme of the struc-ture of the Sun's layers. R4: Schematic represen-tation of the reactions involved in the nuclear fusion in the Sun. R5: Scheme of the Sun with a digest of the processes that occur in it. R6: Scheme of the EM spectrum.	M1: Presentation of information. M2: Make sure that each task is adequately appropriated and understood by the students. M3: Help students overcome their difficulties, for exam-ple, in solving problems involving numerical calcula-tions or in data interpre-tation. M4: Evaluate the knowledge that students already have about the themes to be studied: the Sun, energy, heat and temperature, the concept of atom and its representa-tions. Review these con-cepts and extend the know-ledge about them.

(Contd.)

Physical Situation	*Problem*	*Tasks*	*Resources*	*Teacher Mediation*
		T4: Analyse the process of production, propagation and reception of a radio wave in terms of the associated electric and magnetic fields. [M1, M6; R7, R9] T5: Discuss and characterize EM radiation as a wave or as a beam of particles (photons). [M1, M6; R7, R9] T6: Study the properties of infrared (IR) radiation with a TV and its IR remote control. [M2; R8] T7: Discuss experimental results based on registrations and obser-vations performed by the students. [M3, M6; R9]	R7: Schematic repre-sentation of an EM wave. R8: Electronic equipment (TV or other device equipped with an IR remote control). R9: Overhead projector, blackboard and writing mate-rial.	M5: Make synthesis and schemes of the fundamental information bout the Sun's structure and the production of energy by nuclear fusion in its nucleus [R3 e R4]. Summarize and syste-matize the fundamental information about the particles and EM radiation emitted by the Sun [R5]. M6: Evaluate the ideas that students already have on EM radiation, reformulate, extend and deepen these ideas by helping students analyse some of the less correct aspects under the light of adequate infor-mation and through criti-cal analysis. M7: Give clues for the development of some of the ongoing students' pro-jects, especially those related to EM radiation, and encou-rage the sharing of informa-tion that students may have already gathered in their research. M8. Summarize and systema-tize basic information about the characterization of the various types of EM radiation and the corres-pondent emission by the Sun [R5].

Knowledge to develop:

Understand the importance of the sun for the life on earth and for human activity. Deepen the concept of energy and knowledge of its transfer, transformation and conservation. Understand the relationship between mass and energy. Develop the concept of EM radiation, characterize the various types of EM radiation, their risks and uses. Develop the understanding of how models of the physical reality are built.

Skills and competences to develop:

Distinguish physical reality from its representations. Use models of the physical reality. Perform calculations with numerical data and critically assess the results, using estimates. Perform exploratory experiments and develop competences in the analysis of the correspondent results. Analyse data obtained from scientific instruments and understand how to interpret them. Understand the current limits of physical knowledge on various themes and use the available information to assess the plausibility of one or more possible explanations.

Case 3—'Mediation in Action' in Physics Course in Engineering

The case is described in Viegas, Lopes, and Cravino (2007). With this case we intend to show how the mediation can be made and how the teacher may change from one type to another.

This work, part of a curriculum re-design, based on research in science education, was developed in an introductory physics course in an engineering school of Northern Portugal. The goal was to improve students' competences using physics subject matter and its connections with daily life. The rational is that students will be better prepared to embrace their future profession—engineering—as they are able to recognize, identify, mobilize and interrelate their knowledge with the real problems they are bound to encounter.

Traditionally, in physics teaching, an appreciable time is spent solving exercises on the blackboard, an activity where students do little work. An alternative approach (Viegas, Lopes, & Cravino, 2007) is presented, based on science education research in general, and the FSF in particular, to actively involve students and specially oriented to develop certain important competences in engineering students.

Here the authors were particularly concerned if this competence development approach would affect the final marks and if it would benefit the majority of the students. They were also interested in how students' would percept this new approach and if they would feel comfortable with it.

First, a conceptual network was developed, taking some contexts of use particularly interesting for engineering students (how an elevator works, car accidents and constructions). This network incorporates the interrelations between these contexts and the theoretical models and concepts present in the course contents (basic mechanics).

Mediation in action

Basically, the authors used individual, collaborative and cooperative work in the tasks done by the students meant to promote the development of competencies. The development of autonomous work and student's responsibility was, in this pursuing, also promoted.

Students were invited to develop a project 'How an elevator works', and in each lesson they developed a different task towards their final presentation. This project provided an integrative vision of the course and stimulated the collaborative work in class and after class. It would also imply some cooperative work, because students ought to be organized in order to deliver the final version of the project. No synchronism was imposed on the work of the different groups (proposed problems or project tasks); in fact each group worked at their own pace, achieving their own goals, developing autonomy and responsibility. Respect for their colleagues and their ideas were promoted, in order to include everyone in the daily work.

The success of each individual student's learning achievements was assessed, on a weekly basis, with each student performing an e-learning task.

The teacher's role was to mediate these individual and group achievements, namely in discussing certain issues at crucial moments, encouraging students' performance and giving them permanent feedback on their developments, including in the homework tasks (individual weekly feedback). This took place mainly in the theoretical-practical (recitation) classes. When significant difficulties emerged, a personal consultation would be scheduled with the student for an out of class office meeting with the teacher.

In the theoretical classes (lectures), the teacher used active learning engagement techniques, mainly cooperative work and peer instruction (Mazur, 1997), already tested in previous school years. The major concern was to establish class rhythm, in order to maximize students' attention. The teacher also introduced short self-tests, taken in class and immediate corrected in class by each student's neighbor, while the discussion of the solutions was being made. The students would not only verify the correctness of their answers, but also foresee different interpretations and be able to correct them. They could also gain sensibility to common mistakes they usually make, but to which they do not pay enough attention. Students were not graded based in the marks from these self-tests, only by the corrections they made and mostly by their participation in the process.

The e-learning challenges provided students to work together in complex problems, in which everyone could see each others answers, and could complete them or disagree with them. The teacher would supervise their interactivity and give clues whenever that was felt necessary.

The major modification in the laboratory classes was the almost total abolition of guided experiments. We opted for simpler laboratory devices to demonstrate simple concepts that were being developed in the theoretical classes. The final part of the semester was spent developing a laboratory project, intended to solve a specific problem, in which students, with laboratory material or other materials, should idealized, develop and implement an experiment that could provide the answer to that problem (Neumann & Welzel, 2007).

In this context, six mediation patterns were found:

Pattern A (about presentation of new information). This pattern is composed by the following phases:

(i) Teacher proposes a conceptual question to identify what and how students know about the topic;
(ii) students think about and answer;
(iii) each student discusses with a peer;
(iv) Teacher discusses with class;
(v) Teacher presents information taken into account the previous phases;

(vi) teacher presents a new conceptual question to know the students conceptual level of understanding.

Pattern B (about using knowledge by students). This pattern is composed by the following characteristics:

(i) Teacher proposes a task to students;
(ii) students are organized in small groups and work autonomously in the task to find a solution (each team is not necessarily synchronized with the other teams);
(iii) Teacher support (identifying mistakes and alternative ways of developing ideas, identifying learning outcomes in order to fulfil any evidenced gap, and manage the curriculum, providing help, guidance and explanations in crucial moments, resist the impulse of explaining everything, every time a student has a doubt, but give clues instead, in order to let it be the students to reach out the solution);
(iv) Teacher supervises team discussions, stimulating everyone to participate, awarding grading points mostly for participation and not for their mistakes;
(v) Students give brief presentation of their work to teacher (not to all class) and discussion of the pertinence of the solution they found,
(vi) The teacher visits each group several times in each class.

Pattern C (about Project work). This pattern is similar to pattern B. The differences are:

(i) The project are divided in several tasks and each one of them were developed in the beginning of the class,
(ii) The characteristic (v) of pattern B referred above only occurs in the middle and in the final of project work and the presentation is made to the entire class.

Pattern D (beyond class). This pattern is composed by the following characteristics:

(i) Weekly feedback on the e-learning homework,
(ii) the feedback is characterized by clues for completing it, alert students for major mistakes and stimulate further work;
(iii) teacher participation in the open discussions in the e-learning;
(iv) teacher suggests to some individual students office hours consultation;
(v) maintain a regular attendance in office hours.

Pattern E (about lab-work). This pattern is composed by the following characteristics:

(i) There is synchronism between the theme (chapter) being discussed in other classes and laboratory problems;

(ii) There are autonomous collaborative teamwork in solving the laboratory problems;
(iii) There are collaborative discussion with the teacher supervision;
(iv) Teacher gives weekly feedback on students reports and suggested to each student office hours consultation;
(v) There is a final project work in laboratory (conceive and implement an experiment and obtain the experimental results) with the teacher supervision.

Pattern F (about assessment). This pattern is composed by the following characteristics:

(i) Teacher provides for regularly self-assessment tests;
(ii) Students' work (homework and in classroom) is corrected but mistakes are not graded;
(iii) Provide students feedback on their learning outcomes;
(iv) Diversify assessment tools and give credit for the students participation;
(v) Evaluate how students prepare themselves to the tasks they know they have to face.

As we can see the mediation conducted in this course was mainly dialogic, with some mediation of the types interactive, problem-centred and epistemic.

The results obtained in this case clearly support that, in classes where the learning environment was based on the described mediation:

(i) The academic results were equal or even better than in classes taught in a more traditional approach;
(ii) High level competences were better developed in a larger number of students than in classes taught in a more traditional approach.

Relevance of the FSF's Use in Engineering Education and Conclusions

A variety of good teaching strategies, and research studies that support them, can be found in engineering educational research. Some of the cases encountered can be incorporated into the FSF previously explained. It is believe that this framework (FSF) could easily help in reaching the gains reported on some of them. Science or engineering teachers may try to implement some aspects of this FSF and incorporate the developments to improve their performance over the years, by beginning to structure their courses based on the FSF presented in section 2 and specified in sections 3 and 4, in particular using the tools referred there.

In real life a professional engineer is evaluated by his performance and competence, and is asked to act in different and complex situations that involve analyzing, interpreting and anticipating results, and he should be prepared to do so in college (Perrenoud, 2003). This will only be accomplished if knowledge becomes operative (Astolfi, 1992). For this to happen students must work with knowledge so that it becomes meaningful. Therefore, learning should be directed to the development of competencies that will improve professional performance. In order to do so, teachers must carefully plan their classes around students' knowledge and develop activities that provide opportunities for the growth of both their knowledge but also their competence and their skills useful for their future daily work in other contexts.

Engineering courses all over the world prepare themselves for evaluations of Accreditation Boards Comities (Felder & Brent, 2003; McCowan & Knapper, 2002, Terry, *et al.,* 2002), such as ABET accreditation, in which one of the main concerns is the quality of the graduates in terms of competences acquired, as one can see in one example present in Felder and Brent (2003) when describing these criteria:

- Ability to apply knowledge of mathematics, science and engineering
- Ability to design and conduct experiments, as well as analyze and interpret data
- Ability to design a system, component, or process to meet desired needs
- Ability to function on multidisciplinary teams
- Ability to identify, formulate, and solve engineering problems
- Understanding of professional ethical responsibilities
- Ability to communicate effectively
- Broad education necessary to understand the impact of engineering solutions in a global and societal context
- Recognition of the need for and an ability to engage in lifelong learning
- Knowledge of contemporary issues
- Ability to use the techniques, skills, and modern engineering tools necessary for engineering practice

One knows that some institutions face difficulties in order to obtain such evaluation from their graduates and fresh professionals. By organizing courses and degree cycle/programmes following the FSF, not only these competences, skills and attitudes could be better developed as easily evaluated, and the outcomes specified in Felder and Brent's work (2003) could have (almost) immediate response.

In spite of there being many areas of engineering, these context bases of the FSF should be adequate to each one of them, providing more awareness of their future professional, being an extra effort to show and motivate the students to their area of expertise. Designing the curricula around those contexts of use, this framework provides a unique way of doing engineering, even at the introductory courses. The development of those skills and competences will allow students to accomplish more demanding goals in subsequent courses, since they have been practicing those ideas from the beginning.

Lifelong learning is another subject that worries the engineering professionals (Briedis, 2002). Not only the FS framework could easily be adapted to create post-graduate courses in which they can develop expertise, as the students who develop in this learning environment could be more motivated to learn throughout their lives.

The relationship between college and industry, so dear to engineers (Brisk, 1997) may be accomplished if, for instance, some of the contextual fields are worked out in formative situations as projects, in which professional competences will be better developed. Senior students would gain experience and developed the necessary conceptual fields required, if the discipline organized in this way.

A difficult point will be the moment of change, since these curricular developments based in FSF represent a cut off with the traditional teaching, mainly in introductory courses in which the extensive syllabus frequently tends to create more expositive classes. The contexts of use must be thought to reach the conceptual fields of the students in order to develop the intended contents. Problems and situations must be carefully planed as well, so they can motivate and stimulate students in completing it (nor too difficult nor too easy) and feel the gain by doing it.

And, as already stated, the success of this implementation in classroom is very much dependent on the quality of the mediation provided by the teacher. As there are some professionals who have difficulties generating empathy with students, this should be considered before the huge effort of modifying the entire course.

We believe this tool can indeed be powerful in improving engineering students competences, not only in the first years, in introductory courses, but also throughout the entire course in more advanced courses:

(i) by always considering what the students' already know (from previous courses or from in their real life), by facilitating an integration of knowledge;

(ii) by providing students with real tasks in or out of classrooms, we are preparing them for their real profession of engineering, by training them to solve real problems;

(iii) in developing diversified mediation, teachers will not only, as we have seen, be helping students preparing for their major but also be helping them with the convenient social competences every engineer must possess;

iv) by constructing the knowledge, the students will be preparing themselves, not only for their final examinations, but to apply it throughout their professional careers;

(v) by inducing students in autonomous work, teacher will be preparing students to become competent engineers and not simply straight students. These items are the base of the FSF we described and that must be articulated with one another in the curriculum, or in a broader perspective in the entire degree cycle/programme.

Some relevant aspects of FSF are as follows:

First, All the three cases presented here as examples reported the improvement of students' competences. We could report others. The success of teaching based on FSF is a salient point. The teaching quality was evaluated through questionnaires based on an international standard (the CEQ, Ramsden, 1991) and through validated tests of competences and interviews, namely comparing normalized gains (Hake, 1998).

Second, The curriculum management is very dependent on the teacher's experience, attitudes and knowledge, which have an impact in teaching organization and, above all, in teacher mediation. For example, the study presented by the research team in another chapter of this handbook elucidates the importance of the teacher to implement an intended mediation type. As the FSF predicts, the mediation type change the actual type of teaching in classroom, reducing, eventually, the educational potential of tasks.

Third, FSF as a theoretical framework may be used to:

(i) plan and/or manage the curriculum of courses from different levels of engineering education (in any cycle of Bologna paradigm);
(ii) prepare and/or support the engineering professional development;
(iii) evaluate teaching quality or courses quality, even if they are grounded in other theoretical frameworks.

Fourth, The FSF links theory and practice in an articulated way and is supported in several research studies. The FSF emphasizes what is central to teaching according to the intended learning. Among the multiplicity of researches (in terms of goals, perspectives and concerns) the FSF allows the teacher to concentrate on key-aspects linked among them as figure 12.1 suggest: tasks, mediation, student learning activity, student world, learning outcomes, assessment, competences to develop, conceptual field network, resources and STS context.

Fifth, The FS framework is centred on the student, but takes into account that any education system has certain goals in terms of learning outcomes namely knowledge, competencies and attitudes.

Sixth, Still, the FSF is not a recycling of the old didactical triangle student-knowledge-teacher. In fact, student and knowledge are the two poles of the epistemological structure of knowledge, and the teacher is included in that relationship to influence it in a subtle but effective way.

Seventh, The FS framework is a work in progress, but there are already potential uses for research and for practice. Three practical tools were already developed:

(i) the conceptual field network;
(ii) the network of formative situations;
(iii) and the FS specification table.

We also developed 'mediation in action' as a clarification of how to make mediation operational. On the other hand, other researchers have asked for using FSF in other educational contexts, which is a clear indication of its potential for research.

Notes

1. Evans (2002) defines pragmatisation of research as '(...) *a planned process involving analysis, presentation and dissemination that is directed at transforming research findings into viable, specific ideas and recommendations for policy and practice*' (p. 202).
2. According to Vergnaud (1987, 1991) a conceptual field is a set of interrelated concepts (emphasis on the relational nature of scientific concepts), with a certain dimension and structure, which allows subjects to operate, approach, think and act in a more or less wide class of situations and/or problems.

13

Discovery Based Classroom Projects with Auvs and Rovs

Rustam Stolkin, Richard Sheryll and *Liesl Hotaling*

This paper-chapter describes ongoing efforts to develop a set of educational courses, which teach fundamental engineering principles through the design, construction, programming and testing of underwater robotic vehicles using simple materials. These courses emphasize discovery based learning, creative problem solving, collaborative team work and provide hands on exposure to a real iterative engineering design process.

Why Build Underwater Robots

When students design, build and programme underwater robotic vehicles, they are learning engineering fundamentals which span virtually every engineering discipline. Additionally, students are motivated by an exciting and stimulating design scenario.

There are now a multitude of educational kits, courses, 'camps on disk' and competitions designed to engage young people in science through robotics projects. Predominantly, these projects focus on small, wheeled vehicles moving around on a flat surface. Such projects rapidly reduce to simple exercises in computer programming since the physical construction and applied engineering is often trivial. The authors are regular judges at LEGO robotics competitions. In these competitions. It is often observed the students simply sticking wheels directly onto motors, motors directly onto a controller brick, then programming (often trivially) the vehicle to crash into various objects in order to score points. These activities often do not teach fundamental engineering or scientific principles to the extent which is claimed. This is particularly apparent when students are interviewed about their robot designs and what they have learned while building them.

In contrast, the underwater environment presents unique design challenges and opportunities. The motion of an underwater vehicle, through a three dimensional space with six degrees of freedom, is more complex. Additional engineering issues include gearing, propulsion, drag, buoyancy and stability, electrical circuits and debugging, and how to waterproof electrical components.

Participants must engage in substantial iterative mechanical design, trying out ideas, testing, identifying problems and making modifications, if their robot is to succeed. Additionally, the challenge of creating a robot which can be sent to explore a difficult and inaccessible environment is also far more real and motivating to many students than programming a simple wheeled vehicle to carry out a few simple motions on a floor or table top.

Using pre and post testing we have shown that students tend to substantially increase their understanding of fundamental topics such as buoyancy and gearing when participating in these projects. Students frequently state that they like the opportunities that these projects afford them for real invention and problem solving.

Why Use LEGO?

Our students work with a combination of LEGO and additional simple materials. LEGO is particularly suited to discovery based learning due to its ease and speed of assembly[1, 2]. This speed reduces the time between conception of an idea and its implementation, enabling students to discover through trial and error, rapidly test a range of alternative designs and evolve their designs iteratively by observing the relationship between structure and function. In contrast, when students use conventional materials, the construction process is lengthy and frustrating. Time constraints prevent students from evolving their designs through multiple iterations of testing and modification. Often there is no time allotted for the students to fail, analyse the failure and then modify their design. In contrast 'We know that students will learn most deeply and profoundly when they…have an opportunity to try, fail and receive feedback on their work'[3].

Retention and Recruitment

Enrollment rates in undergraduate engineering programmes are in decline[4] and several studies have found a dropout rate for undergraduate science and engineering students of greater than fifty percent[5]. Student feedback suggests that there is a shortage of genuine opportunities for creative invention within engineering courses and that this can frustrate many talented and motivated students, discouraging the completion of engineering training or the pursuance an engineering career.

The teaching methods described in this paper are intended to provide students with more opportunities to invent and create. Additionally, they enable students to see how the material they learn in science classes is a meaningful set of tools which can solve real problems.

Incorporating these hands on, discovery learning project early in the freshman year is part of an ongoing effort to improve student retention rates. Studies at other institutions[6] have indicated that hands on mobile robot projects using simple materials such as LEGO with undergraduate students, may significantly improve retention rates. We have also incorporated the project into pre-college courses for high school students to help stimulate interest in engineering careers and boost engineering enrollment rates. Over summer 2007, we trained 72 teachers from 36 middle and high schools across New Jersey, who will all implement these projects in their classrooms over the coming academic year. We are hoping to evaluate the effectiveness of such projects for stimulating interest in engineering careers among young students.

Cost

The wire-guided ROV project described below is relatively inexpensive to implement. Start-up costs for materials to enable a team of 4-6 students to complete the project are approximately $200. These materials can then be re-used by successive student teams.

Ongoing work includes extending the projects to include building AUVs with computer control and sensory feedback. This involves additional expense; however we use the LEGO NXT programmable controllers and associated sensors. Sufficient computer control components for the 4-6 student team costs approximately a further $250, however these can also be used for many other classroom and after school activities and can all be reused indefinitely.

Discovery Based Learning

The LEGO underwater robotics classes described are based on 'discovery learning' principles. Discovery learning[7], is a cognitive instructional model in which students are encouraged to learn through active involvement with concepts and principles, and teachers encourage students to have experiences and conduct experiments that permit them to discover principles for themselves.

Although discovery learning is frequently employed in an early childhood development setting, the instructional model offers several advantages to a high school or undergraduate setting. It arouses students' curiosity, motivating them to continue to work until they find answers[8]. Students also learn independent problem solving and critical thinking skills because they must independently analyze and manipulate information.

Students often benefit more from being able to engage in active learning by 'seeing' and 'doing' things than from passive learning by listening to lectures. Tackling material from several perspectives and persevering with unresolved problems improves students' core intellectual skills—they learn how to learn independently. Cognitive development is not the accumulation of isolated pieces of information; rather, it is the construction by students of a framework for understanding their environment. Teachers should serve as role models and facilitators by solving problems with students, explaining the problem solving process and talking about the relationships between actions and outcomes. Observing students during their activities, examining their solutions and listening carefully to their questions can reveal much about their interests, modes of thought and understanding or misunderstanding of concepts[9].

Discovery based learning is a particularly effective means of teaching the iterative approach to engineering design. In contrast, surprisingly little of conventional engineering curricula are devoted to this design process, with the learning experience of engineering students often bearing little resemblance to the activities of professional engineers in industry.

Interesting and Advantageous Aspects of These Projects

These classroom projects have a number of distinctive and useful characteristics:

- These projects are the product of long term collaboration between roboticists, ocean engineers and education experts. They are intellectually and technically substantial and founded on a solid pedagogical footing.
- Projects are short and manageable. They can typically be completed comfortably 5 two hour sessions. This is partly a function of the simple materials, but also of the innovative style in which the courses are taught.
- Projects emphasize discovery learning and inventiveness. Students are not issued with instructions or kits, but given generic materials and set a series of engineering design challenges. Thus every student's solution is very distinct, and unique designs are observed every time the course is run.
- Contrary to common pedagogical assumptions, these projects have been shown to be equally effective when run with undergraduate engineering students and with 12 year old middle school students. The project is helping show that both these groups share many of the same fundamental scientific misconceptions and knowledge gaps and can both benefit from these projects for similar reasons.
- By observing students during these projects, we have revealed a number of severe, fundamental scientific and engineering misconceptions and knowledge gaps. Frequently these were previously assumed by professors and teachers to be well understood subjects amongst their students (and themselves).
- Because the underwater robotics problems are so multi-disciplinary, these

projects themselves form excellent motivating scenarios in which to re-teach and clear up the knowledge gaps observed above.

Remotely Operated Vehicles (ROVs)

Materials

Figure 13.1: Electrical control system built by students, with LEGO compatible end connectors on cables.

Students are provided with a selection of LEGO including several motors, battery boxes and leads, gearing, structural and mechanical components. Also provided, are a selection of plastic propellers (obtainable from hobby stores) mounted on LEGO axles. Additional materials include Styrofoam, modeling clay, a selection of weights (nuts and bolts work well), rubber bands, string and duct tape. A 30 inch deep inflatable pool is used to test the designs, but they can also be tested in smaller pools or large plastic storage tubs. Wiffle balls are specified as the objects to be retrieved and manipulated by the ROVs.

Students are issued a variety of electrical components, with which to create a control system and have the opportunity to learn simple circuit design and debugging. Long control cables are pre-assembled for the students. These cables contain eight wires (enough to control four independent motors) and are terminated with four LEGO compatible end connectors. To build a control system, several three position switches were supplied. Each switch can control a single motor with three possible states, Forward/Off/Reverse. Pre-drilled aluminum boxes were supplied for mounting the switches (figure 13.1).

Procedure

Students are divided into 4-6 person teams. The project typically requires four to five sessions with instructors. In each session the student teams are given progressively more complex, intermediary design challenges. Intermediary challenges initially involve developing simple motorized surface vessels, progressing to fully controllable, submersible vehicles and motorized grabbers. As a final challenge, each team has to use their ROV to retrieve and manipulate objects on the bottom of a pool of water. Note that successive educational stages of the project usually correspond with each added degree of freedom of the robot.

The intermediary design challenges include:

1. Design a surface vessel with a single motor and various propeller options, optimizing gearing ratios to maximize speed in a single direction.
2. Design a surface vessel with steering, using two independently controlled motors. The challenge involved negotiating a figure eight course, around two buoys, in the least amount of time.
3. Develop an electrical control system for four independent motors.
4. Add a third motor to the vehicle, enabling vertical motion in the water column.
5. Design a motorized mechanical manipulator which can grasp specified objects (Figure 13.2)
6. Combine the products of stages 3, 4 and 5 to produce a vehicle which can retrieve the greatest number of objects from the bottom of the pool within a five minute period. Retrieved objects must be deposited in bins at various depths in the water in order to score points. See figure 13.3 for example.

Many of these challenges have a variety of solutions. For example, challenge 2 can be solved using twin propellers, a single propeller plus rudder or a single propeller with variable direction.

In each laboratory session, instructors deliver short, interactive talks. These are limited to around 10 minutes each. On occasions where two talks were delivered in the same session, they are separated by periods of practical work. These short talks are designed to convey the underlying scientific and engineering principles which are necessary to complete each successive stage of the design challenge. Additionally, these talks are designed to show students how the theory that they are studying in mathematics and physics classes relates in tangible ways to the real, practical engineering problems which they are tackling. Talk subjects include:

1. Gearing mechanisms, torque, speed and thrust.
2. Degrees of freedom and number of motors—using two motors to steer.
3. Electrical circuits and control panel design.
4. Buoyancy, Archimedes principle and how to move up and down.
5. Grabbers, graspers and manipulators.

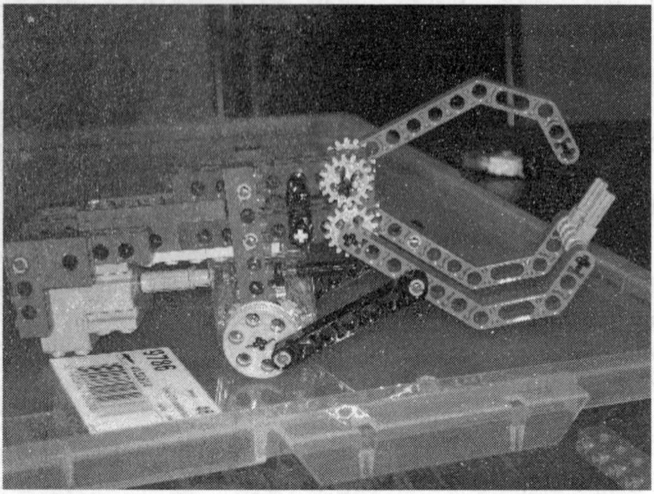

Figure 13.2: Reciprocating mechanical grabber designed and built by high school students.

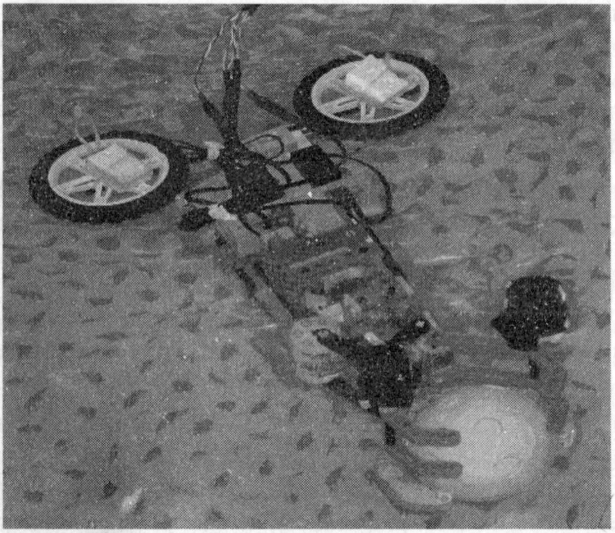

Figure 13.3: Final ROV (incorporating grabber from Figure 13.2) retrieving a ball from bottom of pool.

Results

This project has been run with 30 high school students over summer 2005, approximately 160 undergraduate engineering students from fall 2005 to spring 2007, and with around 70 middle and high school students over summer 2007.

All middle and high school teams, and the majority of undergraduate teams, succeeded in creating remotely operated underwater vehicles which successfully completed the final design challenge. Several important and encouraging features of the student's work were observed:

- Every student team arrived at original and creative solutions to the design problems. Each team's solutions were significantly distinct from those of other teams.
- The iterative engineering design process was highly apparent in each team's work, with solutions evolving through successive cycles of designing, testing and modification.
- Design solutions were achieved through invention, experimentation and discovery and not through didactic, prescribed instructions.
- The structure of the course and the nature of the design challenges successfully induced positive teamwork habits to be developed within each team.
- Students were highly engaged in the work, enjoyed what they were doing and wanted to do more.
- Students took pride in what they created and in their ability to solve significant engineering problems.

Autonomous Underwater vehicles (AUVs)

As a phase 2 project we have been piloting a set of more advanced underwater activities involving sensors and programmable controllers. Students now design, build and test Autonomous Underwater Vehicles (AUVs).

Materials

For programmable robot control, students used the LEGO NXT controller (figure 13.4), sealed inside a plastic box, LEGO robotics sensors, including touch sensors and light sensors (which can be waterproofed using simple materials such as Clingfilm), and the simple icon based NXT-G programming system. Note, programmes can be downloaded through the housing, using Bluetooth.

Experiments with Braitenberg Vehicles

The aim of this phase 2 course was to preserve the educational principles and Progressive, step by step format of our successful ROV course, while exploring ideas of programmable, autonomous robots which respond to sensor stimuli in interesting ways. Our aim is to use these principles to convey basic ideas of feedback systems that enable a robot to interact with a changing world, Figure 13.5.

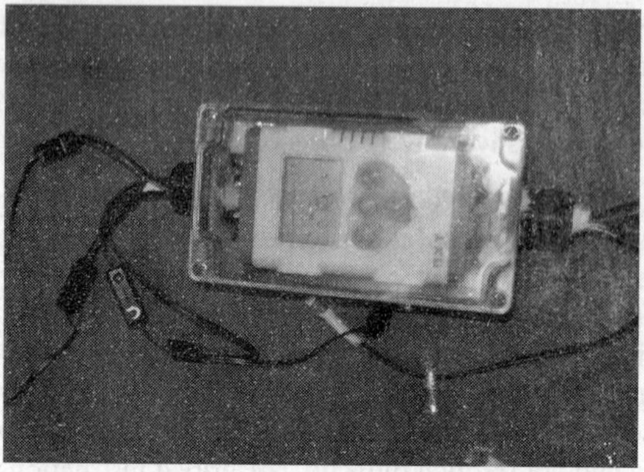

Figure 13.4: The LEGO NXT programmable brick set in a watertight housing. Rubber buttons, set in the housing, enable the controls on the NXT to be pressed. Alternatively a diver's 'pelican' box with snap shut lid can be used. A LEGO plate is bonded to the underside of the housing so that students can add their own LEGO structures and motors.

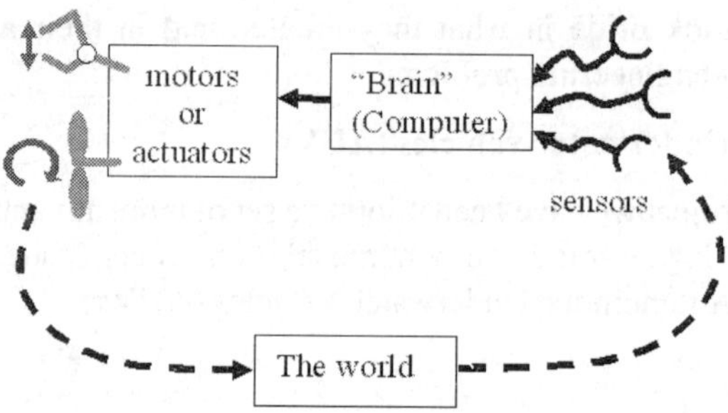

Figure 13.5: An intelligent robot learns about a changing world via its sensors and responds by using motors to intelligently exert changes on the world (or its own position in the world). This leads to an iterative feedback process. Unfortunately many educational robotics curricula do not emphasize this feedback process, but instead have students program a simple pre-determined sequence of actions.

Unfortunately, in our experience, relatively few simple educational robotics curricula emphasize this feedback process, which we believe encapsulates the fundamentals of real robotics. Instead, students are often tasked with programming a simple, pre-determined sequence of events, without creating a robot that genuinely interacts with a changing and unknown environment.

A natural choice of activities, which satisfy all these requirements, was to explore the behaviours of Braitenberg vehicles. 'Vehicles-Experiments in Synthetic Psychology' is a book by Valentino Braitenberg,[10] a famous cybernetician and neuro-anatomist. Braitenberg seeks to explain how the brain may have evolved, how complex behaviours can result from simple mechanisms, and particularly why one side of our brains controls the opposite side of our body. He does this through a series of elegant thought experiments with imaginary robot vehicles which consist of motors connected to sensors. Braitenberg's explanations are profound in their implications for roboticists and neuro-scientists, yet so simple and intuitive that they are immediately accessible to readers of all levels, without any prior knowledge or expertise.

In summer, 2007, as an introduction to ideas of artificial intelligence and robot programming, a pilot group of 33 high school students undertook a practical exploration of Braitenbergian concepts, while building and programming AUVs. Over five laboratory sessions, students gradually evolved their own designs for waterborne 'robotic amoebas' through a series of progressively more complex design challenges. As with our ROV course, students were set a series of progressively more difficult design challenges, gradually adding more degrees of freedom of motion and finally arriving at a fully functional autonomous underwater robot.

For challenge 1, students were given a single motor and a pair of touch sensors. They were told to build a simple vehicle which moves in a straight line across the surface of a pool. When the vehicle touches a wall of the pool, the robot's direction is reversed, figure 13.6. Because the vehicles tend to deviate from straight line motion, this results in a primitive amoeba-like behaviour with the robot repeatedly transecting the pool in a random fashion.

Figure 13.6: A simple 'robot amoeba' uses touch sensors and 'mechanical whiskers' to reverse direction when it encounters the boundary of the pool in which it lives.

Using the highly accessible NXT-G programming system, this behaviour can be generated with a very simple programme, figure 13.7.

For challenge 2, the students begin to implement Braitenbergian ideas. The behaviour of challenge 1 is now modified so that the robot's speed is

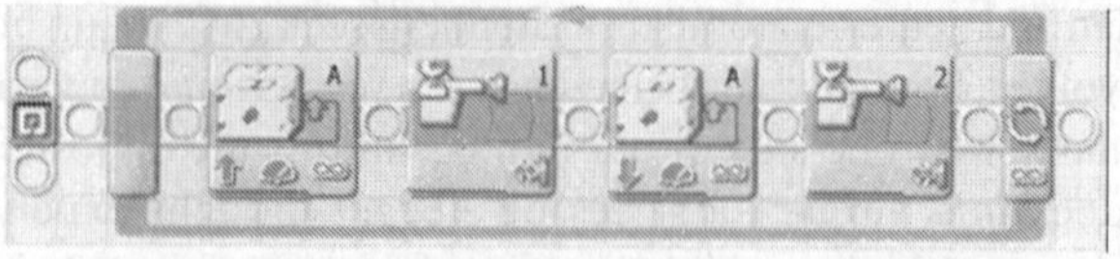

Figure 13.7: Icon based NXT-G programming language. 'Within a continuous loop, move forwards until a touch sensor is bumped, then move backwards until a touch sensor is bumped. Repeat indefinitely.'

proportional to light detected by a light sensor. This implements Braitenberg's most simple robot, which speeds up in bright areas and slows down in dark areas. Now the robots move randomly around the pool area, but dislike light and tend to settle in dark regions. This behaviour can be coded as in figure 13.8.

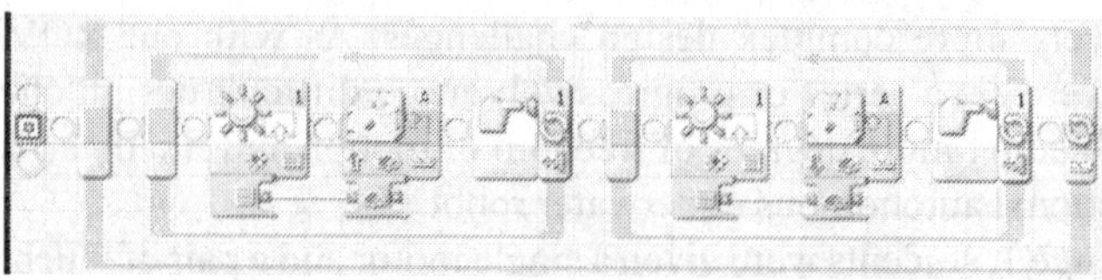

Figure 13.8: 'Move forwards while continually adjusting speed to be proportional to sensed light level. Once a touch sensor is bumped, repeat but in opposite direction.'

We can also explore negative (inhibitory) Braitenbergian relationships between sensed stimuli and motor speed, by setting motor speed equal to '100 minus sensed light level' (where sensed light level is also measured on a scale from 0-100), Figure 13.9.

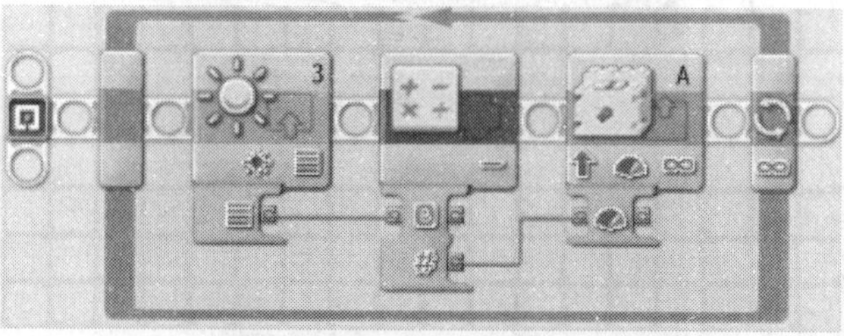

Figure 13.9: 'Continuously monitor light levels. Set motor speed proportional to 100 minus light level.' Hence in bright light, vehicle moves slowly, whereas in darkness the vehicle will move fast.

For challenge 3, students are given a second motor and a second light sensor. They now begin to explore more advanced Braitenbergian attraction and aversion behaviours. By connecting sensors on the robot's left and right sides with motors on either the same or opposite sides, robots can be generated which will either home in on a light source or be repulsed by the source. Braitenberg refers to these behaviours as 'aggression' and 'cowardice'. These behaviours can be easily coded in the NXT-G language by using two parallel threads, one for each sensor/motor pair, figure 13.10.

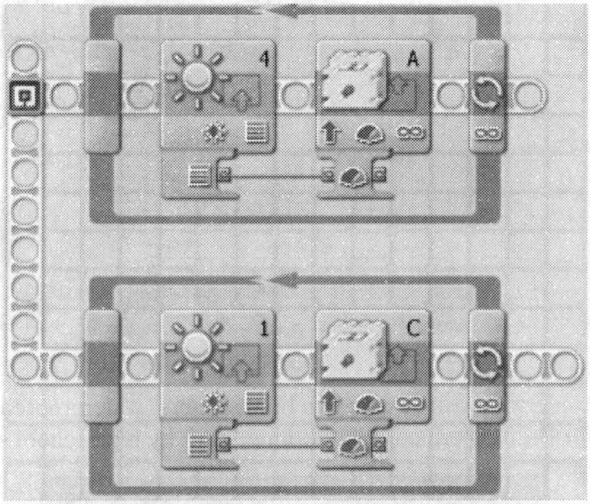

Figure 13.10: 2D Braitenberg attraction and aversion behavior with the NXT-G language. Depending on which side of the vehicle the motors and sensors are placed, this code can result in the 'Aggression' or 'Cowardice' behaviors - robots home in on the light or move to avoid the light

We note that LEGO light sensors have a rather narrow field of view, so that it can be frustrating to try to replicate the scenario envisaged by Braitenberg, where robots are naturally attracted to or averted from ambient regions of brightness or darkness. Instead our students were issued with flashlights. The robots are attracted to or repulsed by the flashlight beams. The students thus can readily observe the Braitenbergian behaviours but are also able to remotely steer their robot around the pool, which they find fun.

Figure 13.11 shows an example of a robot with two light sensors for Braitenberg homing behaviours, built by high school students. This behaviour can also be used to make a robot follow a line of lights, figure 13.12.

For challenge 4, students begin sending their robots underwater, modifying them to dive and surface. Students are given additional motors and learn about buoyancy and Archimedes' principle. They modify the weights and floats on their robots to achieve neutral buoyancy, and can then control depth with motors connected to vertical propellers. The students write a simple programme that demonstrates this capability by repeatedly diving to the bottom of the pool and then re-surfacing, figure 13.13.

The first four challenges were completed in three laboratory sessions. The fourth and fifth laboratory sessions were devoted to a final challenge—to create a robot that can be deployed anywhere in the pool and which will seek out and home in on a light source placed on the bottom of the pool.

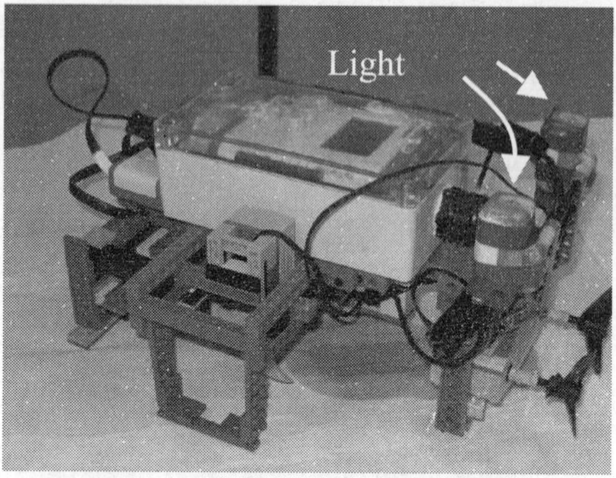

Figure 13.11: Underwater robot with two light sensors (waterproofed with clingfilm) for Braitenbergian light homing, built by high school students

Figure 13.12: Braitenberg's 'aggression' behavior can also be used to follow a line of lights

Figure 13.13: Underwater robot submerged at bottom of pool.

The final challenge was attempted in various ways. Some students tried to extend the Braitenberg behaviours and combine them with search strategies. Some students tried random searches followed by a dive command when a downwards looking light sensor exceeded a threshold. Other students used Braitenberg behaviours to guide their robots across the surface of the pool using a flashlight, followed by a dive command when a downwards looking light sensor exceeded a threshold.

Additional Programmable AUV Activities

The Braitenberg experiments may not be suitable for all students or classrooms. We are currently exploring additional programmable activities such as using pressure sensors and compass sensors with simple feedback loops for automatic depth control and station keeping, and using temperature sensors for transect surveys and data logging activities.

In particular, the technical problems of robustly but accessibly waterproofing the NXT programmable controller introduce expense and complication. Hence, we are also exploring a range of semi-autonomous activities which involve a wire guided vehicle driven from a programmable controller placed outside the water. This also enables the NXT controller's powerful Bluetooth communications capabilities to be fully exploited. Hence, we are exploring robot-robot interaction as classroom activities.

Educational Research

With a major grant from the US National Science Foundation, we have equipped 72 teachers at 36 middle and high schools throughout New Jersey, with enough materials to attempt both ROV and AUV projects in their classrooms.

Over summer 2007, these teachers were trained on the wire guided ROV curriculum. They will attempt this project in their classrooms during Fall 2007 and/or Spring 2008 semesters. Over summer 2008, the teachers will be trained on the programmable AUV curriculum. Curriculum materials have been written to help teachers incorporate the project into conventional core science and mathematics classes at either the middle or high school levels. This is important if teachers are to make use of the project during the school day.

While implementing the ROV project, middle and high school students will be pre and post tested on fundamental topics including electricity, gears and buoyancy.

This kind of testing, with careful observation during project work, has yielded information about serious scientific misconceptions and knowledge gaps in undergraduate engineering students. Over the past two years, we have run the ROV course four times per year (15-20 freshman engineering students each time). Before participating in the ROV course, the majority of our students are unable to answer basic questions about positive and negative buoyancy, show significant lack of understanding of basic gear ratios, and misunderstand basic notions of series and parallel electric circuits. Only one student in two years (a Ukrainian who studied at a Russian high school) has been able to correctly state and understand Archimedes' Principle. Students frequently worry that two 9-volt batteries wired in parallel risks 'burning out the motors with 18Volts'. Immediately following the LEGO ROV course, 50 per cent (up from only 10%) of students correctly answered simple buoyancy questions and the average score on simple gearing quizzes rose from 1.8 correct to 2.6 correct out of three questions.

Collation of anonymous questionnaires also indicates that students feel strongly that these projects have stimulated their interest in engineering, have increased their understanding of a wide range of engineering subjects and programming, and have given them an opportunity to test their inventiveness and develop real problem solving and team work skills.

Summary

Educators and engineers are collaborating to create discovery based educational materials, teaching a wide range of engineering skills and scientific principles through student projects involving underwater robotics.

ROV projects have successfully been implemented with undergraduate engineering students, high school students and middle school students. A follow-on AUV project is being developed and has been pilot tested with high school students. A significant number of teachers have been equipped and trained to implement these projects in their classrooms.

These projects yield significant information about the state of knowledge in our students. The projects form motivating scenarios in which to teach a wide range of scientific and engineering principles in a way which students find meaningful.

Thee projects can help stimulate interest in engineering careers in general, and specifically generate enthusiasm for the field of robotics.

The discovery based learning approach to science and engineering education has proven effective, engaging and stimulating. It is particularly compatible with student projects which emphasize the iterative engineering design process. LEGO components have substantially facilitated the design process by reducing the time between conception of an idea and its implementation.

References

1. Bain. K., Creating a Natural Critical Learning Environment in Large Lecture Classes. Invited lecture, Stevens Institute of Technology. 2005.
2. Engineering Trends. 2005. Synopses of New Reports in Inside Engineering Education on the Engineering Trends Web Site. *Engineering Trends Quarterly Newsletter, Summer 2005.*

3. National Science Board. Science and Engineering Indicators 2004. Chapter 2: Higher Education in Science and Engineering. 2004.
4. Portsmore, M.D. and Rogers, C., Bringing Engineering to Elementary School. *Journal of STEM Education*. Vol 5. 2004.
5. Wang. E., LaCombe, J., and Rogers, C., Using LEGO Bricks to Conduct Engineering Experiments. Proceedings of the ASEE Annual Conference and Exposition. 2004.
6. V. Braitenberg. *Vehicles: Experiments in Synthetic Psychology*. MIT Press, 1984
7. Slavin, R., *Educational Psychology: Theory and Practice*. Allyn and Bacon. 1994.
8. Bruner, J., Toward a Theory of Instruction. Harvard University Press. 1966.
9. Berlyne, D.E., Curiosity and education. In J.D. Krumboltz (ed.), *Learning and the Educational Process*. Rand McNally. 1965.
10. Pomalaza-Ráez, C. and Henry Groff, B. Retention 101: Where Robots Go…Students Follow. *Journal of Engineering Education*. Vol. 91, No. 1, 2003.

14

Study Branches Innovation at the Faculty of Mechanical Engineering

Milada Hlaváèková, Petr Horyl and *Dagmar Juchelková*

Faculty of Mechanical Engineering (FME) VSB—Technical University of Ostrava (VSB-TUO) has been founded in 1950. Town Ostrava had been centre of heavy and mining industry in that time. Because of damping of heavy industry after 1989 and because of environmental problems in town Ostrava, VSB-TUO, Faculty of Mechanical Engineering had to accept changes in industry and adopt these changes to study programme—it means to prepare new study programmes. Applied Mechanics and new study branches Operation and Management in Power Engineering are some of the new successful branches. History, its development and success graduated students in industry and abroad will be described in the chapter.

Introduction

Faculty of Mechanical Engineering VSB—Technical University of Ostrava (FME) has been founded 57 years ago. In that time, town Ostrava had been centre of heavy and mining industry. Traditional study branches were connected with heavy and mining industry. Damping of heavy industry after 1989 and nowadays coming automotive industry and other new and modern international firms to this region has caused needs new study branches at FME.

Applied Mechanics—Branch of Study

Applied Mechanics (AM) is one of these new successful branches. The study branch Applied Mechanics has been founded in 1992. The main target of this specialization has been education of the new specialists with very good knowledge of computational and experimental mechanics. The students of this specialization study applied dynamics, theory of plasticity, mechanics of multibody systems, modern numerical methods, and so on. The students solve in their diploma projects practical industrial problems. The co-operation of the students and teachers of AM with companies is the very good basement for development of study branch and on the other hand it is profitable for industry. A lot of students of AM take part on students study stay abroad. This activity gives them possibility for professional and personal development. The best of them continue their study on Ph.D. level not only in Czech Republic. Our Ph.D. students often work in the famous computational centers.

This chapter is focused to describe the history, main targets of AM specialization. Some of the diploma thesis of the AM students will be described.

The Department of Mechanics and the Department of Mechanics of Materials guarantee AM specialization. The Department of Applied Mathematics share the part of education process too. The education AM specialization for master students has started in 1990. The fist two students finished in 1995. Bachelor study programme has started for the AM specialization in 2001.

The study of mathematical modeling and experiment in the area of linear mechanics is the main goals of the education for bachelor AM specialization. Master degree programme deals with study of nonlinear principles of mechanics of rigid and flexible body or multibody dynamics.

The students receive knowledge from the area of the computer modelling in mechanics (FEM).

On the beginning, just two students studied the AM specialization at 1990. The number of students increases (Fig.14.1). During the time of its existence Applied Mechanics has gradually won firm position and now it belongs to the most difficult fields of study at the Faculty of Mechanical Engineering. The study is supported by modern computer technology that can be applied as a tool in a lot of research and engineering problems as deformation and strength analysis, nonlinear dynamics, linear and also nonlinear buckling, noise propagation and fluid flow modeling. Applied Mechanics attracts students not only by its logic but also by the good and friendly relationship with the teaching staff. Each semester of study is finished by the sport competition and informal meeting that contribute to reciprocal understanding and are highly appreciated by the students.

The AM specialization is one of the most difficult specialization at VŠB-TUO, Faculty of Mechanical Engineering. Because of this study demandingness, the number of AM students is from 1 to 6 per cent from the all graduated students. But, they are traditionally the best students of the Faculty of Mechanical Engineering. Some of the AM graduated students have finished their Ph.D. study abroad (Yokohama University) or their study programme abroad (Imperial College, University of Queen Mary of London and etc.).

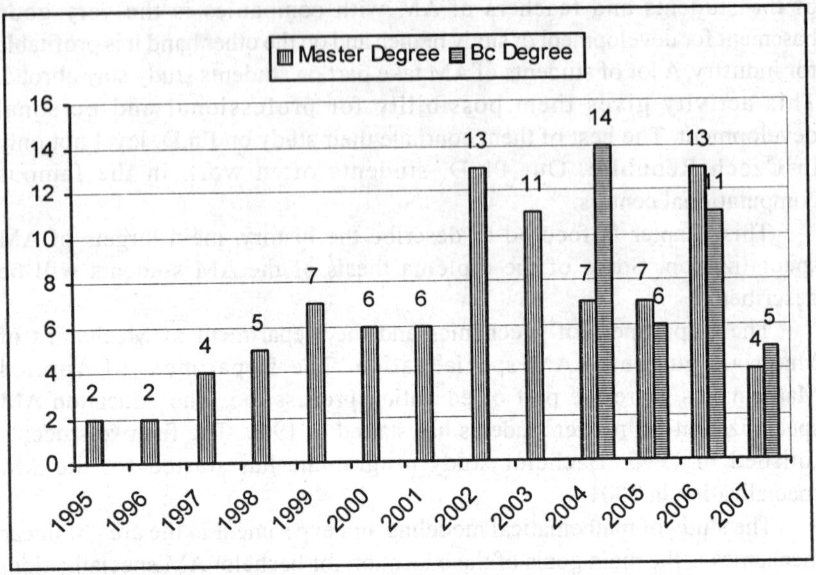

Figure 14.1: Number of Graduated Students

two semesters in 37 countries of EU. In academic year 2006/2007 3 students of AM specialization studied abroad on the base of the S/E programme (2 students in UK, 1 student in Finland). Two AM students were abroad on short practical stay in Finland.

Graduated students are very successful in practice too. They are employees in international companies—Bosch, Visteon-Autopal, Huismann and so on.

The real practical topics for their graduation thesis are very important. The students solve problem from practice, cooperate with workers from industry. They receive a lot of practical knowledge not only from 'university area'.

Examples of Graduation Thesis

Two examples of the latest graduation thesis are in figure 14.2 and 14.3. The students solved hard nonlinear real problems with excellent results. Both problems were solved by ANSYS package. Their graduation theses were among the best thesis at the Faculty of Mechanical Engineering.

Hana Robovska will continue in doctoral study at FME. Ales Vicherek works in Bonatrans Company in Developing Centre.

AM specialization students have also possibility to take part (on the base of the different programme) study stay abroad. For example, on the base of the programme Socrates/Erasmus the students have possibility to study one or Utilization of biogas is very important as the parameter in the Renewable energy strategy. For good results is important a very precise fuel preparation.

Graduation Thesis

Applied Mechanics

Student: Hana Robovská

Supervisor: prof. Ing. Petr Horyl, CSc.

Numerical Solution 3D Model of the Tunnel's Support Clamping Connection

The model of the tunnel's support clamping connection was created by program ANSYS. This system allows us to solve all significant nonlinearities. Clamping connection consists of upper and lower plates and two preloading bolts. The slip resistance of the bolted joint connection was calculated for several magnitudes of a clamping force.

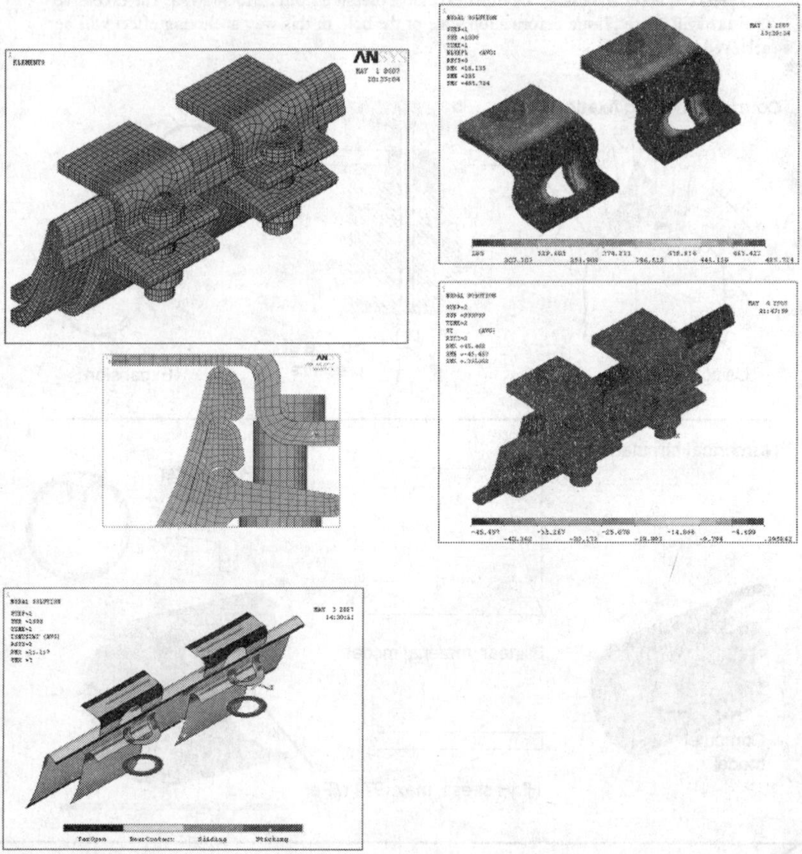

Figure 14.2: Poster of Hana Robovska Graduation Thesis

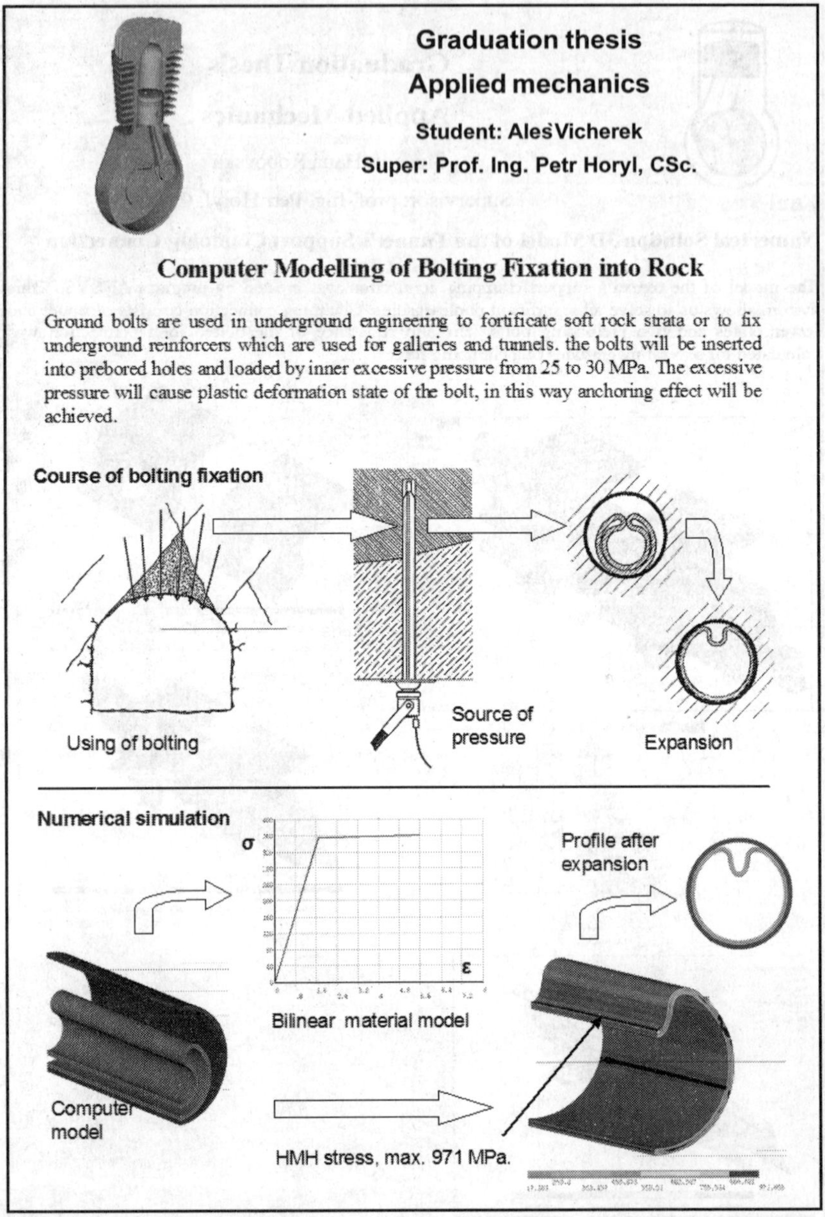

Figure 14.3: Poster of Ales Vicherek Graduation Thesis

Graduation Thesis, Energy Department
Student: Romana Brusová
Supervisor: Prof. Ing. D. Juchelkova, Ph.D.
Biogas Utilization

Fuel Structure:

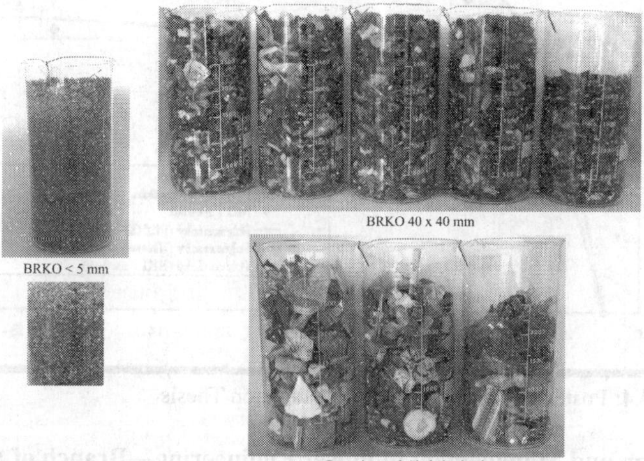

Conversion Technology:

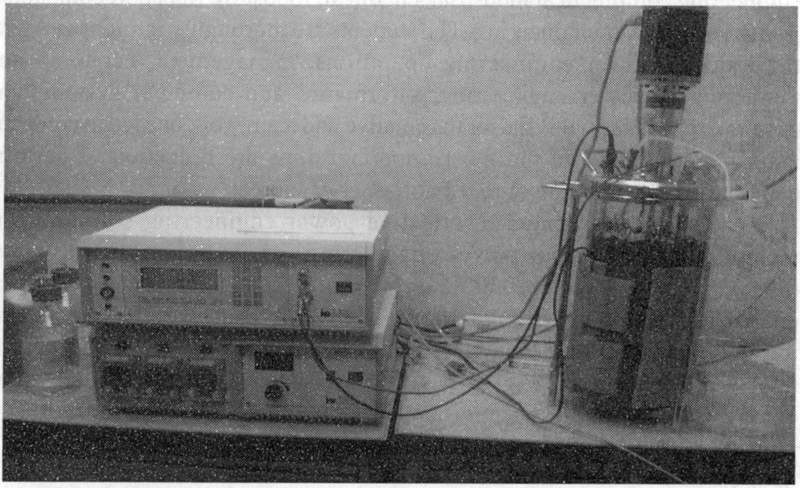

Results:

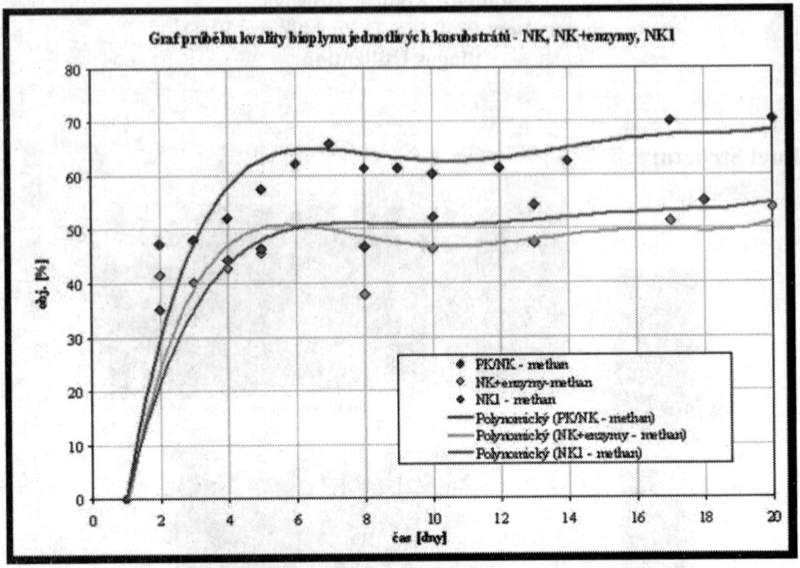

Figure 14.4: Poster of Romana Brusová Graduation Thesis

Operation and Management in Power Engineering—Branch of Study

The study deals with the issue of optimum operation and control of power engineering equipment at industrial, chemical, foodstuff, transport companies, primarily in power engineering. The students are thoroughly familiarized with the issue of power engineering operations, management, economy and marketing in power engineering, informatics and computer systems and development of special skills for the creative and team work needed in company management. Some of the most important aims are reduction of harmful emissions and utilization of renewable energy sources.

The study is oriented to effective power engineering solutions and technologies, industrial power engineering, gas supply systems, water management and recoverable energy sources. The emphasis is laid on enforcement of power engineering legislative in relation to the EU, such as the power engineering law, new price and tax policy, in connection with nuclear power and the environment, energy laws, economical methods of energy utilization. Very important point is close collaboration with the industry.

Conclusion

The necessity of new study branches are confirmed by fruitfulness of the graduated students in the practices. Majority of them received job in industry very quickly. Some of them are in top management of the firms. There is big interest in graduates of technical specialization on the part of industry.

From the experience with new specialization appears:

The foundation of the new specialization was good idea.

It is very important to follow the requirement of practice and adopt and change study programmes. It is function of Faculty management.

We recognize a huge number of students moving to the foreign companies (also abroad).

Part III

Organizational Climate and ICT in Engineering Education

15

In Search of the Academic and Organizational Change in Spanish Universities

Mónica Edwards and *Luis M. Sánchez-Ruiz*

Within the advance in the European convergence process, the majority of the universities are embedded in an important transformation process, reinforcing their three basic missions: education, research and knowledge transference, among their extension and socio-cultural traditional activities (De Woot, 1998; CE, 2003, 2006).

The process of Bologna started in Europe represents the answer to the economic and socio-cultural impacts derived from globalization and the advance of the Knowledge society. The fast development of the globalization and the Information and Communication Technology (ICT) have brought about deep changes in our way of working and living, as the widespread diffusion of ICT is accompanied by organizational, economic, social and cultural innovations. New necessities in the knowledge production and management are originating imbalances between the supply and the demand of job competences, and this has direct incidence in higher educational institutions (CE, 2003; De Grip, Van Loo y Mayhew, 2002; García Aracil, 2003).

In the report *Mobilising the brainpower of Europe: enabling universities to make their full contribution to the Lisbon Strategy* (2005) it affirms that universities need to accelerate the pace of reforms for ensuring a more effective contribution to the Lisbon strategy and the strengthening of the European social model. It identifies three main challenges for European higher education: achieving world-class quality, improving governance, and increasing and diversifying funding (CE, 2005).

On the last decades, Spain has undergone profound social and economic changes that have greatly affected the higher education system. The structural reforms and the intends to modernize and democratize the universities, as well as adapt the higher education system to the socioeconomic needs of the country could be judged as very positive (Ginés Mora y Vidal, 2005).

Despite these approaches the actual academic and organizational culture is not still giving a suitable answer to the new exigencies. For the last two decades in the Spanish case specially, serious problems have appeared in the management of university systems. These problems are related with 'the three e': efficiency, efficacy and equity (Mora, 1998). Thus, institutions show a lack of efficacy, that is, a delay when responding to the society necessities, an absence of efficiency in the use of resources and equity faults.

The tailoring of the structure of different university studies to the European Higher Education Area (EHEA) is one of the major tasks outstanding in Europe's different university systems. The practical implementation of the Bologna recommendations and requirements (new degrees, European Credit Transfer System, quality assurance and accreditation, European Qualifications Framework, etc.) implies not only a conceptual reorganization of the educative systems but a change of paradigm in the academic and organizational culture (Davies, 2000; Ginés Mora, 2006).

Spanish universities are now entering a new period, in which adaptation to the dynamic change and search of high quality will be the most important challenge. Introducing market forces will allow the higher education system to achieve an equilibrium in which the state (representing the whole community), academia (representing the experts in the production process), and the market (as the most effective mechanism to satisfy the needs of students and employers) are able to act in harmony (Vidal y Ginés Mora, 2000). Although the majority of universities are working around these issues, there exist diverse tensions between the national legislation, accreditation, quality assurance and the process of change, both in internal and external contexts.

In this work, we analyze some trends and obstacles that are emerging in the universities related to these issues, particularly in the Spanish case. In first place, we comment the core modernization agenda for universities, intending to identify the critical areas for academic and organizational culture change. Secondly, we present the experience in the School of Design Engineering (Polytechnic University of Valencia) to implement several projects in engineering education. We present the different phases, organizational structure, strategies and planning of tasks, whose objectives were to

(a) establish a curricular structure for competences based professional profiles,
(b) adapt the formative programmes according to the European System requirements;
(c) develop curriculum materials to meet key competences and learning outcomes,
(d) elaborate the Information Package; and
(e) manage an action agenda in the gradual implementation of the changes.

Finally, we comment some of the obtained results, the degree of institutional impact of the actions undertaken and the improvement possibilities in the future.

Modernisation Agenda of Universities in Europe

1. The 'core' modernisation agenda for European universities is to improve and advance in reforms related to the attractiveness, governance and funding (CE, 2005).
2. Attractiveness (curricular reform): Raising quality and attractiveness requires major transformations at universities with a profound curricular renovation, with the implementation of the Bologna reforms and the establishment of a European Qualification Framework (CE, 2006). Universities need better to communicate with society about the value of what they produce, and to invest more in their presence and marketing at home and abroad.
3. Governance reform: Universities are calling for a fundamentally new type of arrangement (or 'contract') with society, whereby they are responsible and accountable for their programmes, staff and resources, while public authorities focus on the strategic orientation of the system as a whole. Also it is necessary enabling institutional modernisation strategies for better system and institutional management. Universities need more autonomy and improve the excellence through internal and external Quality Assurance.
4. Funding Reform: To attract more funding, universities first need to convince stakeholders—governments, companies, households—that existing resources are efficiently used and fresh ones would produce added value for them. Higher funding cannot be justified without profound change: providing for such change is the main justification and prime purpose for fresh investment (Ginés Moray Vidal, 2000).

If universities are to become more attractive locally and globally, profound curricular revision is required—not just to ensure the highest level of academic content, but also to respond to the changing needs of labour markets and socio-cultural demands (Teichler, U. and Schonburg, 2004). The integration of graduates into professional life, and hence into society, is a major social responsibility of higher education.

In this change context, competence and competence-based learning emerge as nuclear concepts in the majority of European universities. The 'New Engineer', besides unquestionable technical skills, must have abilities such as team working, knowledge of foreign languages and cultures, creative thinking, efficient oral and written communication, and appropriate profile for the market needs. Furthermore, future engineers needs to develop habits of life-long learning, must be conscious of their social role and be able to assume their social tasks. It is necessary to graduate professionals that are flexible and open minded to cope with the important changes in the present world; they need to be able to 'learn how to learn' (Hedberg, 2001; National Academy of Engineering, 2005).

Employers demand graduates who are able to operate in complex environments, i.e., environments characterized by ill-defined problems, contradictory information, informal collaboration, and abstract, dynamic and highly integrated processes. Although in Spain employers generally have expressed satisfaction with the technical knowledge and skills of current engineering graduates, they usually affirm that some competences in certain non-technical areas such as communication ability, economics, leadership, teamwork and management are not practically being considered in their formation. In sum, learning needs to encompass transversal skills (such as teamwork and entrepreneurship) in addition to specialist knowledge. Moreover, the potential of Information and Communication Technology (ICT) should be fully exploited in teaching and learning process within framework and perspectives of the lifelong learning.

The current structural and curricular reform provides an opportunity for universities to reflect upon management practices and to review formative programmes and teaching methods with the aim of ensuring their quality. Although the need for reform is obvious, changes are difficult and there is discrepancy between national rhetoric and institutional reality. In several countries it exists a high risk that concepts and tools such as student-centred learning, competences, learning outcomes and curricula development may be implemented haphazardly to comply with existing regulation, without a deep understanding of their pedagogical function (Reichert, Tauch, 2005).

The institutional and academic transformation requires a significant amount of change in attitudes, practices and policies throughout the university community. These attitudes, practices, and policies are what define the academic culture, how people behave and relate to one another, who belongs and how decisions are made, and ultimately what has value and meaning in the organization (Schein, 1992; Chaffee & Tierney, 1988). In a context of an ongoing debate on the crisis of the academic profession, cultural change is a critical issue for planning long-term changes in governance, funding and attractiveness of higher education and a pre-requisite for the successful in 2010 of the Bologna process (Enders, 2001).

Strengths between Governance and Academic Culture

In the document *Delivering on the modernisation agenda for universities: education, research and innovation*, published by the European Commission in May 2006, it affirms that without real autonomy and accountability, universities will be neither really responsive nor innovative. In return for being freed from dysfunctional over-regulation and micro-management, universities need to recognize the importance of accountability and more professional management. Also it consider that it's necessary to adapt the legal frameworks at national and regional levels and to develop new models for governing their research activities, including a higher degree of autonomy and new ways of ensuring internal and external quality and accountability (CE, 2006).

Improving Governance

University governance is related to collective control towards common institutional goals. It could be defined as the way as public and private actors seek to solve university organizational problems. Governance raises questions about who decides when on what. Governance is also related to the institutional capacity to change and to change properly and timely to institutional needs. There are five dimensions in governance:

- State regulation. This dimension refers to regulation by directives; the government prescribes in detail behaviours under particular circumstances.
- Stakeholder guidance. In public higher education systems the government may delegate certain powers to guide to other actors, such as intermediary bodies or representatives of industry in university boards.
- Academic self-governance concerns the role of professional communities within higher education systems. This mechanism is institutionalized in collegial decision-making within universities.
- Managerial self-governance concerns hierarchies within higher education institutions as organizations. Here the role of institutional leadership in internal goal setting, regulation, and decision-making is at stake.
- Competition for resources within and between universities takes place mostly not on 'real' markets but on 'quasi-markets' where performance evaluations by peers substitute customers (Ginés Mora, 2006).

Universities, in words of Burton Clark, move and respond to its environment from the triangle of forces represented by the state, the market and the academic oligarchy (Clark, 1983). In the Spanish case the question of the strengths between governance factors combined with the academic culture is especially relevant, because the actual framework of transformation in Spain is essentially a bureaucratic response in bureaucratic organizations. Universities are bureaucratic organizations, or in words of Mintzberg, professional bureaucracies. The professional bureaucracy relies for coordination on the standardization of skills and its associated design parameter, training and indoctrination. It hires duly trained and indoctrinated specialists (professionals) for the operating core, and then gives them considerable control over their work. Control over his own work means that the professional works relatively independently of his colleagues, but closely with the clients he serves. Most necessary coordination between the operating professionals is handled by the standardization of skills and knowledge—in effect, by what they have learned to expect from their colleagues.

Professional bureaucracy grows bureaucratic cultures which have an internal focus and an orientation towards a stable culture.

Changing the 'Academic' Culture

In this context there are inevitable difficulties in defining cultural change in universities. An emphasis needs to be put on how people think, work and act as a community, their relationships, perceptions and attitudes. The way a system, routine or procedure is shaped depends to a large extent on both the attitudes and the perceptions of the people and organizational structures involved, as well as other external forces.

Cultures serve two critical functions in organizations:

(a) to integrate members so that they know how to relate to one another, and
(b) to help the organization adapt to the external environment.

Daft calls internal integration and it ensures that members of an organization develop a collective identity that allows them to work together effectively. The culture determines how people communicate within the organization, what behaviours are encouraged or discouraged and how power and status is distributed (Daft, 1998). Organization culture is the key to much that happens (or does not happen) in an organization. Culture pervades all the relationships which underpin the organization and influences all its decisions. Changing culture is never easy. It requires understanding and insight into the organization's culture, which depends on self-awareness at an individual level and at the organizational level (Schein, 1992; Astin & Astin, 2000).

Johnson has described a cultural web (Fig. 15.1) identifying a number of elements that can be used to describe or influence organizational culture (Johnson, 1988, 1992). The paradigm in the centre is the set of core beliefs which result from the multiplicity of conversations and which maintains the unity of the culture. The petals represent the manifestations of culture which result from the influence of the paradigm:

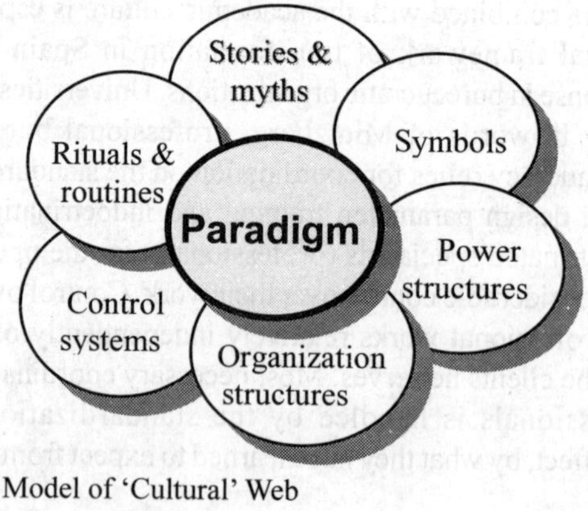

Figure 15.1: The Model of 'Cultural' Web

- *The Paradigm*: What the organization is about; what it does; its mission; its values. Capra defines paradigm in kuhnian sense as a constellation of concepts, values, perceptions and practices shared by a community, which forms a particular vision of reality that is the basis of the way a community organizes itself (Capra, 1997).
- *Control Systems*: The processes in place to monitor what is going on. Role cultures would have vast rulebooks. There would be more reliance on individualism in a power culture.
- *Organizational Structures*: Reporting lines, hierarchies, and the way that work flows through the business.
- *Power Structures*: Who makes the decisions, how widely spread is power, and on what is power based?
- *Symbols*: These include organizational logos and designs, but also extend to symbols of power such as parking spaces and executive washrooms.
- *Rituals and Routines*: Management meetings, board reports and so on may become more habitual than necessary.
- *Stories and Myths*: build up about people and events, and convey a message about what is valued within the organization.

There are many different factors that define an organization's culture, including degree of hierarchy within the organization, degree of urgency (that defines how quickly the organization wants or needs to push decision-making and innovation), people/task orientation, assertiveness/courtesy dimensions, functional orientation, institutional 'personality' issues and values, among others. Cultural change involves new frames of reference, new ways of acting. Cultural change results from actors acquiring new symbolic resources (cognitive frames/paradigms: concepts, knowledge, skills) in changed structural contexts (organizational contexts, work processes) where these symbolic resources are meaningful, deployable and operational (Mintzberg, 1979).

Managing Academic and Cultural Change at Universities

Much has been written on how culture impacts organizational strategies, policies, and programmes. There has been little written, however, on how to assess one's own culture so that appropriate strategies can be developed and implemented effectively.

Whatever strategy used to assess the organizational culture, the process must be honest, thorough, and must focus not on 'what we want to be' as much as 'who we are right now.' Organizations who decide that 'where we are now' is not 'where we want to be,' may also want to look at moving their organization to embrace a different culture prior to initiating new policies and programmes to support the existing culture. Assessing the organizational culture is the first and most important step in developing strategies that support the objectives and goals. Alignment of objectives and plans with organizational culture is a fundamental method of ensuring that the organization will be able to meet and exceed its goals through strategies that support those objectives. Further, by ensuring that the organization is not merely copying 'best practices' from other organizations, they are more likely to develop policies and programmes that will lead the organization toward its goals. In other words, organizations, to be effective, must copy how leading other institutions or organizations think, not by copying what they do.

Organizational change often starts with strategic change, a change in the institution's mission, strategy, and vision, which can lead to changes in the institution's culture and structure. There are various sources of resistance to change. Some of these are lack of information, personal reasons, and emotional issues. One can overcome this resistance by education, facilitation, and negotiation. In addition, there are several steps for change process. Some of the steps are sense of urgency, coalition and commitment, shared vision, empowerment etc.; it is essential to adopt such measures in order to bring effective change in the organization (Daft, 1998).

Recent developments in Spanish higher education have been very positive. Universities have become autonomous and are more in tune to regional needs, their internal structure has become flexible, the whole system has become open and accessible, funds have been poured into the system as never before and market forces have started to play a relevant role. Nevertheless, some perverse effects have begun to emerge. We will focus on some of these negative aspects that deserve deeper consideration: the inadequate adaptation to a mass higher education system, and the negative consequences of the collegial model for governing universities and of regionalization (Montesinos, López & Ginés Mora, 2006).

There is no doubt that the deep process of reflection and intellectual mobilization is worth by itself and, at least at the long run, will be positive for the European Higher Education. The numbers are clear: 66 per cent of all Higher Education Institutions leaders want rapid progress towards the EHEA, 85 per cent of European universities have started curricula reform, 90 per cent have or are planning a two-cycle structure, 75 per cent use a credit system, 70 per cent say that student mobility has increased but… It is yet unclear whether the expected results will be reached. The current educational system of the Spanish State is based on an excessively theoretical lecture and with not very good results, given the high amount of abandonment and of academic failure. Furthermore, this is increased in the case of the technical degrees. Despite these problems a great majority of Spanish universities are still moving between the tradition and the transformation options, being the main obstacles:

- discrepancy between 'EHEA rhetoric' and institutional reality
- lack of clarity in the Spanish legal framework

- scarce of clarity and consensus
- diferences in socio-economic circumstances and institutional support/ commitment
- lack of awareness (students, academics and administrators often unaware of key Bologna reforms)
- weak human factor (absence of teachers and students participation)
- insufficient resources (time/money for real implementation)
- poor participation of the staff
- no background in governance and management experiences at universities

Although the systemic and cultural implications of Bologna reforms are only now beginning to become apparent, it is very important to consider these barriers to improve a real transformation.

Managing the Academic and Organizational Change in the School of Design Engineering

We can affirm that in the past engineering and engineering education was reactive, responding to change. But today, the rapid change signals that it is time to reverse the paradigm. The premise is: if we anticipate the future and are proactive about changing engineering and engineering education, we can shape a significant, dynamic role for our profession. The School of Design Engineering (ETSID) is a good example of dynamic institution which tries to be at the leading edge of educational change and improvement of the European convergence. Within the general plans implemented at the Polytechnic University of Valencia (UPV) since the year 2000 to the present, the School of Design Engineering has being participated in several plans and actions with the aim of strengthening a gradual process of adaptation of engineering degrees to EHEA (Seiz-Ortiz, Sánchez-Ruiz & Ballester-Sarrias, 2004; Ballester, Gimeno, Hurtado & Sánchez-Ruiz, 2005; Edwards, Donderis-Quíles, Sánchez-Ruiz & Ballester-Sarrias, 2006).

The ETSID has been involved in the last decades, and purposefully, in a deep process of global quality assessment and improvement, being the three major fundamental priorities in the centre's policy-making and training scheme:

(a) *Educational Innovation*, to encourage the participation of the teaching staff in educational innovation actions that incorporate the use of active methodologies (new laboratory experiences, project based methodology, new activities and assessment instruments, etc.).

(b) *Close Relationship with the Socioeconomic and Industrial Environment*: The relationship with the industrial environment and companies is very important for the ETSID, since permits us to know the opinion that have the companies of our graduate and the training characteristics that they need.

(c) *International Relations*: Through different international programmes of educational cooperation, ETSID has collaboration, in different levels, with an important number of Institutions within the European Union and other countries. This has permitted to many teachers and students of the ETSID to have direct contact with other models and teaching methodologies, with the consequent benefit that there has reported to the School (Seiz-Ortiz, Sánchez-Ruiz & Ballester-Sarrias, 2004).

In spite of the many obstacles encountered and of the opposing forces that could make the implementation difficult, all the staff works to build up a system that is relevant to the specific context of the industrial engineer, advancing in the European harmonization. The actions for promoting the academic culture change are based on the following key aspects:

- Improving the full faculty participation from 'a bureaucratic' tendency towards a human factor conception
- Achieving the integration of the physical, academic, and human resources.
- Ensuring alignment and coordination of all planning activities and processes.
- Focusing on collaborative planning structures throughout the organization and determine alignment and linkages between them.
- Improving a culture of decision-making more decentralized and focused on the academic planning goals.
- Optimizing the feedback of data, research and trends in co-operation with other Spanish and European institutions.

The Unfreezing-Changing-Refreezing model was applied as the strategy for a proactive approach to the environment, with three stages (Schein, 1995):

- *Unfreezing*: Reducing or eliminating resistance to change by resolving fear and feelings about letting go of the 'old.'
- *Changing* (or moving on to a new level). Moving on to other things through active participation in the change process.
- *Refreezing*: Encouraging recognition of successful change and rewarding people for implementing the change.

The first stages until the process of 'unfreezing' include the following aspects: capitalizing the previous experience in educative innovation, aligning the mission, vision and values of the institution with the involved agents, developing of self-regulation, evaluation and quality indicators, enabling autonomy and flexibility. the Table 15.1 it shows the communication strategies applied (Edwards *et al.*, 2006).

***Strategy* 1**

Considering the human factor, particularly teacher staff and students, as key issues for improving the academic and organizational culture change.

***Strategy* 2**

Raising clearly why and what for the change from a global and local perspective, with a rigorous knowledge about some deficiencies in the Spanish university system. Among them: low performance, high rate of desertion, excessive use of the lecture classes, passive student, etc. [11]-[12]-[13]-[14].

***Strategy* 3**

Showing that the proposed change constitutes an opportunity to improve the formative programme and the teaching-learning system. This change will bring an the improvement of the graduate formation quality and in order to achieve it the key issues are: to advance in coordination with other institutions and European countries, and to improve education, research and management.

***Strategy* 4**

Sharing an institutional slogan: 'Step by step advanced towards the European Higher Education Area', reiterated in presentations, communications, seminars, and internal work papers. This is synthesized in Table 15.1.

Table 15. 1: Communication Strategies for the Culture Academic Change

I.	Human factor: key issue for the exit of the European convergence process. All members of faculty can contribute: directives, teachers, students, administrative ....
II.	The importance of why and what for of changing, reflecting about the need to remove the actual teaching and learning culture.
III.	The change is an opportunity. To mobilize us and to reach a greater efficiency and quality in the formation.
IV.	Slogan to share: 'One step in advance towards the EHEA'. To share a joint vision of the goals to reach and to work in the short and long term.

Working is in progress for managing the change for improving the internal integration (Daft, 1998). Internal integration, as Daft says, ensures that members of an organization develop a collective identity that allows them to work together effectively.

Projects General Description

Projects have been implemented since 2003/2004 course and during three consecutive academic courses with the aim of strengthening a gradual process of adaptation in five degrees of engineering (Mechanical Engineering, Electrical Engineering, Electronics Engineering, Chemical Engineering and Design Engineering). These projects were designed and implemented with the following objectives:

- Review and define the academic-professionals profiles of the actual engineering degrees, through competency-based models of curriculum. It deals with the incorporation of new competences taking care of the needs and opinions of the different stakeholders: employers, academics, graduates, students and other social agents, besides to consider the characteristics of different global, regional and local contexts.
- Adapt the actual degrees and formative programmes to the ECTS recommendations and requirements.
- Promote and coordinate teacher teams for curricula design. The academic staff is changing the courses and subjects organization, including the Information and Communication Technologies uses, active methodologies (case studies, problem-solving, project based learning, etc.), modification of assessment and evaluation of the student performance.
- Elaborate information documents about the study programmes and the results of the students in normalised format (Information Package).
- Develop curriculum materials to meet the key competences and learning objectives, thus achieving an increased incorporation of active methodologies with continuous and formative assessment.
- Use an action agenda with the changes implemented (surveys to institutions, employers, students and administrative staff).

General Organization and Projects Stages

The general coordination at the Polytechnic University of Valencia is held by the Vice-rectorate for the EHEA and the Educational Sciences Institute (ICE). At School of Design Engineering, there is a Deputy Director designed to coordinate the European Convergence Area. Coordinators for each one of the degree courses and student groups were designed, so that the adaptation work carried out by the individual teachers and subjects could be coherent with the overall framework of the institution.

The Projects of Adaptation to EHEA involved all the members of the educative community: directive staff, 210 teachers, 30 administrative personal and approximately 3,500 students. Although the projects started off with a 'bureaucratic' bias in the 2003/04 course, from the 2004/05 course the vision went enriching towards the human factor, being two high-priority objectives added the following ones:

Deepening actions oriented to the awareness and formation of all staff members, considering that the academic culture change involves not only structural issues, but also radical change in methodologies and teaching and learning roles.

Involve teachers and students in a new 'culture to manage the change' towards the new model of education-learning, through the feedback and the exchange of information.

The scheme is a shared management of the change, developing information-formation to be advancing towards a greater involvement of all the faculty members.

The main factors and restrictions that have affected the implementation and development of these projects have depended on the degree of individual staff participation, among the adjustment and reorganization of physical resources. In synthesis, it has been tried to obtain a greater implication of all faculty, with the leadership of the directive equipment and the participation of teachers, students and administrative personnel. The following stages about the planning are indicated:

- Coordinators designation at level of both each degree and each course.
- Coordinators designation by each group of scholarship holders, one by each seven scholarship holders assigned in tasks of support to the teaching staff.
- Design and implementation of materials for formation workshops and seminars for teachers, students and administrative personnel.
- Sequence and temporalization of the predicted actions.

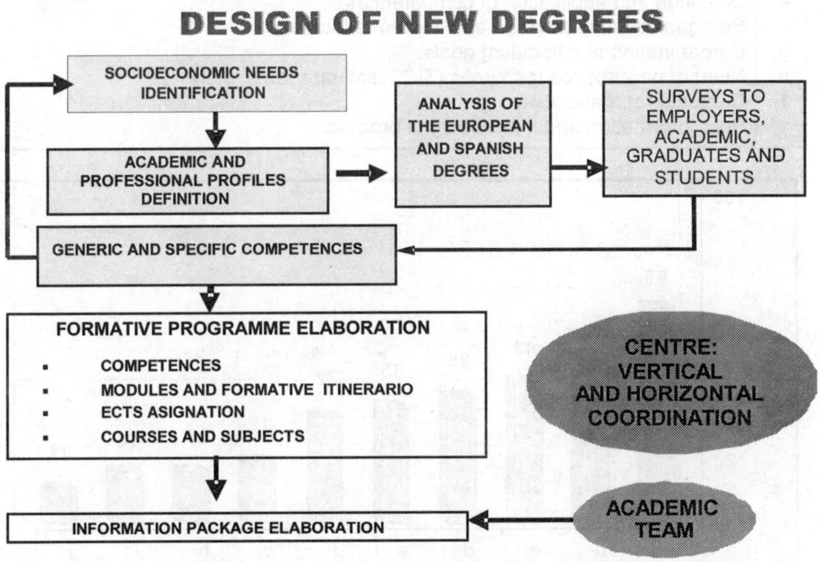

Figure 15.2: Scheme of the Projects of Adaptation to the European Higher Education

Projects have been evaluated by internal and external commissions, pre-established with such purpose. Some examples of the most significant results obtained in the undertaken actions are exposed in the following sections.

Teacher Staff and Students Participation

A diagnosis of situation was made simultaneously with the initial actions undertaken in the projects implementation. Teacher and students' knowledge and participation were analyzed because these aspects are a key factor in the change process (Edwards, Ballester-Sarrias, Fuentes-Durá & Donderis-Quiles, 2005). Surveys to professors and students were applied to evaluate their degree of information on subjects concerning the European convergence and ECTS. The results showed, in general, important lacks of information in the studied sample (37 teachers and 851 engineering students). Table 15.2 and Fig. 15.3 show in decreasing order of importance the obstacles and difficulties indicated by teachers for the adaptation to the European Credit Transfer System.

Table 15.2: Teachers' Perceptions and Opinions about Obstacles and Difficulties for the Adaptation to ECTS

a.	Large classes, with an excessive number of students.
b.	Determination of student workload.
c.	Active methodologies application.
d.	Change in assessment methods.
e.	Definition and application of competences.
f.	Reorganization of physical and human resources.
g.	Determination of curriculum goals.
h.	Need of new spaces resources (TIC, seminar rooms, etc.).
I.	Contents reorganization.
j.	Poor information about the Bologna process.

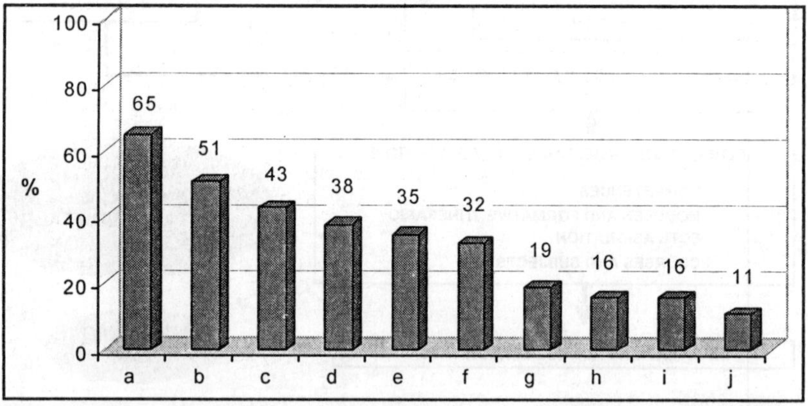

Figure 15.3: Teachers' Perceptions and Opinions About Obstacles and Difficulties for the Adaptation to ECTS

In the student samples, the ignorance on EHEA themes was very high, as it can be observed in Fig. 15.4, which represents the negative answer to the question: 'Do you know the meaning of the expression European Higher education Area?'

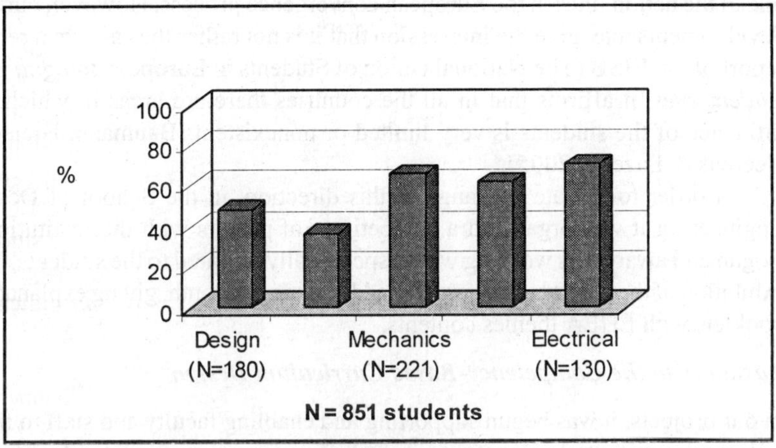

Figure 15.4: Students' Knowledge on the Meaning of EHEA Expression (N = 180 Design Eng.; N = 172 Chemical Eng.; N = 221 Mechanics Eng.; N = 148 Electronics Eng., and N = 130, Electrical Eng.)

The results were similar when the students answered to the question: 'Do you know the European Credit Transfer System?'

It may be observe in Fig. 15.5 that only 37.3 per cent of Design Engineering students responded affirmatively to this question, 15,8 per cent of Chemical Engineering, 14,5 per cent of Electronics Engineering, 8,4 per cent of Mechanics Engineering, and 7,6 per cent of Electrical Engineering.

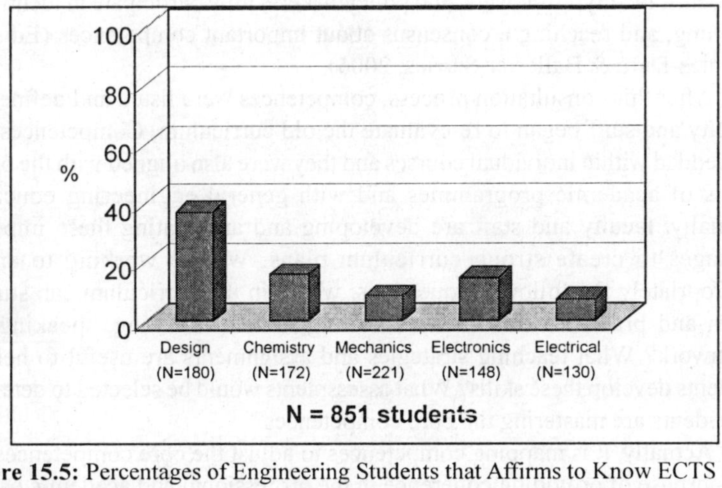

Figure 15.5: Percentages of Engineering Students that Affirms to Know ECTS

These results show a little attention to the students' participation in the process of Bologna. Since the Prague summit in 2001 student involvement is one of the action lines in the European convergence process. However, current developments may give the impression that it is not rather the case. In a recent report of the EISB (The National Union of Students in Europe), *Bologna with student eyes*, it affirms that in all the countries there are areas in which the influence of the students is very limited or nonexistent (Baumann, Bielecki, Heerens & Lazetic, 2005).

In order to initiate a change in this direction, in the School of Design Engineering it was organized a competition of posters with the institutional slogan and awareness working weeks specifically oriented to the students. The exhibition of the rewarded posters was added during a month, giving explanatory booklets with EHEA themes contents.

Advances in the Competency-Based Curriculum Design

In our projects, it was begun supporting and enabling faculty and staff to fully reflect upon potential competences, conducting formal research to identify the most important competences, and reaching consensus. With a directive staff as leader and expert participation, there were realised formal workshops allow faculty and staff to experiment with new ideas about competency-based curricula.

These workshops were usually offered on a regular, consistent basis with follow up discussions and meetings rather than a single event. The *Tuning Project* and the *Engineering criteria 2000* of the Accreditation Board for Engineering and Technology (ABET) were considered in the background (González & Wagenaar, 2003; ABET, 2000). The appropriate stakeholders (students, faculty, employers, and policymakers) fully participate in identifying, defining, and reaching a consensus about important competences (Edwards, Fuentes-Durá & Ballester-Sarrias, 2005).

After this consultation process, competences were listed and defined and faculty and staff began to re-evaluate the old curriculum. Competences were embedded within individual courses and they were also aligned with the overall goals of academic programmes and with general engineering education. Actually, faculty and staff are developing and articulating these important linkages to create strong curriculum plans. We are working to answer appropriately the following questions: where in the curriculum can students learn and practice skills such as writing, critical thinking, speaking, and teamwork? What teaching strategies and assignments are useful to help the students develop these skills? What assessments would be selected to determine if students are mastering the core competences?

Actually, it is mapping competences to adjust the core competences with the purpose of providing coherence in the professional and academic profiles according the recent resolutions of the Ministry of Education about the engineering degrees.

Conclusions

The old and traditional Spanish university system is not likely to be able to face the challenges and requirements of the European Higher Education Area framework. A radical change in governance and academic culture is necessary towards a more competitive, flexible and attractive Higher Education system. This change is a multifaceted endeavour including, among others, structural, legal, curricular, methodological and pedagogical issues. It certainly involves a change in the mentality and roles of students, teaching staff and administrators alike. Over the last years we have built a more flexible organisation by redesigning our jobs and teams to anticipate and respond to the changing needs of our students and clients, the changing nature of information resources and our new strategic context. Preparation is in progress for the next years, assisting staff to make the transition to the new roles for improving quality and excellence in educative model.

After several years of experience in the Projects of Adaptation to the EHEA (since 1999 to the present), it was observed an increase of the number of activities different from the classic lectures: 60 per cent of the hours of teaching are dedicated to activities of practical type (seminaries, teamwork, laboratory, etc.). Also some positive changes in the assessment methods are observed; 42.6 per cent of the subjects are making continuous and formative assessment. However, 15.1 per cent of the subjects continue focusing the assessment in the accomplishment of an only final examination. All these changes are implying a progressive adaptation of the students towards more independent forms of work, and towards a greater implication in group tasks. At present we are working in the curricular development of the new degrees in engineering education proposals, according the ministerial directives and the Dublin and Quality Assurance descriptors.

The principal points to consider for the future are:

- Achieving the integration of the physical, academic, and human resources.
- Ensuring alignment and coordination of all planning activities and processes.
- Focusing on collaborative planning structures throughout the organization and determine alignment and linkages between them.
- Improving a culture of decision-making more decentralized and focused on the academic planning goals.
- Optimizing the feedback of data, research and trends in co-operation with other Spanish and European institutions.

16

Quality Evaluation of the Engineering Education in Brazil

The Method Applied at the Polytechnic School of the University of São Paulo

Giuliano Olguin, Haydée Svab, Ana Cecília Pontes Rodrigues and *Cecília Carmen Cunha Pontes*

The Creation of an International Education Pattern—Is it a Problem or a Solution?

In a world in which interactions among countries are more and more present, international academic relations must be discussed and carefully revised. The Bologna Declaration has pushed this debate, for this, it has already been pointed out some issues concerning Higher Education. The Establishment of a system of credits (such as in the European Credit Transfer System—ECTS) and the promotion of European co-operation in quality assurance with the view of developing comparable criteria and methodologies aims at the increase of education quality in Europe.

The actions proposed by the Bologna Declaration also affect non-European countries. The international programmes of student exchanges, for example, will be affected if the curriculum among the countries does not match.

Each nation has its own ideas about the management of education. It is very hard to create a pattern among different countries since educational systems reflect local society objectives and desires. The identity of each country must be respected. At the same time the increase of the cultural exchange among countries must be pursuit.

In Brazil, there are many laws about education. Since 1996, in Brazil, the Bases and Guidelines Law (Lei de Diretrizes E Bases/LDB), gave definitions to all levels of education parameters. Publications after that one, such as the National Curricular Guidelines (Diretrizes Curriculares Nacionais/DCN), of 2001, have focused on the Higher Education. These laws, allied to a strong process of expansion of the Brazilian Higher Education sector (that happened mostly on private institutions), meant profound changes on Brazilian society. Nowadays the origins of public university have been discussed again.

Therefore, would it be possible to have a worldwide Higher Education system? Would it be possible to have a university without frontiers? How the nation characteristics could be respected in this system?

The Bologna Declaration has generated great discussions that have as result the idea of creating a pattern to regulate the courses, in order to give students the opportunity to study in different countries without causing any damage to its educational result. To assure the educational quality among these countries, institutions are proposed to evaluate the courses in order to check if they are in agreement to the established patterns. In the Declaration of Bologna, some actions have led to 'the establishment of a system of efficient quality assurance, which is recognized among European and non-European countries' (Hortale & Mora, 2004).

During the decades of 80's and 90's, almost all European countries had developed national or regional agencies that carried through the evaluation of the Higher Education. In 1999, as part of the development and implantation of the Bologna Declaration, the European Network for Quality Assurance in Higher Education (ENQA) was created.

In 2001, ENQA developed the Transnational European Evaluation Project intended to develop common systems of evaluation of the courses. However, the ENQA will not be used as a registration instrument ('The Bologna', 2002).

The institutions of Higher Education value will be given in an independent way, following the rules for the country that it belongs to. But it is still very unclear how this ENQA process happens exactly and how these quality patterns are established. Do these patterns reflect the local society characteristics? To what level does society or the community participate on the elaboration and discussion of the results from the evaluation methods?

Complexity of evaluation issue due to the social and cultural diversity in Brazil is already debated. Some authors were raising the following questions:

1— How to promote an evaluation in a national scope, with compatible criteria of comparison, in a big country such as Brazil?
2— How can the same evaluation criteria be valid throughout the country and at the same time respect the identities and diversities of each city and state?
3— How to guarantee the effectiveness of the actions that must be generated from the evaluations results?
4— How to evaluate different areas of the same profession? Should an electrical engineer be evaluated by the same test applied to a mechanical engineer? In this sense, what sort of knowledge should be common to all and what sort should be a specific one?

These boundaries between specificity and general needs to the course identity are very important because these reflect evaluation characteristic and university model. This way, the evaluation and the Higher Education goals remain dissociated. An evaluation method change these courses explicitly or implicitly when creates a concept of quality.

On the other hand, how is it possible to analyze the education quality in relation to specific knowledge, since it is so varied and dynamic? Nowadays technology changes very fast. The professional demands for engineers change constantly, creating the necessity for a dynamic formation, and consequently a necessity for an evaluation that accompanies these fast changes.

So, the economy, culture, and politics also affect what happens inside a classroom and influence the way the quality of education is analyzed. Then, to deal with education, it is also necessary to observe what happens outside the institution. According to Apple (1985), in the United States, 1985: '…the fact that education is through and through a political enterprise withered. The questions we asked tended to divorce ourselves from the way the economic and cultural apparatus of a society operated. A 'neutral' method meant our own neutrality, or so it seemed '(Apple, 1985).

Therefore, these following questions are made:

1. What is the main goal of Higher Education? Who is supposed to define this goal?
2. Within this goal, what does education quality mean? Who is supposed to evaluate this?

Many of the goals of evaluations results are defined from the evaluative process itself that reflects the authors′ desires. That is, who evaluates and how this person or institution sustains the process already points in a certain direction to the evaluation itself. For Freire (1998), 'pedagogical evaluation of students and professors are becoming progressively more dominated by 'top down' forms of discourse that try to pass themselves off as democratic' (Freire, 1998).

This does not mean to be against the evaluation, a necessary instrument, but 'struggle to grasp the theoretical and practical implications of such evaluations. We must see to what extent they may serve as an instrument for enabling teachers who are critical to put themselves at the service of freedom and not of domestication' (Freire, 1998).

It is very important to understand these relations. An educational plan as the Bologna Declaration must be observed very carefully. Who will define the quality of the education in Europe? If the Declaration expands, who will define quality of the education in the world? How these decisions will be taken? How much each country will participate in the decisions?

The main questions behind all these concerns are: How to evaluate Higher Education Institutions? What are the elements present in Higher Education

Institutions? Whether the education takes place only inside a classroom or elsewhere?

In Brazil, most of the universities and specially the public ones work in three complementary areas: teaching, research (in a specific area) and extension (projects that involves society matters). In the Brazilian Federal Constitution of 1988, in the article 207, it is said that universities should obey 'the principle of indissociability between teaching, researching and extension'. This model is still supported almost after 20 years, because, as the university is not only a service supplier, it should somehow give back to the society the investment once made in it.

However, the same Constitution, in the article 209, gives the private institutions the right only for teaching and points out the State the role of evaluator and the power of veto to courses. Ribeiro (2003) says that teaching is public, mainly because its results must spread throughout society, belonging to the sphere of the right which is potentially universal, and not treated as being a privilege which is limited. Also places the research in the noblest place at the academy. That way, two categories are constituted for the Higher Educational Institutions: the institutions that follow the indissociability principle, mostly public institutions and the ones that focus only on teaching, normally private institutions.

By these means, one quality of a Higher Education Institution cannot be measured only by its classes offered; the researches developed and extension must be considered part of an equation. Indicators such as the Top Industrial Managers Europe (TIME) consider these items. On the other hand these three axes are seriously unbalanced.

Martins (2000), also says that: 'surely no legislation has the capacity to implement a indissociability between teaching activities and research in all areas of a certain institution. The professor by himself will become a researcher or vice-versa' (Martins, 2000). In fact, facing the great development and institutional diversification of university teaching, Martins also reinforces that there is a 'hierarchy of institutions' formed from indicators as 'the quality of teaching offered, the heading of the teaching staff, the scientific capacity installed, the organizing formats of these establishments, the reputation and the social and symbolic recognition of the distinctive establishment they make' (Martins, 2000).

So, with all these questions about national and international matters, how is it possible to assure quality of education? In order to understand this question better in Brazil it is necessary to observe the recent changes more deeply.

The National System of Higher Education Evaluation Model and DCNs

The verification process of education quality in Brazil started on July of 1973, with the first officially divulged document—'The evaluation function of making educational decisions'—by the Ministry of Education on evaluation, written by João Batista Araújo e Oliveira and Mariza Rocha. Since then, countless evaluation projects and researches have been developed and applied.

Currently, in Brazil, Higher Education has been evaluated by the Ministry of Education in the entire country. The National System of Higher Education Evaluation (Sistema Nacional de Avaliação da Educação Superior/SINAES) features a proposal of only one nationwide curriculum, for each Higher Education course. For example, all engineering' courses have one test and all law courses have other test. This system established contents and define the quality of education. When you have just one assessment for the entire country, there is a tendency to standardize the education, as well as the professors' actions.

The SINAES, created in 2004, is managed by an autonomous institution—the Anisio Teixeira National Institute of Educational Research (Instituto Nacional de Estudos e Pesquisas Educacionais Anísio Teixeira/INEP). Goals of SINAES are to:

1. Offer a panorama of quality courses and institutions of undergraduate education in the country;
2. Lead to Higher Education improvement;
3. Provide guidance to the expansion of availability;
4. Promote the social responsibility.

Three evaluation axes guide the National System: the institutions, the courses and the students′ performance. The system is comprised of a series of instruments that are coordinated by the National Commission of Higher Education (Comissão Nacional de Avaliação da Educação Superior/CONAES):

1. Self-evaluation (each institution develop an auto-evaluation process);
2. External evaluation;
3. National Examination of Students′ Performance (Exame Nacional de Desempenho de Estudantes/ENADE);
4. Evaluation of the overall conditions of undergraduation courses (census and registration).

These points, in contrast with some evaluation methods from Higher Education Institutions, do not consider or have considered research and extension vaguely. However, give importance to the three aspects would bring incongruence to a nationwide evaluation, since it would go against most of the private institutions that do not develop research and extension. So, as the institutions evaluations are completely unified, but in institutions that are would be a gap in the evaluation process.

All these data serve, initially, for those who have the greater view of educational quality and to guide the Ministry of Education in the regulation of the courses. In unsatisfactory cases, a commitment between the institution and the Ministry of Education is established, in which goals to overcome the difficulties must be accomplished in a certain period of time. In extreme situations, this Ministry may not register or renew the register of a course or an institution.

For Sousa (2003) the evaluation process has become the way to transform the role of the Federal State in the education public management: the State has been assumed the functions of the legislator and appraiser. Afonso (1998) identifies this kind of public government as the 'Appraiser State', which began in 80´s by neo-conservatives and neo-liberal countries. In these cases, the State chooses a competitive ethos, designed by a social neo-darwinism, importing management strategies from the private sector to the public one. The objectives of these strategies are not concentrated in the learning process but in the educational systems results/products, such as the free market in the capitalism.

University of São Paulo (USP) and Polytechnic School (responsible for the engineering course of USP) have been discussing this issue. On November of 2007, USP has organized an event called Seminar on Subjects Courses of Under Graduation Evaluation at the University of São Paulo. Different unities of the university such as Chemistry, Medicine and Administration Schools have shown their evaluative processes that reflect their unique characteristics. In the discussion; many professors said they are afraid to the adhesion of the institution to SINAES.

In this panorama, it is difficult to establish an evaluation system which not suppresses creativity and freedom. So, how to analyze specific realities in a nationwide scope and guarantee the quality of education?

In 2001, trying to face all these questions, the National Curricular Guidelines (Diretrizes Curriculares Nacionais/DCNs) were established by the Chamber of Higher Education, an agency from the National Counsel of Education of the Ministry of Education. These guidelines have to be observed in the curriculum formation of the Higher Education courses in the entire country. As a result, for each course, a minimum curriculum was created to assure minimum quality for the courses and to enable transferences between Higher Education Institutions. Unfortunately, in many cases, due to the enterprises pressures and the industry necessity for a very specialized workforce, the curricula ended up with too many questionable mandatory disciplines. Maybe this will be a problem to the Bologna Declaration because the definition of a minimum curriculum enables the academic interchange and conflicts between the corporative market and governmental interests.

Thus, such discussions are not separable from the social factors that interact with the educational system. For Apple (1988), education is never a neutral assembly of knowledge that simply appears in the schools daily routine.

The structural and educational contents come from a selective tradition, carried through someone or a group that determines what is legitimate knowledge. This knowledge, in its turn, is generated by the social conflicts that organize and disorganize a nation. Many times, the professors do not recognize these relations, because they do not understand education as being relational, as a product of historical social conflicts, placing themselves 'in a separate compartment, one that does not easily allow interaction with the relations of class, gender and racial power that gives education its social meaning' (Apple, 1988).

In Brazil, the path taken from the DCNs was to make the courses:

1. Less homogeneous due to the trend to decrease their length;
2. Putting into practice ways of learning that contribute to reduce the student evasion rate;
3. Implementation of scientific initiation programmes;
4. Inclusion of ethical and humanistic dimensions involved in professional activity in the curriculum.

The DCNs of the Engineering Courses aim at having a contingent of students with the ability of identifying problems and 'propose solutions that are not only technically correct' (Ministério da Educação, 2001), but that may also be considered 'in it's totality a chain of causes and effects of multiple dimensions' (Ministério da Educação, 2001). However, the formation whose priority is the transmission and absorption of an enormous amount of contents instead of the development of abilities is still the predominant model in the Higher Education Institutions in Brazil.

The curriculum proposed by the DCNs of the Engineering Courses also intend to be more flexible, giving more freedom to the institutions and professors. Meanwhile, the ideal curriculum recommended by the Chamber of Higher Education in the document CNE/CES/1.362/2001 has not been reached yet: 'it goes far beyond the conventional classroom activities and must consider complementary activities, such as scientific and technological initiation, ample academic programmes [...], university extension courses, technical visits, scientific events, besides cultural, social and political activities' (Ministério da Educação, 2001).

At the university scenario in Brazil, the desired course structure pointed out by the DCNs has not become true. The desired course structure has to have a pedagogical project that considers not only learning inside the classroom, but also the intellectual stimulation through the development of individual or group projects, especially those capable of integrating different academic background knowledge.

Unfortunately, most of the engineering courses in Brazil are stuck to established contents (30% of basic and 15% of professional contents), emphasizing only teaching instead of fomenting the connection and balance between the components of the tripod teaching-researching-extension, and propitiating better the development of abilities the future engineer has to present.

Methodology of the Education Evaluation at Polytechnic School

Since 2004, the Polytechnic School of the University of São Paulo (EPUSP), in order to verify the quality of education offered, has been developing an evaluation process entitled Evaluation of Education. EPUSP is a traditional institution in the engineering area, founded in 1893, which has 18 undergraduate courses today, 15 departments, 471 professors, 509 administrative employees and nearly 4700 undergraduate students and over 1700 graduate students.

The Evaluation of Education is similar to the Emancipatory Evaluation, proposed by Saul in 1988 and evaluates only the offered education. The research and the extension are not observed although their relation to teaching can be evaluated. The Emancipatory Evaluation is based on three sources: democratic evaluation; institutional critique and collective creation; participative research (Saul, 2006).

Contrasting the bureaucratic studies presented on North-American programmes, the democratic evaluation recognizes the pluralism of values, of students as well as of professors and of the institution. A horizontal dialog is established between participants in order to make all feel well to present each ones point of view and motivations. In this model, the evaluator has as function intermediate the information's exchange of the schools main people, giving importance to the conceptions and reactions concerning school life. 'The evaluative report does not come with recommendations and the evaluator does not think about the misuse that will be made from the collected data' (Barry Macdonald, 1977).

The institutional critique and the collective creation is the methodology of the Emancipatory Evaluation, composed by three stages:

1. Problematization of a determined reality—searching to identify the significant questions from students and professors;
2. Critical retreat—in which a reflection on the educational practice is developed to improve professors and students' awareness;
3. Actions—establishment of actions coherent to the previous discussions to necessarily expose a politic-pedagogical project (Padilha, 2003) that will lead to the rethinking of the organizational structure and will enable a collective and sympathetic construction.

The participative research is based on Borda's (1981) six methodological principles, treated in his article 'Theoretical Aspects of the Participant Research' of 1980:

1. Authenticity and commitment of the appraiser;
2. Non-application of preconceived ideological principles or ideas;
3. Feedback to the participants of the process;
4. Discussion among the collaborators in order to obtain scientific accuracy on what is done in the evaluation field;
5. Rhythm and action-reflection balance;
6. Employment of modest sciences and dialogue techniques that are useful in difficult situations or where there are few resources.

An important remark must be made about the principles of the participative research. The second item is impossible to make, according to Apple, because all the actions come with ideological principles: education is not neutral.

The Emancipatory Evaluation concepts were very important in the construction of the evaluation applied to EPUSP. The experience obtained from methods of evaluation developed in previous years at the Polytechnic School, the results and changes of the nationwide systems of evaluation, the proposal of SINAES and the consequent proposal of self-evaluation commissions creation, besides the knowledge of the educators' and researchers theories in the educational area, have also contributed to the current evaluation system at the Polytechnic School.

The Evaluation of Education at EPUSP has basically five stages:

1— determination of the classroom representatives (Representante de Classe/ RC);
2— elaboration of an opinion questionnaire;
3— the questionnaire application;
4— compilation of the data and the resulting report;
5— meetings between classroom representatives and professors.

The students, professors and the pedagogical coordinator take part in this process.

The pedagogical coordinator, in this method, is similar to an appraiser. Like in the Emancipatory Evaluation, the appraiser has the responsibility to intermediate the exchange of information among the school's protagonists, and to gather people's conceptions and reactions regarding the schools activity.

So, the students act like protagonists and the pedagogical coordinator coordinates the work in the evaluation process. This coordinator promotes the meetings and assists in the activities with professors and students. The coordinator follows most of methodological principles of Borda in the Emancipatory Evaluation.

1—*Determination of the Classroom Representatives (Representante De Classe/RC)*

The first stage of the Evaluation of Education is related to the way the students participate in the process. At the beginning of the semester, the pedagogical coordinator with help of the professors verifies which student has/have an interest in becoming a RC. As a maximum number of RCs per classroom are not stipulated, all those manifesting an interest can effectively become a one. Thus the process does not constitute an election, but rather a collective agreement among the interested parties. Until 2007, the Evaluation of Education was applied in the first four years of the five-year engineering courses; the meetings and activities, described as follows, are divided by year.

2—*Elaboration of an Opinion Questionnaire*

Afterwards, in the Evaluation of Education, there is the elaboration of an opinion questionnaire after a brief period of problematization. Questions that synthesize results of the meetings with RCs, pedagogical coordinator and teachers, when these problems are considered and questions are developed having in mind the reality of the students. The survey is elaborated by the RCs, contemplating aspects that they may consider relevant to the learning process, such as: professor's teaching skill; teaching material; interdisciplinary and contextualized learning.

The professors can also suggest questions to be included in the questionnaire, which will be incorporated upon acceptance of consensus by the RCs. Just the students' and the professors' significant questions are placed in the questionnaire. The pedagogical issues mediate the debate among students and professors. Every semester, the questionnaire is rediscussed. So, the questions change from time to time, reflecting the necessities and characteristic difficulties of a certain period. Some questions remain over time, for example, the professors' didactics—which may enable the construction of a historical series.

The survey that has been applied at the Polytechnic School comprehends quantitative and qualitative questions. For Saul (1988) when an institution uses only quantitative questions, they treats education as merely a technical process. In this case, the evaluation has as objective only to verify if the daily pre-established goals have been reached. In many cases, the results obtained in the quantitative evaluation are addressed only to the responsible authority of the institution, thus serving as support to school planning, many times disregarding the interests and necessities of the students and professors.

On the other hand, qualitative boarding has the purpose to understand a situation where human beings interact and react with conscious and unconscious behaviour when confronted with different opinions, ideologies and positions. The qualitative evaluation does not aim only at comparing observed and quantified data to take care of pre-established objectives. The contents of qualitative evaluation include opinions of different groups, allowing the participants' understandings.

The Emancipatory Evaluation is based only on qualitative data, characterized by participative and dialogical methods, with open interviews, debates, analysis and observations. In this case, the pedagogical coordinator organizes the evaluative work and promotes dialogue to find a critical analysis by the students and professors concerning the schools problems.

On the evaluation process at EPUSP, both qualitative and quantitative data are considered. Students and professors chose this method. So, the objectives of the processes were not determined directly by the school principals

3—*The Questionnaire Application*

Once the questionnaire is elaborated, the third part of the Evaluation occurs: the application of the survey by RCs to all students after eight weeks' lessons. The RCs also assist their colleagues in filling out the questionnaire in case of doubts. Up to the first semester of 2007 the survey was a sheet of paper, front and verse, in which the student filled in pencil or pen. From the second semester of 2007 on, optic sheets were adopted for the quantitative questions and a blank paper for the qualitative.

4—*Compilation of the Data and the Resulting Report*

After the surveys filling, the fourth part starts. With the assistance of a statistical tool (computer software), the mean, standard deviation e graphs are elaborated. Together with these results, the RCs write an essay for each discipline with the respective classroom, presenting an analysis of the numerical results, comments and suggestions of changes. To write this essay, the RC analyzes the numerical data and qualitative issues, mentioning commentaries from the other students, when necessary.

It is worth pointing out that this process also constitutes a moment of learning for the student who has to express himself, read statistical data and write a composition with cohesion, clearness and coherence. Behaviour aspects are also brought up, for many times the students express criticism strongly and many times unnecessarily that may frustrate a professor. That is the main reason why all compositions are read and criticized by the pedagogical coordinator, which points out a productive way to express all complaints. This action is not a censorship but a way to promote better dialogue between students and professors.

The final resulting reports are comprised of essays and also by the mean grades and standard deviations of the evaluated questions, representing solely the opinions of the students on the education quality of EPUSP. In the first two years, they are handed in to their respective professors by the RCs. From the third year on, the evaluation reports are handed in to the Heads of the Department.

5—Meetings between Classroom Representatives and Professors

The last stage, the meetings between RCs and professors, is the product of the Evaluation of Education: the dialogue in the meetings is the main result of this process. In these meetings, the information is discussed and a plan of action is taken. As in the self-evaluation at SINAES, in these meetings the professors' and the students' self-reflection is stimulated. Prompt actions can be taken immediately, modifying the teaching method during the semester. Therefore, the following actions from this evaluation do not necessarily constitute, as in the Emancipatory Evaluation, a politician-pedagogical project, however they do not escape of being part of one.

The Evaluation of Education of EPUSP, different from the Emancipatory Evaluation, uses a qualitative approach, aimed at understanding a situation, such as a quantitative one, that is important for the decision making by school management. This process is repeated every semester, presenting continuity and transformation, accumulating experience of past years without hindering the implementation of new questions.

In 2004, the Education Evaluation was applied only to the first year students at the EPUSP. The evaluation has been advancing each year in the engineering course. In 2006, only part of the third year had been evaluated, and in 2007, the first four years were evaluated.

The participation of 1st year students is already stable around 70 per cent and there is an expectation of similar behaviour with other years' students. The fluctuation of the amount of questionnaires filled out has been due to professors' resistance and mistrust in helping to apply the questionnaires in some disciplines. During the process, with constructive dialogues, this panorama has changed.

With the obtained evaluation data it is possible to notice some particular aspects of EPUSP and others that may be discussed in a global way. One question raised in the last years was the lack of conceptualization in the first year's disciplines of the under graduation course. This aspect could be a specific problem of the curriculum at EPUSP. Another polemic question was the docent evaluations made by the government and private institutions. In most of these evaluations the professor is evaluated only by the research (papers, participation in Congress, guidance of masters and doctors). This is a very common theme in worldwide discussions and may be treated that way since this matter has been approached in scientific seminars and specialized publications.

These aspects are very important and show the impact of the evaluation process, promoting debates and actions to assure the quality of education, respecting the characters of the institution. Besides, they open questions to other universities, countries and educational research groups. In the next sections the lack of conceptualization and the docent evaluation will be discussed.

The Problem of the Lack of Contextualization—A Specific Issue

In 2006, with three-year experience in data collecting, recurrent subjects that indicated bigger problems at EPUSP courses started to appear. One of the biggest problems was the lack of contextualization of the two first year disciplines, such as Calculus, Physics and Chemistry among others, as it was verified in the meetings between RCs and professors. The students mentioned that they feel a lack of approach in the contents of these disciplines with engineering. At the same time they perceived the importance of this theoretical basis. They believe that if professors were able to relate the theory with its application, it would be more motivating for learning and would stimulate greater participation with the students in class.

This factor appeared initially in 2004, when it was noted that in some questions of some of the disciplines, the students expressed dissatisfaction, as are shown in the results of the questions below:

A—'were the frequency of the lessons important for your learning? (0=irrelevant 10=essential)';

B—'Independent from your result on the test, do you feel that you are learning? (0=no 10=yes)'.

These questions were on the questionnaire of the 1st semester of 2004, for the first year's students. The result generated many discussions. At that time it was not possible to diagnose what was not motivating the student, but the questionnaire data have been registered and the process has continued.

In 2005, before the questionnaires application for the students of the 1st year, in the 1st semester, in meetings with the pedagogical coordinator the RCs had already commented the dissatisfaction of the students with some disciplines. Then, the following question was included to verify the students interest on studies:

C—'On an average, how many hours per week have you studied outside the classroom?'

The results of the evaluation show that the problem remains. Disciplines evaluated poorly in 2004 continued to have bad grades.

In other debates, colloquies with the head management and internal commissions of the EPUSP, it was concluded that there was no clarity of intentions in some basic disciplines. Some School professors understood that these disciplines had to display in their curriculum examples of relations between the taught content and applications in engineering, while others thought that the first two year's disciplines had to deal only with the basic concepts, without presenting them application. Without a consensus, the professors who teach basics disciplines, from other institutes out of the Polytechnic School, gave the lessons without showing the application of concepts in engineering.

To evidence the fact, in the 1st semester of 2006 the second year students proposed this question:

D—'Are you able to perceive the relations between the taught content and its application in engineering? (0=I do not perceive relation 10=I perceive relation)'.

From the results and discussions in the meetings it was perceived the importance for students that professors explain, when possible, the application of basic knowledge in the given discipline in the first years, to transform the lesson into a more stimulating content, leading to a greater participation and application.

This aspect was not raised by the RCs of the 1st year of the 1st semester of 2006. The RCs had commented that in that year the professors had already started to show applications of engineering in their lessons, which not necessarily meant that the problem was totally solved. Every year, new professors took classes at EPUSP, and in this rotation it is possible that the class reverted to not having explanations on the applications of basic concepts. A greater resultant action of the dialogues would be a curricular change in a way the course became more motivating for the students.

To sort out these questions, the committee responsible for the first two years of the under graduation course, with the support of the EPUSP Director's office has created a group composed with teachers of several years to discuss the theme. One of the solutions discussed was the elaboration of a 'text-book' of contextualization character, complementary to the bibliography recommended for each discipline. This material is expected to be used in 2009 as didactic support for the disciplines. It is worth pointing out that this work in particular, has been made with no orientation from the DCN's, with no comments on whether the basic disciplines must contextualize their contents.

Perhaps the contextualization is a specific problem of engineering or only of the EPUSP. But this diagnostic is impossible to be implemented as a nationwide evaluation, equal in all courses in all places. Other factors have been also discussed in meetings. A great majority of these factors is specific to the nature of the course. The Evaluation of Education allows us to go into the details of the problem, solving specific problems and generating professors' and students' self-reflection.

Docent Evaluation—A General Issue

As well as evaluating the offered teaching and learning process, the EPUSP has the interest in discussing about a docent evaluation that considers both research productivity indicators and Evaluation of Education. There is a need for an evaluation method that can qualify the professors in both categories, once there are teaching evaluations and ways of measuring the professor's scientific productivity, but shy initiatives to evaluate both and inexistent ones that consider the tripod.

All the process of the EPUSP Evaluation of Education enables an analysis related to the quality of the teaching institution, but it does not consider the research and extension developed by professors. According to Leta and Cruz (2003) in the last 20th century, governments and researchers have organized studies to evaluate the scientific activities and technology in different levels of complexity.

To verify how much a research interferes in the professors´ teaching activities, a research was developed in parallel with the Evaluation of Education. The research, presented at ICEE 2007 (Rodrigues, Pontes & Silva, 2007), treated the analysis from a total of 95 professors who taught at the school, most of them taught the basic subjects common to the first years. In this sample, there are not only professors from Polytechnic School, but also from the institutes that have participation in the formation of the engineering students, such as: the Institute of Physics, the Institute of Mathematics and the Institute of Chemistry.

This analysis was done in two parts: the data obtained from the Evaluation of Education; development of research, data obtained from the *lattes curriculum.*

The first part of the research analyzed the data collected from about 1500 undergraduate students from the first three under graduation years who answered the Evaluation of Education of the EPUSP in 2006. The students answered with natural numbers to the following questions:

1. Grade to your professor's didaction (from 0=very bad to 10=excellent)
2. Grade to your professor's commitment to the student (from 0=very bad to 10= excellent)
3. Grade to your own (student) commitment in relation to the discipline. (from 0= I am not committed to 10= I am very committed)
4. On average, how many hours per week have you studied outside the classroom? (Including works, reports, etc.)?
5. Do you think the test evaluated well the content taught in class? (from 0= no to 10= yes).'—Test applied to the student by the professor to verify the learned knowledge.
6. Is the recommended teaching material appropriate to the discipline needs? (from 0=it is not appropriate to 10= well suited)

In Table 16.1(Rodrigues, Pontes & Silva, 2007), it is possible to observe the proximity between the average and the medium of the questions mentioned before.

Table 16.1: Medium and Averages of the Teaching Evaluation Indicators

Question	*Average*	*Medium*
1	6.69	6.8
2	7.24	7.4
3	6.65	6.8
4	7.16	7.5
5	6.16	7.0
6	6.59	6.6

The second step of this research is a documental one: data obtained from the *lattes curriculum*, a database of academic *curricula vitae* published on the Internet by the National Council for Scientific and Technological Development (CNPq), a foundation linked to the Ministry of Science and Technology. The following data were taken from each professor:

1. Gender;
2. How long s/he has been in the career;
3. Degree (masters, doctorate or post doctorate);
4. Number of concluded supervisions (scientific initiation, undergraduate researches, master and doctorate);
5. Bounds to CNPq through the supporting programme 'productivity scholarship' which aims to distinguish the researcher by valuing his/her scientific production;
6. The number of scientific papers published according to the Qualis classification of journals, newspapers, magazines and conferences publications, a result of the rank made by the Coordination of Higher Education Workers' Improvement (Coordenação de Aperfeiçoamento de Pessoal de Nível Superior/CAPES), and a partition from the Ministry of Education that evaluates the national production on graduate level.

The *Qualis* is the result of a classificatory process of the publications used by the under graduation courses to divulgate the intellectual production of its professors and students. This process was conceived by the CAPES to meet to specific needs of the evaluation system and is based on the information given by its programmes and Collected Data base, that is constantly available at CAPES website.

The classification is made or coordinated by a representative of each area of knowledge in the country and goes under an annual process to be updated. The means of divulgation listed before by the under graduation programmes are categorized in terms of quality—A, B or C and towards the considered circulation of these—local, national and international. The combination of these categories composes nine alternatives of importance to the publication, and by interference of the published paper itself.

The research data was analyzed using descriptive statistics, with techniques of frequency analysis, as well as inferential statistics, exploratory factorial analysis and discriminating Kruskal Wailis analysis, using the software SPSS version 13.1. The variables tested were: scientific productivity, Evaluation of Education and concluded supervisions. The categorical or nominal variables were: gender, CNPq scholarship, degree, and career time.

Before comparing data from Evaluation of Education process with research productivity, some questions must be answered. One activity of research productivity is near the educational action. The supervisions happened in a relation between students and professors. The learning occurred could enlighten other questions. So, are the professors with scholarship the ones with greater productivity and number of concluded supervisions.

As to this question, that is, if professors that receive the scholarship from the research-promoting programme, have greater scientific productivity or more concluded supervisions compared to the others, the fact that the research support is an important factor to the development of science can be observed.

By the Mann-Whitney statistical test, it is possible to observe that the professors with the scholarship have greater scientific productivity and have supervised more students (Rodrigues, Pontes & Silva, 2007).

The results show small differences. Another question is necessary to clarify this matter. Are the professors who produced more and have more supervision concluded the ones with higher degrees?

As to the second question, if the highest qualified professors have greater scientific productivity and more concluded supervisions, this relation proved to be positive, that is, the highest qualified professors have supervised more students and produced more since 2001 (Rodrigues, Pontes & Silva, 2007).

Again, the difference is small. In fact, highest qualified professors have worst results than other above doctorates. With these results, it possibly create a hypotheses, but to dissolve the question, a third question must be made. Are the scientific productivity indicators related to the professor's teaching and didactic quality?

As to the third question, if more productive professors and the ones with more concluded supervisions would obtain better or worse teaching evaluation grades, the Mann Whitney test did not show any statistically significant differences. Showing a lack of relation between teaching and researching criteria.

When trying to establish differences between teaching skills of professors that publish more and supervise more undergraduate and graduate students three questions related to teaching skills from the survey answered, received special attention, these questions were:

1. the one where the student had to grade his/her professor's didactic;
2. the professor's commitment to the discipline;
3. if the student thinks he/she is learning the subject.

The means were made for the teachers with different degrees and teachers with or without the productivity scholarship from CNPq, since the professors that have a degree above doctorate and professors with the scholarship are the ones with greater productivity and number of supervisions concluded. (See mean ranks on Table 16.2 and Table 16.3).

Table 16.2: Mean Ranks

	CNPq Scholarship	*Mean Rank*
Scientific Productivity	No	44.06
	Yes	56.97
Concluded Supervisions	No	43.70
	Yes	57.67

Table 16.3: Scientific Productivity and Concluded Supervisions

	Degree	*Mean Rank*
Scientific Productivity	Doctor	42.32
	Above doctor	57.93
Concluded Supervisions	Doctor	43.54
	Above doctor	56.07

This leads to the conclusion that the teaching skill do not vary in accordance with researching skill therefore, the variables of teaching quality must be different from those of productivity and research quality (Rodrigues, Pontes & Silva, 2007).

Table 16.4: Teaching Grades Means and Standard Deviation for Professors with Different Degrees

Professor's Degree		*Professor's Didactics*	*Professor's Commitment*
Doctorate	Mean	6.942	7.526
	Standard Deviation	1.7016	1.3656
Above Doctorate	Mean	6.124	6.747
	Standard Deviation	1.6607	1.5327

Table 16.5: Teaching Grades Means and Standard Deviation for Professors with or without the Productivity Scholarship

CNPq Scholarship		*Professor's Didactics*	*Professor's Commitment*
No	Mean	6.827	7.410
	Standard Deviation	1.7419	1.4915
Yes	Mean	6.215	6.848
	Standard Deviation	1.6422	1.3998

It may be observed that the professor's evaluation as it is done nowadays, using only or almost only research indicators, does not show correlation with the teaching-quality indicators. That may lead to the conclusion that the principle of indissociability between teaching and researching in the Brazilian university, as mentioned before, cannot be implemented simply by legislation.

Conclusions

In the evaluation system developed at the EPUSP, it is possible to identify specific and general problems. Through dialogue as a result of data analysis from the questionnaires, professors and students participate actively in decisions at the school, by contributing with their personal desires, live experience and motivates for the course improvement. This dialogue generates a collective conscience about the importance of discussion and educational changes, resulting in researches and actions that can modify the educational structure of the institution.

The Evaluation of Education at EPUSP allows educational activities to function dynamically and democratically. These are important factors because an engineering course tends to adjust frequently due to the technological changes in society and the students and professors participate in the evaluation process. And these alterations remain as responsibility of the protagonists of the institution and not of the government, promoting society's participation and diminishing the possible imposition of established models.

The maturation of the students who had been RCs and the increase of dialogue between them and professors were visible in the four years of application of this evaluation. The RCs nowadays participate in many extracurricular activities such as, commissions' representatives at the Polytechnic School, international interchange programmes, scientific initiation, student's movement and others. This singular behaviour might be considered only a reflection of a previous cause, but it can also be consequence of the work carried through.

Another interesting factor is that the professors are closer to the students, listen more and interact more with the school administration. Also, becoming more critical and demanding about the improvements at the Polytechnic School. It is already common to see in the very first week of the term, that some professors demanding RCs. Professors and RCs are organizing some activities outside the classroom, such as technical visits, in order to identify the most motivating external activities for a determined classroom or type of students.

The results of the evaluation, its consequent reflections and actions are also very significant. The changes in the first years' disciplines resulting in more contextualized contents bring a new kind of education methodology. This experience might provoke a chain reaction in other disciplines, promoting the auto-reflection in the professors and the creation of new educational methods. The discussion of the professor's role shows the actual problems and a rethink about the evaluation criteria established by the government and private institutions. A new professor's career development is necessary to change the education in the entire country.

The Evaluation of Education process generated parameters by the discussion about the professor's and university's roles, in a general view. Diagnosing the lack of integration between teaching and research skills, it is possible to foment the university body to get conscience of the relation university-society. Teaching, research and extension are Brazilians universities goals but there is not an evaluation process that demands improvement in these three areas at the same time.

Finally, the evaluation system of the EPUSP respects the identity of the institution and it has already represented an advance in the sense of considering more than the teaching skills. May be this kind of treatment should be implemented to verify the quality in other institutions. This way one can improve quality education and allow students transferences among schools and universities.

17

A New Way to Teach Mathematics in Engineering

New Challenges, New Approaches

Alonso Félix, Rodríguez Gerardo and *Villa, Agustín De La*

The tailoring of the structure of different university studies to the European Higher Education Area (EHEA), an objective forthcoming from the Bologna Declaration, is the major task outstanding in Europe's different university systems. The reform affects not only the structure of university studies, but furthermore leads to European-wide reflection on the suitability of the syllabuses in mathematics subjects and, of greater importance, on the manner in which mathematics is taught. It is now no longer possible to uphold the same approach to teaching mathematics as fifty years ago and classrooms should reflect the technological revolution that has occurred in recent decades.

Taking into account this new frame in which we must develop our teaching activity, it is necessary to reconsider the role of mathematics in engineering schools. It is evident that mathematics will continue fulfilling a double objective in the new university frame. In one hand they will continue being a powerful formative tool and on the other hand they will continue being the support and background of other academic disciplines. Therefore a mathematical basic background will be essential in the new frame of acquisition of competencies. And the methodological changes affect, in an essential way, to the mathematical topics. Let's not forget that, at least in Spain, the trend is from an eminently face to face teaching to a mixed teaching, in which the student, under the supervision of the instructor, must acquire new knowledge across his/her own activity. With this panorama, it is necessary to highlight the importance of e-learning and b-learning techniques in the new academic configuration. Initially the situation is complicated since inertia exists among some mathematics teachers. They try to avoid the deep change inherent to the new system, and prefer to continue with the traditional system of education. In our opinion, it will not be possible.

In this chapter, attempt has been made to present new tools, forthcoming from the European projects Building a European database of mathematical e-learning modules (dMath)[6] and European Virtual Laboratory of Mathematics (EVLM)[4], within the Leonardo da Vinci Programme, which will undoubtedly be an extremely useful tool in favour of the content and methodology review that European society requires. It is convincing that only with the collaborative work between mathematical communities is possible to assume the change that is arriving. Former experiences in this area are well-prominent. These projects, joined to the use of didactic materials, mainly textbooks adapted to our students[8, 9, 10] and the adequate use of CAS[1, 7, 11, 12, 15] will supply a good cocktail to be offered to our students.

The European Higher Education Area: A New Teaching Scenario

In order to find a global understanding of this new paradigm of European university teaching means, we must first outline certain features of the European area that are currently being designed[4, 14]:

- A competency-based teaching offer. Then we can plan and select the mathematical contents for specific students, engineers for example.
- A diversified teaching offer (theoretical and practical teaching, supervised academic activities, independent individual work and so on).
- Concern for the student's overall work, as opposed to the current system in which the only measurement in certain European countries, such as Spain, is the lecture's hours given in the classroom. This work should have a maximum annual volume estimated in 60 European credits (European Credit Transfer System, ECTS). An initial estimate suggests that one ECTS credit is equal to 25-30 hours of student work, including class attendance, laboratories, workshops, individual and group tutorials, individual or group work and assessments.
- Prevalence of student's learning over the lectures provided by teachers.
- Duration of studies that is more adapted to reality.

The demands on the teaching staff, stemming from the European-wide policy of harmonising higher education studies, are basically as follows:

- Teachers should teach things with added value in the labour market (competencies).
- Teachers should adopt a different approach to teaching (methodological innovation).
- The basic criteria for the planning and development of teaching should be students and their needs (students as a referent).

All this involves a greater dedication from teachers to a student's learning process, which should include the teaching hours, planning, material preparation, suggested lines of work, guidance and supervision and, in general, overseeing the student's entire learning process.

This whole situation requires teachers to take special care when planning the following aspects:

1. The competencies that students will acquire individually within the context of the total offer of competencies that are taught in the subject in question.
2. The academic scenarios in which the teacher wants the learning to take place, referring to specialized classrooms (computer rooms, laboratories, audiovisual rooms, etc.), to libraries and other documentation centres, provided that the students can proceed independently within them. In addition, the proper use of e-learning can contribute to the learning process, taking into account:
   - The working process to be followed by the student for the acquisition of these competencies.
   - The system of tutoring-supervision that the teacher has adopted to control the acquisition of competencies on the part of students.
3. The system for assessing the competencies acquired by the student on an independent basis. Assessment criteria should be put in place accordingly (results expected in each stage and overall results of the process) and the evidence regarding each criteria (data collected, generated reports, etc.) liable to assessment, the assessment tools and the assessment dates.

The teacher will be required to provide students with material, deliver lectures, set supervised work or problems, arrange different kinds of tests, use the latest technologies to a greater or lesser extent, etc., in order to generate the number of working hours corresponding to the credits assigned, which are furthermore to be controlled in an effective manner[7].

What to do with Mathematics?

Any University curriculum should be governed by the following two principles:

1. The University must guarantee a supply to its students of the knowledge that will be demanded of them upon their integration into the job market. Consequently, University programmes must adapt themselves to the current needs of society.
2. The training of University students must be scientific and students must receive knowledge in advance of what society will demand of them from a purely formal point of view.

Accordingly, mathematics will continue to be necessary within the basic training of the different types of engineer that European society will need in the future.

It should first be noted that the teaching of mathematics in engineering schools should allow students to acquire sufficient skills to be able to analyse and encounter the best solutions to a given problem as a function of the context within which they will be moving in their later professional lives. The ability to find the 'best' solution of a given problem necessarily passes through being able to analyse all the issues involved in a given phenomenon, physical or economic, such that the acquisition of this skill will necessarily involve the use of mathematics as a practical tool and as part of the way in which students are taught to think about such problems.

Before addressing the change in contents and the methodological change, we must ask ourselves again about the role to be played by mathematics in the training of engineers.

The principles referred to above mark the route to be followed in University teaching, particularly in the field of mathematics. Thus, mathematics should not be isolated from the rest of the sciences but should form an integrating system of several different systems. Only if this aim is achieved, it will be possible to consolidate the mission of the University in society in general; that is, as an innovator of knowledge, thereby preventing scientific and technical stagnation.

To achieve this objective the following guidelines are necessary:

(i) The level of knowledge received through University teaching should allow students to adopt a critical and creative stance when they face with a given problem; it should offer them the necessary reasoning tools (skills) for the solution to such problems. A narrowness of view in the transmission of knowledge could become a severe disease in University teaching.

(ii) Learning the answer to a problem does not provide an intelligent idea of the process of solution since some step will always be overlooked and this will lead to the generation of several questions. The student identifies this step when reflecting on how the solution to the problem is arrived at. Thus, teaching should promote student's criteria, should foster their ability to reason, and should lead them to be able to handle different theories and methods, motivating them to accept or reject them on the basis of such reasoning.

(iii) Scientific advances demand from students the capacity to recycle their knowledge as time progresses and at the same time demand a solid basic training. This should be an objective to be sought. This very dynamic scheme of continuing education means that students must have a sound training in their respective disciplines. Thus, computers may be of great help in this recycling process.

(iv) There is an urgent need to provide teaching with a suitable framework of knowledge, since new contributions to overall human knowledge grow daily and their applications are diverse and complex.

Accordingly, instructors must be in possession of an overall understanding of the subject and of the potential applications of the material taught. With this, it would be possible to make a complete programme that would gather together training and compilation, thus imparting the content of the syllabus selectively and with conceptual depth.

This implies the following:

(i) The instructor must teach mathematics bearing in mind that for his/her students mathematical subjects are a means, but not an end, to their studies. In sum, mathematics is a **service subject**.

(ii) In maths subjects, a field survey should first be carried out to know which parts of mathematics are required and then these should be transmitted in a training-informative way.

(iii) A different type of mathematics should be taught for each science, since their demands differ. Even the same topics should be explained and discussed in different ways, depending on the audience that receives them (this is not usually the case in current study plans since, for example, 'almost' the same mathematics are taught in all engineering studies, without differentiating their particularities). A **functional** edifice should be constructed, with solid mathematical bases.

Without a good teaching strategy, students may arrive at the mistaken idea that mathematics has been introduced in their studies as a kind of 'barrier' of no ulterior use. In general, this strategy involves teaching how to analyse a given situation in abstract terms; that is, modelling a situation. For modelling, three aspects are crucial:

1. Formulation of the problem in mathematical terms. To reach this formulation it is necessary to have an in-depth knowledge of the physical or economic stratum underlying the problem to be solved. In this phase, the mathematical model best suitable to the problem is chosen; that is the appropriate variables are taken and the mathematical problem to be solved is posed. One of the difficulties encountered on passing from the problem to the appropriate language is the need to carry out simplifications of the original problem and here is where it is necessary to discriminate with certainty the magnitudes that may be neglected and those that must be taken into account.
2. Solution of the mathematical model. In this step, the application of mathematics is considered in the most direct sense, together with the theory that will allow that application to be implemented correctly. Then the most appropriate technique known must be applied to solve the problem in question, often with numerical methods.

3. Interpretation and analysis of obtained results. To lend sense to everything that has been carried out, the results should be interpreted through knowledge of the physical or economic problem it is wished to model, contrasting to see whether the results obtained are compatible with the model and with the hypotheses made about it. If the results are not in agreement, the model must be restated.

The different steps are showing in the figure 17.1

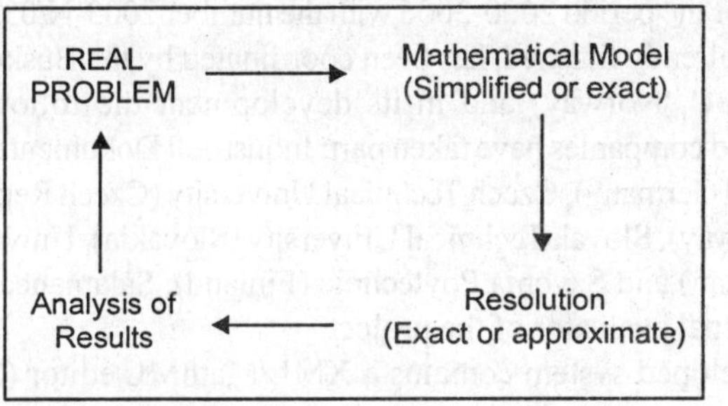

Figure 17.1: Steps

Seeing the characteristics of the EHEA and the aforementioned demands on teachers, certain changes, sometimes of a drastic nature, are required in the traditional approach to teaching. The changes required do not only affect syllabuses, stemming from weaker initial grounding, but in general affect the knowledge of mathematics acquired in the pre-university stages. This is highlighted by different European-wide reports, such as the PISA report, and there is also a need to embrace a methodological change that will allow the addressing of students' new learning needs. The use of the entire potential provided by new technologies applied to teaching may lead to reconsideration of the organisation of different teaching groups, adapting their size to the possibilities of the different computer rooms[15].

Finally, the assessment process need to be changed, seeking mechanisms that assess the whole learning process. New technologies are once again the key instrument, allowing the introduction of well-designed self-assessment processes, guided practical sessions, etc.

To implement all this methodological changes, it becomes indispensable to produce new didactic material to be used by the students in different situations of learning. New material is not reduced to upload the traditional materials and nice power-point presentations on the net. We have to include electronic material, to promote the use of Computer Algebra Systems, on line tutorials, etc. This material will be used according the student's personal needs, it must enhance the mathematical competences and to promote the collaborative work.

In this frame, we will expose the main characteristics of two new European projects that affect in the creation of new didactic materials, providing new tools in the sense mentioned previously. Both projects are focused on the production of new didactic materials to cover the formative needs of our students in the frame of EHEA.

The DMATH Project

A database containing different mathematical modules for the e-learning education has been the main goal of the DMath project[4], financed by Leonardo da Vinci programme for the period 2000-2006 with the number 2003-N/03/B/PP-165.011. This project, already finished, has been coordinated by the Buskerud University Collage (HIBU, Norway) and in its development the following academic institutions and companies have taken part: Industriell Dokumentasjon (Norway), Soft4Science (Germany), Czech Technical University (Czech Republic), Sogndal College (Norway), Slovak Technical University (Slovakia), University Pontificia Comillas (Spain) and Savonia Poytechnic (Finland). Salamanca University has been the external evaluator of the project.

The developed system contains a XML/MathML editor (Sciwriter is the commercial name), the database or data repository (with the working title 'SciLAS System') that is made up from a number of independent modules, each of them containing different files (also known as Reusable Learning Objects), that can be downloaded individually by users of the system, a content management system (Orange) and the package SCORM to download the selected files of the different modules to the local system. User's friendliness is ensured by the interface and the fact that each module will be supported by illustrations and interactive animations in order to visualise the module's content for the user. The mathematical calculations in the modules are done with the Xmath Calculator.

The users of the system are not limited to educational world. Private companies, educational institutions and public offices connected to the education sector could use the different modules in a different way. However the system will also be open to users such as publishers, research scientists, engineers, etc. The database will be an 'evolutionary system' that will be developed by the users, i.e. the users will be able to modify the existing modules and also to create entirely new modules. DMath information can be found at: http://dmath.hibu.no/main.htm.

The different mathematical modules drawn up cover a large part of the mathematical topics in Engineering Schools: Linear Algebra, Calculus in one and several variables, Ordinary Differential Equations, Numerical Methods, Statistics, Modelling, etc.

SciWriter, scientific editor designed for Soft4science, easily allows generating, using menu bars, scientific documents in different formats, especially the ones with the extension.xml[13]. Figure 17.2 shows part of one of

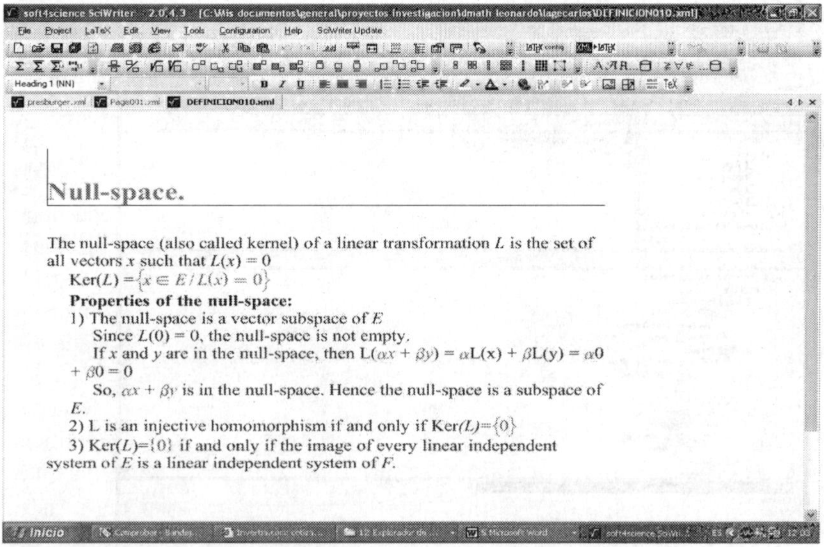

Figure 17.2: Sciwriter Document

the documents created using SciWriter, with the upper menu bars revealing the wide range of options provided by its use.

The database contains mathematical independent modules. It is necessary to do a clear distinction in the modules' author way of working and of the potential users. From the author's point of view, has been divided the content in small units, atoms, to be assembled afterwards in different ways. Different paragraphs: theory, examples, exercises, problems, applications, tests, exercises with web-Mathematica, etc. had been considered.

By assembling atoms we form the molecules that can be used in different modules or units to be offered to the users.

By assembling atoms and molecules in different ways, the users can create their own documents according to the needs and the goals to be reached. Consequently, the versatility is very big and allows adapting to different needs, being able to develop courses with different levels of depth and generating documents to refresh contents, or doing self evaluation, showing applications, etc. The database is organized so that the system is simple to handle. The database structure is shown in figure 17.3. A colours code indicates in every moment the situation of different documents of the unit.

- The padlock symbol indicates that the atom or molecule is in the database and that it can be exported by SCORM, but cannot be modified.
- The green colour indicates that the atom can be published.
- The red colour indicates that the atom is in use and can not be used by other users.

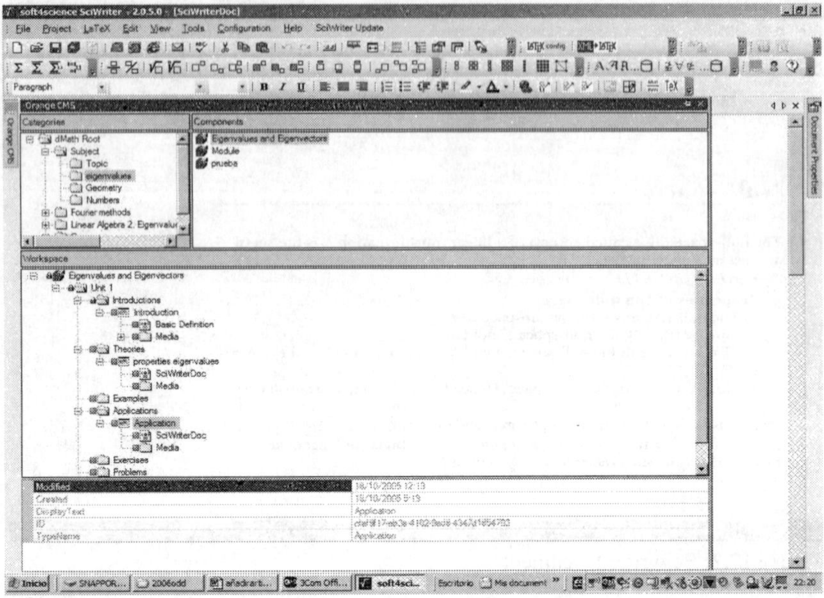

Figure 17.3: Database

- The yellow colour indicates that the file is actually being created by the author and it has not been placed in the database.

Users can select what they like from every unit. The command Export has to be used for it and after that select the atoms/molecules that must appear in the designed unit. Hereby it is possible to adapt and use the documents according to the needs to be covered.

The students have used several modules according to their needs: For example in eigenvalues and eigenvector modules three different possibilities are offered:

- A **theoretical module**, including definitions, propositions, etc. Also selected examples have been chosen. This module has been useful for students in a Linear Algebra Course for enhancing the theoretical aspects of spectral theory.
- A **review module:** In this module only the main theoretical results have been included. The main goal has been to refresh concepts in Spectral theory.
- An **application module**: Several applications have been shown, for example: Leontief models, dynamical systems, Google search algorithm, etc.

One picture after exporting the selected concepts, using SCORM, is shown in the figure 17.4.

All the material developed in the project has been done in English. Though the language should be an aspect without influence for the utilization of the system, the tests carried out among our students reveals the difficulty to use non Spanish material. An idiomatic barrier appears for our students when using this material and this aspect could be the main handicap of this project. It is possible that the following project helps to remedy this fault.

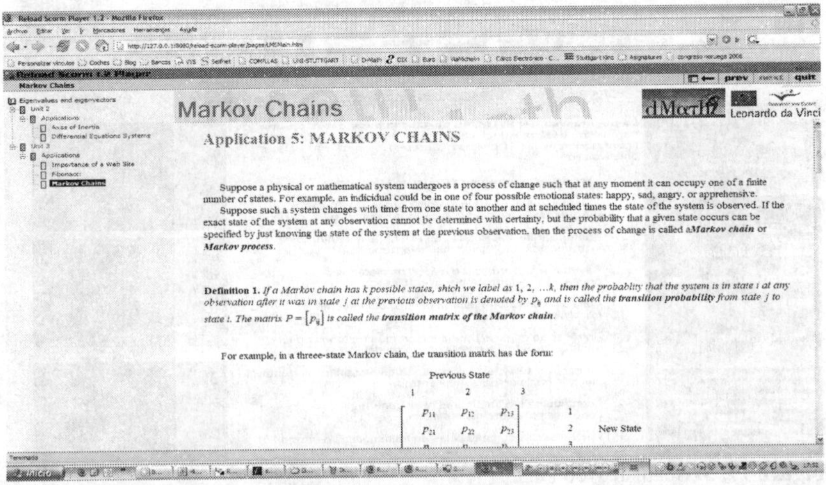

Figure 17.4: An Application Module

All the material developed in the project has been done in English. Though the language should be an aspect without influence for the utilization of the system, the tests carried out among our students reveals the difficulty to use non Spanish material. An idiomatic barrier appears for our students when using this material and this aspect could be the main handicap of this project. It is possible that the following project helps to remedy this fault.

The EVLM Project

The development of an **European Virtual Laboratory of Mathematics** and a Mathematical Centre, which allows the different European users to come in and search for expertise help for different mathematical problems that could arise both in the academic area and in the professional life, are the main goals of the project European Virtual Laboratory of Mathematics (EVLM) [6], also financed by the programme Leonardo da Vinci for the period 2006-2008 with the number 2006-SK/06/B/F/PP-177436. This project is coordinated by the Slovak Technical University (Slovakia) and the following academic institutions are involved: Plodivski University (Bulgaria), Salamanca University (Spain), Tilossilos Ltd. (Finland), Miskolc University (Hungary), University of Limerick (Ireland), Slovak Society for Geometry and Graphics (Slovakia), Coventry University (England) and University of West Bohemia (Check Republic).

In this case, besides the official page of the project being in English, each of the institutions participating in the project has designed its National web page. The Spanish webpage can be found in http://evlmspain.usal.es/ and the front page is shown in the figure 17.5.

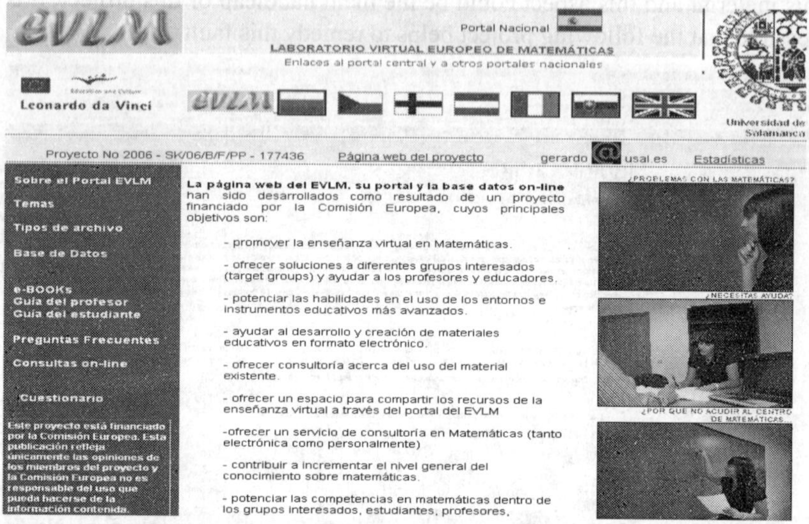

Figure 17. 5: Spanish Web Page

The basic idea of this project is the development of the EUROPEAN VIRTUAL LABORATORY OF MATHEMATICS that will include a net of National Mathematical Centres located in the associate institutions. The EVLM's aim is to promote a better understanding of mathematical topics to be used in other disciplines, with a big component of mathematical background. The home page of central portal (in English) can be shown in the figure 17.6.

Every National Centre will develop a site (in the corresponding language) that will offer a virtual database with information about mathematical resources of virtual learning, elaborated by the partners and other sources (as previous projects financed by the European Union). Besides, the National Centres will offer a consultation service to those who want to know the new results in mathematics and in mathematical teaching.

The EVLM's target groups are:

- Students in a general way (from Secondary School up to PHD degrees). The elaborated resources will be available to get a better understanding of mathematical topics.
- Teachers and instructors. In the EVLM they will find resources for virtual education, the basic handbooks of their use and additional material.

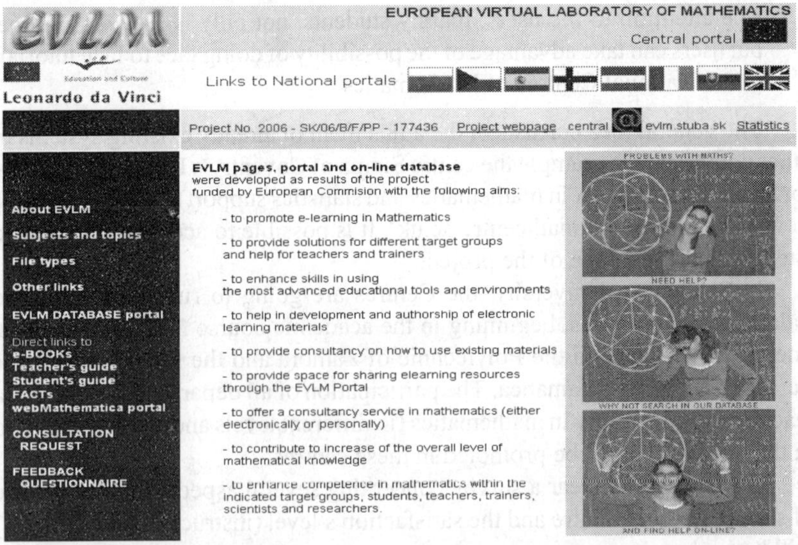

Figure 17.6: Central Portal

- Researchers and scientists not belonging to academic areas. The EVLM will adapt and refresh the advanced mathematical tools necessary for the development of their work.

The final aims of the project are the following ones:

- To develop a catalogue of learning available materials in Mathematics.
- To establish a centralized database that could offer information and links on the catalogued resources.
- To offer an expert service of consultancy (face to face and on line) about the use of these materials.
- To promote the spreading and use of these resources offering the material's translation to the principal languages of the European Union.
- To offer an opportunity to the educational institutions to share with other European institutions the educational materials developed specifically for their purposes (often using funds of European programmes).

It is necessary to remark that EVLM has two fundamental differences respect the previous project DMath:

- The produced materials will be available not only in English, but also they will be in other languages such as Spanish, Slovak, etc., which allows a more comfortable use of the didactic materials for instructors and students.

- The attention to the users, mainly students, not only is realized on-line, but users can take advantage of the possibility of doing face to face tutorials in the National Centres of Mathematics.

The general idea consists of the adjustment of already existing systems of other countries, for example the centre Sigma of Coventry's University (Centre for excellence SIGMA in mathematics and statistics support), that it is possible to visit in http://www.mathcentre.ac.uk/. It is possible to access to the quoted site from the web page of the project.

In Salamanca University, the Centres are going to run in Zamora and Salamanca's campuses, beginning in the academic course 2007-08. The first one of them will be in the Polytechnic of Zamora and the second one in the Science Faculty of Salamanca. The participation of all departments that have a teaching responsibility in mathematics (in different levels and studies imparted in the university) will be promoted in these centres.

During the first year a survey concerning several aspects such as the use of services of this Centre and the satisfaction's level (instructors and students) will be analysed.

18
Clients in Student Software Engineering Projects

Juha Taina

Learning software engineering processes, practices, and methods requires more than classrooms. A fairly realistic software engineering project covering all phases of software development is an important asset of software engineering education. Even a small project can be a very enlightening experience to inexperienced students. In a project students will learn both about the system to be built and about project work more than what could be taught to them in a classroom.

To a certain extent, a software engineering project should be executed in an external real-world environment: in a software company. Yet, in a pure external environment the supervisors of student projects are not teachers. This may affect the learning experience of the project. From the learning point of view, perhaps the optimal solution is to have the projects in a controlled educational environment with real-world clients from software companies.

A good software engineering project offers student's means to learn essential aspects of project work, a chance to practice using software engineering tools and techniques, and especially a safe experience of software engineering without financial risks or schedule overruns. Yet the project cannot be too safe, since safety affects project realism. A 100 per cent safe project is a toy project.

It is fact that students must be allowed to control the project, while professors and other faculty members have as little control over the project as possible but still have means to coach the students when they need it. With this approach the students have a feeling that they run the project while the teachers monitor the project.

In a loosely monitored project, a client has a very important role. The client is responsible for defining a suitable problem domain, expressing requirements, helping in technical issues, accepting finished software, and grading. An interesting question is what type of a client is the best for such projects. The effects to projects that TAs and supervisors cause do not vary much between projects since both TAs and supervisors are university teachers. However, this is not the case with clients because their group is heterogeneous. Intuitively this should affect the outcome of projects, but how much does it do it? How do different types of clients affect student team work? What sort of a client is a good one for a student project? In this paper we try to answer these questions.

Software Engineering Team Projects in the University of Helsinki

The Department of Computer Science at the University of Helsinki is known for its high quality of teaching and research. For example, the Linux operating system was originally developed at the Department of Computer Science. The department is the size of a medium faculty, and it has received several high grades of evaluation both for its teaching and research. In year 2005, we did total 165 person-years and had 175 publications.

Our teaching is based on research and is divided into sub-programmes. The sub-programme of software engineering studies the software and development-process problems related to the manufacturing of large and complex software systems. In addition to courses and seminars, the sub-programme is responsible for the undergraduate software engineering team projects, where students apply what they have learned by developing software for the different needs of varying clients.

The software engineering team project has been a part of our teaching programme since 1985, and since 1990 it has been mandatory for all students majoring in computer science. The project is in the third year of the undergraduate studies. About 100-150 students participate in the student team projects each year. It is often the last course before the Bachelor's thesis.

At the University of Helsinki, Department of Computer Science we have a one-semester software engineering project where 4-7 students form a team to solve a software problem. The students take responsibility of the complete project. Each project lasts for 14 weeks, plus one half-term week in the middle of the project. The project schedules follow closely the teaching periods of the university. The students are expected to work in the project for about 15 hours per week.

A teaching assistant (TA) oversees and when necessary supervises the team. The TA plays the role of a quality manager. A faculty member is a supervisor of all teams. He plays the role of a management group member.

The members of the team control the team work, and they are responsible for all decisions: good and bad. The TA may offer alternatives to the team but the team does not have to follow them. In case of serious conflicts, the supervisor has the final word. However, while the supervisor's advice is sometimes asked, so far teams have been able to settle problems themselves.

Perhaps the most important external member of a project is a client with a realistic software problem. In our case, the projects are arranged in the department, the teachers are assistants and faculty members, but the clients are either from the department or from companies and other departments. Each team has one or more clients. The clients represent actual stakeholders of the created software. They are asked to act the same way they would in a real software project. Most clients are very good at this, thus giving students a very good emulation of real clients.

We call clients from our department internal clients. They are usually Ph.D. students or members from projects that need specific software. We call the clients from companies and other departments' external clients. The clients from other departments usually want a software tool that helps them to do research but that is not necessarily related to their research subject. The company clients typically want a front-end tool to a database.

It is obvious that all external stakeholders affect the course of the project. The TAs that control team work has the strongest role since they are the closest authority to the students, but also the supervisor of all projects has some influence. The TA only inspects the team work and sometimes suggests a reasonable approach. Students are responsible for following the chosen process model and finishing the project on schedule. Even a failed project may be an educational success if the students have learned something from it. This is analogous to real projects where quality assurance team members and managers affect the software projects either implicitly or explicitly.

The software engineering project is performed in teams of 4-7 students. Each team member is responsible for managing a certain area of the project: leading the project, documentation, requirements engineering, design, code structure, testing, etc. The project leader is responsible for maintaining the plan of the project, but every member of the team is expected to inform the project leader of possible issues.

The projects follow either a linear or an iterative process model. The iterative model has three iterations, and teams following the model are expected to write as good documents as the linear model teams. The project covers all phases of the product life cycle from requirements gathering to software delivery.

In the semester before the project, students sign in to the course. They are asked to choose at least three suitable project alternatives from a set of problem definitions. The problem definitions of the projects are real problems from real clients.

A typical product produced in a student project is a well-defined piece of software required by a research group, an administrative software tool, educational software to be used in teaching computer science, or lately more and more often a database front-end application for an external client.

The main programming language in the projects is Java, but lately PHP has gained more interest in the student teams. Other relatively popular languages in the projects are C and C++. Students are not forced to select any language. Usually each team selects their programming language together with their clients.

One week before project deadlines the teams have a demonstration where they introduce their product to public. Each demo usually lasts for 30 minutes. In the demo the students have to explain their work with terms that their audience can understand.

The Department of Computer Science has assigned one senior teacher for supervising all teams. The supervisor allocates students and TAs to teams, educates clients, TAs, and project leaders about their rights and responsibilities, and participates in final grading of the projects. The author of this paper was the supervisor of the experiment teams.

Case study

We analysed a sample of 29 student project teams between summer 2005 and summer 2006 in a case study. The projects had in all 161 students and about 40 clients. One person was a client in three of the projects, two clients were in two projects, and the rest were in one project. We selected all projects that we had on the period above to the experiment.

The teams were categorized according to three client attributes: source, activity, and volume.

The source of the clients is either internal or external. Internal clients are from the department. External clients are from other departments or from companies.

The activity of the clients is either active or passive. Active clients are eager to be in the project and are available almost all the time. They also volunteer to participate in tasks where their presence is not necessity, for instance in late design stages or implementation. Passive clients expect the team to initiate when they are needed. They are available when necessary, but they usually never volunteer for anything.

The volume of clients is either one or many. Some teams had one client that was responsible for all client activities. Some teams had several clients that cooperated in the project.

When the registration to projects was over (and some late students had been added manually), the course prerequisites were checked for students. Those students that fulfilled them were accepted to the course. After that, those problem definitions that gained most interest from students were selected and students were divided into teams according to their preferences. We selected team members so that almost everyone was accepted their most or second most preferred team. This effectively reduced the number of uninterested students in teams. The approach is not optimal to an experiment since students where not selected at random to the teams. However, since students and clients could not select each other, we did not check student skills in the allocation procedure, and practically everyone was allowed to work in a project that they most wanted, we find this approach random enough for client effect evaluation.

During the project, each student kept track of his/her working tasks and used hours of the project. The hours and tasks were stored into a database using a system designed for this. The system forces the students to use predefined classes of tasks.

The classes of tasks that were used in this experiment are as follows:

- Project planning (PRO). This class includes activities related to project management. Student project leaders are expected to update their project plans, follow the schedule and monitor risks. In practice they often more or less neglect these duties.
- Requirements engineering (REQ). This class includes activities related to requirements elicitation and analysis. Each project has a requirements manager whose responsibility it is to nurture requirements and clients. Quite often this works, too, since our teams have relatively good requirements documents.
- Design (DES). This class includes activities related to software design. As our projects usually follow the waterfall model, the design stage should be executed without client's influence. This is not always the case since some very eager clients wish to participate in this stage as well.
- Implementation (IMP). This class includes both programming and unit testing. Students may either programme first and test then or use a modern test-driven approach.
- Testing (TES). This class includes integration and system testing. Sometimes students confuse testing and implementation and also add unit testing here instead of the implementation class.
- User interface tasks (UI). This class has been separated from others in order to calculate how much resources the user interfaces need in our projects. It mostly consists of user interface design and prototyping tasks.
- Project meetings (MEE). This class includes all allocated project meetings.
- Environment learning (ENV). \item[ENV] Learning system and development environments. This class includes tasks related to learning the environment for the new system and the development tools. Typically such subjects as learning CVS or Latex belong to this category.
- Other tasks (OTH). Quite a lot of entries of this class are in a wrong place, but the student who wrote the entry did not figure out a better class for it. However, such entries as finding out how a software license works belong to this class.

The gathered data allows to do all kinds of interesting classifications. We were especially interested to see whether there is a difference between internal and external clients, but at the same time it was relatively simple to add a comparison between teams with one client versus teams with several clients.

The most questionable classification that was used is between active and passive client teams. Unlike the previous classifications, this is not discrete. Few clients are 100 per cent active or 100 per cent passive; they all fall somewhere between. The division to active and passive clients is based on our interviews with TAs and on our own experiences of the teams and the clients. While the partitioning is not absolute, it is not random either. Of the 29 teams, we were unsure of only four teams. We finally evaluated two of those teams to have active clients and two passive clients.

The three classifications above and their analysis is the main contribution of this paper. However, next to these we wanted to find out if perhaps non-client related conditions affect the projects. For this we chose two classifications: project season (spring/autumn versus summer) and team size (4-5 students versus 6-7 students). These two additional classifications gave us valuable information of the team statistics.

Project Results

Each team worked under a TA's supervision. The students were responsible for updating their working hours to the metrics system. Thus, we did not have a controlled experiment.

All teams met their project deadlines. All clients were at least somewhat satisfied with their product. Not all clients used the product after delivery due to various reasons such as software errors (not enough testing) and difficulties installing it to a new environment (lack of maintenance—our projects are finished when their products are delivered).

A summary of all projects and categories is in Table 18.1. It has information about the number of projects of each category, number of students attending projects of each category, the average number of hours per project and per person of each project in each category, and what was the average team size of each category.

Table 18.1: Project Summary

	Projects	*Students*	*Total hours*	*Person hours*	*Team members*
Internal	15	78	1201	228	5.2
External	14	83	1231	208	5.9
Active	18	98	1278	236	5.4
Passive	11	63	1113	191	5.7
Single	15	83	1215	217	5.5
Multiple	14	78	1216	220	5.6
Spring/Autumn	16	93	1290	221	5.8
Summer	13	68	1123	215	5.2
4-5	13	60	1020	221	4.6
6.7	16	101	1374	217	6.3
All	29	161	1215	219	5.6

As can be seen from the table, the authors were quite lucky with the project and student distribution to categories. Both internal/external classification and one/many classification had an optimal number of teams (15-14) and almost optimal number of students (83-78). The active/passive classification could have been more evenly distributed but it is acceptable (18-11, 98-63). The other two classifications are somewhat more evenly distributed than the active-passive classification. By definition, the classification between small teams and large teams has a large difference in the number of participating students.

The internal and external client projects did not have much difference in work averages. The external client projects worked a little more but they also had more team members. The students of internal client teams worked a few hours more per person than the students of external client teams, but again the difference is not very large.

Perhaps the most interesting difference is in fact in the average team sizes. It appears that students preferred external clients, and indeed it shows not only in the actual teams but also in the registration of the course. This can be due to the assumption that external clients cause a more real project (usually true) or that external clients define a simpler software problem (usually not true).

The biggest variation of person hours is between active and passive client teams. The active teams worked as much as 236 hours per person while the passive client teams worked only 191 hours per person. This is clearly the largest difference, especially since the team sizes of active and passive client teams are not very different (5.4 vs 5.7 students per team). It appears that active clients indeed have a strong influence to the working habits of their team members.

There does not seem to be a significant difference between teams with one client versus teams with several clients. Both types of teams worked about the same amount and especially the total numbers of hours per person are surprisingly close to each other. From this statistics it appears that the number of clients does not affect the project results. In a real-world scenario it should affect results since more clients usually implies more stakeholders, which implies more work in requirements gathering.

The other two classifications bring nothing interesting to the total picture. Summer teams are generally smaller than other teams and their members work less. However, these differences are small. Members of small teams do not seem to suffer from the lack of members. Of course small teams have less hours in a project than large teams, but the average hours per person are about equal. Thus, the size of a team does not seem to affect team members' working hours.

A summary of all stages and their hours per project in the three classifications can be seen in Figure 18.1. The additional classifications has been excluded because they are not very interesting here and they make the chart very difficult to read. Those will be used later in statistical analysis.

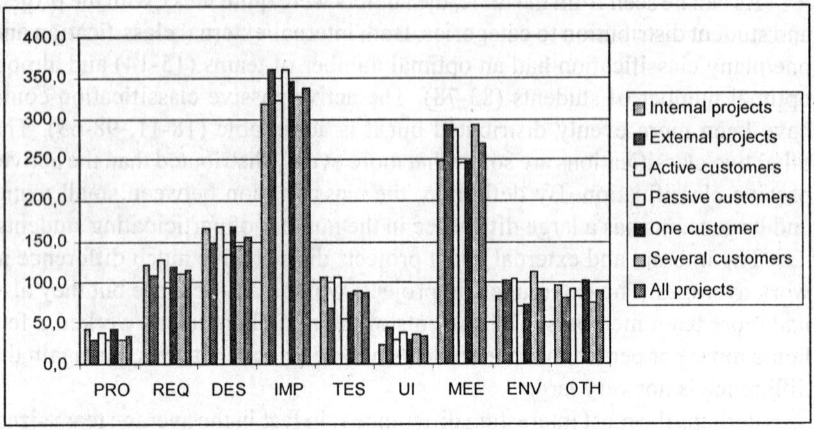

Figure 18.1: Average Project Hours

When internal and external client projects are compared, the biggest differences seem to be in implementation, testing, and meetings. Interestingly, there is no clear difference in requirements engineering which is against expectations. It was expected that the projects with external clients to have longer requirements analysis since external clients are often not as used to expressing requirements as internal ones. One explanation of this can be in the difference in meetings. External client projects have spent considerably more time in meetings, and meetings usually have an agenda. It is probable that at least some of this time has actually been meetings with clients about requirements. But even if requirements and meetings are combined, the external projects are not that much ahead of internal projects. We assume that external clients require more meetings but on the other hand are better in describing their requirements than internal clients. Internal clients explain less and thus project members have to work more with the requirements when the client is not present.

The differences in implementation and testing may be due to wrong expectations of the actual work needed in the implementation stage. Since the design times are about equal, it appears that teams consider software from external clients (e.g. a front-end to a database) to be a simpler task to implement than what it actually is. And when the team misses its implementation deadline, they have to take time from the next stage: testing.

One interesting difference between internal and external projects is in user interface tasks. It appears that projects with external clients use twice as much time to user interfaces than internal projects. The explanation for this is probably in different types of applications. Database front-ends need more user interface design than internal projects where often a simple command line interface is sufficient.

When active and passive projects are compared, the large difference in the total work hours is present in the detailed chart. Projects with active clients have considerably more hours in requirements, design, testing, meetings, and environment issues. These results are not surprising, since an active client is more or less present in all these stages. However, in implementation the projects with passive clients work on the average 40 hours more than the projects with passive clients. Perhaps the influence of active clients make project members concentrate more on specification and design issues, and thus reduce the required implementation time. If this is the case, then this alone is a very good reason to favour active clients, as can be seen from the bar chart. Our projects seem to be closer to agile processes when they should be based on the waterfall model. On the other hand, a similar difference is in the implementation stage between internal and external projects.

Active clients may also have a negative impact to a project if the team members are especially unsure about their skills. This case occurred in our earlier study about cross-cultural software engineering projects. In the project we had two teams cooperating on different countries. One of the teams was filled with very shy people who always relied on their TA. The result was that with an active client the requirements analysis and some of the design was basically a dialogue between the client and the TA.

When one-client and many-client projects are compared, it is noticeable that requirements, design, implementation, testing, and user interface issues have only small differences. However, the differences in meetings and environment issues are large.

One reason for the difference in meeting times was present in our earlier research. In the research analysis was made to determine whether it is a good idea to have female-only student software engineering teams. In the interviews with the team members we found out that sometimes teams with multiple clients suffer from arguments between the clients. Our later interviews with TAs have confirmed this issue. Sometimes when two or more clients are in a project meeting at the same time, they disagree on what they want. While this is a realistic scenario since clients do not always know what they want, it confuses students. They do not have enough experience or authority to deal with this kind of a problem.

The difference in the environment-specific times is a mystery to us. Perhaps multiple clients bring multiple environment problems to solve. When each client has a different view to the problem, someone from the team has to figure out how to combine the views. This could explain why this type of tasks has taken considerably more time with multiple clients.

The previous analysis was based on average project times, but when projects are not equal in size, the statistics can be misleading. This is especially true in average meeting times but also in requirements, design, and implementation stages.

Due to this we normalised projects with their number of members and got member average times for each project. A summary of all stages and their hours per person in all three categories can be seen in Figure 18.2. Again, we have excluded the additional classifications.

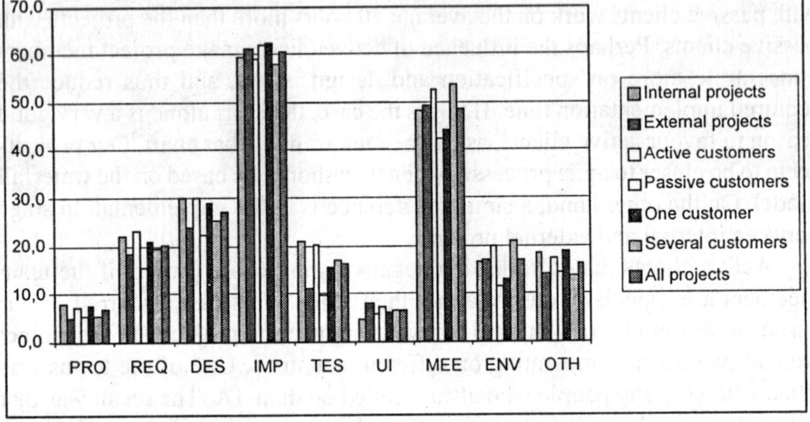

Figure 18.2: Average Student Hours

As can be seen from the figure, some differences vanish in the normalisation, some actually grow. The difference in design between internal and external client projects and active and passive client projects seems to grow while the differences in implementation vanish. Thus, some of the differences in the implementation stage are due to the fact that every member of a project participates actively to the implementation stage while requirements gathering and design are not as evenly distributed among team members. The explaining factor of the implementation time differences seems to be both the team size and the differences in client behaviour. The client influence cannot be completely ignored since it now shows in the requirements, design, and testing stages. Teams with external/passive clients implement more. Members of internal/active client projects specify and design more.

Perhaps excluding implementation, the types of clients do not affect much the work hour percentages. Project planning takes 2-4 per cent, requirements 8-10 per cent, design 11-14 per cent, implementation 25-32 per cent, testing 6-9 per cent, user interface issues 2-4 per cent, meetings 20-24 per cent, environment issues 6-9 per cent, and other issues 6-9 per cent.

The largest variation of the percentages is in implementation. Projects with active clients used 25 per cent of their time to implementation. Projects with passive clients used 32 per cent. The difference between alternatives in other classifications was at most 3 per cent. Table 18.2 summarises these values.

Table 18.2: Percentages of Tasks

	PRO	REQ	DES	IMP	TES	UI	MEE	ENV	OTH
Internal	4	10	14	26	9	2	21	7	8
External	2	9	12	29	6	4	24	8	7
Active	3	10	13	25	8	2	22	8	7
Passive	3	8	12	32	5	4	22	6	8
Single	3	10	14	28	7	3	20	6	8
Multiple	2	9	12	27	7	3	24	9	6
All	3	9	13	28	7	3	22	8	7

t-test Analysis

Next to comparison of numbers, we also made t-tests to all classifications. We used a one-tailed t-test with the assumption that variances of populations are equal. The t-test can be used since all input data is at least on the interval scale.

The null hypothesis was that the sample projects of compared categories are from the same population; that is, the clients do not affect the results and working habits of the projects. We selected our significance level to be 0.05 level of confidence.

T-test to all classifications at a team level was done. Thus, we compared total hours of teams and ignored the fact that the average team sizes were not the same. The results of the team-level t-tests are in Table 18.3.

Table 18.3: t-tests of Project Parameters

	Internal/ External	Active/ Passive	Single/ Multiple	SpAu/ Summer	4-5/6-7
PRO	0.074	0.201	0.087	0.369	0.472
REQ	0.363	0.114	0.377	0.288	0.034
DES	0.292	0.196	0.260	0.365	0.025
IMP	0.167	0.211	0.338	0.101	0.002
TES	0.076	0.030	0.469	0.484	0.345
UI	0.038	0.247	0.342	0.318	0.320
MEE	0.067	0.090	0.059	0.014	0.002
ENV	0.255	0.095	0.057	0.133	0.169
OTH	0.214	0.332	0.047	0.225	0.459
Total	0.417	0.135	0.500	0.126	0.006

In the t-test analysis first of all concentrate was on the two non-client based classifications: spring/autumn versus summer groups and 4-5 student versus 6-7 student groups.

The t-tests of semester differences are not very interesting. The only test where the null hypothesis is wrong at the selected significance level is in team meeting times. Summer teams had considerably shorter meetings than other teams. This could explain some of the differences between one-client and many client teams, since nine of the one client teams were at a summer semester and only three were at other semesters.

The reason for this difference is obviously the time of a year. Students that participate summer projects tend to prefer working alone, for instance on a beach with a laptop, rather than in team meetings at classrooms.

In the t-tests of small versus large teams, the more interesting result is not where null hypotheses fail but where it will not. Actually all null hypothesis should fail since the size of the team should affect the total number of hours of each project stage. This holds true in requirements, design, implementation, meetings and total hours. All the listed stages are large where each team member must participate. Of the others, project planning, testing and user interfaces are tasks that should belong to everyone but perhaps only a few of the project members actually work with these tasks. This could explain why the null hypothesis holds: no matter how many students join the project, only one or two will work on the small tasks.

The environment issues and other issues seem not to be related to team sizes either. This could be due to the students' way to categorise their tasks. It appears that not everyone uses these tasks: one student's client meeting is requirements, for another student it is a system environment meeting.

Ignoring from the other classifications, values that probably depend on the semester of a project or the size of a project, having three t-tests where the null hypothesis fails: testing in active/passive projects, user interfaces in internal/external projects, and other tasks in one client/many client projects. All these have already been covered in the previous analysis.

The t-test results between active and passive client teams are interesting. It was earlier notified that active clients seem to affect requirements, design, implementation, and testing. The effects seem to vanish in the t-tests excluding testing. From a deeper analysis it appears that we had one passive client team with a very large number of total hours in requirements analysis and design. Their client, while passive, was our professor of requirements engineering and their TA was our top design specialist. These external attributes have perhaps affected their working hours. Since the project dealt with only 11 passive client teams, one team can make a difference. When we tried the t-tests without the special team, the results correlated better with the earlier listed averages.

Since it was obvious that the team size affects the result, we normalised the work efforts with team sizes and did the t-tests again. The results of these student-level t-tests can be seen in Table 18.4.

As can been seen from the table, now semester and team size no longer give statistically significant differences. Actually two differences are very close to significance, since the probability that the meeting times of summer teams and other teams are from the same sample are only 0.052 and the probability of other tasks in small versus large teams is 0.053. It is discussed that these differences in the previous analysis. Summer teams simply prefer working outside the classrooms. Another close call is in other tasks of small versus large teams. This difference is more difficult to explain since the other tasks can be anything and also include tasks that actually should belong to some other class.

Table 18.4: T-tests of Student Parameters

	Internal/ External	*Active/ Passive*	*Single/ Multiple*	*SpAu/ Summer*	*4-5/6-7*
PRO	0.030	0.149	0.097	0.165	0.123
REQ	0.223	0.062	0.397	0.465	0.259
DES	0.138	0.087	0.264	0.385	0.211
IMP	0.389	0.335	0.274	0.282	0.250
TES	0.038	0.026	0.373	0.413	0.233
UI	0.093	0.297	0.449	0.477	0.120
MEE	0.399	0.006	0.010	0.052	0.396
ENV	0.491	0.060	0.055	0.175	0.465
OTH	0.100	0.200	0.064	0.071	0.053
Total	0.172	0.018	0.436	0.380	0.432

Next to the earlier covered difference, one new appears in project planning. It appears that internal projects have required more planning than external projects. Some of this difference is due to the fact that external projects had average of 5.9 members in a team while internal projects had only 5.2. Since project planning is traditionally a project leader's task alone, it is natural that on average members in larger teams work less with project management. However, this cannot explain the difference completely since it should then show in the t-test of project planning between small and large teams.

A deeper analysis did not reveal a reason for the difference in project planning. It still appears that projects with internal clients spend more time in project planning than projects with external clients. No obvious reason seems to explain this difference.

We can think of a possible explanation for the listed difference, but it is not a very good and especially it is not validated. First, it is possible that specific internal problem definitions based on complex computer science theories, which attract pedantic students who wish to have good project planning. Since our software engineering project is mandatory to all students, a certain percentage of them just want to pass the project and not to bother with such details as good project planning. The best way to do this appears to be in a project to implement a database front-end: they are the easiest to understand and sound simple. They are not simple, but the students do not know that. On the other hand, however, students with interest in software engineering are perhaps not that interested in internal computer science problem definitions. This is against the previous hypothesis. More research is needed in this subject before we can explain the difference.

Lessons Learned

Student software engineering projects have several factors that affect the results. The role of clients is just one of them. Hence, it is not a surprise that the differences found were rather small. Nevertheless the analysis and previous experiences result some simple points.

First, internal and external clients can be equally good. It depends on what sort of a project is wanted. The time differences in various process stages are mostly not relevant, and even when they are relevant, they usually have simple explanations. It appears that external clients and external problems do not really affect team working habits. An internal project with an internal client can be equally good. Actually the difference is how students see internal and external projects. The external projects are much more popular because students consider them to be more realistic. They might be, but it does not show in working hours.

There seems to be one specific type of projects where external clients are better: user interface projects. It appears that projects with external clients require more user interface planning, design, and implementation. This is probably due to the nature of the external client projects. The internal clients often required a simple user interface and concentrated on the details inside. The external clients were often more interested in the usability issues of the software. However, also internal clients wanted usable software but they also had more difficult internal requirements.

Second, having several clients in a project did not give additional value to our projects. The largest differences were in minor tasks such as meetings, environment learning, and other issues. Regular software engineering tasks did not have a difference. In our projects the clients represented the same stakeholder. Perhaps multiple clients would be more useful if they were members of different stakeholders as well.

Third, active clients result better projects than passive clients while students prefer passive clients. Active clients influence students to specify, design, and test more—and implement less. However, the danger with active clients is that they easily control the project too much. A good active client gives ideas and suggestions but does not force students to do things the way he or she wants. A very good active client can give a positive example especially in requirements engineering and testing. These stages are very important in software engineering. They are also those stages that students in software engineering projects tend to leave for less attention. A good active client requires well tested software, and it shows in the analysis. A good active client also requires students to fully understand what he or she wants from software. In the analysis, this shows in meetings and requirements engineering times.

As a short summary: A realistic student project require, selecting multiple passive external clients. For a controlled student project, selected one active internal client. Fortunately only selecting active or passive clients seems to make a real difference, so other types of combinations can also generate good projects.

The question of the client influence that is wanted to answer is: "What are the characteristics of a good student software engineering team client and how much do they affect the team work?" From our small analysis we answer: "A good client is active but not confusing. A good client represents only one stakeholder. A good client influences the team to spend more time in requirements analysis, design, and testing." There seems to be room for very different types of good clients. Especially the original question whether external clients have better effect on working habits than internal clients does not seem to be true. Both internal and external clients can be equally good.

Conclusion

In general, our experiences with various types of clients have been mostly positive. In spite of the differences in personality and styles, all types of clients have created good software engineering problems and based on the problems, have allowed students to create good software.

Different clients imply different projects. Projects with much freedom have often several passive external clients. These projects are the most realistic ones. Projects with much control have often one active internal client. These projects are the safest ones. Fortunately both safe and realistic projects can be educational, and the number of clients and internal/external clients do not affect students' working habits much.

19

Learning Process Evolution Enhanced by ICT and Educational Technology

Universitat De Valècia Case Study and Open and Collaborative Software Experiences

P. Moreno Clari, V. Cerverón Lleó, Darío Roig and Agustín López

Learning processes, require improvements and technology enhancements. The great development of information and communication technologies (ICT) has forced a dynamic[3] of learning changes which has generated a group in expansion of new students different from the traditional ones[1, 2] with its own necessities. In addition, the latest technological developments and accessibility to communication systems have given to students and teachers the possibility to access to a profusion of information and educational material. Multimedia resources and Internet have opened a vast field to education.

These changes in students and learning materials and resources have changed the education and learning definition[3]. Some current constructivist authors think that learning process is basically collaborative: students, thanks to interaction among them, with their teacher and with their environment, create knowledge. The pupil, in this way, takes part in its formation. All these changes have forced the creation and development of new methods to obtain an effective formation process.

The actual educational system, immersed in a process of European convergence, has the challenge of forming highly prepared people who have the ability to adapt to changes that ICT are introducing. New technologies offer tools for the accomplishment of activities and almost unlimited and ubiquitous access to contents; and they extend the interaction, which in the traditional classroom often is limited by time and space constraints. The simple provision of ICT infrastructures and tools does not ensure the Higher Education alignment neither with these objectives, nor its fulfilment. It is for that reason that plans and actions must be added to equipment and applications.

These plans must be orientated to promote and to improve the Higher Education quality and to generate competences and skills among the students, teachers and staff with regard to an effective ICT use. All these reasons motivated that Universitat de València established a programme whose main objective was designed to take advantage of possibilities which ICT offers to students, in order to increase their active role in the learning process. Its goal was to improve the quality and efficiency of the learning process and to complement the formation in new technologies and their use. To accomplish it, it was necessary for an adaptation of formative profiles to the new and emergent professional careers. At the same time, the conditions which made professors and rest of staff updating their pedagogical and working methods must be generated, by means of using new technologies in those aspects in which they were more useful.

This chapter describes the starting point from which the Universitat de València established the innovation programme and selected and implemented an integrated platform, based in a collaborative international project. The work is centered in the selection process of the learning management system according to the needs of a University with these characteristics[4], the implementation, integration and development process[5] for the largest implementation of the .LRN platform fully open-source (.LRN and OpenACS software, AOLServer as webserver, PostgreSQL database and Linux Debian for the server) to manage the learning and the collaborative work; and the reached situation. Actual blended learning experiences also allow to suggest and to improve the learning management system (LMS) according to the pedagogical and methodological requirements detected in the analysis which has been made.

The last hardware and software improvements which have been made are going to be exposed. The exposition is completed with the obtained results and their evaluation, which study the LMS technical and pedagogical usability, its specifically best valued resources, intend that its use does not suppose an additional effort, thus allowing students and professors to dedicate optimum efforts in the learning process. Finally, conclusions and future work are exposed.

Starting Point Towards Technology Enhanced Learning

Technological and Pedagogical advances in recent years have caused an exponential increase of education based on ICT demand and a revolution in the form to understand the learning process. These changes have forced all the elements involved in the process: students, professors, contents and tools, to adapt to situation; and they have increased the educative panorama complexity. On the other hand, the Higher Education European System is experiencing a deep transformation through the European Convergence Process. Some of the

Spanish University strategies is to accomplish the UE process objectives in ICT have been:

to facilitate all University schools the equipment and facilities to employ ICT;
to develop on-line courses;
to create laboratories to support research and innovation on ICT;
to increase Iberoamerican and European cooperation.

Recent reports about ICT in Spanish University[6] conducted a review of the present situation in university; all considering teaching, research and management matters.

The study also contemplates the existing European e-learning programme and the USA and UK latest initiatives. The report assures that conventional universities face several challenges: the loss of exclusivity; the ICT research implications, which facilitate interchanges between different universities; and its educational implications (changes in the learning process). On the other hand, the Coordination Council of Universities published its work recently, a work which states that in the Spanish universities present situation, which are mainly changing and renovating its educational methodologies, technological innovation, is not the only way, but it represents one of most relevant strategies. The report also gives the successive phases to adequate to future convergence: Impulse (information, motivation, plans design…), teacher's formation and educative innovation (pilot projects, guidelines elaboration…), and diffusion and assessment of best practices and tools.

Universitat de València (UV), one of the largest and most varied in Spain, offers classroom and laboratory learning to 50,000 students in 18 centres. Among them, 6,000 courses from 1,500 subjects are developed. Interested in enhancing the learning process by the use of ICT, a Learning Management System (LMS) was selected, implemented and developed to improve the learning and communication processes for the whole University. In 2003, the Universitat de València had an important ICT infrastructure that supported the more habitual tools. All the professors and rest of university staff had computer equipment and Internet access through RedIris. This fact allowed them to use e-mail (all members in the university community could have an account in the University server), to create and host web pages; and also, give them the possibility of accessing and creating forums, and using other telematic tools.

On the other hand, the students also have computer classrooms, all of them with Internet access (and an incipient wireless network). Students could also request an e-mail account or host at the university's server their personal web pages. In addition, the University worked with different academic and administrative management applications: student's enrolment, files, staff and economic management and also had very important research resources: among these resources, it can be mentioned a supercomputer for scientific calculus.

Nevertheless, the use of ICT was not homogeneous in the different areas and degrees, and its utilisation in the educational activity was not generalized. Different educational and research groups from the Universitat de València took part in several educational innovation aspects by means of the ICT use, from a technical and psicopedagogical point of view; but their efforts should be coordinated. At the same time, it was necessary to have a suitable organisation and institutional support to promote expansion of these experiences to all the University educational activities.

On the other hand, the Universitat de València demanded and impelled at different fronts a renovation and modernisation of its structures and processes according to the European convergence process challenges. In fact, Universitat de València was one of Spain pioneers in experimenting and studying on the consequences of this Higher Education transformation. It was for that reason that it was promoted a call for educative innovation pilot projects to experience and to evaluate new styles and systems of teaching-learning. These projects must accomplish the European convergence criteria. Coordination was the professors' responsibility. They looked for new educational systems which contributed to improve the education at university, the study and working methods, and the relations between professors and students.

The pilot project's objective was to fix the bases and to acquire the necessary organizational experience to outline more extensive plans in subsequent courses. The innovation and convergence programme towards the European Convergence Project had three interrelated fronts:

(i) new technologies implantation in Higher Education;
(ii) changes in the educational methodologies; and
(iii) integration of all the university community in the Information Society.

For that reason, informatization was not only an aim, nor a procedure which virtualized the activity; but an instrument, whose finality was to facilitate and to promote those activities that, by using ICT, really improved the work, communication and interaction between professors and students. In addition, in order to make possible that informatization come to the greatest number of people and activities, it was decided to integrate all the different and dispersed tools which were used until then in a unified learning management, groups and communities system. This LMS (Learning Management System) is described in the following sections.

LMS Selection Process

A Learning Management System (LMS) is something more that a set of isolated web applications. This is a term, which is applied to those systems whose design integrates different aspects such as the tracking of interrelation between educative contents, and its management mechanisms.

The main objective of a LMS is to provide and to manage all the resources of an educational system to the students, taking into account its progress and yield. The LMS are the result of the Computer Based Training evolution. This evolution was made thanks to the existence of new tools for the management and tracking of community members and other communication tools, such as, calendar, assessment, groups, etc. The virtual communities' creation systems must be able to manage dynamic contents. This objective is obtained using a relational database and a programming language. Nevertheless, it's not affordable to repeat this work each time a new project is created, nor for the developer, because of the workload it implies, nor for the client, because of its high cost. So that the best form to take advantage of the work already made, is to conjugate the use of tools as open-source code or a framework, and to foment collaborative work.

A framework can be defined as a re-usable and 'semi-complete' application, with capability of specialized production of applications with personal requirements[7]. Between the benefits obtained with the use of frameworks it can be mentioned modularity, reusability, extensibility, and software version control. A framework can be a solution to a general application or to solve a particular trouble in some concrete domain. It is appropriate to use the term web applications' framework to define development architectures specifically designed to be adjusted to a particular web application' needs in a determined domain, such it can be, the Learning Management Systems.

The University Computer Services (SIUV) was required, by the academicians of the university, to report on the implantation of an e-learning management system to support all the courses in the University. First, needed functionalities and minimum requirements to be accomplished by the evaluated platforms were identified. The following were the demanded minimum requirements:

(a) Scalability: the mean system efficiency should not be affected by the number of courses and users that concur at the same time.
(b) Integration: The platform must allow integration with the existing information systems (i.e. LDAP Authentication, database systems, other academic applications, etc.). In this way, some advantages, commonly present in open source software, were considered. Moreover, the Universitat de València resides in a bilingual region, so the platform interface should be visualized in different languages.
(c) Reliability: use of the platform by others and communication with leading universities guarantee their reliability (UNED-Spain, MIT-USA, U.Galileo-Guatemala, U. Heidelberg-Germany and more)[8, 9].
(d) Standards: catalogue, reusability and migration of the courses between different platforms will be guaranteed using standards in the creation of learning contents (SCORM, IMS).

In order to gather characteristics of each platform, their official sites were visited and their developers were contacted. Later on, specific bibliography search was done considering experiences with similar platforms in other universities of similar size and characteristics than Universitat de València.

Focusing on open-source platforms, Atutor, .LRN, Ilias and Moodle were evaluated. Proprietary WebCT platform, used by the UV until academic course 2003-2004, was also evaluated, and their main weakness were integration and adaptation possibilities, and mainly the cost of licenses which is proportional to the number of students.

The analysis and report[4], conducted on February 2004, recommended the development of a practical case of implementation of the .LRN platform in the University of Valencia. Then, Universitat de València joined the .LRN project[10] because .LRN better meets UV requirements for the learning process and also as information and communication tool for research communities.

The .LRN Consortium represents a collaborative work whose objective is to obtain and improve a LMS the following sections will be exposed the framework and its architecture: OpenACS and, .LRN; the collaboration philosophy: the .LRN Consortium; and the experience of the LMS in the Universitat de València.

Experiences with Open and Collaborative Software

Philip Greenspun proposes a modular set of tools to give a generic answer to virtual communities' necessities (http://philip.greenspun.com/panda/), in the middle of 90's. The set of these modular tools was grouped under the Arsdigita Community System (ACS) name and were released with GNU General Public License (GPL) (http://www.gnu.org/copyleft/gpl.html).

The first database which was chosen was Oracle and the programming language was Tool Command Language (TCL). ACS demonstrated from its beginning to be a very powerful tool and simple to use, with capability to support large projects. Arsdigita disappeared, but thanks to license liberation, the developers' community retook the project. It was in that moment when an ACS version based on the Arsdigita work named OpenACS (http://www.openacs.org/), was developed; using the open code database PostgreSQL (http://wwwpostgresql.org/) . Nowadays it is a ripe project, with more than 7000 members and 10 companies that provide commercial support and development[11].

The present architecture does not depend on the relational database used: can operate with Oracle or Postgres; and has the possibility of operating with other databases, if it is necessary. The last evolution of OpenACS has been denominated dotLRN (http://dotlrn.org/), and constitutes an architecture reconstruction to improve the set of applications and the framework infrastructure.

OpenACS Framework and Architecture

The OpenACS Framework (OACS) is known as application server and it is integrated by a set of advanced tools that allow programmer to develop Web applications which are oriented to define users' communities[12]. In Figure 19.1, OACS Architecture's Infrastructure and services, and the components' distribution functionalities are shown.

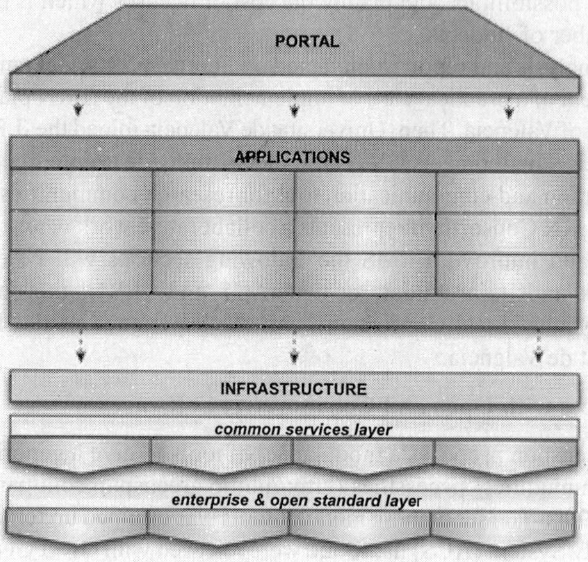

Figure 19.1: Services in OACS Architecture

There is a common layer, named basic services or infrastructure layer, which is supported by the operating system and the relational database where the system information is stored. Linux is used as operating system, because it consumes very few resources and is a very stable and safe operating system. In addition, its cost is practically null and it is maintained by a very active developer community.

Persistency is obtained using PostgreSQL Database, an open code database whose robustness is similar to ORACLE. In addition, PostgreSQL uses *Multi-Version Concurrency Control (MVCC)* to manage the database accesses. Thanks to this, different users can do simultaneous consulting without waiting to the finalisation of one process to start another. This fact adds agility to execution.

Applications use the Infrastructure Layer services: There are different modules which are available through the Web interface. These modules personalise the users' necessities. The modules programming is made by using TCL, Tool Command Language (http://tcl.sourceforge.net/).

This is a multiplatform interpreted programming language which is oriented to applications Web generation. Some applications which are available are:

forums, calendar, news, assessment, storage area, FAQs, Wimpy Point, etc. Figure 19.2 shows the available applications in the ACS core; the applications that can be installed and their organization in the architecture are shown on it.

The portal component is located at the final layer. It is the Web server whose mission is to provide the operation interface and interact with application layer. The Web server technology is AOLserver (http://www.aolserver.com/). It is the software which uses America On Line, AOL, to serve its pages. This company is the greater Internet supplier in the world. This fact indicates that the server can support a considerable workload.

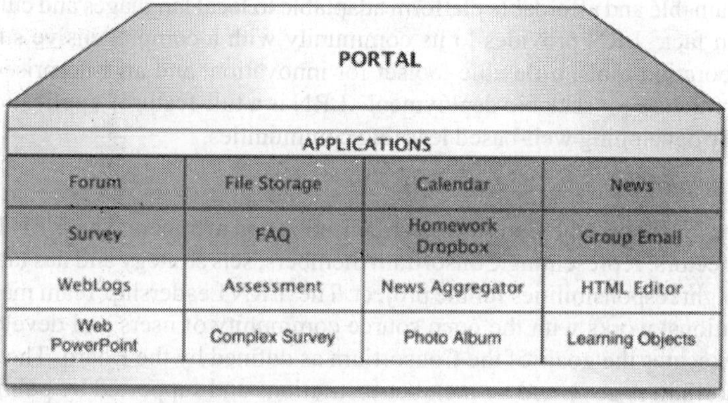

Figure 19.2: Available Applications in the ACS Core

LRN Consortium: Organization and Members

OACS and .LRN Architectures are in continuous evolution and improvement. The implemented and developed modules and functionalities are studied not only by their programmers, but also by a large users' community. The users' community reports the failures they found, the suggested improvements, the new functionalities to implement, etc. This is one of the open code strong points; and it is also the key of the LMS evolution: The large users' community existence improves the product, and this improvement causes that the LMS is chosen by a greater number of new institutions. In this section the philosophy and operation of the cooperation project and community .LRN is described.

.LRN is a global community of educators, designers, and software developers who partner together to drive educational innovation. Because the software is open source, organizations can invest in people and curriculum development instead of licensing and support fees. .LRN is backed by the .LRN Consortium. The .LRN Consortium is a tax-exempted, not-for-profit corporation focused on creating and supporting a freely available suite of web based educational applications to support learning communities. Its mission is to convene a global community of innovative people and organizations in educational technology to share knowledge and applications using open source principles.

Consortium member institutions work together to support each other's deployments and to accelerate and expand the adoption and development of .LRN. The Consortium ensures software quality by certifying components as .LRN-compliant, coordinates software development plans, and maintains ties with OpenACS, the open source toolkit which forms the basis for .LRN. Some of the .LRN Consortium objectives are: to provide the premier toolkit for innovation in educational technology and research collaboration; to support education and research communities with advanced collaboration tools; to provide a scalable architecture based on open industry standards; and to create a sustainable and affordable platform adaptable to local languages and cultures.

In fact, .LRN provides to its community with a comprehensive suite of collaboration tools, a flexible toolset for innovation, and an enterprise-class infrastructure for scalable deployment. .LRN is a full-featured application for rapidly developing web-based learning communities.

Organisation

Figure 19.3 shows the Consortium organisation and members. The .LRN Board of Directors, representing Consortium members, sets strategy and has ultimate oversight responsibilities for the project. The .LRN Leadership Team manages operations, works with the open source community of users and developers, and executes the goals of the Consortium as defined by the Board. The .LRN Consortium is governed by member institutions and supported by public and private sponsors. In consultation with Consortium members, the Board of Directors sets strategic direction and provides financial and operational oversight. In its operations, the Consortium: ensures a reliable release process; supports quality assurance and certification; provides framework for legal due diligence; acts as a clearinghouse for communication; shares best practices with the community; and undertakes marketing and promotion.

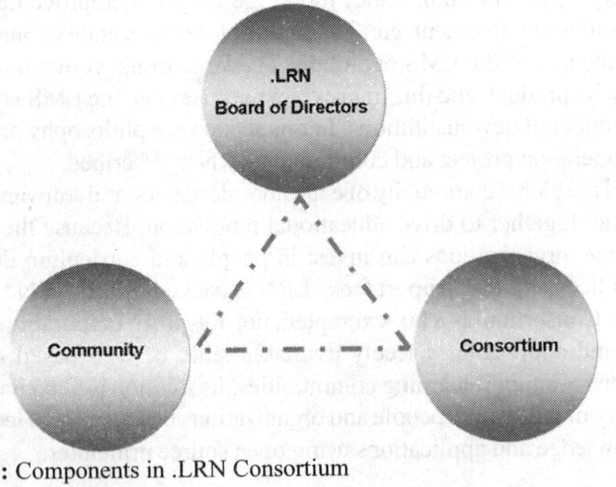

Figure 19.3: Components in .LRN Consortium

Members

Membership in the Consortium is not required in order to use the .LRN software or to participate in the worldwide community dedicated to developing innovative educational software. The principal benefit of membership is the ability to set priorities and influence consortium operations and goals. Any organization, regardless of its size or capability, may join the consortium for a very modest fee. .LRN is built using Open ACS (Open Architecture Community System) (http://www.openacs.org), an advanced enterprise framework for building scalable, community-oriented web applications. The OpenACS 'core' has been in development for nearly a decade. This fact gives OACS a large reliability.

LRN supports learning and research communities for over half a million users in higher education, K-12, and non-profit organizations; which are using .LRN to promote scalable innovation for collaborative education. Some of these organisations are: University of Bergen, UCLA, Galileo University, Harvard JFK, University of Heidelberg, University of Mannheim, MIT Sloan School of Management and Universitat de València.

LMS Implementation and Technological Evolution

'Aula Virtual' is the denomination used for the UV installation and personalization of .LRN. As for the installation, applications available at the Aula Virtual in the first moment were: documents, calendar, news, forum, email and notifications, evaluation-assessment, chat, Learning Object repository system, Wimpy Point (Web presentations), weblogs, photoalbum and FAQ's.

The implantation of the 'Aula Virtual' had been developed progressively, in the following phases:

(a) Analysis: October 2003 — February 2004
(b) Implementation (and translation): February-June 2004
(c) Start-up: academic year 2004-2005
(d) Development and maintenance: since February 2004
(e) Users instruction: courses, user's manual, on-line attention and FAQ: since February 2004
(f) Users support: since February 2004

During analysis phase, workload tests were guided with all UV courses and users, advising of other experienced members of the OpenACS community were asked for, specifically those who had systems similar to ours. The OpenACS and .LRN version that was initially installed corresponds to the branch oacs-5-1 of the CVS. The changes of the branch oacs-5-1 are tested with a weekly regularity in a development platform.

Users are authenticated by three different authentication authorities: LDAP, LOCAL and EXTERNAL:

(a) LDAP authority is verified in the UV LDAP server allowing the use of the accounts that users have created for all e-services in the university. LDAP Authority replaces the .LRN user management used in the rest of authorities.
(b) LOCAL authority is used to create local accounts by the professors and allow them to access their courses with a student role in order to carry out tests when needed.
(c) EXTERNAL authority is used to create accounts for external users who need to join communities supported by Universitat de València research projects.

As it was mentioned before, the platform interface must be available in three languages: Spanish, Valencian-Catalan and English. To accomplish this objective the UV has been participating in the internationalization project of .LRN. The interface also offers the possibility of renaming pages and moving portlets in the new classes, and in addition, user can personalize the following pages: class home, calendar, resources, communication, activities, and information. Figure 19.4 shows the personal access page to Aula Virtual.

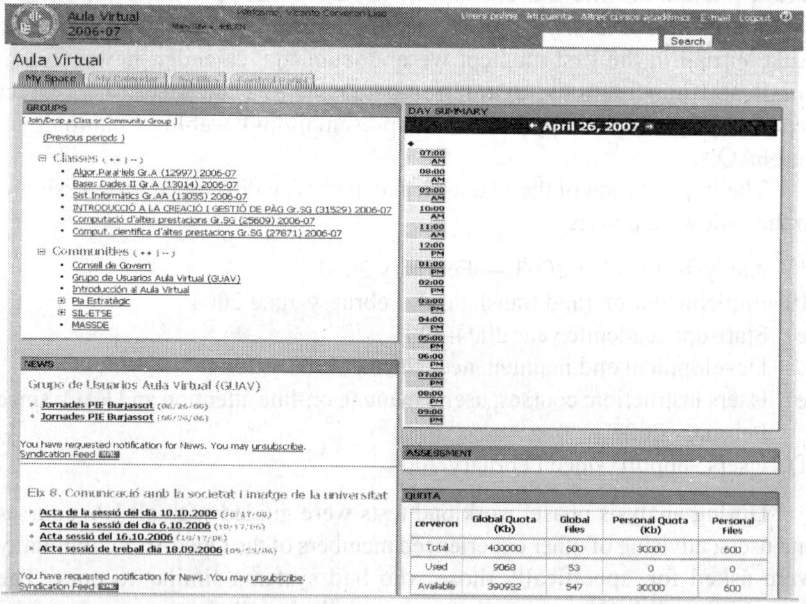

Figure 19.4: Aula Virtual Home Page

Aula Virtual also is a potent tool to workgroup, and has been used by research communities, integrated by Universitat de València and other universities members. This workgroup functionality has been employed by management and strategical groups as it can be observed in Figure 19.5, which shows the LMS use in the working axes of the Universitat de València strategical programme.

Figure 19.5: Aula Virtual Communities

Finally, it must be said, that Aula Virtual constitute the main tool which all Universitat de València community: students, teachers, and personal staff, uses to diffuse news, activities, employment offers, etc., as it can be observed at Figure 19.6.

Figure 19.6: Aula Virtual Communication Use

Integration

Integration with other university applications that show public and private information on the academic courses has been developed using OpenACS packages and .LRN portlets for integration in the courses[5]. Also, batch programmes were made, written in Perl, for the insertion of courses, groups and users, when professors requested it. These batch programmes return, via 'HTTP', the classes teached by a professor and the students registered in their courses, obtaining the information from the academic database. After collecting these data, a package made in OpenACS, named siuvadmin, is invoked. This package uses the creation of courses and users API. Figure 19.7 shows the created courses and groups such they are visualized from the professor personal portal.

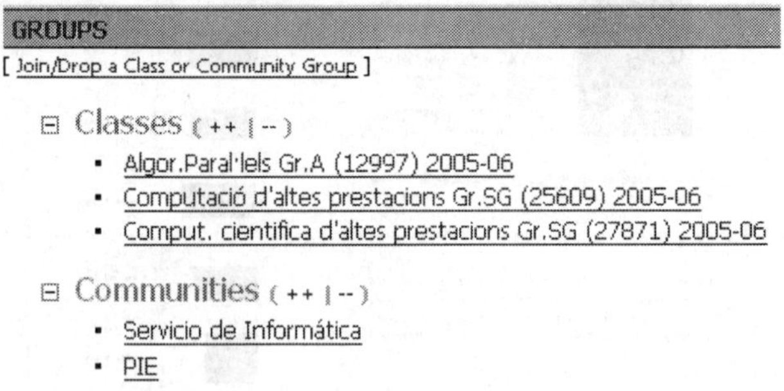

Figure 19.7: Courses and Groups

Figure 19.8 shows an example of the *Asiginfo* package that connects the platform subjects' public part with the UV *Oferta de Curso académico (OCA)* application.

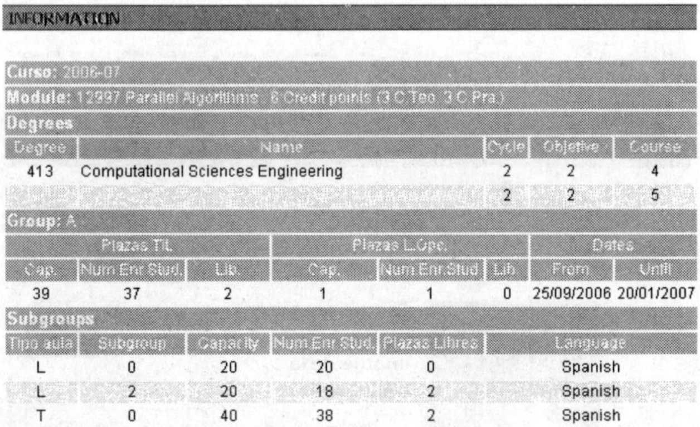

INFORMATION

Curso: 2006-07

Module: 12997 Parallel Algorithms. 6 Credit points (3 C.Teo 3 C.Pra.)

Degrees

Degree	Name	Cycle	Objetive	Course
413	Computational Sciences Engineering	2	2	4
		2	2	5

Group: A

Plazas T.L.			Plazas L.Opc.			Dates	
Cap.	Num.Enr.Stud.	Lib.	Cap.	Num.Enr.Stud.	Lib.	From	Until
39	37	2	1	1	0	25/09/2006	20/01/2007

Subgroups

Tipo aula	Subgroup	Capacity	Num.Enr.Stud.	Plazas Libres	Language
L	0	20	20	0	Spanish
L	2	20	18	2	Spanish
T	0	40	38	2	Spanish

Figure 19.8: Openacs Asiginfo Package

Figure 19.9 shows an example of a .LRN portlet in the private area of a course.

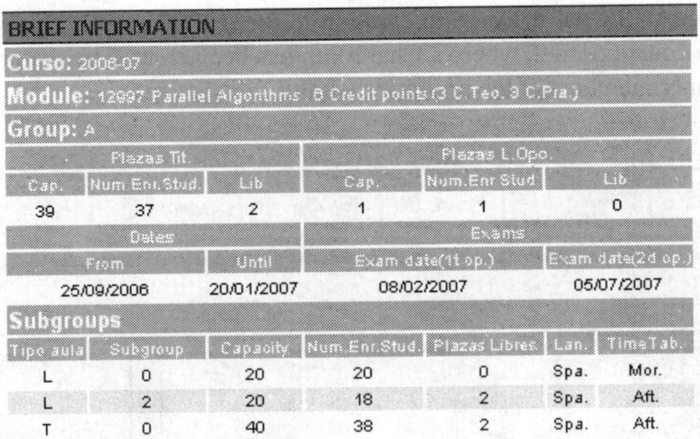

Figure 19.9: Brief Information Portlet

Own Developments and Contributions to .LRN

The users demanded new functionalities and tools, and this fact motivated their development. Among them, we can emphasize the following ones:

Implementation of the interface translation to the Catalan-Valencian and Spanish languages.

Technical support for teachers and students (Technical reference manuals and on-line help).

Development of a space within the .LRN courses where each student has a personal file, replacing classical student cards which professors traditionally asked[13], which was developed from the education Equipment portlet. In this personal file professors can access student data, including his/her photography. The file also allows professors to include commentaries, private or public, referred to the student. Figure 19.10 shows a Personal File and the way to access to the student file information.

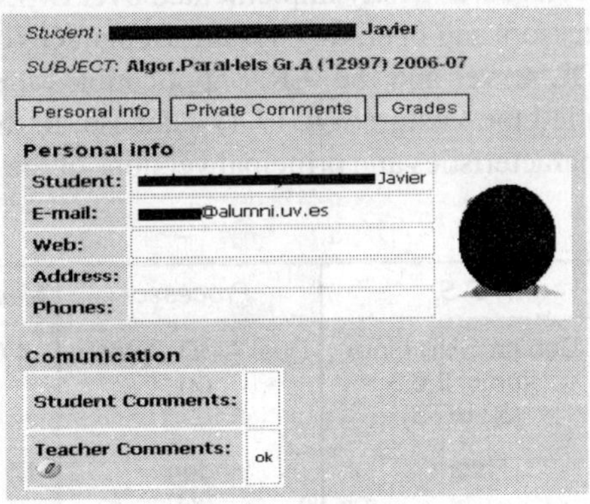

Figure 19.10: Personal File

OpenACS Chat package integration in the .LRN courses. Figure 19.11 shows a course portlet, where a Chat room has been created by the professor where only members of the group are admitted.

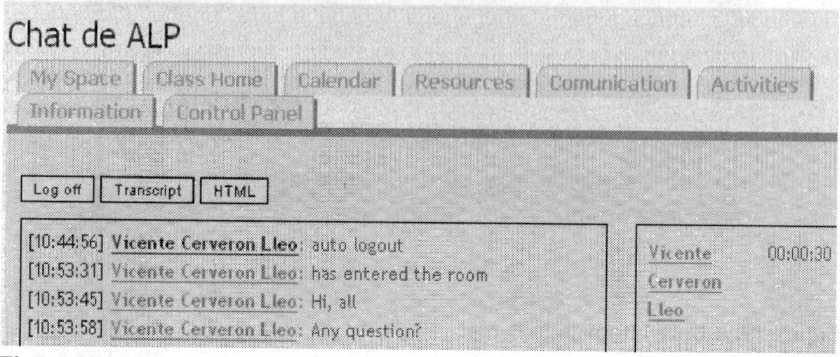

Figure 19.11: Chat Portlet

Possibility of mathematical formulation insertion, introducing symbols, in LaTeX or in ASCIIMath (based in MathML). Figure 19.12 shows a formula insertion using ASCIIMath.

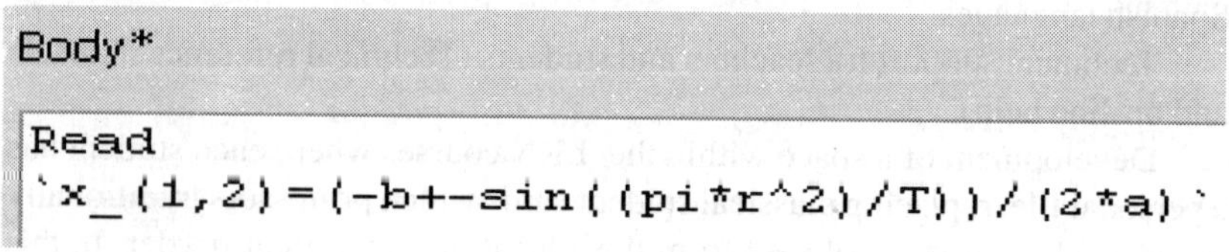

Figure 19.12: Latex Formulae

Aula Virtual's Hardware Evolution

The system architecture was firstly implemented over two servers with AMD Opteron dual processors and operating system Debian GNU/Linux. In one of these, the web AOL server and the .LRN application were installed. In the other, it was installed the PostgreSQL (7.4) database. In the following table there appear the characteristics and principal versions of the products installed in the servers:

Layer	*O.S.*	*Processor*	*Memory*	*Observations*
Web: Aolserver 4.0.5	Debian GNU/Linux kernel 2.6.3 (32 BITS)	Dual AMD Opteron (x1)	4 GB	OpenACS 5.1.4 .LRN 2.0
DB: PostgreSQL 7.4.5	Idem	Idem (x4)	12 GB	

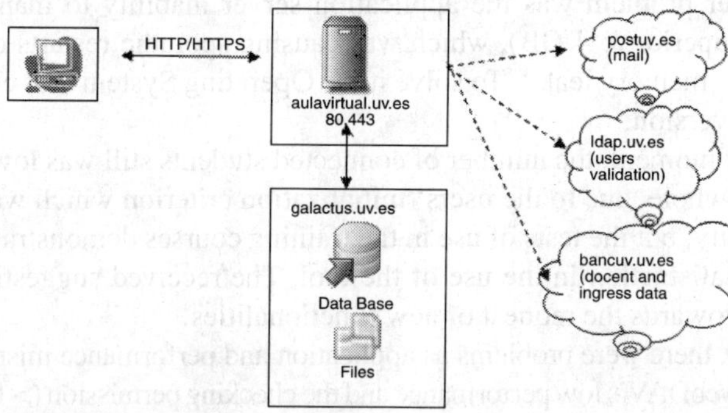

Figure 19.13: Academic Year 2004-2005

The First Cluster of Aula Virtual (Academic Year 2005-06)

There were made tests of performance whose results show scalability problems. These problems were reported to OpenACS's forum, and it was decided to choose the following architecture to install the production platform. The first solution was a CISCO device to balance the load between two web servers. The web servers were connected to the unique database server. The main problem with this solution was synchronization. The configuration of this academic year is shown at Figure 19.14.

Layer	*O.S.*	*Processor*	*Memory*	*Observations*
Web: Aolserver 4.0.5	Debian GNU/Linux kernel 2.6.3 (32 bits)	Dual AMD Opteron (x1)	4 GB	OpenACS 5.1.4 .LRN 2.0
DB: PostgreSQL 7.4.5	Idem	Idem (x4)	12 GB	

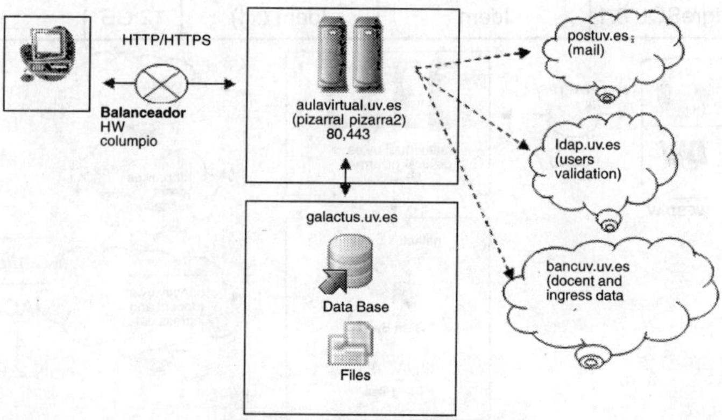

Figure 19.14: Hardware Academic Year 2005-2006

Another problem was the application server inability to manage great memory (superior to 4 GB), which was causing sporadic restarts due to the application 'memory leak '. To solve it the Operating System was changed to the 64 bits version.

At that moment, the number of connected students still was low, a fourth part of the whole, due to the users' initialization criterion which was used at the university; but the tests of use in the training courses demonstrated a high degree of satisfaction in the use of the tool. The received suggestions were orientated towards the request of new functionalities.

Finally, there were problems as application and performance mistakes; as it can be the WebDAV's low performance and the checking permission (> 1.200.000) on the great existing quantity of objects (> 3.200.000) in database. The performance problems usually occurred in the database server because some consultations were monopolizing the CPU's 100 per cent during an excessive period of time. Now, these problems have been solved rewriting the consultations' logic.

Growth and Stability (Academic Year 2006-07)

In the proceeding academic year 15000 students and 750 teachers were reached as Aula Virtual habitual users. The used criterion to consider an Aula Virtual's user is that one to be a user establishes more than 30 meetings in a four-month period. In the first four-month period of the academic year 2006-07 there were made changes in the hardware configuration: the incorporation of a Apache server to deliver the static elements; and the database server updating PostgreSQL 8.1. So, the production servers' configuration was as follows:

Layer	*O.S.*	*Processor*	*Memory*	*Observations*
Web: Aolserver 4.0.10	Debian GNU/Linux kernel 2.6.8 (64 BITS)	Dual AMD Opteron (x1)	6 GB	OpenACS 5.2 .LRN 2.2
DB: PostgreSQL 8.1	Idem	Idem (x4)	12 GB	

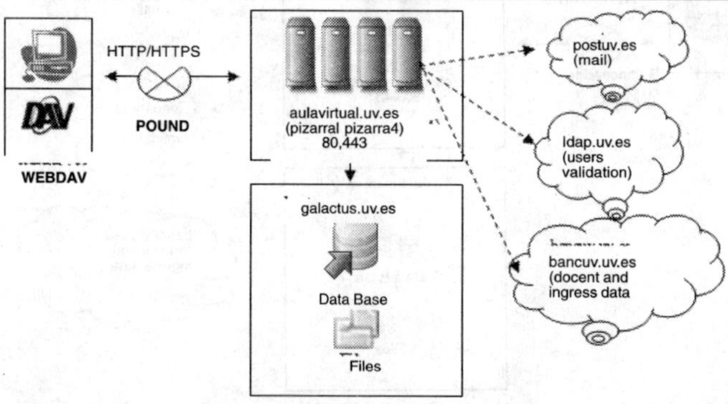

Figure 19.15: Hardware Academic Year 2006-2007

The main problems of this configuration were cluster nodes synchronization failures that forced the modification of some code parts. Another improvement was the existence of two production instances, to allow the access to previous year's information, which were added to the development instance.

In this period of time 500 competing meetings were reached; and were developed the modules: Datamanager, Messenger, Wikipedia and Quotas, which will be explain in the following sections.

Virtualisation and Availability (Academic Year 2007-08)

The 2007-2008 academic year has begun with the following improvements: The number of cluster elements has been increased to six; the web and applications servers have been virtualised (Xen environment) to simplify its maintenance and the new elements management; a multimedia server has been integrated in the general architecture to stimulate the multimedia contents creation at Aula Virtual; a 'heart-beat' solution is going to be incorporated at the balancing load system, so that, another cluster element has the load balance device role in case the principal one does not answer. Finally, the couple Apache + Pound is going to be substituted with a Nginx server.

Layer	*O.S.*	*Processor*	*Memory*	*Observations*
Web: Aolserver 4.5	Debian GNU/Linux kernel 2.6.15 (64 bits)	Dual AMD Opteron (x1)	6 GB	OpenACS 5.3.2 .LRN 2.3.0
DB: PostgreSQL 8.2.5	Idem	Idem (x4)	12 GB	

Aula Virtual's Software Evolution

The OpenACS development system structure creates every module as an independent application with the habitual default parameters and permissions. Usually, students can read and teachers write. To support the default applications installed or to incorporate and parameterize new with permissions: public or private, is the course's teacher decision. The Framework incorporates the based on independent layers development that facilitate its maintenance, presentation, logic and information. In this section, the new developments installed at Aula Virtual, are detailed, grouped by its functionality.

(i) Management Tools

The main lacks in the management system are: the information migration of some modules and the disc occupation control by course documents or users. To solve them, it was developed the Datamanager Tool, which allows to import/export XML information or to copy data between groups (www.ietf.org/rfc/rfc2445.txt). Each new academic year, a new platform instance is created. This instance contains the academic current offer and its responsible teachers. Therefore, the teachers decide what information to export or import among instances or if they have some reusable material to copy between its different matters. News, FAQ, Forums, Card and Blogs are the modules that allow migrating its information. The rest of tools already had the option implemented or due to its caducity it was not necessary to implement it. The information migration between different platforms would be easy because the information is restructured in XML format.

The Quota application allows the platform manager to establish a general control of storage quota for users and groups. Nowadays there is a 100 MB quota as user (50.000 users * 100 = 5 TB) in the personal space and 500 MB as course (10.000 courses* 500 = 4.5 TB). If some courseor user exceeds its quota; it is possible to extend it without considering the general parameters. In the academic year 2006/2007 it was in use a total of 90 GB of disc (600.000 documents).

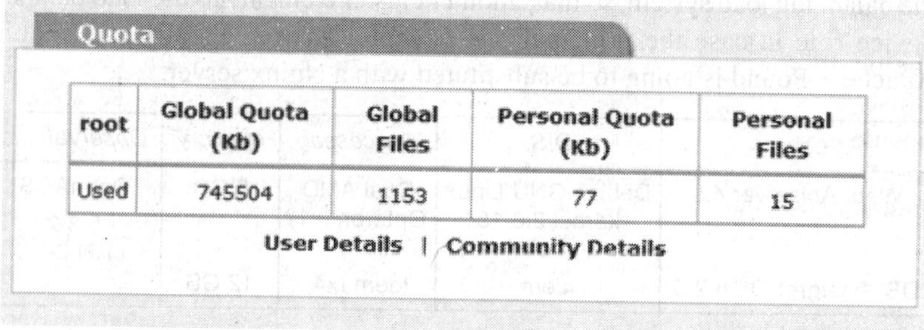

Figure 19.16: Quota

(ii) Communication Tools

This kind of tools is very popular between teachers and students because up to the moment, the communication was via email, with distribution lists and its management was heavy enough. Nowadays, a teacher can send emails to its pupils with a couple of mouse clicks. On the other hand, the facility of use has been increased the massive post office. To avoid this problem and to centralize the communication in the platform, there has been created a new tool of internal communication called Messenger. The teachers can send messages to its pupils and also among themselves.

The personal Blogs are one of the last utilities implemented, now in test phase. The platform was having group Blogs, but due to the users demand, the application has been adapted and improved in order that every user in its personal portal has the possibility of creating its own personal Blog.

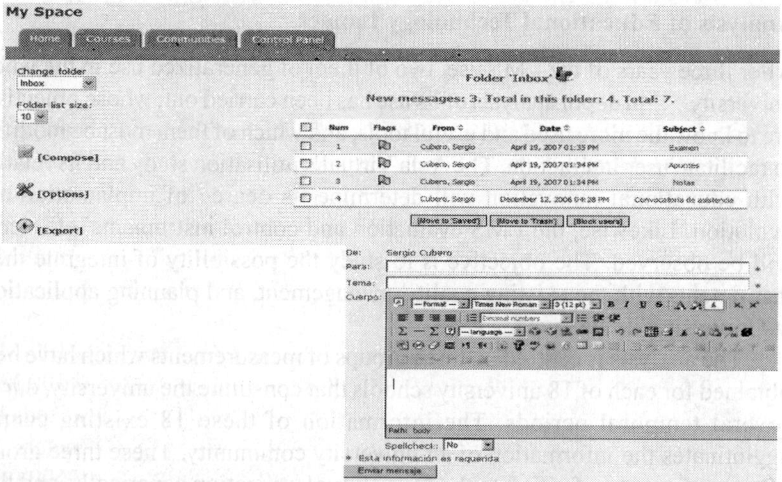

Figure 19.17: Personal Blog

(iii) Distribution of contents, Tools

The platform can show multimedia in a HTML page or of a IMS/SCORM course, but the teacher demands a simpler way to do it. This led to the MMPlayer module creation. This reproduces multimedia resources which are served by the Macroaverage Flash video server. The teacher only must raise up to the platform the multimedia file and the student can reproduce it only acceding to the course. The recommended video and audio format are FLV and MP3 respectively, because they are the files that serve in streaming the Macroaverage server. There have been joined FFmpeg libraries (http://mmedia.uv.es) which codify to the format FLV any other format. The multimedia resources which are established as public are automatically catalogued and it is allowed its access via Web.

Playing one FLV file

Figure 19.18: MM Player

Finally, we can mention the link to Wikipedia (http://es.wikipedia.org/wiki/FFmpeg) which visualizes the definition of the word selected inside the course; and a simple manager of definable by the users' databases, which is very usefully in the research projects that use the platform and need to catalogue bibliographical references, links, images, etc.

Analysis of Educational Technology Impact

After three years of the LMS use, two of them of generalized use in the whole university[14, 15] in depth analysis of its use has been carried out; whose objectives are to know the more used and useful tools, and which of them must be modified to facilitate user interaction. The Aula Virtual's utilisation study and its relation with educational innovation will determine its degree of implantation and evolution. Likewise, the LMS evaluation and control instruments' efficiency will be observed. The objective is to study the possibility of integrate these instruments with the existing quality, management, and planning applications at Universitat de València.

The analysis is centred on three groups of measurements which have been obtained for each of 18 university schools that constitute the university, during several temporal periods. The information of these 18 existing centres agglutinates the information of all university community. These three groups of measurements refer first to the Aula Virtual utilization generically, and they include the study of the variables: **avprof** (teachers), **aval** (pupils) and **avasig** (subjects); and the use of its tools, whose variables of study are: **doc** (documents), **forum**, **notic** (news), **correo** (mail) and **activ** (activities). On the other hand they are confronted by the set of the educational innovation plans in the study centres, whose analysis measurements are: **IECURS** (educational innovation courses), **IECOORD** (number of coordinators on innovation), **IEPROF** (number of teachers on innovation) and **IEAL** (number of pupils on innovation), and **PIES** (number of educational innovation projects). And thirdly, overall education quality indexes (in Spanish, índices de Financiación Ligada a Objetivos-FLO) are analyzed school by school. The quality indexes which are included in the study are: **TABAN** (abandon rate), **TAD2C** (admissions in the first or second preference rate), **ISADC** (satisfaction of the pupils with the received teaching), **TMEC** (months of students stay in international programmes of interchange) and **NSSP2C** (school/centre acceptance).

Once the descriptive study of these variables has been realized, a complex set of summary measurements have been elaborated to contemplate the relevance and influence of the different variables of every group. New summary variables will be those whose psicometric behaviour has been the best. After it, the relation between new variables of the different groups is explored, to obtain useful information about how the three axes of approximation to Higher Education European System (HEES) convergence and learning processes improvement are related.

Descriptive Results

The analysis has been carried out by evaluating two academic years. In the **2004/2005 academic period,** blended learning courses were activated on requests (after explicit expression of interest from the involved professors and lecturers). 600 requests were received which generated the creation of 2,662 courses with 1,890 groups and 35,400 users with a student role. Beside 18 communities (collaborative groups) associated to research projects were opened. Simultaneously connected users' average between 8:00 and 24:00 hours was 40 with peak values of 80 users.

For the **2005/2006 academic year** all courses in the Universitat de València were opened for blended and technology enhanced learning, giving a personal account to all students and professors and lecturers. In addition, a utility to import the previous course contents was implemented. Figures from this academic period were: 48,199 students involved, 3,256 professors and lecturers, 8,197 courses, 41 communities (research groups sharing information and communication resources). General activity results indicate that 1,420 professors and 29,553 students had employed to the platform more than 10 times; 871 and 18.604 had done it more than 30 times. This fact represents a utilization of 55 per cent basic users and 33.5 per cent habitual users (There are study centres where the percentage doubled). These data are specially valuable considering that the use of the Aula Virtual is voluntary as much for the teaching staff as for the student, who has alternative ways to follow and pass the matters, courses and activities. In fact, the use of 'Aula virtual' is not obligatory but improves traditional teaching[16]. Statistics of use of different modules show that the tool more used is **Documents** and the less used is the one of **Activity-Evaluation**, as can be observed at Figure 19.19.

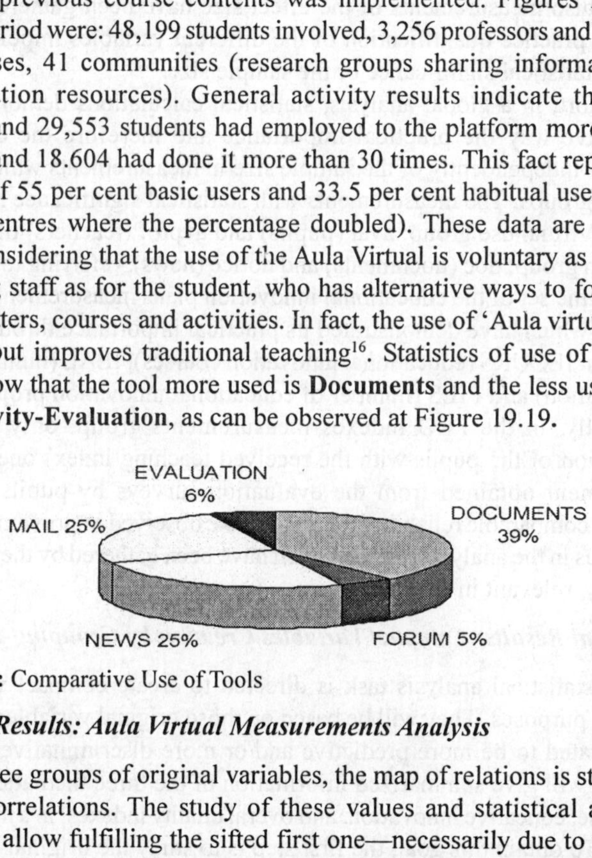

Figure 19.19: Comparative Use of Tools

Inferential Results: Aula Virtual Measurements Analysis

From the three groups of original variables, the map of relations is studied by Pearson's correlations. The study of these values and statistical associate significance allow fulfilling the sifted first one—necessarily due to the great number of contemplated variables—which annotates the most relevant aspects. At the same time, having treated about linear correlation coefficients, the study of every couple of correlated variables association has been carried out by means of a dispersion graph. From all considered variables that show significant correlation, only two do not show a linear correlation with the rest: an innovation indicator **(PIES)** and the FLO indicator **TAD2C**.

The indicator values have been gathered in different temporal periods, and they include two or even three courses. For that reason it is interesting to know if there are significant differences between the values depending on the different analyzed times. The objective is to establish whether improvement between courses has been relevant in statistical terms and it not has been produced randomly. This analysis phase has been made with the SPSS 14 Linear General Model Module of repeated measurements ANOVA. Moreover, the Huyhn and Feldt correction verifies the necessary suppositions to use the statistical tests as there may exist homogeneity problems in the variable variance. Besides, also measurements of the effect size have been gathered. This fact reflects a practice quantification of the different variables importance, apart from its statistical significance or the sample size.

In short, in a global analysis, statistical calculations demonstrated in a quantitative way the practical importance and therefore the comparative capability independently of the sample size in measurements which belong to the three groups. The measurements with statistical significance have been in the Aula Virtual use group: aval (pupils) and avprof (teachers) of generically utilization group; doc (documents) and notice (news), referring to its tools use group. In the set of the educational innovation plans measurements group, the variables which have demonstrated its practical importance through the years have been: IECURS (educational innovation courses), IEAL (number of pupils on innovation) and PIES (number of educational innovation projects).

Finally, in the FLO indexes measurements group, only the ISADC (satisfaction of the pupils with the received teaching index) one, which is a measurement obtained from the evaluation surveys by pupils, presents a statistical comparable reliability. Therefore, the observed improvements through the courses in the analyzed period which have been gathered by these indicators are, really, relevant in statistical terms.

Inferential Results: Compact Variables Creation by Grouping Indicators

Another statistical analysis task is directed to create compact variables for summary purposes. They will be based on those original variables which have demonstrated to be more predictive and/or more discriminative. These new variables will give summarized information of the three thematic areas: Aula Virtual use, educative innovation, and overal quality indexes, in a more efficient manner. To obtain this goal, the first step is to study the original composition of variables, and its possible grouping in one or more by each group, by means of the Principal Components Analysis (PCA). This kind of study forces a factor and studies the explained variance percentage, and also uses the sedimentation graph. The results which have been obtained indicate a totally different behaviour for each of three variables groups.

The Aula Virtual use variables have been assigned to two components. The first component is named **Platform Implantation**: it is explained in a 46.42 per cent in the 2005 course and in a 33.74 per cent in the 2006 course. In both courses this component includes the variables **avprof** (teachers), **aval** (pupils) and **activ** (activities), but in 2006 **avasig** (subjects) is added to the factorial solution. The second component of this factorial solution with orthogonal components (varimax rotation) is named **Tools**: it is explained in a 25.41 per cent in the 2005 course and in a 30.08 per cent in the 2006 course; it is formed by contributions of the variables **doc** (documents), **forum**, **notic** (news) and **correo** (mail); but in the 2006 solution the variable **forum** is not included.

The educative innovation variables offer a very clear one-factor solution, which is explained in a 94.03 per cent in the 2006 course and in an 89.8 per cent in the 2005 course. In both cases the new variable is formed by the variables **IECURS** (educational innovation courses), **IECOORD** (number of coordinators on innovation), **IEPROF** (number of teachers on innovation) and **IEAL** (number of pupils on innovation), that is to say all educational innovation indicators less **PIES**, which has been those discarded previously because of its not linear behaviour.

The third group of variables, those belonging to overal education quality indexes, has not offered any factorial solution consistent across the different courses. There is no solution with considerable explanation percentages nor interpretable. For this reason its use is kept as indicators and it is not proposed a summary global indicator.

Inferential Results: Compact Variables Analysis

The last phase of analysis raises new Pearson's correlation mould with these summary variables. The correlation tries to offer a more interpretable and direct information oriented to have good decisions in the Aula Virtual environment. The Pearson's linear correlations mould studies the association between the new key indicators, relating them for couples.

High and positive relations have been obtained in every measurement in the successive years; but the Aula Virtual component **Tools** is excluded because it presents a very low correlation (0.072) in successive years. This fact can be explained because the different Universitat de València study centres have applied different politicies to spread the new available modules as much as its improvements. As for the interfamily correlations (measurements belonging to different families in successive courses): in general, the Aula Virtual implantation is related to the educative innovation projects and the student success index also can be related to the Aula Virtual implantation. As for specific relations, it is necessary to emphasize that **TMEC** (months of students' stay in international programmes of interchange) in the 2005 course it predicts the 2006 course educative innovation in almost 40 per cent; or that the 2004 course's **TABAN** (abandon rate) can predict the 2005 course variable **Tools** in 25 per cent.

Finally, linear predictive regressions of the Aula Virtual use during last courses have been realized. The results offer significant regressions to predict the platform implantation, but not to predict the component **Tools**. This last aspect can be more linked to the educational peculiarities of every centre. For that reason, technical work must be centred on improving the different tools, by maintaining a close contact and communication with those centres/schools with highest use of those tools. On the other hand, the implantation criteria must be guided by general actuation programmes, centred on University's decisions; because implantation has resulted related to innovation, and to overall education quality indexes.

Conclusions and Future Work

Universitat de València is the largest in Spain adopting an open source platform linked to educative innovation for blended learning. The evaluation process shows a high degree of use of Aula Virtual, even being voluntary. This fact evidences clearly that both, professors and students, have found real utility and new possibilities using the LMS. The Aula Virtual use helps to establish methodologies and parameters to plan and to evaluate the on-line learning incorporation in learning processes, always according to the European convergence process criteria; and also promotes the technological and pedagogic collaboration. This collaboration is based on transference and reutilization of educational materials and formative resources among all universities in Higher Education European Area or in the rest of the world.

There are two Aula Virtual modules which are being improved in short term to be used in educative innovation. They are the less and the most used tools: Assessment-Activity, and Documents, respectively. The improvement of these modules can help to its generalized use at all the university, and to its use related to innovation future analysis that must be made in the near future to continue helping the new learning-teaching processes.

Activities and assessment modules allow the distribution of tasks between homework, practices and exams, the weighted distribution in the final evaluation note of each one of these tasks, etc.; but some defects which were detected. It is clear that many different situations are presented. The current work in progress tries to gather all the possibilities to reach that assessment-activity application can be used by all professors who want to manage students' evaluation by using Aula Virtual. There are two phases in the programmed work. In first phase, all possible forms of evaluation that can occur in the different university courses must be compiled and an algorithm, which takes into accounts all of them must be defined. The algorithm will reach the solution using a logical sequential flow. In the second phase, a module whose start point is the existing Aula Virtual' tools will be developed. This software module will have to be able to implement the algorithm which has been defined on the first step. The result will be a new module which gathers all the evaluation styles of a subject and it will finish with its final grade. Finally, necessities to export results to other university applications will be identified; and also these applications will be integrated with the new module.

As for the Aula Virtual Documents tool improvement, the Universitat de València LMS has not the possibility of dynamic content creation, which could be visualized, and edited at the platform. At present, an active collaboration between University of Galileo and Universitat de València is maintained http://openacs.org/xowiki/Simple_Content_development_tool, in order to create a content creation tool for Learning Objects, related to the .LRN LORS package. The use of this package will allow to create adaptative and collaborative learning models, and, on the other hand, to create re-usable contents; not only in different courses and groups of one institution, but also in other LMS. This interoperability will be guaranteed by using standards in contents creation.

Finally, the generalization in use of the blended learning and ICT in the teaching activity will depend decisively on the pedagogical work. This means that it must be developed new courses and activities to instruct in the use of the tool; and also to inform the university community about ICT use and LMS environment didactical potentialities.

References

1. Lee, W., Owens, D.L. (2003), 'Multimedia-Based Instructional Design: Computer-Based Training', *Web-Based Training, and Distance Learning*, Pfeiffer (Wiley), USA, 2000.
2. Wong, H.K., 'How to Improve Student Achievement (1)', Harry K. Wong Publications, USA.
3. Pallof, R.M., Pratt, K., 'Collaborating Online: Learning Together in Community', Jossey-Bass (Wiley), USA, 2003.
4. Roig, D., 2003. 'Evaluación de plataformas de Teleformación para su implantación en el ámbito universitario', *Proyecto final de carrera de Ingeniería Informática*, Universitat de València, 2003.
5. Vázquez, J.A., Roca, S., López, A., Roig, D., Cubero, S., 'Implantación de .LRN en la Universitat de València. Integración de la plataforma y desarrollos propios' *Foro hispano de .LRN. Congreso de usuarios y desarrolladores de .LRN*, 2005.
6. CRUE, 'Las tecnologías de la Información y las Comunicaciones en el Sistema Universitario Español', A report conducted by Senén Barro (USC Rector), 2004.
7. Calvo, P.A., 'Introduction to e-commerce system', *Pearson Education*, 2002.
8. S. Ros, J. Gonzalez-Boticario, R. Pastor, M. Rodríguez-Artacho. M, Un modelo de organización para la producción de cursos virtuales, Jornadas sobre el uso de las TIC en la UNED, Madrid, Spain, April 2005.
9. O.C. Santos, J. Gonzalez-Boticario, C. Barrera, aLFanet: An adaptive and standard-based learning environment built upon dotLRN and other open source developments, Foro hispano de .LRN. (see [2]), Madrid, 2005.
10. Essa, A., Cerverón, V., Blessius, C., '.LRN: An Enterprise Open-Source Learning Management System', *Educause 2005,* Orlando (USA), 2005.

11. Demetriou, N., Koch, S., Neumann, G., 'The Development of the OpenACS Community', *Open Source for Knowledge and Learning Management: Strategies Beyond Tools,* Miltiadis Lytra, Ambjorn Naeve, Idea Group Publishing, Hersey, PA, 2006.
12. Boticario J.G., Raffence E., Aguado M., Arroyo D., Cordova M.A., *et al.* (2004) 'An active collaborative framewok for improving e-learning practices'. On Proceedings *21st Worls Conference on Open Learning and Distance Education, ICDE*, 2004.
13. Soler-Lahuerta, F., Cubero, S, López, A., Roig, D., Roca, S., 'Desarrollo del módulo fichas en la estructura de la UVEG para la herramienta groupware .LRN', *Foro hispano de .LRN, Congreso de usuarios y desarrolladores de .LRN,* Madrid, 2005.
14. Moreno, P. and Cerverón, V. (2006). '« Aula virtual »: an e-learning management platform of Universitat de València development based on Open Code and Collaborative Software', *M-ICTE, IV Conferencia Internacional sobre Multimedia Tecnologías de la Información y Comunicación en Educación*, November, Sevilla, 2006.
15. Moreno, P., Cerverón, V., 'Plataforma tecnológica para potenciar los procesos de enseñanza-aprendizaje: desarrollo en la Universitat de València basado en software libre y colaborativo', *SIIE 06. VIII Simposio Internacional de informática aplicada a la enseñanza,* León, 2006.
16. Vázquez, J.A., Roca, S., López, A., Roig, D., Cubero, S., 'Implantación del software .LRN open source de ayuda al aprendizaje en la Universitat de València', II *Congreso de Software Libre de la Comunidad Valenciana*. Castellón, 2005.

20

Enhancing Teaching and Facilitating Learning Using ICT

Shyamal Majumdar

During the past few years, the world has witnessed a phenomenal growth in communication technology, computer network and information technology. Development of new broadband communication services and convergence of telecommunication with computers have created numerous possibilities to use a variety of new technology tools for teaching and learning system. The integration of computers and communications offer unprecedented opportunities to the education systems with its capacity to integrate, enhance and interact with each other over a wide geographic distance in a meaningful way to achieve the learning objectives. The growth of these communication and computer systems, their ease of use, the power and diversity of information transfer allow teachers and students to have access to a world beyond the classroom[1]. It has the potential to transform the nature and process of the learning environment and envision a new learning culture. Interactivity, flexibility and convenience have become the order of the day in the ICT supported environment. ICT opens up opportunities for learning because it enables learners to access, extend, transform and share ideas and information in multi-modal communication styles and format. It helps the learner to share learning resources and spaces, promote learner centered and collaborative learning principles and enhance critical thinking, creative thinking and problem solving skills.

Not only mastering ICT skills, but also utilizing ICT to improve teaching and learning is of utmost importance for teachers in performing their role of creators of pedagogical environments. While literature provides some evidence of the effectiveness of using ICT in technical considerations, little is known about which learning strategies and pedagogical framework should be used for education and training. How to construct these electronic teaching and learning environments so that they are based on specific epistemologies or knowledge bases? What will be the new vision and guiding principles of teacher development for pedagogy-technology integration? As we become increasingly supported by ICT, teaching and learning will not be the same as before. We will have to make use of the rich and exciting opportunities offered by the new technologies in education to reach our new goal and vision. To appreciate the integration of ICT in teaching and learning, we need to understand the major paradigm shifts in education in recent years.

Paradigm Shifts

Education around the world is experiencing major paradigm shifts in educational practices of teaching and learning under the umbrella of ICT enabled learning environment. Whereas learning through facts, drill and practices, rules and procedures was more adaptive in earlier days, learning through projects and problems, inquiry and design, discovery and invention, creativity and diversity, action and reflection is perhaps more fitting for the present times. The major hallmark of this learning transition is from teacher centered to learner focus paradigm.

During the last three decades, the changes in educational environment have been phenomenal. The model, focus, role of the learner and technology has been changed drastically from traditional instruction to virtual learning environment as depicted below.

Changes in Teaching-Learning Environment

Model	Focus	Role of Learner	Technology
Traditional	teachers	Passive	Chalk & Talk
Information	Learners	Active	Personal Computer
Knowledge	Group	Adaptive	PC + Network

Shifting the emphasis from teaching to learning can create a more interactive and engaging learning environment for teachers and learners. This new environment also involves a change in roles of both teachers and learners. The role of the teachers will change from knowledge transmitter to that of facilitator, knowledge navigator and sometime as co-learner. The new role of teachers demand a new way of thinking and understanding of the new vision of learning process. Learners will have more responsibilities of their own learning as they seek out, find, synthesize, and share their knowledge with others[2]. ICT provides powerful tools to support the shift from teacher centred to learner centred paradigm and new roles of teacher, learner, curricula and new media. The major shifts have been described in a tabular form below.

All these changes taking place in learning and teaching demand a new learning environment to effectively harness the power of ICT to improve learning. ICT has the potential to transform the nature of education: where,

Changes in Teachers' Roles	
From	*TO*
Transmitter of Knowledge	Guide & Facilitator of Knowledge
Controller of Learning	Creator of Learning Environment
Always Expert	Collaborator & Co-learner
Learning to use ICT	Using ICT to Enhance Learning
Didactive/Expository	interactive/Expenential/Exploratory

Changes in Learnerrs' Roles	
From	*TO*
Passive Learner	Active Learner
Reproducer of Knowledge	Producer of Knowledge
Dependent Learner	Autonomous Learner
Solitary Learner	Collaborative Learner
Solely Learning content	Learning to learn/Think/Create & Communicate

Changes in Curricula and Delivery	
From	*TO*
Single Sense Stimulation	Inquiry Based
Single Media Application	Multi Sensory Stimulation
Delivery of Information	Multimedia Application
Monologue communication	Exchange of Information
Analogue Resources	Dialogue & Collaborative
	Digital Resources

Changes in Curricula and Delivery	
From	*TO*
Single Sense Stimulation	Multi Sensory Stimulation
Single Media Application	Multimedia Application
Delivery of Information	Exchange of Information
Monologue Communication	Dialogue & Collaborative
Analogue Resources	Digital Resources

when, how and the way learning takes place. It will facilitate the emergence of responsible knowledge society emphasizing life long learning with meaningful and enjoyable learning experiences.

Creating New Cultures

The integration of ICT into the very idea of teaching and learning always places pedagogy over technology. It is not the only concern to master ICT skills, but rather it involves using ICT to improve teaching and learning. The major emphasis of ICT infusion in pedagogy should be such that it tends to improve learning, motivate and engage learners, promote collaboration, foster enquiry and exploration, and create a new learner centered learning culture. It permits the move from reproductive model of teaching and learning to an independent, autonomous learning model that promotes initiation, creativity and critical thinking with independent research. Learners are expected to collect, select, analyze, organize, extend, transform and present knowledge using ICT in authentic and active learning paradigm. Teachers are expected to create a new flexible and open learning environment with interactive, experiential and multimedia based delivery system. ICT should help teachers and learners to communicate and collaborate without boundaries, make learners autonomous and allow teachers to bring the whole world into classroom activities. It is ultimately important to understand the roles of ICT in promoting educational changes. A basic principle is that the use of ICT changes the distribution and ownership of information resources in the space of teaching and learning and thus changes the relationship among educational participants[3]. While designing any innovative teaching and learning environment using ICT, the teacher should always keep the learning at the centre of all activities, pedagogy should be at the heart and integration of pedagogy-technology should be the central focus.

Pedagogical Practices using ICT

Mere learning ICT skills is not suffice, but using ICT to improve the teaching and learning is the key for pedagogy-technology integration. But the question is how we can combine these two.

Consider a scenario of a young teacher who has just started to use ICT for his daily classroom activities of teaching and learning. To start with he or she needs to prepare lesson plans and compile lesson materials for the classroom lecture. To prepare such materials one has to go through the act of drafting phase, editing phase, revising phase and finally publishing the lesson plans and course contents. Word processor can be a great help to accomplish this task in a professional and productive way to avoid repetition, duplication of manual work and concentrate on quality of the course materials.

The teachers also need to make lists of the name of the students for monitoring and recording their academic performance and to analyze and perform a statistical analysis to take some corrective measure if any, in the lesson plan, delivery of instruction. Spreadsheets can be a good choice for creating class lists, recording their performance and executing statistical analysis upon them.

While delivering the class lectures, any innovative teacher needs to draw diagrams, show pictures, animate some objects to explain critical concepts, even play some video clipping of real time operation. All these multimedia applications can assure very productive, interesting, motivating, interactive and quality delivery of classroom instruction. Presentation software like power point can be a good choice for teachers for performing such tasks.

In spite of the best efforts of teachers there will be a number of learners who will not be satisfied with the pace of instruction of the teachers. There may be a fast learner, average learner and slow learner. In a classroom environment it is impossible to satisfy all categories of learners with their specific learning styles. It is in these situations, teachers become helpless in a conventional teaching and learning environment. One way to solve such situations is to create interactive multimedia based instructional materials where learner is given control to review the topic at their own pace and in accordance to their individual interests, needs and cognitive processes. As such, multimedia courseware can be of great help to teachers to meet the challenges of such situation. With availability of user friendly authoring tools, it is now possible to develop multimedia courseware by any young teachers to support drill and practice to master basic skills, simulate complicated situations, produce individualized instruction with multimedia elements with built-in evaluation questions and scores. Such multimedia courseware can produce profound changes in the learning outcomes when it is being used along with face-to-face instruction.

Learners always look for flexibility in time, space, place, content selection and delivery of instructions. It was quite impossible to satisfy such requirements in earlier times due to non-availability of proper tools. It is now feasible and possible to implement open and flexible learning strategies using ICT as tools. Flexible access to content and learning resources via network across conventional class rooms, homes and community centres is the defining characteristic of what has come to be known also as distributed learning. Learning any time, anywhere with synchronous and asynchronous communication across space, time and pace is the key to web based instruction. With the availability of online tools, it is now possible to create content websites, online education to support and assist face to face instruction in an innovative way. Communication with e-mail, searching for information, locating a proper website is now the key to success. Developing online and offline learning resources using various learning management system software/tools will become one of the key competencies of modern day teachers. Searching, locating and categorizing knowledge and information via internet have opened new vistas in implementation of flexible learning strategies.

As such starting from the productivity software to specialized educational software, there are numerous examples of various applications of the ICT tools in the teaching and learning system. Therefore, preparation of teachers to face the challenges of an ICT enriched teaching and learning environment is crucial. First teachers need to be equipped with the fundamentals of ICT tools and sufficient understanding on the integration of these tools in teaching and learning and secondly efforts must be oriented towards changing mind set and developing positive attitudes towards ICT application in teaching and learning. Understanding the changing role of teachers from instructor to facilitators, teacher lead instruction to learner-centered instruction is the key for successful implementation of pedagogy-technology integration for teacher development.

In designing learning materials using ICT productivity tools certain pedagogical principles needs to be considered carefully. Mere ICT tools by themselves do not make good pedagogy. The moot question is how should the learning environment is designed using ICT as tools? What pedagogical principles would take the advantages of the best practices and unique environment afforded by this new ICT tools. These were the central questions which needed to be addressed The use of ICT should satisfy the diverse needs of all kinds of learners characterized by all kinds of socio-cultural conditions including the diversity of multiple intelligences. Teachers should continue to learn through their lives new ways of using technology for the growth of their learners as well as the very systems of education. The critical question in education is—in what ways ICT can enhance learning and teaching practices. Broadly ICT tools help to open up opportunities for learning by enabling four major key processes in transforming teaching and learning as follows:

- Access ideas and information from diverse sources through searching, locating, selecting, and authenticating material in a wide range of multimedia forms;
- Extend ideas and information through processing, manipulating, analyzing and publishing material in different multimedia forms;
- Transform ideas and information into new or different forms through synthesizing, modeling, simulating and creating material in many multimedia styles and formats; and
- Share ideas and information across local, national and international networks by interacting electronically with others in actual and/or delayed time.

Access, extend, transform and share represent key processes by which students learn and become independent learners and self-starters. Through the processes learners express their creativity and imagination. These processes can be applied in all areas of learning and in all levels of education. There are three broad categories of educational software namely, Generic tools for learning, Content-based resources and Interactive instructional courseware. Starting from productivity tools to simulation and modeling, there are various generic tools that help learners to access, extend, transform and share information. Content-based resources help learners to access a vast source of educational resources that effectively can be integrated with the curriculum objectives. Interactive instructional coursewares are basically self-paced learning materials. These programmes are helpful to learners to control their learning at their own place and convenience.

The integration of ICT with teaching and learning has produced some of the significant positive gains in learners' knowledge, skill and attitudes by providing the following key advantages:

- Explore and represent information dynamically and in many forms
- Become socially aware and more confident
- Increase motivation
- Communicate effectively about complex processes
- Develop better understanding and broader view of processes and systems
- Greater problem solving and critical thinking skills.

A Few Emerging Topics in ICT Integration

Multimedia

The pedagogical strength of instructional multimedia is that it uses the natural information processing abilities that we already posses as humans. Our ear and eyes, in conjunction with our brain, form a formidable system for transforming meaningless sense data into information. The old saying that' a picture is worth a thousand words' often understates the case especially with regard to moving images, as our eyes are highly adapted by evolution to detecting and interpreting movement. The major challenge in designing instruction through multimedia is, therefore, the choice of media and their application for optimising human learning with respect to the learning objectives. Multimedia courseware development process[4] is the systematic approach to the analysis, design, development, implementation and evaluation of learning materials. Instructional design aims for a learner-centered rather than the traditional teacher-centered approach to instruction, so that effective learning can take place. There appears to be an increasing realization by teaching faculty that in particular situation, multimedia courseware can offer a pedagogical improvement on traditional teaching methods by providing the learners with following advantages:

- Exercise more effectively and efficient control over their own learning.
- Secure real time assessment and feedback.
- Secure more information on their own learning.
- Obtain situational appropriate learning assistance.
- Obtain more individualized learning assistance.

E-learning

The link between distance learning and telecommunications is becoming even stronger, yielding new solutions to old problems, innovative educational resources and new teaching/learning practices. One of the most innovative and promising outcomes of this relationship is e-learning and online education, notably a process whereby teachers and students are linked up in an electronic media/computer network[5].

The concept of e learning and how it relates to effective use of ICT is critically important for teacher education, because it places the focus firmly where it should be—jointly on pedagogy and the new ICT. The term e-learning, or learning via electronic media, nicely combines this twin concept: first, the changing focus of pedagogy to learning and, second and the new technologies stretching beyond the walls of the traditional classroom. In other words, e-learning for teacher development is learning about, with, and through all electronic media (i.e., ICT) across the curriculum to support student learning. ICT is the means, and e-learning and the effective integration of pedagogy and ICT constitute the goal. There are a number of benefits to e-learning. These include any time learning, anywhere learning, asynchronous interaction and group collaboration.

Blogs

Blogs or classroom web logs are becoming increasingly popular with teachers and teacher education. Many experts predict that blogs will eventually become more successful teaching tools than websites[6]. A blog is a web page made up of usually short, frequently updated posts that are arranged chronologically-like a 'what's new' page of a journal. The contents and the purposes of blogs vary greatly from links and commentary about other websites to news about a company/person/idea, photos, poetry, mini-essays, project updates, even fictions. A crucial blog mission is to link to other web sites, or, sometimes even other blogs.

Many blogs are personal. Others are collaborative efforts based on a specific topic or an area of mutual interest. The use of blogs in instructional settings is limited only by one's imagination. There are many ways teachers can use blogs, some of them include content-related blog, networking and personal knowledge sharing, instructional tips for learners, course announcements and readings, annotated links etc., most importantly for the purpose of knowledge management. Learners can also take part in blogs by reflective writing, assignment submission, collaborative work, e-portfolios and sharing course-related resources. For teachers, blogs are attractive because it needs little efforts to maintain, unlike more elaborate classroom web sites. Teachers can build a blog or start a new topic in an existing blog by simply typing text into a box and clicking a button. Such ease of use is the primary reason to predict that blogs are more successful teaching tools than web sites.

Pedagogical Content Knowledge

Pedagogy cannot exist in isolation to contents. In fact, there is a new beginning to appreciate that the two intertwined into what is described as Pedagogical Content Knowledge (PCK), and is an essential tenet in the current thinking about teacher education. The term content refers to far more than factual information. It encompasses all aspects of a subject: concept, principles, relationships, methods of inquiry and outstanding issues. According to National Science Teachers Association (NSTA)[7], meaning of content to a science teacher is (a) Concepts and principles understood through science, (b) Concepts and relationships unifying science domains, (c) Processes of investigation in a science discipline, and (d) Applications of mathematics in science research. Similarly, the pedagogy component includes actions and strategies of teaching, organization of classroom experiences, providing for diverse learner needs, evaluation and implementation based on learner's prior notions, and transformation of ideas into understandable episodes. The NSTA Standards accurately identify major problems with respect to pedagogy and contents. It states:

> [There is] '….a poor match between learner needs and teaching methodology', …….'in many traditionally taught courses the emphasis is on learning large amounts of information at a rapid pace', ……and …… 'division of knowledge, for convenience into disciplines, fields and sub fields'…… that ……'may contain the development of linkages among concepts across fields'.

This is similar to what Shulman[8] had observed, 'the key to distinguishing the knowledge base of teaching lies at the intersection of content and pedagogy'. The blend of content and pedagogical knowledge include understanding why some learners experience difficulties when learning a particular concept, while others find it easy to assimilate knowledge about useful ways to conceptualize and represent a chosen concept. The basic principles of PCK is to make teaching and learning

(a) Engaging and motivating,
(b) Interactive,
(c) Contextual,
(d) Reducing cognitive load,
(e) Scaffolding and, finally,
(f) Collaborative[9].

With ICT, there are better ways and opportunities to make above principles more realistic learning experiences. ICT encourages interactions, development of collaborative culture, utilization of active learning and introduction of feedback in proper context. ICT can bring abstract concept to life by bringing into the teaching and learning the real world experiences through simulation, modelling, capturing and analyzing real event.

All instructional designers agree on the need for effective planning of the design and development process. The success of the process largely depends on the preparation of a document, often called a lesson plan with essential elements such as clear indications of what will be done, how it will be done, when it will be done and, more importantly, how technology is going to be used. Let us take a simple example of pedagogical content knowledge with high ICT integrated approach as described below[9]:

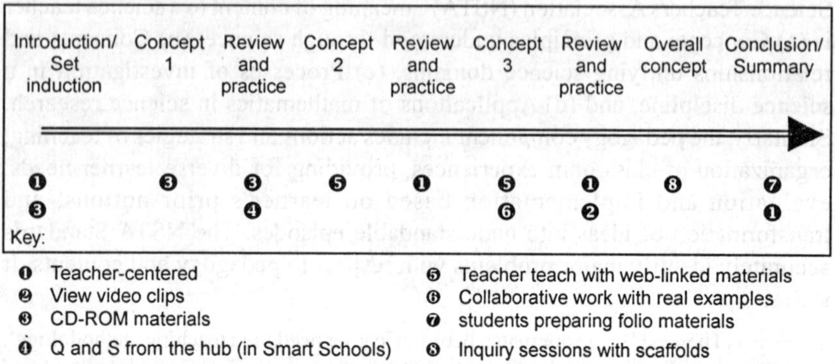

Figure 20.1: Pedagogy with ICT Integration

Figure 20.1 illustrates a higher degree of embedding ICT in teaching learning process. Such an ICT-enabled environment creates a good integrated teaching and learning with ICT that fulfils good pedagogic principles as described above.

It has been observed[2, 10] that several prominent theories such as constructivism, socio cultural concept, situated cognition, multiple intelligences, distributed cognition, problem based learning etc., play an important role in designing learner centred environment. Each of these theories is based on the same underlying assumptions that learners are active agents purposefully seeking and contributing collaborative knowledge within a meaningful context. ICT offers various tools to implement above theories to create rich and engaging learning environments.

Stages of Web Development Continuum in Teaching and Learning System

A framework[11] of use of the Web has been suggested as continuum approaches. These levels represent continuum from basic occasional use to advanced continual use. They are: (1) informational, (2) supplementary, (3) complimentary (4) hybrid and (5) total.

Level 1: Information Web Use

The informational level of Web use is the most common and easiest to manage. Informational Web use consists solely of providing relatively stable information to the student. Typically, this information is administrative in nature and may not convey course content directly. Students may access this information from time to time during the course for reference purposes, but they would not be expected to review it on a frequent basis.

Level 2: Supplementary Web Use

The supplemental level of Web use is becoming more common, is more useful than the informational level and is only slightly more difficult to manage than the information level. The key difference between Level Two and Level One is that the supplemental level actually provides course content information for the learner. As the name suggests, however, this information is not critical to the course; it is intended as an addendum to the core content. Level Two consists of the instructor placing course notes and other handouts on the Web.

Level 3: Complimentary Web Use

Essential refers to the fact that the student cannot be a productive member of the class without regular Web access. The essential level of Web use is still fairly uncommon today. At this level, the student obtains most, if not all, of the course content information from the Web. At this level, one might think, for lack of a better example, of the Web replacing textbook in the course

Level 4: Hybrid Web Use

The communal level of Web-based instruction is only just beginning to receive widespread use. At this level, classes meet face-to-face and online. Course content may be provided in an online environment or in a traditional classroom. Ideally, students generate much of the course contents themselves. This level goes beyond basic HTML and requires the use of other online tools, such as Internet chat, bulletin boards and perhaps one—and two-way desktop video.

Level 5: Total Web Use

At this level all of the course content and course interactions occur online., this level should be seen as a sophisticated, constructivist virtual learning community. While it may include some degree of traditional content presentation, student practice, feedback and assessment practices found in traditional distance instruction, it is often comprised of learner-centered, constructivist pedagogues. At this level, both instructor and students must have a high level of technical expertise and sophisticated learning strategies.

Conclusion

As we become increasingly supported by ICT, teaching and learning will not be the same as before. We will have to make use of the rich and exciting opportunities offered by the new technologies in education to reach our training goal and mission. One of the objectives of the present paper is to provide better understanding and appreciation of the role of ICT in teaching and learning system. Several view points of integrating ICT in teaching and learning system has been discussed. Learning is not a transfer of knowledge, rather an active construction. This paradigm shifts give the learners a completely new role that was not earlier described in the transmission model of teaching. Technology and teacher professional development in its use are best introduced in the context of broader educational reform which embraces a shift away from teacher-centred, lecture oriented towards learner centred, interactive and constructive learning environment. Multimedia and ICT can play the role of catalyst for such educational reforms. Multimedia courseware can promote effective instruction that is more engaging; learner centred, interdisciplinary and more closely related to real life events and processes and adaptive to individual learning styles and needs. It also encourages higher order thinking skills and help to construct knowledge socially. Thus teacher professional development in the use of interactive technology should embody and model the forms of pedagogy that teacher can use themselves in their classroom.

References

1. Majumdar, S. (1997). Network based flexible learning: Prospects and challenges in the 21st Century: Invited keynote address at the International Conference of Vocational Education and Training (IVETA '97), Helsinki, Finland. August 24-28.
2. Resta, P. (Ed.). (2002). Information and Communication Technologies in Teacher Education: A Planning Guide. UNESCO, Paris.
3. Zhu, Z.T. (2003). On Educational Informatization and the transforms of educational cultures, in Journal of Global Chinese Society of Computers in Education, Vol. 1.
4. Phillips, Rob (1997). The Developer's Handbook to Interactive Multimedia: A practical guide for educational application. London: Kogan Page.
5. Majumdar, S., and Park, M. (2002). Pedagogical Framework for On-line learning, Published in the book entitled 'Transforming TET Institution: The CPSC way: Book published by CPSC, ISBN: 971-8557-70-9.
6. Glenn, D. (2004). Scholars Who Blog, Chronicle of Higher Education. http://chronicle.com/free/v49/i39/39a01401.htm.
7. National Science Teachers Association, (1998). CASE Draft Standards for the Preparation of Teachers of Science, http://www.nsta.org/nstapubs
8. Shulman, L., (1987). Knowledge and Teaching: Foundations of the New Reform. Harvard Educational Review 57.
9. Ng, W.K., (2005). Pedagogical Principles and Instructional Design of Lessons Using ICT, Presentation to Expert Meeting on Training Modules on the Effective Use of ICT in Teaching and Learning, Bangkok, Thailand. January 20-21.
10. Witfelt, C. (2000). Educational Multimedia and Teachers' Need for New Competencies to Use Educational Multimedia. Education Media International, 37 [4].
11. Harmon, W, S and Jones, G M. (1999). 'The Five levels of Web use in education: Factors to consider in planning online courses' Education Technology Nov-Dec, 1999, pp. 28-32.

Part IV

Revisiting Curricula and Allied Issues in Engineering Education

21

Pre-Engineering Degree Programmes in USA

An Investigation

Xin-Ran Duan

After the industrial revolution took place in England in the mid-eighteenth century, some engineering schools were established in France, Germany and Britain. The first American engineering school was the U.S. Military Academy at West Point, New York, established in 1802[1]. Today in the US there are hundreds of engineering schools offering a variety of engineering disciplines and degree programmes.

Advances in technology fuel the economic growth of the United States and the industrialized nations. However, the shortage of employees with adequate science, mathematics and engineering skills at all levels, created a major impediment to continued national economic growth. Increasingly, new jobs in many fields require an array of mathematical, scientific, technical and engineering skill. Therefore, raising the level of skills of all Americans is vital, because many societal issues have become grounded in mathematical and scientific principles[2].

To train tomorrow's engineers is a significant task for engineering community in facing the challenge in the 21st century[3,4]. The Pre-Engineering programmes have been developed in secondary education for years. PLTW (Project Lead The Way) is a good example of Pre-Engineering programme for public high schools. Currently, more than 300 schools in 26 states offer PLTW courses taught by trained teachers. The Pre-Engineering curricula sponsored by PLTW have provided training in design, digital electronics and computer integrated manufacturing[5].

Another example for the secondary education is DAPCEP (Detroit Area Pre-College Engineering Programme), operating for 23 years in the state of Michigan. Hill[6] reported that, 'About 80 percent of DAPCEP's high school graduates attended universities and colleges across the country. And more than 56 percent of those who attended college pursue degrees in mathematics and science—way above the national of 23.5 percent, according to the National Science Foundation.' In addition to the above programmes, many more other Pre-Engineering programmes are also available in second education.

To connect the secondary education and increase transferring opportunities for engineering education, many institutions of higher education offer Pre-Engineering degree programmes for high school graduates. At the college level, the Pre-Engineering associate degree is a special degree programme of study designed to prepare students for transferring into a four-year university in engineering disciplines beyond their two-year associate degrees. The course offerings include general education, introduction of engineering, and transfer requirements. Upon successful completion of the programme, the students with an associate degree in Pre-Engineering will be academically prepared to start a third year of study at their chosen universities to pursue a Bachelor of Science in engineering major. A variety of engineering disciplines include aerospace, agricultural and biological, architectural and construction, chemical, civil, computer, electrical and electronic, environmental, industrial, material, mechanical, nuclear, general engineering, and other engineering fields. The Pre-Engineering programmes are available in both two-year and four-year institutions. And more new Pre-Engineering programmes are developed by university faculty members.

In addition, Pre-Engineering programmes have strengthened technical education. Why? Scarella *et al.*[7] explained in their report: 'Pre-Engineering education has a direct correlation to technology education', and 'technology education has provided both the career exploration and skill development for students to enter the engineering profession.' The second reason is that 'across this nation, there is a serious shortage of engineers and engineering technologists.' 'Another important factor for career and technical educators is that engineering provides advanced career path for technology education students.' For example, the South Carolina Advanced Technological Centre of Excellence (SCATCE) has developed a Pre-Engineering technology programme, known as 'Technology Gateway' in the technical college system in South Carolina[8, 9].

On the other hand, as a part of transferring curricula, the Pre-Engineering programmes have increased transferring opportunities in higher education. Transferring is one of the key issues in higher education and has been for a long time. 'The pressure on colleges and universities to adopt standard formule for transferring credits has grown in recent years along with the number of transferring students. More than half of students graduating from four-year public institutions began their undergraduate studies at another institution, according to the Association of American Colleges and Universities. In addition to traditional 'vertical' transfer from two-year to four-year institutions, colleges and universities face increasing numbers of 'horizontal' transfers between institutions of the same kind, transfers from online or corporate education programmes into traditional universities, and transfers from foreign to U.S. institutions.'[10]

Specifically, Bradbum and Hurst's study[11] indicated that quite a good transfer rate for community college students who expect to earn a bachelor's degree or higher at a four-year college or university was thirty-six percent[9]. Duan[12] addressed that transferring from two-year institutions into four-year institutions is a good option for students. They could start their engineering training at a two-year programme, then finish two more years of training at a university and become engineers in their chosen career. Obviously, attention was paid to the Pre-Engineering studies in engineering education.

The purpose of this study is to introduce the Pre-Engineering degree programmes in the US to international educators to enhance science, engineering and technology education worldwide. This study investigated a variety of Pre-Engineering programmes in post-secondary education in the US in terms of the classifications of degrees and curricula; then analyzed and compared the offerings, and finally an associate degree model curricula for Pre-Engineering programme was proposed.

Methodology

In addition to the literature search, review of the Pre-Engineering programmes on the Internet is a primary approach for this study. It was found through the electronic search that hundreds of colleges and universities offer Pre-Engineering degree programmes in the US. The GOOGLE search engine was used for this study[13]. For example, on a computer using 'pre-engineering' as a key word for GOOGLE search, about 497,000 items could be immediately received in 0.12 seconds; but, using 'pre-engineering degree programmes' as key words, about 213,000 items could be received also in 0.12 seconds.

In the search process, only 70 institutions offering Pre-Engineering degree programmes were randomly chosen; they were the both two-year and four-year institutions. All the 70 institutions' published Pre-Engineering curricula were printed out and collected for references in this study. These institutions included two-year technical colleges, two-year community colleges, four-year public state universities and colleges, and four-year private universities and colleges. Based on an analysis and comparing all the data, the researcher indicated curriculum and degree classifications, and then developed a curriculum for associate's degree Pre-Engineering programmes.

Findings

Several significant findings have emerged in this study. First, the classification of Pre-Engineering programmes in American higher education was figured out. Table 21.1 provides a summery of classification for Pre-Engineering degree programmes. There are five types of Pre-Engineering degrees; three of them are associate degrees: AS (Associate of Science), AA (Associate of Arts) and APE (Associate of Pre-Engineering), requiring 60-70 credits to award a degree. These three associate degrees may be offered in both two-year and four-year duration. However, most associate degrees are offered in two-year.

In the category of four-year institutions, there are two options for students to earn an engineering degree in 4 to 5 years. The first option is a 3-2 Pre-Engineering programme towards a Bachelor's degree in an engineering discipline within 5 years (BA or BS). This option requires 3 years of study in a liberal arts school, and then 2 years of study in an engineering school. For the first 3 years of study, more than 70 credits could be achieved.

Another option is a 2-2 Pre-Engineering programme. This option requires 2 years of liberal arts, science and mathematics courses plus another two years of study of engineering courses; a Bachelor of Science in an engineering discipline could be awarded.

Table 21.1: Types of Pre-Engineering Degree Programmes in the U.S.

	Programme Type	*Degree*	*Credits*	*Yrs.*
1.	Associate	AS (Associate of Science)	60-70	2
2.	Associate	AA (Associate	60-70	2
3.	Associate	of Arts)	60-70	2
4.	*3-2 Pre- Engineering	APE (Associates	>70 for first 3 yrs.	5
5.	**2-2 Pre-Engineering	of Pre-Engineering)	>60 for first 2 yrs.	4
		towards a Bachelor		
		towards a Bachelor		

Notes: * 3 years in Liberal Arts School, 2 years in Engineering School, 2 degrees (BA, BS) could be awarded.

**2 years of Liberal Arts, Science and Math courses; 2 years of engineering courses, BS is awarded.

Among these 70 randomly selected Pre-Engineering programmes, there are community colleges, technical colleges, public state universities, and private universities. Table 21.2 provides 8 good examples of institution-settings with institution's name, location, classification, title of degrees offered, required credits, and individual institution's website[14-21]. Three community colleges offer AS, AA and APE, respectively; a state technical community college offers an AS; they are listed in Table 21.2. In addition, two state universities, one independent university, and one four-year independent college are also listed in Table 21.2.

It is obvious that all the Pre-Engineering programmes require course studies in the following areas: mathematics, natural and physical science, English composition/oral communication, computer competence, humanities, behavioural/social science, and introduction to engineering. The required course credits vary from college to college, university to university. In general, 60-70 credits are required to achieve an associate Pre-Engineering degree during a period of two years.

Table 21.2: Samples of Pre-Engineering Degree Programmes

	COLLEGE	*TYPE*	*DEGREE*	*CREDITS*
1	Red Rock Community College Colorado	2 yr. Community College	AS	60
2	Lake Sumter Community College Florida	2 yr. Community College	AA	60-62
3	Chattanooga State Technical Community College Tennessee	2 yr. Tech. Community College	AS	60
4	Salt Lake Community College Utah	2 yr. Community College	APE	63-69
5	Missouri Southern State University Missouri	4 yr. Public University	AS	65-66
6	Weber State University Utah	4 yr. Public University	APE	> 60
7	Illinois Wesleyan University Illinois	4 yr. Private University	3/2 for a BA or BS	>20 in residence Dual Degree Programme
8	Hillsdale College Michigan	4 yr. Private College	2/2 for a BS 3/2 for BA and BS (2 degree programme)	2 years of liberal arts 2 years of engineering 3 years at Hillsdale

A Proposed Model Curriculum

Based on an analysis and comparing the data from these 70 randomly selected Pre-Engineering programmes, the researcher proposed a model curriculum containing 68 credits for 20 courses. Table 21.3 shows the breakdown of a total of 20 courses with credits.

Table 21.3: Pre-Engineering Curriculum for Associate Degree

CATEGORY	*CREDIT HOURS*
MATHEMATICS	15
College Algebra	4
College Calculus I	4
College Calculus II	4
Differential Equations	3
NATURAL and PHYSICAL SCIENCE	16
College Chemistry	4
College Physics I	4

(*Contd.*)

CATEGORY	*CREDIT HOURS*
College Physics II	4
Introductory Biology	4
COMPOSITION/ORAL COMMUNICATION	9
Fundamentals of Public Speaking	3
English Composition	3
Technical Writing	3
COMPUTER COMPETENCE	3
Computer Fundamental for Technology	3
HUMANITIES	6
Introduction to Philosophy	3
Introduction to Ethics	3
BEHAVIOURAL/SOCIAL SCIENCES	6
Principles of Macroeconomics	3
Introduction to Psychology	3
INTRODUCTION TO ENGINEERING	13
Technical Graphics	3
CAD Fundamentals	3
Introduction to Engineering and Technology	3
ENGINEERING MECHANICS	4
	Total: 68

For Mathematics, 4 courses are listed for a total of 15 credits: College Algebra, College Calculus I, College Calculus II, and Differential Equations.

For Natural and Physical Science, 4 courses are required to reach a total of 16 credits: College Chemistry, College Physics I, College Physics II, and Introductory Biology. Three courses are required for a total of 9 of credits in English Composition/Oral Communication: Fundamentals of Public Speaking, English Composition, and Technical Writing.

Only one course in Computer Competence is required: Computer Fundamental for Technology with 3 credits. Humanities require 2 courses for 6 credits: Introduction to Philosophy, and Introduction to Ethics.

Similarly, Behavioural/Social Science also requires a course for 6 credits: Principle of Macroeconomics, and Introduction to Psychology.

Finally, 4 courses are in the area of Introduction to Engineering: Technical Graphics, CAD Fundamentals, Introduction to Engineering and Technology, and Engineering Mechanics. A total of 13 credits are required.

In summary, a total 68 credits for 20 courses are required to accomplish an associate Pre-Engineering degree. All the details are shown in Table 21.3.

What would be a good plan within a two year period to accomplish an associate Pre-Engineering degree? A suggested study plan is shown in Table 21.4.

In order to achieve a two-year Pre-Engineering degree within a period of two years as full-time student status, the students have to take 5 courses each semester not including summer tem; on average, 17 credits is assigned for each semester.

Table 21.4: Suggested Study Plan for Pre-Engineering Associate Degree

FRESHMAN YEAR		*SOPHOMORE YEAR*	
First Semester		*Second Semester*	
College Algebra	4	College Calculus II	4
College Chemistry	4	College Physics I	4
English Composition	3	Introduction to Psychology	3
Engineering Graphics	3	Introduction to Philosophy	3
Computer Fundamentals for Technology	3	Introduction to Engineering and Technology	3
	17		**17**
Second Semester		*Second Semester*	
College Calculus I	4	Differential Equations	3
Introductory Biology	4	College Physics II	4
Fundamentals of Public Speaking	3	Principals of Macroeconomics	3
Technical Writing	3	Introduction to Ethics	3
CAD Fundamentals	3	Engineering Mechanics	4
	17		**17**
			Total: 68

Clearly, as a result of this study, the proposed model curriculum provides some guidelines and directions as a template for a variety of Pre-Engineering degree offerings. Individual institutions may make necessary adjustments for a specific degree curriculum to meet student needs and community demands.

Conclusion

This paper addressed the importance of Pre-Engineering programmes, reviewed a variety of Pre-Engineering programmes at high schools and at college level in the United States. The following conclusions may be made:

1. The Pre-Engineering degree programme in higher education is a specifically designed curriculum for high school graduates and college freshmen to prepare them for transfer into a four-year university engineering discipline for a bachelor's degree. How do we train tomorrow's engineers better? Pre-Engineering degree programme is one of college effective offerings. The programme not only increases transfer opportunities for students, but also advances in engineering education to impart the basic skills in science, mathematics and engineering for tomorrow's engineers. Currently, the Pre-Engineering degree programmes are offered by hundreds of colleges and universities in the US, which benefits engineering education.
2. In this study, only seventy published Pre-Engineering curricula were randomly chosen and collected for research. As a result of this study, a proposed model curriculum was developed. The model curriculum may work and be deliverable for an individual institution with necessary adjustment to accommodate some course changes. Also, it may be considered as a template in training for tomorrow's engineers.

3. A systematic study in Pre-Engineering programmes was made in this paper. As a preliminary programme of engineering, the Pre-Engineering programme is significantly important towards engineering disciplines. A better curriculum can attract more students. Hopefully, more young high school graduates who are interested in science, mathematics, engineering, may start their college studies with a Pre-Engineering programme; then transfer into an engineering discipline; and finally become tomorrow's engineers. Clearly, this move would advance engineering education and boost the economical growth.
4. This study on Pre-Engineering degree programmes in the United States could be beneficial and helpful to international educators to enhance understanding, exchange, and development in science, engineering and technology education to meet the global needs.

References

1. Yurtseven, H.O. (2005). 'Impact of Accreditation on Internationalization of Engineering and Technology Education in the United States,' *Innovations: World Innovations in Engineering Education and Research.* Edited by Aung, W. *et al.*, ISBN: 0-9741252-2-9, pp. 423-429, iNEER, Arlington, VA, 2005.
2. Brown, S.I. (1999). 'Making a Difference in Science and Engineering Education,' *Mechanical Engineering,* Vol. 121, No. 5, p. 36.
3. Wiebusch, B. (2001). 'Engineering Education Changes,' *Design News*, Vol. 56, No. 24, p. 13.
4. Valenti, M. (1996). 'Teaching Tomorrow's Engineers.' *Mechanical Engineering,* Vol. 118, No. 7, pp. 64-69.
5. Mathias-Reigel, B. (2001). 'Early to Engineering,' *ASEE Prism,* Vol. 11, No. 2, p. 45.
6. Hill, K. (2000). 'DAPCEP: A Model Engineering Programme that Attracts Other than Repels Students,' *Tech Direction,* Vol. 59, No. 7, pp. 29-30.
7. Scarcella, J. Rogers, G.E., and Olson, J. (2004). 'Technology Education Division Report,' *Techniques (Association for Career and Technical Education),* Vol. 79, No. 5, pp. 44-45.
8. Craft, E.L., and Mack, L.G. (2001). 'Developing and Implementing an Integrated Problem-Based Engineering Technology Curriculum in an American Technical College System,' *Community College Journals of Research and Practice,* Vol. 25, No. 5/6, pp. 425-439.
9. Reese, S. (2001). 'Excellence in Engineering Technology Education,' *Techniques. Alexandria,* Vol. 76, No. 4, pp. 26-27.
10. 'Transferability of Credits Increasingly at Issue,' *Academe,* Vol. 87, No. 5, September/October 2001.
11. Bradbum, E.M., and Hurst, D.G. (2001). 'Community College Transfer Rates to 4-Year Institutions Using Alternative Definition of Transfer,' *Education Statistics Quarterly,* Vol. 3, No. 3, pp. 1-8. Available: http://www.nces.ed.gov/programs/ Quartlt/vol 3/3 3/9 7.asp.
12. Duan, X.R. (2006). 'A Proposed Transferable Curriculum for Mechanical

Engineering Technology Programmes,' *Proceedings on International Conference for Engineering Education and Research 2005: Exploring Innovation in Education and Research,* Tainan, Taiwan, March 1-5 2005. Also, *Innovations 2006: World Innovations in Engineering Education and Research.* Edited by Aung, W. *et al.*, ISBN: 0-9741252-5-3, pp. 141-149, iNEER, Arlington, VA.

13. Available from Web: http://www.google.com
14. Available from Web: http://www.rrcc.edu
15. Available from Web: http://www.lscc.edu
16. Available from Web: http://www.chattanoogastate.edu
17. Available from Web: http://www.slcc.edu
18. Available from Web: http://www.mssu.edu
19. Available from Web: http://www.weber.edu
20. Available from Web: http://www.iwu.edu
21. Available from Web: http://www.hillsdale.edu

22

Engineering Undergraduates — Development Communication Skills in English

An Analysis of the Structural and Interactional Aspects of Teleconferences in the Ideels Telematics Simulation Project

Penny Macdonald and David Perry

In the last few decades, and in most areas of knowledge related to education, there has been a shift in emphasis from environments where the teacher is the absolute controller of the classroom dynamics, to a much more learner-centred focus where the participants (i.e. the students) take an active part in their own learning process.

The field of language learning has been no exception to this. Indeed, one could argue that it has been one of the pioneers of learner independence (especially within the teaching of English as a Second or Foreign Language). It has been seen that teaching pedagogy swing from the behaviourist methods of the 60s, with their emphasis on habit-formation brought about by imitation, reinforcement and repetition, to the more eclectic, Communicative Approach to language learning where the focus is on helping learners to make optimum use of both receptive and productive skills to achieve real, and realistic, communicative goals in the target language.

Critics of the Communicative Approach argue that there is too much emphasis placed on fluency to the detriment of accuracy, but research into interaction in the language classroom has shown that students do benefit from task-oriented activities involving negotiation of meaning[7, 13, 15, 21] and that this is also beneficial for increasing awareness of the form of the language[8, 17], for testing hypotheses, for the syntactic processing required for producing language and for improving grammatical competence[10, 15, 20].

The importance of interaction with peers (including those with a lower level of proficiency) should not, therefore, be underestimated, especially as many learners do not have any other opportunity for practising outside the classroom. Prior to the more widespread adoption of more communicative modes of teaching, the amount and type of typical language exposure in a traditional class was often limited to exchanges between the teacher and a student with the following pattern, called I+R+F (initiation, response and feedback):

Teacher (initiates the exchange): Where do you live?
Student (responds): I live in Valencia.
Teacher (provides corrective feedback): Yes, you live in Spain.

Hardly an authentic model for language use outside the confines of the classroom!

In the Communicative Approach, classroom activities are designed to provide opportunities for students to use the target language to interact with their peers in a more meaningful way; to encourage language use which involves more authentic objectives mirroring those which might be expected in real life encounters. Of course, one cannot escape the fact that these activities take place and develop in a classroom; as in the theatre they require the suspension of disbelief — which in our experience all students are more than happy to engage in — nevertheless, to borrow a phrase from Skehan[18], well-designed tasks require the language learner to operate at the 'cutting-edge' of his or her language proficiency.

Computer Mediated Communication

Numerous studies have documented the positive effects of Computer Mediated Communication (CMC), so we will limit ourselves to mentioning a few of these. Several researchers[3, 1, 12, 19, 22] have noted that the amount and type of language production increases, especially in comparison with face to face activities or group work carried out in the classroom. It is not difficult to imagine how much more (and more meaningful) language is produced in the relatively anxiety-free environment provided by networked computers when compared with the I+R+F situation mentioned above. Finally, it is semi-permanent, and therefore provides researchers with a rich source for investigation of many different aspects of authentic language production.

Naturally, CMC is not without its drawbacks. One is that there can be a tendency for a lack of coherence in the structure of the 'dialogue', more so when there are many participants, so that following the different threads of the sequences is not always straightforward. The difficulty is increased when we take into account the fact that the participants are trying to follow the flow of interaction in a language that is not their mother tongue. A further criticism is that participants cannot make use of the nonverbal behaviour which is such a fundamental part of face to face communication. However, by using *emoticons*, certain punctuation signs, and diminutives some affective aspects that would otherwise be missing can be incorporated. Lastly, the increased fluency required of the participants to keep up with the pace of the postings can obviously affect the grammatical accuracy or choice of vocabulary, but the fact of having a written record of the production can be used a posterior to analyse the language used and design materials to bring any language points requiring clarification to the students' notice.

CMC in English for Specific Purposes Programmes

Most language programmes which have been developed specifically for students of the different engineering degree courses emphasise the acquisition of skills which will, in principle, help the students understand the scientific articles and technical texts related to their field of study, and develop strategies for note-taking, report-writing and other study skills. There is less time, as a result, for involving the students in activities to practise their interactional skills in the target language. The situation described in this paper involves students from various academic backgrounds taking part in a telematics simulation which we believe not only promotes intercultural communication among tertiary education institutions, but also encourages students to participate in meaningful exchanges and has led to benefits in the development of their communication skills.

Aims of Research

Studies that have been carried out into the type of language produced in human-human interaction mediated through the computer[5, 4] suggest that we are dealing with a new variety of language which shows characteristics typical of both spoken and written forms. In the case of a teleconference like the one we describe, although the discourse is written, in many instances structures and forms of oral interaction are used. As Johanyak[11] notes, in many computer mediated activities, students engage in 'writing' discussions in which multiple conversations occur almost simultaneously, switching from a more formal writing mode, to more colloquial, informal chatting from one turn to another. He also points out that the medium used, in this case computer technology, limits to a certain extent the language users' rhetorical options for communication, although the writing itself is still determined by the participants own textual constructions, based on the individual, cognitive and contextual experiences they have brought to the technology.

The aim in the research was to try and determine the characteristics of students' online written production, how the structure resembles that of conversational patterns in face to face interaction, and how the interaction promoted a series of sequences in which the students had to delay the main topic being dealt with in order to negotiate meaning. In order to do this, certain terms has been originally used by Conversation Analysis (CA) to describe the structural aspects of interactive communication, taking into account the turn-taking system, opening and closing sequences, etc. whilst on the interactional-meaning level it has been established which negotiation routines were most used, how repair was carried out and what role punctuation plays in the course of the simulation.

The dynamics of Telematics Simulations

The Polytechnic University of Valencia, Spain, has participated in the Project IDEELS, a Curriculum Design Initiative carried out under the auspices of the European Commission's Socrates programme, which has developed a series of telematics simulations for educational purposes. Coordinated by Dr. Janet Sutherland at the University of Bremen, the interdisciplinary, intercultural communication project IDEELS involves several tertiary institutions in Europe. The participants take on specific roles, negotiate, and make an attempt to deal with the problems that the fictitious federation, Eutropia, faces through discussion and cooperation firstly, within their own group, and latterly with others, in order to come to an agreement on a general policy statement.

Here attempt is made to describe a teleconference on the theme of Tertiary Education Policy (the web page for the IDEELS Telematics Simulation is http://www.ideels.uni-bremen.de.) Participating universities were:

- University of Bremen, Germany
- University of Bergen, Norway
- Nord-Trondelag College, Norway
- University of Nice, France
- The Polytechnic University of Valencia, Spain

The students were from different academic backgrounds ranging from English Philology to Telecommunications, Computer Science, Psychology, Multi-media Pedagogy and English as a Foreign Language (EFL). The language used throughout the simulation was English.

The topic the students were to debate about was: University Education in Eutropia, and more specifically, State Educational Policy, state funding — where this comes from, which degrees to offer, student intake, entry requirements, fees, and the use of Information and Communication Technology. The dynamics of the simulation are as follows:

1. The teams are formed, involving representatives of the different regions of Eutropia (Northland, Bardland, Coastland, etc. and various non-governmental organizations, citizens' groups, trade union associations, the media, etc.). Once the groups have themselves established a set of guidelines for their Internal Briefing Document, they then elaborate their own Policy Statement which is sent to all participants, after which they start to communicate with other groups in order to create alliances for the

online teleconference. These negotiations are carried out by sending messages, by e-mail, through OPUSi, the computer based communications system developed for the simulation by the students of Computer Science at the University of Bremen.

2. The online teleconferences are scheduled and barring any last-minute technical hitches, all the different institutions will log on at more or less the same time. During the synchronous conference, participants will generally communicate either with all the other groups, or they may 'whisper' by sending messages to a particular group, or to members of their own group. At the end of the conference, an agreement is reached, and the whole event ends with a less formal post-simulation conference.

In this simulation the teams are logged on for 5 teleconferences adding up to a total of almost seven and a half hours online.

The Structure of the Teleconference

Like other types of social interaction that have been studied, it has been found that the teleconference is a mode of communication with certain structural characteristics which mirror those of face to face interaction, in the sense that they are rule-governed and the participants create meaning through language and through the individual interpretation of the interaction as it develops on the screen. In the study attempt is made to give examples of how the participants in this online teleconference organize their linguistic behaviour, and how it is to a certain extent conditioned by the medium they are using and the type of event they are participating in, but how they actually use different strategies to try and overcome any apparent difficulties.

I. Turn-taking

In face to face interaction, turn-taking is usually organized so that the present speaker can either give up or maintain a turn at a transition relevant place, or talk can be taken over by another participant who self appoints him/herself as next speaker. This often comes about through certain interactional devices such as question-answer, and greeting-response pairs, when one speaker asks another a question the turn is given to the interlocutor in order that s/he may respond to the first part. Signals that also may be given in face to face interaction to indicate speaker change include a whole range of non-verbal signs involving gaze, body posture, etc. Due to the absence of non-verbal signals in CMC, we have noted that the participants in the teleconference used the following strategies to indicate speaker change; although technically speaking when a participant presses 'enter' s/he is giving up the floor:

When one participant makes a direct question to the whole group (note that participants' contributions have not been corrected):

- <2:449:1>this is a test from Team D — Anybody out there?
- <220:491:5> who wants to evaluate the Bardland paper? Any volunteers?

Turns are also passed on by asking a question or making a comment to a previously specified message number as in:

- <1077:491:31*> #27

And how about the students of 30 years of age or over?

(the last number indicates the chronological order of the postings.)

Indeed, due to the very fast apparition of postings on the screen, which can, nevertheless, be paused by participants in order to look more closely at a turn, the dynamics of the interaction probably make it necessary to write a reference to whom the message is addressed, in order to maintain some sort of coherence since there are often several different sequences going on at any one time during the conference.

However, unlike face to face interaction were found numerous examples where the first part of an adjacency pair of the type question-response does not actually get answered such as the following:

- <1138:491:64> #60 How is your suggestion about measuring 'life-experience'? Shouldn't we rather be talking about 'work-experience'

On the other hand, there may often be multiple responses to a first part comment such as:

- <1218:490:101> Changing into statement 5, we believe that three years are enough for a good education in the most of degrees and one for job internship
- <1225:491:105> #101 Three years—without the practical semester and the exam phase? Do you think this is a good idea? Cathy
- <1226:486:106> #101 4 years + 1 year practice + half year preparing the final exam
- <1232:485:110> #101 It depends on what you study (issue)?

It was also noted that unlike conversation between 2 or more participants, the second part of an adjacency pair may not be answered, due to the time lag, until several turns later, the average being between 5 and 10 turns,

- <1278:486:139> #137 we think everyone should study that he wants and can choose his subject combination
- <1287:491:144> to 139 Does this include extremely useful combinations like Ethnology, Hebrew and Fine Arts?

and the maximum it was found that 46 turns later with the following sequence:

- <2621:1180:106> in Nice the university of letter has too much students so the department of psychology has moved away that's why a
- <2667:1198:133> that's why what?

However this question does not get answered as the topic has moved on and participants probably do not know what this posting actually refers to.

The following is an example of a 'whisper' where a group member sends a message to another person in the same group which is not seen by any of the other groups, and curiously enough we do have an example here of adjacency, in fact the number of the postings actually coincides, meaning there was a split second between turns:

- <1172:491:82> Can I answer to #80? Nicola?
- <1173:491:82> sure, go on.

When one participant makes a question to certain members of their own group they are passing on turns to their conference-mates:

- <227:491:5> Nicola and Anne! What shall we do?
- <232:491:15> to sven from gayle. your answer please

Another way in which the medium influences the turns is that in face-to-face interaction the person who is giving up their turn would never had a need to identify themselves. Whilst whispering, however, this is a necessary requirement in this sense, making it more like written communication in a letter or e-mail:

- <236:491:12> Anne: sorry Ce, was me

The participant identification, however, can be confusing from the researchers point of view, as the name of the sender is sometimes written before the turn, as in the last example, or after, as in the next posting:

- <234:491:10> I would do the Northland paper. Rebus

A common feature of face to face interaction is the phenomenon of interruption. Normally, participants cannot interrupt one another as it is technically impossible to respond to a message when it hasn't actually been finished and sent by another participant [11, 26]. A turn can last for as long as one person wishes to write, although in the data for the study, the turns were, in general, short, except when a group was sending its opening/policy statement which was nearly always a pre-prepared text. It is interesting, therefore, to observe that the participants themselves can perceive that interruptions do take place as in the following:

- <2940:1190:63> to all groups, please try to follow the conversation. don't interrupt
- <2949:1980:67> #63 we're so sorry!

This particular message also gives the impression the participant is angry — punctuation, as shall be commented on later, can show varying degrees of emotion in the writer — making up for the lack of nonverbal cues in this type of conference.

II. Opening and Closing Sequences

In interaction there are certain rituals that open and close the different types of communicative encounters we have. These vary depending on the type of communication (telephone calls, service encounters, email, public speech, etc.), and tend to be culturally bound. In the teleconference each team has to have an opportunity to say they are 'present' identify themselves, and greet the other participants:

- <990:486:2> Hi everybody! Coastlanders are here.
- <992:490:3> Hello every country of Eutropian Federation:

Likewise, the closings follow similar patterns with the pre-closing and closing sequence often in the same turn:

- <1392:491:217> Time is up! Let´s continue the discourse through messeage centre! Midlanders would like to say 'bye-bye´ to all the other delegations and we hope to hear from you soon! Keep up with messages and memos!

However, interaction continues with the following:

- <1400:485:219> goodbaye. We have a snowstorm to attend
- <1402:486:220> Lucky you!
- <1404:486:222> Bye bye! The Coastlanders

III. Negotiation of Meaning

Negotiation in a language learning context refers to the modifications or adjustments that take place during conversations between native speakers (NSs) and non-native speakers (NNSs), or exclusively between NNSs, in order to allow for a better understanding of the discourse at hand. The research work that has already been done on conversational adjustments in NS/NNS[7, 14] and NNS/NNS[8, 15] interaction confirms that negotiation certainly gives learners the *opportunities* to attend to L2 form and to relationships of form and meaning[15]. Participants co-construct meaning using various resources such as comprehension checks, clarification requests, direct questions, and repetition and non-verbal cues. It has also been suggested that not only are these modifications essential for the understanding of the interaction, but also following Swain[20], the modified output that the learner is encouraged to do during negotiation i.e. the reorganising of the syntax to make form and meaning clearer, also contributes to the acquisition of the target language. There is undoubtedly little negotiation going on in many language classrooms, even now, and therefore the authors maintain that the type of intercultural communication described in the research is beneficial for language acquisition.

As noted by Pica[15] most of the speech modifications concern lexis, requiring changes to be made through repetition, replacement by synonyms, paraphrase, etc. This is certainly confirmed in our data. In face to face interaction between learners of a foreign language the two main incidences of actual communication breakdown involve non-target language like pronunciation, and non-recognition of the vocabulary. Very rarely would a grammatical error, such as dropping the third person singular-s, (she go* to the university.) or the use of a non-existent form for an irregular past tense (she goed* to the university) actually impede communication. They may notice the error, and this may be beneficial, but learners will normally avoid correcting their peers unless the classroom task actually requires them to do so. It is potentially a face threatening act and participants will not purposely offend their interlocutors by showing they know less than themselves. The type of sequence which has been found more frequently are comprehension checks and clarification requests concerning the ideas or content, and were not seemingly triggered through non-understandings, or misunderstandings from a strictly linguistic or grammatical point of view. Gass[6] has indicated that during interaction semantic comprehension occurs prior to syntactic comprehension, and this is probably decisive in the sense that if a word is understood in the context, its morphological characteristics take second place as regards meaning. On the other hand when students are engaged in other tasks, such as information gap, jigsaw activities, the task is actually designed so that more intense language negotiation must be carried out in order to complete them.

Varonis and Gass[21] have described the typical pattern involved in the structure of negotiation sequences. There is normally a word or expression that triggers the need for negotiation. This is followed by an indicator on the part of the interlocutor that there is a communication problem. A response ensues which attempts to clear up the problem and this may be followed by an optional reaction to the response.

- <2325:490:193> nk you for being so fast Midland (trigger)
- <2329:491:195> What exactly does nk mean?;-) (initiator)
- <2332:490:195> Sorry we meant thanks. (response)

In the following case we have a clarification request:

- <2650:1180:121> We think the number of students mustn't depend of the fact that they are rich or not. Here we don't need to pass an exam to go to university we only need the 'baccalaureat'

- <2655:1191:124> What is 'Baccalaureat'?
- <2658:1180:127> 'Baccalaureat' is high school exit exam

In fact this question is answered by three different messages giving an idea of the cooperation that actually goes on while negotiating meanings.

Explanation requests are slightly different and require more elaboration, such as in the following:

- <1081:486:33> #27 students over 30 can of course study, but under different conditions
- <1086:491:37> #33 Please specify 'different conditions'!

As we mentioned above, there are very few examples of grammatical errors being corrected in this negotiation process. The following is one of these:

- <2916:1197:49> For 30. if there are fewer student in university there are no selection for enter, but less students can't enter in the university. Are you agree?
- <2925:1190:54> To Oliver: speak correctly, please. We´re not agree, we just agree

This second message was first sent as a whisper and then immediately to all the groups. In neither case was it responded to.

In conversational interaction, repair follows patterns depending on who initiates the repair and who actually carries this out[16]. During the IDEELS conference we have observed the following types in our data:

(a) Other-initiated other repair, in this case the error is pointed out by one group and the actual repair is carried out by another.
   - <2585:1189:81> #69, Nowadays, the situation is better than before about university access but the buildings are destroied
   - <2586:1201:81> destroied?
   - <2594:1198:88> #82 destroyed = in poor repair

(b) The normal type of repair, though, is other initiated self repair, as in:
   - <2954:1198:69> how much is 100000 pesetas in euros??
   - <2971:1180:79> #68it's 37 349 euros
   - <2982:1198:86> are you crazy??37 349euros???
   - <2993:1180:95> it's a mistake, we are sorry

(c) In the case of self-initiated self repair the writer has seen the mistake and sent a message to do the repairing for him/herself:
   - <2729:1180:172> #163, like this God will give you all you need and in addition the CHRETIENTY !!!!!
   - <2740:1150:176> Sorry 'CHRISTIANITY'

(d) Sometimes the trouble spot is indicated but no repair is carried out. This may be due to the fact that it is not managed 'locally', i.e. repair in face to face conversation is normally carried out in the same or immediately subsequent turns:

- <3121:1182:172> Will you oay more fees?
- <3127:1181:176> #172 What is oay?

IV. Expressing Emotion

We would like to mention a feature observable in our data which has been the subject of debate when the affective factors involved in CMC are taken into account. Due to the lack of non-verbal cues in the interaction, participants have developed strategies to show their emotions using the most obvious means they have at hand — the keyboard. We will review the use of some of these and show how the medium need not be as impersonal as it has been attributed to be.

Exclamation marks are used very frequently and seem to 'lighten' the discourse, making it more immediate and spontaneous. They express both surprise and happiness and we have observed they are often used to mitigate turns expressing disagreement:

- <3297:1182:278> I don't think so!

Or denial

- <1177:486:84> #79 we have never said it!

Or they emphasise intentions:

- <1868:491:11> I'll do my very best!!! Nicola

Question marks are not only used for enquiry, but for expressing doubt and sarcasm

- <3942:1401:86> #48 pardon?
- <1726:491:93> …and the screet of sepllinge???

There are however fewer full stops than would be expected and commas are hardly used at all. Uppercase letters are used, as the very participants perceive them, to express shouting in the sense of anger, frustration, as in

- <3151:1198:191> please say to who you are answering otherwise we wont get out of here!!
- <3161:1189:195> ooooooooooh don't shout you are not alone and can you talk nicely please j

They are also used to mitigate criticism as in

- <2232:491:134> OOOOOOHHHHH wee little northies….

Ellipsis points are very frequent in the teleconference, sometimes for indicating that the present turn is giving up the floor, or after certain expressions as in written language (hmm…/yeah…)

- <398:486:20>any volunteers? i already wrote the opening statement…
- <164:449:30> hmm… that's probably the best way to keep a secret!

Lastly we mention the phenomenon of emoticons. These are frequently used by the participants, and in many different contexts. They express agreement, solidarity, irony, amusement, sadness, etc.

- <4754:447:56> indeed J
- <1516:486:20> Irene… okay…that was our first step. I am proud of youJ
- <1908:491:26> Dear Northies,

  You really do agree with all statements, sounds kind of boring.;-))
- <3531:1182:401> hehehe J
- <3505:1189:395> The best is having fewer students and for that it means more fees…:-(

Conclusion

Similar to the results presented in Blake[2], much evidence of negotiation has not been found as regards the strictly grammatical features of the discourse that the participants in the teleconference co-create. However, there is a great deal of interactional negotiation going on throughout, giving students practice with the management of meaning-making both as regards specific lexical items, and in the structural aspects of the genre it belongs to i.e. quasi-synchronous online discussions. The conference we have analysed is only part of a corpus of a total of 82 000 words which, with future study, it is expected, will also reveal interesting features of this fairly recent mode of communication, certainly as regards pragmatic aspects of CMC, issues related to gender and ethnicity, topic structure, and affective factors, to mention a few. Pending also is the research which compares different types of CMC, namely the language production in both asynchronous and synchronous modes.

Apart from the advantages we have mentioned from a linguistic point of view, especially considering the status of English as an international language used by, and between, more and more NNS in all parts of the globe, we feel that as the opportunities become more widespread for involving students from all fields of Tertiary education in CMC, there can only be positive outcomes for establishing virtual links between different cultures, and for fomenting tolerance and negotiation as reasonable objectives to be aimed at in the real life scenario as well.

References

1. Beauvois, M.H. (1992). Computer-assisted classroom discussion in the foreign language classroom: conversation in slow motion. *Foreign Language Annals* 25, pp. 455-464.
2. Blake, R. CMC (2000). A window on L2 Spanish interlanguage. LLT Journal 4, pp. 120-136,.
3. Bump, J. Radical (1990). Changes in classroom discussion using networked computers. *Computers and the Humanities* 24, pp. 49-65.
4. Collot, M. and Belmore, N. Electronic language (1993). A new variety of English. In J. Aarts, P. de Haan, and N. Oostdijk (Eds.) *English Language Corpora: Design, Analysis and Exploitation.* Amsterdam: Rodopi.
5. Ferrera, K., Brunner, H. and Whittemore, G. (1991). Interactive written discourse as an emergent register. *Written Communication* 8, pp. 8-34.
6. Gass, S. (1997). *Input, interaction, and the second language learner*. Oxford: Oxford University Press.
7. Gass, S. and Varonis, E.M. (1985b). Variation in native speaker speech modification to non-native speakers. *Studies in Second Language Acquisition* 7, pp. 37-58.
8. Gass, S. and Varonis, E.M. (1994). Input, interaction and second language production. *Studies in Second Language Acquisition* 16, pp. 283-302.
9. Herring, S. (1999). Interactional Coherence in CMC. *Journal of Computer-Mediated Communication* 4.
10. Izumi, S. and Bigelow, M. (2000). Does Output Promote Noticing and Second Language Acquisition? TESOL Quarterly 34, pp. 239-278.
11. Johanyak, M.F. (1997) Analyzing the Amalgamated Electronic Text: Bringing cognitive, social and contextual factors of individual language users into CMC research. *Computers and Composition* 14, pp. 91-110.
12. Kern, R. (1995). Restructuring classroom interaction with networked computers: effects on quantity and quality of language production. *The Modern Language Journal* 79, pp. 457-476.
13. Long, M. (1980). *Input, interaction and second language acquisition.* Unpublished doctoral dissertation. University of California, Los Angeles.
14. Long, M. (1983). Linguistic and conversational adjustments to nonnative speakers. *Studies in Second Language Acquisition* 5, pp. 177-193.
15. Pica, T. (1994). Research on Negotiation: What Does It Reveal About Second-Language Learning Conditions, Processes and Outcomes? *Language Learning* 44, pp. 493-527.
16. Schegloff, E.A., Jefferson, G. and Sacks, H. (1977). The preference for self-correction in the organization of repair in conversation. *Language* 53, pp. 361-382.
17. Schmidt, R. (1990). The role of consciousness in second language acquisition. *Applied Linguistics* 11, pp. 129-158.
18. Skehan, P. (1998). *A Cognitive Approach to Language Learning.* Oxford: Oxford University Press.
19. Sullivan, N. and Pratt, E. (1996). A comparative study of two ESL writing environments: a computer-assisted classroom and a traditional oral classroom. *System* 29, pp. 491-501.

20. Swain, M. (1985). Communicative competence: some roles of comprehensible input and comprehensible output in its development. In S. Gass and C.G. Madden (Eds.) *Input in Second Language Acquisition*. Rowley, MA: Newbury House.
21. Varonis, E.M. and Gass, S. (1985a). Miscommunication in native/non-native conversation. *Language in Society* 14, pp. 327-343.
22. Warschauer, M. (1996). Comparing face-to-face and electronic communication in the second language classroom. *CALICO Journal* 13, pp. 7-26.
23. Wilkins, H. (1991). Computer Talk: Long distance conversations by computer. *Written Communication* 8, pp. 79-113.

23

Transitional Changes as Driver for Reengineering Curricula for Electrical Engineering Education in Serbia

Case of the Autonomy Province of Vojvodina

Djuro Kutlaèa and Vojin Šenk

Autonomous Province of Vojvodina (APV) lies in the Pannonian plane, ideal for agricultural production. Natural resources of APV, such as oil and gas, provide higher standard of life as compared to other parts of the Republic of Serbia (RS). This attractivity enabled the number of inhabitants of the province to be disproportionatly higher than necessary for using the aforementioned resources. The surplus of inhabitants is concentrated in larger cities such as Novi Sad, above all, as well as Zrenjanin, Subotica, Sombor, Kikinda, Panèevo, Vršac, Sremska Mitrovica and others. The existence of important educational institutions in these centres, and, above all, the University of Novi Sad as core high education (HE) centre in APV, enables the rise of relatively skilled resources. Retention in the country and employment of these high-quality human resources is thus the priority of the development of APV. The use of the infrastructure of these cities, above all that of Novi Sad, constitutes a ohance to attain these goals. In Research and Development (R&D) domain this infrastructure has to be significantly improved by building innovation activity institutions such as the Science & Technology (S&T) Park in Novi Sad, business incubators, innovation centres etc. The Information and Communication Technology (ICT) sector, as a generic one, has a key role in this domain. It cannot only employ human resources educated to work in the sector, but, because it is inherently multidisciplinary, enable the employment of specialists in all other sectors.

APV is encountering a multitude of challenges on the road of developing a vivid market economy. Investment and business environments improve as new laws are being introduced, new institutions are being established, and new development policy is implemented. Majority of old industry is subject to radical changes and restructuring, meaning that in foreseeable future it will not be able to contribute to growth and employment. The ICT industry in APV is currently in a phase of fast growth but there are lots of unused potentials in other sectors that can use ICT to their own advantage. The ICT industry, thus, constitutes a huge chance and possibility of AP Vojvodina to approach European integrations and standards, and for the economy in APV to realize an outbreak into the global market.

ICT sector, especially software industry, has extremely spread all over the world in the last ten years, and brought many possibilities for business development and entrepreneurship. It is expected that this growth will continue, since technology and communications enable access to global market and new business opportunities to both small and big companies. Globally, this sector usually exhibits the following main characteristics (EITO, 2004)[1]:

- it provides quality employment to computer literate bachelors and technical personnel;
- starting obstacle for market entry, i.e. financial expense, is usually small in regard to the one in other sectors, which facilitates the occurrence of many innovative companies;
- the markets, especially the ones for special purpose software and for computer technology services, are still fragmented and versatile, which allows a wide spectrum of possibilities for small specialized companies in a multitude of subsectors;
- small companies can also export final products, if they have good connections with international markets, since the export canal is simple (Internet connection); and
- International companies are in constant search for cheaper solutions and access to knowledge that can make them competitive; this helps the global spread of technologies to the countries in development and transition.

Review of the papers dealing with issues such as ICT and globalization, and its consequences toward education and employment, particularly in developing and so-called transition countries; lead us to the following four findings, which are of importance for research presented in this paper:

Outsourcing

Outsourcing has number of impacts for both the company and the involved countries. This process that typically begins as part of a company's cost saving initiatives eventually affects the social structure and economics of the involved countries. Main impacts which is of particular concern for our research is impact of outsourcing on the engineering practices as well as on engineering education in APV. As it is pointed out in the literature, 'the more traditional and routine engineering tasks will continue their migration to lower cost countries. This suggests that the 'next generation' of engineers in the highly developed countries may need skills different than those from less-developed countries, and in many cases, skills different than what they currently possess'[2]. Direct consequence of the outsourcing processes in the field of ICT, is change which implies that ICT professionals should have not only a high level of technical skills and analytical ability, but also capabilities and knowledge of system integrations, communication, organization and motivation skills combined with the ability to work across cultures[2].

Team-work and Software Engineering

Additional requests for software professionals are result of move from individual software development toward team work. 'New graduates know few of the 'best practices' characterizing professional software engineering (SE) (e.g., use of software processes, measurement and analysis, team building, requirements engineering and high-level development methods, quality engineering, software maintenance, and testing). Unfortunately, with the increasing demand for software engineers and other computing professionals, many of these issues are obscured and it is difficult for many computing educators to understand and appreciate the importance of software engineering education. This problem is exacerbated by the fact that employers are so desperate to get graduates with any computer skills that mismatches between curricula and industry needs may be overlooked'[3]. Combination of business skills with computer science and other ICT topics in university curricula become general trend in HE reform[4].

Management of Technology (MOT)

Fast technological development implies another issue in industry, issue of integration of existing, more traditional and obsolete technology, with new, mostly ICT based technologies. 'Unfortunately, there have often been important mismatches between the graduates of universities and the skills needed by today's technology based organizations ... The National Research Council defined MOT as 'linking engineering, science, and management disciplines to address the issues involved in planning, development, and implementation of technological capabilities to shape and accomplish the strategic and operational objectives of an organization'[5].

Higher-education Reform

Authors' suggest the 'education reforms, under the context of globalization, could be characterized by a finance-driven reform emphasizing decentralization, privatization and better performance'[6]. Further pressures comes from growing concern for 'value for money' and 'public accountability, and 'situated in a far more competitive global marketplace, modern universities have to expand their commercial and business arms to reach out to the private sector for generating additional funding'[6]. University — industry networking has integrated users, producers, entrepreneurs and policy-makers with university staff in knowledge production process, implying that 'in an asymmetrical way, the university through these institutional innovations is also co constitutive of its industrial environment'[6]. Also, reform of HE system in direction of Bologna process, suggest: 'In the Bologna system, the first half of the first cycle … maintains … general un-oriented training. Afterwards, the future bachelor choices a "major" orientation, the programme of which is constituted of entrance courses into the elected speciality, preparing the student for the Masters degree in the same domain. This is smoothed by the concept of 'minor' orientation, in addition to the major one, which allows certain flexibility to an eventual further re-orientation.'[7].

In Serbia and APV, this sector is rising, unlike many others, while the Government of Serbia is preparing the implementation of e-management programme on the state and regional level, and the economy and public companies are trying to modernize administration business and the work process. It is encouraging that foreign companies are coming to APV to produce for both domestic and international market[8]. Small private companies earn by export to specialized markets, and universities and institutes have initiated the creation of university innovation centres, incubators, science and technology parks and new innovative (spin-out) companies, focused on international cooperation.

The paper elaborates changes which are being and should be done in order to build new curricula for electrical engineering education in Serbia. It is based on surveys organized in the APV, the richest part of Serbia, with economy based on traditional sectors such as agriculture, as well as on emerging software industry, telecommunications and pharmaceuticals. Building innovation infrastructure with business incubators all around Vojvodina and Science and Technology Park in Novi Sad, faces Vojvodina with fast growing economic activities, but with lack of high educated human resources too. ICT sector is among leaders in growing sectors, with almost 100 per cent of export of all products and services. During 2006 the authors of this paper were engaged in creation of ICT development strategy in Vojvodina[9]. Visits, interviews and surveys were conducted in order to build information reach foundation for this strategy. Particular attention is paid to knowledge, skills and positions of already employed electrical engineers: how employers evaluate existing engineers. We will present the main findings and lessons learned during this research, which are inputs for on-going changes of curricula for electrical engineering education in Faculty of Engineering (Faculty of Technical Sciences) within University of Novi Sad (FTS UNS).

Background

World economy includes processes that change conditions and rules in global competition, and transition towards knowledge based economy is one of its most prominent features. ICT and software industry sectors are the best representatives of a new technology revolution based on knowledge. The World Economy Forum defines competitiveness as a blend of factors, policies and institutions determining the level of productivity in the country and thus establishing the level of development that a country can achieve in conditions where knowledge-based economy is being established and functions[10]. By the WEF methodology, developed in 2001, the Growth competitiveness index (GCI) is defined, encompassing three components represented by three indices[10]:

1. A component describing quality of macroeconomical environment — represented by the Index of macroeconomical environment,
2. A component describing the state of institutions in a country — represented by the Index of public institutions,
3. A component describing the importance of technology and innovations, i.e. the level of technological readiness — represented by the Index of technological readiness (or Technological index), comprising the following three indices:
   - Innovativeness index,
   - Technology transfer index,
   - Information-communication technology index.

However, the data for Serbia and Montenegro in this WEF report (the report does not contain separate data for Serbia, and for APV), are not favourable. The position of the state union has deteriorated from 2004 to 2005, measured by the Networked Readiness Index Rating: in 2004 it was in the 79th and in 2005 on the 80th place (of 104 countries ranked)[11]. According to the data on the Growth competitiveness index of Serbia and Montenegro, it was in 80th position (out of 117) in 2005, improving its position in comparison to 89th place in 2004. The position regarding the Index of technological competitiveness is somewhat better — 68th (75th place in 2004), whereas the position regarding the Index of macroeconomical development is quite worst — 111, which is worser than 102nd place in 2004. Regarding the third component of the aggregate index of state competitiveness, the Index of public institutions, Serbia and Montenegro was at the 69th place (out of 117) in 2005 (85th place in 2004)[10].

The WEF report for 2005/2006 emphasizes the importance of education and acquisition of particular skills, as well as the level of training of employees, in the new conditions of global economy and ICT development. Reduced transportation and communication costs have stimulated large multinational companies to move their production and development facilities into the parts of world where there is a favourable combination of knowledge and abilities of the employees and cost of their work, as well as political and social stability (outsourcing). Such a combination existed during the transition process in most countries of Central and Eastern Europe (CEE) during the nineties, causing twice as fast economical growth as in the rest of Europe[10].

In order to better understand the influence of ICT on the development of economy and the society in general in the countries of CEE, especially in the new Europian Union (EU) member states as well as countries candidates for EU membership, several studies of this phenomenon have been conducted in the past years, coordinated on behalf of the EU by the Institute for Prospective Technological Studies (IPTS) in Seville. The aim of these studies is creation of a range of national monographies on the development and establishment of information society, including analysis of positive and negative effects and influences in the countries of CEE. A synthetic report for a group of CEE countries that were analyzed points at three main challenges that will influence the development of information society in Europe in this decade[12]:

1. A change in conditions of competition pressure — a potential of ICT for economic development;
2. Growing divisions in the society — the influence of ICT on society groups and society segmentation, so called digital division;
3. Appearance of new problems related to economical growth and demography — influence of ICT to transition and reforms in education.

Results of those studies are grouped into two main findings[12]:

1. ICT can help countries, new EU members, to reach the level of economical development of original EU countries before its expansion (so called EU 15);
2. There is a potential for economical growth based on ICT in sectors that do not use ICT as well.

These findings have stressed the need for more intensive use of ICT in certain branches of industry and public sector as well as creation of economical and industrial environment in which the business sector would invest more in ICT, resulting in faster economical growth and establishment of an information society in CEE countries, in line with the Lisbon strategy for increasing EU competitiveness[13].

Gloomy WEF findings related to the state of competitiveness of Serbian economy are nevertheless encouraging as regards trends. 80th place in 2005 is much better than 89th place in 2004, with even more significant improvement regarding the Index of technological competitiveness (68th place in 2005 compared to the 75th place in 2004). Namely, by its content, the Index of technological competitiveness describes the potential of an economy for its further development. Since ICT is one of the key factors of the Index of technological competitiveness, an analysis of the competitiveness of this particular sector comes as a logical subject of investigation. Table 23.1. shows some of the most important indicators of ICT industry development in the world and in the region.

Table 23.1: Some of the Most Important Indicators of ICT Development and Application of ICT in Economy and Society

Year 2002	*IT costs/GDP [%]*	*IT costs per capita [EUR]*	*No. of PCs per 100 HE employees*	*No. of PCs per 100 inhabitants*
Greece	1.38	169	63	10
EU	3.22	723	83	28
Western Europe	3.26	745	85	29
Japan	3.48	903	49	39
Sweden	4.88	1,216	113	54
USA	4.77	1,362	141	83

Year 2002	*IT costs in millions [EUR]*	*Participation [%]*	*IT/GDP [%]*	*IT costs per capita [EUR]*
Romania	719	6.2	1.5	32
Bulgaria	312	2.7	1.8	40
Poland	3,992	34.5	2.0	104
Slovakia	757	6.5	2.4	141
Hungary	1,958	16.9	3.5	193
Czech Republic	2,620	22.7	3.3	254
Slovenia	507	4.4	2.1	255
CEE total	11,555	100.0	2.3	111
Western Europe total	286,740	100.0	3.1	735

If Romania, the country with the lowest investments in IT equipment per capita in this table, is considered a reference point for APV, it can be calculated that the minimal investment of industry and public sector in ICT is about 64 million EUR. If the entire CEE is considered a referent point instead, the minimal investment rises to 222 million EUR. If the calculation is performed with regard to investments in Western Europe, the sum amounts to 1.47 billion EUR.

Methodology

The purpose of creation of ICT development strategy in Vojvodina, launched in 2006, was to bring up objective facts and competitive possibilities for companies of ICT industry in AP Vojvodina, so it could fit to modern market course in an adequate way and compete both at home and on the global market[9].

The authors of this paper were engaged in creation of this ICT development strategy in APV, preparing the methodology and conducting main research and other activities in order to identify main problems and obstacles as well as to propose set-up of priorities (projects and programmes) in the field of ICT, crucial for development of economy and society of APV in next 5-10 years. Methodology is consisting of:

- Survey of existing ICT companies in APV, including questionnaires, interviews and on-site analysis of company's performance;
- Set of brainstorming sessions, devoted to analysis of present situation and generation of possible directions for future developments in ICT sector in APV; and
- Use of Delphi method for setting-up of priority programmes and projects;
- Presentation of achieved results, in order to collect responses from all interested stakeholders, as well as to promote proposed set-up of priorities (projects and programmes).

In this survey, primary data comes from statistical research computed in the course of preparation of this document, while the secondary data comes from existing statistical reports. The sample used for the survey was provided by the Chamber of Commerce of Serbia and came from the list of registered companies in ICT area in APV. Checking these data, 43 active companies were identified in the field of software industry with 497 employees, 4 in the field of telecommunication with 71 employees, and 32 companies in the field of hardware industry with 517 employees, which are 79 companies with 1085 employees' total. By direct insight — visits, interviews and analysis of gathered questionnaires in these companies, a sample of 14 companies were treated with 399 employees, which is 37 per cent of all employees in ICT industry in APV.

For this survey, 'A questionnaire for surveying competence, competitiveness, and cooperation and characteristic development trajectories of companies in the ICT sector in AP Vojvodina' was developed, which consisted of the following segments[9]:

1. General company data;
2. Company profile data — for identification of competence of the company;
3. Business and company growth data — for identification of competitiveness of the company;
4. Strategic company partnership data — for identification of cooperativeness of the company;
5. Company business effects data;
6. The opinion of the accountable manager of the company about the quality of human resources in the company — current state and trends in the period 1995-2006;

7. The plan for further development of the company — what will the accountable manager do to make the company do improve business in the period 2006-2008 (2010), in the following fields:
   - Technology development,
   - Home market,
   - Global market,
   - Development of the company human resources;
8. What does the company expect from the state — what do they expect the state will do to improve business conditions for companies in APV;
9. Is the company satisfied with available communication infrastructure;
10. Data of the people who answered the questionnaire.

For the purpose of this paper, findings and results are presented, which are of relevance for analysis of human resource potentials in APV, regarding to education and training of electrical engineers within higher education system in APV.

Findings

I. Software Industry in APV — Survey' Findings

Analyzed companies of the ICT industry are, regarding the number of employees, in the category of micro/small/medium companies. They have exceptionally good qualification structure, with more than 80 per cent of employees who have finished university. Employees on software development with university education make more than 50 per cent of the employees altogether. The trend of employment rise is particularly encouraging. It can be observed that in the year 2006 is the break-out one, because the number of employees is more than doubled, with an intention to continue the trend in 2007 as well. It indicates the ever improving state of this sector.

Table 23.2: Distribution of Analyzed Companies by Size and Education of Employees

Employees — status December 31st — plan for 2007	*2001*	*2002*	*2003*	*2004*	*2005*	*2006*	*2007*
All employees:	44	53	96	120	186	399	494
Rise in the number of employees— previous year = 100%	100%	120%	181%	125%	155%	215%	124%
Number of employees with university education	38	44	76	109	165	373	467
Employees with university education as % of all employees	86%	83%	79%	85%	85%	93%	94%
Number of software developers with university education	22	24	50	75	100	271	351
Software developers with university education-% of all employees	50%	45%	52%	59%	52%	68%	71%

Most of the analyzed companies of the ICT industry are relatively young, founded after year 2000 (see table 23.3). They are mainly companies in private ownership.

Table 23.3: Distribution of Analyzed Companies by Year of Founding

The year of founding	*Before 2000*	*2000*	*2001*	*2002*	*2003*	*2004*	*2005*	*2006*
Number of companies	2	1	2	2	3	2	2	0
% of analysed companies	14.3%	7.1%	14.3%	14.3%	21.4%	14.3%	14.3%	0%

Main activities of the analyzed companies are: (a) selling of own products/ services; and (b) outsourcing. 12 products/services were identified for both activities (see table 23.4). When the activity of a company is selling their products/services, the predominant are: Real-time system management software; Web applications; Communication software; Production management, ERP (Enterprise Resource Planning). Regarding outsourcing, the predominates are: Web applications, ERP. Note that the analyzed companies are concentrated on lesser number of products/services, when their activity is just their selling. Larger dispersion is noticed concerning outsourcing.

Table 23.4: Distribution of Analyzed Companies by Activities

Sort of products/services:	*Participation in selling their products/services:*	*Participation as outsourcing:*
Enterprise resource planning (ERP):	19.58%	14.55%
Web applications:	19.58%	23.18%
Real-time system management software:	17.50%	2.73%
Communication software:	17.08%	7.27%
Embedded software:	6.25%	11.36%
Porting — adaptation of SW to a new hardware platform:	5.42%	7.27%
Consulting:	5.42%	16.36%
Testing:	5.00%	4.55%
Support:	2.92%	2.73%
System software:	0.83%	0.00%
Implementation:	0.42%	5.45%
Middleware solutions	0.00%	5.00%
Altogether:	100%	100%

Year after year, revenue of these companies, on home and foreign market, is observed to grow. Even though these companies are not particularly willing to disclose data about their business, the collected data suggest that the majority as well as the most important buyers/users of products/services of these companies are abroad. Since the average total labor cost is 50 per cent (out of total turnover), the one applied from the competition from the EU countries, we can conclude that the main source of competitive advantage is the quality of products/services of our companies, since the labor cost in Romania and Bulgaria is two times lower than here.

Most companies founded so far are small companies. Figure 23.1 show that companies with a small number of employees have large dispersion of income per employee, because they work on a project basis, i.e. for larger projects professionals are engaged part-time, whereas there are chunks of time without any projects, or those that are in a start-up phase are competing charging extremely low prices. Income per employee is virtually constant for enterprises having 60-110 employees.

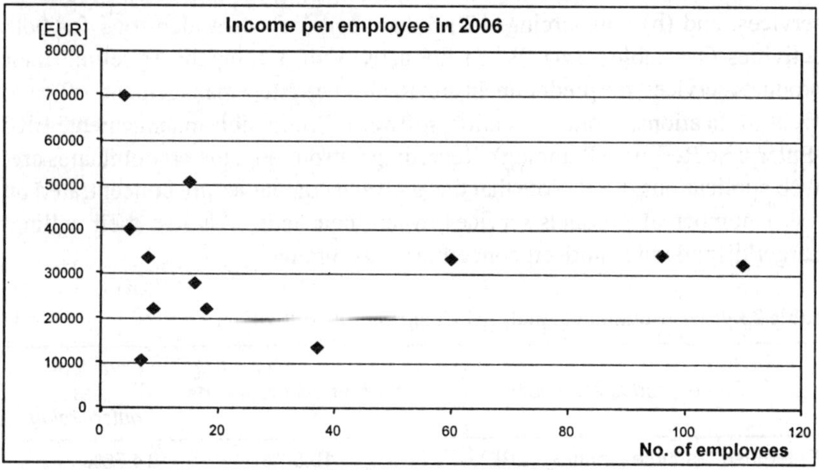

Figure 23.1: Income Per Employee in ICT Sector (Based on a Sample of Companies)

Software tools/programming languages that are mostly used are JAVA and C++, which shows the nature of the majority of applications that are being developed in these companies, and at the same time it also shows what kind of knowledge do the graduated experts need to have (see table 23.5).

The previous conclusion is confirmed by the evaluation of the sources of competitive advantage of the analyzed ICT companies: (a) Regarding the global markets, the predominant source of the competitive advantage is good quality; (b) Regarding the home market, the specialized expertise in the sector are the most important (see table 23.6).

Important information for strategic positioning and development of the companies in the ICT sector is the evaluation of competitive disadvantage: (a) Regarding the global market, the most important source of competitive disadvantage is poor marketing; (b) At home, the most important sources of competitive disadvantage are poor marketing and high prices of products/services, implying that the market is still underdeveloped (see table 23.7).

Table 23.5: Software Tools/Programming Languages that are Used by Employees in Work

Software tools/programming languages that are used in work	*Number of employees that use this tool*
JAVA	189
C++	154
Eclipse/NetBeans, JavaScript, HTML	44
Microsoft .NET (ASP.NET, C#)	14
Database, SQL	12
WebSphere Development Studio	10
Other: Delphi, ASP, Basic	6
Matlab	4
Progress 4GL	2
CVS, ClearCase, Bugzilla, ClearQuest, MS Project	1
SUN Forte	1
OS Windows 95/98/2000/2003/XP/CE; Linux	1
OS in Linux, Symbian, Nucleus	1
PHP	1
Enterprise Architect	1
Altogether	441
Number of employees with university education	271
Number of tools per employee	1.63

Table 23.6: Sources of Competitive Advantage of the Analyzed ICT Companies

Evaluation of importance of sources of competitive advantage (1–no significance; 2–small significance; 3–significant; 4–very significant; 5–exedingly significant):	*Importance for the home market*	*Importance for the global market*
Good quality:	3.89	4.57
Meeting milestones:	3.38	4.36
Specialized expertise:	4.44	4.21
Software design capabilities:	3.78	4.14
Programming capabilities:	3.78	4.07
Reputation:	3.44	4.00
Access to global partners and sources:	3.13	3.91
Competitive price of products/services:	3.33	3.57
Diversification of products/services:	3.38	3.23
Proximity to key markets:	3.00	2.92
Access to clients and contacts at home market:	4.11	2.09

Table 23.7: Sources of Competitive Advantage of the Analyzed ICT Companies

Evaluation of importance of sources of competitive disadvantage (1–no significance; 2–small significance; 3–significant; 4–very significant; 5–exedingly significant):	*Importance for the home market*	*Importance for the global market*
Poor marketing	3.50	3.69
Shortage of programmers and designers:	2.70	2.92
High price:	3.40	2.77
Low quality:	2.10	2.62
Poor design capabilities:	1.90	2.23
Limited programming skills:	1.90	2.15
Limited expertise in specific areas:	2.30	2.00

The most important type of relationship with foreign partners is R&D outsourcing contracts, with significant presence of license agreements (see table 23.8). This finding should influence the institutions assigned with the task of governing the science and technology development, indicating that there exists a significant portion of the innovation system in the APV that is, at least not publicly, a part of R&D system, i.e. is not the beneficiary of regional subvention programmes.

Table 23.8: Relationship with Foreign Partners of the Analyzed ICT Companies

Relationship with foreign partners (all applicable modes at the time of filling the form):			
Totally owned by the foreign partner:	14.29%	R&D agreement:	35.71%
Joint venture:	35.71%	Joint development:	35.71%
Producer:	14.29%	Authorized distributor:	0.00%
Authorized reseller of the system:	7.14%	System integration contract:	0.00%
License agreement:	28.57%	System partner:	7.14%
Vendor that provides a support before selling:	0.00%	Joint production:	7.14%

ICT companies in APV look for foreign partners in order to solve the problem of finding the customers, again stressing the aforementioned conclusion about the poor marketing as the primary source of their competitive disadvantage.

The final finding indicates a large discrepancy between the development of the home and global ICT market. Global market poses more constraints, not only regarding prices and deadlines, but especially regarding quality. Home market, as stated before, is preoccupied more by the price than quality of ICT products/services.

II. Human resources in SE

Human resource (HR) **quality** in SW companies in APV (an overview of statements of analyzed companies):

- These are good programmers, dedicated to their work;
- Having in mind the exceedingly complex requirements of the software components used and realized, there is a shortage of very talented programmers, as well as experts in this complex field (digital signal processing, linguistics, math…);
- Regarding skilled managers, it is difficult to find people who are capable of acquiring this fairly complex matter and at the same time remain persuasive when communicating to people;
- Quality of experts is on a very professional level, with a stress on the personal wish to improve the working environment and continuous professional improvement;
- HR of the ICT companies are their most valued assets;
- Development of human resources has been initiated from the R&D centre at the Faculty of Engineering (FTS), University of Novi Sad (UNS);
- Regarding the beginners—junior programmer positions — the engineers coming from the FTS-UNS, are capable of a fast introduction into the work process, with those from the Faculty of Science (FS) from the same university, close second. Recent changes in curricula have enabled the students to acquire practical experience, working on the university projects, which proved to be very useful;
- The shortage of people in the sector is a consequence of huge increase in demand;
- The price of quality experts have significantly grown in the last 12 months;
- Practical cooperation between FTS-UNS, and ICT companies — strategically investment into people during their studies and focusing them on areas that will ease employment after finishing them. Thus, there is a direct correlation between the quality of studies on this faculty and the quality of human resources employed now or in the future at the companies, justifying the intense focus of the companies on the improvement of the studies on the FTS-UNS;
- Some thoughts on theme 'Which are the qualities needed for a Junior Programmer?':
  - Intelligence (IQ) is very important; genius is not needed, but high IQ is more than useful;
  - Perseverance, will to learn new things (even an extreme IQ is useless if the person is lazy and disinterested);
  - Ethic/moral values, sincerity, openness (sounding maybe trivial, this is still of utmost importance);
  - Everything is possible to learn/change, if one is persistent and willing to learn;
  - Communication:

    — Not too many people, especially those that have recently finished their studies, are capable of actively listening. Listening here means not being obedient to orders, but active participation in the conversation and reasoning (as opposed to just nodding without any understanding what it is about);

- — Asking questions when something is not clear, without fear/shame that the question is stupid;
- — Open communication about problems encountered; if something does not go, one should ask and tell the problem, usually there is a more experienced person that will give a helping hand;

- *Pragmatism*: Experience with beginners says that they usually try to solve the problem in highest possible generality. The other usual problem is that people are tied to a certain tool or environment, and tend to neglect any other possibility including more efficient work environments;
- Excellent knowledge of foreign languages (primarily English);
- Last, but not least, one should have the basic knowledge based on the projects management finished during studies.

- Insufficient number of quality programmers for Java and .Net technologies;
- During the period 1995-2006 we observed a declining trend of available high-quality people, which can partly be attributed to increased demand. Currently not too many high-quality people finish studies;
- Specificity of the business and long-term projects implore ICT companies to 'build their own personnel', employing new human resources immediately after finishing their studies, and than gradually introducing them into their development teams;
- In 90 per cent of cases, the company employs students who finish electrical engineering at communication and signal processing direction or those who finish studies at computer engineering direction of the Faculty of Engineering in Novi Sad. Knowledge obtained there enables active participation in the training programme which is organized by the company for candidates for the job. We have observed that the studies at the faculty have to be improved by introducing a closer cooperation with the companies so as to enable the students to acquire practical experiences in the environment of their future employers. This would enable students to cope with real problems from everyday life of an engineer, and let them learn the requirements and norms of work in the industry.

HR **development** in SW companies in APV (review on individual reports of analyzed companies):

- In the company they work in few different ways to ensure and maintain quality of employees: scholarship for the most talented students, mentoring work, number of international projects and good team organization;

- In company they expect to double a number of employees in next two years by developing partnership with the biggest companies in that field;
- Growing marketing team, selection end optimization of development team — the goal is to low expenses;
- In company they expect increasing of the number of employees and, also, quality and competence of new employees. That will reach by improving cooperation with university and foreign partners. Cooperation with foreign partners means trainings and educations of employees, in partner's company or in houses that are specialized for that field. There is knowledge management system in company that provides internal education. It is expected to continue with that practice;
- Employees participation in conferences, scholarships for master or doctoral study, mentoring programme for new graduates;
- The most important thing is training of employees' competence in selected fields: project management, quality control and managers' skills and techniques, and continuous technical and professional improvements;
- Scholarship for students on last years of studying;
- Student practice;
- Training in foreign countries for employees;
- In company are needed qualified and motivated people, together with continuous education and information on new technology and trends in SW technology, and certification of leading professionals.

III. R&D and Educational Institutions in the ICT Sector in APV

The most significant R&D and higher education institutions in the ICT sector in APV are located within the University of Novi Sad:

- The Faculty of Engineering (FTS),
- The Faculty of Sciences (FS).

Table 23.9: Human Resources for Research and Development in the ICT Field in APV

Human Resources	*FTS*			*FS*	*Total*
	E1	*E2*	*Total*		
Professors	15	10	25	5	30
Associate Professors	10	6	16	1	17
Assistant Professors	7	7	14	1	15
Assistant Teachers	29	22	51	6	57
Junior Assistant Teachers	17	10	27	4	31
Junior Researchers	7	—	7	1	8
Curricular and research staff — Total	85	55	140	18	158
Students — year I	400	84	484		
Average number of graduations per year	204	51	255		
% of graduated (out of total no. of enrollees)	51 %	61 %	53 %		

Total number of teaching staff is 158, and number of students is close to 2000. Number of graduates is close to 300 every year. Human resources available for research and development, as well as education of students within undergraduate and graduate courses in the ICT field in APV, are given in Table 23.9.

IV. SWOT Analysis of HR in the ICT Sector in APV

Following the overview of the current state in companies and research/educational institutions in the ICT sector in APV, a synthesis of the score is given in the form of SWOT tables (tables 23.10, 23.11, 23.12 and 23.13).

Table 23.10: SWOT Analysis — Human Resources in the ICT Sector in AP Vojvodina

STRENGTHS — particularities of ICT	*WEAKNESSES — particularities of ICT*
➢ High qualification structure of employees ➢ Programmers mostly use JAVA and C++ ➢ Programmers are taught to use a very wide array of software tools ➢ Programmers are dedicated to their work ➢ Quality of human resources at a high professional level ➢ Capability of fast absorption of new knowledge, efficient use of the Internet and a logical approach to problem solving are the typical traits of young ICT experts	➢ Lack of programmers and other ICT specialists ➢ Lack of managers to run ICT business ➢ It takes 3-6 month for experts who have finished studies to be able to perform given tasks in their companies with success ➢ Some people have lost interest and motivation for work owing to the difficult situation in the country ➢ Lack of quality programmers for JAVA and .Net ➢ A decrease in the number of available quality experts and graduate ICT specialists can be seen ➢ Lack of inventiveness and innovativeness
OPPORTUNITIES — particularities of ICT	*THREATS — particularities of ICT*
➢ Increase in employment rate since 2005. ➢ FTS and FS are quality faculties for education of ICT specialists ➢ FTS has developed practical collaboration with ICT industry companies ➢ ICT companies organize training of their employees ➢ Programmes for fast training of the people with medium education for software jobs ➢ Including people with lower education or abilities into services via ICT infrastructure ➢ Awarding scholarships to students of final years of ICT studies	➢ Cost of quality people has risen significantly since 2005. ➢ Attitude towards job and absence of professional ethics ➢ Lack of interest in studies of technical sciences ➢ Underdeveloped infrastructure for specialized training of ICT professionals ➢ Lack of specific knowledge and abilities required for ICT business: ICT project management, marketing and PR in ICT etc.

Table 23.11: SWOT Analysis — Infrastructure in the Area of R&D in the ICT Sector in APV

STRENGTHS — particularities of ICT	*WEAKNESSES — particularities of ICT*
➢ Tradition of high quality education in the area of technical, mathematical and other sciences ➢ Innovative-entrepreneurial potential at the University well developed ➢ International cooperation in the area of ICT research and development well established ➢ Price of RD resources in the ICT sector still competitive	➢ Inadequate potential of high education in the area of technical, mathematical and other sciences compared to the needs of APV ➢ Inadequate regional distribution of RD infrastructure in the ICT sector in APV
OPPORTUNITIES — particularities of ICT	*THREATS — particularities of ICT*
➢ A high level of competence of local human resources as well as potential for cooperation with foreign and local ICT companies and RD organizations ➢ EU programmes for regional RD cooperation in the field of ICT ➢ Potential and needs of the ICT market in APV and Serbia	➢ Political situation in the city, APV and the republic, slowing down and/or obstructing the development of the ST park at the University ➢ Cheap outsourcing — RD projects not defined in accordance with local needs — in case international cooperation is not commercially based ➢ Unstable economical and political situation in the country ➢ Brain drain

Table 23.12: SWOT Analysis of the ICT Industry in AP Vojvodina

STRENGTHS — particularities of ICT	*WEAKNESSES — particularities of ICT*
➢ ICT companies are mostly young, founded after 2000, and mostly owned by private parties ➢ Good qualification structure, with more than 80% of employees with high education ➢ ICT companies launch their products and services mostly in the following areas: software for real-time system management, web applications, co-mmunication software, production management and enterprise resource planning (ERP) ➢ ICT companies outsource mostly in the areas of web applications and ERP ➢ ICT companies are typically concentrated on a smaller number of products/services, and their key activity	➢ Most companies do not have an international quality control certificate ➢ The most important cause of weak competition at markets abroad is weak marketing ➢ The most important cause of weak competition at the local market is the high price of products/services. ➢ Local ICT companies look for foreign partners for solving the problem of finding a market, due to the lack of their own marketing potentials ➢ Local ICT market usually pays attention to the price of ICT products/services rather to their quality

(*Contd.*)

STRENGTHS — particularities of ICT	WEAKNESSES — particularities of ICT
is the actual sale of these products/services ➤ Income of these companies on both local and foreign markets grows each year ➤ The major buyers/users of products/services of these companies are located abroad	➤ In case of outsourcing, a larger dispersion in engagement can be noted, i.e. acceptance of a much larger number of product/service development projects
OPPORTUNITIES — particularities of ICT	**THREATS — particularities of ICT**
➤ Gross price of work of employees in local ICT companies is about 50% compared to the competition in EU countries, leading to the conclusion that the major source of competitiveness is actually the quality of products/services offered by our companies, since the price of the same work in Romania or Bulgaria is about half the price here. ➤ As to the local market, the main source of competitive advantage is a specialized expertise in a certain area.	➤ Foreign partners demand a quality control certificate according to ISO 9001 and CMMI/level 3 or higher ➤ Access of Romania and Bulgaria to the EU, since these are countries with the same geographical position, but lower cost of work ➤ Crisis in the ICT sector in the EU (bankruptcies of certain traditional partners of our companies) ➤ Foreign ICT product/service market is more demanding regarding price, deadlines, as well as quality ➤ Appearance of some new players at the market (Belarus, Moldavia)

Table 23.13: SWOT Analysis of the ICT Sector in APV — Synthetic Table

STRENGTHS	WEAKNESSES
➤ Well developed ICT market ➤ Expert staff in ICT sector ➤ Diverse products/services ➤ An increase in the number of ICT SMEs ➤ Active innovative behaviour	➤ Absence of foreign companies ➤ Lack of inflow of new programmers and designers
OPPORTUNITIES	**THREATS**
➤ Attracting new students to the ICT area ➤ Planned industrial infrastructure ➤ Legalization of 'gray' economy ➤ Presence of large ICT companies in neighbo-ring regions in Hungary and Romania, owing to their plans for expansion into Serbia/APV ➤ Readiness of local government to deal with issues important for economic development, as well as consciousness of ICT development	➤ Illegal outsourcing ➤ Brain drain ➤ Political instability in the country ➤ Possible instabilities at target markets, especially in Germany ➤ Increase in the price of quality human resources ➤ Increase in the need for communication infrastructure not covered by providers of broadband communication services

Recommendations of the Survey Concerning the Curricula for Electrical and Computer Engineering Education

Interviews, on-site visits and written remarks, both from ICT companies and from university staff, lead us to propose institutional as well as infrastructural recommendations, regarding education and training of electrical engineers and other professionals, who are of primary concern for development of ICT sector in APV[9]:

- Organizing guest engagement of professors from the universities abroad for a period from 6 months to a year (financed by provincial authorities). Priority should be given to our acknowledged experts, due to the language issue;
- Organizing courses at university with foreign lecturers and exchanging experiences with colleagues from abroad. Participation in organizing thematic courses for needs of enterprises;
- Reform of university curricula in direction of introduction of different management courses within technical studies, such as: project management, marketing management, quality management; business communication; professional ethics; etc.
- Introducing entrepreneurial education;
- Supporting inventiveness and innovativeness of ICT professionals;
- Supporting the function of an S&T Park as an integrator of domestic firms having a similar but complementary profile, so that they could apply for getting projects of a greater significance. Projects being referred to are the ones for the domestic market and financed by EU institutions, whose terms eliminate smaller and relatively new domestic firms;
- Organizing a business incubator in Novi Sad and in other cities in APV, particularly in the field of ICT;
- Founding a Training centre of secondary school pupils in JAVA and C++ tools. This centre would provide an efficient—from 6 to 12-month — training of new programmers, prepared to get involved in development projects of ICT industry in APV immediately. A similar solution gave results in Timisoara (Romania);
- Reforming the secondary education system in to the effect of encouraging team work, creativity, active listening and reasoning in the course of conversation;
- Bring in insurance against employees' professional responsibility, which is a prerequisite for making some international contracts;
- Simplifying customs regulations on temporary import of ICT equipment;
- Including people with lower educational profile or capabilities in providing services through ICT infrastructure, without the additional education being necessary;
- Encouraging a mathematical way of thinking at the earliest age possible,

by helping the activities of Archimedes and the like, by organizing competitions in mathematics at all levels regarding age, schools, local self managements, counties, APV (the goal is to include as many young people as possible, and furthermore, the competitions in logics, algorithms, and the like develop curiosity and capabilities to be significant in the later work in ICT sector);

- Starting technological foresight programmes in ICT field (there is the example of Austria, which defined specific priority sectors, e.g. ferrous metallurgy, which can realize their competitiveness at most by using ICT. A similar approach to defining development priorities and the role of ICT should be adopted by APV as well);
- Participation in the expenses of patent protection abroad;
- Building of broadband telecommunication infrastructure for Internet, connecting end-users of all kind (R&D, health, cultural and educational institutions, government and other public institution, companies, and individuals).

Reform of the Electrical and Computer Engineering Education at the Faculty of Engineering

In 2005, a new curriculum was introduced at the Faculty of Engineering. The teaching process was aligned with the Bologna recommendations, with so far not brilliant results regarding the number of students that pass exams in due time, and even more regarding the residual knowledge and understanding of the learned contents. This is largely due to the fact that elementary and high-school education in the nineties crawled down and introduced the culture of memorizing without understanding the learned material. Having one semester instead of two-semester subjects, coupled with two or more mid-term exams, which is normally an excellent idea, eased the task of those students who just memorize and reproduce. Understanding the subject as a whole is now never checked due to partial examining the knowledge.

On the other hand, there is good news as well. The number of hours for computer skill-based subjects was nearly doubled, with lots of work done in laboratories on practical problems. Entrepreneurship has been introduced through the UNESCO chair for entrepreneurship. Students are introduced to inventions, innovations, and business planning. Internships are introduced in high-tech firms, implying more practical skills for those students willing to acquire them. Multidisciplinarity is encouraged. Wherever possible, tuition is coordinated and tightly correlated with R&D work in the spin-out companies from FTS. Thus, there is a sound belief that long-term the process will improve the capabilities of human resources generated at FTS to be included in R&D activities upon completion of their studies. The first results will be observed by the end of 2009, when the first generation finishes their BSc studies, and in 2010, when those who enroll to MSc studies get their diploma.

References

1. 'EITO — European Information Technology Observatory (2004)', ISSN 0947-4862, Eggebrecht-Presse KG, Mainz.
2. Bidanda B., Arisoy O., Shuman L.J. (2006). 'Offshoring manufacturing: Implications for engineering jobs and education: A survey and case study', *Robotics and Computer-Integrated Manufacturing*, Vol. 22, pp. 576-587.
3. Hilburn T.B., Hislop G., Bagert D.J., Lutz M., Mengel S., McCracken M. (1999). 'Guidance for the development of software engineering education programmes', *The Journal of Systems and Software*, Vol. 49, pp. 163-169.
4. Kitchenham B., Budgen D., Brereton P. and Woodall P. (2005). 'An investigation of software engineering curricula', *The Journal of Systems and Software*, Vol. 74, pp. 325-335.
5. Nambisan S. and Wilemon D. (2003). 'A global study of graduate management of technology programmes', Technovation, Vol. 23, pp. 949-962.
6. Ka Ho Mok. (2003). 'Fostering entrepreneurship: Changing role of government and higher education governance in Hong Kong', Research Policy, Vol. 34, pp. 537-554.
7. Eugène C. (2006). 'How to teach at the university level through an active learning approach? Consequences for teaching basic electrical measurements', Measurement, Vol. 39, pp. 936-946.
8. Moore, K. and Kutlaca, D. (2003). 'An Overview of the Information and Communications Technology Sector in Serbia and Profiles of Selected Companies', OECD Investment Compact for South East Europe and The Stability Pact for South Eastern Europe, OECD, Paris, http://www.investmentcompact.org/general/library.htm.
9. Vojvodina, A.P. (2006). 'Basic Directions of Technology Development for the Computer engineering, Communications and Automated systems Sector', Faculty of Technical Sciences, University of Novi Sad.
10. 'Global Competitiveness Report (2005-2006). Executive Summary', World Economic Forum, http://www.weforum.org/site/homepublic.nsf/Content/Global+Competitiveness+Programme%5CGlobal+Competitiveness+Report
11. 'Global Information Technology Report (2005-2006). Executive Summary', World Economic Forum, http://www.weforum.org/site/homepublic.nsf/Content/Global+Competitiveness+Programme%5CGlobal+Information+Technology+Report
12. Piatkowski, M. (2005), 'The potential of ICT for the development and economic restructuring of the new EU member states and candidate countries', European Commission, Joint Research Centre, Technical Report EUR 21589 EN.
13. European Commission (2000). 'Presidency Conclusions — Lisbon European Council', Press Release No. 100/1/00, Lisbon, 23-24.

24
Engineering Education: From European to Polish Perspective

Lidia Zakowska

General Trends in Engineering Education

We live in a time of revolutionary change. Not only the world relying increasingly on technology for economic growth and job development, but the nations are making the difficult transition of refocusing a significant amount of their technology investment from national security to international economic competitiveness. At the same time, we view technology as important in helping solve many difficult societal problems, from creating environmentally-sustainable development and improving communications, to devising more effective and cost-efficient health care systems. Communication developments alone are leading to profound redefinitions of such concepts as 'community,' 'library,' 'corporation,' and even 'university.'

Within this technological context, engineers play an ever more significant role. They develop new manufacturing processes and products; create and manage energy, transportation and communication systems; prevent new and redress old environmental problems; create pioneering health care devices; and, in general, make technology work. Through these activities, engineers create a huge potential for the private sector to develop national wealth. The nation with the best engineering talent is in possession of the core ingredient of comparative economic and industrial advantage.

And just as important as their specific technical skills, engineers receive valuable preparation for a host of other careers in such areas as finance, medicine, law and management. These professions require analytical, integrative and problem-solving abilities, all of which are part of an engineering education. Thus, engineering is an ideal undergraduate education for living and working in the technologically-dependent society of the twenty-first century.

One of the strengths of engineering education is the broad spectrum of engineering schools whose development has been unconstrained by a single, centrally-prescribed mission. Schools of engineering range from highly research-intensive institutions to those that focus largely on undergraduate education, with many variations in between. Even with the considerable differences in missions, undergraduate engineering education programmes maintain universal core curriculum content and minimum standards through the accreditation board for engineering and technology, a national partnership between academics and practicing engineers. Additionally, most engineering schools have forged close relationships with industry and benefit from annual assessments of their programmes by external advisory boards that have strong industry participation.

While engineering education has served the nation well, there is broad recognition that it must change to meet new challenges. This is fully in keeping with its history of changing to be consistent with national needs. Today, engineering colleges must not only provide their graduates with intellectual development and superb technical capabilities, but following industry's lead, those colleges must educate their students to work as part of teams, communicate well, and understand the economic, social, environmental and international context of their professional activities. These changes are vital to the nation's industrial strength and to the ability of engineers to serve as technology and policy decision makers.

Most important, engineering education programmes must attract an ethnic and social diversity of students that better reflects the diversity of the European Universities and takes full advantage of the nation's talents. Not only does the engineering profession require a spectrum of skills and backgrounds, but it should preserve its historical role as a profession of upward mobility.

In response to these needs, engineering colleges throughout the countries are experimenting with new approaches to curricula, rethinking traditional teaching modes, and developing innovative ways to recruit and retain students from underrepresented groups. Each includes a variety of schools ranging from predominantly undergraduate institutions to the most research intensive. The consortia are working to redesign curricula and improve teaching methodologies, each offering a different perspective and strategy.

European Strategy for Modernization of Universities

A European Commission Communication of 10 May 2006 urges Member States to press on with the modernisation of Europe's universities. The aim is to increase universities' contribution to the Lisbon Agenda for more growth, and more and better jobs. Europe's 4000 universities have enormous potential, much of which unfortunately goes untapped because of various rigidities and hindrances. The Commission is urging Member States to free up the European Universities's substantial reservoir of knowledge, talent and energy with immediate, in-depth and coordinated change: from the way in which higher education systems are regulated and managed, to the ways in which universities are governed. This Communication is the fruit of joint work by the Directorates-General for Education and Culture and Research, and covers all the activities of Europe's universities, from their delivery of education, their research activities, through to their potential as drivers of innovation.

'Knowledge and innovation are the engines of sustainable growth in Europe today, and universities are crucial for achieving the goals set out by the European Council. However, there are important weaknesses in the performance of European higher education institutions compared to those of our main competitors, notably the USA. Although the average quality of European universities is rather good, they are not in a position to deliver their full potential to boost economic growth, social cohesion and more and better jobs. The Commission invites national decision makers to set out measures that would enable universities to play a full role in the Lisbon strategy', as expressed by Ján Figel, European Commissioner for Education, Training, Culture and Multilingualism.

Education and Science in European Union

Education and science are areas where the European Union's role is limited to supporting national governments. In education, the policy was mainly developed in the 1980s in programmes supporting exchanges and mobility. The most visible of these has been the ERASMUS, a university exchange programme which began in 1987. In its first 20 years it has supported international exchange opportunities for well over 1.5 million university and college students and has become a symbol of European student life. There are now similar programmes for school pupils and teachers, for trainees in vocational education and training, and for adult learners in the Lifelong Learning Programme 2007-2013. These programmes are designed to encourage a wider knowledge of other countries and to spread good practices in the education and training fields across the Europeon Union. Through its support of the Bologna process the European Union is supporting comparable standards and compatible degrees across Europe.

Scientific development is facilitated through the European Union's Framework Programmes, the first of which started in 1984. The aims of European Union policy in this area are to co-ordinate and stimulate research. The independent European Research Council allocates Europeon Union funds to European or national research projects. The Seventh Framework Programme (FP7) deals in a number of areas, many of which are connected with engineering.

Since January 2000 the European Commission has set its sights on a more ambitious objective, known as the European Research Area; extensively funding research in a few key research areas. This has the support of all member states, and extends the existing financing structure of the frameworks. It aims to focus on co-ordination, sharing knowledge, ensuring mobility of researchers around

Europe, improving conditions for researchers and encouraging links with business and industry as well as removing any legal and administrative barriers.

Several associations and organizations are involved in engineering education cooperation in Europe. European Society for Engineering Education (SEFI) is the first example of an association directly linking the institutions of higher engineering education, hence independent of national or community filters in establishing its policy, as an international forum for discussing problems and identifying solutions relating to engineering education. SEFI was founded in 1973 as a non-profit making organisation under Belgian Law. It is the largest network of higher engineering institutions and of individuals involved in engineering education in Europe. SEFI has the mission to contribute to the development and the improvement of the engineering education in Europe. The society serves as a European forum and should be considered as a service to European institutions, academic staff, students and industry.

Apart from the European Society for Engineering Education, there are several European associations and initiatives linking engineering education goals. One of those is CESAER—the Conference of European Schools for Advanced Engineering Education and Research—a non-profit-making international association of leading European Engineering Universities, Colleges and Schools. CESAER, is an association of leading European Universities engaged in advanced engineering education and research and dedicated to research lead teaching. They are determined to make the offer of engineering education curricula across Europe truly perceived as a wide spectrum of education possibilities with a variety of educational processes and objectives, and to avoid it being leveled out in a common monolithic 'engineering' academic field. Members are convinced that the progress of the European Union in all respects requires further and increased contributions from the educational side. They are committed to the development of the best possible human asset in engineering on which Europe can capitalize to overcome its challenge and to the development of the European Area for Engineering Education and Research. This would enable them to respond to the changing demands of the European society in a global environment.

CESAER was established in 1990 and now has a membership of sixty universities in western and central European countries. The main objectives of CESAER are to provide 'High Quality' Engineering Education in Europe and to improve links between its members in Research as well as in Postgraduate and Continuing Education. To this end, CESAER aims to:

- Encourage the training of engineers with broader educational experience, including linguistic abilities, developed by attendance at two or more European leading engineering institutions;
- Increase the awareness of engineering graduates to the specific needs and opportunities of future European industrial and economic cooperation.

This includes the strengthening of the cultural background of engineering graduates in view of their increasing responsibility for the construction of a humanistic neotechnic civilisation;

- Maintain the advantageous diversity and the standards of the highest levels of engineering education in Europe;
- Secure international validation and acceptance of the qualification of university educated engineers;
- Promote further collaboration in engineering education, research and development between leading European universities.

CESAER Plans

- To promote interaction among its associates and with those organizations or individuals, public and private, that may make substantial contributions to high-level engineering education in Europe and academic research, especially in its application to industry and services.
- To develop further with industry innovative patterns for co-operation, and to disseminate the social and industrial benefits of education and research and development provided by universities.
- To support and to disseminate the idea that society needs advanced engineering education connected with research and technological development and that therefore appropriate support has to be given to such education.
- To further explain how research-oriented engineering institutions are key factors in the development of engineering research and innovative technology that lead to new services and products.
- To provide the European Union and national governments with guidance and feedback on how to develop an efficient European system for engineering education and research.
- To set a profile picture of engineering graduates from different European countries and from a variety of institutions providing education in the field of engineering for the benefit of students and employers.
- To define indicative standard requirements for resources and for assessing innovative management systems and educational models.
- To promote cross-European and international-oriented academic and professional recognition and quality assessment.
- To foster a European dimension in education through cross-European engineering curricula, course content and academic mobility.
- To aim for implementation of the European Credit Transfer System (ECTS) throughout its membership and to promote the exchangeability of study programmes and the compatibility of academic calendars.
- To emphasize the importance of languages in engineering education.

- To facilitate networking in Research and Development, postgraduate and continuing education amongst its members.
- To promote the development of continuing education.
- To disseminate best practices and to promote benchmarking.
- To support its member institutions in their drive for excellence.

CESAER Pursues Its Aims through

- Consultations between the members on a regular basis concerning the aims of the Conference;
- Development and implementation of programmes of multinational engineering education at undergraduate, postgraduate and professional levels;
- Discussion of educational objectives, methods and course content among the members and with external partners, particularly national and European industries;
- Co-operation with European and national governmental institutions, agencies and other university networks;
- Identification and development of solutions to specific problems and deficiencies which hinder the achievement of the aims of Conference;
- Facilitating the exchange of information between the members—on course objectives, content, modes of presentation and other matters.

History of Polish Education in Engineering

Early History

Higher education in Poland started in the middle ages. Education has been of prime interest to Poland's rulers since the early12th century. The catalog of the library of the Cathedral Chapter in Krakow dating from 1110 shows that Polish scholars already then had access to western European literature. In 1364, King Kazimierz the Great founded the Cracow Academy, which would become one of the great universities of Europe. The list of famous scientists in Poland begins in earnest with the polymath Nicolaus Copernicus, who studied there.

In 1773 King Stanislaw August Poniatowski established the Commission of National Education, the world's first ministry of education. The National Educational Commission was the central education authority in the Polish-Lituanian Commonwealth. Because of its vast authority and autonomy, it is considered the first ministry of Education in history and an important achievement of the Polish Enlightenment. The basic reason for its creation was that in Poland and Lithuania education was almost entirely controlled by the Jesuits. Although the Jesuit schools were fairly efficient and provided the Polish youth with a good education, they were also very conservative. In addition, in 1773 the pope decided to close down the Jesuit order, which could have resulted in a complete breakdown of education in the Commonwealth. After the third partition of Poland, in 1795, no Polish state existed. The 19th and 20th centuries saw many Polish scientists working abroad.

In 1826 the first technical university was established in Warszawa, which is now the largest technical university in Poland. Polish students have studied in university since the fourteenth century. From 1919-1939 universities were focused primarily on arts, science, and engineering. Education was based solely on Humboldt's model of university combining research and teaching. This model incorporates a strict hierarchy of authority and a considerable degree of autonomy for its governing bodies.

Post World War II

In the first half of the 20th century, Poland was a flourishing centre of mathematics. Outstanding Polish mathematicians formed the Lwow School of Mathematics. The events of World War II pushed many of them into exile. Today Poland has over 100 institutions of post-secondary education — technical, medical, economic, as well as 500 universities — which are located in most major cities. They employ over 61,000 scientists and scholars. Another 300 research and development institutes are home to some 10,000 researchers. There are, in addition, a number of smaller laboratories. All together, these institutions support some 91,000 scientists and scholars.

Many higher education institutions were established after World War II. At the end of communism (1989), there were 820 institutions in Poland, about 20 of them being engineering oriented. In the 1990s a two-tier system was reinstituted. The first tier was considered to be vocational rather than academic. The two-tier system was instituted in Poland well before it was suggested by the Bologna Declaration.

After 1989 higher education in Poland changed dramatically. Borders were opened for free mobility, autonomy of universities in curricula and management. New laws concerning higher education, convertible Polish currency, easy communication, (telephone and internet), and access to European education and research programmes made higher education more accessible.

The Present Time

As of 2001 there were 1,224,600 students enrolled in the publicly funded universities and colleges. In the private universities and colleges there were 519,100 students. This number has quadrupled over previous enrollment figures. This rise in the rate of enrollment in higher education strongly influences the qualification level of the youngest age group making up the workforce.

Considering that an individual's active life lasts about forty years, more time is needed to raise the level of adult education. In a 1995 census 6.8 per cent of the Polish population have higher education.

The impact of the Bologna Declaration on education in Poland made the diploma supplement mandatory for all diplomas in Poland. Polish universities then pushed for the European Credit Transfer System which was a quality assessment and accreditation programme. There had been no official national system of credit transfer and accumulation in Poland previously. Therefore, a credit-point system was introduced for particular specialization.

The promotion of mobility had a goal to reach 10 per cent. The obstacle in student mobility is differences in the organization of the academic year in European countries. The number of students coming to Poland is about 10 times lower than other countries and the need for other European languages was evident. Warsaw had 300 students in English and in Technical University of Lodz there were 500 students in English and French.

Belonging to the European co-operation in quality assurance, Poland is trying to solve the problem of quality and accreditation in a highly professional way. The process of accreditation of study programmes at Polish higher education institutions has been significantly accelerated. There are 2 faces: the state-controlled accreditation and the academic community-owned accreditation. For Poland, belonging to the European family is very important. Lifelong learning and promoting the European higher education area is their primary concern, they also believe that the European higher education area is best promoted by following the Bologna Declaration priorities and does not need any further comments.

Public Versus Private

The Polish People's Republic concentrated on the opening of new universities in the major cities. Poland started setting up vocational and pedagogical schools and university-branch-campuses. Private universities and colleges became more easily accessible to young people from the country and from working-class families than were the public higher educational institutions. The location is one of the most important criteria in choosing a university. This is due to costs for travel and room and board often exceed the costs of tuition at a private university located close to a student's place of residence.

Education in Poland is one of the few sectors that were not restructured after the ending of the communist era. The systems in use for managing public universities and colleges vary substantially from those used in the private sector. The costs of instruction in public universities and colleges are higher than those in private institutions. The globalization of public life and the perspective of Polish membership in the European Union are pushing Polish graduates to choose to work abroad. It is inevitable that children from poor families and from small villages have practically no possibilities to enter admission competition and to take entrance examinations. Private higher education institutions, located close to the homes of such candidates, are more easily accessible to them.

Poland has been at the forefront of the development of the private higher education sector. Private educational institutions provide education to students for a fee; not for profit and usually invest their financial surplus in the development of themselves and their facilities.

Private higher education institutions are devoid of the burden of collective management. Their decisions are made by the rector or presidents. The senate and the faculty council are entirely advisory bodies which confer the academic degrees. Private institutions can respond rapidly to the changing needs of educational demand and labour market needs.

The majority of private higher educational institutions offer 3 year courses of study for a Bachelor's degree. Only about twelve institutions offer a 5 year course of study which leads to a Master's degree and only one has obtained the right to confer the doctorate degree. There are now 12 private institutions that occupy top positions relating to the standards of tertiary education which are published every year by many institutions.

Private higher education institutions are decidedly more expensive for students than are the public. Private institutions are more flexible and definitely offer higher quality services than do their public counterparts. The public institutions are taking note and are taking measures to reduce these proportions. Nearly 100 per cent of private institutions are funded from tuition fees and not from the state budget. They are dependent on their markets.

The effects of globalization and education are enormous. Education used to be regarded as a non-tradable service however; private provision of education is huge business in many nations. The technological developments like the Internet and cheaper telecommunications combined with increased acceptance on non-traditional educational settings (remote learning) may well broaden the scope of international trade in education services in the coming years and at this point has created the potential for fast growth.

Globalization has heightened the demand for education, which has also increased many private higher education institutions however; globalization may also lead to an erosion of national regulatory frameworks for education. In a globalized environment where businesses and workers find themselves operating more often in foreign environments, the national character of educational frameworks will potentially cause problems.

By 2010 Poland is hoping that the number of people enrolled in higher education should rise 35-40 per cent and 40-45 per cent in 2020. These increases will raise new challenges for higher education in regards to its accessibility, particularly for the inhabitants of villages and small towns. Ideally Poland wants to decrease the differences in the level of civilization between the country regions and the various social groups. With the spreading effects of the metropolises, the situating of universities and colleges in the medium-sized cities offers a chance to establish education centres of high quality and the possibility of creating innovative processes. The large well-equipped private higher education institutions with increasingly stable staff are expected to prosper.

The ultimate goal for private institutions is to have official recognition of university status. The majority of institutions educating such specialists will be forced to diversify their offerings, which are bound to increase their costs. Higher education in Poland is trailing many European countries. They need to adapt to the changing labour market which will generate a larger demand for postgraduate, supplementary and retraining studies. By doing this it will increase the role of higher education in the fostering of regional development; the creation of regional innovation networks and a cultural atmosphere.

It is not easy to maintain the national traditions, habits and historical experience and at the same time fulfill common European priorities. The private higher education institutions are not as well treated as public institutions. Only the large national universities can guarantee high-quality education, while private schools require special supervision.

Women in Engineering Education in Poland

From early '90s the number of women studying at universities raised five times, while men only four times. There are more women studying at those faculties, which were regarded as typically males, like technical ones. The new GUS state statistics report on 'Women in Poland' describes high educational ambitions of polish women. It has been revealed that 65 per cent of graduates are women, also 70 per cent of post-graduate students. Polish women do not afraid of studying engineering, if they create 31 per cent of all students at technical universities.

In Poland there are 2 per cent more woman studying at universities than the mean rate in the European Union. However, only 7 per cent of key positions in engineering scientific board members are represented by women.

The fact that more women are working to obtain engineering degrees overall does not necessarily correlate with an increase in women working in the key jobs in engineering research and education. Many factors affect the development of academic career in engineering. Women's and men's path tend to diverge as women are promoted more slowly and as they abandon engineering work for other fields. This seems to be true even for women who have no children and few household responsibilities. Many girls are influenced by stereotypes that certain jobs are for men only. Much talent is being wasted if women turn away from engineering careers, and as women in engineering universities become discouraged by discriminatory treatments.

At universities, a women's place in a team may be determined by preconceived ideas rather than her actual knowledge and abilities. Stereotypes still exist, which is compound by different ways of communicating. Women can feel that pushing their ideas strongly is unacceptable in men dominated engineering community. With these disadvantages it can be difficult for women to play the key roles that lead in turn to promotion opportunities.

Career paths in scientific research are often associated with the gaining of varied experience in foreign countries. Women's careers and opportunities are often adversely affected when they are not free to travel to attend conferences, or to take up a research long-term visit abroad. Undoubtedly varied experience is important, and efforts must be made to develop women's skills and talents through opportunities that fit their circumstances, such as short visits instead of a longer posting or assignment to international teams in their home country. A women's career development may be affected by her taking time out when children are young and it can be difficult to return to a position comparable to those held by others who have not taken time off and have been steadily advancing in their careers. It may be difficult for women to comply with rules to complete the requirements for a qualification and research degree within a fixed number of years from the commencement date.

Exceptional women may reach high positions, but the statistics show that there is a considerable discrimination. To retain best women in the engineering higher education workforce, they must be given equal opportunity to be successful and to advance. A supportive workplace climate is vital: one that is safe and free of discrimination, where clear polices are in place to support the work-family balance of all, and where opportunities exist for career development and advancement.

Innovations and Creativity in Engineering Education

In this chapter a new concept of education and practice in engineering design is discussed. The innovative concept, called VISUAL DESIGN, involves modern 3D/4D computer visualisation not only as a designing tool, but also as a philosophy and a method to reach the goal. Dreams and fears behind the successive implementation of this concept into teaching and practice of engineering design are presented and evaluated.

Introduction towards Changes

Engineering education is undergoing major reforms, when teaching procedures are being changed. New predictions on engineering education developments and challenges are caused by the rapid progress in information technology. Recent and continuous advancement in computer graphics, simulation and virtual reality as well as Computer Aided Design (CAD) software development made it indispensable to introduce Computer Aided Learning (CAL) into everyday teaching practice at technical universities. The role of graphical language and visualisation in modern teaching of engineering design is growing.

The future engineering education must be more holistic and more integrative. It is expected that in addition to the normal engineering and technical competence, engineers of the 21st century must demonstrate the ability to function on multi-disciplinary teams. They must identify, formulate and solve engineering problems, but also understand professional and ethical responsibility. They are expected to communicate effectively, to understand the impact of engineering solutions in a global and societal context. They must recognize the need for career-long learning, showing in-depth knowledge of contemporary issues and understanding how they affect the practice of engineering.

After many years of abstract learning on technological—scientific base, when economy was the main target in development, a need to harmonise construction and environment has been recognised. Engineering design in democratic societies in the 21st century must become an open process that is sensitive to the protection of natural and human-made environment. It is indispensable to consider fully the aesthetic, scenic, historic, and other cultural values, along with the safety and mobility needs. In order to achieve good design, creative thinking and fluent communication of designers with environmentalists and the public is essential.

New Perspectives of Engineering Graphics as International Language

Engineering graphics seems to be the only intercultural, universal language of engineers. Technical drawings and drafting were studied for long semesters and the skills of accurate and detailed drawing were assumed as the most important engineering skill.

Engineering world has changed dramatically, when time-consuming hand drawings gave way to computer drafting. Numerous graphical software are being used in the process of engineering education, especially for designing purposes. Despite the existing differences between many software programmes, the idea of straight and easy communication is still the same. Less labor, better effect. Only positives, one may say.

There are some fears, however. There are some unanswered questions. What kind of problems related to CAD and CAL the university teachers and students observe at civil and transport engineering departments in Poland? Why restricting drawing lessons only to computer aided classes may be dangerous for some important engineering traits? To what extent can engineer forget hand-drawing skill, without lowering her/his creativity?

The current academic discussion covers all the problems mentioned above, with the aim to find a solution suitable for European engineer of the 21st century.

Research-based Facts and Fears

Continuous advancement in computer graphics, simulation and visualisation as well as Computer Aided Design (CAD) software development made it possible to introduce Computer Aided Learning (CAL) into everyday teaching practice of engineering design at technical universities. The role of advanced computer graphics on creativity in modern teaching of road planning and design is discussed based on practical observations and also on the experimental research studies. What kind of role does spatial imagination play in design work, while using CAD/CAL methods?

A series of experimental research studies has been carried out in Poland in order to investigate the role of CAL in creative design work. The experts method employed in this research allow the author to compare the attitude of practitioners to spatial imagination, creativity and new tools in design work (CAD).

The main objective of this research was to find out the impact of using CAL and CAD methods in the process of education on the future career and success in engineering practice of engineers who represent faculty of architecture and civil engineering. The first studies in this series has been conducted at Cracow University of Technology by the author in early 1995 (Boryczko & Zakowska, 1996), during 1996-1997 (Zakowska & Boryczko, 1997) and during 1998-2000 (Zakowska, 1999, 2001).

Apart from the numerous interesting results received and published, some additional experience was gained last years while teaching at experimental courses for transportation at civil engineering faculty.

The main goal in designing the study was to show the current 'state of art' of computer aided learning and the expected effects of teaching process on the future engineering career. The study based on a survey, using a questionnaire developed during earlier research of this series (Zakowska & Boryczko, 1997) in consultation with a psychologist researcher.

80 respondents took part in the survey. They represented two engineering faculties: architecture and civil engineering. The subjects were drawn from the student body and professional engineers, aged from 19 to 55 and they were grouped into four categories of professional experience, namely: none—1st year students (aged 19-21), little—0-5 years' experience (aged 25-30), medium—10-15 years' experience (31-40), large—over 15 years' experience (over 40). Respondents were asked to express their opinions on the future of engineering practice in the context of using CAL and CAD. The results of the survey underwent statistical analysis using ANOVA and the EXCEL programme. Three independent variables constructed (1) the amount of professional experience of subject, four levels of experience; (2) sex, two levels and (3) engineering specialisation of respondents, two levels. Two dependent variables related to the future career in designing practice formed the items designed and stated in the questionnaire (Zakowska 1999).

Respondents were asked to express their opinions on the following points:

- The use of CAD methods in engineering design (the importance of the ten selected individual items on fluency in practical engineering computer aided design), 10 items, and

- The future of engineering practice (in the context of using CAL and CAD), 2 items.

Results: CAD Methods (the Future of CAD in Engineering Design)

The respondents were asked to rate the effect of the ten items, as listed below, on the fluency in using CAD methods:

(1) Inborn technical capabilities,
(2) Knowledge of foreign languages,
(3) Broad theoretical basis of engineering knowledge,
(4) Large engineering practice,
(5) Knowledge of computers,
(6) Proper spatial imagination,
(7) Ability to abstract thinking,
(8) Readiness to changes and to technical progress,
(9) Open mind thinking,
(10) Ability to individual work.

The first analysis covered mean ratings of all subjects, neglecting specialisation, sex or experience, and has revealed the basic tendencies in ratings of the importance the items in fluent use of CAD and CAL.

With respect to CAD methods, all respondents rated the proper spatial imagination of engineer the highest (mean rating 8.79). Readiness to changes and technical progress received the second highest mean ratings. The third, next most important characteristic appeared to be the ability to abstract thinking.

Surprisingly, the computer knowledge was not the dominant trait on this level of analysis.

The more detailed analysis, in which the experience and age of subjects was implemented, has shown that the knowledge of computers is a significant trait among the youngest respondents (not experienced in designing work first grade students). For all other respondents this item turned out to be less, or rather not important.

It is significant that the same age group showed an importance of spatial imagination. The individual ratings of spatial imagination were also very high on every level of subjects' manipulation, as sex, age and engineering specialisation.

Further analysis in groups of respondents' specialisation has shown, that (item 8) readiness to changes was very important for architects (mean rating 9.13—the highest assessed item), though slightly less important for civil engineers (mean rating 8.35).

Results: Future of engineering practice in relation to the use of CAD methods.

The respondents were asked to assess, in the ten points rating scale (1—for total disagreement and 10—for entire, full agreement), the two following questions:

(1) Wider implementation of computer methods in engineering design process makes engineering work easier and more effective, and
(2) Use of computer methods makes that engineering designing process is no longer recognised as a typically men profession.

Interestingly, men and women do not diverse in their opinion on "engineering as typically men profession' as much as some other groups of respondents' manipulation.

The study revealed that the most important items as regards the appeal of the profession were need of special talents and access to new technology, giving the opportunity for self-fulfilment.

The belief that engineering is a male preserve is changing among young men, whereas women in all age groups clearly believe it is not. The profession is, however, assessed as one that needs special talents.

Students, as well as practising engineers of both sexes, found spatial imagination to be an essential trait for a successful career in the engineering profession.

It has long been claimed (Zakowska, 1986), that creativity and spatial imagination are extremely important in an engineering education and career. These study results demonstrate that spatial imagination is still rated highly by students and professionals of architecture and civil engineering specialisation. Creativity was evaluated highly only by architects, especially female ones. It is positive that young architects find creativity to be essential in their job.

It is understandable, that not all engineers desire the same amount of imagination and/or creativity in his/her everyday work. Architects and most civil engineers (especially those involved in road designing work) have to rely on their creative talents, closely related to their spatial imagination. It can be hypothesised, that use of computers and, as a consequence, easy access to the immediate drawing on the screen, makes the youngest engineers and students neglect the above regarded precious character traits.

Visualization seems to be the most effective way to harmonize designed construction with its surrounding. It is also the easiest way of communication between parties. Visualization in engineering design, as advanced computer graphics, real-time simulation and animation or virtual reality is becoming the key technology and a norm (not an exception) in modern design process. Visual engineering design is a chance for creating user-and environmental-friendly man-made environment of 21st century, provoking innovative thinking for full consideration of all objectives.

The Future of Engineering Education and Engineering Professor

It is time to conclude on what the major challenges are for the engineering professor at the beginning of the 21st century. The universities and their faculties are struggling to meet the challenge, become more efficient and cost-effective and at the same time, responding to the pressure to improve what they do. The rate of change will only quicken. The effective life of a given product design, once measured in years, is now measured in months, particularly for high tech products.

Today's small engineering design team using powerful CAD/CAM tools, perhaps working at different locations through telecommunication, now can do more design work than a hundred or more engineers of decades ago. And in the future the number of engineers 'displaced' by increasingly powerful analysis and design tools will be even greater. Does this suggest that there will be a lesser need for engineers in the future that we have had in the past? If the engineers of the future were to do only the same kinds of jobs that the engineers of the past have done, the answer would perhaps be 'yes.' But engineers of the new century will be serving a much broader range of industries and societal needs than in the past—and as a result the demand can be expected to increase. These new 'industries' which seek engineers will want people with good analytical skills, are good at modeling and the use of computers, have good problem solving skills, and understand technology in the broadest sense. The new opportunities tend to be in the service sector such as: banking and finance; entertainment/media; legal and intellectual property; management and consulting; marketing; and health care—as well as entirely new approaches to manufacturing and other more traditional expectations of the engineering profession.

For the engineer of the 21st century to take advantage of these new opportunities, the engineering education must become more holistic. The following (Bordogna, 1997) writings provides an example of what it is about (Table 24.1).

The professor of tomorrow must see this expanded role for engineers and modify the engineering education process to meet these needs. This need has been recognized by Smerdon (1999) as the most important challenge for university professors, involved in engineering education.

Education has been a process of transferring knowledge, information and techniques to a student. The professor's knowledge has traditionally been shared verbally and visually with the sitting (perhaps dozing) student. In today's world, this process is not likely to satisfy a student's quest for learning. It is possible now for the students to get the information they need at the time they want it, and from wherever they want to get it. So each university and each professor in the next century will have to adapt to the student desires regarding learning—

or the students will go elsewhere for their education. The professor of tomorrow must adapt to the learning styles of the individual students, not focus on her/his own style of teaching.

Table 24.1: Components of the Holistic Engineering Education of the 21st Century

Analytic (Science) Model. 1960-90	*Integrative Model. 2000 and Onward*
Vertical (In-depth) Thinking	Lateral (Functional) Thinking
Abstract Learning	Experiential Learning
Reductionism-Fractionation	Integration-Connecting the Parts
Develop Order	Correlate Chaos
Understand Certainty	Handle Ambiguity
Analysis	Synthesis
Research	Design/Process/Manufacture
Solve Problems	Formulate Problems
Develop Ideas	Implement Ideas
Independence	Teamwork
Technological — Scientific Base	Societal Context, Ethics
Engineering Science	Functional Core of Engineering

The professor of tomorrow must become more innovative in his or her approach to education. Engineering education is big business and those professors who cannot or will not change to meet the needs of the students should be displaced.

Professors of tomorrow must look at the market and determine what the students want. The immediate relevancy of the coursework which universities provide to the student's goals will become increasingly important. The engineering professor of tomorrow must focus on student needs and not the professor's desires.

25

Spiral Curriculum to Facilitate Student Learning and Development

M.L. Wolfe, T. Wildman, K. Mallikarjunan, V.K. Lohani and J. Connor

This chapter is a product of an interdisciplinary curriculum development project being conducted at Virginia Polytechnic Institute and State University (Virginia Tech) in Blacksburg, Virginia, USA. The disciplines involved include several engineering disciplines, as well as education. The primary participants are from the Departments of Engineering Education and Biological Systems Engineering, and the School of Education.

This introduction provides a brief description of the university and academic structure within which the curriculum development project is being conducted. An overview of the project is also given. Subsequent sections of the chapter provide the rationale for selecting a spiral curriculum approach, a description of the specific curriculum steps being undertaken, and a discussion and conclusions related to the spiral curriculum.

Virginia Tech is a publicly supported, comprehensive, land-grant university, serving the Commonwealth of Virginia, the nation, and the international community by generating and disseminating knowledge in the humanities, arts, social sciences, scientific, and professional disciplines through instruction, research, and extension. The university enrolls about 26,000 undergraduate and graduate students and offers approximately 200 degree programmes, including more than 70 bachelor's degree programmes through its seven undergraduate academic colleges and about 120 master's and doctoral degree programmes through the Graduate School and the Virginia-Maryland Regional College of Veterinary Medicine.

The College of Engineering (CoE) offers Bachelor of Science (B.S) degrees in 15 programmes, administered through 13 departments. Freshmen (1st year students) enrolled in the College of Engineering are in General Engineering. In the sophomore (2nd) year, students move into one of the 15 degree programmes. The General Engineering programme is administered by the Department of Engineering Education (EngE). The EngE department teaches two freshman level engineering courses that all freshmen in the college are required to take. In addition, the department provides advising for all freshmen (approximately 1300 students each year) and offers a PhD programme in engineering education.

The Department of Biological Systems Engineering (BSE) offers the B.S. degree in BSE. The students have the choice of focusing in one of two options: bioprocess engineering or land and water resources engineering. The bioprocess option was established in the mid-1990's to provide engineers to design and develop engineering systems and equipment to produce food, fuels, pharmaceuticals, plastics, construction materials, and other products from biological materials. There are approximately 40 students in the bioprocess option.

The mission of the EngE department is 'to be inventive, inclusive, interdisciplinary, and international as cutting-edge research and scholarship is conducted, primarily in the emerging discipline of Engineering Education, simultaneously developing and delivering meaningful and memorable learning experiences for future engineers and educators.' In fulfilling this mission, EngE faculty members actively seek collaborations with other disciplines to advance engineering education.

The first initiative in this regard began in 2003 when a group of engineering and education faculty received a planning grant from the United States National Science Foundation (NSF) under its Bridges for Engineering Education programme. This project created an active team of engineering and education faculty interested in exploring use of educational theories for improving engineering pedagogy within the CoE. The engineering-education team pursued a Department Level Reform (DLR) grant from the NSF in 2004 in collaboration with BSE faculty members, as well as individual faculty members from several other disciplines throughout the university. The group decided to focus efforts on the bioprocess option in BSE, including the freshman year. Several characteristics of the bioprocess option made it a good choice. It is a relatively new option with a small number of students. A significant number of new faculty members have joined the bioprocess engineering programme since it was initiated, thus bringing new ideas and perspectives. And perhaps most importantly, several BSE faculty members were very interested in reforming the bioprocess curriculum based on new insights from other disciplines as well as insights gained from administering the programme for several years and from alumni.

The project was funded (US$ 1,082,944) by the NSF beginning in 2004, for four years. The goal of the project is to undertake department level reform of General Engineering (GE) and Bioprocess Engineering at Virginia Tech. The specific objectives are to:

- Reformulate the existing General Engineering and Bioprocess Engineering curricula using theme-based spiral curriculum design and improved pedagogical methods;
- Train faculty in the use of learning centered pedagogical techniques;
- Develop a continual assessment plan to measure the impact of the reformulated curricula, faculty improvement activities, and student learning; and
- Disseminate the results of the curricular reformulation and pedagogical changes to peers within and outside Virginia Tech.

This chapter focuses on the first objective, specifically on the reformulation of the bioprocess engineering option in the BSE department.

The Drive to Reform Engineering Education

Reform is a concept that probably has been too readily applied to education, perhaps in part because of the persistent idea that we can always steer the process to better results. Inevitably, many if not most reform movements tend to circle back to a few fundamental ideas that have been difficult to dislodge from the public consciousness. Examples might include getting students to work harder, specifying more precisely what is to be learned, testing more frequently for results, and increasing accountability. In many ways, the more threatened the department feel from poor results the more conservative becomes department's approach to change.

The reform spotlight is now shining brightly on the engineering profession, and educators once again must negotiate the pressure for change against the inertia of traditional behaviour. Part of the calculation in deciding to do something different is an assessment of the stakes: 'What happens if nothing happens?' An example of this dialogue about change and the need for it appeared in the October 2006 special edition of the Journal of Engineering Education. In the introduction to this issue, the needs side of the equation spoke to the competitiveness of the emerging global economy and the idea that engineering itself has changed in ways that make it imperative to consider alternatives to the traditional educational paradigms. For example, few now believe that engineering is primarily about applying well-formed technical knowledge to predictable problems. New engineers entering the workforce will more likely be working in contexts that involve complex collaborations around problems that are inherently 'messy' in nature and perhaps only solvable through knowledge and technologies that were simply not part of their recent educational experiences. These and other considerations are now opening the door to more serious consideration of educational alternatives.

Of course, the other part of the calculation about doing something different is finding a new direction that is likely to produce better results. And it is here that leaders in the field of engineering education are beginning to notice the importance of educational research and theory. Not only is it important for engineering to produce its own viable educational research arm, but since engineering education involves the same learning mechanisms as any other educational domain, it would seem to make good sense to consider as well the large fund of research on human learning in general (see, for example *How People Learn,* published by the National Research Council, 1999).

When a large group of colleagues at Virginia Tech decided to apply for one of NSF's *Department Level Reform* projects, we too were faced with the decision of choosing a curricular and pedagogical direction that made sense in our own context and that was supportable in terms of good educational theory. Part of this chapter is thus devoted to telling the story of how the authors chose to think about student learning, and how we have begun to conceptualize a curriculum that will achieve the outcomes we wanted.

Curricular Considerations—from Linear to Spiral

Human learning, like any other natural phenomenon, has its own architecture and trajectory, and it has been the business of educational research to discover the important patterns. These patterns do not remain static, but changes in practice may lag for years behind new research. For many decades, and especially since World War II, the dominant shape of American education has been defined by a particular kind of relationship between research, professional practice, and teaching. Donald Schon, author of *The Reflective Practitioner* (1983), describes this dominant approach to professional education in terms of the model of *technical rationality*. In Schon's words, technical rationality, emanating from a positivist philosophy, may be defined as 'instrumental problem solving activity made rigorous by the application of scientific theory and technique' (p. 21). This model was thoroughly embraced by higher education, especially in the professional schools, and the results are evident in the hierarchical curricular priorities given to basic science first, applied components second, and attention to other human and cultural matters third. This dominant mindset—that the problems of humankind will yield to technical solutions—has been slow to change despite a steady decline of confidence in the professions since the 1980s. Situations involving complexity, uncertainty, conflicting values, instability, and the like are highly troublesome to professional practitioners, including engineering educators. To those seeking the high ground in a system based on technical rationality, the tendency is to adopt narrow technical practices (e.g., systems analysis, mathematical modeling) to convert messy soft problems into hard ones amenable to scientific analysis. Donald Schon poses the dilemma this way:

> In the varied topography of professional practice, there is a high, hard ground where practitioners can make effective use of research-based theory and technique, and there is a swampy lowland where situations are confusing 'messes' incapable

> of technical solution. The difficulty is that the problems of the high ground, however great their technical interest, are often relatively unimportant to client or to the larger society, while in the swamp are the problems of greatest human concern. Shall the practitioner stay on the high, hard ground where he can practice rigorously, as he understands rigor, but where he is constrained to deal with problems of relatively little social importance? Or shall he descend to the swamp where he can engage the most important and challenging problems if he is willing to forsake technical rigor? (p. 42)

Schon goes on to point out that technical rationality depends on agreement about ends—about the problem to be solved. Yet, practitioners cannot get to problem-solving without first engaging in what is clearly a non-technical process, which is the business of deciding the boundaries to be investigated, naming the problem, and framing the context in which it will be approached. The ongoing debates about human and animal cloning, and genetically altered foods are just examples of such complexity, and many others appear routinely.

Two features of Schon's analysis seem important in the context of the quest to seek alternative pathways to professional education. One concerns the way the authors view professional knowledge and practice. The authors need to recognize that their perspectives on knowledge and knowing influence the messages their students receive and in turn shape how they view themselves as knowers and professionals. This dynamic will be discussed later in the context of explaining the particular curriculum model chosen for DLR project.

The second feature concerns how, and how teaching take place methodologies are influenced by the institutional bureaucracies in work spectrum. Here we may be forced to acknowledge that our organizations for learning are themselves highly technical, highly dependent upon specialized expertise, and highly susceptible to the dangers of hardheaded rationality, over-management, and detached technical justification for decisions.

Universities, like other bureaucratic entities, are systems in which tasks are prescribed, routines are learned, policies are developed, and strategies are created. Universities in this regard are inherently conservative in that they value predictability and stability. This stability, and its protection by the system, may be positive in that it preserves good educational practice, but it may be negative in that it might also protect bad practice or stifle innovation and creativity. Within universities, the modern efficient transmission of knowledge has long required a system of controls, standards, and objective measures of progress and proficiency that all teachers and students in the system are expected to honour. The cynical view of this structure is that teachers and students quickly learn how to optimize the 'system' to their own advantage by playing the game of delivering and receiving the specified chunks of material meted out in fixed credit courses. Each gets so good at this that the real purpose, learning, is easily evaded in favour of satisfying the technical requirements of the system.

Now is the place in this narrative where mentioned that the curriculum framework most suitable to the model of technical rationality is the general linear curriculum. Familiar to all, the linear model is the frame around which most courses of study are formed, and to which faculties and students alike must adhere. The chief idea is that the curriculum is designed mainly to deliver knowledge and produce skills deemed necessary for some future endeavor such as business, law, engineering, or education. Once the content is decided upon, the curriculum itself can be organized in a linear, sequential, and hierarchical fashion. One of the key pedagogical concerns, then, is to arrange things so that the instructional trajectory moves from simple to complex, so that students will presumably always be confronting material for which they have some prior grounding. So arranged, the curriculum moves ahead steadily under the assumption that students acquire knowledge and skill and then retain it in some usable fashion for future needs. Of course, learning problems do arise but these can be handled with appropriate sensitivity to whether students have actually 'gotten it' as they move from course to course and level to level. And, once students successfully exit the programme with the required number of credits they will then be equipped with the technical expertise to negotiate what life presents to them, at least in professional terms. Or, so we would like to think!

As early as the 1960s, alternatives to the general linear model were beginning to emerge—the principal idea being that learners simply do not advance in their development in a straight-line trajectory. Jerome Bruner, writing in his book The Process of Education (1999), proposed that a learning curriculum ought to be capable of engaging students of any age in any subject matter and do it in an intellectually honest manner. This proposal at the time seemed radical, and indeed may still appear somewhat farfetched, mainly because it does not make the usual assumption that education is preparation for some future endeavor that is not yet within the reach of learners at a beginning stage. Bruner's argument took a different stance—that education involves legitimate participation in the important work of any discipline of choice. Further, such participation should start early. Bruner's idea was that learners—even beginners—could engage successfully with the central problems and questions inherent in any discipline if those key questions could be represented in a manner that invites real experimentation and inquiry. One key to this idea is that the learning curriculum could be arranged so that the central questions, or themes in a discipline, could be addressed at a basic level and then returned to again and again as learners advance in their knowledge and intellectual capacity. The learning trajectory is thus represented as a spiral rather than the linear pathway that is suggested under the model of technical rationality. As learners participate in increasingly complex investigations, organized carefully around the major themes of choice, they acquire in a more natural way the knowledge they need because it is connected to problems of real import and interest, and they acquire also the full intellectual apparatus associated with being the scientist, historian, or engineer rather than learning about their chosen discipline. In particular, it is this notion of learning to be something, rather than leaning about something, that has captured the imagination of investigators and teachers in current engineering education project.

Since Bruner first proposed that the key to successful learning lies in more artful curriculum building, it has been seen a number of decades of research into human learning that now allows a more complete fleshing out of this idea. At the time Bruner first suggested the notion of a spiral curriculum, the psychology of learning was just transitioning from a behavioural tradition to a whole new set of theoretical constructs centered on the metaphor of learners as information processors. Human memory took centre stage in this movement. So, instead of focusing on how learners learned to behave in complex ways through drill and practice, aided by selective reinforcement focus was shifted on how people acquire complex knowledge and how that knowledge could be represented in memory so that it would always be available and accessible when needed. This became quite a complex story, because it turns out that learners do not simply store verbatim what they hear or see; rather they construct their own unique representations (memories) that are guided substantially by what they already know (prior knowledge). Invariably, these representations, or understandings, are flawed by their incompleteness and they often contain misconceptions that are extremely difficult to dislodge and fix. Astute educators recognize this type of learning as a building process, and they know that any curriculum that has learning as its objective must contain provisions to double back to build on, elaborate, and correct what students have acquired at any given point in time. This means that learning is inherently a recursive process, involving both construction of meaning and reconstruction at a later time in a course of study. Followers of the traditional linear curriculum, then, are taking it as an act of faith that students will engage in these self correcting actions on their own, but this is only a safe bet with the most mature of learners. This means curriculum design needs to adjust and accommodate for new insights into learning so that students can receive the support and guidance they require along the way. In other words, we need a learning curriculum, not a teaching curriculum.

The spiral curriculum that we have been working toward seeks to do more than ensure that students have the ability to acquire knowledge and skill. Developments in learning research over just the past two decades have moved beyond the primary emphasis on cognition and memory to focus on learning as a culturally, socially situated phenomenon. This research emphasizes that learning always occurs in some type of context or culture (Brown, 2006, Lave, 1988). Classrooms and campuses represent a distinct type of culture for student learners just as companies that make products or sell services, provide a distinct culture for workers who are also engaged in an ongoing learning process

(Wenger, 1998, Wildman, 2005). The more we learn about the role of context in learning, the more we understand the limitations of formal educational processes that are essentially context free as is the case with most classroom and textbook learning. Jerome Bruner has weighed in on this in two of his more recent books, Acts of Meaning in 1990 and The Culture of Education in 1996, and there are numerous other sources that have documented the importance of context and the social dynamics of learning.

Formal schooling environments tended students not to think very much about the impact of the cultural setting in terms of how it supports and shapes the learning process. Inside schools it is simply taken for granted that what students need to know about any discipline can be stripped from its natural context and learned as a codified body of facts, rules, and principles. It is assumed that once students enter a professional or real-life domain they will simply apply what they have learned in schools to the new context. This assumption of transferability has now become one of the major issues because of the growing realization that knowledge gained in classrooms does not easily and reliably transfer to situations outside of schools. To understand why this may be the case it is useful to examine some of the differences between a purely cognitive orientation to learning, and what we now know about the nature of learning that occurs in authentic social contexts. Here are five of the main ideas.

1. There tends to be a great deal of support for learning when it occurs in rich social contexts involving authentic cultural practices. This support includes other people, tools of the trade, stories that develop around the practice itself, and well structured ways that people actually participate in the practice in question. Learning in schools tends to be more of a solo process, and we tend not to acknowledge and sometimes even allow those supportive elements that are taken for granted outside of school. The important thing to know is that physical settings, people, tools, and shared discourse are all important in scaffolding the learning in question.
2. Learning in natural cultural contexts will likely be defined differently than it is in schools. Rather than focus on what can be stored in memory, researchers looking into real settings (Wenger, 1998) tend to notice how people participate in the practice in question. In other words, learning involves acquiring particular roles that are important to the practice, and that may be seen in relation to roles that other people play. A well functioning design team, for example, would have participants playing different roles, and the roles played would change as people become increasingly mature or central to the practice. The learning trajectory then, is not so much about knowledge as it is about effective participation.
3. Learning involves identity development. This is something we tend not to think about or evaluate in schools, but as people become adept at the roles they play in social settings they begin to develop an identity as a

particular type of practitioner. In essence, they know who they are as a practitioner, and this is actually one of the major outcomes of a learning trajectory that is more richly contextual.

4. Learning in cultural contexts tends to be immediate rather than future oriented. This is because learning in social contexts is a natural part of doing, rather than preparation for the 'doing' that may occur in the future. We know from much experience in schools that learning that has no utility value is difficult for many reasons, including lack of motivation. This fact is not lost on teachers who are constantly struggling to find ways to make classroom learning more relevant.
5. Finally, the way that learning is documented in our formal programmes tends to be through a certification process of testing, grading, and transcripts. Outside of school the emphasis is on the emerging roles that people can play, their expanded repertoire of skills, and the ability of entire communities of learners to advance together in a shared enterprise.

Collectively, these characteristics suggest that it may be necessary to re-engineer parts of our existing educational system, and in doing so begin to take on a new mind-set with regard to our responsibilities as educators.

If we stop for a moment to summarize the various considerations now at work in our curriculum redesign project, we can quickly see that more is involved than just rearranging existing curriculum components. We are attempting to work with a new set of assumptions about how we position and engage students in their own education. Some of the key considerations are as follows:

First, we need to recognize that our purpose is not simply to 'get across' to students what they 'need to know' about a given discipline or profession. Rather, the more important mission is to develop in students an appetite for exploration and discovery and a realization of their own powers to create knowledge on their own and with others in active communities of practice.

Second, we need to create opportunities for authentic engagement near the front of the curriculum. The more typical model is to allow participation in real projects only at the end—as capstone courses—after students have acquired all the prerequisite knowledge and skill they may need. A revised model, putting authentic engagement near the beginning would better allow what the preponderance of research suggests we need, which is more 'learning in context.'

Third, we need to re-engineer significant chunks of the traditional linear curriculum into a project space that allows students prolonged opportunities to work with colleagues in a team environment in which there is opportunity for professionally relevant social interaction.

And fourth, we should focus our efforts in curriculum building on a few powerful themes that allow learning in depth and opportunities to discern the deep underlying structure of the discipline, rather than spending so much time attending to the surface features.

Spiral Curriculum Development for Bioprocess Engineering

There is not a prescribed method for developing a spiral curriculum, and university models are scarce. We therefore developed our own step by step process for development and implementation of a spiral curriculum. The process was led by a core group of faculty members under the auspices of the project funded by the NSF. The project had a project director, from the EngE department, and four principal investigators, with two from the BSE department, one from the School of Education, and one from EngE. Additional BSE, EngE, and other faculty members were affiliated with the project at different levels.

As indicated previously, bioprocess engineering is a formal option offered within the B.S. degree in Biological Systems Engineering, with approximately ten BSE faculty members specializing in the bioprocess area. The spiral curriculum development process for bioprocess engineering was led by the two BSE faculty members who were project investigators for the NSF project, with much assistance from the other Project investigators on the project. This group is referred to as the 'core development team.' The full BSE faculty has responsibility for developing and administering the curriculum so it was essential to involve the full faculty in the curriculum development process.

When developing the DLR project proposal, we identified sustainability as the overall theme for the curriculum. The cross-cutting skills of communication, teamwork, life-long learning, research experience, and laboratory experience are woven throughout the curriculum. A schematic representation of the spiral curriculum is seen in Figure 25.1.

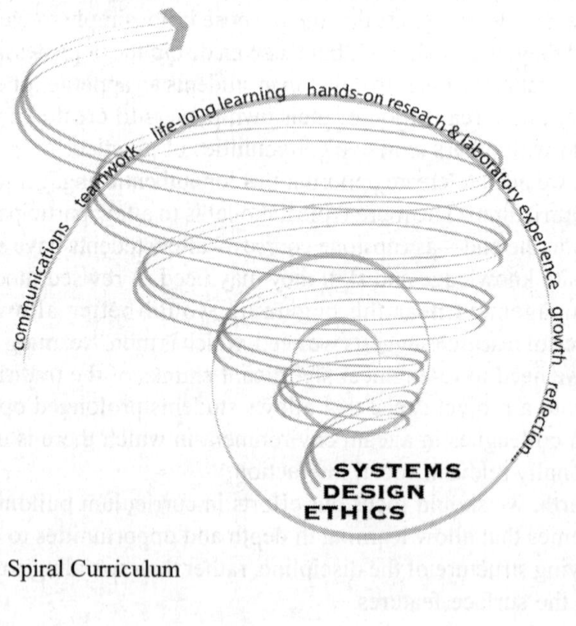

Figure 25.1: Spiral Curriculum

The approach was the spiral curriculum development as a design problem: 'design a spiral curriculum for bioprocess engineering.' The process followed evolved over time. We broke the activity into steps and developed the process as we went. As a result, we developed a seven-step process for developing a spiral curriculum:

1. Identify outcomes to be achieved
2. Develop concept maps
3. Identify knowledge for each outcome at different levels
4. Develop learning objectives
5. Develop learning modules
6. Incorporate the modules to existing courses
7. Develop new courses to include the modules

Each of the steps is described in the following sections.

Step 1. Define Overall Outcomes

In developing the spiral curriculum, we started with a blank slate and asked the question 'What do bioprocess engineers need to be able to do when they graduate with the B.S. in Biological Systems Engineering: Bioprocess Engineering option?' Our faculty brainstormed and listed many items that students should be able to do by the time they graduate. Our goal was to identify the high level outcomes, so we continually asked 'why do they have to be able to do that?' about each proposed outcome until the answer was 'because they are bioprocess engineers.' Looking at the similarities of various skills that a bioprocess engineer should have, we narrowed the list to four, high-level outcomes:

1. Design a bio-reactor;
2. Design a processing system and optimize the process conditions;
3. Select units (components) in a processing system and design a processing-plant layout; and
4. Control the processing system.

   As we moved through the rest of the steps of developing the curriculum, we affirmed that these four outcomes remained the appropriate ones related to bioprocess engineers. As we developed the curriculum, we added a fifth outcome that is important for all engineers:

5. Possess professional skills, such as communication, team-working, and familiarity with ethical and professional responsibilities.

After we identified the overall outcomes, we considered how the general spiral approach might be applied to each outcome. For example, a general spiral for the first outcome, design a bio-reactor, could be described as follows. First, the students would work with simple reactions, e.g., enzyme catalyzed hydrolysis, in a test-tube in the earlier levels, which could be followed by a complex reaction involving mechanisms to start/stop the enzyme reaction in a beaker. In the higher levels, students would learn to design a bioreactor and conduct experiments in laboratory/pilot scale bench reactors. The students' knowledge could then be extended with a field visit to a bioprocessing industry where they could see full-size bioreactors (Figure 25.2).

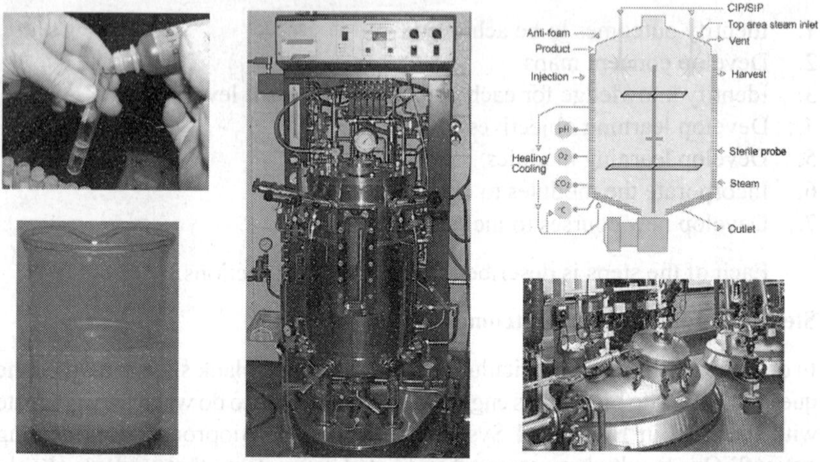

Figure 25.2: Spiral Concepts for a Reactor Design

These overall visions of the spiral approach for each outcome provided a context for focusing our efforts as we proceeded through the spiral curriculum development.

Step 2. Develop Concept Maps

For each of the outcomes identified in step 1, we identified the subject matter expertise that would be needed to attain each of the outcomes. We used the term 'concept map' to describe the resulting diagrams (Fig. 25.3). The concept maps provided a visual representation of the knowledge areas and interrelationships that would need to be included in the curriculum to enable students to attain the outcomes. At this step, we focused on the general knowledge areas and identified those knowledge areas that are common to multiple outcomes and should be explored further through their own concept maps (noted with a lightning strike in fig. 25.3) and those that are unique to a single outcome.

Step 3. Identify Knowledge for Each Outcome at Different Levels

For each subject matter knowledge areas, identified in step 2, we identified the specific topics about which students need to be knowledgeable to attain each outcome. We identified those knowledge areas for three levels of the curriculum, i.e., level II representing the sophomore year, level III the junior year, and level IV the senior year. As an example, consider the knowledge area of 'unit operations,' an important area for outcome 2, design a processing system, since processing systems are comprised of unit operations. Here categories of unit operations about which students needed to be knowledgeable are defined. Then we divided the unit operations in each category into levels II, III, and IV by considering the level of difficulty in learning about the unit operation and when it would be appropriate to include the topic in the curriculum (Table 25.1).

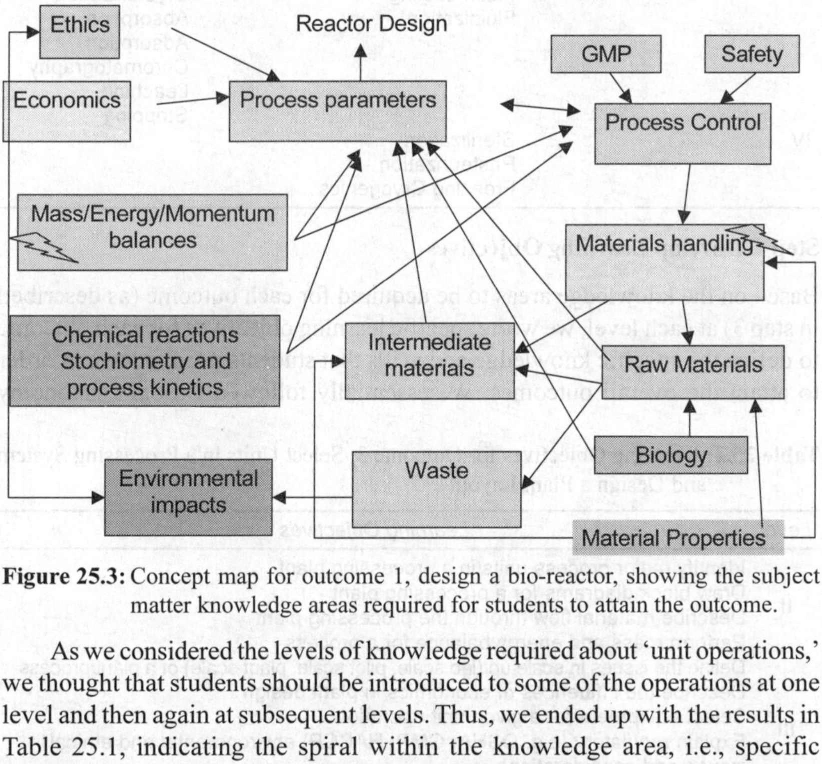

Figure 25.3: Concept map for outcome 1, design a bio-reactor, showing the subject matter knowledge areas required for students to attain the outcome.

As we considered the levels of knowledge required about 'unit operations,' we thought that students should be introduced to some of the operations at one level and then again at subsequent levels. Thus, we ended up with the results in Table 25.1, indicating the spiral within the knowledge area, i.e., specific operations that will be revisited at more in-depth levels as students move through the curriculum.

When we conducted this step, we thought of the three levels as sophomore, junior, and senior; however, later we realized that these are actually knowledge levels and did not have to correspond to years in the curriculum. A student just needs to acquire knowledge level II for a particular area before moving onto level III in that area. This recognition helped to maintain flexibility as we moved through the subsequent steps of curriculum development.

Table 25.1: Needed Topics at Different Levels for the 'Unit Operations' Knowledge Area

Knowledge Level	*Unit Operations*		
	Mechanical	*Thermal*	*Mass Transfer*
II and III	Size reduction Sieving Filtration Centrifuge	Evaporation Distillation Drying: spray, drum, freeze, thin layer, deep bed fluidized bed	Extraction Precipitation
III and IV	Cyclone Sorting	Heat exchangers: types, design and selection Flash cooling Fluidization	Membrane separations Crystallization Absorption Adsorption Chromatography Leaching Stripping
IV		Sterilization Pasteurization Freezing Cryogenics	

Step 4. Develop Learning Objectives

Based on the knowledge areas to be acquired for each outcome (as described in step 3) at each level, we wrote specific learning objectives for each outcome to define the specific knowledge and skills that students need to have in order to attain the overall outcomes. We essentially followed Bloom's taxonomy

Table 25.2: Learning Objectives for Outcome 3, Select Units in a Processing System and Design a Plant Layout

Level	*Learning Objectives*
II	Identify major process units in a processing plant Draw block diagrams for a processing plant Describe material flow through the processing plant
III	Perform mass and energy balance for a process Define the issues in scale up (lab scale, pilot scale, plant scale) of a plant/process Describe the influences of economics in plant design Select equipment for a given unit operation Explain regulatory (e.g. OSHA, GMP, HACCP) environmental and ethical issues and considerations Explain international/global issues related to manufacturing
IV	Design a plant layout for processing Perform economic analysis of the plant design Select equipment needed to optimize the flow of the material through the plant Design control systems Simulate the processes and process control using software such as SuperPro Implement a plant management plan — Safety and SOP Incorporate regulatory compliances and environmental/ethical issues into the plant design Function effectively as a team member with other elements of plant management team

with increasing cognitive levels as we moved from level II to III to IV. For example, learning objectives for outcome 3, select units in a processing system and design a plant layout, are given in Table 25.2.

Step 5. Develop Learning Modules

We used the term 'learning module' to describe a combination of learning activities that would facilitate student achievement of a set of learning objectives. Each module also included activities to assess student learning. Because we had an existing bioprocess engineering curriculum, faculty members had already developed and were implementing a number of learning activities on many of the subjects that are included in the spiral curriculum. To capitalize on existing material and to maximize efficiency, we started this step by comparing the learning objectives developed in step 4 ('spiral learning objectives') to the learning objectives of existing courses in the curriculum. The results indicated which spiral objectives we were likely to already have some learning activities for and which ones were new.

We developed module-building teams for different groups of learning objectives. A team typically included a BSE faculty member already teaching in the respective area, an EngE faculty member, an education faculty member, and additional BSE faculty members and graduate students. Each team developed modules to facilitate student learning of a group of learning objectives.

The first learning module that we developed was 'Introduction to Systems' that focuses on level II learning objectives related to outcome 2, design a processing system. We took learning activities that were already being conducted in the course, i.e., two laboratory exercises, and added a few other activities, i.e., in-class lecture and individual and group exercises, and assessment of student learning. The learning module included the following learning activities:

- Individual assessment of student knowledge — pre-test
- In-class presentation — to give context for the terminology
- In-class group activity — each group identifies processes/systems
- In-class group activity — compile examples and discuss
- In-class introduction — to laboratory exercise on 'extraction and refining of cottonseed oil'
- Group laboratory exercise — conduct 'extraction and refining of cottonseed oil' experiment
- In-class introduction — to laboratory exercise on 'hydrologic systems'
- Group laboratory exercise — conduct 'hydrologic systems' experiment
- Individual homework and group laboratory reports
- Individual assessment of student knowledge — post-test.

Step 6. Incorporate the Modules into Existing Courses

This is an activity oriented step.

Step 7. Develop New Courses to Include the Modules

Curricula at Virginia Tech are comprised of courses, so it was necessary to group learning modules into courses. Figure 4 illustrates the concept of grouping learning modules into courses. When feasible, our first step was to incorporate learning modules into existing courses; otherwise we will develop new courses comprised of one or more learning modules.

We incorporated the first learning module that we developed, 'Introduction to Systems,' into an existing sophomore course, Introduction to BSE. This was straightforward because the major activities, the two laboratory exercises, were already part of the existing course, so the structure of the course did not require change. This initiated the process of converting the two-semester sequence of sophomore courses in the curriculum to be comprised of well-defined learning modules to accomplish all of the level II spiral objectives. As of this writing, we are continuing to develop the learning modules for incorporation in existing courses.

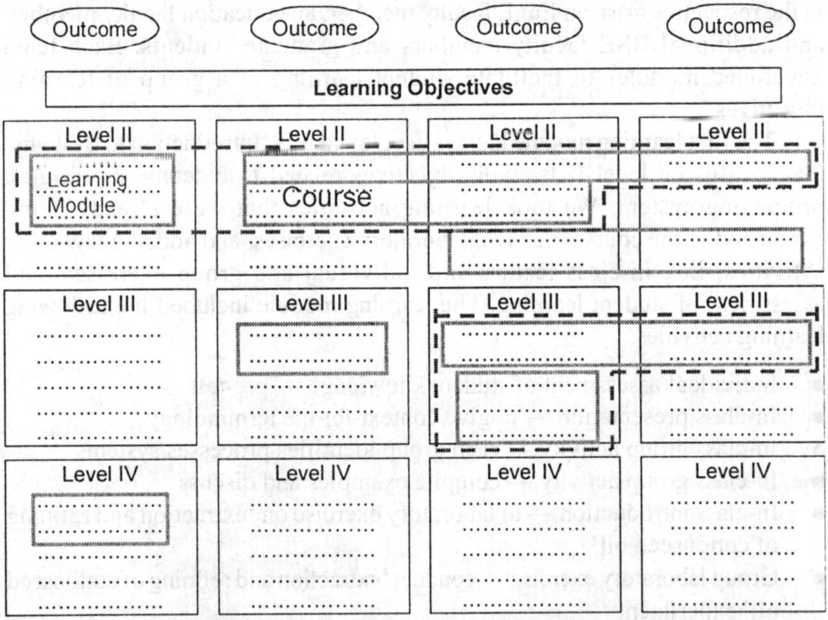

Figure 25.4: Combining Learning Modules into Courses

When we compared the spiral objectives to the learning objectives for existing courses, we identified some spiral objectives that are not included in existing courses. For example, a number of the learning objectives for outcome

4, control a processing system, are not included in the non-spiral curriculum. Thus, we needed to develop modules for those spiral objectives. For level II, those modules will be incorporated into the existing sophomore sequence of courses. For levels III and IV, some of the modules will be grouped into a new course that is being taught for the first time in the current semester (spring 2008). The other level III and IV modules will be incorporated into existing courses, particularly the Plant Design course.

Discussion of the Process

Steps 5, 6, and 7 are not necessarily distinct steps. In our experience, we found them to be more iterative. We did not develop all of the learning modules and then incorporate them into existing or new courses. Rather we developed a module and implemented it. This helped guide our development of the next module. These steps helped the core development team develop guidelines for the broader module teams to be used in developing subsequent learning modules.

The learning modules provide the context for incorporating the authentic learning experiences that were described previously. It is a challenge to develop authentic learning experiences rather than academic exercises. In developing the learning activities, we ask ourselves 'what does a bioprocess engineer do on the job?' How can we replicate that here?' One good source of ideas is the BSE departmental advisory board, which is comprised of representatives of a number of companies.

As described in the introduction, the bioprocess curriculum begins in the common freshman year and then continues for the next three years within the biological systems engineering department. Therefore, it is important that the themes and pillars of the spiral curriculum are initiated in the freshman year. As mentioned earlier, at Virginia Tech, there are approximately 1300 freshmen in engineering. Only about 15-20 of them are going to pursue bioprocess engineering. We chose the spiral theme and cross-cutting skills to be ones of importance to engineers of all disciplines, so initiating the curriculum in the freshman year is possible and could help set the stage for other engineering disciplines to adopt many aspects of the spiral curriculum.

We are in the process of developing and implementing course learning modules. It is an iterative process to ensure that the learning modules fit together well, provide authentic learning experiences, and facilitate student achievement of the learning objectives and overall outcomes of the programme.

While we have not completed the development and implementation of the spiral curriculum, we have already seen benefits to our programme. It has been very educative for our faculty to look closely at what we want to achieve in the bioprocess curriculum. Taking a fresh look at the desired outcomes has given us a context in which to review our current curriculum. We have identified effective aspects of the existing curriculum that are easily modified for inclusion in the spiral curriculum. We have also identified some aspects of the existing curriculum that do not have a place in the spiral curriculum.

One of the major benefits has been the focus on developing learning activities to facilitate student achievement of learning objectives. We are exploring a much wider array of learning activities than we have used across the curriculum before. Faculty interaction in developing the learning activities has been beneficial to both the individual faculty members and the curriculum. Including faculty from outside the BSE programme in developing activities has also been beneficial, by bringing different perspectives to bear.

We are looking forward to completing implementation of the spiral curriculum. Its format is such that it facilitates continuous improvement over time. Individual learning modules can be improved or whole segments of the spiral could be improved, if such improvements were dictated by the assessment processes.

Bibliography

Accreditation Board for Engineering and Technology (ABET). 2000. *Engineering criteria 2000* http://www.abet.org. 2000

——, (2002), *Criteria For Accrediting Engineering Programmes: Effective for Evaluations During the 2002-2003 Accreditation Cycle,* http://www.abet.org

Adams, Donald and W. Chapman. (1998). 'Education and National Development in Asia: Trends and Issues', *International Journal of Educational Research, 29(7): 581-602.*

Afonso, A.J. (1998). Políticas educativas e avaliação educacional: para uma análise sociológica da reforma educativa em Portugal (1985-1995). In *Cadernos de Pesquisa da Fundação Carlos Chagas* (n. 108). São Paulo: Fundação Carlos Chagas.

Ahlstrom, G. (1982). *Engineers and Industrial Growth,* London: Groom Helm.

Albett, Jonathan and Ivar-Andre Slengesol. (2000). 'Education in Crisis: The Impact and Lessons of the East Asian Financial Shock. 1997-1999' Washington DC: World Bank, Human Development Network.

Alonso, F. García, A. García, F. Hoya, S. Rodríguez, G. Villa, A. de la: 'Some unexpected results using computer algebra systems'. International Journal of Computer Algebra in Mathematics Education, 2001. Volumen 8, número 3. Páginas 239-252.

Aman, C., Poole, G., Dunbar, S., Maijer, D., Hall, R., Taghipour, F. and Berube, P. (2007). Student learning teams: viewpoints of team members, teachers and an observer. *Engineering Education*, 2(1), 2-7.

Anderson, B; Bach, F. (2005). On designing and evaluating teaching sequences taking geometrical optics as an example. *Science Education*, 89, 196-218.

Apple, M.W. (1985). *Education and power.* New York: Routledge.

——, (1988). *Teachers and texts: a political economy of class and gender relations in education.* New York: Routledge.

Arons, A.B. (997). Teaching Introductory Physics: USA, John Wiley & Sons, Inc.

Arthur, C. (1993). *Why Graduates Won't Wear Science,* New Scientist, March 27.

Astin, A.W. and Astin, H.S. (2000). *Leadership Reconsidered: Engaging Higher Education in Social Change.* Battle Creek, MI: W.K. Kellogg Foundation.

Astolfi, J.-P. (1992). L'école pour apprendre. Paris: ESF.

——, Darot, E., Vogel, Y. and Toussaint, J. (1997). Pratiques de Formation en Didactique des Sciences [Teacher Education Practice in Science Education]. Paris: De Boeck and Larcier.

Audacity website (2007). audio software, http://audacity.sourceforge.net/

Augar, N., Raitman, R., Zhou, W. (2004). Teaching and Leaning online with wikis. *Paper presented at the International Conference on Web-based Learning, ICWL, 2004*, Beijing.

Augustine, N. (1994) (chair). *Engineering Education for a Changing World,* ASEE.

Aulich, Sen. T.G. (Chair), (1990) *Priorities for Reform in Higher Education, Report of the Senate Standing Committee on Employment, Education and Training,* Canberra: Australian Government Publishing Service.

Australian Science and Technology Council [ASTEC] (1996). *Matching Science and Technology to Future Needs—Key Issues for Australia to 2010,* Canberra: Australian Science and Technology Council.

Backer, Gary S. (1964). 'Human Capital', New York: National Bureau of Economic Research.

Ballester, E., Gimeno, A., Hurtado, E. and Sánchez-Ruiz, L.M. (2005). *Implementing the European Higher Education Area at the Universidad Politécnica de Valencia (Spain).* En Moscinski, J.Y. Maciazek, M. (Eds.). Proceedings of the International Conference on Engineering Education ICEE 2005. *Vol.1*, 130-134.

Barnes, C. and Tynan, B. (2007). The adventures of Miranda in the brave new world: learning in a Web 2.0 millennium. ALT-J, 15:3, 189-200.

Bartholo, R. (2003). 'O Diálogo nos Rigores do Pensamento: Notas sobre Conhecimento e Verdade a partir de Emmanuel Lévinas'. *Revista Tempo Brasileiro*, vol. 152, jan.-mar. 2003, pp. 43-73.

Basu, Aparna. (1972). '*Essays in History of Indian Education*', New Delhi, Concept Publication.

Baumann, A. Biolcki, N. Heerens y P. Lažetic. (2005). *ESIB's Bologna Analysis 2005—Bologna with student eyes.* ESIB (The National Unions of Students in Europe). Bergen, Norway.

Beder, S. (1989). *Towards a More Representative Engineering Education.* International Journal of Applied Engineering Education, Vol. 5, No. 2, pp. 173-182.

Bell, B. (2005). Pedagogies developed in the Learning in Science Projects and related theses: *International Journal of Science Education*, Vol. 27, pp. 159-182.

Benjamin, C., Keenan, C., (2007). Implications of Introducing Problems Based Learning in a Tradionally Taught Course. *Engineering Education*, 1(1), 2-11.

Bennett, J. (2003). Teaching and Learning Science. *A Guide to Recent Research and Its Application*. London: Continuum.

Bennett, J; Kennedy, D. (2001). Practical work at the upper high school level: the evaluation of a new model of assessment. *International Journal of Science Education*, 23(1), 97-110.

Beswick, D., Julian, J., and Macmillan, C. (1988). *A National Survey of Engineering Students and Graduates,* Cęntre for the Study of Higher Education, University of Melbourne, Australia.

Bogantes, B. (1993). La cooperación en el enfoque centrado en la persona. En *La cooperación en los grupos: Un modelo de trabajo centrado en la persona.* (pp. 44-65). Universidad Iberoamericana, Ciudad de México.

Bohart, A. (2000). Carl Rogers' Helping System: Journey and Substance. *British Journal of Guidance and Counselling, 28* (2), 297.

Bong, M. and Skaalvik, E.M. (2003). Academic self-concept and self-efficacy: How different are they really. *Educational Psychology Review, 15* (19), 1-40.

Bordogna, J. (1997). Making Connections: The Role of Engineers and Engineering Education. The Bridge, NAE, 27 (1), pp. 11-16.

Boryczko M., Zakowska L. (1996). A Research based Study on the Position of Women in the Engineering Community in Poland. The 7th International Conference on Engineering Computer Graphics and Descriptive Geometry (Proceedings), Cracow 1996, Vol. II, PK, Poland.

Bot, L., Gossiaux, P.B., Rauch, C.P. and Tabiou, S. (2005). 'Learning by doing': a teaching method for active learning in scientific graduate education. *European Journal of Engineering Education*, 30(1), 105-119.

Bothwick, S. and Murphy, T. (1998). *Supply and Demand for Scientists and Engineers,* Department of Education, Employment, Training and Youth Affairs, Canberra: Australian Government Printing Service.

Bowring, Philip. (2000). 'East Asia's Revival of hope', International Herald Tribune (January), Reprinted in '*The Asian Age*', 10th January, p. 18.

Box, V.J., Munroe, P.R., Crosky, A.C., Hoffman, M.J., Kauklis, P. and Ford, R.A.J. (2001). Increasing Student Involvement in Materials Engineering Services Subjects for Mechanical Engineers. *International Journal of Engineering Education.* 17(6), 529-537.

Bradley, S., Middleton, A., and Nunnington, N. (2006). Media interventions: designing video and audio to stimulate learning activity. Proceedings of DIVERSE (Developing Innovative Video Resources for Students Everywhere) Conference: Enriching e-learning using video and multimedia (both face-to-face and at a distance). Glasgow.

Braham, J. (1992). *The Silence of the Nerds?* Machine Design, Vol. 64, No. 17, p. 77.

Brand, J.P. (1998). *Direcção e Gestão de Projectos*. Lidel Ed.

Brandão, C.R. (1981). *Pesquisa participante.* São Paulo: Brasiliense.

Briedis, D. (2002). Developing Effective Assessment of Student Professional Outcomes. *International Journal of Engineering Education.* 18(2), 208-216.

Bringslid, O. *WebMathematica: Interactive Mathematics on the web.* First European Workshop on MathML and Scientific e-contents. Abdus Salam International Centre for Theoretical Physics (ICTP), Trieste, Italy. November 2002.

Bringslid, O. *Xmath: Mathematical e-Learning Project in the EU Minerva Action.* First European Workshop on MathML and Scientific e-contents. Abdus Salam International Centre for Theoretical Physics (ICTP), Trieste, Italy. November 2002.

Brisk, M.L. (1997). Engineering Education for 2010: The Crystal Ball Seen from Down Under (an Australian Perspective). *Global J. of Engineering. Education*, 1(1).

Brittain, S., Glowacki, P., Van Ittersum, J. and Johnson, L. (2006). Podcasting lectures. *Educause Quarterly*, Number 3, 2006. Available online at: http://www.educause.edu/ir/library/pdf/eqm0634.pdf, Last accessed: 1/3/2007

Brown, G. (2001) Assessment: 3. A guide for lecturers. Assessment series, LTSN Generic Centre.

Brown, J.S. (2006). New environment for the 21st century: Exploring the edge. Change. September/October.

——, Collins, A., and Duguid, P. (1989). Situated cognition and the culture of learning. Educational Researcher, 18, 5-11.

Bruner, J. (1990). Acts of meaning. Cambridge, Mass.: Harvard University Press.

——, (1996). The culture of education. Cambridge, Mass.: Harvard University Press.

Buber, M. (1982). *Do Diálogo e do Dialógico.* Tradução de Newton Aquiles Von Zuben. Editora Perspectiva, São Paulo, 171.

Bucciarelli, L. (1996). *Designing Engineers.* Cambridge: The MIT Press.

Butler, C. (1987). *The Case of Engineering,* in Linklater, P. (ed) *Education and the World of Work: Positive Partnerships,* Milton Keynes: SRHE, Open University Press.

Capra, F. (1997). *The Web of Life: A New Synthesis of Mind and Matter.* 1997. London: Flamingo.

Carlsson, K. (1990). The Percentage of Women on Study Programmes in Technology at Lulea and in the Rest of Sweden 1980-1989, Lulea University, Sweden.

Carnoy, Martin (Ed). (1995). *International Encyclopedia of Economics of Education.* Oxford: Pargamon.

Carr, H.E. (1964). *Studies in Revolution,* New York: Grošsett and Dunlap.

CE (Commission of the European Communities). (2006). *Recommendation of the European Parliament and of the Council on the establishment of the European Qualifications Framework for lifelong learning.* Brussels, 5.9.2006. COM (2006) 479 final.

——. *Delivering on the modernization agenda for universities: education, research and innovation.* Brussels, 10.5.2006. COM (2006) 208 final.

——. (2003). *The role of the universities in the Europe of knowledge.* COM(2003) 58 final. Brussels, 05.02.2003.

——. (2005). *Mobilising the brainpower of Europe: enabling universities to make their full contribution to the Lisbon Strategy.* Brussels, 20.4.2005. COM (2005) 152 final.

CESEAR, and SEFI (2005). Engineering Education and Research and the Bologna Process—On the Road to Bergen 2005: Belgium.

Chaffee, E.E. and Tierney, W.G. (1988). *Collegiate Culture and Leadership Strategies.* New York: Macmillan.

Chickering, A., and Ehrmann, S.C. (1996). Implementing the Seven Principles: Technology as Lever, AAHE Bulletin, October, pp. 3-6. Available online at: http://www.tltgroup.org/programs/seven.html, Last accessed: 7/1/2008

Clark, B. (1983). *The Higher Education System. Academic Organization in Cross-National Perspective.* University of California Press.

Cohen, L., Manion, L., and Morrison, K. (2000). Research methods in education. 5th edition.Routledge and Falmer, London and New York.

Consortium Linking Universities of Science and Technology for Education and Research (CLUSTER): www.cluster.org

Cooper, N.J. (2000) Facilitating Learning from Formative Feedback in Level 3 Assessment, *Assessment and Evaluation in Higher Education*, 25:3, 279-291

Costa, N., Marques, L. and Kempa, R. (2000). Science Teachers' Awareness of Findings from Education Research. *Research in Science and Technological Education*, 18(1), 37-44.

Coutinho, C.P.; Bottentuit Junior, J.B. (2007a). Collaborative Learning Using Wiki: A Pilot Study With Master Students In Educational Technology In Portugal. *Proceedings of World Conference on Educational Multimédia, Hypermedia e Telecommunications (ED-MEDIA)*. Vancouver, Canadá.

——, (2007b). Blog e Wiki: os futuros professores e as ferramentas da Web 2.0. In M.J. Marcelino and M.J. Silva (Org.), *Actas do IX Simpósio Internacional de Informática Educativa* (SIIE 2007), pp. 199-204. Porto: ESE-IPP.

Cravino, J.P. (2004). 'Ensino da Física Geral nas Universidades Públicas Portuguesas e sua Relação com o Insucesso Escolar—Caracterização do Problema e Desenho, Implementação e Avaliação de uma Intervenção Didáctica,' vol. Doctoral dissertation. Vila Real: Universidade de Trás-os-Montes e Alto Douro.

——, Lopes, J.B. (2003). The teaching of introductory Physics courses in portuguese public universities. Conference Proccedings: Teaching and Learning in Higher Education: Trends and Innovations. University of Aveiro, pp 1-12.

Cross, H. (1980), *Engineers and Ivory Towers*, New York: Ayer Company Publishers.

Cross, N. (1999) 'Intelligence in Design'. *Design Studies*, vol. 20, n. 1, jan. 1999, pp. 25-39.

Crouch, C., and Mazur, E. (2001). Peer Instruction: Ten Years of Experience and Result: *Am. J. Phys.*, Vol. 69, p. 970-7.

Daft, R.L. (1998). *Organization Theory and design*. 6th Edition South-Western College Publishing. Cincinnati, Ohio.

Davies, J. (2000). *Cultural Change in Universities in the Context of Strategic and Quality Initiatives*. http://www.eua.be/eua/jsp/en/upload/Strategic_Manag_Uni_institutional_Devlpt.106932239787, 7.pdf

De Woot, P. (1998). *Managing Strategic Change in the University*. International Seminar on Strategic Management and Quality of Universities. Universitat Politècnica de Catalunya. Barcelona, 19-21 January 1998, 39-55.

Deans, J. (1999). *The Educational Needs of Graduate Mechanical Engineers in New Zealand*, European Journal of Engineering Education, Volume 24, No. 2, June, pp. 151-162.

Department of Education and Employment (2000). *An Assessment of Skills Needs in Engineering*, Nottingham, UK: DEE Publications.

Department of Education, Training and Youth Affairs (2000),(A), *Undergraduate Characteristics—Engineering and Surveying*, http:/www.detya.gov.au/tenfields/engineering/under.html

Department of Employment, Education and Training (2005). *Selected Higher Education Statistics 2004*, DEET, Canberra: AGPS.

——, (1998). *Selected Higher Education Statistics 1997*, DEETYA, Canberra: AGPS.

Department of Labour and National Service (1973), *Survey of the Australian Engineering Profession-1971*, Canberra: Australian Government Printing Service.

Didier, C. (2000). *Engineering Ethics at the Catholic University of Lille: research and teaching in European context.* European Journal of Engineering Education, 4, Vol. 25, pp. 325-331.

Diedrich, G. (2000). *Private Communication,* Hamburg, Germany, July.

Dietrich, G. (1996). *Getting People's Perceptions Closer to Reality,* Civil Engineer *Australia,* May.

Direction General for Education and Culture. *ECTS Users' guide*, Bruxels, 17-08-2004.

Ditcher, A.K. (2001). Effective Teaching and Learning in Higher Education, with Particular Reference to the Undergraduate Education of Professional Engineers, *International Journal of Engineering Education.* 17(1), 24-29.

dMath: http://dmath.hibu.no/main.htm

Dowell, E., Baum, E., and McTague, J. (1998). *The Green Report: Engineering Education for a Changing World,* American Society for Engineering Education: http://www.asee.org/publications/html/green.htm

Durcholz, P (1979). *The Hidden Career: How Students Chose Engineering.* Engineering Education, Volume 69, No. 7, p. 721.

Education Services and Globalization. National Education Association Higher Education. Retrieved November 28 from http://www2.nea.org/he/global/intl-sect2.pdf.

Edwards; M., Fuentes-Durá, P. and Ballester-Sarrias, E. (2005). *Competences of engineers: compared vision of graduates, employers and academics.* ICECE 2005. Madrid, September 2005.

——, Donderıs-Quíles, V., Sánchez-Ruiz, L. and Ballester-Sarrias, E. (2006). *Approach to the European Higher Education Area in the School of Engineering Design.* International Conference on Engineering Education (ICEE 2006), 23-28 July 2006. San Juan, Puerto Rico.

Edwards-Schachter, M; Ballester-Sarrias, E.; Fuentes-Durá, P. and Donderis-Quiles, V. (2005). *Perceptions et avis du professorat espagnol sur le processus de convergence.* 22ème Congrès de l'Association Internationale de Pédagogie Universitaire. Genève.

Ellis, R.A. (1991). *Engineering and engineering technology degrees,* Engineering Education, pp. 34-44.

Elms, D.G. (1992). *Formation of the New Engineer,* in Duggan, T.V. *International Quality and Environmental Issues,* Vol. 1, Proceedings of the Third World Conference on Engineering Education, Portsmouth, 20-25 September, Southampton: Computational Mechanics Publications.

Enders, J. (2001). *Academic staff in Europe. Changing contexts and conditions.* Information Age Publishing.

Engle, R.A., and Conant, F.R. (2002). Guiding Principles for Fostering Productive Disciplinary Engagement: Explaning an Emergent Argumentin a Community of Learners Classroom: Cognition and Instruction, Vol. 20, pp. 399-483.

Etkina, E. (2000). Weekly reports: A two-way feedback tool. *Science Education*, 84(5), 594-605.

European Commission (DG Research), European Charter for Researchers and code of Conduct for the Recruitment of Researchers: http://ec.europa.eu

European Commission WiS database: http://epp.eurostat.ec.europa.eu

European Federation of National Engineering Associations (FEANI): www.feani.org

European Network for Quality Assurance (ENQA): www.enqa.net

European Round Table of Industrialists (ERT): www.ert.be

European Society for Engineering Education (SEFI): www.sefi.be

European University Association (EUA): http://www.eua.be/eua/

Evans, L. (2002). Reflective Practice in Educational Research: Developing Advanced Skills. London: Continuum.

EVLM. http://evlmspain.usal.es/

Faqueti, M.F.; Alves, M.B. (2006). Wikis e o bibliotecário de referência: novos ambientes de aprendizagem. Retrieved from http://www.snbu2006.ufba.br/soac/viewpaper.php?id=333

Fawcett, A. and Roberts, P. (2001). *The Institution of Engineers Australia—At the Turn, Remaking for Relevance.* Transactions for Multi-disciplinary Engineering, vol. 25, pp. 51-63.

Felder R.M., Woods D.R., Stice J.E., and Rugarcia A. (2000). 'The Future of Engineering Education II. Teaching Methods that Work,' *Chem. Engr. Education*, 34, 26-39

Felder, R.M. (1995).We never said it would Be Easy: Chem. Engr. Education, Vol. 29, pp. 32-33.

——, (1997). Beating the Numbers Game: Effective Teaching in Large Classes, ASEE Annual Conference: Milwaukee, WI.

——, (2004). Teaching engineering at a research university: problems and possibilities: *Educación Química*, Vol. 15, pp. 40-42.

——, (2007). Research on Teaching and Learning Engineering, in Lecture, A. o. C. E. A., editor, Department of Chemical and Biological Engineering, University of Missouri-Rolla.

Felder, R.M. and Brent, R. (2003). Designing and Teaching Courses to Satisfy the ABET Engineering Criteria. *Journal of Engineering Education*, 92(1), 7-25.

——, (2003). Learning by Doing. *Chemical Engineering Education*, 37(4), 282-283.

——, (2007). Active Learning: Methods from the Analytical Sciences, ACS Symposium Series 970, Chapter 4: Cooperative Learning. P.A. Mabrouck, ed. Washington, DC: American Chemical Society.

——, (1999). How to Improve Teaching Quality: *Quality Management Journal*, Vol. 6, p. 9-21.

——, (2007). Cooperative Learning, in Mabrouck, P.A., editor, Active Learning: Models from the Analytical Sciences: Washington, DC: American Chemical Society, ACS Symposium Series 970.

Felder, R.M., Woods, D.R., Stice, J.E., and Rugarcia, A. (2000). The Future of Engineering Education II. Teaching Methods that Work: *Chem. Engr. Education*, Vol. 34, pp. 26-39.

Filipkowski, A. (2003). The Implementation of the Bologna Declaration in Poland. *European Journal of Engineering Education*. 28(2). pp. 237-245.

Finniston, M. Sir (1980) *Engineering Our Future.* Committee of Inquiry into the Engineering Profession, London: HMSO.

Florman, C.S. (1994). *The Existential Pleasures of Engineering,* London: Souvenir Press, p. 13.

Florman, S.C. (1996). *Non-Technical Studies for Engineers: The Challenge of Relevance,* European Journal of Engineering Education, Volume 21, No. 1, pp. 249-258.

Franco, A. Franco, P. García, A. García, F. González, F.J. Hoya, S. Rodríguez, G. Villa, A. de la (2000). 'Learning Calculus of Several Varibles with New Technologies'. *International Journal of Computer Algebra in Mathematics Education,* Vol. 7, No. 4. pp. 295-309.

Freire, P. (1998). *Pedagogy of freedom: ethics, democracy, and civic courage.* Lanhan: Rowman & Littlefield Publishers, Inc.

Freyre G. (1987). *Homens, Engenharias e Rumos Sociais* (Prefácio do Autor), São Paulo: Record, pp. 9-19.

García Aracil, A. (2003). *A Labour Market Analysis for European Higher Education Graduates.* Doctoral Thesis. Facultat d'Économía. Universitat de València. 2003.

García, A. García, F. López, A. Rodríguez, G. Villa, A. de la: CÁLCULO I: Teoría y problemas de Análisis Matemático en una variable. Third edition. 688 pages. With CD. Ed. CLAGSA. Madrid. 2007.

——, de la: Ecuaciones diferenciales ordinarias: teoría y problemas: 432 pages. With CD. Ed. CLAGSA. Madrid. 2006.

——, de la: 'A course of ODE with a CAS'. Proceedings del Congreso: Technology and its Integration in Mathematics Education. TIME-2004. Montreal (Canadá). http://time-2004.etsmtl.ca/

——, *Una propuesta de innovación educativa: Una enseñanza integrada del cálculo infinitesimal en las escuelas de ingeniería.* Proceedings XIII Congreso de Innovación Educativa en las Enseñanzas Técnicas. Maspalomas (Gran Canaria) September 2005.

García, A.-López, A. Rodríguez, G. Romero, S. Villa, A. De La: Cálculo II: Teoría y problemas de funciones de varias variables. Second edition. 648 pages. With CD. Ed. CLAGSA. Madrid. 2002.

Gibbs, G., and Simpson, C. (2004). Conditions under which assessment supports students' learning. *Learning and Teaching in Higher Education,* Issue 1, 2004-05.

Gijlers, H., and Jong, T.D. (2005). The relation between Prior Knowledge and Students' Collaborative Discovery Learning Process: J. of Research in Science Teaching, Vol. 42, pp. 264-282.

Gil-Perez, D., Furió-Mas, C., Valdés, P., Salinas, J., Martinez-Torregrosa, J., Guisáosia, J., González, E., Dumas-Carré, A., Goffard, M., and Pessoa de Carvalho, A. (1999). Tiene sentido seguir distinguiendo entre aprendizaje de conceptos, resolución de problemas de lápiz y papel y realización de prácticas de laboratorio? [Does it make sense to go on making a distinction among conceptual learning, pencil and paper problem solving and laboratory practical work?]. Enseñanza de las Ciencias, 17, 311-320.

Ginés Mora, J. (1998). Financing higher education: innovations and changes. Editorial, *European.*

——, (2006). *Changes in the governance of European universities.* CHES Seminars. London, 21st. November 2006.

——, and Vidal, J. (2005). Two decades of changes in Spanish Higher Education: learning the hard way. In A. Amaral, A. Gornitzka and M. Kogan (Eds.), *Reform and change in higher education: renewed expectations an improved performance.* Springer, 136-152.

——, (2000). Adequate Policies and Unintended Effects in Spanish Higher Education. *Tertiary Education and Management, Vol. 6, No. 4,* 247-258.

Glover, I.A., and Herriot, P. (1982). *Engineering Students and Manufacturing: Chalk and Cheese?* Energy World, April, p. 8-12.

Goldman, L.S. (1991). *The Social Captivity of Engineering,* in Durbin, T.P. (ed) Critical Perspectives on Non-academic Science and Engineering, pp. 121-145, Betlehem: Lehigh University Press.

——, (2004). *Why do we need a philosophy of engineering: a work in progress.* Interdisciplinary Science Reviews, 29 (2), pp. 163-176.

González, J. and Wagenaar, R. (Eds.). (2003). *Tuning Educational Structures in Europe.* University of Deusto and Groningen: Deusto.

Gordon, G. (2000). Comparability of postgraduate academic qualification: Some issues, challenges and experiences: Higher Education, Vol. 40, pp. 377-388.

Gorecki, R. (2001). The University of Warmia and Mazury in Olsztyn as an Agent of Regional Development and Higher Education in Poland. Higher Education in Europe. 26(3). Retrieved November 28, 2007 from http://www.cepes.ro/publications/pdf/hee_eng_pdf/he4_03.pdf.

Gorsky, P., Caspi, A., and Trumper, R. (2006). Campus-based university students' use of dialogue: Studies In Higher Education, Vol. 31, pp. 71-87.

Goss, E. (1969). 'Change in Technological and Scientific developments and its Impact upon the Occupational Structure', in Perrucci, R., and Gerstl, J. (eds.) *The Engineers and the Social System,* New York: John Wiley and Sons.

Grinter, S. (1955), (chair). *Report of the Committee on Evaluation of Engineering Education,* Journal of Engineering Education, Vol. 46, pp. 25-60.

Guay, F., Vallerand, R.J., and Blanchard, C. (2000). On the assessment of situational intrinsic and extrinsic motivation: The situational motivation scale (SIMS). *Motivation and Emotion, 24* (3), 175-213.

Hake, R. (1998). Interactive-engagement vs traditional methods: A six-thousand-student survey of mechanics test data for introductory physics courses: Am. J. Phys., Vol. 66, pp. 64-74.

Hammersley, M. (2002). *Educational Research, Policymaking and Practice.* London: Sage.

Hampton, S.E., and Reiser, R.A. (2004). Effects of a theory-based feddback and consultation process on instruction and learning in college classrooms: Research in Science Education, Vol. 45, pp. 497-527.

Haq, M.S. (1975). *Education and Development Strategy in South and South East Asia,* Honolulu: East-west Centre.

Hardy, D.J. (1992). 'Educating Engineers for Positive Environmental Action,' in Duggan, T.V. ed) ' International Quality and Environmental Issues', Vol. 1,

Proceedings of the 3rd World Conference on Engineering Education, Portsmouth, 20-25 September, Southampton: Computational Mechanics Publications.

Hedberg, J. (2001). *The role of the Global Engineer—An European view. Educating the Engineer for the 21st Century.* Proceedings of the 3rd Workshop on Global Engineering Education. Kluwer Academic Publishers.

Heitmann, G., John. V., Van Oort, J.H. and Waszczyszyn, Z. (1995). *Educating the Whole Engineer. The Role of Non-technical subjects in Rngineering Curricula,* Cracow University of Technology, SEFI Curriculum Development Group, pp. 135-140.

Heller, P., R.Keith, and Anderson, S. (1992). Teaching problem solving through cooperative grouping. Part 1: Group versus individual problem solving: Am. J. of Phys., Vol. 60, pp. 627-636.

Hendriks, P.G. and Van Snippenburg, L.B. (2002). Measuring motivations for media exposure: A thesis. *Quality and Quantity, 36* (3), 259-276.

Hewton, E. (1975). Project Work in Universities: Physics Education.

Hilton, R., and Lee, I. (1988). *Educating Scientists and Engineers,* Office of Technology Assessment, United States Congress, OTA Report Brief, Superintendent of Documents, Washington, DC: United States Printing Office, June.

Hoadley, C.M. and Linn, M.C. (2000). Teaching science through online, peer discussions: Speak Easy in the Knowledge Integration Environment. *International Journal of Science Education,* 22(8), 839-857.

Hortale, V.A. and Mora (2004), J.G. Tendências das reformas da educação superior na Europa no contexto do processo de Bolonha. In *Educação e Sociedade* (Vol. 25, pp. 937-960), Campinas: Codes.

Hotchkiss, E.W. (1935). *Social Sciences in Engineering Schools,* Journal of Engineering Education, (XXVI), p. 94.

Howard, D. (2005). *Albert Einstein as a Philosopher of Science.* http://www.physicstoday

Huang, S. (2000). A Quantitative analysis of audiotaped and written feedback. *Tunghai Journal,* Vol. 41 pp. 199-232.

Huband, L.F. (2007). *A Better World Through Engineering.* Prism, Summer, p. 6.

Hudson, L. (1975). *Human Beings,* London: Cape.

Hutchinson, A.M., Follman, K.D., Sumpter, M. and Bodner, M.G. (2006*). Factors Influencing the Self-Efficacy Beliefs of First Year Engineering Students,* Journal of Engineering Education, January, pp. 39-47.

Hutton, P.S., and Gerstl, E.J. (1995). *The Effects of Background and Training on Success in Engineering,* in Semler, G.E. (ed) The Engineer and Society, London: Institution of Mechanical Engineers, p. 142.

——, and Lawrence, P. (1982). *German Engineers: An Anatomy of a Profession,* Oxford: Clarendon Press.

Illich, I. (2002). *En el Viñedo del Texto. Etología de la lectura: un comentario al Didascalicon de Hugo de San Víctor.* México: Fondo de Cultura Económica.

Jakobeit, Cord. (1999). 'The World Bank and Human Development', *Development and Cooperation,* No. 6 (Nov/Dec): 4-5.

Jimenez-Aleixandre, M.P. (1996). Dubidar para aprender. Vigo. Ediciόns Xerais de Galicia.

Johnanson, R. (1999). Rethinking the Red Ink: Audio feedback in the ESL Writing Classroom. Texas Papers in Foreign Language Education, 4(1), 31-38

Johnson, G. (1988). Rethinking Incrementalism. *Strategic Management Journal, Vol. 9,* 75-91.

——, (1992), Managing strategic change—strategy, culture and action. *Long Range Planning, Vol. 25,* 28-36.

Johnson, P. (1996]), (chair). *Changing the Culture: Engineering Education into the Future,* Barton, ACT: Institution of Engineers, Australia.

Johnston, C. (1994). *Profession moves to convert conservatism to social relevance,* Campus Review, November 24-30, p. 13.

Journal of Education, Vol. 33, Nn° 1, 59.

Kearney, M. (2004). Classroom Use of Multimedia-Supported Predict-Observe-Explain Tasks in a Social Construtivist Learning Environment: Research in Science Education, Vol. 34, pp. 427-453.

Keil, B. *Authoring MathML and e-Learning Content with SciWriter and SciLAS.* Second European Workshop of MathML and Scientific e-Contents. Kuopio (Finland). 16-18 September 2004. http://dmath.savonia-amk.fi/secondWorkshop/servlet/Home/program.html

Khan, A.R. (1998). 'The Impact of Globalization on South Asia and Growth and Poverty in East and South East Asia in the Era of Globalization', in A.S. Bhalla (ed.), *Globalization Growth and Marginalization.* pp. 103-124 and 125-148. London: Macmillan.

Kirkup, G. and Kirkwood, A. (2005). Information and communications technologies (ICT) in higher education teaching—a tale of gradualism rather than revolution. *Learning Media and Technology,* 30(2), 185-199

Kirschner, P.A., van den Brink, H. and Meester, M. (1991). Audiotape Feedback for Essays in Distance Education Innovative Higher Education, 15(2), *Spring/Summer.*

Koen, V.B. (1984). *Toward a Definition of the Engineering Method,* Engineering Education, Vol. 75, 3, pp. 150-158, Washington, DC: American Society for Engineering Education (ASEE).

Kolasinski, M. and P. Lisiecki. (2003). The Strategic Role of Public Relations in Creating the Competitive Advantages of Private Higher Education in Poland: The Example of the School of Banking in Poznan. Higher Education in Europe. 28(4) Retrieved November 28,

Koliopoulos, D. and Ravanis, K. (2000). Élaboration et évaluation du contenu conceptuel d'un curriculum constructiviste concernant l'approche énergétique des phénomènes mécaniques [Elaboration and evaluation of the conceptual content of a constructivist curriculum about an energy approach of mechanic phenomena]. Didaskalia, 16, 33-56.

Krueger, R.A., and Casey, M.A. (2000). *Focus groups: a practical guide for applied research* (3rd edition). Sage Publications, Inc., Thousand Oaks, London, New Delhi.

Lafarga, J., and Gómez del Campo, J. (Eds.). (1986). *Desarrollo del Potencial Humano: Aportaciones de una psicología humanista, Vol. 3.* México: Trillas.

Lang, J.D., Cruise, S., McVey, F.D. and McMasters, J. (1999). *Industry Expectations of New Engineers: A Survey to Assist Curriculum Designers. Journal of Engineering Education*, 88, 1, pp. 43-51.

Larson, M.S. (1979). *The Rise of Professionalism: A Sociological Analysis*, Berkeley, CA: University of California Press.

Lave, J. (1988). Cognition in practice. Cambridge, UK: Cambridge University Press.

Laws, P.W. (1997). Millikan Lecture 1996: Promoting active learning based on physics education research in introductory physics courses. *American Journal of Physics*, 65(1), 14-21.

Layton, T.E. Jr. (1976). *American Ideologies of Science and Engineering*, Technology and Culture, 17, No. 4, pp. 688-701.

——, [1971], *The Revolt of the Engineers: Social Responsibility and the American Engineering Profession*, Cleveland: The Press of Cape Western University.

Leach, J. and Scott, P. (2003). Learning science in the classroom: Drawing on individual and social perspectives. *Science and Education*, 12(1), 91-113.

Lee, M., McLoughlin, C. and Chan, A. (2007). Knowledge creation processes of students as producers of audio learning objects. Proceedings of ALT-C 2007, Nottingham, UK.

Lemke, J.L. (1997). Cognition, Context, and Learning: A Social Semiotic Perspective. In David Kirshner and James A. Whitson (Eds.) *Situated Cognition: Social, Semiotic, and Psychological Perspectives* (pp. 37-56). New Jersey: Lawrence Erlbaum Associates.

——, (2005). Research for the Future of Science Education: Multiple sites, media and goals. Invited paper presented at the VII Congreso Internacional sobre Investigación en la Didáctica de las Ciencias, Granada, Spain.

Leta, J. and Cruz, C.H.B. (2003). A produção científica brasileira. In *Indicadores de ciência, tecnologia e inovação no Brasil* (p. 1-616). Campinas: Editora da UNICAMP.

Leuf, B. and Cunningham, W. (2001). *The Wiki Way: Quick Collaboration on the Web*. Addison-Wesley Ed. Boston.

Liaison Committee of the Associations of University Graduate (CLAIU) Engineers of the European Union: www.claiu.org

Locke, R.R. (1984). *The End of the Practical Man: Higher Education and the Institutionalisation of Entrepreneurial Performance in Germany, France and Great Britain—1880 to 1940*, in McKay, J. (ed), Industrial Development And The Social Fabric, London: JAI Press Inc., Volume 7.

Lopes, J.B. (2004). Aprender e Ensinar Física [Learn and teach Phiscis]. Lisboa: Fundação Calouste Gulbenkian.

——, (2004). Aprender e Ensinar Física: Textos Universitários de Ciências Sociais e Humanas: Lisboa, Fundação Calouste Gulbenkian, 430 p.

Lyotard, F.J. (1984). *The Postmodern Condition: A Report on Knowledge*. Minneapolis: University of Minnesota Press.

Macdonald, B.A. (1977). A political classification of evaluation studies. In: Hamilton, D. *et al.* (orgs). *Beyond the numbers game*. Hampshire: Macmillan Education Ltd.

Mann, R.C. (1919). *The American Spirit in Education*, US Bureau of Education Bulletin, No. 30 (1919) p. 50.

Manzini, E. (2002). Sustainable solutions. New business ideas and new ideas on business'. In: *Encyclopaedia of Environmental Management Strategies*. Sangyo Chosa-kai, Tokyo.

——, (2007). 'Design, social innovation and sustainable ways of living. Creative communities and diffused social enterprise in the transition towards a sustainable network society'. August-September 2007. DRAFT. Ezio. DIS-Indaco, Politecnico di Milano.

——, Vezzoli, C. (2002). *O Desenvolvimento de Produtos Sustentáveis*. São Paulo: USP, pp. 41-62.

Marques, C.M.; Lopes, J.B.; Carvalho, M.J. (2005). Mediação do trabalho prático de química no ensino universitário: uma experiência de integração no currículo. Conference Proceedings. Enseñanza de las Ciencias, 2005. Número extra. VII Congreso.

Martin, J. and Solbes, J. (2001). Diseño y Evaluación de una propuesta para la Enseñanza del concepto de campo en Física [Design and evaluation of a proposal for teaching the concept of field in physics]. Enseñanza de las Ciencias, 19(3), 393-403.

Martins, C.B. (2000). O ensino superior brasileiro nos anos 90. In *São Paulo em Perspectiva* (vol. 14, pp. 41-60). São Paulo: Fundação Seade.

Mathew, S. and Earnest, J. (2004). Laboratory-Based Innovative Approaches for Competence Development. *Global Journal of Engineering Education*. 8(2).

Mayer, J.D. and Cobb, C.D. (2000). Educational policy on emotional intelligence: Does it make sense? *Educational Psychology Review, 12* (2), 163-183.

Mazumder, Tapas. (1998). Economics of Indian Education: The Emerging Policy, and Finance' *Asian Development Review, 15(2): 86-130.*

Mazur, E. (1997). Peer Instruction, a user's manual: New Jersey, Prentice Hall, 253 p.

McCowan, J.D. and Knapper, C.K. (2002). An Integrated and Comprehensive Approach to Engineering Curricula, Part One: Objectives and General Approach. *International Journal of Engineering Education*. 18(6), 633-637.

McGregor, D. (1960). *The Human Side of Enterprise,* New York: McGraw-Hill.

Meltzer, D.E., and Manivannan, K. (2002). Transforming the lecture-hall environment: The fully interactive physics lecture: American Journal of Physics, Vol. 70, pp. 639-654.

Meng, P. (2005). Podcasting and vodcasting: Definitions, discussions and implications. A White paper by IAT Services at University of Missouri. Available online at: http://edmarketing.apple.com/adcinstitute/wp-content Missouri_Podcasting_White_Paper.pdf, Last accessed: 5/12/2005

Meroni, A. (ed.) (2007). *Creative Communities. People Inventing Sustainable Ways of Living*. Edizioni POLI.design.

Miles, M. and Huberman, M.A. (1994). Qualitative Data Analysis (second edition). Beverly Hills: Sage Publications.

Ministério da Educação (2001). CNE/CES/1.362/2001. Brasília: Conselho Nacional de Educação.

——, (2001). Diretrizes curriculares nacionais. Brasília: Conselho Nacional de Educação.

Mintzberg, H. (1979). *The Structuring of Organizations*. New Jersey: Prentice Hall.

Moesby, E. (2005). Curriculum Development for Project-Oriented and Problem-Based Learning (POPBL) with Emphasis on Personal Skills and Abilities. *Global Journal of Engineering Education*. 9(2).

Moll, L. (2002). Through the Mediation of Others: Vygotskian Research on Teaching. In V. Richardson (Ed.), *Handbook of Research on Teaching* (fourth edition, pp. 111-132). Washington: American Educational Research Association.

Monteiro, B.G. (2004). *A Centralidade da Peça-piloto no Processo de Desenvolvimento de Roupas de Malha: Um Estudo de Caso*. PhD Thesis in Engenharia de Produção, COPPE/UFRJ.

Montesinos, P., López, M. and Ginés Mora, J. (2006). *The challenge of University management: University 3rd mission and continuing Engineering Education opportunities*. 10th IACEE World Conference on Continuing Engineering Education (WCCEE), April 19-21 2006, Viena, Austria.

Moore, G.E. (1977). Individualizing Instructional feedback: A Comparison Modes in University Classes, Paper presented at the Annual International Conference for Individiaulized Instruction, West Lafayette, Indiana, USA.

Moorehouse, C.E. (1964). *Engineering Courses in Australian Universities,* The Australian University, 2.

Morrow, R. (1994). *Issues facing Engineering Education.* Journal of Engineering Education, 83 (1), pp. 15-18.

Moura, A. (2006). Produzir uma webquest num wiki. In A.A.A. Carvalho (org.) *Encontro sobre Webquest: programa, Resumos, e Workshops*. Braga: CIED, Universidade do Minho pp. 61-71.

Muller, H.D., and Collet, M. (1995.) *How to make a Manager out of an Engineer,* in Krueger, R.E., and Kulacki, A.T. Proceedings of the Fourth World Conference on Engineering Education, Saint Paul, Minnesota, Vol. 3.

National Academy of Engineering (2005). *Educating the Engineer of 2020.* The National Academies Press. Whasington, DC.

——, (2005a). 'Recommendations' in *Educating the Engineer of 2020: Adapting Engineering to the New Century.* Washington, D.C.: National Academy Press, 2005, pp. 51-58 (pdf available at http://www.nap.edu).

——, (2005b). 'Getting to 2020: Guiding Strategies' in *Educating the Engineer of 2020: Adapting Engineering to the New Century*. Washington, D.C.: National Academy Press, pp. 17-31 (pdf available at http://www.nap.edu).

——, Activity 7 (2004). *The Philosophy of Engineering—defining engineering and the constituent parts; educating engineers and the public on the meaning and impact of engineering.*

——, (2004). *Technological Context of Engineering Practice in The Engineer of 2020: Visions of Engineering in the New Century*, Washington, D.C.: National Academy Press. pp. 7-25 (pdf available at http://www.nap.edu).

National Engineers Register (1994), *Engineering Manpower in Profile,* Washington, DC: National Science Foundation.

National Research Council, (1999). How people learn: Brain, mind, experience, and school. Washington DC: National Academy Press.

National Science Foundation (2004). *An Emerging and Critical Problem of the Science and Engineering Labor Force: A Comparison of Science and Engineering Indicators.* www.nsf.gov/sbe/srs/nsb0407/stat.htm

Neumann, K. Welzel, M. (2007). A new labwork course for physics students: Devices, Methods and Research Projects: *Eur. J. Physics*, Vol. 28, pp. 61-69

Nicol, D.J., and Macfarlane-Dick, D. (2006). Formative assessment and self-regulated learning: a model and seven principles of good feedback practice. *Studies in Higher Education,* Vol. 31, No. 2, April 2006, pp. 199-218

Noakes, N., and Lomas, C. (2005). Narrowcasting 101: using blogs, podcasts, and videoblogs in Higher Education. EDUCAUSE Live! webinar, July 21, 2005. Archive available online at: http://www.educause.edu/LIVE0514, last accessed 4/12/2007

Noble, F.D. (1984). *The Forces of Production: A Social History of Industrial Automation,* New York: Alfred. E. Knopf.

Nortcliffe, A.L. and Middleton, A. (2007). Audio Feedback for the iPod Generation. In *Proceedings of International Conference on Engineering Education,* Coimbra, Portugal, 2007

Novak, G.M., Patterson, E.T., Gavrin, A.D., and Christian, W. (1999). Just-in-time teaching: blending Active Learning with web technology: NJ, Prentice Hall, Upper Saddle River.

O'Reilly, T. (2005). What Is Web 2.0?—design patterns and business models for the next generation of software. Available online at: http://facweb.cti.depaul.edu/jnowotarski/se425/What%20Is%20Web%202%20point%200.pdf, last accessed 26/03/07

Ortega, L. and Mariño, E. (1997). Cambio y autorrealización en los grupos de crecimiento de Desarrollo Humano. En *Cuadernos de Investigación en la División de Ciencias del Hombre, Transformación y Cambio, Salud Integral y Calidad de Vida*: México: Universidad Iberoamericana.

Padilha, P.R. (2003). Projeto político-pedagógico da escola: por uma escola mais alegre, prazerosa e aprendente. In *Revista Pátio,* Nº 25, 2003. Porto Alegre: Artmed Editora.

Panitz, T. (s/d). *Collaborative versus cooperative learning: a comparison of two concepts which Hill help us understand the underly nature of interactive learning.* Retrieved from http://home.capecod.net/~tpanitz/tedsarticles/coopdefinition.htm.Consulted 12/12/2007.

Papaneck, V. (1973). *Diseñar para el Mundo Real.* Madrid: H. Blume Ediciones.

Papanek, Gustav. (1988). The New Asian capitalism: An Economic Portrait' in P.L. Berger and H.H.M. Hsiao (Eds.), *In Search of an Asian Development Model,* pp. 27-80. Brunswick: Transaction Books.

Parlamento Europeo. Las universidades y la enseñanza superior en el espacio europeo del conocimiento, September 2002.

Paulsen, M.B., and Wells, C.T. (1998). *Domain differences in the epistemological beliefs of college students,* Research in Higher Education, 39(4), pp. 365-384.

Pea, R.D. (2004). The social and technological dimensions of scaffolding and related theoretical concepts for learning, education, and human activity. *The Journal of the Learning Sciences*, 13(2), 423-451.

Pearson, P.H. (1974). Conceptualizing and measuring openness to experience in the context of psychotherapy. En D.A. Wexler and L. North Rice (Eds.), *Innovations in client-centered therapy* (pp. 139-170). New York: John Wiley & Sons, Inc.

Penin, L. (2006). *Strategic Design for Sustainable Social Innovation in Emerging Contexts: Framework and Operative Strategies.* PhD Thesis, Politécnico de Milão. Milão.

Perrenoud, P. (2003). Porquê construir competências a partir da escola? Porto, ASA Editores, S.A., 124 p.

—, (2003). Porquê construir competências a partir da escola? 2ª ed. Porto: ASA Editores, S.A.

Polman, J.L. and Pea, R.D. (2001). Transformative communication as a cultural tool for guiding inquiry science. *Science Education*, 85(3), 223-238.

Powell, J.J. (1998). Reducing Teacher Control, in D.Boud (ed.), *Developing Student Autonomy in Learning*, Kogan Page, London, 109-118

Prandy, K. (1965). *Professional Employees: A Study of Scientists and Engineers,* London: Faber and Faber.

Qian, Y. (2007). Meaningful Learning with Wikis: making a connection. In R. Craslen *et al.* (Eds.). *Proceedings of the 18th International Conference of the Society for Information Technology and Teacher Education, SITE 2007*. Chesapeake, VA: AACE, 2093-2997.

Race, P. (1999). Why assess innovatively? In Sally Brown and Angela Glasner (eds.) *Assessment matters in higher education*. The Society for Research into Higher Education and Open University Press, Buckingham.

Ramsden, P. (1987). Improving Teaching and Learning in Higher Education: the case for a relational perspective: Studies in Higher Education, Vol. 12, pp. 275-286.

——, (1991). A Performance Indicator of Teaching Quality in Higher Education: The Course Experience Questionnaire: Studies In Higher Education, Vol. 16, pp. 129-150.

Redish, E., and Steinberg, R. (1999). Teaching Physics: Figuring Out What Works: Physics Today, Vol. 52, pp. 24-30.

Redish, E.F. (1994). The Implications of Cognitive Studies for Teaching Physics. *American Journal of Physics*, 62(6), 796-803.

——, (2003). Teaching Physics with the Physics Suite: USA, John Wiley & Sons, Inc., 216 p.

Reichert, S. and Tauch, C. (2005). *Trends IV: European Universities implementing Bologna*. 2005. European University Association (EUA).

Reiser, B.J. (2004). Scaffolding Complex Learning: The Mechanisms of Structuring and Problematizing Student Work. *Journal of the Learning Sciences*, 13(3), 273-304.

Ribeiro, R.J. (2003). *A universidade e a vida atual:Fellini não via filmes*.Campinas: Campus.

Richards, J. (1992). *Poor Image Prevails,* Professional Engineering, January 9, Southampton: Mechanical Engineering Publications.

Richardson, W. (2006). *Blogs, Wikis, Podcast and other powerful Web tools for classrooms*. Thousand Oaks, CA: Corwin Press.

Ritti, R.R. (1971) *The Engineer in the Industrial Corporation,* New York: Columbia University Press.

Rodrigues, A.C.P., Pontes C.C.C., Silva, D. (2007). Proceedings from ICEE 2007: *The moving frontiers of Engineering*. Coimbra, Portugal: University of Coimbra.

Rodriguez, G, Villa, A. Could the computers change the trends in Mathematics learning?. A Spanish overview. Proceedings Applimat 2005. Slovak University of Technology Bratislava (Eslovaquia) February 2005.

Rogers, C.R. (1978). Condiciones necesarias y suficientes del cambio terapéutico de la personalidad. En J. Lafarga and J. Gómez del Campo, J.F. (Eds.), *Desarrollo del potencial humano: Aportaciones de una psicologia humanista, Vol. 1* (pp. 79-92). México: Trillas.

Roldão, M. d. C. (2003). Gestão do Currículo e Avaliação de Competências: Lisboa, Editorial Presença, 89 p.

Rompelman, O. (2000). 'Assessment of student learning: evolution of objectives in engineering education and the consequences for assessment', *European Journal of Engineering Education, 25* (4), 339-350.

Rotheram, B. (2007). Using an MP3 recorder to give feedback on student assignments, Educational Developments, Issue 8.2, June, pp. 7-10, Staff and Educational Development Association, London.

Roy, R. *et. al.* (2006). Attitude of the Working Engineers Towards Distance Mode of Instruction. *Indian Journal of Open Learning; 15* (3), 225-235.

——. (2002). 'Information Based Instruction (IBI) and Future', *Journal of NEIES*, IX (I): pp. 150-158. Shillong.

Royal Academy for Engineering [RAE] Seminars (2007). *AI and IT where philosophy and engineering meet. Metaphysics and Engineering-Engineering and Environmental Philosophy.*

RShepard, L. (2002). The role of classroom assessment in teaching and learning. In V. Richardson (Ed.), *Handbook of Research on Teaching* (fourth edition, pp. 1066-1101). Washington: American Educational Research Association.

Ruiz, M. (2007). Attitudes and values in engineering students: the Human Development Scale. Paper presented at the International Conference on Engineering Education — ICEE 2007, University of Coimbra, Portugal, 3-7 September.

Rust, C. (2001). A Briefing on the assessment of large groups. LTSN Generic Centre. Available online at: http://www.heacademy.ac.uk/resources/detail/ourwork/tla/assessment_series, Last accessed: 10/01/2008

Sadler, D.R. (1989). Formative assessment and the design of instructional systems. Instructional Science, 18, 119-144.

Santamaria, F.G.; Abraira, C.F. (2006). Wikis: posibilidades para el aprendizaje colaborativo em Educacion Superior. In L. Panizo *et al.* (Eds.) *Proceedings of the 8th International Symposium on Computers in Education*, (Vol. 2), pp. 371-378.

Saul, A.M. (2006). *Avaliação Emancipatória: desafios à teoria e à prática de avaliação e reformulação do currículo*. São Paulo: Cortez Editora.

Savinainen, A., Scott, P. and Viiri, J. (2005). Using a bridging representation and social interactions to foster conceptual change: Designing and evaluating an instructional sequence for Newton's third law. Science Education, 89, 175-195.

Schein, E. (1995). Kurt Lewin's Change Theory in the Field and in the Classroom: Notes Toward a Model of Managed Learning. *Systems Practice*, http://www.solonline.org/res/wp/10006.html

Schein, E.H. (1992). *Organizational Culture and Leadership*. (2nd Ed), San Francisco: Jossey-Bass Publishers.

Scholtens, H.N. (1991). Dutch Policies to Increase Participation of Women in Engineering Education: An Overview and Evaluation, in Proceedings of SEFI'91 Annual Conference, New Perspectives on the Dissemination and Synthesis of Engineering Knowledge, Marseilles, pp. 176-172.

Schön, D.A. (1983). *The Reflective Practioner*. Usa, Basic Books, Inc.: Cambridge, 1983.

Schons, C.H.; Silva, F.C.C. and Molossi, S. (2007). O uso de wikis na gestão do conhecimento em organizações *Revista Biblios* Ano 8, No. 27, Jan-Mar. Retrieved from http://www.bibliosperu.com/articulos/27/27_13.pdf Consulted a: 20/12/2007.

Schultz, Theodore W. (1975). 'The Value of the Ability to Dill with Disequilibria', *Journal of Economic Literature*, 12(3) (September): 827-846.

Schultz, Theodore W. (1990). *'Restoring Economic Equilibrium'*, Cambridge: Basil Blackwell.

Schwartz, L.; Clark, S.; Cossarin, M. and Rudolph, J. (2004). Educational Wikis: features and selection criteria. *The International Journal of Research in Open and Distance Learning, Vol. 5 (1).* [Online]. Retrieved from 24/01/2007 from http://www.irrodl.org/index/irrodl/article/view/163/244.

Scott, P.H., Mortimer, E.F., and Aguiar, O.G. (2006). The Tension Between Authoritive and Dialogic Discourse: A Fundamental Characteristic of Meaning Making Interactions in High School Science Lessons: Science Education, Vol. 90, pp. 605-631.

SEFI (2002), *The Bologna Declaration and Engineering Education—a Discussion Paper*, Brussels, Belgium: European Society for Engineering Education.

Seiz-Ortiz, R., Sánchez-Ruiz, L.M. and Ballester-Sarrias, E. (2004). *Training the New Engineer in the Europe of Knowledge and convergence. The case of the School of Design Engineering in Valencia.* Proceedings of International Conference on Engineering Education. University of Florida, October 17-21, 2004.

Sen, Amartya. (2000). Development as Freedom: Oxford University Press. New Delhi.

Shaufeli, W.B., Salanova, M., González-Fomá, V., and Bakker, A.B. (2002). The measurement of engagement and burnout: A two sample confirmatory factor analytic approach. *Journal of Happiness Studies, 3* (1), 71-92.

Shulman, S.L. (2005). *If Not Now, When? The Timeliness of Scholarship of the Education of Engineers,* Journal of Engineering Education, January, p. 11.

Siemens, G. (2004). *Uma teoria de aprendizagem para a idade digital. Competências profissionais.* Retrieved from http://www.webcompetencias.com/textos/conectivismo.htm Consulted a 20/12/2007.

Silva, A. (2007). 'Identificação e Replicabilidade de Casos de Comunidades Criativas para Promoção de Inovação Social, a adoção desse Instrumento de Design Estratégico na Formação em Design'. Submitted to XXIII PRÊMIO JOVEM CIENTISTA. CNPq, Brasil.

Sinclair, G. and Tilson, W. (1979). *Improved goals for engineering education.* Proceedings: Frontiers in Engineering Education Conference, pp. 252-258.

Skobrook, S. (2006). *The role of pre-entry practices and induction strategies in relation to student retention.* Strategy Guide Resource of the PROGRESS Project, University of Huli: http://www.engsc.ac.uk?downloads/progress/shobrook.pdf

Smerdon, E.T. (1999). Global Challenges in Engineering Education. Proceedings of the 28th International Symposium Engineering Education in the Third Millennium, Band 1, Vol. 1, pp. 20-26. Leuchtturm Verlag.

Solomon, D.S. (1996). *An Engineer Goes to Wall Street,* Technology Review, Vol. 94, No. 1, p. 28.

Sommerville, I. (2004). Chapter 22: Verification and Validation. In *Software Engineering* 7, Pearson Addison Wesley, 515-536

Sousa, S.M.Z.L. (2003). Possíveis impactos das políticas de avaliação no currículo escolar. In *Cadernos de Pesquisa da Fundação Carlos Chagas* (n. 119, pp. 175-190). São Paulo: Fundação Carlos Chagas,

Stinner, A. (1990). Philosophy, thought experiments and large context problems in the secondary school physics course. *International Journal of Science Education*, 12(3), 244-257.

Strawbridge, S. (2001). Carl Rogers. *The Psychologist, 14* (4), 182-185.

Streeten, Paul. (1998). 'Globalization: Threat or Opportunity?' *Pakistan Development Review,* 37(4) (Part 1: Winter): pp. 51-83.

Szablowski, J. (2001). The Role of Private Universities and Colleges in the Spatial Restructuring of Higher Education in Poland. Higher Education in Europe. 26(3). Retrieved November 28, 2007, from http://cepes.ro/publications/pdf/hee_eng_pdf/he3_01.pdf

Task force on Higher Education and Society. 2000. *Higher Education in Developing Countries*: *Peril and Promise*. Washington DC: World Bank.

Teichler, U. and Schonburg, H. (Eds.). (2004). *Comparative Perspectives on Higher Education and Graduate Employment and Work—Experiences from Twelve Countries.* Kluwer Pub.

Terry, R.E., Harb, J.N., Hecker, W.C. and Wilding, W.V. (2002). Definition of Student Competencies and Development of an Educational Plan to Assess Student Mastery Level. *International Journal of Engineering Education*. 18(2), 225-235.

Thematic Network Teaching and research in Engineering in Europe (TREE): http://www3.unifi.it/tree/

Thulstrup, W.E. (1999). *Secondary School-University Interface: Science and Engineering,* Global Journal of Engineering Education, Vol. 3, 1 p. 9-20.

Tiberghien, A., Jossem, E. and Barojas, L.J. (Eds.) (1997). Connecting Research in Physics Education with Teacher Education. International Commission on Physics Education.

Tilak, J.B.G (2001): 'Education and Development', *Indian Social Science Review,* 3(2): pp. 219-266. New Delhi.

Tonke, E. (2005). Making the case for a Wiki. *Ariadne,* 42 (online journal). Retrieved from www.ariadne.ac.uk/issue42/tonkin, consulted the 28/11/2007.

Top Industrial Managers Europe (T.I.M.E.): www.time-association.org

Treagust, D. (2003). The role of submicroscopic and symbolic representations in chemical explanations. *International Journal of Science Education*, 25(11), 1353-1368.

Turns, J., Atman, C.J., Adams, S.R. and Barker, T. (2005). *Research on Engineering Student Knowing: Trends and Opportunities.* Journal of Engineering Education, January, pp. 27-40.

UNDP. 1999-2003: *Human Development Reports*, New York, Oxford University Press.

UNESCO (1968). *International Conference on Trends in Teaching and Training of Engineers—Recommendation of the Commission,* Final Report, Paris: UNESCO Press.

UNESCO (1970). *The meeting of Experts on Engineering Education*, Final Report, July 21-24, Paris: UNESCO Press.

UNESCO (1974). *International Seminar on the Role of Social Sciences and Humanities in Engineering Education,* Bucharest, September 1972, Paris: UNESCO Press.

UNESCO Institute for Statistics (UIS): www.uis.unesco.org

UNESCO, 2007. Science, Technology and Gender: An International Report. Science and Technology for Development series.

Valero, P. (2002). The myth of active learner: from cognitive to social-political interpretations of students in mathematics classrooms. In P. Valero and O. Skovsmose (Eds.), *Proceedings of the third International Mathematics Education and Society Conference* (pp. 489-500). Copenhagen: Centre for Research in Learning Mathematics.

Vergnaud, G. (1987). Les fonctions de l'action et de la symbolisation dans la formation des connaissances chez l'enfant [Functions of action and symbolisation in the formation of knowledge in children]. In J. Piaget, P. Mounoud and J.P. Bronkart (Eds.), Encyclopédie de la Pléiade Psychologie (pp. 821-844). Paris: Gallimard.

——, (1991). La théorie des champs conceptuels [The theory of conceptual fields]. Recherches en Didactique des Mathématiques, 10(23), 133-170.

Vermunt, J.D., Verloop, N. (1999). Congruence and friction between learning and teaching. *Learning and Instruction*, 9, 257-280.

Vesilind, A.P. (1991). *The Social Role of Engineers: A Philosophical Perspective*, Engineering Education, April, pp. 376-9.

Vidal, J. and Ginés Mora, J. (2000). Changes in Spanish Universities: Improvements and Unsolved Conflicts. *Planning in Higher Education, Vol. 29, No. 1,* 15-23.

Viegas, C., Lopes, J.B. and Cravino, J.P. (2007). Real Work in Physics Classroom: Improving Engineering Students Competences. *Proceedings of the 2007 ICEE*, Coimbra-Portugal.

Vygotsky, L.S. (1962). Thought and language. Cambridge, MA: MIT Press.

Watson, J.C., Goldman, R.N., and Warner, M.S. (Eds.). (2002). *Client-centered and experiential psychotherapy in the 21st century: Advances in theory, research and practice*. London: PCCS Books.

Weil-Barais, A. (1994). Heuristic value of notion of zone of proximal development in the study of child and adolescent construction of concepts in physics. *European Journal of Psychology of Education*, 9(4), 367-383.

—— and Dumas-Carré, A. (1998). Les Interactions Didactiques, Tutelles et/ou Médiation [The didactic interactions, monitoring and/or mediation]. In Dumas-Carré, A. and Weil-Barais, A. (Eds.), Tutelle et Médiation dans l'Éducation Scientifique. Bern: Peter Lang.

Weingart, P. (1978). *The relation between science and technology — a sociological explanation,* in Weingart, P., Krohn, W., and Layton, E.T. (eds.) Sociology of Sciences Yearbook: The Dynamics of Science and Technology, Dordrecht: D. Reidel.

Wenger, E. (1998). Communities of practice: Learning, meaning, and identity. Cambridge: Cambridge University Press.

White, R.T., and Gunstone, R.F. (1992). *Probing Understanding*. London: Falmer Press.

Wijekumar, Kay (s/d). *Implementing Collaborative Learning in Web-Based Course Design and Management systems.* [Online]. Retrieved from http://ieeexplore.ieee.org/iel5/7507/20425/00943862.pdf. Consulted the 24/01/2007.

Wildman, T.M. (2005). From the outside in: Lessons in learning beyond the school walls. About Campus, 10 (1), 16-22.

Wilenski, H. (1964). *The Professionalization of Everyone,* American Journal of Sociology, 70.

——, (1964). *Varieties of Work Experience,* in Borrow, H. (ed) Man in a World of Work, Boston: Houghton-Miffin.

Williams, B. Sir (1988). *Review of the Discipline of Engineering,* Canberra: AGPS.

Wilson, R. (2005). *Projections of Occupations and Qualifications,* DfEE and Institute of Employment Records, Warwick, UK: University of Warwick.

Windham, C. (2007). Confessions of a podcast junkie. *EDUCAUSE review*, May/June 2007. http://www.educause.edu/apps/er/erm07/erm0732.asp, Last accessed: 5/31/2007

Woolnough, B.E. (1991). *The Making of Engineers and Scientists,* Oxford University, The Department of Educational Studies.

Yates, A. (2000). *Discussion Paper on Raising the Status of Engineers,* The Institution of Engineers *Australia,* Sydney.

Yeomans, S.R. and Atrens, A. (2001). A Methodology for Discipline-Specific Curriculum Development. *International Journal of Engineering Education.* 17(6), 518-528.

Young, P. (2000). 'I Might as Well Give Up': self-esteem and mature students' feelings about feedback on assignments. *Journal of Further and Higher Education*, Vol. 24, No. 3, 409-418

Yrjänheikki K., and Takala, M., (2001). *Engineering education facing new challenges in the learning society: case Finland.* ASEE '21st Century Engineer', Nov 2-3, 2001.

Zakowska, L. (1986). Spatial Imagination as a Necessary Criterion in the Engineering Profession (in Polish), AGH Scientific Journal, Technology of Education, Cracow.

——, (1999). Modern Teaching of Civil Engineering Design and Creativity of Students. Proceedings of the 28th International Symposium Engineering Education in the Third Millennium, Band 2, pp. 900-904. Leuchtturm Verlag.

——, (2001). Dreams and fears behind computer aided visual road design (CAD) and learning (CAL) processes. CALIE'01, International Conference on Computer Aided Learning in Engineering Education, 8-10 November 2001, Tunis, Tunisia.

—— and Boryczko, M. (1997). Subjective assessment of influence of CAL and CAD on the professional skills of engineers — a case study, 4th International Conference CAEE97 (Computer Aided Engineering Education (Proceedings), Akapit Krakow, 273-279.

Zañartu, L.M. (2003). Aprendizaje Colaborativo: uma nueva forma de dialogo interpersonal y em red. Contexto Educativo. *Revista Digital de Educacion y Nuevas Tecnologías,* 28(v). Retrieved from http://contexto-educativo.com.ar/2003/4/nota-02.htm, Consulted the 14/12/2007.

Zaoual, H. (1999). 'The Maghreb Experience: A Challenge to the Rational Myth of Economics'. *Review of African Political Economy*, vol. 26 n. 82, dec. 1999. pp. 469-478.

——, (1999). 'The Maghreb Experience: A Challenge to the Rational Myth of Economics'. *Review of African Political Economy*, vol. 26 n. 82, dec. 1999. pp. 469-478.

——, (2005). *Nova Economia das Iniciativas Locais: uma Introdução ao Pensamento Pós-Global*. (translation by Michel Thiollent), Rio de Janeiro: DP & A Ed.References
——, (2005). *Nova Economia das Iniciativas Locais: uma Introdução ao Pensamento Pós-Global*. (translation by Michel Thiollent), Rio de Janeiro: DP & A Ed.
Ziman, J. (1991). *Reliable Knowledge: An exploration of the grounds for belief in science,* Cambridge: Cambridge University Press.

Zussman, R. (1985). *Mechanics of the Middle Class: Work and Politics Among American Engineers,* Berkely: University of California Press.

Contributors

Albert E. Segall is presently Associate Professor of Engineering Science and Mechanics at the Pennsylvania State University. He was previously Director of Engineering Programmes and Associate Professor of Mechanical and Manufacturing Engineering at Washington State University, Vancouver. He received is his Ph.D. in Engineering Science and Mechanics from the Pennsylvania State University.

Agustín López is Adjunct Professor of Law and the current Director of the Administrative Hearing Programme for the University of San Diego"s School of Law. He oversees hearing officers who preside over administrative hearings for the City and County of San Diego, City of Coronado, City of Encinitas, and San Diego State University.

Alonso Félix is a teaching assistant of Applied Mathematics Department in Pontificia Comillas University.

Ana Cecília Pontes Rodrigues is presently associated with Escola Politécnica da Universidade de São Paulo.

Andrew Middleton is presently Senior Lecturer of Academic Innovation Learning & Teaching Institute at Sheffield Hallam University.

Anne Nortcliffe is Member of Faculty of Art, Computing, Engineering and Science at Sheffield Hallam University.

Beany Guimarães Monteiro is Professor at Department of Industrial Design of the Fine Arts School in Federal University of Rio de Janeiro. She has experience in design, product project and her work comprises the areas of Production Engineering, Sustainable Development, Social Innovation and esthetics, having as an important methodological reference the emphasis on the key role of dialogical relations and local social actors, participation in social and environmental projects and Computer Aided Design-CAD-, for textile industry. She is coordinator of Interdisciplinary Laboratory of Social Interest Design (Industrial Design, EBA/UFRJ).

C.M. Marques is associated with Department of Chemistry of University of Trás-os-Montes e Alto Douro (UTAD), at Vila Real Portugal.

C. Viegas is associated with Instituto Superior de Engenharia do Porto (ISEP), Porto, Portugal.

Cecília Carmen Cunha Pontes is associated with Centro Estudos Rurais e Urbanos at São Paulo.

Ana Cecília Pontes Rodrigues is associated with Escola Politécnica da Universidade de São Paulo.

Clara Pereira Coutinho is Associate Professor at the Institute of Education and Psychology, Minho University, Braga, Portugal. She teaches Educational Technology and Research Methods in Education in Graduate and Post Graduate Teacher Education Programmes. Her areas of current research and interest are Educational Multimedia, Web 2.0 in Teacher Education and Research Methods in Educational Technology.

Claudio Borri is Vice Dean for International Relations and Full Professor of Computational Mechanics of Structures at Facoltà di Ingegneria, Università di Firenze. He is President of SEFI 2005-07 and President of IFEES 2006-08 — President of Thematic Networks E4 and TREE.

Dagmar Juchelková is Professor of VŠB-Technical University of Ostrava at Poruba, Czech Republic.His significant contribution is in the area of low active waste, waste combustion, waste composition and utilization, emissions from combustion processes, fludized bed boilers, co-combustion, alternative fuels and biofuels.

Darío Roig is a member of faculty at Servei d''Informàtica, Universitat de València. Vicent Andrés Estellés, Burjassot (Valencia.) Spain.

David Perry is member of faculty of Polytechnic University of Valencia, Department of Applied Linguistics, Camino de Vera, Valencia, Spain.

Djuro Kutlaèa is Professor at Faculty of Security Studies, University of Belgrade. He is also the Deputy-editor of "INFO" national journal for ICT.His recent projects are in setting-up of national programme in the field of basic research (2001-2002); creation of concept of national innovation system (2003-2004); feasibility study for setting-up of S&T park MPI (2005-2007); research on innovation capacity in Serbia (2006-2010).

Edson Pedro Ferlin is currently a Chair Professor in the department of Computer Engineering, Positivo University (UP). He was professor of the PUCPR and SPEI Faculty since 1996. His research interests include computer architecture, parallel computing, microprocessors and reconfigurable computing. He is reviewer of national and international journals and conferences.

Elisa Guberti is Doctor in Languages at the Università di Bologna. Since 2001 she is Head of the International Relations Office at the Faculty of Engineering of the University of Florence. She acted as Project Manager within E4 Thematic Network and is presently playing the same role for several European funded projects both under the LLP and the TEMPUS actions. She is co-author of several scientific papers dealing with engineering education.

Francesco Maffioli is Professor of Operational Research at the Politecnico di

Milano since 1980. He was also visiting professor at the Université Libre de Bruxelles (ULB). His fields of scientific activity are: combinatorial optimisation, mathematical programming, computational complexity, and telecommunication network design. He is very active within SEFI and was President from 1995 to 1997. Within the SOCRATES II programme of the European Commission, he co-ordinated the Thematic Network "Enhancing Engineering Education in Europe" (E4), has chaired the Synergy Group on Engineering of the TUNING project, and is now the Scientific co-ordinator of TREE Thematic Network.

G. Diercks-o"brien is member of faculty at Department of Automatic Control, Mappin Street, University of Sheffield, UK.

Giuliano Salcas Olguin is currently the Pedagogical Advisor at the Polytechnic School of the University of São Paulo. He is responsible for the evaluation of the quality of education and elaboration of educational projects.He is the coordinator of a research group on engineering education (Saltimbancos). His research explores the methods of assessment of educational institutions (curriculum, pedagogical project, performance of students), the purpose and concept of Higher Education (goals, law, relationship with the market) and the various methodologies of Engineering Education.

Haydée Svab is member of faculty of Escola Politécnica da Universidade de São Paulo.

Joaquim Bernardino De Oliveira Lopes is currently the professor of Department of Physics at University of Trás-os-Montes e Alto Douro (UTAD) at Portugal.

Jeff Connor is Associate Professor in Engineering Education Department, Colege of Engineering of Virginia Tech.

José P. Cravino is member of faculty in the Department of Physics, University of Trás-os-Montes e Alto Douro (UTAD), Portugal.

John Anthony Rossiter, D.Phil, worked as an academic at Loughborough University and now the University of Sheffield where he is a Reader in Automatic control and systems engineering. His main research interest is predictive control where he has contributed several concepts to the community that are now widely adopted. Increasingly he is now taking an interest in educational issues and how to give the highest quality education to students. His interests cover pragmatic issues such as effective staff support and encouragement along with individual innovations in his own teaching.

João Batista Bottentuit Junior is a professor at Faculty of Maranhão (FACAM), Brazil. He is Master in Multimedia in Education by University of Porto, Portugal, is Post-graduate in Teaching in Higher Education by Catholic Pontifical University of Minas Gerais, Brazil and Administration of Information Systems by Federal University of Lavras, Brazil. He is also, graduated in Data Processing Technology by University Center UNA, Brazil. Currently is Ph.D. student in Education (in Educational Technology) at Institute of Education and Psychology of Minho University, Braga, Portugal.His areas of interest are Computer Science, Technology Education, Engineering in Education and Information Systems.

Josef Rojter, a doctorate in the area of application of engineering practice, have had an extensive experience in industry, industrial consulting and research, and academia.Preently he is associated with School of ACME, Faculty of Health, Engineering and Science, Victoria University, Melbourne, Australia.His area of interest includes the epistemology of engineering and the application of engineering knowledge to the world of professional engineering practice.

Juha Taina is currently professor of Software Engineering at the Department of Computer Science of University of Helsinki. His research interests include empirical software engineering, software testing, and software engineering education.

Parameswarakumar Mallikarjunan is Associate Professor of Biological Systems Engineering at Virginia Tech, Blacksburg.

Linda Gray is member of faculty in the Department of Automatic Control, Mappin Street, University of Sheffield at UK. Educated at the University of Kansas, she subsequently worked as a senior computer programmer at the University of Sheffield. After becoming increasingly more interested and involved in teaching and student support, she became a University Teacher. Her interests include improving the student experience, taking account of the very diverse backgrounds, needs and aspirations of students in Higher Education today.

Lidia Zakowska is a member of faculty in Cracow University of Technology, Warszawska Street at Krakow, Poland.

Liesl Hotaling is Director of Education for the Beacon Institute, a global center for interdisciplinary research, policy-making and education regarding rivers, estuaries and their connection with society. She was formerly Assistant Director for the Center for Innovation in Engineering and Science Education (CIESE), Stevens Institute of Technology.

Milada Hlaváèková is associated with VŠB-Technical University of Ostrava at Poruba, Czech Republic.

Luis Manuel Sánchez Ruiz has been affiliated with Polytechnic University of Valencia, Spain where he became Full Professor of Mathematics in 2000. He had graduated and received his Ph.D. from University of Valencia and been a Visiting Professor at the University of Florida, Gainesville, USA. His current research interests include Functional Analysis from both theoretical and applied points of view. As former Academic Co-ordinator of Mediterranean University of Science and Technology, he has been responsible for several research projects granted by the Spanish Ministry of Education.

Mary Leigh Wolfe is presently Professor of Biological Systems Engineering at Virginia Tech, USA.

Mariana Ruiz Morales is a full-time Professor at the Engineering Department in the Universidad Iberoamericana, Mexico. Her projects deal with methods to enhance the educational experience and environment friendly processes. She has several publications in the areas of Agroindustry and Engineering Education.

Mónica Edwards Schachter is working at the Institute of Innovation and Knowledge Management of Valencia and is consultant in curricular development and teacher training at the School of Design Engineering of Valencia (Polytechnic University of Valencia) and the Informatics Faculty of The Polytechnic University of Madrid (Spain). Her current research interests are curriculum design, technology integration, academic and cultural organizational change, and evaluation.

Nestor Saavedra holds a position of Full Professor of Physics at Computer Engineering Department of Positivo University, at Curitiba, Paraná State, Brazil. He leads the Experimental Physics and Electronic Instrumentation team and his present interests are about computer-assisted experiments at both, scientific and didactic laboratories.

P. Moreno Clari is currently the member of faculty at Dpt. d"Informàtica, Universitat de València, Spain.

Paira, Anjana is a doctoral research scholar in the Faculty of Education in Visva-Bharati, Santiniketan, India. Her research interest is zoomed over education for development of the ethnic population, with special reference to their indegenious technology.

Penny Macdonald is currently a member of faculty at Polytechnic University of Valencia, Department of Applied Linguistics, Camino de Vera, Valencia, Spain.

Petr Horyl is currently holding the position of Profesor in The Faculty of Mechanical Engineering at VŠB — Technical University of Ostrava.

Rajarshi Roy is Assistant Profesor of Education in National Institute of Technical Teachers" Training & Research, Kolkata, India.

Richard Sheryll is a Research Associate in Ocean Engineering at Stevens Institute of Technology. He is an experienced design engineer specializing in the development of novel underwater machinery, such as deep-ocean sampling systems for retrieving exotic life-forms from the bottom of the deep ocean trenches.

Roberto Bartholo is Professor at the Production Engineering Programme at Federal University of Rio de Janeiro. His work comprises the areas of Production Engineering, Sustainable Development, Social Innovation and

Ethics, having as an important methodological reference the emphasis on the key role of dialogical relations and local stakeholders, participation in social and environmental projects. He is coordinator of Laboratory of Technology and Social Development (Production Engineering, COPPE/ UFRJ)

Rodríguez Gerardo is associated with Universidad de Salamanca, Escuela Politécnica Superior de Ingeniería, Campus Viriato, Cardenal Cisneros, Zamora, Spain.

Rustam Stolkin is a Research Assistant Professor at the Center for Maritime Systems, Stevens Institute of Technology. He received a MEng degree in Engineering from Oxford University and a PhD in Robotic Vision from London University. Dr. Stolkin is an interdisciplinary engineer with diverse research interests including underwater robotics, robotic vision, artificial intelligence, sensor systems, science writing and journalism, and engineering education. He is a member of the Institute for Electrical and Electronics Engineers, the Robotics and Automation Society and the American Society for Engineering Education.

Shyamal Majumdar is presently holding the position of Director General at Colombo Plan Staff College, Manila, Phillippines. Apart, he holds his substantive position of Professor at National Institute of Technical Teachers" Training & Research, Kolkata, India. Dr. Mazumder was the Regional Vice President of Asia & Pacific Region IVETA.

Terry M. Wildman is Professor of School of Education at Virginia Tech, Learning Sciences & Technology at Blacksburg, USA.

V. Cerverón Lleó is associated as member of faculty at Institut de Robòtica, Universitat de València, Paterna (Valencia) Spain.

Vinod K. Lohani is Associate Professor in Engineering Education Department, Colege of engineering of Virginia Tech. His area of specialization is in Agricultural Engineering and Civil Engineering with special focus on Irrigation Water Management.

Valfredo Pilla Jr. has been with Positivo University at the Department of Computer Engineering. His research interests are in the areas of evolvable hardware, reconfigurable computing, biomedical engineering, pattern recognition and education in engineering.

Villa, Agustín De La is full professor of Applied Mathematics Department in Pontificia Comillas University. He has participated in several projects of investigation financed by autonomic, national and European organizations. His current research interests include image processing, applied mathematics and new technologies in education.

Vojin Šenk is full Professor since 2003 in the Faculty of Engineering in the University of Novi Sad. He is currently lecturing a number of courses related to Information and Communication Theory, as well as

Entrepreneurship in the high-tech area. His recent projects include coordinating the national competition for best technology innovation in Serbia and a feasibility study for setting-up of S&T parks in Serbia.

Xin-Ran Duan is the Dean of Science, Engineering and Mathematics Division at Holyoke Community College, Massachusetts, USA. Prior he was a Full Professor and Chair of Technology at Ivy Tech State College, Columbus, Indiana. Dr. Duan has been working in higher education for over twenty five years. Professor Duan received the President's Award for Excellence in Instruction in 2002 and an award plaque for Excellence from the College's Board of Trustees in 2003. He is a member of iNEER (the International Network for Engineering Education and Research), ASME (American Society of Mechanical Engineers), AAUP (American Association of University Professors), NAIT (National Association of Industrial Technology), CADA (Council of Academic Division Administrators) in Massachusetts, and MASGC (NASA Massachusetts Space Grant Consortium).

Index